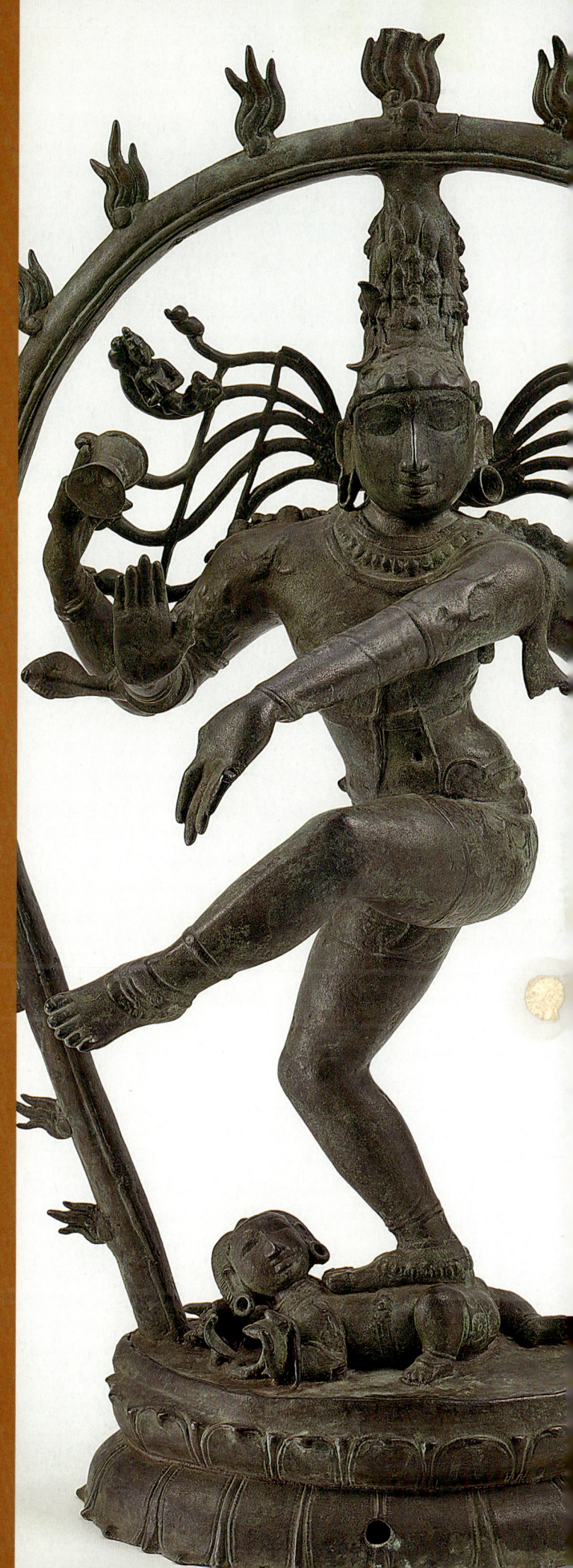

The
Thief
Who Stole
My Heart

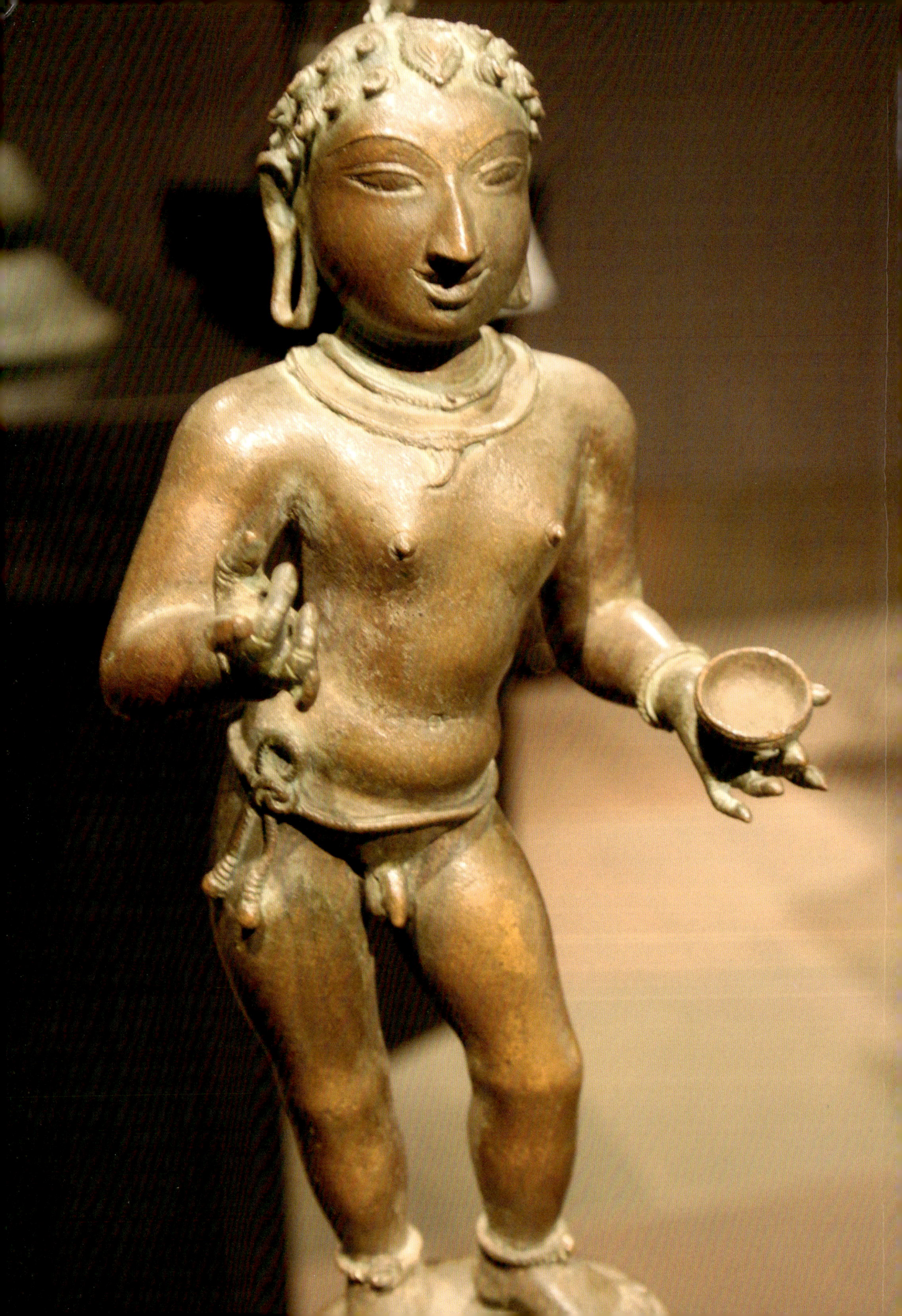

The Thief Who Stole My Heart

The Material Life
of Sacred Bronzes from
Chola India, 855–1280

Vidya Dehejia

Princeton University Press
Princeton and Oxford

The A. W. Mellon Lectures in the Fine Arts
National Gallery of Art, Washington
Center for Advanced Study in the Visual Arts
Bollingen Series XXXV: Volume 65

Copyright © 2021 by Board of Trustees, National Gallery of Art, Washington
Requests for permission to reproduce material from this work should be sent to permissions@press.princeton.edu
Published by Princeton University Press, 41 William Street, Princeton, New Jersey 08540
In the United Kingdom: Princeton University Press, 6 Oxford Street, Woodstock, Oxfordshire OX20 1TR
press.princeton.edu

Jacket illustrations: (*front*) Detail of Marriage of Shiva and Uma (Kalyanasundarar), ca. 1012, Art Gallery, Thanjavur; and (*back*) Detail of Uma as Consort of Shiva with Bull, Tiruvenkadu temple, Nagapattinam district, 1012, Art Gallery, Thanjavur.
Frontispiece: child saint Sambandar who sang of Shiva as "The Thief Who Stole My Heart," ca. 1100, Norton Simon Museum, Pasadena
Illustrations in front matter: p. i, detail of fig. 4.16a; p. ii, fig. 7.17a; p. vi, detail of fig. 9.7
Chapter opening illustrations: p. xii, detail of fig. 0.1; p. 8, detail of fig. 1.6; p. 36, detail of fig. 2.9; p. 66, detail of fig. 3.9; p. 88, detail of fig. 4.1a; p. 128, detail of fig. 5.4a; p. 164, detail of fig. 6.5; p. 192, detail of fig. 7.1; p. 220, detail of fig. 8.5a; p. 248, detail of fig. 9.7; p. 266, detail of fig. 4.21

All Rights Reserved
ISBN 978-0-691-20259-4
Library of Congress Control Number: 2020950584

This is the sixty-fifth volume of the A. W. Mellon Lectures in the Fine Arts, which are delivered annually at the National Gallery of Art, Washington, and organized by the Center for Advanced Study in the Visual Arts. This volume is based on lectures delivered in 2016. The volumes of lectures constitute Number XXXV in the Bollingen Series, supported by the Bollingen Foundation.
British Library Cataloging-in-Publication Data is available
Designed by Jo Ellen Ackerman / Bessas & Ackerman
This book has been composed in Vesper Pro and Source Sans Pro
Printed on acid-free paper. ∞
Printed in Italy
10 9 8 7 6 5 4 3 2 1

For Jay

with thanks for his companionship,
insight, encouragement, and humor
on my journey through Chola India

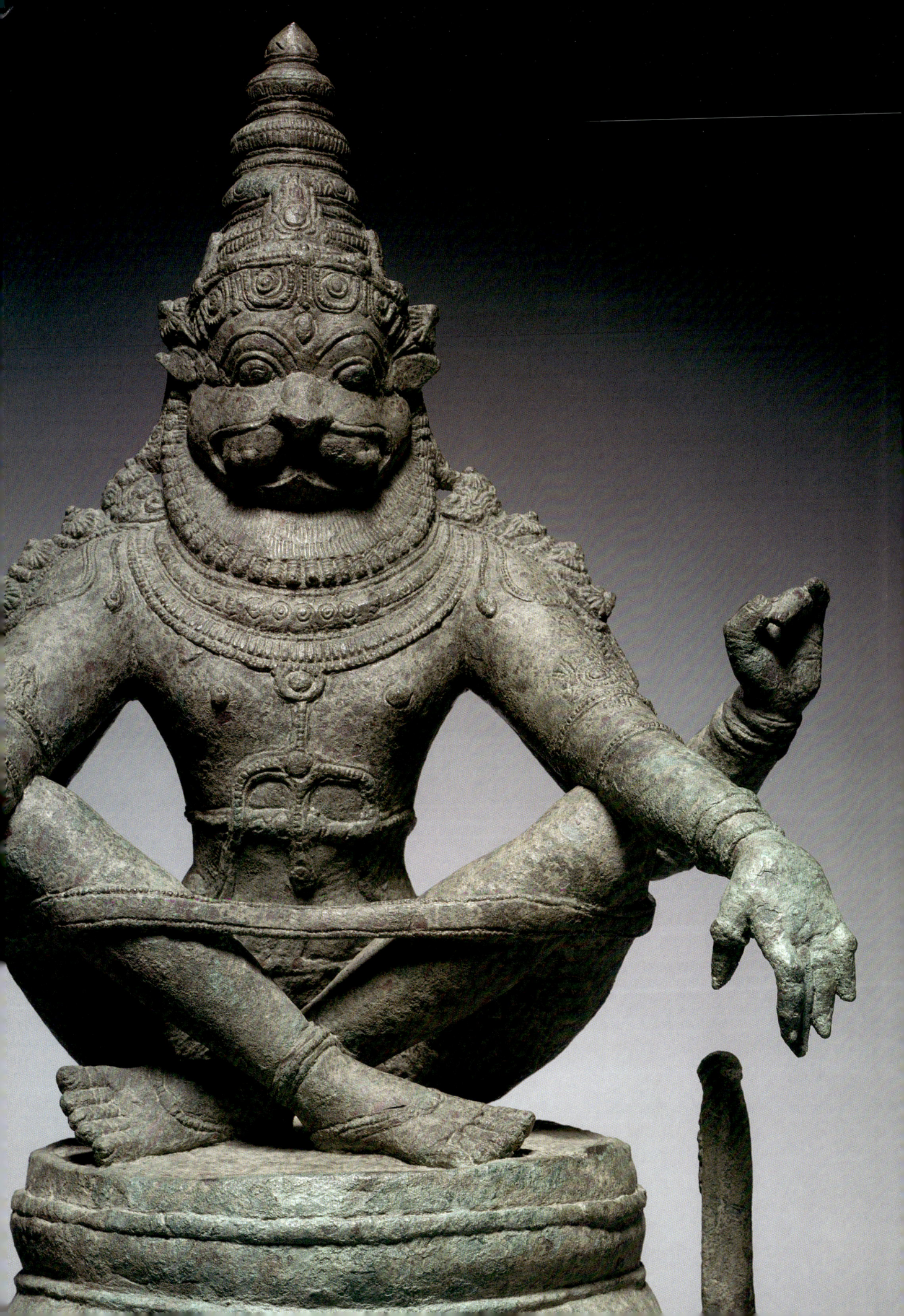

Contents

Acknowledgments viii

Introduction: Chola Bronzes and the Thief Who Stole My Heart 1

1 Gods on Parade: Sacred Forms of Copper 9

2 Battling for Empire and Shiva as Victor of Three Forts: 855–955 37

3 Writ in Stone: Temple Walls as Inscribed Archives 67

4 Portrait of a Queen and Her Patronage of Dancing Shiva: 941–1002 89

5 The Tiruvenkadu Master and Ten Thousand Pearls Adorn a Bronze: Eleventh Century 129

6 Chola Obsession with Sri Lanka and Hindu Bronzes from the Island: Eleventh Century 165

7 The Silk Route of the Ocean and Temple Art in the Days of Rajaraja II: Twelfth Century 193

8 Evolving Manifestations of the Goddess, the God Vishnu, and the Buddha 221

9 Worship in Uncertain Times and the Secret Burial of Bronzes: Thirteenth Century 249

10 Reviewing the Chola Achievement a Millennium Later 267

Appendix A: Main Rulers of the Chola Dynasty: A Tentative Genealogy 272

Appendix B: Assemblages of Sacred Bronzes: Inscriptional Evidence 273

Appendix C: Tenth-Century Chola Yoginis in Context 277

Appendix D: Trace Metal Analysis on Five Chola Bronzes, by Matthew L. Clarke, Nicole C. Little, and Donna K. Strahan 282

Glossary 286

Notes 288

Index 316

Photography and Copyright Credits 322

Acknowledgments

With Chola bronzes widely acknowledged as standing at the very top of South Asia's aesthetic pyramid, it is natural for the reader to assume that Chola temples, sculptures, bronzes, and their historical milieu have been researched in considerable depth, and that a plethora of books and monographs have been published on the subject. The fact that this is not so may come as a surprise to many. Perhaps researchers have been deterred by the enormous scope of the Chola artistic heritage. After all, the Chola period covers some four and a half centuries of amazing artistic creativity, with temples, stone sculptures, bronzes, jewelry, music, dance, and literature produced in a geographically expansive area of south India. One way of conveying the richness of the period is to point out that over one thousand stone temples were built during this period, and that each temple housed on average twelve to fifteen bronzes.[1]

During the 1960s and 1970s, S. R. Balasubrahmanyam recorded the architectural features of the many temples built during the Chola period in four volumes that each contain a brief reference to their stone sculptures, and an occasional mention of their bronzes and their inscriptions.[2] The French Institute of Indology made the decision to focus on comprehensive monographs devoted to three of the four royal temples.[3] More recently, Padma Kaimal has focused on temples built by chieftains during the first hundred years of Chola rule, and has contributed substantially to the dialogue on Dancing Shiva, both in stone and bronze.[4] Chola bronzes per se were studied by four early scholars interested in south India: Douglas Barrett identified many early Chola bronzes in temples (1965); P. R. Srinivasan catalogued the Madras Museum's bronze collection (1963); C. Sivaramamurti wrote a more general book on south Indian bronzes (1963); while R. Nagaswamy has highlighted bronzes still in worship in temples and newly discovered finds.[5] All have displayed an almost exclusive focus on dating Chola bronzes and on their iconographic identification. No contextual study exists of these most admired and highly coveted works of bronze art.

Equally surprising is the fact that the standard history of the Chola dynasty, written in 1938 and revised in 1954 by the doyen of Tamil studies, Nilakantha Sastri, remains the standard work on the subject.[6] Recent scholarship has focused on individual strands within the wider field of historical studies. Noboru Karashima and Y. Subbarayulu, for instance, have studied inscriptions that yield information on revenue assessment, land holding and land transfer, and taxation, producing the first computerized concordance of such terms in Tamil. They have used such inscriptional material to produce a wide-ranging picture of Chola administration at village and town levels.[7] Tansen Sen's facility with the Chinese language and his access to Chinese texts has resulted in his substantial contribution to the field of Indian Ocean studies.[8] Kenneth Hall, George Spencer, C. Champakalakshmi, and Kanakalatha Mukund among others have looked closely at trade contacts and war, while Leslie Orr's focus on epigraphy has enabled her to highlight the role of women as active participants within the temple scenario.[9] Significant work on the sacred context of Chola bronzes comes from Richard Davis,[10] while Indira Peterson, David Shulman, and Vasudha Narayanan are among those who have translated the hymns of the Tamil saints,[11] thereby greatly expanding our appreciation of the ancient sacred milieu. I am especially indebted to Indira Peterson, who graciously permitted me to use several of her translations, and who went out of her way to produce, for this work, the very first English translation of Gandaraditya's hymn on Shiva dancing at Tillai or Chidambaram, as well as a verse from Sambandar's poem on Tirukonamalai (Trincomalee) in Sri Lanka.

I am deeply grateful to the National Gallery of Art and to its Center for Advanced Study in the Visual Arts (CASVA) for having provided me with the opportunity to delve more deeply into the subject of Chola bronzes in order to present the 65th A. W. Mellon Lectures in the Fine Arts. My work relating in one way or another to Chola material has early beginnings. Forty years ago, I began a study of the Tamil saints, the sixty-three *nayanmar* of god Shiva and the twelve *alvars* of god Vishnu, when I realized that every single Chola temple, and those of later date, housed images of these saints. While these were most often of bronze, I discovered that large temples frequently housed a second set of saints' images in stone, while even small temples with restricted funding had images of the saints painted on their walls. My study began at a time prior to the publication of translations of the saints' hymns by the scholars just mentioned. Encouraged by A. K. Ramanujan, my mentor for a brief time before he died, I immersed myself in the hymns of the saints written in "middle" Tamil, translating many poems largely in order to understand the iconography of the saints and to appreciate the important role they played in the temple ritual cycle. *Slaves of the Lord: The Path of the Tamil Saints* (1988)[12] was followed up, at the encouragement of A. K. Ramanujan, with my translation of the poems of a Vishnu woman saint as *Āṇṭāḷ and Her Path of Love: Poems of a Woman Saint from South India* (1990).[13] To present the Polsky Lectures at the Asia Society in New York in 1987, I turned to Chola sculpture in stone and bronze, and to Chola temple architecture, combining these with the material available from existing translations of Chola inscriptions to present a more rounded picture of the period.[14] Eight years as a museum professional at the Freer and Sackler Galleries of the Smithsonian Institution in Washington, DC, induced me to organize a major loan exhibition of Chola bronzes for the Sackler Gallery, titled *The Sensuous and the Sacred* (2002);[15] this was followed up a few years later with an exhibition for the Royal Academy in London, succinctly titled *Chola* (2006).[16] The A. W. Mellon Lectures have provided me with the exceptional opportunity to unearth new material and to present a myriad of details on the unique societal role that Chola bronzes played during the four and a half centuries of Chola rule, a pivotal role that they continue to hold in Tamil society to this day.

I owe a debt of gratitude to all the scholars mentioned earlier who provided a solid grounding for the field of Chola studies, and to several other noteworthy researchers who are acknowledged specifically in the notes of the various chapters that follow. Here, I would like to acknowledge my deep indebtedness to epigraphy scholar Marxia Gandhi, who has been my partner in the venture of unearthing and reading unpublished Chola inscriptions. We traveled together to several temples, spending days correlating published inscriptions with those inscribed on the temple walls, and finding, as so often happens, several errors and inexplicable variations. We made trips to the offices of the Epigraphical Survey in Mysuru, where we read inscriptions, sometimes from the original rubbings that were taken from temple walls as many as a hundred years ago. Her willing partnership and her scholarly generosity made this voyage of discovery truly enjoyable.

In Sri Lanka, I owe a deep debt of gratitude to Jagath Weerasinghe, who generously took me under his wing, vouchsafing for me with the director of the Colombo National Museum, the director general of the Department of Archaeology, and the director general of the Central Cultural Fund, and thus enabling my successful visits to the sites and museums at Polonnaruwa and Anuradhapura, and to the Colombo National Museum. I am grateful too for their permission to use photographs of images in their museums in this publication. Dr. Weerasinghe introduced me to Dr. Arjuna Thantilage, who had recently completed his dissertation on an archaeo-metallurgical study of a select group of Sri Lankan bronzes, Buddhist and Hindu.[17] It was Dr. Thantilage's generosity in sharing his dissertation with me that allowed me to explore the possibility of Sri Lankan copper having been the source for Chola bronzes. Dr. Thantilage, Dr. Sudarshan Seneviratne, and Dr. Jagath Weerasinghe have evidence that Sri Lankan copper from the Seruwila belt was worked on an industrial scale and was definitely exported in an early period. Their research has made it possible to begin assessing the possibility that nearby Seruwila might have constituted a major source for the large amounts of copper involved in a changeover from wooden processional images to those made of copper-bronze under the Cholas. To these scholars I am deeply grateful. My thanks go also to Dr. Donna Strahan, director of the Smithsonian's Freer Gallery of Art in-house laboratory, for her willingness to pursue an inductively coupled plasma (ICP) test on select samples of five Chola bronzes, one from the Asia Society in New York, one from the Norton Simon Museum in Pasadena, and three from the Freer Gallery of Art. I had not anticipated the difficulties in conducting such a test in a laboratory in the United States with Seruwila copper having been tested in a facility in Sri Lanka, nor had I realized the crucial importance of using the identical scale of variables. Seruwila as the source of copper for Chola bronzes is a very strong possibility for reasons explored in chapters 1 and 6; yet it must remain a hypothesis until cooperation on an international scale enables testing of both Seruwila ore and Chola image samples in the very same lab.

My sincere thanks go to the Department of Hindu Religious and Charitable Endowments (HR&CE) of the Tamil Nadu State Department for its cooperation, especially in view of the fact that I was working in Tamil Nadu at an awkward time when major smuggling scandals dominated the scene, causing authorities to view with suspicion anyone who wished to study temple bronzes. Photography in the temples and museums of Tamil Nadu was made possible through the courtesy of individual temples and museums, and the HR&CE. For help in securing permission to publish images of bronzes from temples and museums in India, I must mention the generous help I received in Chennai from Sriram Panchu, and from N. Ram of *The Hindu* and his wife, Sudha, and also from Delhi-based Jyoti Sagar and his Chennai colleague Aarthi Sivanandh.

I owe a debt of gratitude to my *athimber*, M. S. Swaminathan, the renowned "green revolution" savant, who put me in touch with the Rice Research Institute at Aduturai; there, Dr. Rajendran and Mrs. Saraswati took me in hand, introduced me to a range of Public Works Department offices that handled irrigation at various points, and initiated me into the details of rice cultivation. It would have been difficult to appreciate the importance of irrigation canals set up in Chola times without this first-hand exposure in the field. I am grateful to the Ratnasabhapati Bronze Workshop in Swamimalai, whose owners and staff showed me details of wax working and bronze casting, answering with great patience my many questions on the subject. My deep gratitude goes too to the many museums in the United States and Europe, and to individual private collectors, for their permission to study and photograph their Chola bronzes. I would like to mention several scholars for their personal interest and their input, including Milo Beach, Frederick Asher, Bob Brown, Padma Kaimal, Leslie Orr, Tamara Sears, and Subhashini Kaligotla, and I am immensely grateful for the valuable suggestions from the readers of my manuscript. I am indebted to Lydia Tugendrajch, friend and art enthusiast, for her constant insistence on readability, and to Arathi Menon for help with the nitty-gritty of my project.

At the Center for Advanced Study in the Visual Arts, I must mention in particular Dean Elizabeth Cropper and Associate Dean Therese O'Malley for their valuable input into the lectures themselves, and to Cynthia Ware and Emiko Usui for their involvement with the manuscript. My thanks go to Mary Reilly for her deft handling of the maps, and my sincere appreciation to various members of Princeton University Press.

The mandate of the annual A. W. Mellon Lectures in the Fine Arts is to address an interested but nonspecialist audience, and this book addresses that same audience while, hopefully, providing new avenues and new ideas that my peers within the field of South Asian art may feel inclined to follow up. In keeping with that aim, I have avoided the use of diacritical marks, using, instead, a system of spelling that I believe will enable readers to pronounce names of towns, temples, and patrons as closely to the sound of the original as possible. In the single instance of my translation of the Tamil poems of woman saint Andal, at the insistence of a publishing house, I have used the Tamil lexicon system; I find, however, that only practiced users of the Tamil lexicon system are able to read such words correctly. An example is the name of child saint Sambandar, which I trust will be read and pronounced by most readers phonetically as "some-bun-dur"; the Tamil lexicon system demands that it be written in English as Campantar, a form that only scholars of Tamil will read and pronounce correctly. With Sanskrit letters and especially with "s," I have avoided diacritical marks and used "sh" instead, thus avoiding the accent above "S" in Siva (Shiva) and the dot below the "s" in Visnu (Vishnu). I understand that this may be a controversial decision, but I do it in the interests of making the book more accessible to a wider audience.

A final word about the visuals. There are more Chola bronzes in temples than in museum collections, and photography in temples is difficult, restricted, and often prohibited. Few museums in India have a visual archive of their own from which one can order images, and generally they do not permit scholars to use tripods or special lighting, or grant permission to open glass cases for photography. If you appreciate the images of bronzes in the Thanjavur Art Gallery, the credit goes to Mr. Sanjeev Trivedi, a close friend and an accomplished photographer who took the photographs on my behalf. I trust readers will be forgiving generally of the visual quality of a small sample of crucial images that I have chosen to include in this book because of their intrinsic significance.

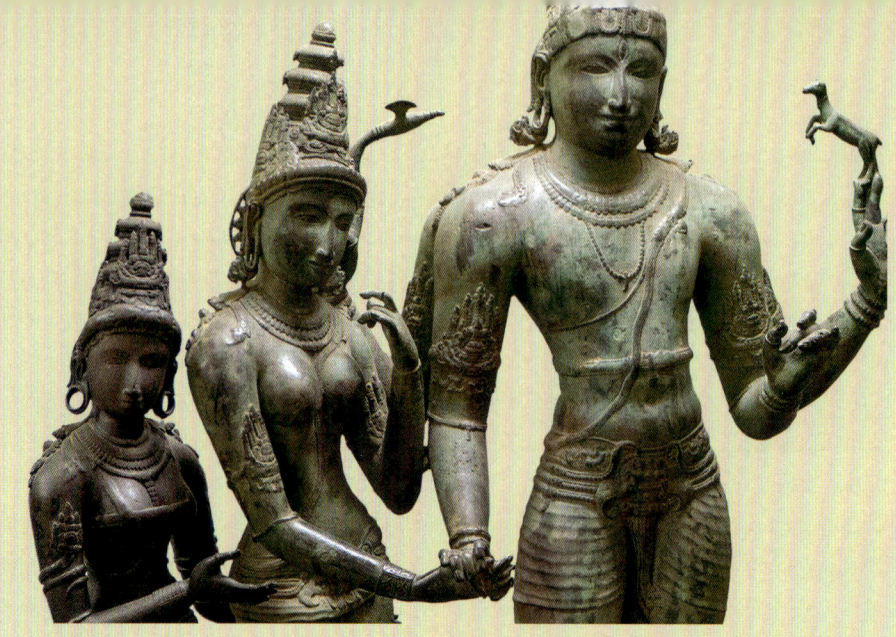

Introduction
Chola Bronzes and the Thief Who Stole My Heart

He wears a woman's earring on one ear;
riding on his bull,
crowned with the pure white crescent moon,
his body smeared with ashes from the burning-ground,
He is the thief who stole my heart.
SAMBANDAR, HYMN 1, VERSE 1[1]

An unnamed Master, equal in stature to Donatello of early Renaissance Florence, created the original wax model for this impressive four-piece bronze group (fig. 0.1a). His work captured my imagination, lured me into finding out more about him, and as you will see in chapter 5, has not yet released me. Living in Chola-ruled south India, this Master was attached to a foundry where he oversaw the translation of his original wax model into the finished bronzes, of solid metal, that you see here. The centerpiece of the group represents the supreme god Shiva taking the hand of his bride Uma in marriage. To the right is god Vishnu, the other major god of the Tamil-speaking region of south India, who in south India alone is regarded as Uma's brother, while Vishnu's consort, goddess Lakshmi, is portrayed here in the role of the bride's friend and confidante. The Master has captured a fleeting tender moment, giving us a confident and eager bridegroom with a shy and hesitant bride. This poised bridegroom is none other than the paradoxical Hindu god Shiva, ascetic of ascetics, whose normal garb is tiger skin, serpents, and skulls, while the crescent moon adorns his hair arranged in dreadlocks. Myth speaks of him being interrupted from intense yogic meditation, and opening his eyes only to fall in love with Uma.

In this bronze composition, four-armed Shiva stands relaxed as the handsome bridegroom, with a diadem holding back his matted locks piled high on his head in an elegant arrangement. He wears pendant earrings shaped like the mythical aquatic *makara*, a series of necklaces, a brahmanical sacred thread that diagonally crosses his chest, and a high waistband above his short, tight dhoti; large armlets, an elbow band, bracelets, anklets, and rings on eight toes and fingers further adorn him. With his front right hand, he reaches out confidently and takes his bride's right hand in marriage. Note the way in which the master artist has positioned a very young, timid Uma to stand hesitantly, a few steps behind the powerful bridegroom, with her shoulders curving inward just a trifle as if to shield her vulnerable body. Notice too how well the master artist has captured the hidden understanding of a sensitive moment by the bride's confidante, who uses both hands to gently urge the innocent and exceedingly bashful bride to move toward Shiva (fig. 0.1b). How extraordinary that he should have bothered to capture this delicate moment, this sensitive communication that is all but invisible in full frontal view! None but us fortunate few who can see the image from this angle a millennium after it was created may appreciate the empathy displayed by the sculptor in his perceptive portrayal. In the Western world, we speak of God having made man in his own image; in the Tamil-speaking region of south India we may speak, without the slightest suggestion of disrespect, of artists and poets making the gods in their own image.

The bronzes are evocative, sensitive, and exceedingly sensuous in their portrayal of a smooth idealized body that has none of the emphasis on muscularity that we see in sculptures of the Greek and Roman classical period or in those of Renaissance Europe. Chola bronzes signal a direct and appealing path to the divine through an appreciation of the beauty of the body of god, and propose a rapturous engagement with that beauty that is intended to capture your heart and soul. The poet-saints of south India, whom we will encounter frequently in the chapters that follow, presented that beauty to their devotees in ecstatic verses that describe the glory of god's body. They address Shiva in

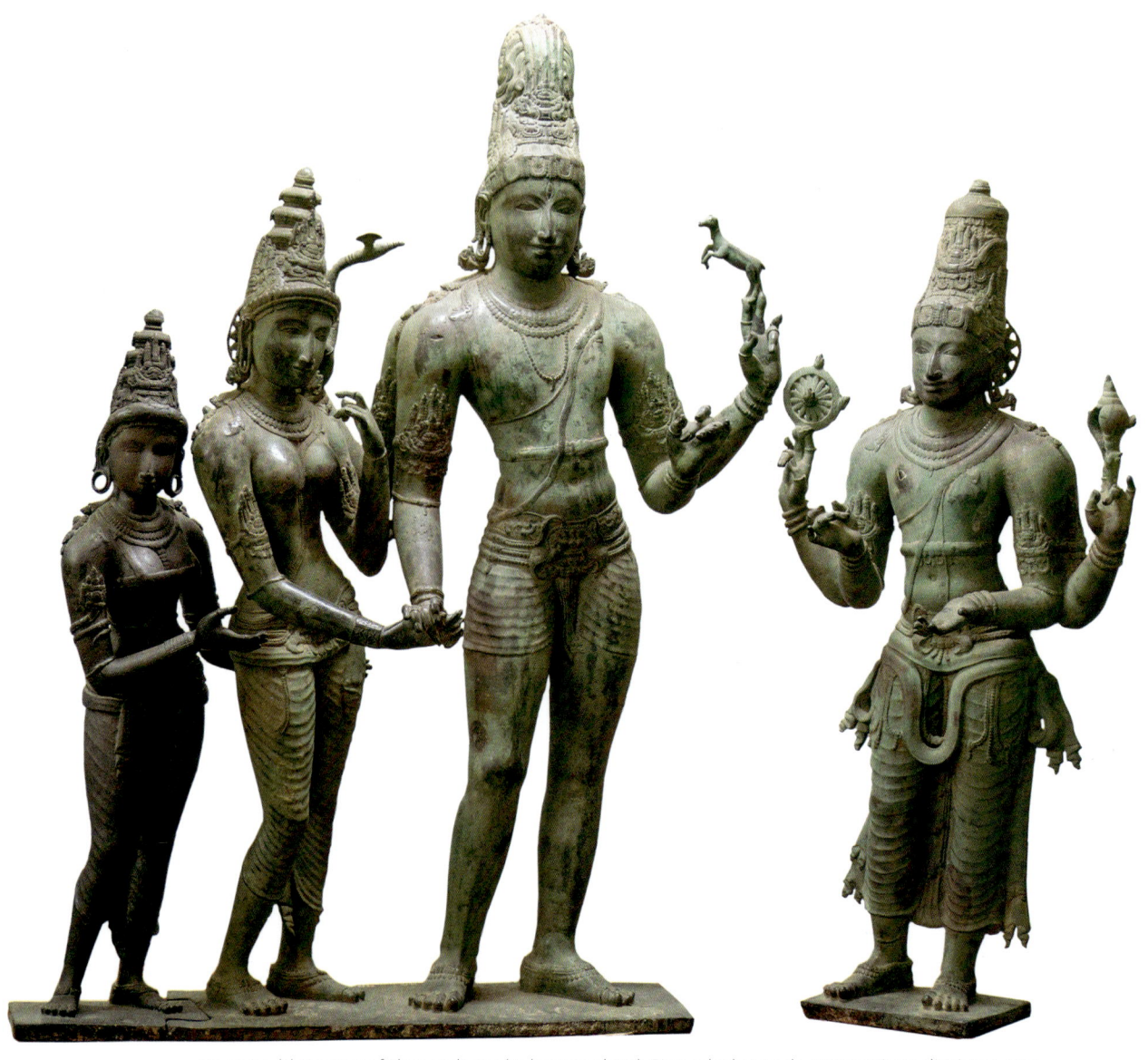

Figure 0.1. (a) Marriage of Shiva and Uma (*Kalyanasundarar*), Tiruvenkadu temple, Nagapattinam district ca. 1012, Art Gallery, Thanjavur. (b) Rear view of Marriage of Shiva and Uma (*Kalyanasundarar*) (fig. 0.1a), detail.

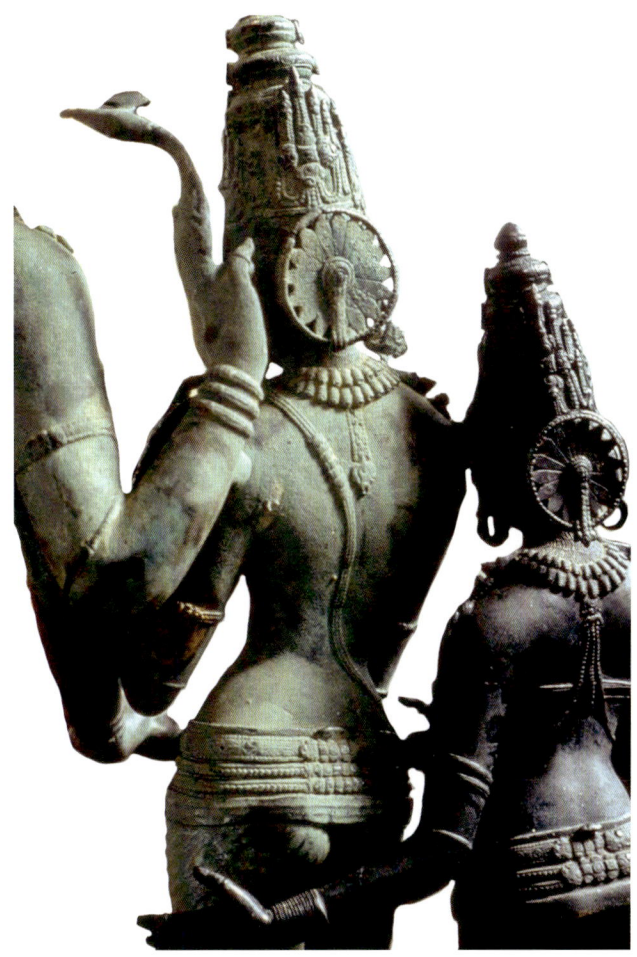

their hymns as "god with the golden form" and "you who take for your color the sunset's brilliant hue." He is

> "My pearl, my precious gem,
> glittering branch of coral, bright flame."²

Saint Appar applauds the radiance of Shiva:

> "Youth who shines as a ruby,
> as a cluster of emeralds!
> Being who enters my heart,
> stirring memory!"³

Equally mesmerizing are phrases describing Shiva's consort Uma. "She moves in beauty like the swan," "her flawless gait mocks the peacock's grace," she has "feet soft as cotton down," a "waist small like gathered lightning," breasts "fresh as new-born lotus buds."⁴

Artists creating bronzes during the Chola period translated this poetic ecstasy into the exquisite images that we will examine throughout this book. In the context of Indian devotional worship, the sacred and the sensuous are to be viewed as a continuum, and not as two concepts that are divorced from one another. Sheer physical perfection of form was viewed as a reflection of spiritual beauty and inseparable from transcendence and divine supremacy. A well-formed and attractive body was both a sign and a result of moral perfection.[5] In the context of the religions born in India, whether Hindu, Buddhist, or Jain, spiritual beauty and bodily splendor went hand in hand.

In this book, we will indeed acknowledge and delight in the sheer physical beauty of Chola bronzes, created to evoke the verbal picture conjured up by child saint Sambandar, who called Shiva "the thief who stole my heart" in the first verse of his first hymn that opens the entire Tamil "canon." We will move, however, beyond the sensuous to ask questions of this material that have not been asked before. I propose to treat the bronzes not merely as exquisite masterpieces created by talented wax modelers and accomplished metal casters but also as material objects that interacted in meaningful ways with human activities, and with socioeconomic and religious practices. Chola bronzes are sacred images commissioned by temples for festival worship; curiously, few scholars have shown any interest in ascertaining the number of bronzes that were created for such rituals during the Chola period, or to establish the number of temples built to house these images. T. V. Mahalingam's set of volumes of inscriptions, arranged district-wise within Chola territory, and then town-wise within each *taluka* subdivision of a district, provides us with the raw material to enable such a count.[6] For instance, a total of 311 temples were built in the three districts of Tiruchirappalli (henceforth, Trichy), Thanjavur, and Nagapattinam that form the heart of Chola territory along the lower reaches of the Kaveri river.[7] On average, each temple would have housed twelve or so bronzes to fulfill its ritual cycle, resulting in a total of around 3,700 sacred bronzes in just the three districts that will be our focus. What were the circumstances that permitted the creation of so many temples and such large numbers of exquisite bronzes in spite of the constant warfare that the Chola monarchs undertook to retain and expand their empire? Inscriptions indicate the prime position held in Chola times by rice paddy; rice was the measure by which wages were paid to temple employees, and rice was the measure by which goods were bought in the town markets. What made possible the rich agricultural wealth that enabled donors to commission large numbers of bronze images and to further adorn them with lavish jewelry? What was the source of the precious and semiprecious materials used to create the lavish gold jewelry, embedded with pearls and coral, rubies and diamonds, that was gifted to adorn every temple's sacred bronzes? Could the quest for pearls have instigated Chola wars with their southern neighbors, the Pandya kings of Madurai, and with the rulers of island Sri Lanka? In the context of Chola financing of temples and their bronzes, it is also important to note that south India, and Sri Lanka, are located halfway along the lucrative ocean trade route from Aden to China. The ports along the Chola coastline, and those in Sri Lanka, collected valuable taxes, levies, and customs duties from the merchant ships that docked at their ports, thereby enhancing the wealth of their treasury.[8] To what extent was female patronage a force to be reckoned with, not just of the wealthy elite and of early Chola queens, but also of the *anukki* or "intimate" of more than one Chola king?

Another major issue relates to the source of copper used to create Chola bronzes that laboratory testing affirms to be anywhere from 90 to 98 percent copper.[9] A fact that we have all ignored thus far is that there is no copper at all that may be profitably mined in the granitic region of Chola territory, the state known today as Tamil Nadu. My quick calculations reveal that temples in just the heart of Chola territory, in the same three districts of Trichy, Thanjavur, and Nagapattinam mentioned earlier, would, on the basis of twelve sacred bronzes per temple, require 153 tons of copper for their sacred images.[10] Where did the bronze casters and their patrons suddenly procure the large quantities of copper required to create their sacred images? Why do so many Chola bronzes display the green patina that forms when copper is subjected to high humidity, while others have a darkened hue?

Food offerings made to the sacred bronzes are an unexplored aspect that has been bypassed thus far but opens up an entire area within the field of sensory studies.[11] Temple inscriptions frequently list the exact quantities of the various ingredients required for daily food offerings, and specify the additional delicacies needed for important festivals, giving us a fascinating picture of the nature of contemporary taste. The fact that food offerings are referred to by the term *tiru amudu*, or "sacred nectar," is relevant, and equally important is the fact that these same inscriptions often specify that once the food has been ritually offered to the bronzes, it should be distributed to temple employees and devotees. Accompanying such ritual worship of the bronzes were the sacred hymns chanted by specialized hymn-singers to the accompaniment of an array of musical instruments that included the reverberation of the blown conch shell and the pounding beat of drums, all of which worked together to create a pulsating surround-sound vibration that aroused an emotional response from temple devotees.[12] We will touch on some of these areas of inquiry as we embark on a journey of discovery through four centuries of Chola art and culture. While I will not be able to do justice to all the issues I am raising about the sacred bronzes created during Chola rule, my intent is to open up the field and encourage further productive exploration.

No complete inventory of Chola inscriptions exists, although a digitization project, limited to records relating to Buddhism, was initiated some years back.[13] A prime resource for Chola epigraphs remains T. V. Mahalingam's eight volumes of inscriptions that contain a tantalizingly brief English summary of each record.[14] Using his volumes as a basis, and looking only at areas and periods controlled by the Cholas, we find no fewer than 1,083 temple sites; in actuality, the number of temples is greater, since the entries under some towns list records in both a Shiva and a Vishnu temple. Adding up the inscriptions listed in these volumes, we come up with somewhere between eleven thousand and twelve thousand inscriptions, written largely in the Tamil script and language. Like a richly textured yet clinging mantle, these inscribed records cover the stone walls of the several hundred temples that dot the deltaic plains of the Kaveri river, running seamlessly across the light projections and recesses of temple walls. Only the inscriptions on Rajaraja Chola's Great Temple at Thanjavur have been published fully in English translation, while the greater number of the remaining records are available only in the form of a brief English synopsis, mostly in T. V. Mahalingam's volumes. Thanks to the impetus provided by the invitation to deliver the Mellon lectures, I have been able to delve into carefully selected examples of such material, located in the offices of the Epigraphical Survey of India in Mysuru either as rubbings from the temple walls or as hand-written copies of such rubbings. A careful scrutiny of these Tamil inscriptions enabled me to unearth valuable information that animates and informs my present study. What I have uncovered is just the proverbial tip of the iceberg. With the majority of inscriptions on Chola temples untranslated, and over half unpublished, this trove of documents presents a largely neglected corpus for future research. The most frustrating issue for an art historian writing after three decades in the field is that this inscriptional material is in full view and plain sight for anyone walking around a Chola temple. The nature of such documentation is quite amazing. For instance, at the Neyttanam temple along the Kaveri river, some 7 miles north of the Chola capital of Thanjavur, an inscription cut into the south wall of the main *mandapa* tells us exactly where to look to find detailed instructions regarding the performance of a particular festival.[15] It specifies that these stipulations are inscribed along certain precise sections of base molding, and along specific areas beneath the temple eaves; the inscription serves almost as a footnote system, or perhaps one might better describe it as a card catalogue and a library all in one. While this rich archive of inscriptions plays an important role in this book, there is much to be done before we reach the point where the inscriptions truly illuminate our understanding of Chola art.

Thus, my prime source material for this study are the Chola bronze images themselves, which I have examined in person over the years, using photographs for later comparative study to reinforce conclusions regarding their creation. Today, after having been eclipsed for some years, the self-evident centrality of the art object is back in play, and connoisseurship is acknowledged as an essential tool that no art historian can afford to ignore.[16] Art historians must and do pay attention to fine visual distinctions, to rhythm, to the recurrence of stylistic details, to regularity or lack of regularity of motifs, to a distinctive way of depicting, say, drapery folds, or a lion-head clasp on a jeweled belt. The defining words on connoisseurship are still those of nineteenth-century scholar Giovanni Morelli: "As most men who speak or write have verbal habits and use their favorite words and phrases involuntarily and sometimes even inappropriately, so almost any painter [substitute sculptor] has his own peculiarities which escape from him without him being aware of them."[17] The intuitive judgment that is part of connoisseurship is not some nonrational process; as Sydney Freedberg wrote while explaining critic Bernard Berenson's procedure, such intuition is merely the process by which a connoisseur enters data into her mental bank of remembered comparables, analyzes it, and arrives at a solution.[18] More recently, David Freedberg, with his interest in the relationship between art and neurosciences, speaks of "thin-slicing" as the new term for that "critical part of rapid cognition . . . whereby you instantly select out a particularly indicative detail as characteristic."[19] The interdisciplinary nature of connoisseurship is today a recognized reality, as is the fact that a vital layer of solid archival material underlies good connoisseurship. The quintessential part of the process remains close looking over an extended period of time. It is only close looking, such as my collaborator and I engaged in during our years of fieldwork on *The Unfinished: Indian Stone Carvers at Work*, that enabled us, for instance, to recognize the hand of a specific "Animal Master" at the Pallava site of Mamallapuram.[20]

Before we turn our focus to Chola bronzes, let us take a quick look at what was happening in the rest of the world when these sacred bronzes were created in south India. In 850, as the Cholas came into power, the Abbasids of Baghdad controlled Central Asia, North Africa, and Spain, while the Tang dynasty ruled China; Europe, by contrast, was at a low point in its cultural history. By 985, when Chola ruler Rajaraja ascended the throne, the Fatimids of Egypt had replaced the Abbasids, and the Sung dynasty was in power in China. When Rajaraja completed his great temple, 210 feet high, at the capital of Thanjavur in the year 1010, the Romanesque churches of Europe were not yet built; work on the Cathedral at Pisa, for instance, would start in another fifty years, and continue for almost three centuries. As Chola power came to an end in the thirteenth century, the Gothic cathedral in Europe was reaching perfection with the completion of Notre Dame in Paris. The period of 425 years that intervened between the start of the Chola dynasty in 855 and its demise in the year 1280 was truly a momentous one for global art and architecture. So onward to south India and the Kaveri river.

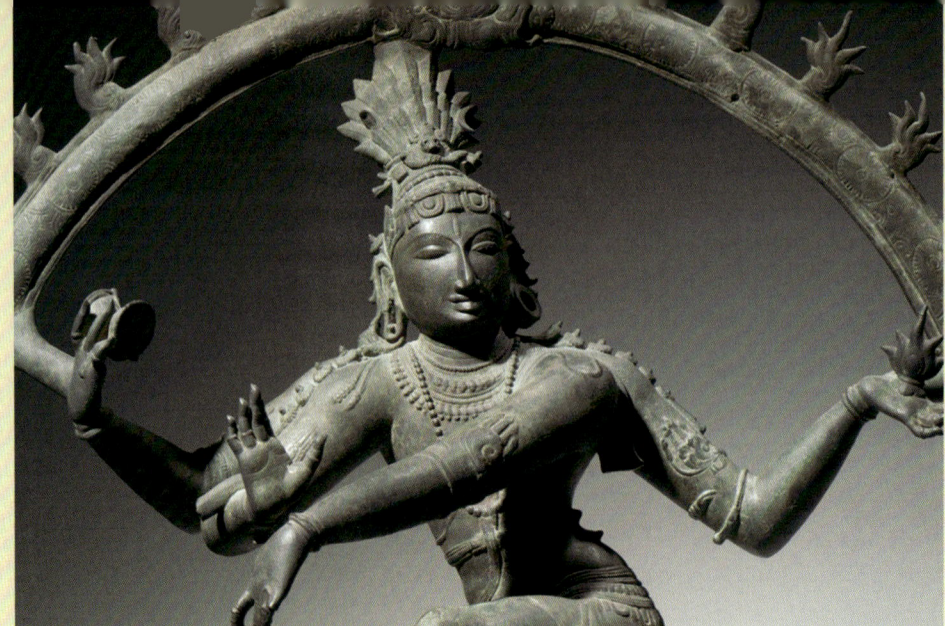

Gods on Parade
Sacred Forms of Copper

1

Vijayalaya Chola
He, the light of the solar race, took possession of Tanchapuri (Thanjavur) which was picturesque to the sight, as beautiful as Alaka (god Kubera's town), whose high turrets had reached the sky, and the whitewash of whose mansions appeared like the scented cosmetic applied to the body—just as he would grasp by the hand his own wife who has beautiful eyes, graceful curls, a cloth covering her body, and sandal paste as white as lime, in order to sport with her.
THE TIRUVALANKADU COPPER-PLATES, YEAR 1018[1]

Aditya Chola
Rajakesari by whom the row of large temples of Shiva, as it were banners of his own victory, lofty and unacquainted with defeat, were built of stone on the two banks of the Kaveri from the Sahya mountain, inhabited by the lordly elephants . . . even to the ocean which has the moon playing on the folds of its big restless waves.
ANBIL COPPER-PLATES OF SUNDARA CHOLA, YEAR 960[2]

In the mid-ninth century in the Tamil-speaking region of south India, an upstart with an ego and sound military strategy took a city by storm—the city of Thanjavur. His name was Vijayalaya Chola, and we know nothing of his antecedents except that he had the audacity to take the name Chola, which belonged to a renowned dynasty that had faded from the scene some centuries earlier. By around 1030, Vijayalaya's successors expanded their area of influence from the immediate vicinity of the town of Thanjavur to encompass all of south India, the Maldive Islands, and much of Sri Lanka (map 2). They also made naval forays across the Bay of Bengal to the island of Sumatra and the Malaysian peninsula that were under the control of the Srivijaya dynasty. Chola royalty proved themselves to be politically shrewd and ambitious; their kings and queens were refined and cultured, and deeply invested in the religious ethos of Hinduism, especially in the devout worship of god Shiva. They encouraged the building of temples and sponsored some of the most inspired images of their deities in the medium of bronze. There is nothing quite like these sacred bronzes anywhere else in India; there is no parallel tradition of bronze processional images in northern, western, or eastern India.

During the first century and a half of Chola rule, their heartland was territory along the sacred river Kaveri in the low-lying, Tamil-speaking country of south India. This is rich agricultural land of rice fields interspersed with coconut groves, banana plantations, and sugar cane fields, an area where the very idea of a forest or of barren land is unknown. Villages and towns dot the region, being separated one from the other by no more than 2 or 3 miles, and each village and town had its own temple that was the focus of religious, social, economic, and political activities. It is this area known as Chola-mandalam, comprising the districts of Trichy, Thanjavur, and Nagapattinam, lying largely south of the Kaveri river, that is the focus of this book.

Dozens of stone temples of graceful proportions and moderate size were built in the delta of the Kaveri river during the first century of the Chola presence. Each consists of a small square sanctum housing a stone image of the deity, topped with a modest tower that rises on average to a height of 30 feet. Directly in front of the sanctum is an attached half-hall (*ardha-mandapa*) that connects with a larger rectangular flat-roofed hall (*mandapa*) to accommodate devotees (fig. 1.1). The exterior walls of the sanctum as well as of the *ardha-mandapa* and *mandapa* carry finely crafted stone images of gods and devotees carved on separate slabs of stone that are inserted into niches in the stone walls. What is quite extraordinary and quintessentially Chola is the manner in which all available space on these walls is covered with inscriptions pertaining to the temple and written in the Tamil language and script (fig. 1.2). Neither their predecessors, the Pallavas, nor their successors, the Vijayanagara emperors, placed such a plethora of inscriptions on their temple walls. The largest number of these epigraphs speak of gifts to the temple—of lamps; of cows, sheep, or lands to provide ghee to burn in these lamps; of sacred bronzes; and of jewelry to adorn these bronzes. But they also record a range of other information pertaining to the temple in a most general and wide-ranging way, such as the remission of taxes on gifted land, the repair of canals and sluices on temple lands, the construction of roads to facilitate temple festivals, and even details on thefts of temple jewels together with the judgment passed on the offenders.

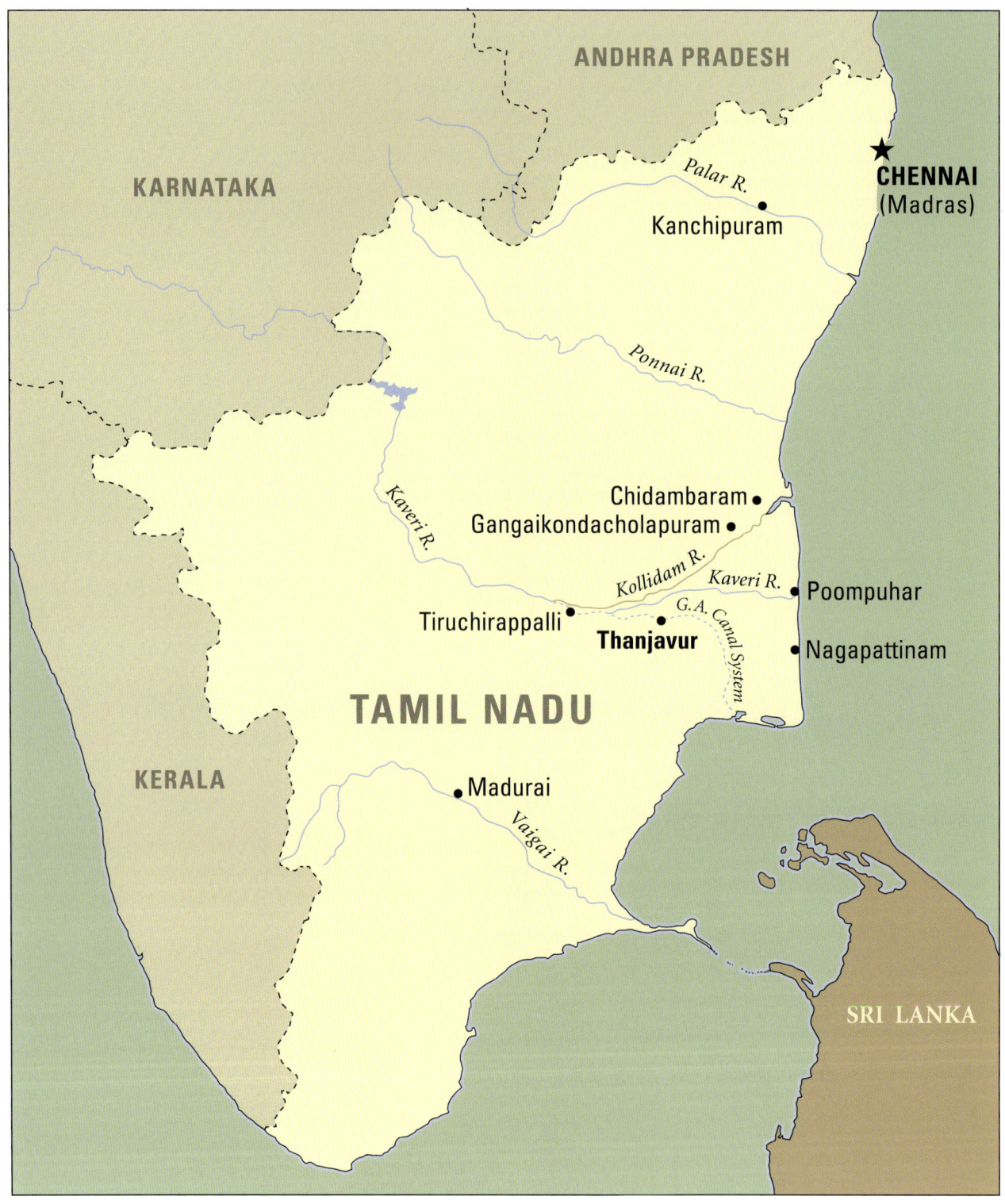

Map 1a. State of Tamil Nadu with its modern capital of Chennai (previously Madras) and the Chola capital of Thanjavur in the Kaveri river basin.

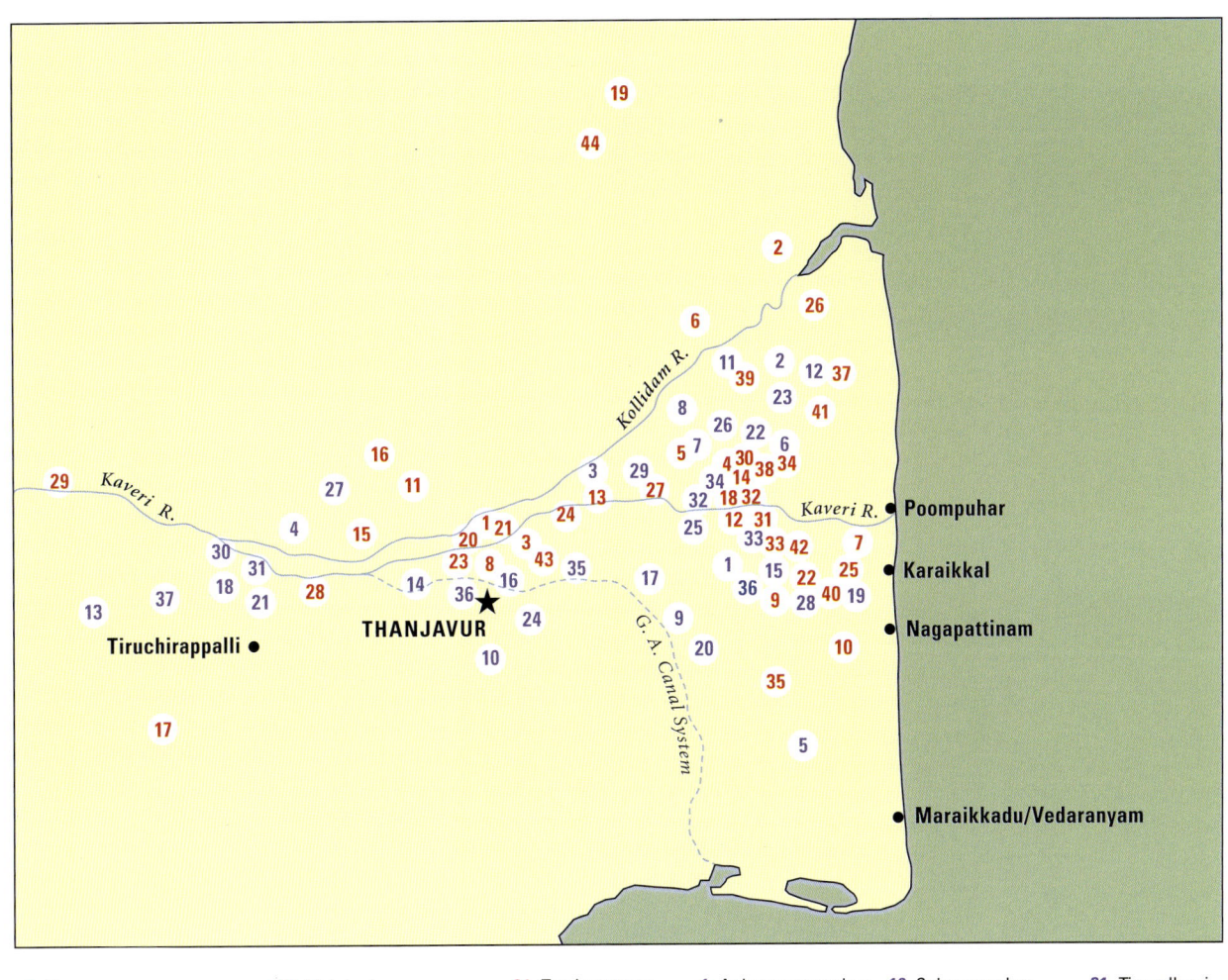

1. Aiyaru	**16.** Melaipalavur	**31.** Tandantottam	**1.** Achyutamangalam	**16.** Sulamangalam	**31.** Tiruvellarai
2. Chidambaram	**17.** Muvar Koil, Kodumbalur	**32.** Tribhuvanam	**2.** Avalivanallur	**17.** Tiruchattrimurram	**32.** Tiruvelvikudi
3. Chottruturai	**18.** Nallur	**33.** Tirucherai	**3.** Kalitattai	**18.** Tiruchendurai	**33.** Tiruvidavayil
4. Darasuram	**19.** Navalur	**34.** Tiruvaduturai	**4.** Kannanur	**19.** Tiruchengatankudi	**34.** Tiruvisalur
5. Esalam	**20.** Neyttanam	**35.** Tiruvaymur	**5.** Korukkai	**20.** Tirukkalar	**35.** Udaiyalur
6. Gangaikondacholapuram	**21.** Palanam	**36.** Tiruvarur	**6.** Kottur	**21.** Tirukkarkuti	**36.** Ukkachi
7. Kadaiyur	**22.** Paruthiyur	**37.** Tiruvenkadu	**7.** Kovilvenni	**22.** Tirukodikaval	**37.** Vayalur
8. Kandiyur	**23.** Poonturutti	**38.** Tiruvidaimaradur	**8.** Manambadi	**23.** Tirumananjeri	
9. Karaiyaviram	**24.** Pullamangai	**39.** Tiruvindalur	**9.** Mannargudi	**24.** Tirumandurai	
10. Keelaiyur	**25.** Sembiyan Mahadevi	**40.** Vadakkalathur	**10.** Niyamam	**25.** Tirupamburam	
11. Kilaipalavur	**26.** Sirkali	**41.** Valampuram	**11.** Pandanallur	**26.** Tirupanandal	
12. Konerirajapuram	**27.** Shivapuram	**42.** Valuvur	**12.** Punjai	**27.** Tirupattur	
13. Korangaduturai [Aduturai]	**28.** Solagampatti	**43.** Vedikudi	**13.** Ratnagiri	**28.** Tirupugalur	
14. Kumbakonam	**29.** Srinivasanallur	**44.** Vriddhachalam	**14.** Sendalai	**29.** Tiruvalanjuli	
15. Lalgudi	**30.** Swamimalai		**15.** Senganur	**30.** Tiruvannaika	

Map 1b. Detail of Kaveri river basin with schematic listing of temples featured in this book. Red numbers indicate temples of significance for bronzes, architecture, and sculpture, while blue numbers indicate temples cited primarily for their inscriptions.

GODS ON PARADE   11

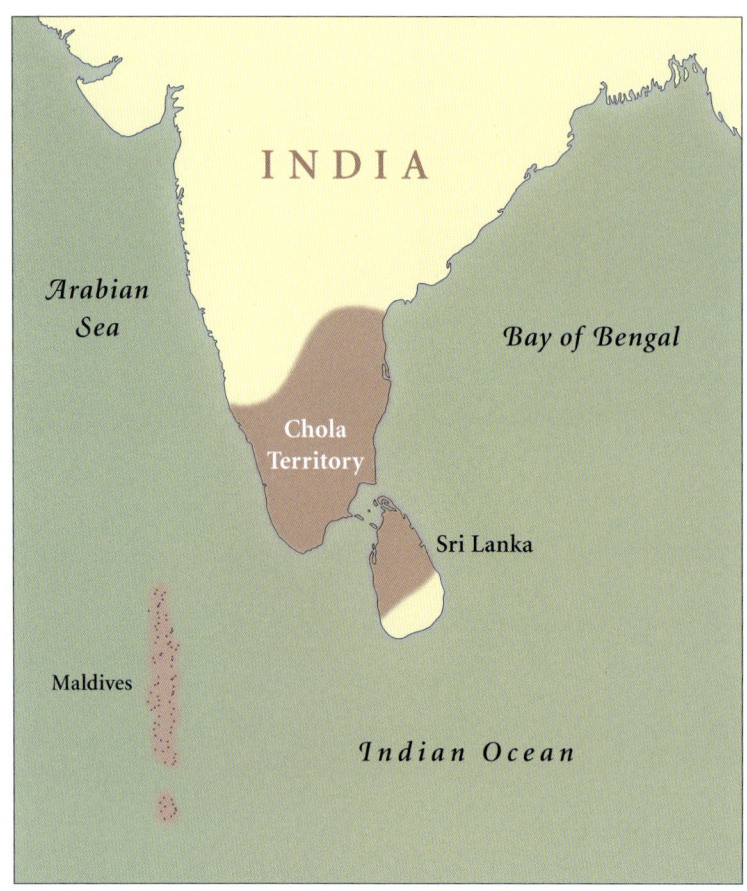

Map 2 Chola kingdom at the height of its power, ca. 1030–1070.

Each temple possessed an entire set of bronze images that numbered anywhere from ten to forty-five depending on the wealth and generosity of the donors supporting the temple (fig. 1.3).[3] The medium-size temple of Tiruvaduturai, built largely by a lay devotee who gave himself the title of *Kattrali Pichchan*, or "Stone temple enthusiast," with Chola king Parantaka claiming the completion of the shrine tower, commissioned twenty-five bronzes of which two were portrait lamps of two major temple patrons.[4] My epigraphy collaborator, Marxia Gandhi, and I were fortunate in finding an unpublished and unknown inscription on the Tiruvaduturai temple walls that named each bronze and provided the measurements of all but one portrait lamp. The group included all major forms of Shiva accompanied by his consort Uma. The largest images were of Dancing Shiva, and of Shiva with the bull, both measuring 41 inches; Shiva as the Begging Lord stood 29 inches tall; while saints Sambandar, Appar, and Sundarar measured approximately 16 inches.[5] Rajaraja's royal temple at Thanjavur possessed some sixty-six bronzes, about which we get information from an entire series of inscriptions on the temple. Published as early as 1918, these records describe each bronze, give us the measurements of most of the images, and provide details of the jewels presented to adorn each bronze.[6] The largest bronze at Thanjavur, still in worship in a small shrine within the temple grounds, is a bronze of the Expert Dancer, approximately 40 inches high, apparently gifted by the emperor, although its size is not specified in the inscription.[7] The next largest Thanjavur bronze is Shiva as Victor of Three Forts, measuring 38½

12   CHAPTER 1

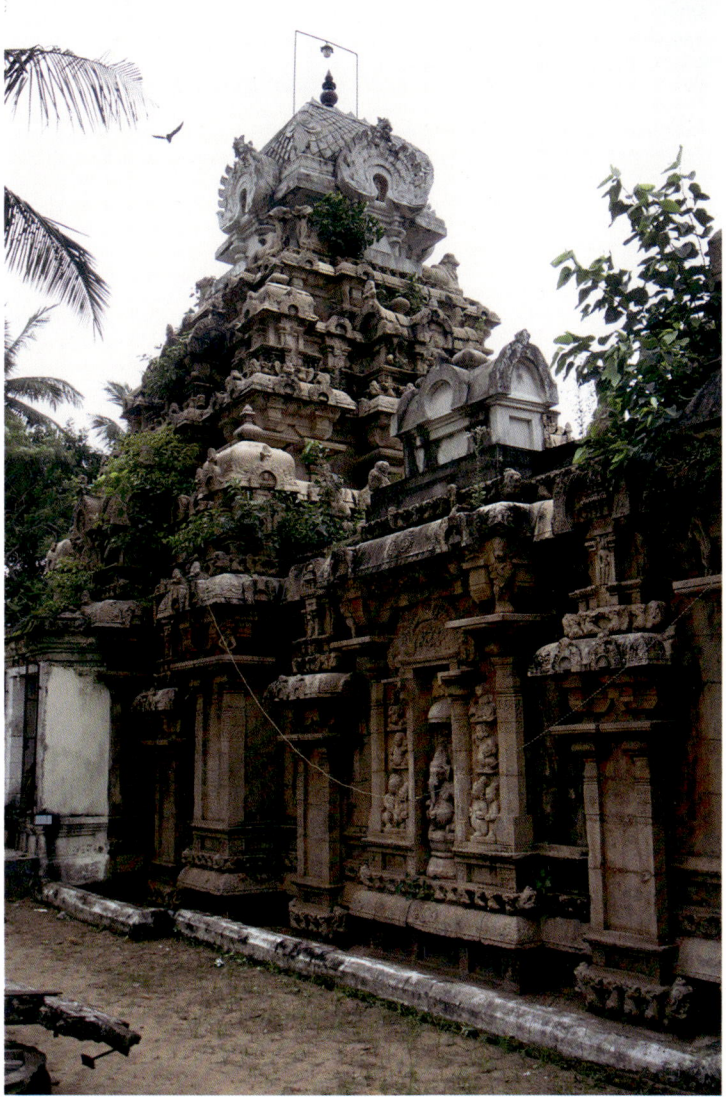

Figure 1.1. Pullamangai temple, Thanjavur district, ca. 930.

Figure 1.2. Inscriptions on the walls of Nageshvara temple, Kumbakonam, Thanjavur district, ca. 910.

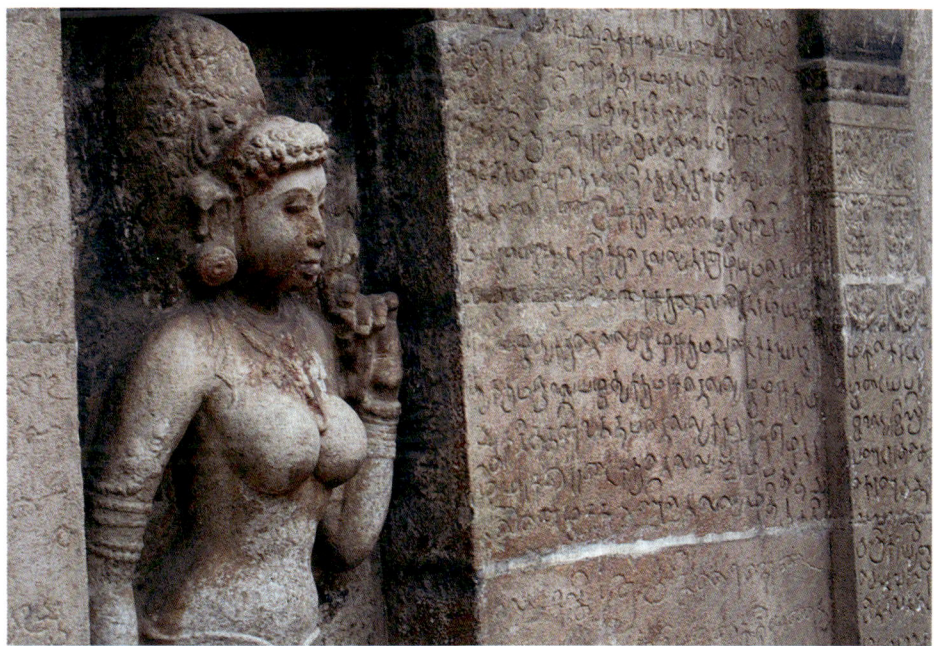

inches, with Shiva as Begging Lord at just over 29 inches. Every Chola bronze was portable and intended to be carried in procession through temple and town during the festivals celebrated at each temple. Each bronze has circular or square holes in the lotus-shaped base on which the figure stands, while its rectangular lower pedestal frequently has additional lugs against its four ends, so that carrying poles may be threaded through them. In the case of small bronzes, these poles rest on the shoulders of those who carried the images in procession. With major heavy bronzes like the Marriage group that we examined as an introduction to the art of the Chola bronze, shorter poles were used to secure the images onto the backs of a range of wooden animal *vahanas*, or vehicles, that would be placed on carts and wheeled along as part of the procession, in a manner similar to the floats seen in today's many festive parades across the world.

But what was the need at all for portable images? Sometime during the sixth or seventh century, well before the emergence of the Cholas, the emphasis in the Tamil country shifted from the immovable stone image occupying the sanctum of a temple to portable festival images (*utsava murtis*) that now became a vital part of the religious life of the Tamil people. In a shrine to Shiva, the immovable sanctum image was always an aniconic *linga*, the symbol of god Shiva (fig. 1.4). In all other parts of India, such an immovable stone image remained, and still remains, the sole focus of Hindu temple worship. But Tamil India came up with an innovative concept that resulted in a novel visualization of its deities. Like royalty, or like the pope for that matter, the deities were visualized as giving audience, inspecting the temple premises, celebrating birthdays and wedding anniversaries, and setting out on festival processions to the beach, riverfront, or a coconut grove. Homage continued to be paid to the sanctum image, the original or core image known as *mula vigraha* or root-image. But now portable deities, originally created of wood, became crucial to Tamil worship; these perishable portable images were supplanted during the Chola period by more permanent metal images.

The bronzes created by artists during the period of Chola rule are indeed exquisite forms, but they are more than mere epitomes of beauty (fig. 1.5). They played a fundamental role in the ritual and social life of the citizens, a role that remains as crucial today as it was during the Chola period. As portable processional images, Chola bronzes are vital for the performance of ritual festivities that are facilitated and conducted by a range of temple functionaries. But the success of a festival depends equally on the active participation of the residents of that town or village. While these festivals are sacred observances that require the engagement of temple priests, they also partake of the nature of carnival. Consider, for instance, the festival in which bronzes of Shiva and his consort, together with Shiva's ritual weapon, the trident, are taken for a dip in the waters of the ocean, or in river waters if the ocean is too far distant. Today, this is celebrated each year in the lunar month of *Masi*, or February–March; in 2016, the festival was held on the 22nd of February. The winter chill of the 70s Fahrenheit in Tamil Nadu, which brings out sweaters and shawls in Chennai, has departed; the sharp heat of April with temperatures in the high 90s Fahrenheit is yet to come. It is a day for everyone to accompany the god to the beach for their own dip in the waters. In Chennai today, the images from the town's main Kapalishvara Shiva temple are taken in procession to the Marina, the grand beach of Chennai. The god is richly adorned with silks and jewels, flower garlands, and

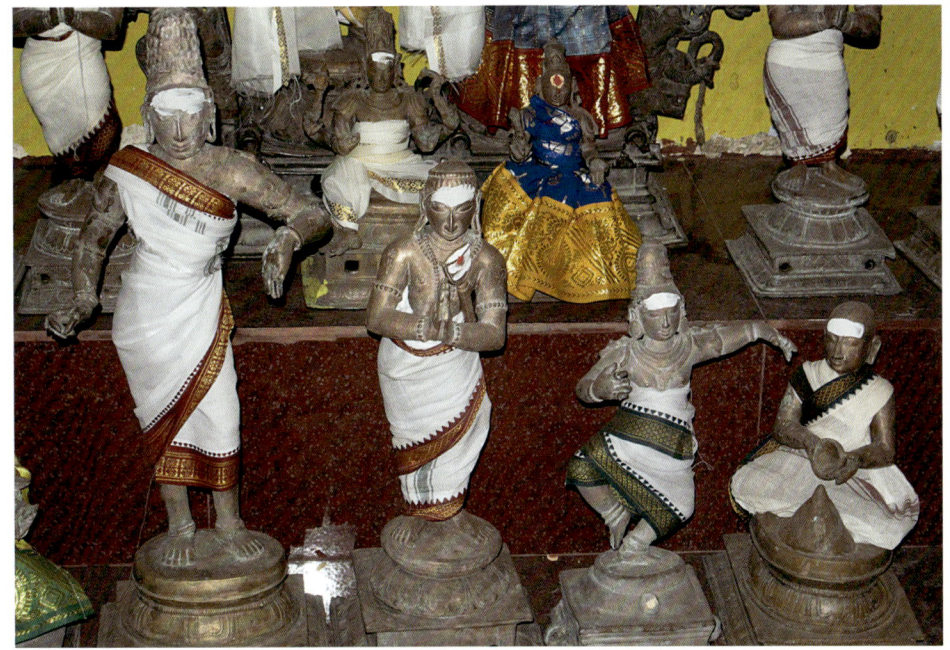

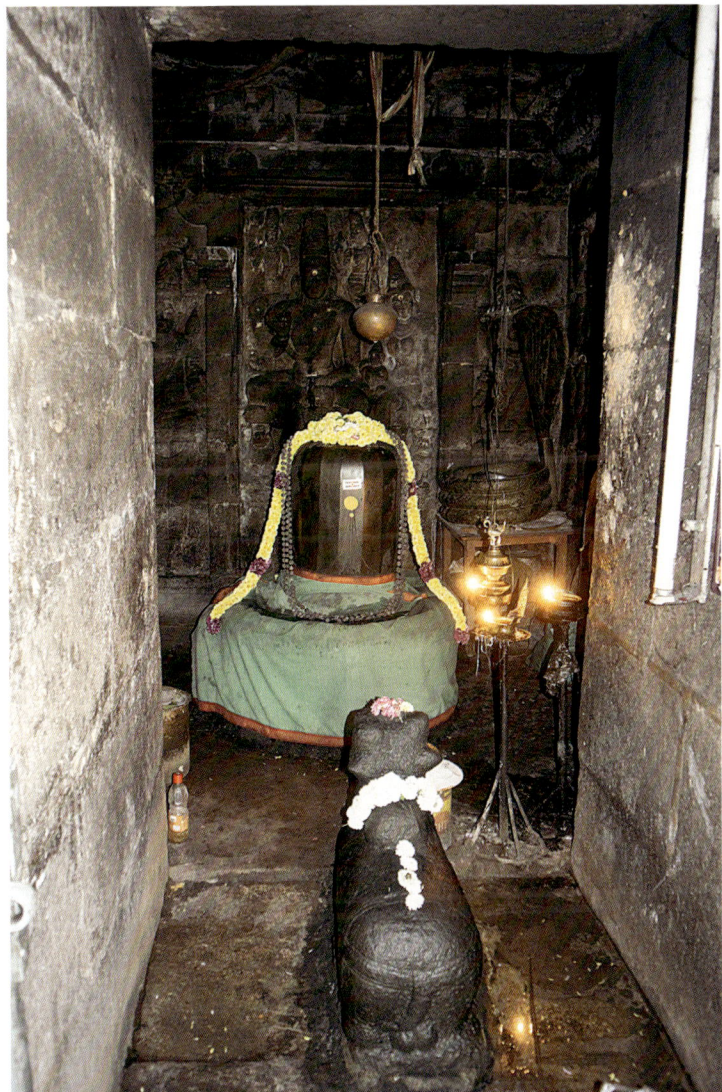

Figure 1.3. Temple bronzes of varying dates, Kilaipalavur temple, Trichy district.

Figure 1.4. Aniconic image: immovable stone Shiva *linga* in temple sanctum, Kanchipuram, pre-Chola period.

GODS ON PARADE   15

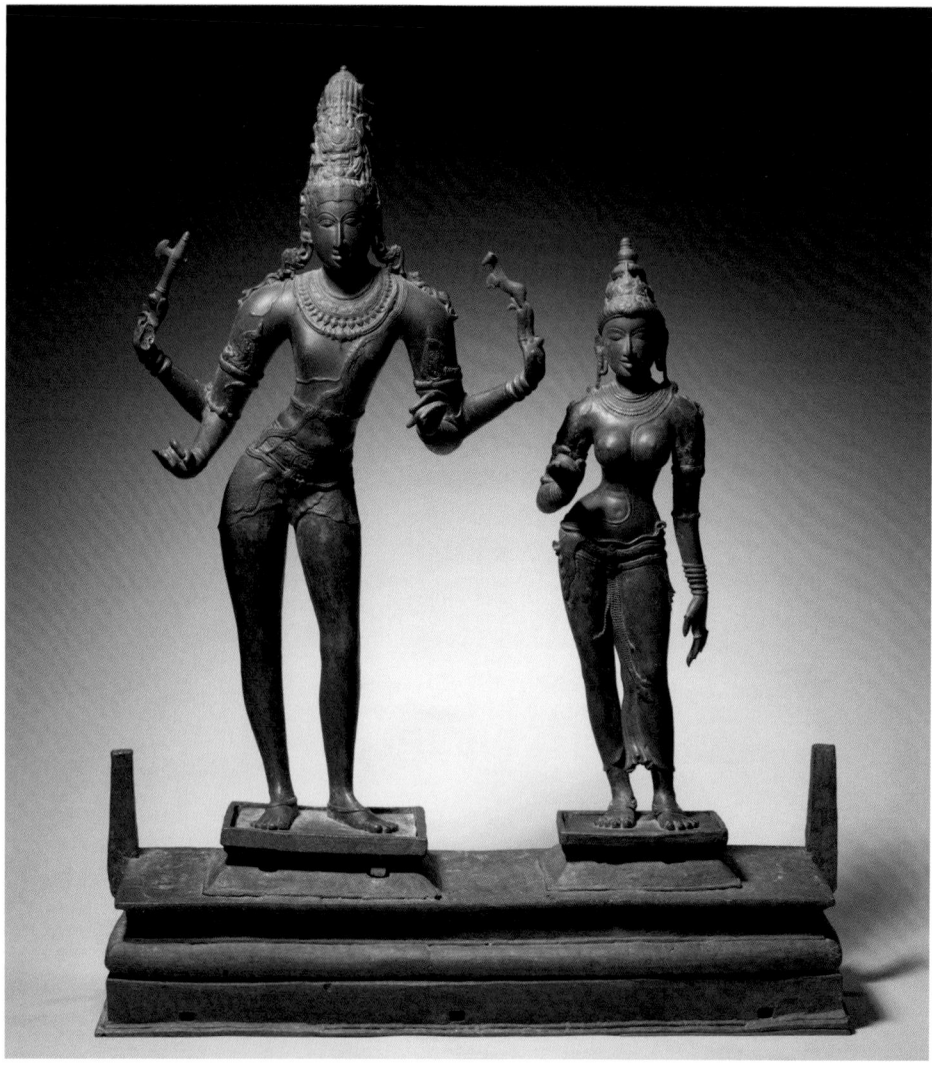

Figure 1.5. Shiva with Uma, ca. 955, The Cleveland Museum of Art, John L. Severance Fund.

aromatics, and is accompanied by musicians and dancers. The citizens too wear their finest garb, enjoy the celebratory food prepared by the temple kitchens for the festival, and partake in the joyous light-hearted atmosphere that the festival promotes.

That such a procession to the ocean was celebrated during the Chola period is evident from numerous inscriptions. Perhaps the best-known instance is an inscription of minister Naralokaviran, who served both emperor Kulottunga I (r. 1070–1120) and Vikrama Chola (1116–1135). Naralokaviran cleared a road from the temple at Chidambaram to Killai-on-the-Sea to facilitate the procession of taking the bronze of Shiva as Wondrous Dancer to the beach (fig. 1.6). Since the festival started from the temple's south entrance, the minister adorned that gateway with multiple lamps. At Killai, we read that Naralokaviran constructed a hall to shelter Dancing Shiva, planted a garden along the seashore, and dug a large freshwater tank for the use of devotees who accompanied the festival procession.[8] The continued importance of such a beach festival is seen from an inscription of the thirteenth century in the temple of Tiruvidaikali at a time

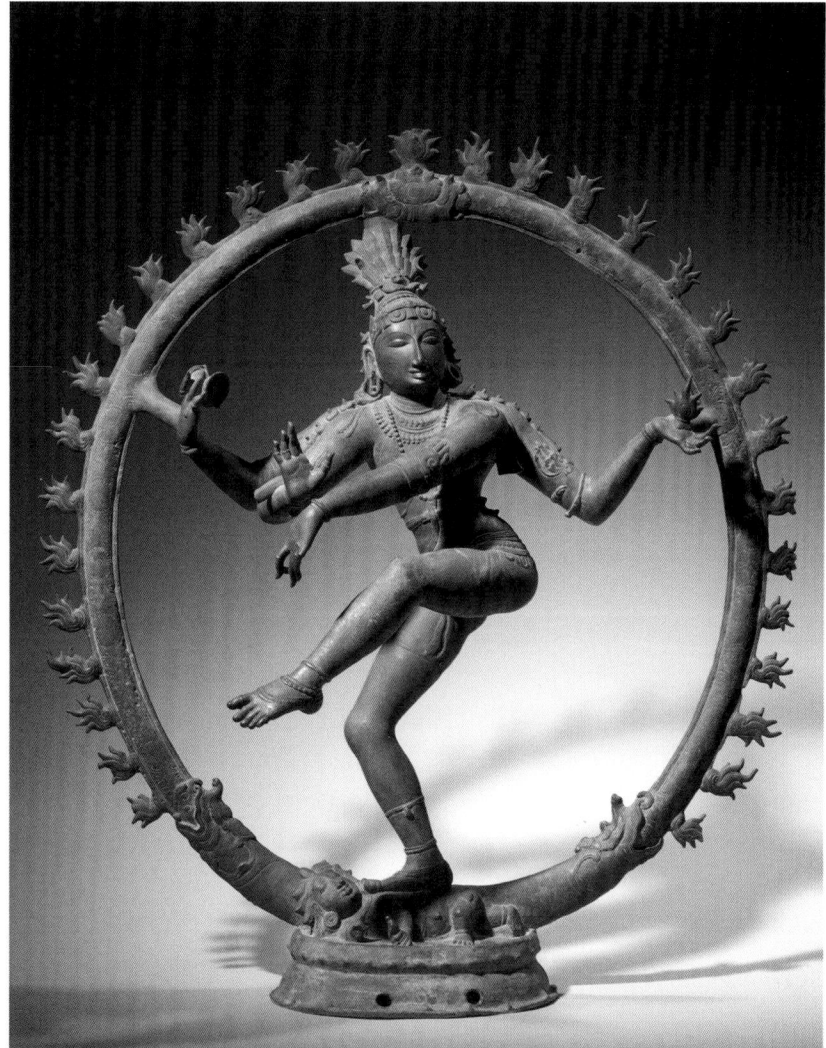

Figure 1.6. Dancing Shiva, ca. 1100, The Cleveland Museum of Art, Purchase from the J. H. Wade Fund.

when Chola rule was coming to an end. It records a gift of land to enable building a road from the temple to the oceanfront in order to take the bronze image of the god for sea bathing on festive occasions.[9]

Chola temple inscriptions frequently carry detailed instructions regarding temple festivities. An extensive inscription at the Tyagaraja temple at Tiruvarur in the coastal belt, dated in 1140 during the reign of king Kulottunga II, in which the monarch set aside three villages to serve as resources for certain temple festivals, speaks of as many as fifty-six days in a year being celebratory festival days.[10] The list is fascinating and emphasizes the many days of each year set aside for people to take off from their routine activities. The new moon day (*amavasya*) of each month, and the first day (*sankranti*) of eight of twelve months are listed as festival days and hence guaranteed holidays, or more accurately holy-days. Additionally, the full moon days of the five months of *Markali* (December–January), *Tai* (January–February), *Chittirai* (April–May), *Adi* (July–August), and *Avani* (August–September) were days of festive celebration, as were two days of an eclipse (*grahana*), and

GODS ON PARADE   17

one day described as "a sacred day of new clothes for the deity." The inscription speaks finally of three festivals, each extending over multiple days, described as "sacred days on which the deity rose and emerged to view the sacred streets"[11]—in other words, these were festival processions outside the temple. These comprise a six-day festival in *Aipashi* (October–November), a six-day festival in *Adi* (July–August), and the most important of all, a ten-day festival known as *brahmotsavam* in *Panguni* (March–April) that involves a sacred bath of the bronze deities on its final day. The *brahmotsavam* (brahma festival), described by one scholar as "an annual 'renovation' or 'recreation' of the temple,"[12] is the one festival that even the smallest and least endowed of temples will somehow procure the funds to celebrate. The Tiruvarur inscription concludes with a list of the payments made to all those who facilitated the celebration of these holy-days, specifying the measures of rice to be paid to the various persons who performed duties during these fifty-six festival days. Apart from the ritual priests and their assistants, the list includes those who were paid to carry the deity in procession, supervisors to ensure the appropriate performance of the festival, those who delivered perfumes to anoint the sacred bronzes, the musicians who played a variety of instruments during the celebrations, gardeners who tended the flowers in the temple gardens, those who created garlands of blossoms to adorn the bronzes, the washerman who washed sacred clothes, the potter who equipped the temple kitchens, the suppliers of firewood for these kitchens, the cleaning women, and an accountant. The lengthy list of monies to be dispensed to the various members of the temple staff ends on a practical note, with the accountant setting aside three coins for unaccounted items, for extras, and for wastage.

Far from being a drain on the economy, temple festivals actually served to redistribute wealth and improve socioeconomic conditions. Temple kitchens prepared food from ingredients provided by a range of wealthy devotees; this food was ritually offered to the stone sanctum image and to the bronze deities, after which it was distributed to temple employees and to devotees who participated in the festival. The infrastructure of the area was improved, since roads were widened or newly constructed to accommodate temple processions. The productivity of the region was enhanced; the profile of temple and patron was elevated. One such instance is recorded at the temple of Tirupanandal, where an inscription of the year 1146 during the reign of Rajaraja II speaks of a gift of land to construct a new road to take a temple bronze in festival procession to the Kollidam river. It informs us that 750 coconut palms were planted on both sides of the road and were to be appropriately tended; the income derived from the sale of the coconuts was set aside for a variety of temple expenses including oil lamps to illuminate the premises.[13] Another inscription, dating to the year 1210 during the reign of Kulottunga III, records an undertaking by the local brahmin *sabha* to widen the road along which the bronze festival image of the deity of the Tiruvaymur temple was taken to the *toppu*, or cultivated garden.[14] Temple festivals were also occasions for the performance of music, dance, and drama, and inscriptions speak of grants of gold, rice, and clothes to performers who enacted scenes from dance-dramas during major festivals. We hear of at least three varieties of dance-dramas (*kuttu*) performed in Chola temples—*chakkai,* which is a dance-drama performed today in Kerala on the west coast, *ariya* (northern?), and *tamula* (Tamil?). In the temple of Kilaipalavur, an actor named Adalaiyur-chakkai was given gold, rice, and a set of clothes

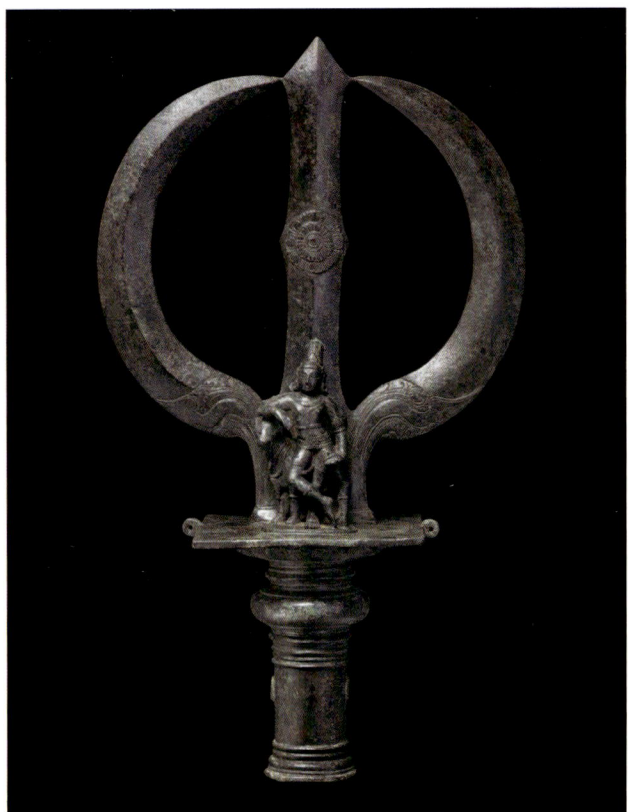

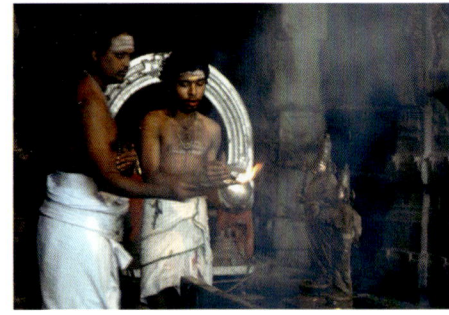

Figure 1.7. Shiva's Trident Weapon Personified as *Astra Devar* (Lord Weapon), ca. 1050, private collection.

Figure 1.8. Evening *sribali* puja.

as payment for enacting three scenes of *Chakkai kuttu* during the festival days in the month of *Aipashi* (October–November).[15] In the year 960, at the important temple of Tiruvidaimaradur on the south bank of the Kaveri, an officer named Parantakan Muvendavelan met with other dignitaries in the dance hall (*nataka shala*) of the temple to make provisions for the performance of a dance-drama in seven parts that was described as *Ariya kuttu*. The performer, a certain Tiruvelai-arai-chakkai, was to dance the first part at the *Tai* (January–February) festival, three parts on three consecutive days after bathing the deity (presumably at the *brahmotsavam* in *Panguni*, or March–April), and the final three segments starting the day after the *Vaikhashi* (May–June) festival.[16] At the Manambadi temple, an inscription of 1088 informs us that the merchant body (*nagarattar*) and the temple authorities set aside a gift of land as an endowment for dance-drama performances (*kuttattu kani*). The performer was to enact the *Tamula kuttu* on five occasions during the festival in the month of *Chittirai* (April–May).[17]

The various celebratory processions center around bronze images that are specific to each festival. For the nightly ritual of *sribali* puja that occurs every single day of the year, the participating image is either a bronze of Shiva's trident weapon personified as *Astra Devar* (Lord Weapon) or alternatively the beneficent image of Shiva as Lord crowned with the Crescent Moon (*Chandrashekhara*) together with his consort Uma (figs. 1.7 and 1.8). This daily reenactment requires small images that may be carried in a light palanquin on the shoulders of two priests as they walk the image around the temple. That the image for this ceremony was often Shiva's trident, which frequently carries a sculpted image of the god along the base of its triple prongs, is seen from an inscription dating to 897. It speaks of the dedication of a *sribali* image that weighed 25 *palam*, while

GODS ON PARADE   19

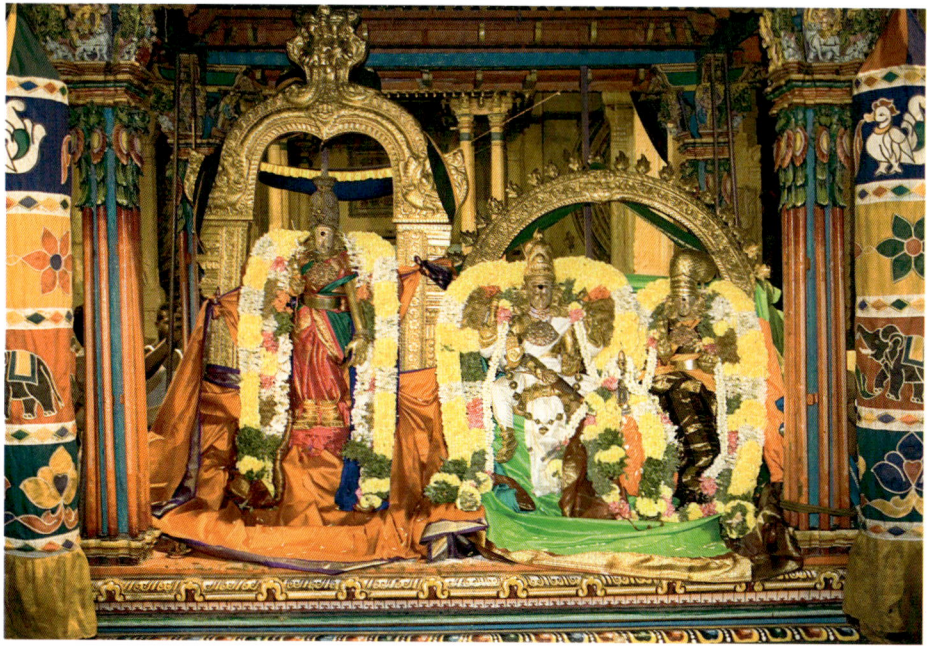

Figure 1.9. Images of Uma (left) and *Somaskanda* (right) dressed and adorned for a temple procession (bronze faces, hands, feet, and shoulders covered with gold-plated metal *kavachas*), Minakshi temple, Madurai, 2015.

its pedestal (the tall bronze handle for the trident) weighed all of 80 *palam*.[18] Bronzes used for the annual celebration of the marriage of Shiva and Uma must necessarily be those that reflect the ritual involved and portray Shiva taking Uma's hand in marriage, as in the marriage group we encountered in the introduction (see fig. 0.1). To use any other image of Shiva and Uma standing beside each other as a loving couple, such as an image of *Tripura Vijaya* (Victor of Three Forts) with Uma, would be incorrect (see fig. 1.5). For the ten-day annual *brahmotsavam* festival celebrated across the Tamil country, the featured image is a seated group of Shiva and Uma together with their infant son, Skanda, known as *Somaskanda* (*sa* [with] Uma and Skanda), preceded by their elder son, elephant-headed Ganesha. The necessity for temples to possess an entire series of bronzes of Shiva, in his various manifestations, is evident. At the end of each festival, the featured bronze is set aside in a hall adjoining the sanctum until it is required for the same festival in the following year, month, week, or day.

An amazing continuity of some 1,400 years is seen in the festival cycle, from at least the seventh century, if not earlier, into the present day, as is evident in festival processions of bronzes where, to this day, we see them richly adorned with gold, rubies, pearls, silks, and flower garlands (fig. 1.9). In a way, nothing much has changed, and yet changes are manifest in the huge television screens placed outside especially popular temples so that the masses, who wish to participate in the celebration but are unable to find space within the temple premises, may view the proceedings from outside the temple walls. Today, at the important temple town of Madurai, roughly 120 miles south of the Chola capital of Thanjavur, the celebration of the marriage festival of god Shiva and his consort, known locally by the name of Minakshi (carp-eyed One), attracts such massive crowds that the temple has taken to broadcasting the proceedings on television, thus taking the event into every home where the elderly and infirm, as well as toddlers, may comfortably watch the ritual proceedings. Moving the sacred into homes is not without a level of ambiguity, but appears to be taken very seriously, as witnessed by the fact that the devout place a garland around the television set. Easy and direct access to a sacred temple ceremony that would have been difficult to view in the temple itself with its tight crush of devotees is thereby provided to a vast public in a modern version of the village street.

In this chapter, we will first consider the saints of the Tamil country and their poems that testify to the changing concept of the deity reflected in temple festivals, a concept that necessitated the creation of portable images. We will then explore the novel introduction of copper that made Chola bronze images possible. Last, we will examine the process of creating these images through use of the direct lost-wax process that results in solid and heavy metal images. We will see that the Master's original wax image is melted away, and the clay mold is broken open to release the metal image, making each Chola bronze a singular piece that cannot be replicated.

The Saints of Shiva (*Nayanmar*) and Vishnu (*Alvars*)

A discussion of the changing concept of the deity requires turning to a group of holy men and women who lived between the years 500–800 of this era and who may be called saints. Unlike the saints of the Western tradition, these were not lone, solitary hermits; indeed, several traveled together. They were not renunciants and several were married. They were not intercessors between devotees and god, although devotees tend to relate specially to one or another saint. Hagiography speaks of sixty-three saints devoted to Shiva who called themselves *nayanmar*, or leaders (fig. 1.10), and twelve saints dedicated to god Vishnu who were known as *alvars*, or those who dived deep (into the divine). Three

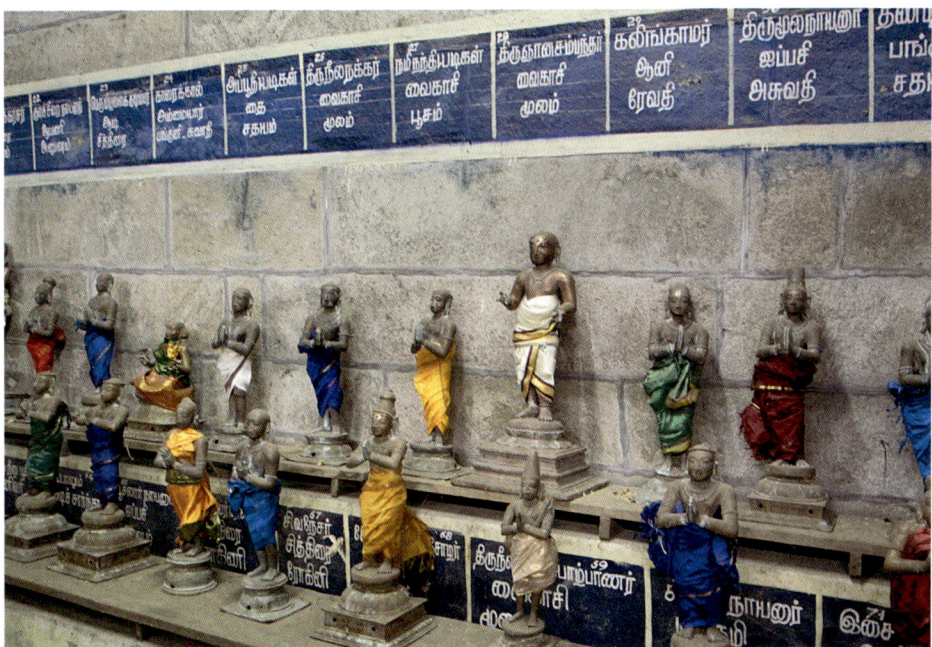

Figure 1.10. *Nayanmar*: 63 Saints of Shiva, Tiruvidaimaradur temple, post-Chola bronzes.

of the sixty-three saints of Shiva caught the popular imagination and came to be known as the Revered Three, or *Muvar*. They lived prior to the creation of our bronzes, and between them composed 700 hymns that comprise the sacred body of hymns known as *Tevaram* that is recited in Tamil temples. By the Chola period, the saints had entered the repertoire of temple bronzes and themselves became objects of reverence. Their hymns only rarely expound philosophy; rather, they extol the feats of Shiva, and speak repeatedly of Shiva's irresistible beauty. Child saint Sambandar's very first hymn, which opens the entire Tamil "canon," carries as the refrain of each verse his celebration of Shiva as "the thief who stole my heart" (*en ullam kavar kalvan*).

In the early centuries of the current era in Tamil Nadu, prior to the time of the saints, temples built of brick and wood were few and far between and found only in a few larger towns known as *urs*. The shrines that existed in village after village consisted generally of a stone *linga*, the emblem of Shiva, beneath a hallowed tree in an open space (*turai*). During the lifetime of the saints, wood and brick structures began to be constructed around these sacred shrines, and such enclosures frequently included the sacred tree within the temple. Sambandar and Appar lived during the seventh century within the area that later became Chola-mandalam, and they traveled within their home territory from one sacred site to the next, usually no more than a few miles apart, and sang of the Shiva enshrined at each site, praising his many manifestations.[19] They located Shiva in a banyan forest (*alan-kadu*), where peacocks dance (*mayil-adu-turai*), where monkeys play (*kurang-adu-turai*), in the sacred white forest (*tiru-ven-kadu*). Today, these vivid and expressive terms, and a multitude of other similarly evocative phrases, remain the names for what have now become small towns whose descriptive names give us a glimpse into the ancient environment. The saints' role in providing Shiva with a local Tamil habitation was of crucial significance. Indian myth, as narrated in classical Sanskrit texts, speaks of Shiva as the god of the snow-bound Himalayan mountain of Kailasa to the far north. The Tamil saints relocated Shiva to the lush and humid plains of the Tamil country and praised him in the local Tamil tongue.

The saints' hymns frequently describe festivals at these various sacred sites in which portable images of deities were carried in procession. A verse from a hymn of saint Appar, dedicated to Shiva at Tiruvarur, close to Appar's own hometown of Tirupugalur, provides a vivid picture of the festival cycle in the late seventh century.

> *He goes on his rounds*
> *amid the glitter of a pearl canopy*
> *and gem-encrusted golden fans.*
> *Devoted men and women follow him*
> *along with Virati ascetics in bizarre garb...*
> *Such is the splendor of Atirai day*
> *in Arur, our Father's town.*[20]

A verse from child saint Sambandar on a temple procession, also of the late seventh century, speaks of the temple-car that continues to play a central role in festival processions:

The Lord of Citticcaram shrine in Naraiyur
goes resplendent in ceremonial dress,
as his devotees and perfected sages
sing and dance his widespread fame,
and the sound of festival drums
beaten in the streets where the temple-car is pulled
spreads on every side.[21]

There were no processional bronzes in the seventh century when these hymns were composed, and early festival images were most likely created of wood; indeed, an inscription of the third century speaks of the dedication of a wooden image of eight-armed Vishnu for a temple sanctum in the adjoining state of Andhra.[22] Festival images were ritually bathed with a variety of liquids including milk, honey, and water from the local sacred Kaveri river, after which they were dressed and adorned. With repeated anointing and bathing, such wooden images would need frequent replacement, and with wooden processional images one appreciates even more the need for soft silk drapery, rich jewelry, and colorful and fragrant flower garlands.

The Introduction of Copper Festival Images (*Sheppu Tirumeni*)

The three revered saints, the *Muvar*, lived during the Pallava dynasty (ca. 550–728), whose kings ruled from the town of Kanchipuram and were in power in south India before the Cholas came on the scene. Large processional bronzes were not created during the time of the Pallavas; all we have are small bronzes of god Vishnu, never of Shiva, that are clearly objects of personal devotion. Typical examples are standing images of Vishnu that measure 8 inches or so inclusive of their pedestal, and seated Vishnu images 4 to 5 inches in height (fig. 1.11). Clearly, festival images of the Pallava period continued to be created in wood. Around the year 855, however, a dramatic change occurred that involved the introduction of copper on a scale never before seen in Tamil Nadu. Now began the creation of what temple inscriptions describe as "sacred forms of copper," or *sheppu tirumeni*. A technical study of a group of four Chola bronzes in the Los Angeles County Museum reveals that they have a copper content that varies between 90 percent and 95 percent, with the remaining 5 or 10 percent being comprised of roughly equal quantities of tin and lead.[23] All Chola bronzes are solid bronzes, so that an image of Dancing Shiva from the Cleveland Museum, a little under 4 feet tall together with its aureole, weighs 257 pounds (see fig. 1.6).[24] Chola bronzes are extremely heavy pieces of solid metal; bronzes from just about every other part of the world are hollow and thus far more economical in their use of metal. The Pallava standing bronze at 8 inches, inclusive of its pedestal, is diminutive relative to the size of the Chola dancing Shiva, just under 4 feet tall, without its missing rectangular lower pedestal.

Pure copper has an exceedingly high melting point of 1,084 degrees Centigrade, and is difficult to cast, as it has a tendency to trap bubbles of gas; however, the addition of 10 percent of tin lowers the melting point to 950 degrees and creates the perfect alloy known worldwide by the term "bronze."[25] Tin itself is rare, and the majority of known

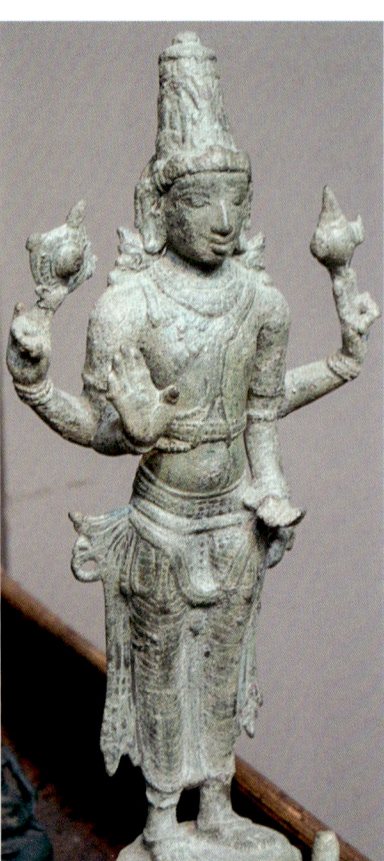

Figure 1.11. Pallava-period Vishnu within a shallow wooden drawer, private collection.

tin deposits are in southeast Asia; this fact, together with the discovery of the Dong Son copper drums belonging to the second millennium BCE, has caused some scholars of metallurgy to suggest that bronze itself may have been discovered in mainland and/or island southeast Asia.[26]

In the course of three years of intensive field research devoted to preparing the 65th A. W. Mellon Lectures in the Fine Arts, I discovered that there is absolutely no copper that may be easily or cost-effectively extracted in Tamil Nadu itself, and that no one has a clue regarding the source from which copper was obtained to create this multitude of Chola bronzes. It is extraordinary that such an important issue has been overlooked by all of us without so much as a second thought. How, and from where, was copper procured in sufficient quantity to revolutionize the creation of processional images and, indeed, the production of the many copper-plate inscriptions issued by Chola monarchs? The Tiruvalankadu copper-plate charter of emperor Rajendra consists of thirty-one sheets of copper that, together with its seal-ring, weigh 203 pounds; the recently discovered Tiruvindalur copper plates of emperor Rajadhiraja, of the year 1065, consists of eighty-five sheets of copper that, together with their seal-ring, weigh 330 pounds.[27] The main sources of copper in India are Rajasthan and Bihar, both in northern India; a 1975 report informs us that 56 percent of India's copper comes from Bihar, 40 percent from Rajasthan, and very small quantities from Karnataka and Andhra.[28] Information of this nature is gathered from ore-crushing pits, from smelting sites that leave behind large slag heaps, or from remains of furnaces. Bihar was probably the source of the pure copper bolts that connected the famous Ashokan stone columns and their capitals; the bolt from the Rampurva lion pillar, now in the Indian Museum Calcutta, is just over 2 feet long and has a circumference of 14 inches at the center and 12 inches at its ends.[29] Copper deposits in Karnataka in south India, such as that at Ingladhal in Chitradurga, have yielded copper ores with only 0.81 percent of copper;[30] such deposits just cannot be gainfully mined. Professor K. Srinivas of the Department of Mining and Geology at Anna University in Chennai shared with me the information that over 30,000 tons of low-grade ore, with a copper content of as much as 5 percent (as against the 0.81 percent in Karnataka), would be required to yield the 153 tons of copper that I proposed in the introduction as necessary to create bronzes for Chola temples in the three districts of Trichy, Thanjavur, and Nagapattinam.[31]

It is useful to look more widely at trade networks and to consider the possibility that Chola bronzes depended on the import of copper into south India. A Greek sailor's log of the first century CE, *The Periplus of the Erythraean Sea*, mentions copper as an import into Barygaza, today's Broach, a port north of Bombay. However, the text is somewhat contradictory, as another passage speaks of the export of copper, presumably from northern India. Lionel Casson, in his new 1999 translation of the text, starts his section on metals with the caveat, "The information provided by the Periplus on metals presents difficulties"; he continues with the comment, "The greatest puzzle is presented by copper"; and concludes, "In a word . . . attempts to resolve the problem are mere guesswork."[32] Early indigenous texts have little to tell us on this issue, but Amarasimha's Sanskrit lexicon, attributed to the sixth century, refers to copper as *mlechcha mukha* ("foreign-face").[33] A thirteenth-century metallurgical-cum-medicinal text, the Sanskrit *Rasa Ratna Samuchchaya*, which would date toward the very end of the Chola period, speaks of two categories of copper, one from Nepal and the other from *Mlechcha*, or a foreign country.[34]

A substantial proportion of the cache of letters found in the Cairo Geniza deal with the India trade and were written by Jewish merchants in Aden to their counterparts in south India. They contain tantalizing hints regarding the use and reuse of copper. One group of twelfth-century letters is addressed by Joseph Ben Abraham, based in Aden, to Abraham Ben Yiju, who owned a bronze factory in the town of Mangalore on India's west coast. Copper, in the form of both bars and damaged utensils, was sent from Aden to south India for conversion to new products—a ten-cornered tray, a water jug, a candlestick—and then shipped back to Aden. I give here an abbreviated extract from one such letter sent from Aden to Mangalore:

In Your Name, O Merciful
I have sent to Sheikh Abraham . . . in the ship of the ship-owner Mahruz—may God ordain its safety—a bag containing copper . . . Total weight: 53½ lbs.

. . .

If God decrees that it arrives safely, please have made for me a ten-cornered tray the same size as the one sent to you . . . a table jug should fit into the center of the tray. . . . The table jug should weigh 8 lbs, more or less, and the tray about 4 lbs. Furthermore a small candlestick . . . As to the remainder of the copper, please sell it, and with its proceeds pay the craftsman's fee. With the balance buy me, your servant, a small quantity of fresh betel nuts, or, if they are not available, cardamom or turmeric.[35]

Raw material—in this case, copper—was sent to India for processing, and a finished product was returned. This would seem to represent one of the earliest recorded instances of outsourcing, something we consider to be a late twentieth-century phenomenon. Why would traders ship copper from Aden to Mangalore if copper was readily available in south India? If available, was it just too expensive and therefore cheaper to ship to India? Another possibility is that copper may have served a dual role, being used also as ballast for ocean-trade vessels. Among the many discarded documents that turned up in the Cairo Geniza is a set of accounts written on a piece of Aden paper. We learn that craftsmen were not paid wages as such; rather they were paid by piece-work, and the payment depended on the weight of the copper used to make the piece; it also confirms that trays, jugs, and candlesticks used a variation on the lost-wax process.[36]

My consultations with expert colleagues in the fields of geology and metallurgy, from Australia and London, from Denver and New York, including scholars like Paul Craddock, Vince Piggott, and Ian Glover among others, indicate that pinpointing the source of metal is perhaps the single most difficult task to achieve. Their generosity in sharing information, articles, and personal opinions born of years of study is something for which I am most grateful. Their initial suggestion was that I leave the source of copper as an unresolved issue to be researched in a possible future collaborative project that might draw together experts in various fields. Yet, recently, I have found an unexpected and exciting possible source for Chola copper—in neighboring Sri Lanka—thanks to the work of Arjuna Thantilage[37] and his Sri Lankan colleagues, Sudarshan Seneviratne and Jagath Weerasinghe, all scholars of archaeology and metallurgy. Could access to a nearby source of copper have been one of the additional reasons for the Chola obsession with Sri Lanka, a subject whose ramifications we explore in detail in chapter 6?

The Seruwila copper belt in northwestern Sri Lanka is close to the port of Trincomalee and within easy access of the major city-centers of Anuradhapura and Polonnaruwa (map 3). It has yielded archaeological evidence of copper ore extraction on an industrial scale during the first millennium, when Thantilage finds two distinct phases of extraction that indicate a movement from a centralized site in the earlier period to multiple village sites. Excavations of the first phase have yielded several massive slag heaps, each 30 to 40 feet high and extending 1,500 to 2,000 feet in length, upon which local residents have built their houses in recent years. The second phase has yielded a large number of "village" sites of copper extraction, and a recent C14 date from a mass of carbon taken from one such furnace site, some 20 feet high, has yielded a date of 990–1050 CE. The period covered by the two phases appears to be fourth century BCE to the end of the eleventh century CE. Recently, Thantilage has also found evidence that the processing of already extracted raw material continued into the thirteenth century.[38] Sri Lankan scholars are certain that Seruwila copper was exported; their only uncertainty is the destination of the copper exports. Backing up this evidence of extensive Sri Lankan copper working are several early brahmi inscriptions in the area dating between the first century BCE and the second century CE. One reads "Cave of copper-smith Roniguta, son of Tisa" (*tabakarat tisaputa ronigutasa lene*), while another labels a cave as belonging to coppersmiths Pusa and Sumana (*tabakara pusasa sumanas ca lene*).[39] Other inscriptions speak of a "great copper-working guild," a copper industry minister (*tambakara attana*) who donated

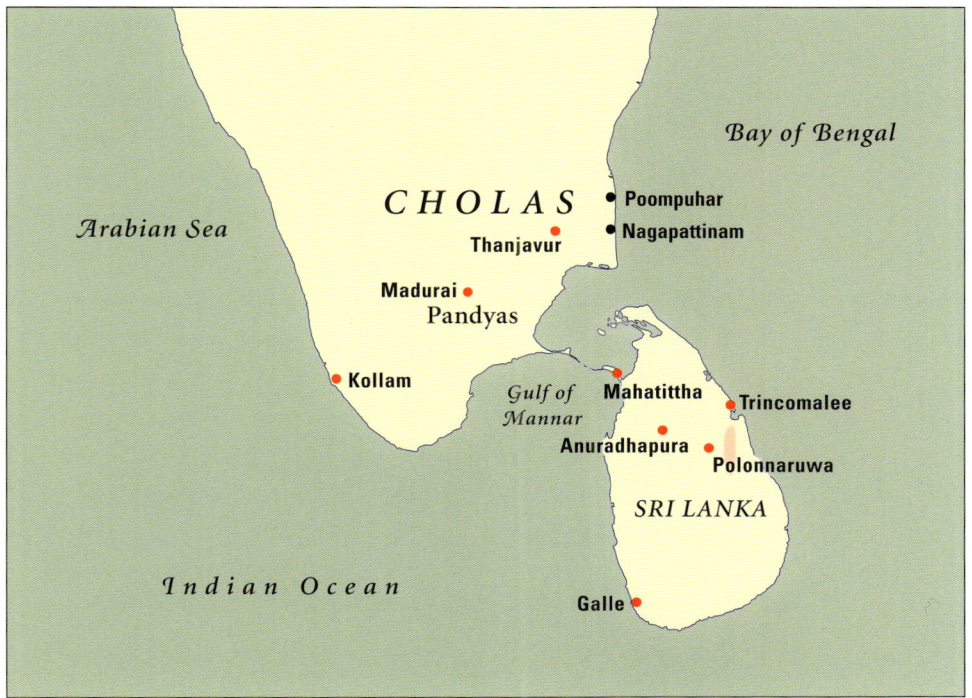

Map 3 The Cholas and Sri Lanka with the Seruwila copper belt (in orange).

income to a local Buddhist temple, and of customs collection from the metal production area.[40] A Lankan text on the Buddha's relics, the *Dhatuvamsa*, or Lineage of Relics, refers to a port named Ilankaturai that Thantilage and his colleagues have located. They have also traced an ancient trade route that connects Seruwila to the road linking the port of Ilankaturai to the early capital city of Anuradhapura and, additionally, have uncovered the ancient support stones of a 600-meter stone bridge across an intervening lagoon.[41]

So where are we with this exciting possibility that Chola bronzes were created with copper acquired from Sri Lanka? Thantilage has demonstrated that Sri Lankan Seruwila copper (S1) has a clear and exceedingly rare trace element of 0.3 percent to 0.5 percent of cobalt-nickel.[42] I was able to persuade three US museums to provide samples from select Chola bronzes to attempt a minimally invasive test known as ICP (inductively coupled plasma) to see whether the samples yield the cobalt-nickel signature trace element that may prove conclusive. I found to my dismay that ICP metal testing was not something that laboratories in the United States undertake routinely. However, with the cooperation of Donna Strahan, head of the Freer Gallery of Art's lab, and members of its staff, it has been possible to procure results that show high trace levels of cobalt-nickel in three of the five bronzes (see appendix D). It appears, however, that the only way to ensure the accuracy of such testing is for both Seruwila copper ore and the copper samples from Chola bronzes to be tested in the same laboratory under the same conditions, with identical calibration, a project that would require cooperation on an international basis. Even if this becomes a possibility, experienced metallurgists have expressed the opinion that trace elements may exist in one area of a copper belt and not in another, and they state, quite definitively, that pinpointing the source of an ore is a near impossibility.[43] So for the moment, it appears that my proposal that Seruwila was one source of copper ore for

GODS ON PARADE

Chola bronzes must remain a strong possibility, based on compelling and persuasive circumstantial evidence, but not a proven fact. However, the shift from wood to the large-scale creation of sizable copper sculptures certainly suggests that a new and readily available supply of ore had been identified.

A few words are in order on tin, a metal necessary to create bronze, and a substance known to be widely prevalent in southeast Asia, including Thailand. A Tamil inscription from Takua Pa in southern Thailand, a trading post apparently settled by Tamil merchants, has been dated to the ninth century on paleographical grounds. It speaks of the construction of a tank named Sri Avani Naranam that was placed under the protection of three bodies—a well-known Tamil merchant guild named Manigramam, a military unit (?) named Senamukam, and another body whose name is in a damaged area of the inscription.[44] It seems quite possible that southeast Asia was the source of tin, of which only small quantities were required, to produce bronze in India; however, tin is also found in the Bastar tribal belt of central India.

The Earliest Bronze Processional Images

An elegant duo from a Shiva temple at Vadakkalathur, a town in the Chola coastal belt, which represents Shiva taking Uma's hand in marriage, might well be the earliest known Chola processional bronze (fig. 1.12). Standing on an 8-inch-high pedestal, Shiva is a slender figure, 27 inches tall, who reaches out with his right hand to grasp Uma's right hand in marriage; Uma, standing 20 inches tall, lingers behind Shiva, not looking him in the face but preferring to turn away bashfully. Shiva stands with his left lower hand in the gesture of protection and benediction, while his two rear hands hold his emblems, the battle-ax and a pet antelope, and a pet serpent rears above his shoulder. He wears a short dhoti held in place with a large decorative clasp and is richly adorned with necklaces, waistband, sacred thread, armlets, elbow bands, bracelets, rings, anklets, and toe-rings. His matted locks, piled high on his head, are held in place by a diadem, as he stands resting his weight on his right leg. An exceedingly slender and youthful Uma, wearing a long skirt that clings to her limbs, seems to linger behind. A diadem frames her face, and her long hair is arranged in an elaborate chignon twisted into the form of a figure eight. Large earrings, multiple necklaces, armlets, bracelets, and anklets adorn her body.

It will become evident from the chapters of this book that the body, whether divine or human, is invariably the body adorned. Elsewhere, in a book devoted to the subject of adornment, I have demonstrated that the body of the artistic tradition of India is always ornamented with a lavish range of jeweled ornaments, with cosmetics and fragrant pastes, with flowers and fine fabric.[45] The importance of ornament in the Indian artistic tradition cannot be stressed enough. Ornament is auspicious; ornament is protective; ornament makes the body complete, whole, beautiful, desirable. To be without ornament is to provoke the forces of inauspiciousness, to court danger, even to create danger. Such a belief is clarified in poems that speak of armlets protecting the arms, necklaces screening the neck, earrings sheltering the ears.

A ninth-century Tamil poem, written at the precise time that Chola processional bronzes first began to be made, is of relevance in its description of the manner in which

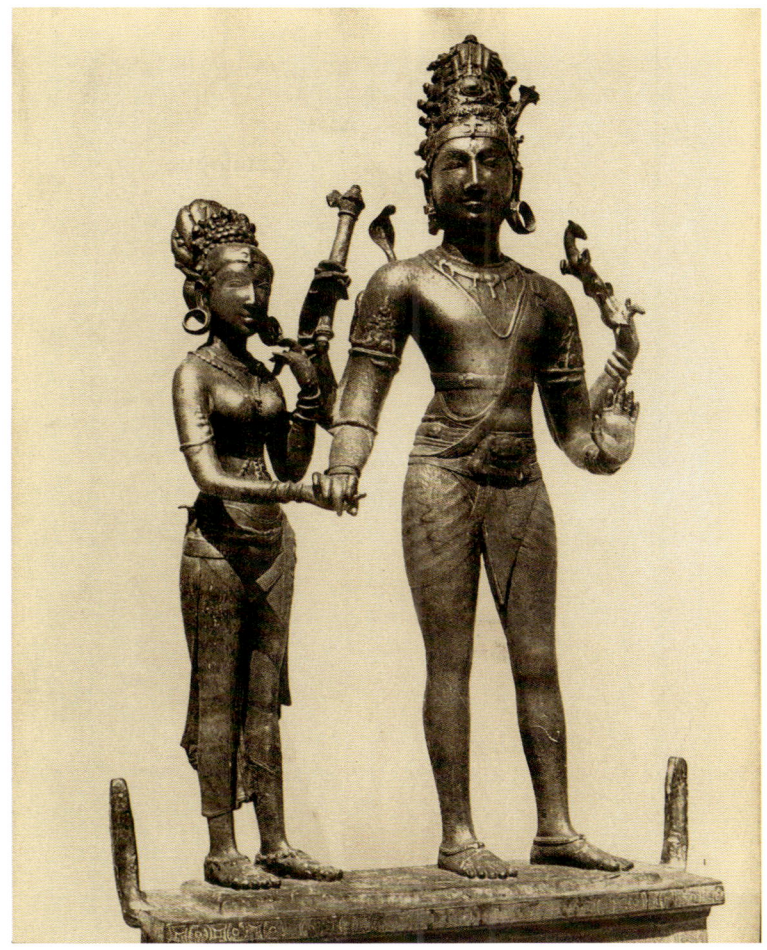

Figure 1.12. Shiva Taking Uma's Hand in Marriage (*Kalyanasundarar*), Vadakkalathur temple, ca. 860.

Uma adorns Shiva before he embarks on his processional route. Here is the relevant portion in Blake Wentworth's translation:

*She decked him with a garland fashioned by the irrepressible god of love
and dusted him with wholesome fragrant powders;
Taking up cool sandalwood prepared by ladies accomplished in their art
she applied it to his worthy chest.
She clothed him in silk fresh
with the scent of wish-giving trees
and tied golden anklets on his feet,
She placed on his head a crown set with a sparkling crest-jewel
and on his forehead a shining plate bright with gems.
She graced his ears with sea-monster earrings made of unpierced rubies
and taking up a necklace of large diamonds,
a fine necklace of huge pearls threaded with gold, and a shining victory garland,
she wreathed his holy chest and it shimmered in their light.*

She tied armbands around his eight mighty arms
and buckled on a belt that delights all who see
She bound a waist-cord about him, placed bracelets on his hands
and adorned his body with elegant designs.[46]

It is thus sumptuously adorned that Shiva emerges to meet his devotees, and it is similarly richly adorned that his consort Uma will emerge in procession. Every bronze we examine in the chapters of this book is richly adorned in the bronze itself. But, as we will see in chapter 5, devotees vied to make gifts of sumptuous gold jewelry set with rubies, diamonds, crystals, corals, and pearls to further adorn the bronzes.[47] Clearly, you could not have too much of a good thing.

This early marriage duo comes from the hands of a sensitive sculptor, similar to this modern master or *sthapati*,[48] who works with a mixture of paraffin wax (*melugu*) and the resin of the *shal* tree (*kunguliyam*) that is processed with the addition of groundnut oil (fig. 1.13a). For the necklaces, armlets, belts, and other adornment, this prepared wax is further mixed in a 50/50 proportion with beeswax to create a more malleable texture suitable for carving details of the beads, jewels, clasps, and fabric. The master craftsperson creates the forms piece by piece, independently modeling the torso, arms and legs, hands and feet, the face, the crown or headdress, and then joins them (fig. 1.13b). Beside him is a flame in which he softens the wax units to mold them better, and a tub of cold water into which he places a finished piece. When satisfied with his work, the artist adds wax struts to connect arms and legs to the torso (fig. 1.13c) and lets it settle overnight in a bath of cold water for a small image, and for several days for large pieces. Then commences the addition of the first layer of extra-fine clay from the Kaveri river, known as *vendal mun*, which is mixed and allowed to "sour" for a day just as is done with the batter for south India's popular breakfast dishes, *idlis* and *dosas*. Craftsmen emphasize the importance of expertly and delicately applying this first layer of clay over every portion of the wax image; only then will the final bronze emerge to perfection and reflect accurately the work of the wax master (fig. 1.13d). This critical job is entrusted only to those with extensive experience. Workers of lesser caliber then apply several further layers of clay to create a mass that no longer provides even a hint as to the nature of the image enclosed. When the clay-enclosed image is fired, the liquid wax flows out of an opening left at the bottom, resulting in a hollow mold that exactly reflects the original wax image. Note that the Master's original wax image is melted and gone forever.

Metal casters now heat the copper, to which they have added small quantities of tin and lead, until it reaches the prescribed consistency that indicates to them that the correct temperature has been reached. It is quite extraordinary that even in the twenty-first century, the metal casters use no thermometers, mechanical gauges, protective clothing, spectacles, or even footwear (fig. 1.13e). Meanwhile, other workers watch over the clay mold that has been slowly heated in a pit packed with coals so that it may withstand the heat of the metal it is about to receive. The clay mold is placed head down into a receiving pit, and the molten metal is poured in through the opening at its base from which the wax exited. The pouring is a skilled process, and metal experts have to ensure that air is not trapped anywhere and that the molten metal flows evenly through the

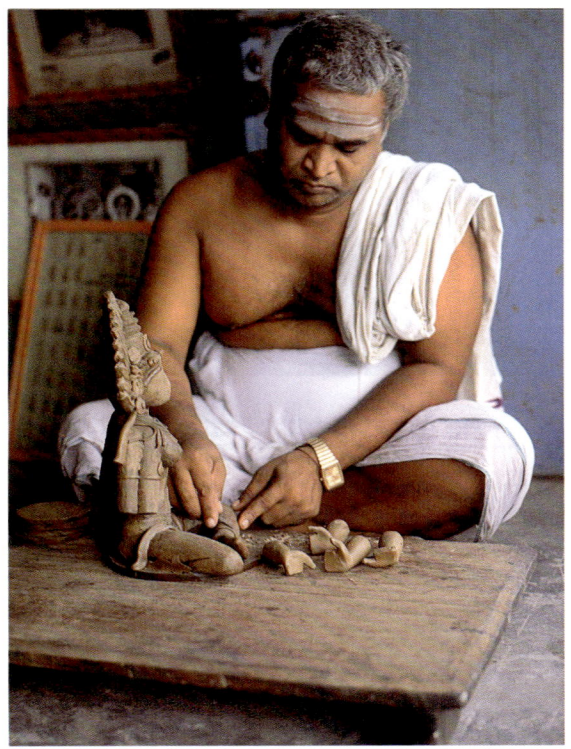

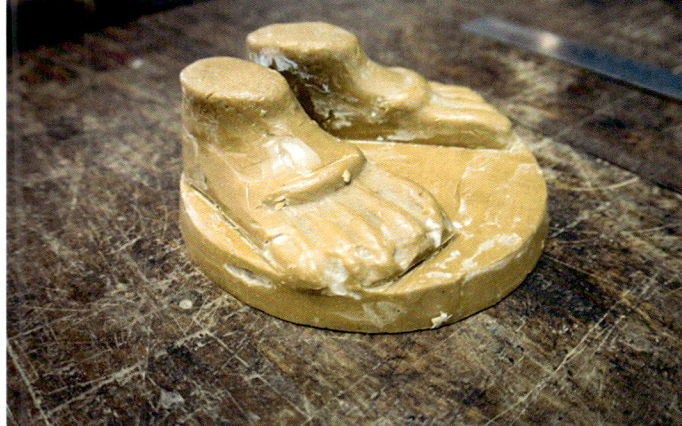

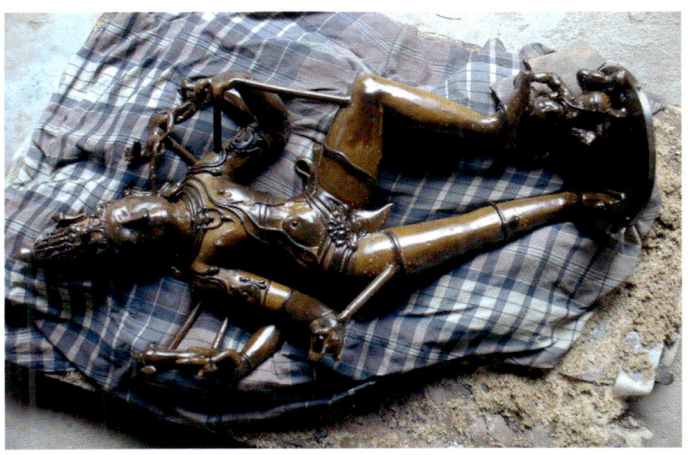

Figure 1.13. (a) A *sthapati*, or master. (b) Feet and base plate modeled separately. (c) Mid-progress: wax image complete, with struts to connect the torso and appendages. (d) Application of *vendal mun* (Kaveri river clay) over the wax image. (e) A metal caster firing the image.

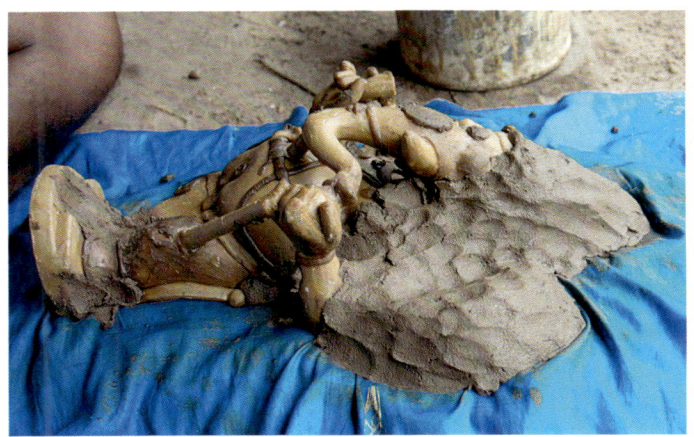

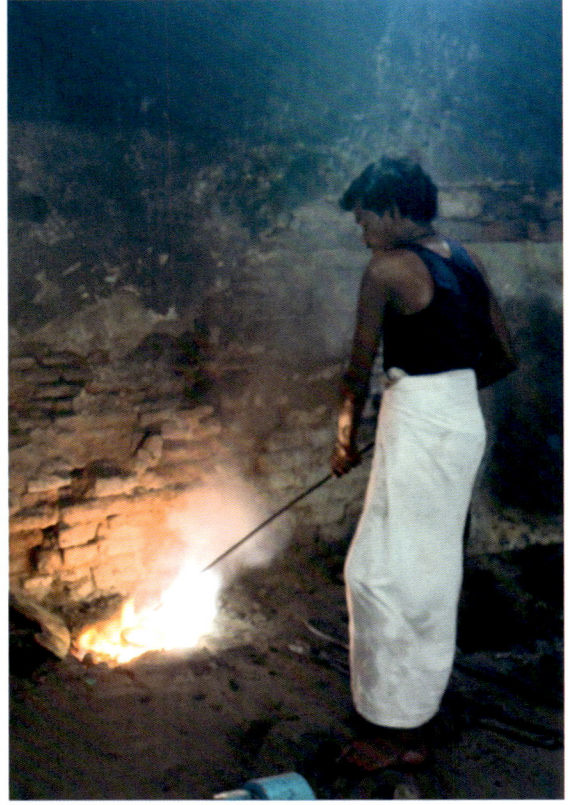

GODS ON PARADE

connecting struts into each section of the mold. The metal-filled mold cools for several days before it is broken open. Initially, the workers use large hammers; later, gentle strokes of a chisel reveal the image. If the crucial first layer of clay was expertly applied, little needs to be done except to chisel away the metal struts that connect limbs and torso, and smooth the surface to remove the "skin," a dark surface that results from the process of firing. The faces of modern images are routinely left with the "skin" intact to await the arrival of the Master himself, who usually returns at this stage to apply the expert touch of his chisel to ensure the hint of a smile or the perfection of an oval face.

Modern bronze casters at the town of Swamimalai in the coastal belt, who speak of their hallowed ancestry, continue to this day to create sacred bronzes for new temples, whether these are in Pittsburgh or Delhi, in Chennai or Kauai. They now take certain shortcuts like leaving a band of plain clay to represent a necklace, and then use cold chiseling, after the metal image emerges from the mold, to carve the details of individual beads, the decorative details of drapery, and other ornament. The relative sharpness created by such extensive cold chiseling reveals itself to the eye and to the touch as distinct from the softness of details created in wax itself that one encounters on original Chola bronzes.[49]

All Chola bronzes are the product of this direct lost-wax process in which the mold must be broken to release the image. There is no mold left for reuse, so each Chola bronze is a singular piece that may not be replicated in any mechanical fashion. Of course, the wax modeler could create a closely similar piece for another patron, modeling it once again, from scratch, in wax. But multiples or replicas are just not possible with the Chola process. By contrast, bronzes from the Greek and Roman world, Renaissance bronzes, and more modern Rodin bronzes are cast hollow. In this indirect lost-wax process, the original model is retained; it is preserved, it is reserved, thus encouraging the creation of replicas and multiples. This procedure is so obvious in the context of Greek and Roman statuary that Carol Mattusch casually remarks of bronze: "That is, after all, the nature of the medium."[50] Of public sculptures of standing heroes, of which "there are still 3000 in Rhodes, and no fewer believed to exist at Athens, Olympia, and Delphi," she says, "The best way to make such a commission was, of course, by serial production."[51] It is likely that some of my readers are familiar with the Roman process in which the original image, often made of wood, is covered with a single layer of clay or plaster that is applied in a number of easily removable sections to create a clay mold of the original. When dry, the sections of the clay mold are removed from the original work of the artist, which is put away and remains untouched and reusable, allowing for the future creation of multiple replicas, as we see to this day with "new" Rodin bronzes. The sections of the clay mold are then reassembled and fired; the interior of this clay model is then coated with a thin layer of beeswax, which, in turn, is covered with a second layer of clay that, when heated, permits the thin layer of wax to melt and flow out through the series of sprues and funnels added in wax. Molten metal is poured into this slim hollow matrix, resulting in a relatively fragile, hollow metal image, frequently no more than 0.2 to 0.4 inch thick, and very different indeed from solid Chola bronzes. An image of Uma from the Asia Society, standing 3 feet tall, weighs 93 pounds (fig.1.14), while a slightly smaller Shiva-Uma bronze duo from the collection of the Cleveland Museum of Art weighs 240 pounds together with its 8 1/2 inch pedestal (see fig. 1.5).[52] Bronzes from southeast Asia

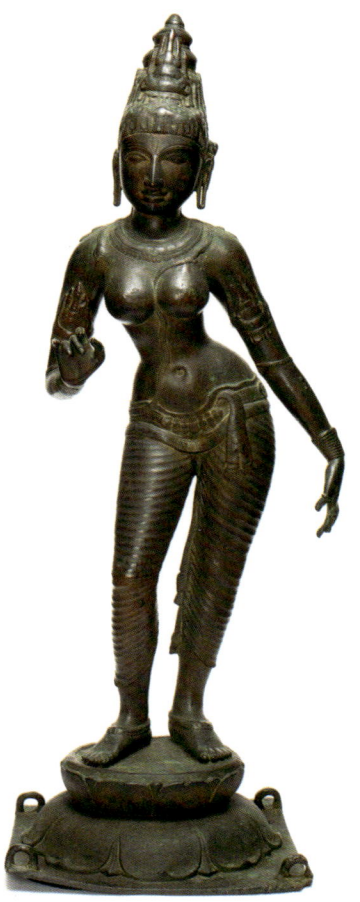 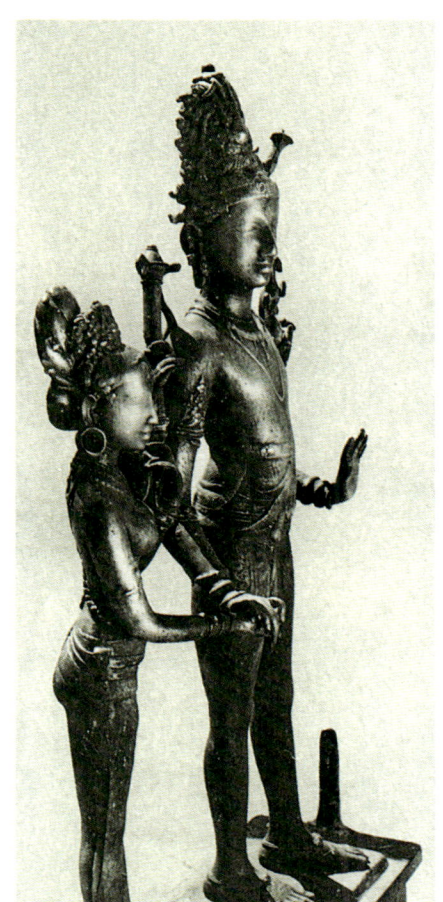

Figure 1.14. Uma, ca. 1012, Asia Society Museum, New York, Mr. and Mrs. John D. Rockefeller 3rd Collection.

Figure 1.15. Side view of Shiva Taking Uma's Hand in Marriage (*Kalyanasundarar*) (see fig. 1.12), Vadakkalathur temple, ca. 860.

use a variant on the direct hollow lost-wax process in which a wax model is created over a substratum of clay that remains within the metal image. Here too, there is no possibility of the reuse of a model and hence no possibility of the creation of exact replicas; these southeast Asian images are lighter than Chola bronzes, although still singular pieces.

The marriage duo from the coastal temple at Vadakkalathur belongs to the very first generation of Chola processional bronzes, perhaps as early as 855/860. And what a dramatic start they represent. No evidence exists of hesitant beginnings. Where did this Master come from? Where is his other work? Might it emerge from an underground burial site? Since the entire art of processional bronzes was in its infancy, we must assume that the artist who created this couple in the mid-ninth century trained as a sculptor in a wood- or stone-carving workshop. The markedly flattened form of the images that is strikingly evident in side view is noteworthy; it is almost as if the figures were extracted from a bas relief in stone or wood (fig. 1.15). It is likely that this flattened treatment was characteristic of the wooden processional images that preceded these first bronzes; indeed, a parallel treatment of flattened backs is seen to this day in the local Tamil craft tradition of *marapachi*, or wood dolls, which are carved from a type of medicinal wood. In this bronze pair, one might say that we are witnessing the birth of the Chola bronze. The terminology of Pallava-Chola transition, sometimes used to describe these images,[53] is fraught with problems. Any transition must surely assume a robust tradition in an earlier phase that then morphs into a slightly variant tradition in the later phase. Since there is no Pallava tradition of sizable processional bronzes, I suggest abandoning such terminology altogether.

The Shiva temple at Tandantottam, also in the coastal belt, once housed this exceedingly slender image of a youthful Shiva posed in exaggerated contrapposto, a posture favored by artists in India to suggest graceful movement (fig. 1.16). This might seem outlandish to those accustomed to the idea of verisimilitude, but it must be stressed that sculptors and painters in India never subscribed to the concept of mimesis. Additionally, considerable importance was given in India to the concept of beauty in motion.[54] Think of the very idea of a dancing deity, of a supple Shiva with a finely toned body who dances the world into creation, or of heroic Shiva who dances a frenzied dance of triumph after having defeated threatening forces of evil. The Tamil concept of Shiva, combined with Chola aesthetics, is indeed a thing apart. In this image from a temple in the extended coastal belt, Shiva stands in relaxed splendor, with a playful serpent looking over his right shoulder. This Shiva, whom we will discuss further in the next chapter, belongs to a date somewhat after the marriage couple we just examined, perhaps around the year 875. These two early bronzes, and several others that we will soon examine, were created for temples along the coastal belt that extends some 65 miles north to south along the Bay of Bengal. The area comprises the delta of the Kaveri river and, moving from north to south, includes the four port towns of Poompuhar, Karaikkal, Nagapattinam, and Maraikkadu that were clearly of strategic importance to the early Chola monarchs, newly established in the Kaveri delta.

I conclude with a reminder of the captivating beauty of Shiva (fig. 1.17, a detail of fig. 1.12). Child saint Sambandar's first song, and the descriptive refrain of its verses of Shiva as "the thief who stole my heart" is familiar to many in the Tamil-speaking area. They can recite it pretty much in the way in which Christians are familiar with the 23rd psalm, "The Lord is my shepherd." Here is Sambandar's first verse in its original Tamil:

> *Thodudaiya sheviyan, vidai eri, or thu venmati shudi*
> *Kadudaiya shudalai podi pushi, en ullam kavar kalvan—*

In English, it reads somewhat prosaically:

> *He wears a woman's earring on one ear;*
> *riding on his bull,*
> *crowned with the pure white crescent moon*
> *his body smeared with ash from the burning ground,*
> *he is the thief who stole my heart . . .*[55]

Tamil and English, as linguists point out, are "unequal languages."[56] Like other Indian languages, Tamil has no need for articles, while several pronouns and auxiliary verbs are

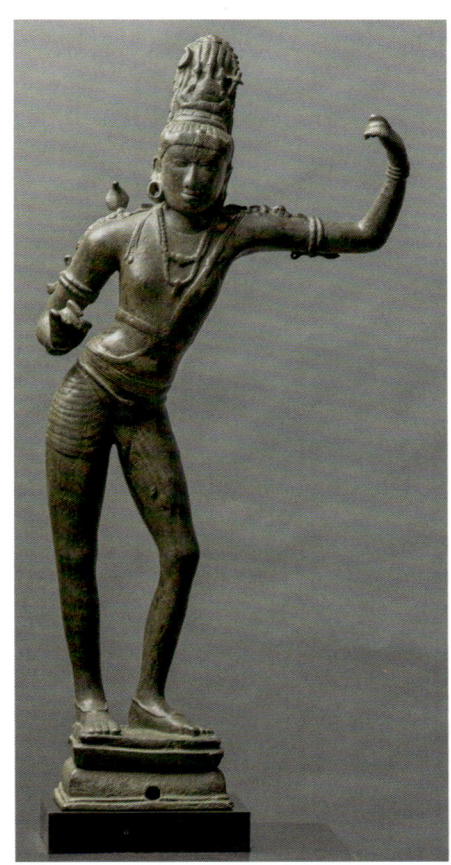 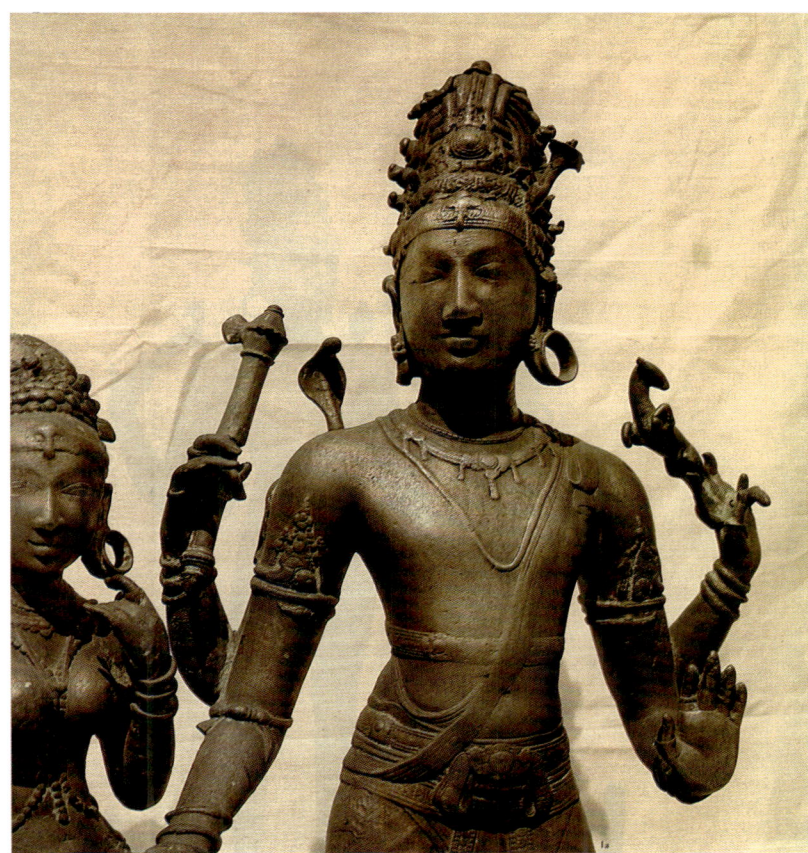

Figure 1.16. Shiva as Victor of Three Forts (*Tripura Vijaya*), Tandantottam, ca. 875, Norton Simon Museum, Pasadena.

Figure 1.17. Detail of Shiva Taking Uma's Hand in Marriage (*Kalyanasundarar*) (see fig. 1.12), Vadakkalathur temple, ca. 860.

part of word endings, making it possible to convey deep meaning in just a few syllables.[57] Rabindranath Tagore, the famous Bengali poet and Nobel prize winner for literature, who was himself responsible for early translations of his own work into English, is believed to have expressed his frustration with the process by remarking that reading Bengali poetry in translation gave about as much pleasure as making love to a woman through the services of an intermediary! Yet, the Chola sacred image can be seen as Tamil poetry in bronze.

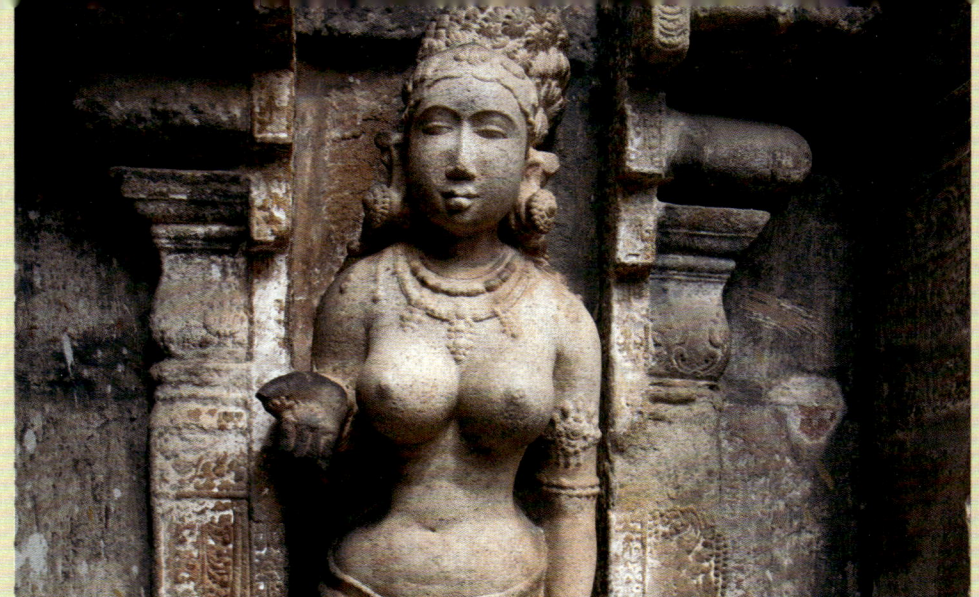

Battling for Empire and Shiva as Victor of Three Forts

855–955

2

Svasti sri. The Chola who captured Tondainadu, the Rajakesari [king-lion] who defeated [those with] many elephants, together with the Chera king Sthanu Ravi, honored Vikki Annan with the family title of "Sembiyan Tamil-Vel," and bestowed on him a throne, flywhisk, palanquin, drums, bugles, elephants, mansion, royal allowance. His wife, Kadamba Madevi gave to the Shiva of the Neyttanam temple a perpetually burning lamp and 100 sheep; these in the protection of the temple's Shiva Brahmins [pan maheshvara rakshai].

SOUTH WALL OF *ARDHA-MANDAPA*, NEYTTANAM TEMPLE[1]

The fleeting glimpse of Chola history from chapter 1 merits elaboration here to better understand the dynamics of the first hundred years of Chola rule when three kings, Vijayalaya, Aditya, and Parantaka, were seeking to retain hold over their kingdom. We encountered the founder of the dynasty, an upstart chieftain who wielded little power; the few inscriptions dated in his reign appear to be on "hero-stones" rather than on temples. One such from his third year (858?), located 63 kilometers north of Thanjavur, commemorates the death of a local cattle guardian, and refers to Vijayalaya as "Supreme-Lion [Parakesari] who captured Thanjavur."[2] His successor Aditya Chola threw off Pallava overlordship and assumed the title "King-Lion [Rajakesari] who captured Tondai-nadu," the name for Pallava territory. The evocative inscription on the Neyttanam temple, cited earlier, encourages us to imagine the celebration of a later victory against the interior region of Kongu. Led by military general Vikki Annan, the armies of Aditya and those of his Kerala ally, Chera king Sthanu Ravi, had been victorious in a major battle; in acknowledgment of the general's pivotal role in this victory, the two rulers had bestowed upon him an unprecedented group of honors, and the honorific title of "Tamil Chola Hero." In gratitude, the general's wife, Lady Kadamba, made a gift to the Neyttanam temple in her husband's honor and arranged for her commemorative gift to be engraved on the temple wall in clear Tamil letters.

Royal copper-plate charters of later Chola monarchs, quoted at the start of chapter 1, glorify these first two rulers of the dynasty. The Tiruvalankadu copper plates of Rajendra Chola dated to 1018 speak of the ease of Vijayalaya's capture of Thanjavur, "just as he would seize by the hand his own wife . . . in order to sport with her."[3] The Anbil copper plates of Sundara Chola dated to 960 praise Aditya by whom "a row of large temples of Siva, as it were banners of his own victories, lofty and unacquainted with defeat (collapse) . . . was built with stone on the two banks of the river Kaveri from the Sahya mountain . . . even to the ocean."[4] While the immediate purpose of a royal copper-plate charter was to record a substantial gift by Chola monarchs, usually of villages or a parcel of land to a temple or to a group of brahmins, the introductory portion was used to proclaim the glory of Chola descent from divine sources and to commemorate the achievements of each historic ruler. The claim of the eulogy writer of a later Chola monarch to the effect that Aditya was a builder of many temples surely contains a degree of hyperbole in its desire to create distinction for an ancestor; that was a necessary role for a court poet employed to write such panegyrics. By pointing out that certain early temples described as "Chola," such as those at Melaipalavur and Kilaipalavur, were in fact constructed by a Palavettaraiyar chieftain, Padma Kaimal has issued a necessary corrective to the overemphasis on Chola royalty as the exclusive source of early Chola temple construction.[5] At the same time, it is surely significant that Palavettaraiyar chieftain Kandan Maravan dated his temple inscriptions in the regnal years of the Chola monarchs; by so doing, he accepted the overlordship of the Cholas who, in turn, permitted him and other chieftains to retain direct hold of their small principalities. Aditya Chola may not have built dozens of temples along the river Kaveri from the mountains down to the ocean, but I find it difficult to agree with the proposition that Aditya may not have built a single temple.[6] I propose that this suggestion needs reevaluation in the context of facts, inscribed in stone, that I have recently unearthed.

The third Chola ruler, Aditya's son Parantaka, ascended the throne in 905, and his lengthy reign of fifty years was filled with repeated battles. To the south, he fought with the Pandyas of Madurai and rulers of Sri Lanka; to the north, he battled against the powerful Rashtrakutas, who dealt Parantaka a crushing blow in the year 949, when they killed his favorite son, Rajaditya, the crown prince and his chosen successor. A unique feature about Chola royalty is their foresight in making it customary for father and son to rule jointly for a few years, a policy that resulted in a routine overlapping of reign dates. In addition, at their coronation, successive rulers assumed the alternating titles of either Rajakesari (King-Lion) or Parakesari (Supreme-Lion).

This hundred-year period between 855 and 955, packed with repeated battles against kingdoms to both north and south, witnessed the appearance, for the very first time in bronze, of memorable portable images of Shiva that had hitherto been created of wood. There is nothing tentative about the workmanship of these first processional bronzes. Despite the political instability of a struggling and nascent Chola kingdom, skilled artists working in wax modeling workshops that were attached to metal foundries produced stately bronzes of rare elegance that convey an assured sense of artistic maturity. Certain moments in time generate unprecedented originality and creativity, and the early Chola period is one such rare moment. In the Chola country, god Shiva became the intense focus of unquestioning devotion for all who contributed toward the enrichment of the temples, whether they be chieftains, princes and princesses, queens, kings, military officers, merchants, or a range of women donors of varying status. Temple statistics indicate that of the 311 temples in the extended Kaveri delta (the present-day districts of Tiruchirappalli, Thanjavur, and Nagapattinam), 295 honor god Shiva, while only 16 are dedicated to god Vishnu.[7] The intensity of the focus on Shiva appears to have been conducive to the creation of finer and finer bronze images of a relatively restricted group of manifestations of Shiva. While the direct lost-wax technique by which the bronzes are produced rules out the possibility of replication, temple bronzes that belong to the same general period of time bear a striking similarity to each other. Apart from the fact that the most favored images were those that followed established tradition, the similarity evident among Chola temple bronzes within each half century during the Chola period is explained by the fact that several bronzes were made in the same workshop and most likely by the same family of artists.

This chapter will start by identifying some of the earliest temples built during the time of the Cholas, and in particular explore a group known as the Sacred Seven (*sapta sthala*) located within close proximity of the Chola capital of Thanjavur. Largely ignored and uninvestigated as a group, no one has seriously studied the numerous inscriptions they carry that, I believe, reveal the involvement of Aditya Chola. We are devoting time to these early temples because it was for ritual worship in such temples that devotees commissioned the bronze images that were housed beside the temple sanctum; without the devotees who participated in temple processions of the bronzes, and without the priests who enabled these temple festivals, there would be no bronze portable images. The greater part of this chapter will then explore a small sampling of the early festival bronzes created during the initial hundred years of Chola overlordship from 855–955. During this period, a very large number of images were created of Shiva as Victor of Three Forts, a manifestation that appears to have had especial appeal for devotees whose monarchs were battling intensively for empire. Into this discussion of early bronzes, I shall weave my suggestion of the possibility of distinguishing between a coastal workshop and an interior capital workshop, a distinction based largely on the proportional system used, and on a few distinctive stylistic traits.

Housing Sacred Bronzes: The Earliest Temples of the Sacred Seven

In the 13th year of king Parakesarivarman, when the king was at Palaiyaru, Pudi Kuttan of Pullamangalam reclaimed land at Palanam in Nalur-nadu, and [made] an endowment for . . . food offerings and . . . to the lord of the temples of Palanam, Aiyaru, Neyttanam, . . . , . . . , Vedikudi, and Arrukunram [Poonturutti].

—NORTH WALL, CENTRAL SHRINE, PALANAM TEMPLE[8]

Seven finely proportioned stone temples of modest size stand along the banks of the Kaveri river and its tributaries, between 7 and 13 kilometers north of Thanjavur (map 4). These temples are at the junction of two routes, one east-west along the Kaveri river and four of its tributaries, and the other running northward from Thanjavur, the newly established Chola city, to Palavur, center of the Palavettaraiyar chieftains,[9] and beyond. The northernmost of these seven temples is at Aiyaru, or Five Rivers, and is known as the Pancha-nadishvara, or "Lord of the Five Rivers," the Kaveri itself and four tributaries, the Arisalar, Vennar, Vettar, and Kudumurutti. The Sacred Seven is celebrated today as a tightly related group in which the Aiyaru temple's bronze processional image of Shiva as *Chandrashekhara* (the Lord with the moon in his locks), accompanied by his consort, is carried in procession to the other six temples. Today, this procession takes place on the second day after the full moon of the month of *Chittirai* (April–May), and follows an elliptical route visiting, in topographical sequence, the temples at Palanam, Chottruturai, Vedikudi, Kandiyur, Poonturutti, and Neyttanam before returning to home-base at Aiyaru (fig. 2.1 a–g). Inscriptions in two of these temples suggest that this custom dates back a thousand years. The Palanam record, quoted earlier, speaks of an endowment of land, most likely in the year 983, for offerings in the temples of Palanam, Aiyaru, Neyttanam, Vedikudi, Attrutali (Poonturutti), and at two other sites whose names are in a damaged portion of the inscription. The grant was made by an individual named Pudi Kuttan from the nearby town of Pullamangai, with the sanction of the king

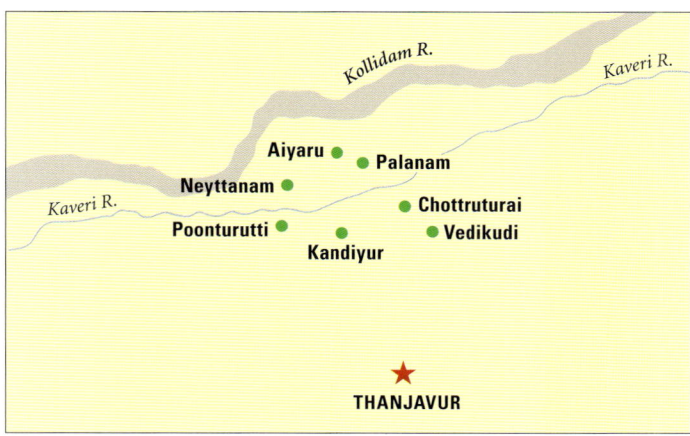

Map 4 The Sacred Seven along the Kaveri river and its tributaries.

BATTLING FOR EMPIRE 39

Figure 2.1. The Sacred Seven group, end of the ninth to end of the tenth century.

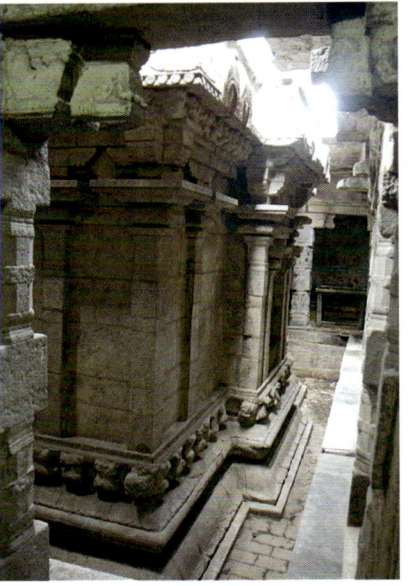

(a) Aiyaru temple (enclosed within later additions), Thanjavur district, late ninth century.

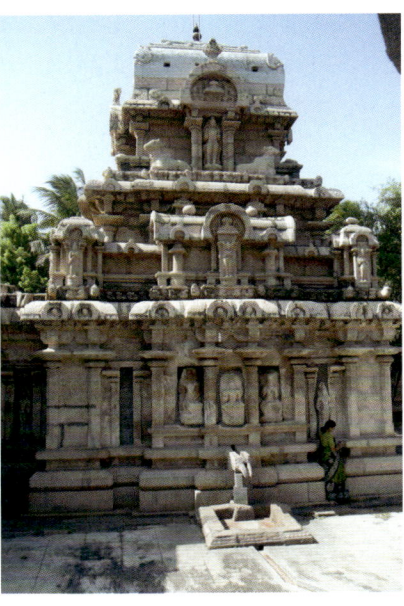

(b) Palanam temple, Thanjavur district, late ninth century.

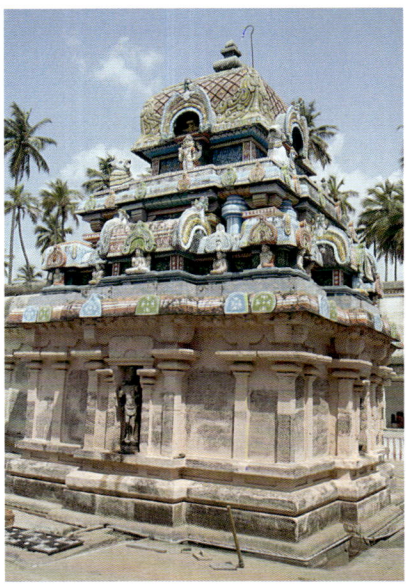

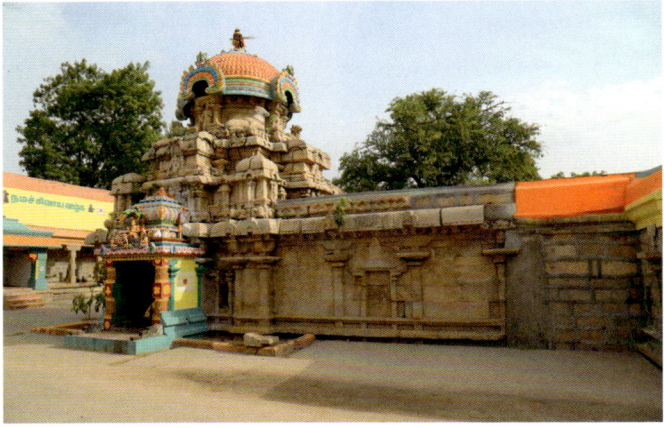

(d) Vedikudi temple, Thanjavur district, tenth century.

(c) Chottruturai temple, Thanjavur district, late ninth century.

(almost certainly Uttama Chola), who was camping at Palaiyaru.[10] A second inscription, this time of the year 1000 from the Chottruturai temple, speaks of an endowment given by an officer with the title Vagaiyili Muvendavelan for sacred food to be prepared on the day of Vishakam in the month of *Vaikhashi* (May–June), when the deity of Aiyaru came to their village.[11] None of these seven temples carry a foundation inscription to tell us which chieftain, royal prince, queen, official, or other individual or group might have been responsible for their construction. Such reticence on the part of patrons appears to have been the norm with temples erected within the territory of the Cholas; even the

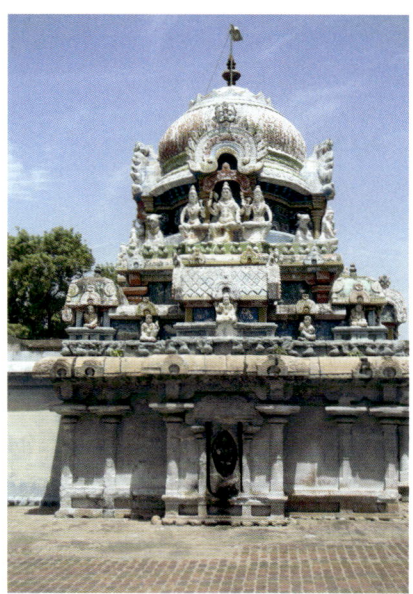
(e) Kandiyur temple, Thanjavur district, late ninth century.

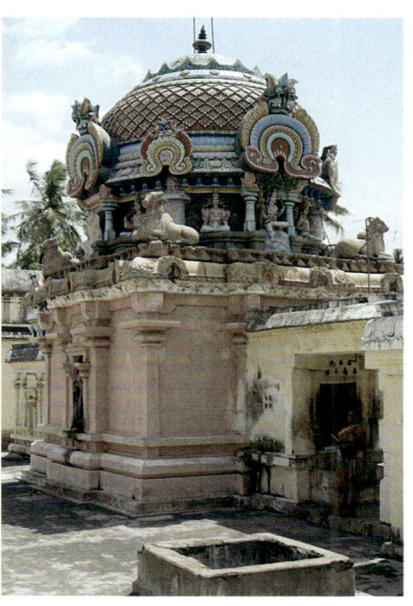
(f) Poonturutti temple, Thanjavur district, late ninth century.

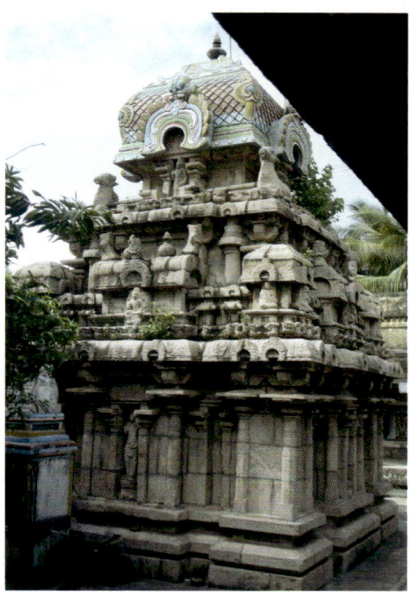
(g) Neyttanam temple, Thanjavur district, late ninth century.

famous royal temple at Gangaikondacholapuram has no foundation inscription and is assigned to Rajendra Chola on the testimony of his Esalam copper-plate inscription. The notable exceptions to this silence regarding temple building comes from families of *araiyars*, a term that might be translated "little kings" or chieftains. For instance, records of the *araiyar* chieftains of Palavur, the Palavettaraiyars, speak of their direct role in temple construction in two temples in and around their center of Palavur. There is also the donative inscription of the Vel chieftain of Kodumbalur, Bhuti Vikarama Kesari, who, together with his two wives, built the Muvar Koil at Kodumbalur, and a record of his daughter, Nangai Bhuti, who married a Chola prince and constructed a temple at Tiruchendurai.[12] The Muttaraiyar chieftains, centered at Niyamam, which is not far from Thanjavur, and who are presumed to have controlled Thanjavur, are less in evidence as temple builders, although we have records of their gifts to existing shrines. Despite their supposed connection with Thanjavur, no Muttaraiyar inscription has been found in that town itself.

Regardless, for the moment, of the actual builders of the temples of the Sacred Seven, a scrutiny of the inscriptions that cover their walls reveals the close involvement of the "Chola royal family" with the maintenance and administrative running of the temples. Before we move to examples of such involvement, commencing with those that reveal the earliest chronological dates, it is important to reiterate that these seven sites were already celebrated in the songs of the *nayanmar*, who composed their hymns roughly between 650 and 800. These were sacred sites whose glory was sung by the Tamil saints (*padal petra sthalam*), where structures of wood, combined perhaps with brick, existed. The saints frequently link three or four of these sites together in their verses. Appar, for instance, asks the lord the name of his original town and sings "What town do you really come from? Is it Turutti, or Palanam, or Neyttanam?"[13] Or again, he praises Shiva as

BATTLING FOR EMPIRE 41

> *Our light in Corrutturai, pure gem in Turutti,*
>
> *King of Palanam on the river, our rare gem in Alavay* [not part of the septad],
>
> *Sliver of moon in Neyttanam . . .*[14]

The *Tevaram* corpus of hymns of the Revered Three devotes six hymns to Shiva at Neyttanam, six to Shiva at Palanam, six to the lord of Chottruturai, and as many as eighteen hymns to the lord of Aiyaru.[15]

Sometime in the latter half of the ninth century, perhaps as soon as Aditya felt that Thanjavur and its immediate vicinity was securely under his control, but apparently prior to the 885 battle of Sripurambiyam at which he likely declared himself independent of Pallava overlordship, these temples were converted to the stone structures that exist today as small well-balanced temples of the *ekatala*, or single-story order (see fig. 2.1a–g).[16] Perhaps it is this very fact of their conversion from brick to stone, as opposed to their brand-new construction, that explains why none has a foundation inscription. Could it be that no one claimed their construction because, after all, a temple already existed at the site, albeit in brick and wood, occasionally with stone jambs to frame the shrine doorway? Perhaps the stone version of such a temple was thought of more as a renovation than a new foundation. For instance, the earliest inscriptions at Neyttanam that record gifts of gold for lamps, and engraved on the left and right doorjambs into the shrine, are from Pallava king Nandivarma of Tellaru fame (in his tenth year, or 856) and from king Maranjadaiyan, also known as Varaguna Pandya, together with his queen and his son Parantaka, with the gift executed in the year 866 through an official, Venbanattu Velan.[17] These two inscriptions at Neyttanam are gifts made to the earlier brick temple that carried stone doorjambs flanking the shrine entrance. When the entire temple was rebuilt in stone, the inscribed stone doorjambs were merely relocated into the new stone temple. The regular occurrence of stone doorjambs to flank shrine entrances in brick temples may be surmised from the recurrent inscriptions of the ninth-century monarchs Varaguna Pandya and Nandivarman of Tellaru fame, found engraved on such doorjambs and not in other locations.[18] The only other stone found in a few early wood and brick temples are stone pillars such as those found in temples dedicated to Kala Pidari or Kali.[19] Varaguna Pandya also gifted gold for a lamp at the temple in Chottruturai, while in 890 Pallava Nripatunga made a gift to a goddess temple in the town of Kandiyur.[20] This explanation for the lack of foundation inscriptions has exceptions, since it appears that chieftains made it a point of recording temple construction. Palavettaraiyar chieftain Kandan Maravan claimed to have constructed a stone temple at Kilai-paluvur despite the fact that it was built at ancient *Alandurai*, sung of by saint Appar, where a shrine of brick and wood surely stood. At any rate, the numerous inscriptions on the walls of the *sapta sthala* temples—63 at Neyttanam, 101 at Chottruturai, 51 at Vedikudi, and in that range at the other four sites—do not proclaim the identity of their founders. The inscriptions record only the many donations to an already existing and already functioning temple.

The evidence that leads me to emphasize royal involvement in these temples is inscriptional in nature. The earliest in date are two important inscriptions at the Neyttanam temple that belong to the reign of Aditya I (see fig. 2.1g). The first, quoted at the start of this chapter, speaks of Madevi Kadambadevi, wife of general Vikki Annan, who gave a perpetual lamp to Shiva at Neyttanam to commemorate the bestowal of a range of honors on her husband by Aditya Chola (*tondainadu pavina cholan palayanai kokandan ayina Rajakesari*) jointly with the Chera king Sthanu Ravi (*Cheraman Ko thanu Eravialum*). The year in which the gift was made is not specified, but the inscription on the southern wall of the *ardha-mandapa* at Neyttanam remains clearly readable today. Setting aside the issue of whether or not Aditya was responsible for the construction of this temple, we can say with certainty that the sanctum and *ardha-mandapa* of the temple were sufficiently complete during his reign for such an inscription to be cut into the stone of the *ardha-mandapa*'s south wall. A second inscription on the Neyttanam temple, inscribed on the south wall of the shrine itself, indicates that Aditya's son Kannaradeva[21] (who died early and never ruled the kingdom) was associated with this temple. Dated in the year 8 of the reign of a Rajakesari (which corresponds with the year 878–879 if that Rajakesari is Aditya), it speaks of a gift from Adittan Kannaradeva, son of the ruling Chola king (*Adittan Kannaradeva Cholaperumanadigal makanar*). The prefix Adittan to the name Kannaradeva is the standard Tamil formula for stating any individual's father's name; here, it clarifies that Kannaradeva is Aditya's son and that he is the son (*makanar*) of the ruling Chola king (*chola peruman adigal*).[22] We read that in the year 878–879, prince Kannaradeva gave gold to the temple to ensure a *nonda vilakku*, a perpetually burning lamp, to illuminate the temple premises; clearly, the shrine of the stone temple of Neyttanam, on whose south wall this inscription is engraved, was constructed prior to 879. A third inscription, this time in the adjoining temple of Aiyaru (see fig. 2.1a), adds an interesting piece of information along the same lines. A woman named Kadambavitari, who identifies herself as foster-mother (*tati*)[23] of the prince Kannaradeva, gifted gold for a perpetually burning lamp in the Aiyaru temple, no more than 2 miles north of Neyttanam, in the year 20 of Rajakesari (891 for Aditya).[24] Despite the absence of a dedicatory inscription, I find the fact of these three inscriptions—the first of Kadambamadevi mentioning Aditya who captured Tondainadu, the second a gift of Aditya's son, prince Kannaradeva, and the third a gift of Kannaradeva's *tati*, to be strong pointers to the possibility that the Neyttanam temple was built with the blessings of, if not by, Aditya Chola. Also of relevance is the fact that Adittapuram is the name of the market town mentioned in two inscriptions at Neyttanam: one speaks of a gift of gold for lamps from the trading community (*nagarattar*) of Adittapuram,[25] while a second speaks of a similar gift of gold from a merchant belonging to the Manigramam, a major trading guild, of Adittapuram.[26] Additionally, it makes perfect sense that temples erected during the early phase of attempted consolidation of an incipient monarchy would be located close to their new capital of Thanjavur.

The continuing participation of Chola princes in this group of seven temples after the time of Aditya appears to be a further pointer to royal association with the Sacred Seven. Inscriptions reveal the involvement of three sons of Aditya's successor Parantaka,[27] prince Arikulakesari, prince Uttamasili who never ascended the throne, and Arinjaya who appears to have ruled jointly with his brother Gandaraditya and, upon his brother's abdication, jointly with his own son, Sundara Chola. At the Neyttanam temple, in the twenty-fourth year of Parantaka (930), who is referred to by his known moniker as king Parakesari who captured Madurai (*Madirakonda Koparakesari*), prince Arikulakesari (*Cholaperumanadigal Sri Parakesari vanmar makanar Parantaka Arikulakesariyar*) gifted gold, specified to be *Ilakasu* (Sri Lankan money), that was entrusted to the town council to be used for a perpetual lamp as well as for ghee to keep the lamp burning.[28] A second son of Parantaka, *pillaiyar* Uttamasili, gave a gift of gold and land for a perpetually burning lamp to the temple at Kandiyur, an endowment that was seemingly renegotiated in the year 932.[29] Prince Arinjaya (*Parantaka Arinjikai*) similarly gifted gold for a lamp to the temple at Poonturutti as well as ghee to keep it burning.[30] A final gift of interest here is that of Pandan Kali, foster-mother to Parantaka himself; her gift to the temple at Palanam, made in Parantaka's thirteenth regnal year of 918, was to be used to feed ten brahmins daily and also to pay the expenses of the temple cooks, potters, and other servants.[31] These four gifts to four temples of the septet, three by three different royal princes during the reign of their father Parantaka, and one by Parantaka's own foster-mother, further suggest a "royal" relationship with a "family" temple.

What about the role of royal women? A case has been made to the effect that during the first hundred years of the dynasty, the contribution of "Chola" queens should be considered in terms of their natal families, generally of chieftain status, rather than of the Chola line into which they married.[32] The argument is strong and convincing in the cases cited, of which there are a limited number, but its applicability may have been overstated. Inscriptions from this group of seven temples suggest that the princesses who entered into these marital alliances, and indeed their mothers too, appear to display an independent connection to Chola religious institutions. Vayiriakkan Tribhuvanamahadevi, queen of a Rajakesari, made a gift of gold to the temple of Poonturutti;[33] her mother, Kadupattigal Tamaramettiyar, made gifts to Palanam[34] and to Chottruturai.[35] The gift to Palanam was made in the year 23 of Rajakesari, leaving us with only Aditya and Rajaraja as Rajakesaris who ruled that long. By the year 23 of Rajaraja, his inscriptional preamble (*meykirti*) was well established; its omission in this record may be a pointer to Vayiriakkan being a queen of Rajakesari Aditya. Queen Tennavan Mahadeviyar, perhaps also an Aditya queen, made a gift in the year 17 of a Rajakesari to the temples at Neyttanam[36] and Palanam.[37] She displays a continued interest in the Palanam temple, making two further gifts in the years 8 and 10 of a Parakesari, with these inscriptions specifying that Tennavan is the queen of Ko Rajakesari.[38] I read Tennavan's gifts as having been made initially in the reign of Aditya, a Rajakesari, and continuing into the reign of Parantaka, a Parakesari, at which time it became necessary for the inscription to clarify that the donor was the queen of the previous king, a Rajakesari. Mullai Nangaiyar, mother of a Parantaka queen named Cholamahadevi, gave gifts to four of the temples of the Sacred Seven—to Neyttanam, Chottruturai, Palanam, and Poonturutti—in the same year of 909.[39] A second Parantaka queen Chola Sikhamaniyar, daughter of Nanguri Nangaiyar of Mayilapil, made a gift at Aiyaru, while her mother made a gift in her daughter's name at Chottruturai.[40] These multiple gifts to the temples of this early Chola cluster from various early queens and their mothers suggest that, apart from links that must indeed have existed between the queens and their natal families, there was also a strong desire to establish an association of influence with the family they entered through a marital alliance.

Another set of inscriptions that I would like to bring into the picture as we investigate possible royal involvement in this Kaveri river septad of temples involves the *bhogiyar*, or concubine, of a Chola king. The temples at Poonturutti and Neyttanam carry inscriptions, one dated in the year 11 and the second in the year 14 of a Rajakesari, that speak of gifts of gold by Nangai Chattapeymanar, *bhogiyar* of the ruling Chola king (*Cholaperumanadigal*), to be used for a perpetual lamp in each temple. At Poonturutti, the conditions of her gift were fulfilled.⁴¹ At Neyttanam, however, the temple authorities diverted her funds to build a *namana mandapa*, or bathing hall (for the bronze processional images). The inscription tells us that the king himself intervened and donated land purchased from the assembly of the town of Perumpuliyur in order to fulfill his *bhogiyar*'s original intention.⁴² Another ruling king's *bhogiyar*, Nakkan Aiyaradigal of Rajamarttandapuram, a part of Niyamam, donated gold for a perpetual lamp at the Aiyaru temple in the seventeenth year of a Rajakesari. The inscription tells us that the *nagaram*, or market town, of Shivapuri, which received the money, agreed to supply the necessary quantity of ghee for burning in the lamp.⁴³ It is debatable as to whether we should interpret the involvement of a ruling king's *bhogiyar* in gifts to a temple as signifying the involvement, in one way or another, of their royal "lords."

A final significant group of stakeholders in this septad of temples is the *srikaryam* officers who were in charge of overseeing temple administration; their role included checking the accounts of the temple and levying fines for offenses when deemed appropriate. From the phraseology used in the inscriptions, it appears that these officers received sanction to implement their decisions by the king or chieftain in question. In the year 931, a *srikaryam* officer, Bavataya, scrutinized the accounts of the Neyttanam temple with the direct sanction (*srimukam*) of the king Parantaka and levied fines accordingly.⁴⁴ In the year 11 of a Rajakesari, Ayyan Kamakkodanar investigated the affairs of the temple (*devadana*) of Neyttanam and collected fines from three members of its administration, using the gold collected as fines to make gold diadems for the deity.⁴⁵ A *srikaryam* officer with the title Minavan Villattur Nattukon appears repeatedly in inscriptions at the Sacred Seven. In the year 10 of Parakesari, an inscription at Neyttanam speaks of his investigation of the village, the merchants, and the temple.⁴⁶ We encounter him again at Vedikudi, where, in the year 990, during the reign of Rajaraja, he made arrangements for the nighttime *sribali* service.⁴⁷ We meet Minavan Villattur Nattukon a third time at Chottruturai in the year 991 as the officer who, with the blessings of Rajaraja, investigated the lamp service; in the following year, he investigated the food offerings at the same temple and levied fines on those found wanting in their execution of the task.⁴⁸ These various official investigations appear to suggest an interest and an involvement by the king in the affairs of this group of temples. In conclusion, I should mention the twenty inscriptions of chieftains, either with the suffix *Vel* or *araiyar* (as in Palavett-araiyars and Mutt-araiyars), that record donations of gold or land for perpetual lamps; these comprise only 2 percent of the total of about four hundred records in the seven temples of this sacred septad.⁴⁹

These various inscriptional records from the Sacred Seven, viewed together as a discrete group, lead me to propose that this cluster of seven temples was rebuilt in stone during the reign of Aditya I, and the temples owe their current appearance (when the original survives) to work done toward the end of the third quarter of the ninth century. Not a single inscription contains information about the builders of these temples. The inscriptions of Aditya's own son, Kannaradeva, and of three sons of his successor Parantaka, princes Arikulakesari, Uttamasili, and Arinjikai, indicate a close connection, and continued interest, of members of the "royal family" in these seven temples. So too do the inscriptions of the kings' *bhogiyars*, and their many queens and mothers-in-law. The fact that these temples carry inscriptions from the king's *srikaryam* officers, who were authorized to levy fines on individual members of the temple administrative officers including the accountant, together with a reference in one such inscription to the *srimukham* or sacred face of the king, further emphasizes a degree of royal interest in this group of temples.

Before we leave the Sacred Seven, it is useful to return to the theme of the use of stone in place of brick, and turn to the Vedikudi temple, in which five inscriptions repeatedly specify that it is a stone temple (*kattrali*)[50] (see fig. 2.1d). The market town associated with Vedikudi is Parakesaripuram, whose merchants seem to have had a significant role to play in the temple's donations, and perhaps even its construction. Is the Parakesari to whom the town refers Parantaka Chola? Inscription 7 speaks of the merchants of Parakesaripuram as having decided that the record should be cut into the stone of the stone temple (*kattraliyil kalmel vettu enraruli cheyya parakesaripurattu nagarattar . . .*). Inscription no. 11 similarly informs us that the officer of the stone temple of Shiva mahadeva (*tiru kattrali mahadevar*) of Parakesaripuram, as well as the town residents, ordered that the gift of queen Vanavanmahadevi should be cut into the stone (*kalmel vettu enru*). Inscription nos. 10 and 11 refer to gifts to the mahadeva of the stone temple (*tiru kattrali*) of Parakesaripuram. Inscription no. 14, badly damaged, is the most intriguing of all; it speaks of the *nagarattar* or trading community of Parakesaripuram as having installed the *mukattodu*, or crowning-stone of this stone temple (*ikkattrali mukattodu yitta nagarattar*).[51] The repeated emphasis in these inscriptions on Vedikudi being a stone temple indicates the importance assigned during the early phase of the Chola period to converting preexisting brick temples at a variety of sacred spots (*padal petra sthalams*) to stone structures.

It is relevant to mention that inscription no. 15, and a few others at Vedikudi, give the impression of being a consolidated copy of earlier gifts. A cluster of inscriptions along the lowest section of the base moldings (*jagati*) start with the words *svasti sri*, records a gift, and ends with a dash-like stop mark; it then continues once again with *svasti sri,* and lists another gift, once again ending with a stop-mark, and so on. What is missing is the standard formulaic introduction at the start of each gift, which contains the name of the king, his regnal year, the exact topographical location of the temple to which the gift was made, as well as the name of the god of the temple.[52] The implication is that when the brick temple at Vedikudi was converted to a stone structure, some of its earlier inscriptions were reengraved on stone as a consolidated cluster. When we turn to chapter 4 and queen Sembiyan's contributions to Chola architecture and sculpture, we will see that she frequently tells us in her inscriptions that she converted an earlier temple to a stone structure, and that she ordered the earlier inscriptions to be reengraved on the stone temple. An inscription of her grand-nephew, emperor Rajaraja,

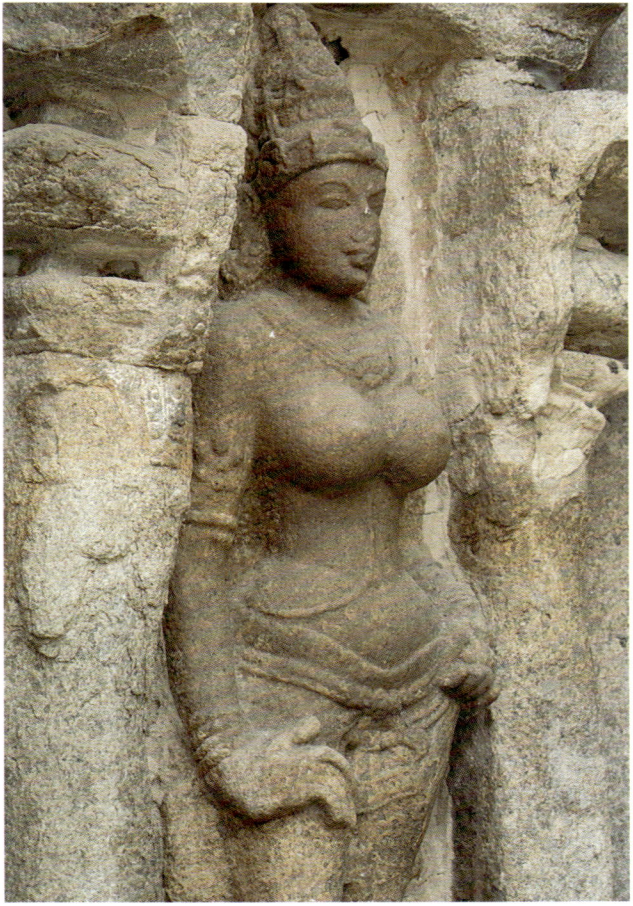

Figure 2.2. A less weathered stone image from Vedikudi temple, Thanjavur district.

recounts a similar conversion, and reengraving, at the site of Tirumalavadi.[53] An even later instance of rebuilding is recorded in the year 1110 during the reign of emperor Kulottunga, when a Bana chieftain petitioned the king and received permission to remove the old and dilapidated brick structure and rebuild the central shrine and its *mandapa* in stone.[54]

It is unfortunate that the once glorious sculptures on the Vedikudi temple have suffered such severe weathering as to disguise the quality of the workmanship. It is necessary to look at the only existing well-preserved image to remind ourselves that the others—so badly worn—were also smooth and elegant once (fig. 2.2). There is no stone at all along the Kaveri basin, so the nearest granite quarries are in the vicinity of Tiruchirappalli, some 40 miles distant. It might appear that the granite at Mamallapuram, or indeed that of the Kalugumalai outcrop in the Madurai region, is of vastly superior quality. But this may be an incorrect assumption. Rather, we may remind ourselves that Mamallapuram and Kalugumalai are rock-cut monuments in which the topmost weathered surface of the stone was removed to expose and carve unweathered rock below.[55] The same could not happen in any uniform manner with constructed monuments where quarried rock would be taken first from the surface, and where an image sculpted from

BATTLING FOR EMPIRE

such exposed rock would readily lose its topmost layer of weathered surface. Whether an image retains its onetime elegance or has lost it to weathering may depend on the particular slab of stone given to a sculptor. As a rock outcrop continued to serve as a quarry, the chances improved of a sculptor getting unweathered stone from deeper within the rock face.

Do these seven temples have architectural features in common that tie them together as a group? Considering the fact that we are speaking of a phase of large-scale conversion of earlier brick temples to stone, which coincided with a new dynastic takeover, it should not surprise us to find several details in a state of flux. Features like a band of mythical lion-like *yalis* along the upper level of the base moldings, or the presence or absence of angular versus curved moldings, or the occurrence of lotus petals or their lack thereof along the moldings, is neither uniformly present nor uniformly absent in temples of this septad. However, we may note the absence from all seven temples of two significant features that are routinely seen in temples built later, during the time of Parantaka, like those at Pullamangai, Tirunamanallur, and the Nageshvara at Kumbakonam. None of the Sacred Seven carry decorative bracket figures of dancers who rest their feet on the *palagai*, or upper flat platform above the raised pilaster running up the walls, and are then slotted within the overhanging eave. A second feature that appears in the Parantaka-period temples and are absent in this septad are the series of boxed scenes from the Ramayana and from sacred myth that are inserted at two levels along the base moldings. The upper level is seen along the recessed band between the topmost *pattigai* molding and the niches on temple walls that carry figures of deities; the second set is lower down between the *pattigai* and the curved or sloping *kumuda* moldings. Only Vedikudi among the Sacred Seven carries boxed panels, but these are without narrative content and feature either vegetal scrolls or dancing figures. Vedikudi is also the only temple of the Sacred Seven that introduces side niches to flank the central niche featuring a deity; all others of the septad have plain walls to flank the central niche. It would seem that Vedikudi was the last of the Sacred Seven to be converted to stone and that it introduces, somewhat tentatively, features that were soon to become standard features. We should point out that temples of the Aditya-era Palavettaraiyar chieftains at Kilaipalavur and Melaipalavur, as also those of a Vel chieftain at Kodumbalur and that of his daughter at Tiruchendurai, similarly lack these two characteristics, featuring neither bracket figures nor boxed scenes from epic and myth.

Before we leave the temples of the Sacred Seven, let me raise a crucial question that has somehow bypassed us all. First, the facts. Using T. V. Mahalingam's volumes of inscriptions as the basis, we find that the two present-day districts of Thanjavur and Nagapattinam have 220 inscribed temples of the Chola period.[56] At twenty-five of these temples—and a more thorough search will likely reveal some further examples—it is possible to find individual donors who claim construction: these include two *araiyan/araiyar* chieftains, a Vel chief, a chieftain from Tondai, officers, a *pandita*, a merchant, merchant guilds, and no less than four different individuals who call themselves *Kattrali Pichchans* (stone temple fanatics). The given name of the stone temple fanatic at the Tiruvaduturai temple is missing, even though he features in five inscriptions, one of which is in the nature of a label to his small portrait image.[57] The given name of the stone temple fanatics at the other three temples survives: at Tirumananjeri, he is Aruran Kamban; at Kalitattai, he is Parantaka Siriyavelan, the king's commander-in-chief; and at Tiruvelvikudi, he is Srika, son of Tiruvaiyaru Yogiyar.[58] The Tiruvelvikudi temple inscription carries intriguing information to the effect that one-quarter of the temple construction was paid for by two well-known and established merchant guilds, the Valanjiyar and the Disai Ayiratti Ainurruvar, while the rest was funded by Tiruvaiyaru Yogiyar and his son Srika, known as *Tirukattrali Pichchan*.[59] The inscriptions at Tiruvelvikudi reveal further information on what one might today refer to as crowd-sourcing: we read that three members of the Gandaraditya military regiment gifted three stones on the temple wall, a scribe in the revenue department made a gift of a doorpost, while single stones were gifted by various individuals.[60] On occasion, an individual's gift to the temple, whether of sheep for a perpetual lamp or of ritual vessels for use in puja, is engraved on a slab of stone and the inscription specifies that the inscribed stone too was the gift of the donor.[61]

If we set aside these twenty-five temples that specify their patrons,[62] we are left with 195 temples in the two districts of Thanjavur and Nagapattinam, of which fourteen carry royal inscriptions: ten are of queen Sembiyan Mahadevi, one of Rajaraja's queen Dantisakti, and three are the well-known monumental royal temples at Thanjavur, Darasuram, and Tribhuvanam.[63] We are left then with the burning issue of the patronage and authorship of the remaining 181 temples. Why did no one claim their construction? Why do the earliest records at so very many sites commence with gifts to an already functioning temple? Since chieftains like the Palavettaraiyars and Vels left inscriptions claiming construction of temples, should we assume that it was customary for chieftains, and chieftains alone, to state their involvement in building temples? Should we then assume that the 189 temples without such claims were not built by chieftains? Last, under these circumstances, it may be appropriate to return to the Anbil copper plates, which state that Aditya built many temples along the Kaveri, in order to reassess the suggestion that Aditya may not have built a single temple.[64] Royal copper-plate charters contain much hyperbole and should be interpreted with care; but if we discard some of their statements as downright falsehoods, we seem to be left in the uncomfortable position of having to decide how to separate the inscriptional wheat from the chaff.

An Excursus on Lamps

Many gifts to these temples, royal or otherwise, starting with those of prince Kannaradeva and his foster-mother, are for perpetually burning lamps. Gifts of lamps may sound like a petty matter, but they were not; in fact, inscriptions suggest that this is one of the burning issues (pun intended) in the Chola period when lamps to illuminate the way within enclosed temples was a huge priority. The interiors of temples are always dark and need illumination day and night. Perpetually burning lamps that stayed alight night and day required a major infusion of funds to ensure a steady supply of ghee to keep the wicks burning. A tenth-century Sanskrit text from central India lays out dramatically the importance of a gift of light when it speaks of Shiva's gift in return of the light of knowledge. Halayudha's hymn to Shiva in seventy-one verses, inscribed on the walls of a temple at Mandhata on the banks of the river Narmada, admittedly some 1,600 kilometers north of the Kaveri river, speaks thus in its twenty-seventh verse:

> *O Three-eyed Lord! To the person who offers You a lamp that rends the darkness of Your temple with blazing light, You in turn give that light of knowledge that needs no further illumination and that splits the dense darkness of delusion in the night of terrifying illusion.*[65]

It is noteworthy that roughly half the records in any one temple in the Kaveri delta are for perpetual lamps.[66] At Neyttanam, just over half of the sixty-three inscriptions are gifts to ensure adequate illumination. Thirty of the sixty-two inscriptions at the temple of Kilaipalavur,[67] constructed some 20 miles north of this septad by the Palavettaraiyar chieftains, are gifts of either sheep, gold, or lands to ensure adequate illumination. Of the forty-six inscriptions at the companion Palavettaraiyar temple at Melaipalavur, twenty-two are gifts of land, gold, or sheep for perpetual lamps. Princes, queens, merchants, and other monied individuals gave gold or land for *nonda vilakkus*; even more numerous are gifts of goats entrusted to shepherds whose responsibility was to convert the milk to ghee to keep those lamps burning day and night. The range of social variation among lamp donors is strikingly demonstrated at the Tiruvidavayil temple, where money for lamps came from a washerman (*vannan*) at one end of the economic strata and from the chiefs of Thanjavur and Kottur at the other end.[68] The importance of illumination is further emphasized in two inscriptions of the time of Rajaraja, where his *srikaryam* temple officer, Minavan Villattur Nattukon, at the instigation of the king, made arrangements for appropriate lighting for the nighttime *sribali* service in which the portable bronze of the deity is taken around the temple. At Vedikudi, one of the temples of the septad, we hear of thirty portable lamps for this purpose, with four people assigned the task of carrying them around the temple to illuminate the path of the god and his devotees.[69] At Chottruturai, Minavan made provision for fifty iron lamps, assigning eight persons who lived in temple housing to carry them around the temple, with four pipers, three gardeners, one cook, and eight cleaning persons to further assist in the ceremonies.[70]

Early Bronzes of Shiva as Victor of Three Forts

> *When the three citadels, unmoored,*
> *flew about wreaking destruction*
> *in heaven and on earth,*
> *oppressed by their assault,*
> *the frightened gods, led by Ari [Vishnu] himself*
> *sought his protection.*
> *Then, moved by compassion, the gracious savior*
> *kindled his deadly arrow with fire,*
> *shot fire from the snake that was his bowstring,*
> *bent his mountain-bow to its fullest,*
> *and reduced the citadels to ashes . . .*
> —APPAR, HYMN 4[71]

In the yr 20 of Parantaka, queen Kokkilanadigal, who installed the processional image of the Lord who Burned the Three Forts [Tripura-dahanam] *in the temple at Tiru-turutti, gifted paddy to make food offerings to this Beauteous Lord of the Three Worlds* [Tripura Sundarar], *and gold to burn a perpetual lamp in front of him.*

—*KUMUDA* BASE MOLDINGS, WEST WALL OF CENTRAL SHRINE, POONTURUTTI TEMPLE[72]

Victor of Three Forts is a manifestation of Shiva that appears to have held special significance during the first century and a half of Chola rule, when war was a constant and recurring fact of life. While the third Chola monarch, Parantaka, ruled for all of fifty years, the loss of his eldest son and crown prince, slain in action on the battlefield in the year 949, makes it clear that Chola control over a vulnerable kingdom, centered in the Kaveri river delta, was still far from assured. During this perilous period, Shiva's warrior-like manifestation as Victor of Three Forts, holding a bow in his upraised left hand and an arrow in his lowered right hand, proved to be an inspiration for Chola queen Kokkilan, and for the families of the chieftains and officials who made gifts of bronzes to temples. According to the myth celebrated by Appar in one of many verses that praise Shiva as Victor of Three Forts (*Tripura Vijaya*), the god once took this war-like form in order to destroy the fortified cities of three lethal demons who threatened the stability of the universe; Shiva used but a single arrow to penetrate and destroy all three forts, one of gold, the second of silver, and the third of iron. The bow and arrow that were cast separately and placed in the hands of these images are generally missing today. The large-scale commissioning of bronze images of Victorious Shiva, apparent in the number of images that survive of this manifestation, appears motivated by the desire for an exemplary deity who would serve as archetypal model for victorious warfare and the defeat of Chola enemies.[73] While it might be coincidence, it is interesting to note that in the early tenth century, the Cholas too were fighting three sets of enemies—the rulers of Lanka and the Pandya kings to their south, and the Rashtrakuta monarchs to the north.

Bronzes of Shiva as Victor of Three Forts outnumber surviving images of other forms of Shiva and appear to have been commissioned in temple after temple. While keeping in mind the vagaries of survival, it is relevant to turn to the inscription of 925 of Parantaka's chief queen Kokkilan, mother of crown prince Rajaditya, cited earlier. She dedicated an image described as "Handsome One of the Three Worlds" at Poonturutti, one of the temples of the Sacred Seven; in case there should be any doubt about the exact form the image took, she clarified in her inscription that her dedication was a metal processional image of the "Lord who burned the Three Forts."[74] Ironically and tragically, her son, crown prince Rajaditya, was later slain on the battlefield. With this royal commission as an inscriptional placeholder, we will examine some of the earliest bronzes of Victor of Three Forts. Threaded through this discussion will be an exploration of a related issue that has not been raised thus far. As I revisited temples in the Kaveri delta during the past six years to look at bronzes, and as I rechecked museum collections around the world, it appeared to me that during the first century of Chola rule it is possible to distinguish between the hands of two workshops, located only some 50 to 70 miles apart. I was drawn deeply into this material that has not been studied before in this manner, and I happily leave it to a generation of future scholars to decide whether or not to agree with me. What I am calling the "Coastal workshop" existed in the vicinity of the port town of Nagapattinam and produced images for a number of temples in the area. Coastal images are exceedingly slender and sinuous, with a proportion of elongated torso to lower limbs that makes them seem very tall, and with faces that tend to be perfect ovals. The "Capital workshop" operated in and around the Chola capital of Thanjavur, and extended inland beyond Trichy. These images display a somewhat different proportionality with a more compact torso and broader shoulders that make them seem more solidly grounded, and with a square touch to their faces. Such distinctions are apparent on both bronzes and stone sculptures of this early period when sizable bronze processional images began to be made for the very first time.

Some of the earliest bronzes of Shiva come from temples in the coastal belt, with its four ports of Kaveripoompattinam, Karaikkal, Nagapattinam, and Maraikkadu, control of which were clearly of crucial importance to the early Chola monarchs. The Shiva temple at the southernmost port of Maraikkadu carries a set of thirty-eight inscriptions belonging to the reign of Parantaka, who conducted several campaigns to Sri Lanka from this port. Interestingly, until recent peace in Sri Lanka, the swampy marshes near Maraikkadu formed the illicit entry point for those involved in one way or another with the Tamil Liberation Army.[75] Let us start by revisiting the superb image of Shiva and Uma as bridegroom and bride that we considered in the previous chapter, where I proposed that the bronze couple represents the birth of the phenomenon of Chola processional bronzes. This marital couple serves as a key benchmark against which to consider bronze images of the first hundred years of Chola overlordship (see fig. 1.12). Standing 27 and 20 inches above their common pedestal, the duo was created soon after the year 855 for a temple at Vadakkalathur in this coastal belt. A diadem, a standard and favorite adornment of the Chola period, frames the face of Shiva and Uma; a decorative clasp treated as a double *makara*-head and topped with a rounded medallion holds back Shiva's matted locks, which are arranged in towering splendor, with each set of dreadlocks ending in a ringlet-like curl. The crescent moon adorns Shiva's locks on one side, the trumpet-flower[76] stands upright on the other, while a fully open lotus blossom crowns the very top. Shiva wears a single large earring in his left ear, while his friendly serpent looks over his right shoulder. The lowest of his three necklaces is arranged to rest on his chest in a soft V formation, and this V-shape is echoed further down by the triangular flap of his short dhoti, which is wrapped around his hips and held in place by a decorative belt with simple fabric loops at either end. A brahmanical sacred thread and a high waistband encircle his torso, and Shiva wears elaborate armlets, an elbow band, bangles, anklets, and rings on eight of ten toes and fingers.[77] Uma is likewise richly adorned.

If we turn now to look at an evocative bronze of seated Shiva, 2 feet high, from a temple at Keelaiyur in this same coastal belt (fig. 2.3), one is struck by its many resemblances to the divine bridegroom. These include the precise manner in which the matted locks are piled high, and the diadem and double *makara*-head clasp that hold the locks in place, although here the circular medallion is converted to a skull. A ring adorns one ear, but now a dangling earring is seen in the other, and the longest of three necklaces rests softly on the chest in a V formation. There is the same high waistband and similarly draped sacred thread with the same simple belt and soft fabric loops at either end to hold

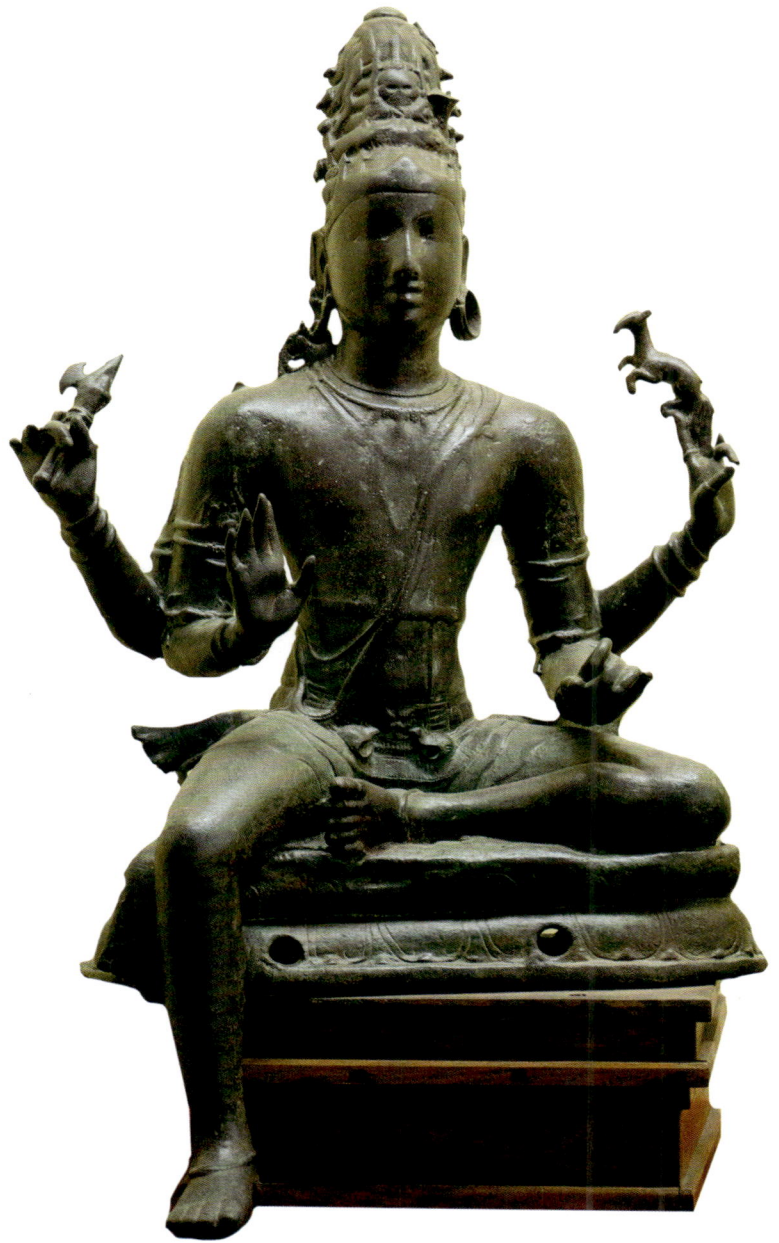

Figure 2.3. Seated Shiva, "Coastal style," Keelaiyur temple, Nagapattinam district, ca. 890, Art Gallery, Thanjavur.

the dhoti in place. The snake peeping over Shiva's right shoulder is broken but partially visible in frontal view. And last, we encounter that undefinable heart-wrenching beauty of the exquisite oval face with a hint of a smile that the artist has succeeded in capturing. The main difference in the treatment of the Keelaiyur image is that the body of Shiva has moved away from the drastically flattened form, reminiscent of bas relief sculpture, that characterized the first marriage couple, where it seemed almost as if the images had been sliced away from a bas relief. Shiva's body has now acquired a degree of three-dimensionality that is inherent in the technique of wax-modeling—a change that appears to have occurred within a period of about twenty-five years.

A standing Victor of Three Forts from the same coastal temple, 30 inches high, reveals a similar stylistic idiom, though it comes from the hand of a second sculptor who has inverted from left to right the placement of the trumpet flower and crescent moon, as well as of the two ear ornaments (fig. 2.4). This second artist favored a patterned fabric for Shiva's short dhoti, and gave him a triple-strand sacred thread, and arranged his necklace in a rounded format. Notice the puzzling fact that the bronze casters did not file away the metal rod joining Shiva's left shoulder to the prancing antelope held in his rear left hand. While these connecting channels are a necessary part of the bronze casting process, such rods were filed away in the finishing process, and we see them primarily in the rare instances of bronzes discarded due to a casting flaw.[78] The smooth surfaces of this bronze Shiva make it clear that it was an image in worship and by no means a discarded bronze. The answer lies perhaps in the fact that the artist finishing the bronze felt that the almost horizontal leap of the little pet antelope could do with this additional support, and hence refrained from removing it. The rod would have gone unnoticed during temple worship when the image was adorned with silks, jewelry, and flower garlands.

An image of Shiva as Victor of Three Forts from the Calico Museum of Textiles, 24 inches high, also belongs to the Coastal style, and is closer to the marriage couple in the somewhat flattened handling of the body (fig. 2.5a, b). At the same time, the artist has rounded out the buttocks somewhat as his experience grew with free-form wax modeling, which strongly encourages three-dimensionality. While several details of headdress, waistband, and fabric ties to hold his dhoti are familiar from the divine bridegroom and the two Shivas from Keelaiyur, one might note the U-formation of the longer of his two necklaces, and the unusual simplicity of his armlets that are mere bands of fabric tied into a simple knot on the rear of his arm rather than the more elaborate jeweled armlets seen on the previous three images. The apparently effortless splendor of the image almost disguises its mastery.

Slightly inland, but still within the Coastal workshop zone, is a captivating Shiva of Three Forts from a temple at Tandantottam. I will refer to its wax modeler as "Master of the off-kilter substyle" (fig. 2.6). Standing poised with one arm raised high to hold the bow, this Shiva, 30 1/2 inches tall, appears almost off-balance. And yet, this solid metal image, weighing an estimated 90 pounds, is totally stable. Exceedingly slender, and standing on his right leg with his right hip thrust outward, and with his body in exaggerated contrapposto of a type we have not yet encountered, this two-armed Shiva is totally comfortable with his seemingly precarious posture. High, matted locks display the usual trumpet flower, the crescent moon, and the medallion resting on a double *makara*-head ornament placed above his diadem. We see the familiar large ring in one ear and a dangling ear ornament in the other, with the serpent looking over his right shoulder. Two features seen also in the Victor from the Calico Museum are the manner in which the longer of his two necklaces is treated as an elongated U-shape, and the fact that his armlets are those same unadorned fabric bands tied in a plain knot at the rear. The enchantment of this image is enhanced by what seems an unbalanced stance but that, in fact, reflects the artist's comfort level with the wax image he modeled, and his confidence that the resulting bronze would be totally stable. He pushed the limits of the stance—of that there is no doubt—but he knew his materials sufficiently, both wax and bronze, to be

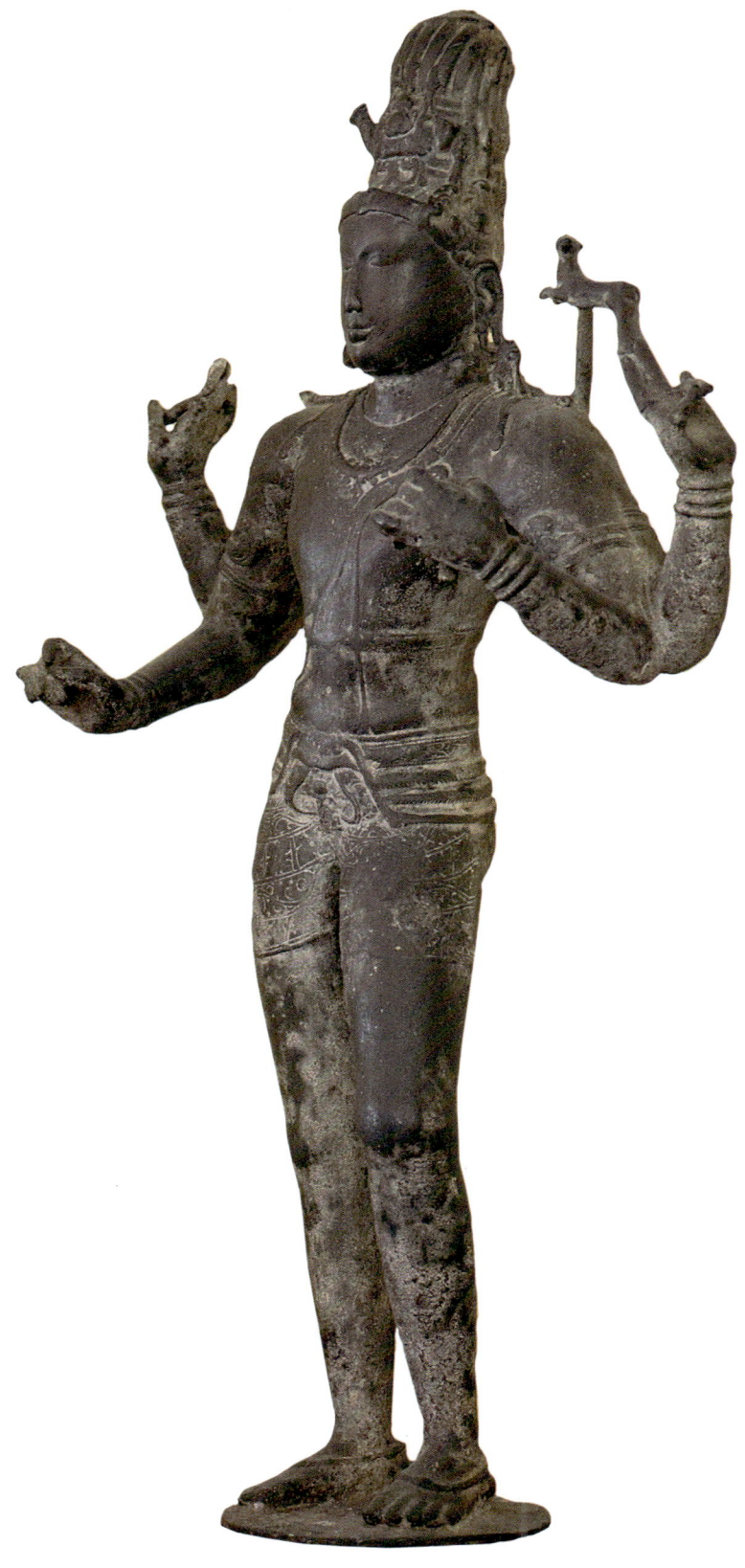

Figure 2.4. Victor of Three Forts (*Tripura Vijaya*), "Coastal style," Keelaiyur temple, Nagapattinam district, ca. 890, Art Gallery, Thanjavur.

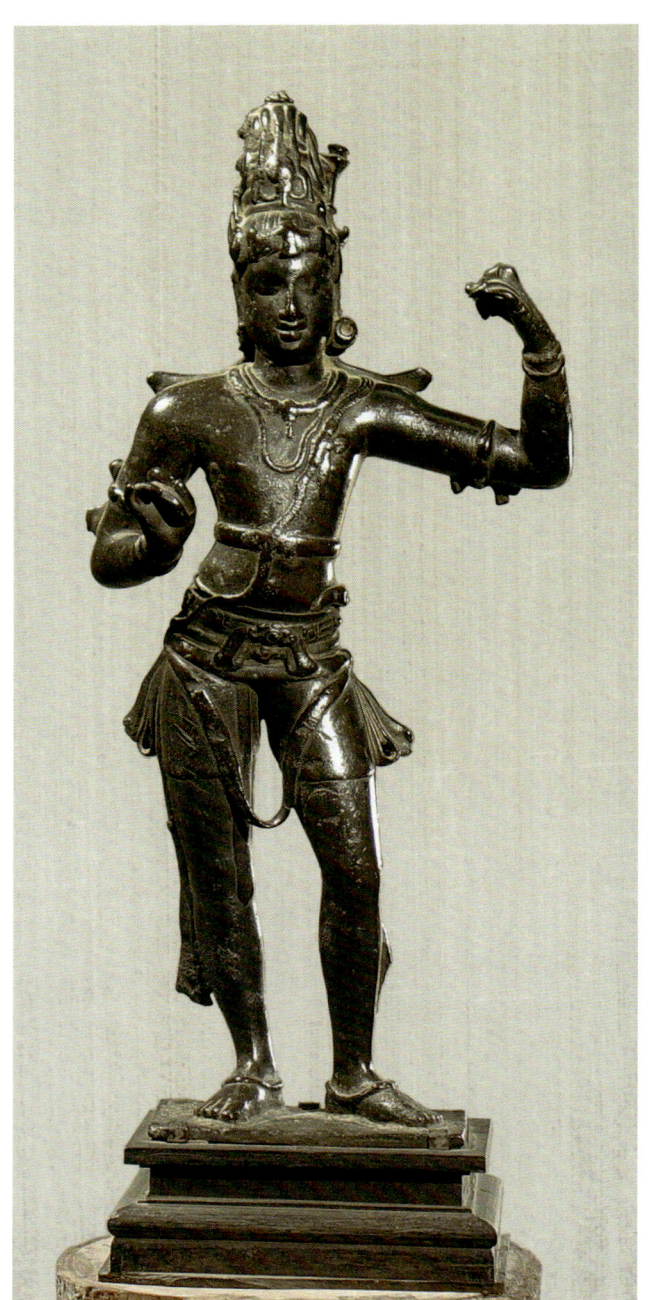 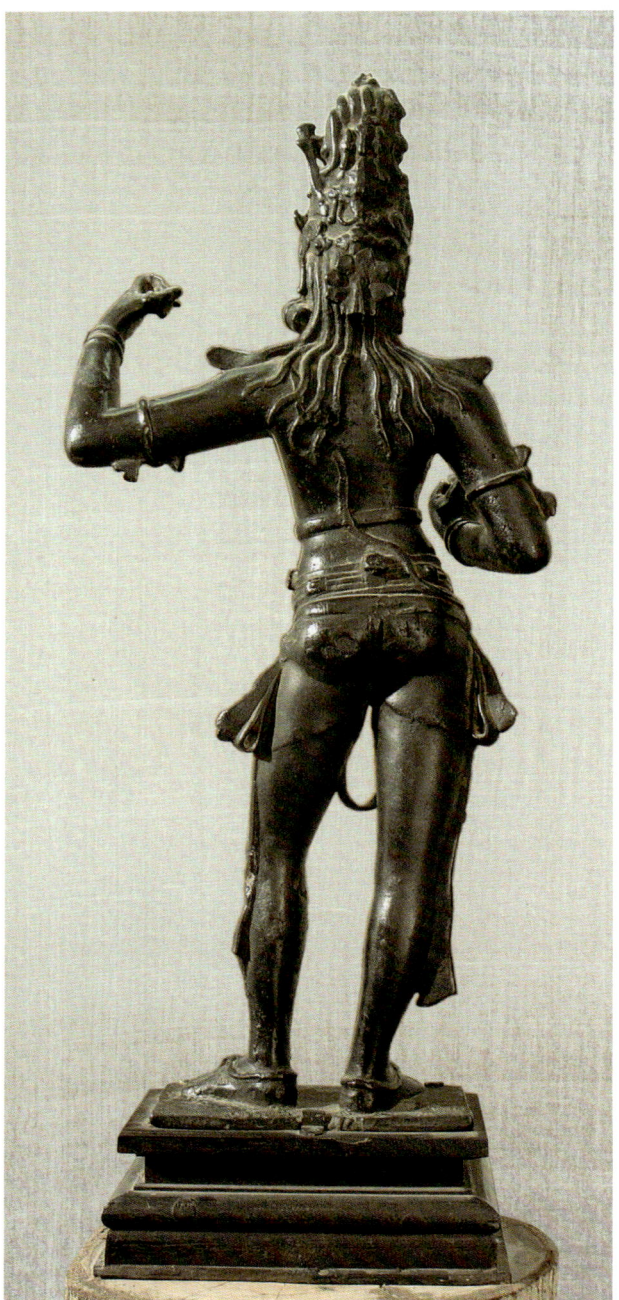

Figure 2.5. (a and b) Shiva as Victor of Three Forts (*Tripura Vijaya*), "Coastal style," ca. 875, The Calico Museum of Textiles and The Sarabhai Foundation Collections, Ahmedabad.

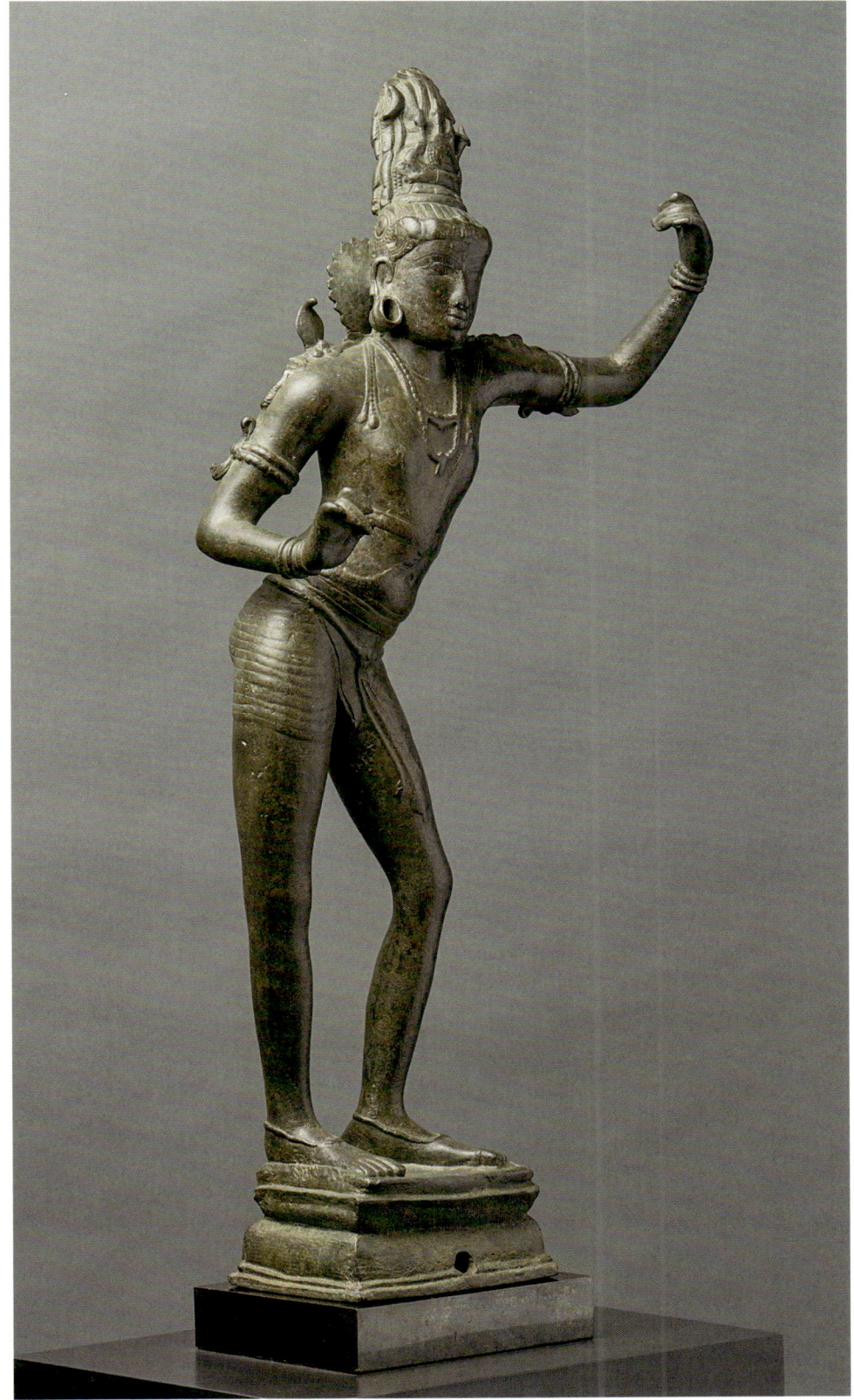

Figure 2.6. "Master of the Off-Kilter Substyle," Shiva as Victor of Three Forts *(Tripura Vijaya)*, Tandantottam, ca. 875, Norton Simon Museum, Pasadena.

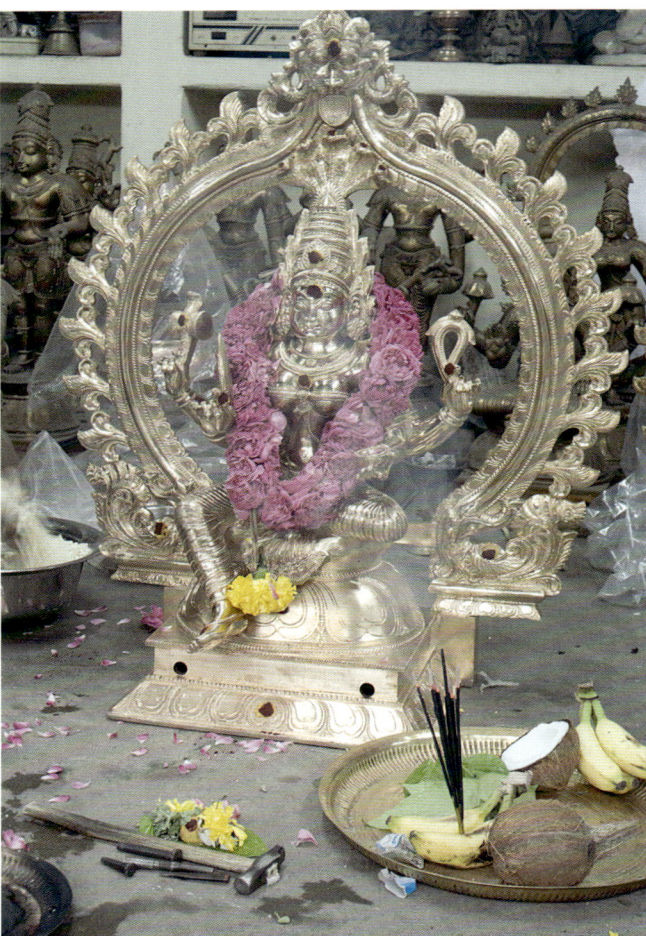

Figure 2.7. Ritual consecration of newly cast bronze image of goddess Kali in bronze workshop in Swamimalai; note the sanctification of hammer and chisels.

sure he was on safe ground. In chapter 4, we will encounter the work of descendants of this "Master of the off-kilter substyle."

In the context of donors who commissioned bronze images from master artists, we should point out that wax modelers were attached to workshops that had a foundry equipped with a range of mud ovens in which the clay-covered wax images were baked, and with fire pits in which metal was melted in order to pour into the hollow clay molds. Master modelers rarely moved from one foundry to another; rather, it was the patrons who moved around to commission images from one or another foundry renowned for its wax modeler. This continues to be the case to this day and temple priests bring donors to the famous bronze workshops at Swamimalai in the coastal belt. When the commission is ready, priests and donors return to the workshop to collect the sacred image. They perform the initial ritual sanctification of the image in the bronze workshop itself, and only then take it back to their own temple, which might easily be 50 to 100 miles away. Chisels and hammer are part of this ritual puja in which the master artist symbolically opens the eyes of the image and thus "enlivens" the deity, who is now pronounced ready to receive devotees (fig. 2.7).

The many early bronzes from the coastal belt (map 5) speak both to the sanctity of the sites of that area as well as to the strategic importance of ports during early Chola rule.[79] Thanjavur, while serving as the Chola administrative and military center, was a newly settled town without an ancient sacred shrine praised in song by the saints. In fact, a major Shiva temple was built there for the first time only around the year 1000 by emperor Rajaraja. Prior to that date, the cluster of small temples that comprise the Sacred Seven are representative of the Capital style.

We move inland now to consider an image of Shiva as Victor of Three Forts, standing 3 feet high, from a temple at Solagampatti (fig. 2.8), roughly 25 miles west of the Chola capital of Thanjavur. The image represents work of the very same period that we have been examining from the coastal workshops, but it comes from the hands of an artist with a slightly different though equally assured style that I am terming the Capital style. Shiva's face is a broad U-shape rather than the oval faces we have encountered along the coast, and the width of the shoulders and their straight and level line is more marked. The iconography and adornment are largely familiar. Curiously, the standard high waistband that normally adorns the male torso is absent, resulting in a somewhat awkward and unwieldy treatment of the waist area contrapposto that is so smoothly handled in other instances. The simple fabric bands that held the dhoti in place are replaced here by a floral metal clasp. In a variation on images of the Victor of Three Forts examined thus far, this artist introduced a crouching dwarf-like figure upon whose back Shiva rests his left foot. Representing Mushalagan, the egotistic demon who must be controlled, this little figure, holding a serpent in one hand, is portrayed here as a nonthreatening creature whom Shiva has well under control. The positioning of the tall slender god to stand at a slight angle to his rectangular pedestal is engaging. Two damaged stumps on the rectangular pedestal

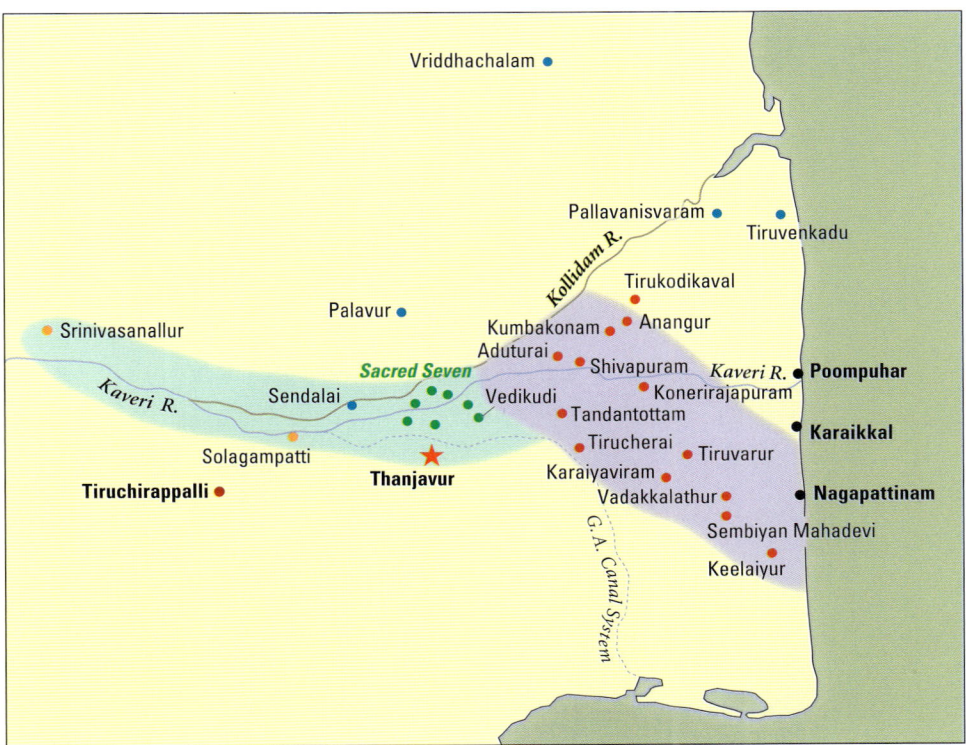

Map 5. Schematic rendering of "Coastal style" temples (purple zone) and "Capital style" temples (blue zone): ca. 855–985.

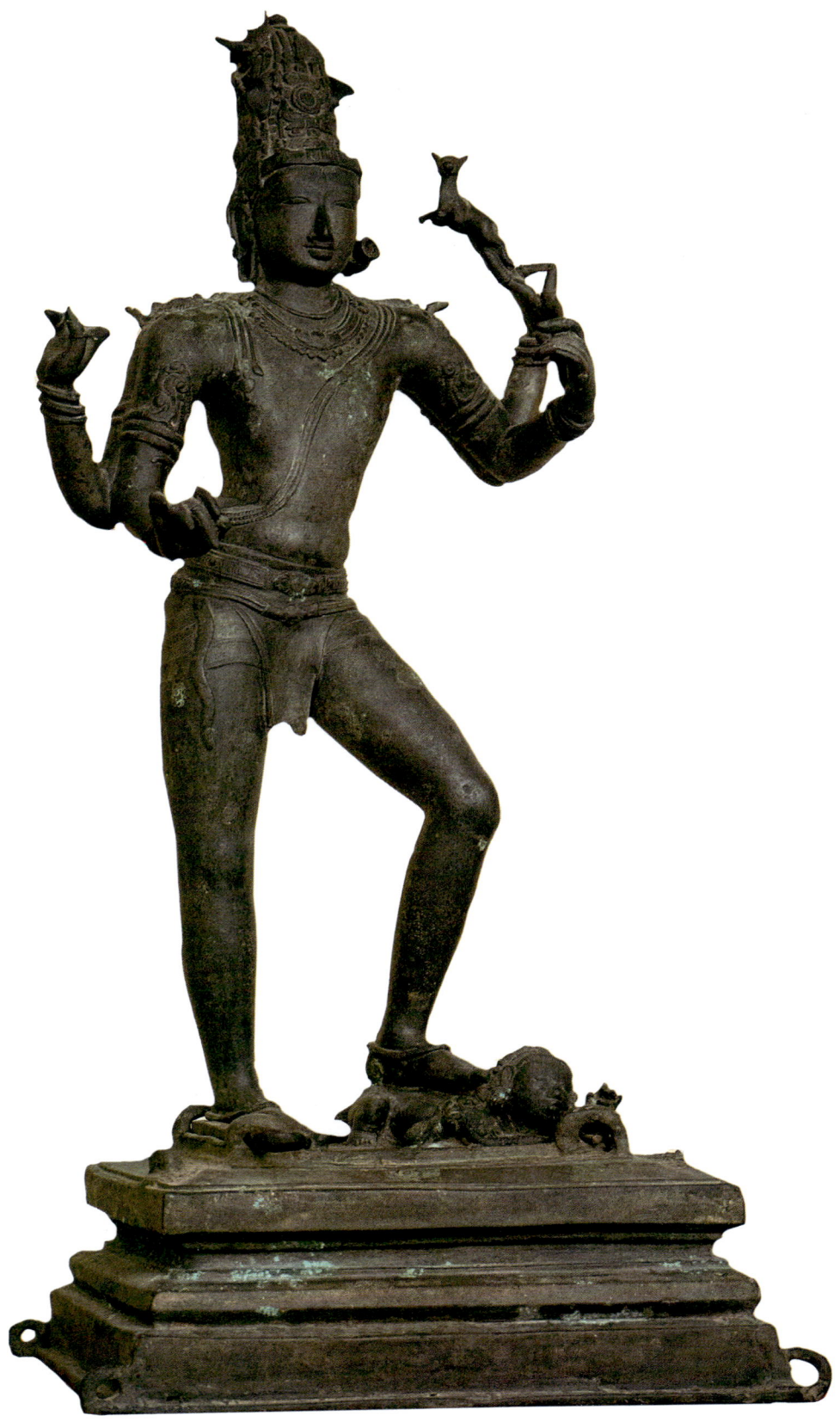

Figure 2.8. Shiva as Victor of Three Forts *(Tripura Vijaya)*, Solagampatti temple, Thanjavur district, ca. 890, Art Gallery, Thanjavur.

once held the flame-tipped aureole that framed and enclosed this and all other bronzes, thereby emphasizing their sacred significance.

A comparison of this well-preserved Capital style bronze with the two Keelaiyur Shivas reveals a blurring of details on the two images from Keelaiyur (see figs. 2.3 and 2.4). Such blurring clearly indicates that the images have remained in worship since their creation some 1,100 years ago, being lustrated regularly with a range of liquids and unguents including milk, yogurt, honey, sandal paste, and water, during which the priests' right hand moved from crown to foot in a sweeping motion typical of a right-handed person. Bronze images were further subject to ritual cleansing upon their return to the temple after have been taken in procession beyond the temple grounds, when they would be rubbed down with the olive of the palm tree, which brings the sheen back to copper, as indeed to silks and gold thread. Years of ritual worship, and of purificatory renewal for further worship, have smoothed, rounded, and blurred the profile of the nose, eyes, lips, diadem, and several other original details. By contrast, the bronze from the interior capital region was recovered only recently from its underground burial spot and so its details are crisper and sharper, and match more closely the original vision of its artist. A second difference between the two sets of images is apparent in their color, with those from the coastal temples being dark in color, while the recently unearthed bronze is green in hue. Having stood in the temple where they were exposed to air since their creation over a thousand years ago, the Keelaiyur bronzes have acquired a dark hue caused by oxidation. By contrast, the green hue reflects the patina acquired by copper when exposed to humid conditions or buried in moist soil. The image with the green patina was buried in 1310, some four hundred years after it was created, an issue that we will bypass here and leave as a mystery to unravel in chapter 9.

During this early period of 100 years, between 855 and 955, a close stylistic relationship is seen between the work of wax modelers and stone carvers who were creating images with the same iconography and, importantly, of similar size. A comparison of two stone queens from the Nageshvara temple in the coastal belt with a dated bronze of Uma from Karaiyaviram, also in the coastal zone, will make the point. The stone queens from the Nageshvara stand poised and sinuous, with long slender legs and arms, soft upraised breasts, delicate oval faces, and exquisite smiles (fig. 2.9). They are the work of assured craftsmen creating imagery in the Coastal style in the early tenth century, the date of the earliest gifts to an already functioning Nageshvara temple. The Karaiyaviram bronze Uma, also in the Coastal style, has a perfect oval face with a hint of a smile, a supple form with a gentle, soft curve to her full breasts, and slender hips that could be thought of as wide only by comparison with the waist that is so very narrow (fig. 2.10). She stands on a circular lotus base that carries an inscription that states that she was created in the eleventh year of Parantaka Chola, corresponding to the year 917. She is not, however, a royal commission; the monarch's regnal year is mentioned solely to fix the date of the dedication, and the inscription gives us the name of the donor, Katanagan Nagattaraiyan, a chieftain from Sellur.[80] The bronze Uma and the stone queens reveal a close similarity in the treatment of their proportional systems; both have elongated torsos, lithe swaying bodies with softly rounded breasts and gently sloping shoulders, and faces that are tapered ovals.

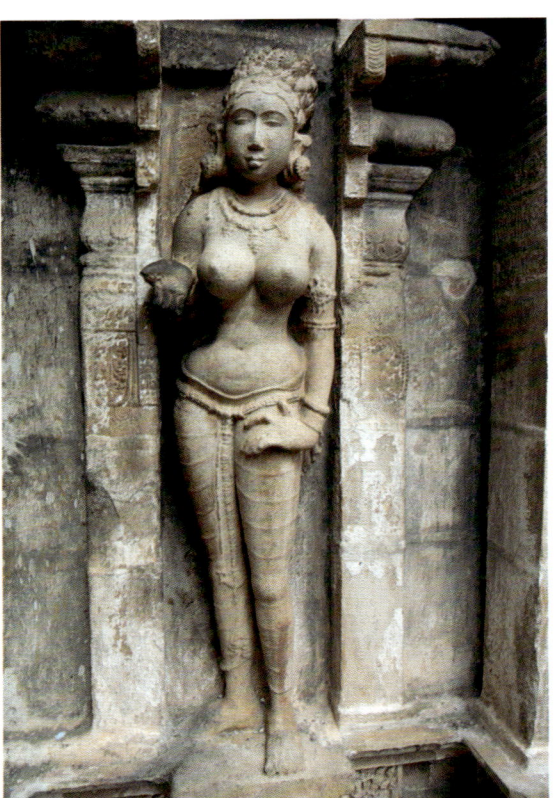

Figure 2.9. Stone queen from Nageshvara temple, Kumbakonam, Thanjavur district, ca. 910.

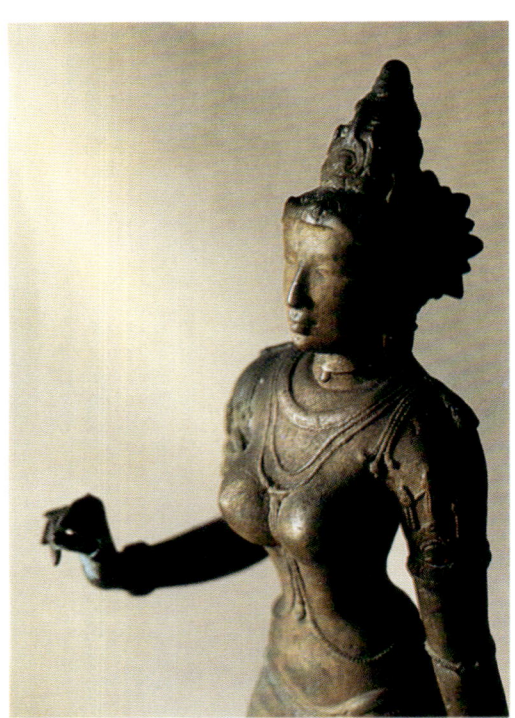
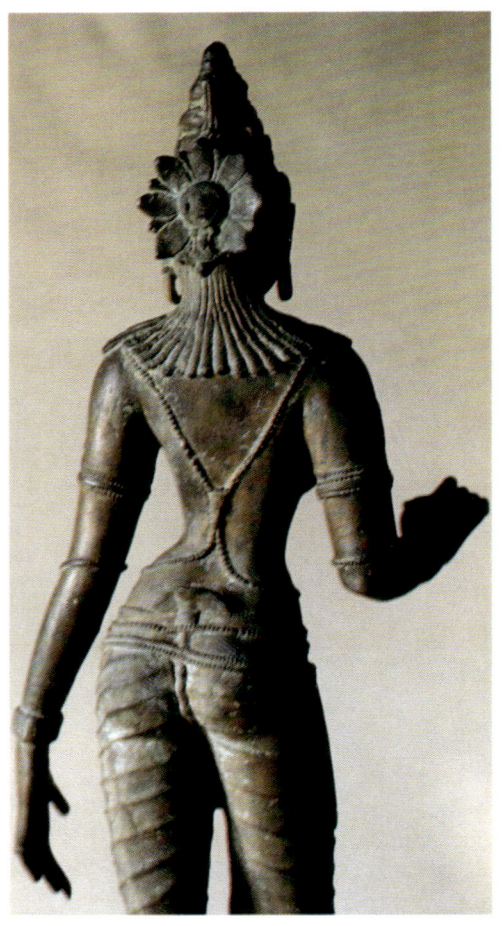

Figure 2.10. (a and b) Uma, Karaiyaviram temple, Nagapattinam district, 917.

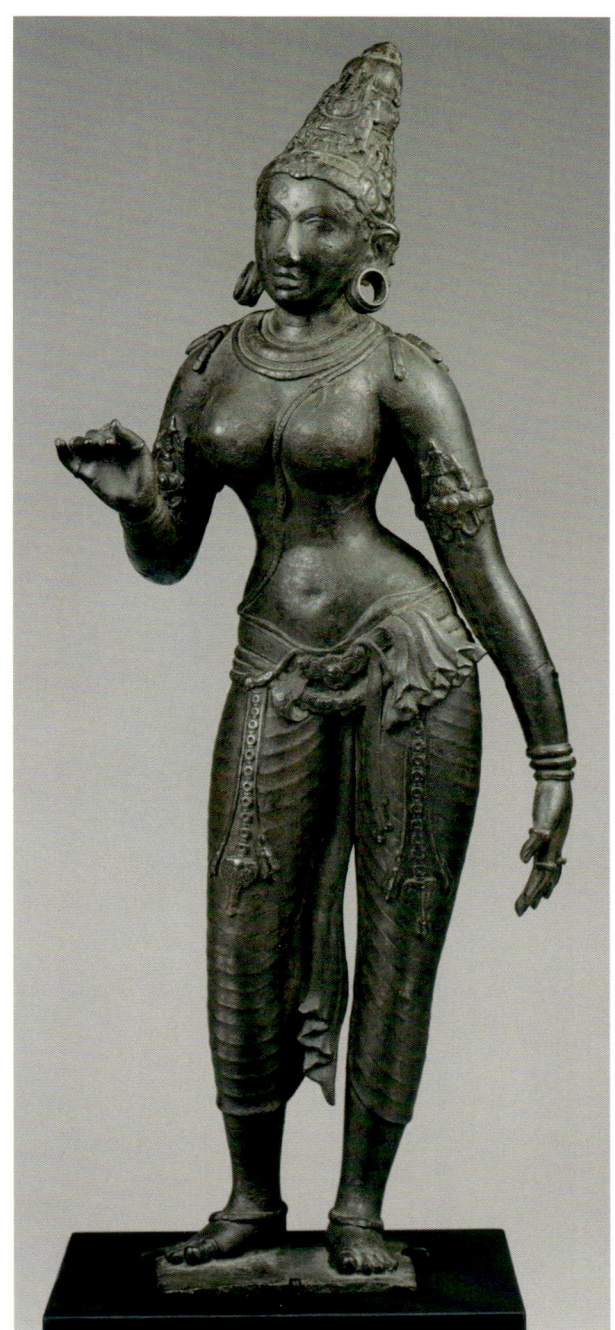 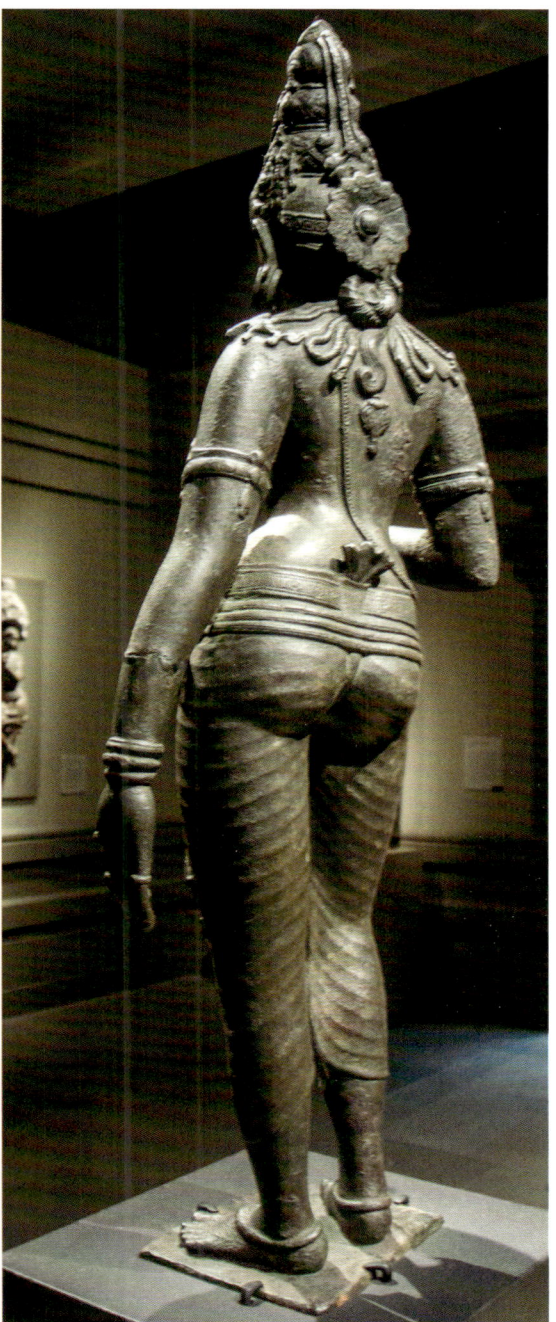

Figure 2.11. (a and b) Uma, "Capital style," ca. 900, The Metropolitan Museum of Art, New York, Bequest of Cora Timken Burnett, 1956.

By contrast, a bronze Uma from the Metropolitan Museum of Art displays a broader face, and wider shoulders, while the more compressed proportion of torso to lower limbs are characteristics of the inland capital area (fig. 2.11a, b). She may be compared with a stone figure of Shiva as Half Woman from Poonturutti (fig. 2.12), one of the temples of the Sacred Seven near Thanjavur, which is also representative of the Capital style. Both the bronze Uma and the stone Half Woman of the Capital style display a compact torso, broad shoulders, and a U-shaped face. The long skirt worn by both images is held in place by fabric bands that extend below a floral clasp. The untidy arrangement of pleats along the left thigh of both images is striking, but that is a characteristic of many tenth-century images, regardless of whether they belong to the Coastal or the Capital style.[81]

Two final comparisons, first of bronze Umas from Capital and Coastal styles, and then of stone images from Coastal and Capital styles, will help support the point I wish to make. The bronze Uma from the Metropolitan Museum of Art is created according to the central proportional system that favors a shorter torso and less extended lower limbs that result in a body more compact and less sinuous than the Coastal bronze Uma from Karaiyaviram whose inscription places her in the year 917 (see fig. 2.10). A similar comment may be made about the stone image of Shiva as Half Woman from Poonturutti that represents the Capital workshop (see fig. 2.12) as compared to Shiva as Half Woman from the Nageshvara temple in the coastal belt (fig. 2.13). Both images belong to the early 900s, but the Coastal workshop gives its image a delicate oval face, narrower shoulders, and a distinctly sinuous outline, all of which contrast with the more "grounded" image from the Capital workshop. The Coastal versus Capital distinction is apparent in images fashioned during the first hundred years of Chola presence, when artists creating bronzes trained in the same sculpture workshops as those working in stone, and where craft specialization had not yet arisen.[82]

The bronzes examined in this chapter make it evident that the constant battles fought by Chola kings Aditya and Parantaka did little to inhibit the creativity of their stone sculptors and wax modelers, who created outstanding images in two lightly varying stylistic modes. Warfare did, however, influence the choice of imagery in that Shiva's warring form as Victor of Three Forts became a favored god, serving as an abiding model at a time when bloody battles were the order of the day. This popularity of Shiva as Victor of Three Forts continued into the reign of the great emperor Rajaraja, who, some forty years later, captured much of south India, the Maldive Islands, and all of northern Sri Lanka, making the name Chola a force to be reckoned with. In building his great temple at the capital of Thanjavur (fig. 2.14), Rajaraja ordained that every one of the stone images in the thirty-two niches on the upper level of his temple walls should feature Shiva as Victor of Three Forts. All the images are four-armed, holding bow and arrow in two front hands with the trident and a second arrow in the rear hands, and all have serpents knotted around their hips. The eight images at the corners of each face of the sanctum, and the ten images on the south and north walls of the *ardha-mandapa*, depict Shiva with one foot raised and placed upon a pedestal that in several instances has been carved into a lion-head.[83] In posture, they resemble the Victor of the Capital style from Solagampatti, whose raised leg is placed upon the head of a dwarf demon. The remaining twelve images of the Victor, four against the central section of each of the south, west, and north faces of the sanctum, depict him with both feet planted firmly on the ground, as seen in the majority of bronzes examined here. Rajaraja's authority and domination over an expanded Chola empire was assured by the time he built the Thanjavur temple. The repeated emphasis on this manifestation of Shiva may be read as Rajaraja Chola's celebration of the grace bestowed upon him in his military campaigns, and as a thanksgiving for Victor Shiva's blessings.

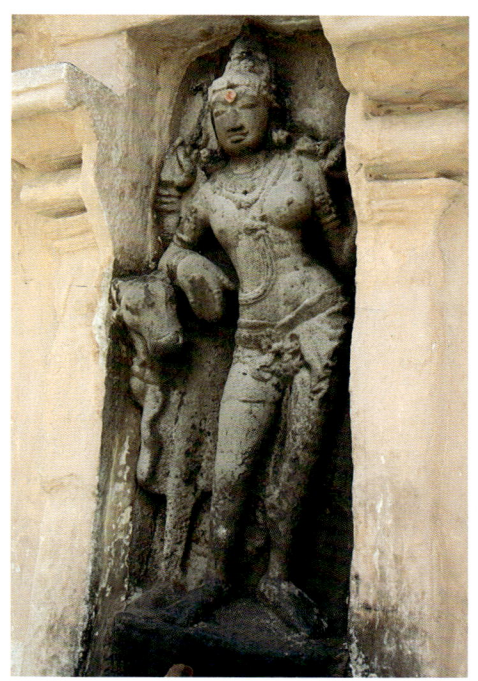
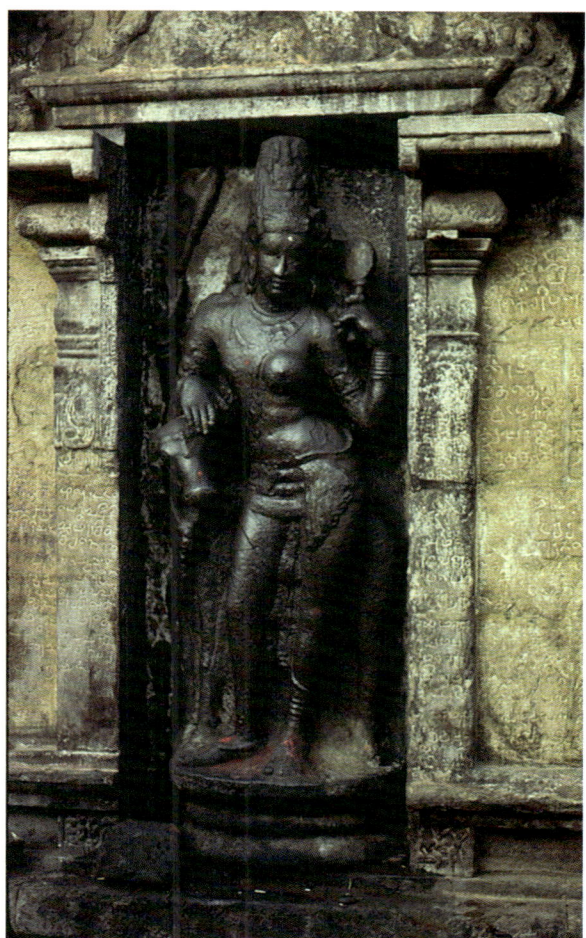

Figure 2.12. Shiva as Half Woman, "Capital style," Poonturutti temple, Thanjavur district, early tenth century.

Figure 2.13. Shiva as Half Woman, "Coastal style," Nageshvara temple, Kumbakonam, Thanjavur district, ca. 910.

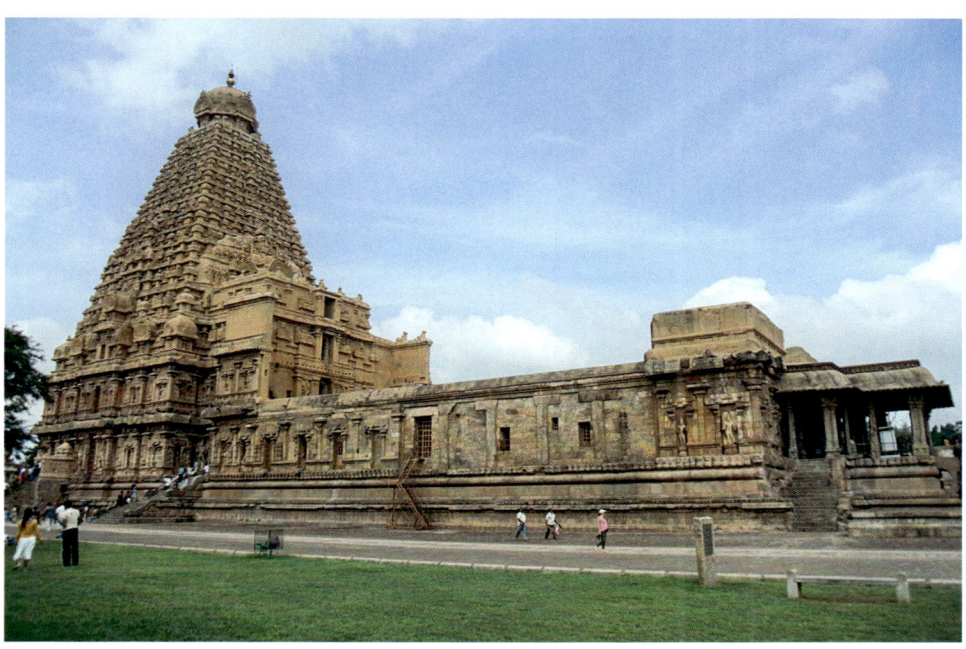

Figure 2.14. Rajaraja Chola's Great Temple, Thanjavur, ca. 1010.

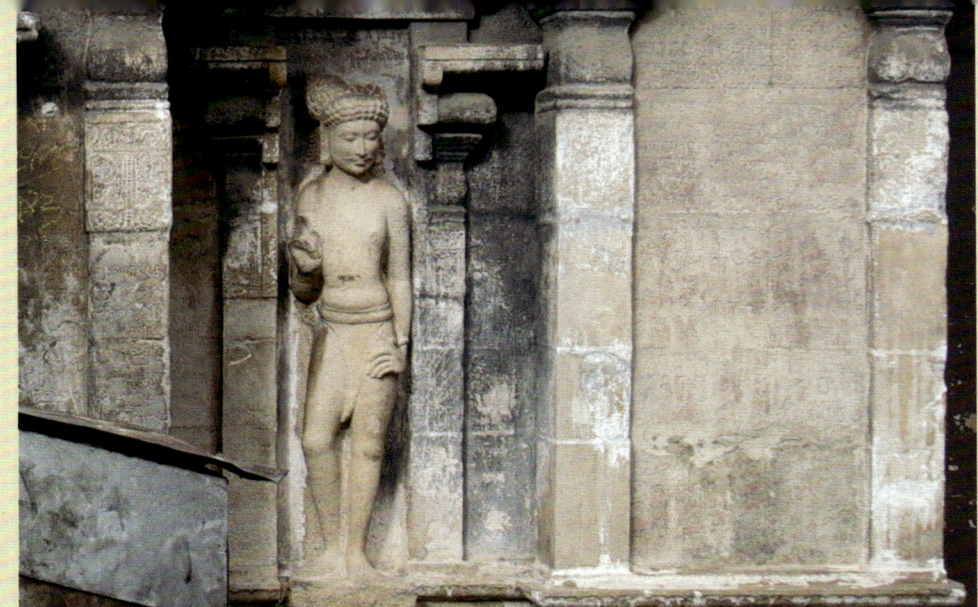

Writ in Stone
Temple Walls as Inscribed Archives

3

We, the administrative authorities, undertake to celebrate the seven-day sacred festival in Vaikhashi [May–June] as per instructions cut into the stone [kallil vettinapadi]; on the south side of the great temple, to the west of the exit (of the ardha-mandapa), along the uttiram, podigai, *and* virkandam; *and on the exterior of the image bathing hall to the east; on its south wall, along the* jagati, *on the* pattigai, *and along the recessed neck of the* pattigai, *and below this along the* kumuda *molding. . . . As per the inscriptions cut in stone [vettinapadi], I, Kavalamoli Madevan, undertake to perform the sacred festivals of Vaikhashi [May–June] and the ten-day festival in Chittirai [April–May]. Entrusted to the protection of the temple priests.*

SOUTH WALL, MAIN *MANDAPA*, NEYTTANAM TEMPLE, YEAR 930[1]

This inscription on the Neyttanam temple, one of the cluster of the Sacred Seven that we examined in the previous chapter, records an undertaking to perform two major festivals at the temple, and it points us to the exact location of two other sets of inscribed records that lay out stipulations regarding their performance (see fig. 2.1g). It tells us that one set of specifications is engraved on the south wall of the temple's *ardha-mandapa*, and may be found in three descending levels below the eave—on the *uttiram* (uppermost level), and on the *podigai* and *virkandam* (platform and neck of the pilaster below) (fig. 3.1). The second set of stipulations is engraved on three levels of the base moldings along the south side of the image bathing hall; here again, the record is precise in telling us that the record is inscribed on the *jagati* (the lowest rectangular molding), on the vertical panel and the recessed neck-transition of the *pattigai* (the uppermost narrow molding), and on the curved *kumuda* molding between (fig. 3.2). The start of this record, not quoted earlier, informs us that these two festivals were funded through gold obtained from a fine levied on those members of the town assembly who had failed to attend a meeting convened by the royal *srikaryam* officer in charge of temple affairs. Some of the gold was used to make a diadem for Shiva, and the rest was set aside to celebrate the two multiday festivals at the Neyttanam temple. This "prime" inscribed record, which makes reference to two other inscribed records, is indicative of the manner in which inscriptions were regularly and routinely engraved along temple walls and moldings. Such records were also written on palm-leaf archives, but the detailed instructions on where exactly to find the inscribed stipulations would have been helpful to an official or adjudicator who wished to locate a record without having to work through the archives or scrutinize every single inscription on the temple walls.

A tight mantle of inscriptions covers the outer walls of Chola temples, where every nondecorated surface was utilized to cut into stone a permanent record of an entire range of dedications (fig. 3.3). These epigraphs, clearly considered important in their time, demand our attention; indeed, it seems to me that any study of the architecture, sculpture, or bronze art of the temples that ignores the stone inscriptions, so visually dominant and so liberally covering temple walls, would be a partial and incomplete exercise. In this chapter, we will look at the purpose these epigraphs serve and explore the manner of their addition to the temples over the reign of successive Chola monarchs. We will consider in detail one temple, the Nageshvara at Kumbakonam, in order to try and comprehend the sequence in which records were cut into the stone of temples. We will then briefly consider three other temples, whose inscriptions indicate that they were constructed early in the reign of Parantaka, in order to demonstrate the manner in which merchants, officers, and other individuals continued to make gifts through the reigns of successive Chola kings until the very end of the thirteenth century, when Chola dynastic rule ended. Every inscription on a temple relates in one way or another to the temple itself, and celebrates donations to the temple, speaks of rules pertaining to temple administration, or records infringements of rules and the punishment meted out to offenders. In concluding, we will consider briefly a second category of inscriptions in the form of royal charters that were inscribed on sheets of copper. These copper-plate inscriptions commence with Chola genealogy, trace the royal line down to the king issuing the charter, and list his accomplishments especially in the realm of battle; only then

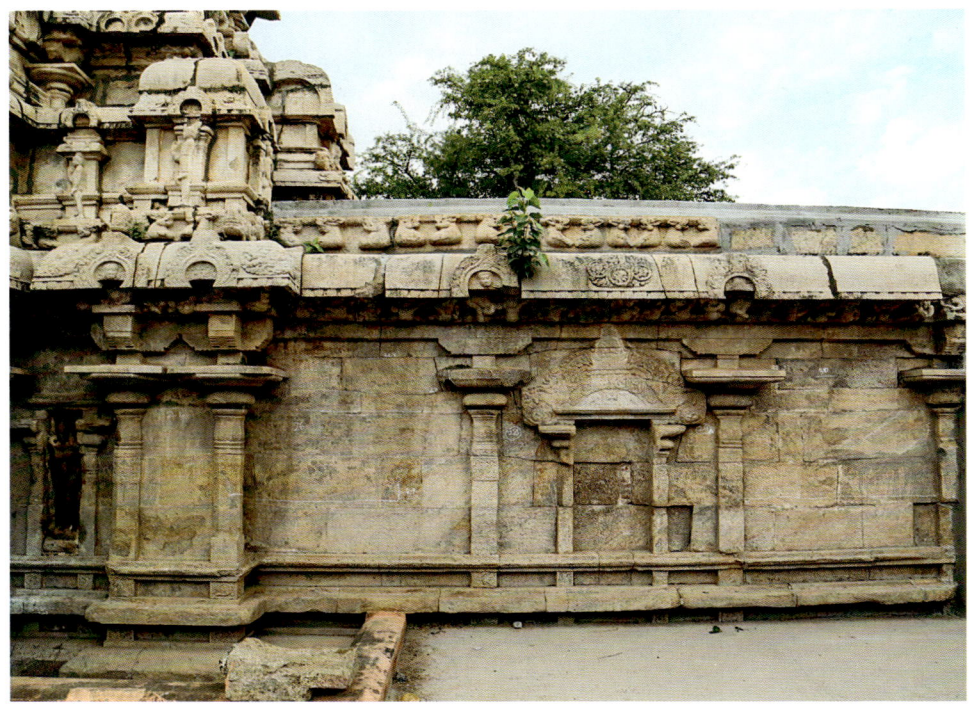

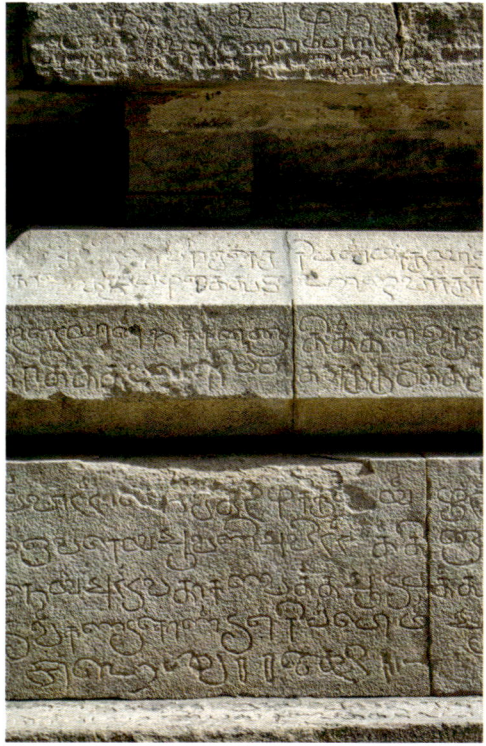

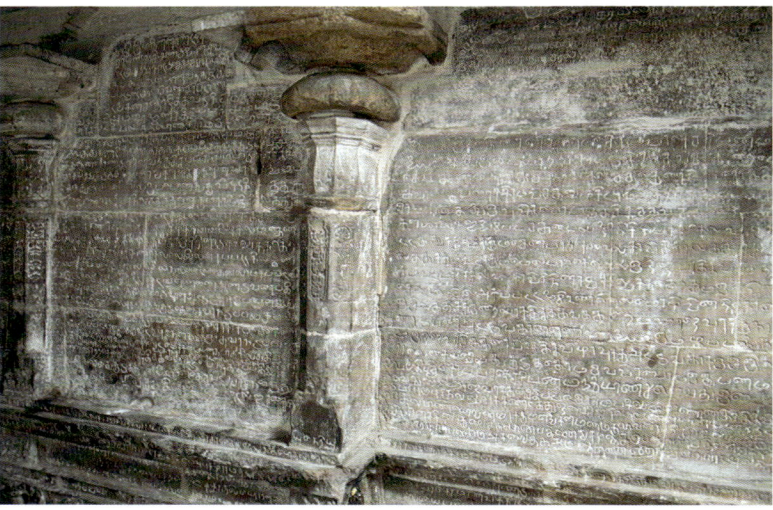

Figure 3.1. Inscriptions on walls of the Neyttanam temple, Thanjavur district, end of the ninth century. Note especially those below the eave.

Figure 3.2. Inscriptions along the base moldings of Neyttanam temple, Thanjavur district, end of the ninth century.

Figure 3.3. Inscriptions on the walls of Shiva temple, Lalgudi, Trichy district.

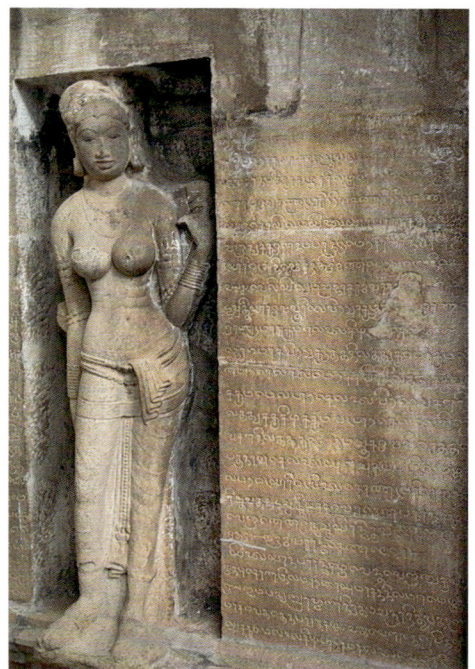
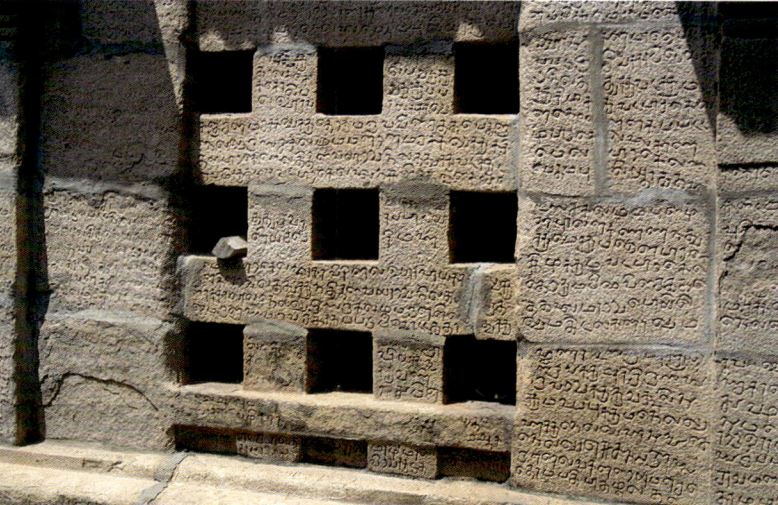

Figure 3.4. Inscriptions on the walls of Nageshvara temple, Kumbakonam, Thanjavur district.

Figure 3.5. Inscriptions along grille window at Neyttanam temple, Thanjavur district.

do the inscriptions turn to the reason for the grant, which is a royal gift, usually of land and villages to a temple or to a group of brahmins.

Inscribed Temple Walls

Walking around the walls of early Chola stone temples makes one intensely aware of the fact that inscriptions cover all available spaces, flowing seamlessly around niches that carry sculpted figures, and across the light projections and recesses of the temples' walls (fig. 3.4).[2] They are placed too along the various levels of base moldings, and are even inscribed along trellis windows (fig. 3.5). These records comprise a massive readable "archive" when well-meaning but wrongly directed sandblasting has not obscured the Tamil letters; they reveal fascinating information of relevance that I use throughout this book to discuss the temples, their bronzes, and their ritual worship.

    Scholarship on India has often regretted India's lack of a sense of history, complaining that there were no chroniclers who kept track of events, and that it was only with the coming of Islam that historical archives came into existence in India. Certainly, it is true that as far as India's artistic heritage is concerned, we have no equivalent of, say, Vincent of Beauvais, who wrote enthusiastically about his Beauvais cathedral. And regrettably, there was no Vasari to leave us details about artists and their works. But what, in fact, do we mean by a sense of history?[3] In Tamil Nadu, starting around the year 850 when the Cholas appeared on the scene, inscriptions of local import, historical and otherwise, began to appear in large numbers on the walls of every single temple in the Kaveri delta. Approximately 13,000 inscriptions are to be found on the walls of temples constructed during the period of Chola rule.[4] Of these a mere 1,000, largely from the walls of Rajaraja Chola's Great Temple at Thanjavur, have been available for the past hundred years in a complete English translation.[5] Another 11,000 are accessible in the form of a frustratingly brief English synopsis, collected together in a set of eight volumes published by T. V. Mahalingam between 1987–1992.[6] Additionally, several volumes of a series published as *South Indian Inscriptions*, starting as early as 1891 and continuing to the latest volume dated to 2012, carry the text in the original Tamil with no translation either into English or into modern Tamil. Last, there are a few important publications by the Tamil Nadu State Department of Archaeology, the French Institute of Indology,[7] select articles in *Epigraphia Indica*, which is largely devoted to Sanskrit inscriptions, and some important but scattered studies in the journals or occasional publications of specialized institutes. Roughly two-thirds of the corpus of Chola inscriptions has never been published in its entirety. Such inscriptions are available to scholars and researchers in the form of original rubbings taken from the temple walls, or as hand-transcribed copies of these rubbings, both housed in the offices of the Epigraphical Survey of India in Mysuru.[8] The inscriptions, often formulaic in nature, are written in the Tamil script of the ninth to thirteenth centuries, which differs considerably from modern Tamil, while a small number of records are written in both Tamil and Sanskrit. Temples in our focal area of the Kaveri river basin account for roughly 5,000 inscriptions that, by and large, record gifts to already functioning temples.[9] A survey of the complete corpus of inscriptions on any individual temple reveals, as we shall see, that temples constructed early in the Chola period continued to receive active patronage throughout the four centuries of Chola rule.

These inscribed temple records provide us with a treasure trove of material that sheds light on multiple aspects of the times from sociopolitical circumstances, through the economics of agriculture, irrigation, and trade, to the religious milieu within which the temples functioned and, incidentally, to temples and bronzes. We learn from the inscriptions of the wide range of individuals, residing in different towns in the vicinity, who were involved in supporting sacred rites, rituals, and ceremonials within the temples. They made gifts of bronze images of deities, gave jewels to adorn the bronzes, and donated land or cash for a range of temple activities from lighting permanent lamps in the temple and providing "sacred" temple food, to paying for aromatics, perfumes, silks, and flower garlands to adorn the deities, and ensuring the proper irrigation of temple lands and coconut groves. The list is seemingly endless, and provides ample material for several studies that I trust will be undertaken in the future.

In the midst of these varied details, we hear of fascinating semijudicial issues related to temple management. One such issue concerns the misbehavior of two temple priests, *bhattars*, at the Shivapuram temple. Their list of misdemeanors commenced with taking a pearl necklace of the goddess Uma and giving it to a concubine. The various irregularities of which they were accused include keeping false accounts for the perfumed unguents used in worship, of hostile behavior when asked to pay their land taxes, of collecting 50,000 coins by illegal means, of stealing rice, and of defying royal orders. The temple priests, the *srimahesvaras*, met with the town residents, the *urar*, and pronounced the two priests guilty of a crime, both against god Shiva (*Shivadroha*) and against the king (*rajadroha*). They were sentenced to excommunication, and their property, both immovable and movable, including their servants, was handed over to the state.[10] Another intriguing temple inscription from Achyutamangalam, dated to the year 1207, gives expression to the principle that the United States today classifies as "eminent domain," whereby a city or state is entitled to take over privately owned property for certain necessary, common-interest, purposes. The inscription records an agreement made by the Somanathadeva temple that had the sanction of the Chola king, Kulottunga III. It was agreed that the street in front of the temple was not wide enough to accommodate the grand processions of bronze deities now being conducted by the temple. The authorities, who had been empowered to demolish the houses on one side of the street fronting the temple in order to widen the street, were now required to make adequate repairs and alterations to the alternative housing that had been provided for the dispossessed house owners.[11]

Adding Inscriptions to the Nageshvara Temple, Kumbakonam

In the 28th year of Ko Rajakesari, Danapati Arangan aka Panchavan, headman of Karuvur in Mililaikuttram, gave 20 gold coins to the Lord of Tirukirkuttram [the Nageshvara temple] . . .

—BILINGUAL INSCRIPTION: SANSKRIT FOLLOWED BY TAMIL[12]

A sustained study of all the inscriptions engraved on any single temple,[13] treating them as material objects, raises a number of pertinent questions regarding the placement of such records. Who decided on the exact spot along the walls or base moldings where an inscription should be placed? Was the south wall of a temple, that is encountered first by a visitor circumambulating the shrine, a preferred location? Was space at eye level along the walls a donor's first choice for an inscription? To address some of these issues, I have chosen to examine the Nageshvara temple at Kumbakonam, located on the north bank of the Kaveri in the extended coastal belt (fig. 3.6). Its inscriptions indicate that the temple was constructed soon after Parantaka (905–955) came to the throne, and the fifty-four records cut into the walls of the sanctum and the attached *mandapa* were added over a period of roughly 125 years. Space ran out on the main temple during the reign of emperor Rajendra, with the result that some inscriptions dated in his reign and records dated in the reigns of later rulers had to be inscribed on enclosing walls, subsidiary shrines, and subsequently on the *gopuram* gateway. The stone sculptures on the walls of this temple are true masterpieces. The dignity and bearing of the two female figures on the south wall of the shrine suggests their identity as aristocracy or royalty, while the sensuous and assured treatment of the figures speaks of the hands of accomplished stone carvers (fig. 3.7). Equally striking are images on the rear wall of the shrine that feature "portraits" of two male aristocrats; a striking mustached male has the poise and confidence of a courtly figure (fig. 3.8), and was probably carved by the same talented stone sculptor responsible for the "queens" on the south wall.

Earliest among the dated inscriptions on the temple is the damaged and partly incomplete inscription cited at the start of this section, which is engraved along the base moldings beneath the elegant image of the mustached male on the rear west wall of the Nageshvara temple. It encourages us to imagine the scenario of an engraver, who knew how to write

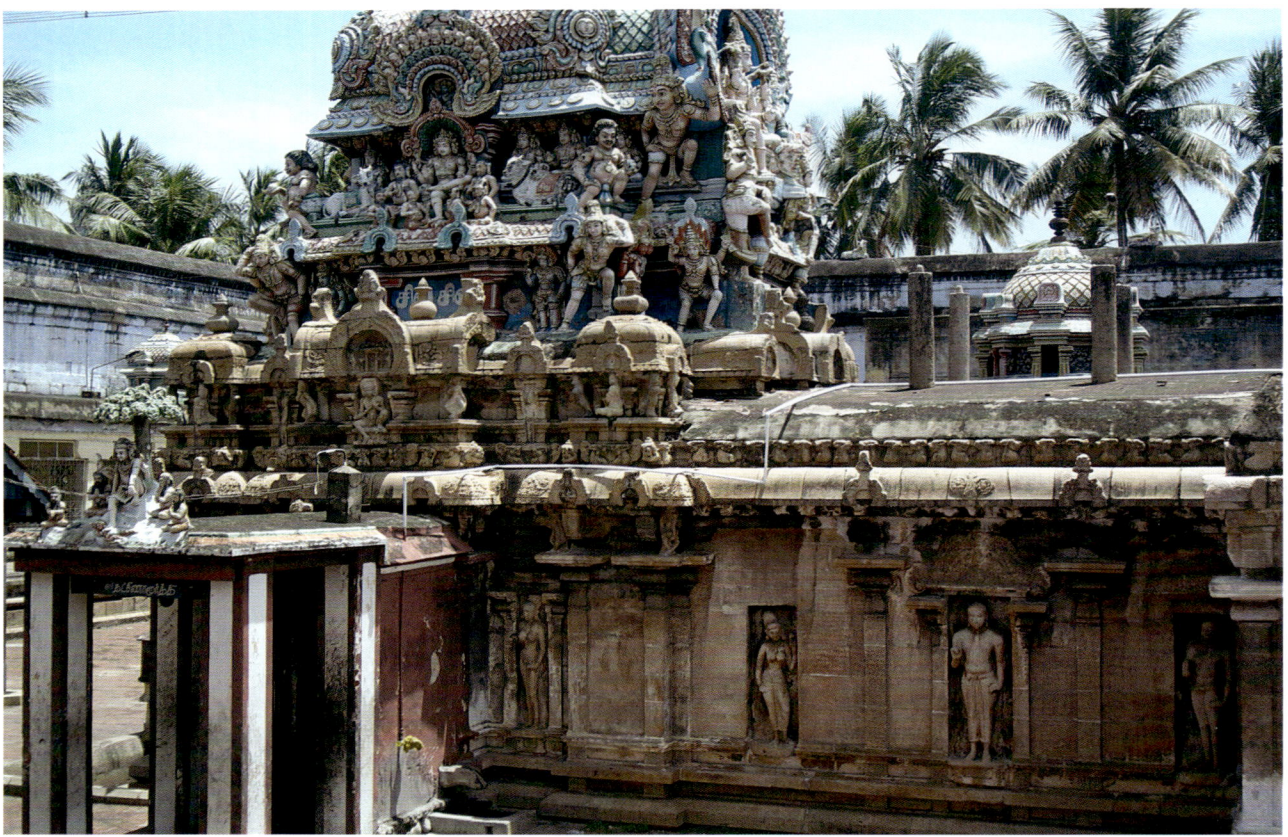

Figure 3.6. Nageshvara temple, Kumbakonam, Thanjavur district.

both Sanskrit and Tamil, walking around the recently completed temple with chisel and hammer in one hand and a single palm leaf carrying the dedication he was to engrave. The surfaces of the temple were free and available for inscriptions; why did he chose to cut the letters so low down along the base moldings rather than at eye level where it could be seen easily? Was his choice perhaps dictated by his desire to compel the donor, who titled himself *danapati*, or lord of gifts, to bend down low to read his dedication (fig. 3.9)?

To demonstrate the apparently random placement of stone inscriptions on walls that, as yet, had nothing inscribed on them, I will focus on the south face of the Nageshvara temple, turning to the rear west wall and the north wall only to reinforce the information gained from a close scrutiny of the temple's south face. Three inscriptions, indicated by the green lines drawn along three different sections of this south wall, indicate the earliest inscriptions that belong to the reign of Parantaka Chola (905–955) (fig. 3.10). Let me clarify that none of these records are royal inscriptions, but rather gifts from a varied population of donors who used the regnal years of Parantaka's reign to mark the precise date of their gifts. The first of these runs almost the full length of the base moldings, and is inscribed along the vertical edge of the sloping *kumuda* molding. It records a gift of land to the temple by a chieftain named Villavan Peraraiyar; the record is badly damaged and missing several portions that include its precise date.[14] Two other inscriptions placed along the south wall belong to the reign of Parantaka. Engraved on the *mandapa* wall, between a queen placed in an

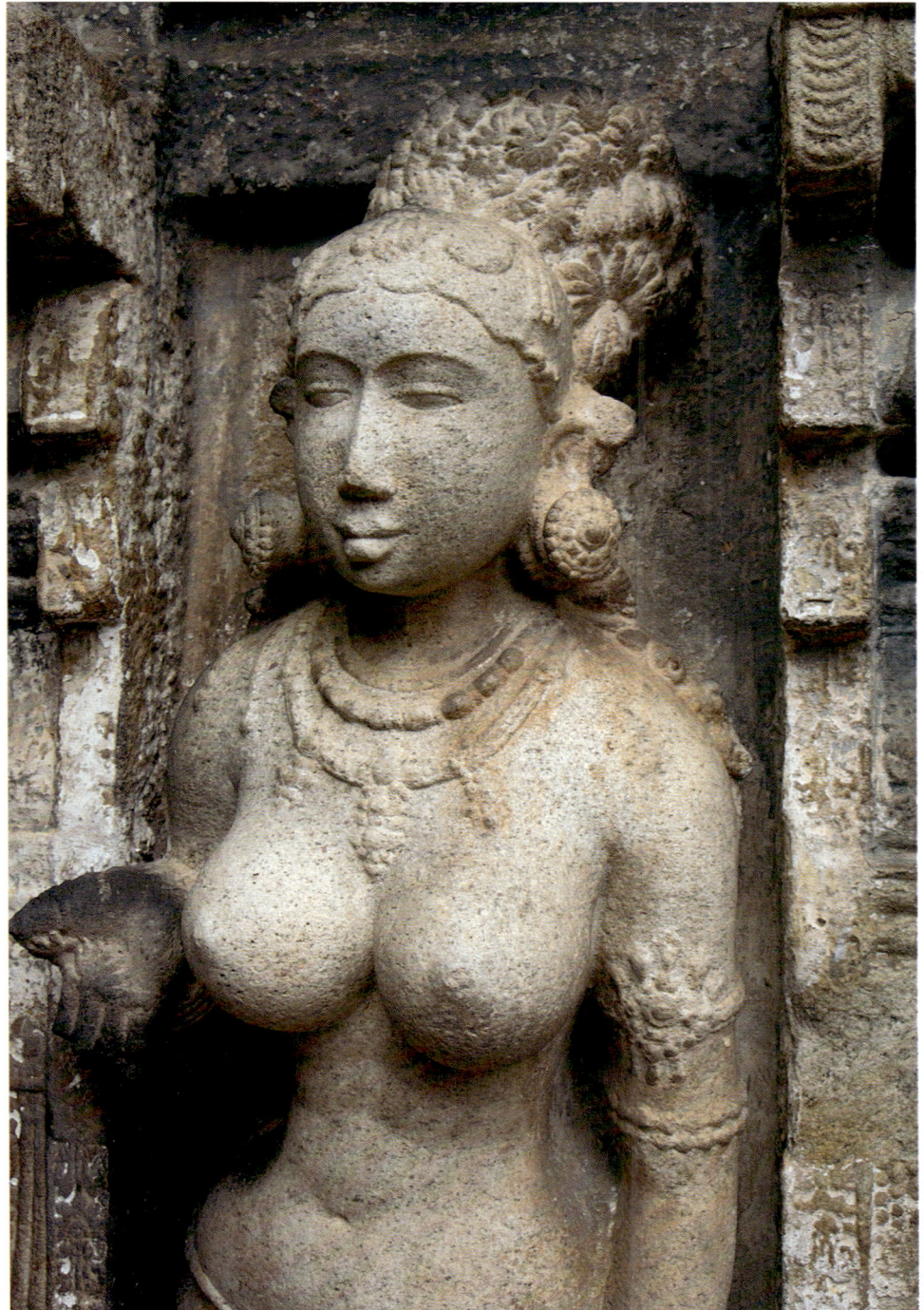
Figure 3.7. Queen, detail from south wall of the Nageshvara temple, Kumbakonam, Thanjavur district, ca. 910.

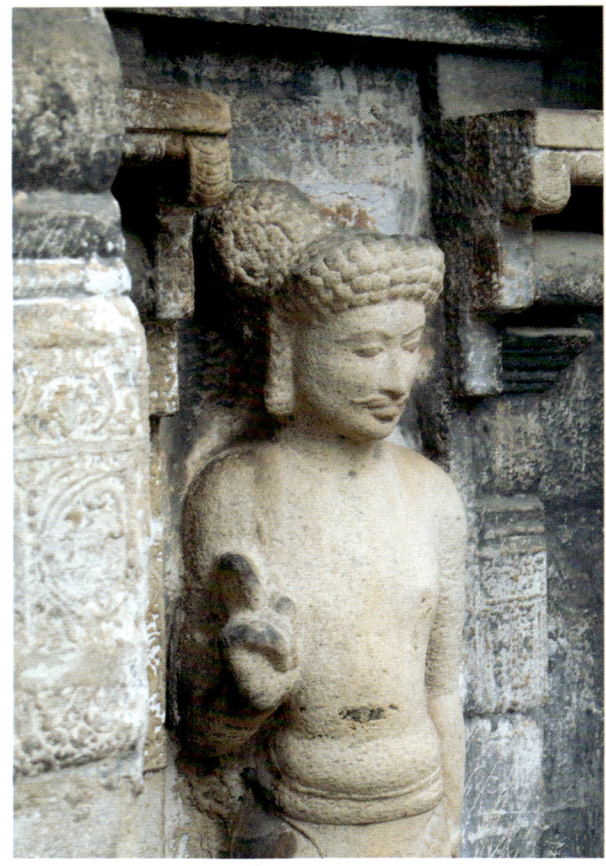

Figure 3.8. Aristocrat, rear west wall of the Nageshvara temple, Kumbakonam, Thanjavur district, ca. 910.

Figure 3.9. Inscription of Danapati Arangan in the twentieth year of Parantaka Chola (marked in green), rear west wall of the Nageshvara temple, Kumbakonam, Thanjavur district, 925.

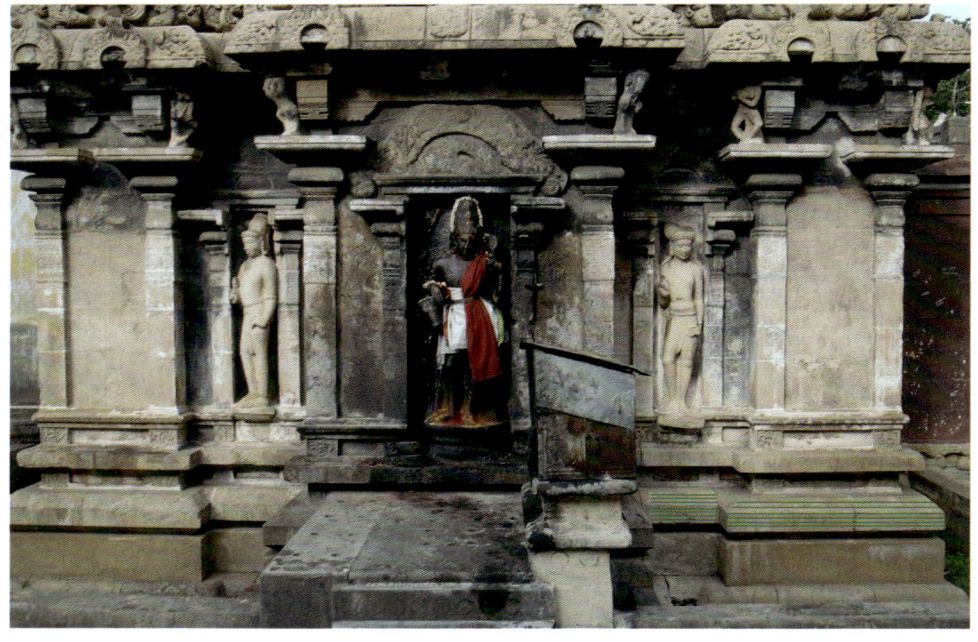

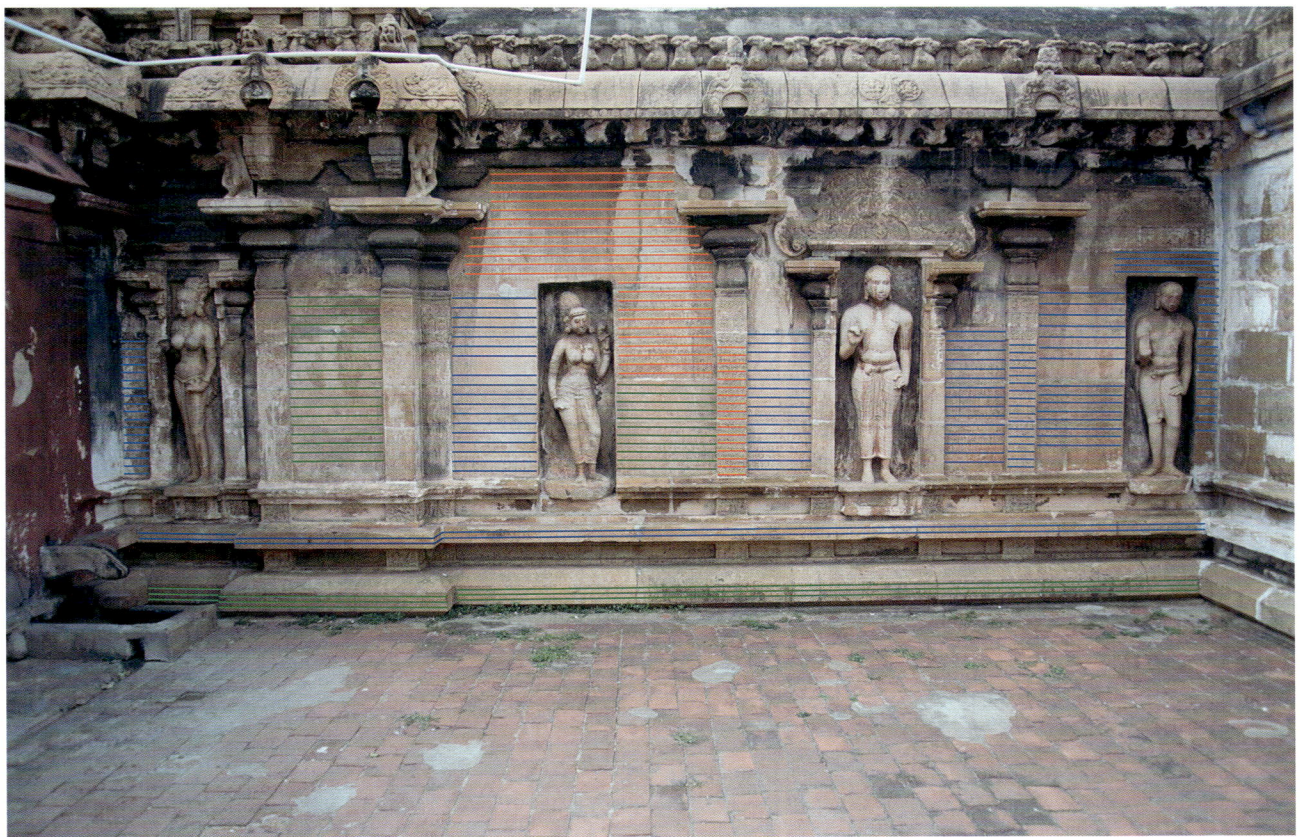

Figure 3.10. Inscriptions from three periods, south wall of the Nageshvara temple, Kumbakonam, Thanjavur district: the time of Parantaka Chola (905–955; in green); between Parantaka Chola and Rajaraja Chola (955–985; in blue); and the year 1015 (in red).

undecorated niche and the figure of a standing sage beneath a decorative archway flanked by pilasters, one inscription dates to 943 and records a gift of ninety sheep for a perpetual lamp by Mainjan Kavaiyan; it provides the names of two shepherds who received the sheep and agreed to supply the ghee necessary for burning the perpetual lamps.[15] The inscription along the *ardha-mandapa*, to the right of a queen enclosed by pilasters, is a gift of land from a temple priest, Bhattan Mahadevan Narayanan, for a perpetual lamp, and for camphor and the perfumed *sitari* root, and represents a donation made during the fortieth year of Parantaka (946).[16] It is difficult to find any logic in such a placement of inscriptions upon a totally blank wall; why not inscribe all three along the moldings, or all three upon the walls?

A relevant factor in reading inscriptions is the universal Indian ritual of *pradakshina*, or circumambulation, which requires devotees to walk around the temple and its sanctum prior to approaching the image within for ritual worship. Since both the Tamil and Sanskrit scripts run from left to right, in the same manner as English, a devotee walking around the temple in the ritually appropriate clockwise manner would encounter the end of a line of inscription before its start. This is especially striking with the record of chieftain Villavan Peraraiyar that runs the entire length of the base molding along the south

WRIT IN STONE 75

side of the temple. Anyone wishing to read it would have to walk to the start of the inscription, and then move from left to right along the south wall, in counterclockwise manner; additionally, since the inscription is in three lines, the reader would have to repeat this maneuver twice more. In other words, it is clear that reading inscriptions and the rite of worship were not connected; temple inscriptions were archival in purpose, were intended to record gifts to the temple, and had no direct religious function. It is doubtful too whether literacy was at a level where visitors to a temple could read the inscribed records. Probably they were read by only the donors, priests, and adjudicators of disputes on the use of the numerous recorded gifts of land, gold, bronzes, and jewelry.

A similar situation confronts us when we turn to the rear west wall of the sanctum, which contains three inscriptions of the time of Parantaka. One is the bilingual record with which we commenced this section, inscribed on the sloping *kumuda* molding below the mustached aristocratic male image. The second inscription, recording a gift of ninety-six sheep for a perpetual lamp, is on the lowest *jagati* molding beneath the central niche that carries Shiva as Ardharnari leaning against his bull; the record is partly hidden today by the platform constructed to give the priests easy access to the niche containing the stone image of Shiva as Half Woman. The third record, dated in the forty-sixth year of Parantaka, or 951, occupies the entire wall space on the far-left wall of this rear space and records a gift of sheep. On the north face of the temple, the inscriptional situation is even stranger, since we find only a single record dated in the reign of Parantaka that makes provision for sacred food at noon. This is inscribed on the *kumuda* molding along the *ardha-mandapa*, beneath the figure of a princess or queen within a plain undecorated niche; the start of the record is today subsumed within the later enclosure built around the Durga figure on the adjoining *mandapa* wall.

Returning to the south face of the temple that is our focus, the second cluster of inscriptions, marked in blue, belong to the years 955–985 that intervened between the death of Parantaka and the accession of emperor Rajaraja (see fig. 3.10). Of the monarchs who ruled in those thirty years,[17] we have seven, perhaps eight, records on this south wall of Aditya Karikala and four of Uttama Chola. The inscription along the vertical band of the *pattigai*, or uppermost level of the base moldings, appears to have been the first to be added after the end of Parantaka's reign. Dating to the year 3 of a Rajakesari, and hence most likely to the year 953 during Gandaraditya's reign, it speaks of the sale of land to the temple by the town assembly to repay 500 *kalanju* of gold as part of the penalty (*dandam*) of 3,000 *kalanju* levied on them by Parantaka.[18] The remaining eight inscriptions are largely on the temple walls, where more than one runs across lightly raised pilasters. They come from a varied group of donors, several of whom sponsored the burning of perpetual lamps, and include a member of a military regiment who gave ninety sheep to provide for a lamp, a generous gift from a merchant (*vyapari*) to provide food for brahmins with details of the ingredients to be provided for this meal, and a gift of a perpetual lamp from Eran, wife of Bhattan Mahadevan whom we encountered as a donor during the reign of Parantaka.[19] Here too, no logic is apparent in the exact placement of the records. A similar lack of planned execution is apparent with the large number of records belonging to the period 955–985 on the west and north faces of the temple. For instance, one might imagine that queen Viranaraniyar's gift of land for a flower garden to provide the garlands required for temple worship would be located in a prominent place.[20] She was, after all, daughter of a Muttaraiyar chieftain and consort of Uttama Chola. But her record is inserted into the narrow space to the proper right of the mustached male and completed on the lower half of the pilaster enclosing the image. Her second gift of ninety-six sheep for a perpetual lamp is not located on the same face of the temple;[21] it is on the north wall, this time in a prominent location to the immediate right (for the viewer) of the central Brahma niche.

By 985 when Rajaraja became king, space for inscriptions was running out along the walls and base moldings of the main temple. The single record marked in red on the south face of the temple dates to the year 1015 during the reign of Rajendra and belongs to a woman donor who made a generous gift to the temple of land, rice, coins, and a house plot (see fig. 3.10). The gift was to ensure that her Darling Lord (*chella piran*), would be honored every day with a garland of red lotuses as well as a noonday meal that, it was stipulated, must include rice, dal, ghee, and betel nuts—a meal that, of course, would then be distributed to temple employees and devotees.[22] Despite the shortage of available space, the engraver was enterprising and managed to engrave Vasudevan Mahadevi's record on this south face of the temple. He commenced his inscription across the entire available space above the niche carrying a sculpted image of a "queen." He stopped on encountering a previously engraved inscription—the blue lines to the left of the female image—and continued his task on the wall to the viewer's right of the image. There, he was forced to stop halfway down upon encountering an even earlier inscription—in green. He turned to a lightly raised pilaster farther to the right and inscribed the remaining text down its narrow vertical space.

A single inscription of the time of Rajaraja is found engraved on the west wall of the shrine, along the pilaster to the far left of the projection that encloses the image of Shiva as Ardhanari. None are to be found on the north wall, where space was clearly exhausted. All inscriptions later than the third year of Rajendra I could no longer be accommodated on the walls of the main temple; they were added on the enclosing *prakara* walls, on other small shrines, and, as the temple premises were expanded, later records were placed on the entrance gateway.[23]

Studying the distribution of inscriptions on the walls of the Nageshvara, one might suggest that there was an overall preference for using the south wall that devotees and other visitors would encounter first upon circumambulating the temple. On the other hand, while there was ample space on the south wall for all the inscriptions of the time of Parantaka, we have seen that three inscriptions dated in his reign are placed on the west wall and one on the north wall. The only inscriptions that suggest a logical and planned placement are a set of four gifts from an officer named Koyil Mayilai, known also as Parantaka Muvendavelan or Madhurantaka Muvendavelan; belonging to the second, third, fifth, and tenth years of Aditya II Karikala, they are inscribed beside each other on the north face of the temple.[24]

Why were temple walls treated as if they were the public records office? Each inscription commences with the statement that the gift in question was "given to the lord of the *devadana* of Tirukudamukkil (Kumbakonam), in Tirukirkottam, in Pambur Nadu, on the north bank of the Kaveri." The only change in this repetitive statement that is part of every single inscription is that the lord of the temple is alternately referred to as *swami*, *mahadevar*, or *perumanadigal*. Otherwise, the formula of *vadakarai pamburnattu devadanam tirukudamukkil tirukirkottatu (swamikku/mahadevarkku/perumanadigalikku)* is repeated fully. Such wording would be superfluous if these gifts were recorded solely on the stone of the temple itself. The repeated emphasis on the very specific topographical location of the temple suggests that the records were written first on palm leaves, or *olai*, housed in a records office; they were then copied in their entirety onto the stone temple walls, together with the wording that specifies the precise location of the temple. Palm leaf has clearly not survived the hot and humid climate of Tamil Nadu. It is important to note that the officer in charge of inscribing records was known as *tirumandiram olai* even when he was in charge of cutting inscriptions on stone rather than writing them on palm leaves. The question that arises, of course, is why it was considered necessary at all for gifts to be inscribed onto the walls of the temples that were the beneficiaries of such gifts. Possibly the fragility of palm leaf was acknowledged at the time. Additionally, since the original gift documents would require revisiting as and when disputes arose regarding the many items given to a temple, it would appear that inscribed stone constituted both a highly reliable record-keeping system as well as one that was right out there in the open for all parties to consult freely.[25] Last, there is also the issue of the legitimacy and protection that documentation on a temple wall must have provided.[26]

Three Tenth-Century Temples and Continuing Chola Patronage

A perusal of the entire series of inscriptions on a temple—on its sanctum, *ardhamandapa*, main *mandapa*, its adjunct shrines, enclosing wall, and its entrance gateway—indicates that just about every temple built during the period of Chola rule continued to receive gifts from a wide section of the population until the very last days the Cholas. Its donors all followed the practice of citing the regnal year of the ruling king to clarify the exact date of their gifts, which included new bronzes with jewelry to adorn them, perpetual lamps with the oil or ghee necessary to keep them burning, and fresh endowments for continuing ritual worship, particularly during the many festivals that the temples celebrated. We will here consider three temples built during the time of Parantaka Chola (905–955), whose precise regnal year is mentioned in the gifts inscribed on their walls, and briefly follow the histories of these temples until the Pandyas made inroads into erstwhile Chola territory during the thirteenth century.

Tirunavalur (Tirunamanallur)

Toward the north of the small Chola kingdom as it existed in the days of Parantaka Chola, in today's South Arcot district, is the Tirunavalur temple, built in stone by Parantaka's queen Kokkilanadigal to honor her son, crown prince Rajaditya. It carries ninety or so inscriptions along its walls that relate a mini-history of the dynasty in a way that few other Chola temples do. A third of the temple's inscriptions belong to the phase of its inception and consist of thirty-two records dated in various years of the reign of Parantaka Chola, identified specifically as King Parakesari who captured Madurai (*madiraikonda ko parakesari*). The earliest inscription on the walls of Tirunavalur belongs to prince Rajaditya himself, and is dated in the year 16 of his father Parantaka, and thus to 921/22; by that time, the Tirunavalur temple was already a functioning entity. The record specifies that Rama with the Kodanda bow (*Kodandaraman*, a reference to the Rama avatar of Vishnu, is a name by which Rajaditya was known), son of the ruling Chola king, gave a gift of 400 sheep for four lamps to be kept perpetually burning in the temple of Tiruttondishvara, alias Rajaditta-Ishvaram, at Tirunavalur.[27] An important record of the year 28 of Parantaka, or 933, belongs to Chitrakomalam, a female attendant of queen Kokkilan, mother of Rajadittadevar, who gave an *Ila*, or Sri Lankan lamp, to the temple, together with ninety sheep to provide the ghee to keep the lamp burning perpetually. Inscribed on the south wall of the *mandapa*, this record informs us that it was queen Kokkilanadigal who caused the temple to be built of stone, although it does not specify the year when the queen built the temple.[28] An inscription on the same south wall, dated a year later, records the gift of 100 sheep for a lamp from a follower of Rajaditya and seemingly ends with the usual phrase that it is in the protection of the temple's priests. It then adds a statement to the effect that the record was inscribed by a resident of Tiruchengatankudi (his name is in a damaged portion of the record) who built the Navalur temple, and thus appears to refer to the architect who actually constructed the temple.[29] The remaining thirty inscriptions dated in the reign of Parantaka record gifts from those in a close circle around prince Rajaditya, largely of lamps and of sheep to provide ghee for keeping the lamps lit night and day. As a measure of their open allegiance to the crown prince, these gifts came from his physician, his accountant, his chief accountant, his oil supplier, and his own queen Mahadeviadigal, who was daughter of chieftain Iladaraiyar. Especially interesting are gifts from various members of his *parivara* (regiment), including those who identify themselves by specialty as horse trooper, elephant trooper, or as Malaiyali (Kerala) members of his regiment. By the thirty-ninth year of Parantaka, or 944, when gifts of this nature cease, we may assume that the newly built temple was completely equipped for worship, with all its lamps and other ritual necessities.

The year 949 witnessed the disastrous Chola battle at Takkolam against the Rashtrakutas to their north, who were aided by their allies, the Gangas of Andhra. By all accounts, crown prince Rajaditya was killed by the Ganga king, who mounted the elephant that the crown prince was riding and speared him, so that Rajaditya was known in all future inscriptions as "lord who 'slept' on the elephant." Tirunavalur's inscriptions testify to this breakdown in Chola fortunes in that it carries four records that are dated in the regnal years of the victorious Rashtrakuta king Krishnadeva III, of which the earliest belongs to his nineteenth year, or 958. While Krishnadeva's records in his own territories, to the northwest of the Cholas, are in the Sanskrit language and the northern devanagari script, those in Navalur are in the Tamil language and the Tamil script; additionally, he adopted the Tamil title of "Kannaradeva who took Kanchi and Thanjai (Thanjavur)."[30] Another three inscriptions dated in his regnal years, all placed on the south wall of the *mandapa* in front of the main shrine, record gifts of gold for lamps or of sheep to provide ghee, and are dated in various years of Krishnadeva. The latest belongs to 967, the very year in which the Cholas reestablished their claim to territory they had lost temporarily, though ignominiously, to the Rashtrakutas. It should be noted here that inscriptions dated in the twenty-first to the twenty-ninth regnal years of Krishnadeva III also occur farther north in Chola territory at Saluvankuppam in the Kanchipuram district and on stone slabs near temples in the more northern Cuddalore and Chinglepet districts. These records vary from gifts of oil for festival lamps, through payment to drummers during the daily *sribali* ceremony, to food offerings to the deities.[31]

The next set of inscriptions at Navalur commence with the third regnal year of a Parakesari, who appears to be Aditya II, known as Karikala. They are varied in nature and speak of water rights of temple land, the construction of a *mandapa*, an eastern gateway, a shrine to Chandesha, the gift of a gold diadem, and of money to employ four sweepers and two garland-makers.[32] The temple inscriptions continue with those dated in the reigns of Rajaraja I and Rajendra I; they are largely official in their phraseology and are gifts of villages to the temple to ensure the continuation of regular worship. A record from a military official speaks of a gift of a gold diadem for the "Dancer [*kuttar*] who was pleased to dance" in the temple, clearly a bronze Dancing Shiva.[33] Another gift of jewelry came from Rajendra's military commander, who gifted three necklaces, one of pearls, and one of gold inset with eighteen crystals and two sapphires to the "Expert Dancer" (*Adavallar*), to whom he also gave a bracelet embedded with crystals and pearls.[34] A smaller number of inscriptions of Kulottunga I, Vikrama Chola, and later rulers follow. The final inscriptions on the temple are those of the year 1285, when Chola power had ended, and are dated in the reign of Vikrama Pandya III. One records a royal gift of a village to the temple from the conquering Pandya ruler; a second is another royal gift of a village, this time to forty-four brahmins for reciting the Vedas during the early morning service.[35]

This brief review of the inscriptions engraved on the Navalur temple, and indeed those inscribed on other shrines in territory held by the Cholas, demonstrate the continuing patronage given to temples throughout the four centuries of the Chola presence. Two features set the Tirunavalur inscriptions apart. The first is the very large number of gifts from prince Rajaditya's circle of devoted followers at the time that the temple was constructed, that appear to stand as a testimonial to their devotion to the prince. The second is the evidence of Rashtrakuta Krishnadeva III's occupation of the area for almost ten years, during which time gifts to the Navalur temple were dated, not in Chola regnal years, but in those of the Rashtrakuta king.

Maraikkadu (Today's Vedaranyam)

> *We know his place*
> *where the fruit of the coconut*
> *and long palmyra palms*
> *falls into the sandy gardens*
> *while ships at sea*
> *lurching over conch and brilliant oysters*
> *bend their high masts in worship*
> —SUNDARAR, HYMN 71[36]

Close to ninety inscribed gifts exist on the temple at ancient Maraikkadu, the southernmost point of the Kaveri deltaic region. Thirty-eight of these are dated in the reign of Parantaka, identified clearly as King Parakesari who captured Madurai, and range from a record in his seventh year (913) to his forty-third year (949), which marks the disastrous battle of Takkolam. Thirty-three of these inscriptions record gifts connected with ensuring the burning of perpetual lamps in the temple and refer to a ghee measure named Tiru-maraikkadan after the town and its temple; the remaining five inscriptions speak of gifts of gold for food offerings, for a fly-whisk, and gold to ensure that a brahmin priest, well-versed in both the Vedas and the intricacies of ritual (*archana vidhi*), conducted the necessary ritual services at the temple.[37] One interesting inscription, partly in verse, and dated to the year 939, records the successful return of the donor after a campaign in Sri Lanka that resulted in the defeat of the Sinhalese king.[38] A gift of 900 *Ilakasu*, or Sri Lankan coins, made two years earlier, speaks of the close relationship that existed between this southernmost port and Lanka.[39] Two records testify to a connection with royalty; one speaks of a gift from the children of a woman who worked at the great palace in Thanjavur,[40] while the second speaks of a gift from the children of a woman who worked for queen Kilanadigal (obviously queen Kokkilan, mother of Rajaditya).[41] Parantaka's overall territorial authority clearly extended from at least the northern town of Tirunavalur in South Arcot district to Maraikkadu located on the coast well south of Nagapattinam. One may assume that this temple was constructed early in Parantaka's reign, prior to the gift of 913; the possibility that a few inscriptions belong to the reign of his predecessor Aditya may not be ruled out.

Maraikkadu's temple inscriptions continue with those of Rajaraja, and reveal a spurt of activity during the reigns of Kulottunga III and Rajaraja III; these largely testify to the declining state of affairs in the thirteenth century that will be our subject in chapter 9. The Maraikkadu inscriptions, like those at Navalur, demonstrate that a temple built during Chola rule was likely to receive patronage throughout the reign of the Cholas.

The Story of Tiruvidaimaradur

An example of the astounding number of inscriptions that might be inscribed on the walls of a temple is provided by the temple at Tiruvidaimaradur in the deltaic region of the Kaveri river, which once carried 147 inscriptions dated in the regnal years of the entire range of Chola kings. It is fortunate for us that these inscriptions were published in the *Annual Report on Epigraphy* for the years 1895 and 1907, since not a single inscription remains intact. The temple has been completely renovated, and its old stone walls replaced by newly cut stone, so that nothing survives of the original structure or its inscriptions except for a couple of broken stones that carry traces of writing. Its 147 inscriptions commence with those of Parantaka and end with those of the Chola enemy, Vikrama Pandya; ranging over the years 905–1286, they stand testimony to the continued importance of temples, and of this one in particular, throughout Chola rule. Several royal orders are recorded in this temple, which appears to have been a site of personal significance for Vikrama Chola (r. 1118–1135), since frequent mention is made of the monarch being personally present in one or another hall of the temple when making gifts.

The earliest inscriptions at Tiruvidaimaradur, thirty-two in number, are dated in the reign of Parantaka and record varied gifts to the temple including lamps, food offerings, payment to musicians, gold diadems to adorn the bronzes, gold for a variety of purposes from repairing a channel branching off from the old course of the river to keeping a garland of lamps burning every day between the twilight worship and the closing of the temple after the night service.[42] One inscription reports the theft of a golden bowl and a gold diadem and speaks of the cost of replacing these.[43] Forty-one inscriptions are dated in the reigns of the monarchs between Parantaka and Rajaraja and speak of a similarly wide range of gifts including, for instance, a sword with a sandalwood hilt given by a military officer.[44] Inscriptions often specify that coins, or *kasu*, were Sri Lankan coins (*Ilakasu*) that appear to have had currency in Chola territories. One such gift of Sri Lankan gold coins came from the maidservant of queen Kokkilan, mother of crown prince Rajaditya, who was slain in battle with the Rashtrakutas. Her gold was to be used for ornaments to adorn a bronze of Uma and consisted of a marriage necklace, a necklace of twenty-seven pearls, and a pair of pearl-studded armlets.[45] Several other records speak specifically of gifts of jewelry to temple bronzes. The officer of Sacred Works, a certain Pallavaraiyar from Inganadu, made a gold crown (110 3/4 *kalanju*) for Shiva using cash realized from the sale of areca nuts from the temple garden.[46] The same *srikaryam* officer, Pallavaraiyar of Inganadu, also set up of a bronze image of the Dancing Lord together with several gold ornaments to adorn him. The inscription in question explains that a merchant had previously presented money to the temple for the express purpose of digging a water tank. However, the townsfolk and the brahmin *sabha*, consisting respectively of 300 and 400 persons, met and decided to divert the use of that money to create a gold necklace to adorn the Dancing Lord. They then named their Dancing Shiva as "Lord of the 700" (persons who made that decision).[47] A gold handplate to enhance the raised hand of dancing Shiva is among the gifts from a merchant-trader named Kanari Tonri.[48] Money for a regular supply of plantains for the worship of a bronze Ganesha came from the military community of the town;[49] interestingly, it is specified that this group, whose main connections must have been with island Sri Lanka, gave Sri Lankan money (*Ilakasu*). Inscriptions recording gifts for the performance of dance and music highlight the importance of such activities in the temple's festival cycle. One such speaks of members of the temple hierarchy being assembled in the theater (*nataka shala*) and hearing the order of a high official, Parantakan Muvendavelan, who made provision for all seven parts of a dance known as *Ariya kuttu*, or Arya dance (northern?), to be performed on different occasions during the year. The dancer to whom payment was made was a specialist named Kirti Maraikandan, also known as the dancer of the *chakkai* mode from Tiruvellarai (*Tiruvellarai chakkai kuttan*).[50] Another record speaks of a gift to enable payment to a musician to sing *deshi* (local Tamil?) songs before the lord of the temple.[51] The names of the dancers make it clear that dance dramas were performed by male dancers.

Twelve gifts were made during the time of the emperors Rajaraja and Rajendra. A maidservant of Rajaraja's queen Vanavan Mahadevi, residing in Thanjavur, gifted a number of jeweled items to the goddess Uma including a marriage necklace and a pearl ornament.[52] Another queen, Panchavan Mahadevi, gifted a small golden image of Shiva and Uma together that weighed just over 12 pounds.[53] An inscription of this period alerts us to the importance of a royal visit to the temple. When queen Panchavan Mahadevi visited the temple, she was waited upon by the Sacred Works officer, the priests of the temple, the brahmin *sabha* of the town, and the merchants of the town. She visited the recently established *champaka*-tree-laden temple garden known by the name of the great dowager queen Sembiyan Mahadevi, and made a grant for the services of a gardener.[54] Testifying to the importance of trade guilds, we read of a construction by a military officer, in front of the temple, that was placed under the protection not of the temple authorities but of the influential merchant guild, the Five Hundred of the Thousand Directions, whom we shall encounter in chapter 7.[55]

While there is no break in the pattern of gifting at Tiruvdaimaradur, we see a monarch's direct personal involvement with the temple when we turn to inscriptions dated to the reign of Vikrama Chola (1118–1135). We read, for instance, that while Vikrama Chola was seated along with his queen on his throne-couch in the hall called Eka-nayakam (The One Leader), in the big courtyard in front of the temple, he ordained that the village of Vannakudi be endowed, tax-free, to the temple.[56] Another inscription informs us that this order was entered into the tax registers (presumably of palm leaf), and that it was also engraved in stone and signed by seven revenue officers.[57] Another direct order of the king, while he was seated on the royal seat named after him in the hall known as Tyagasamudram within the temple, was to the effect that 160 and 240 lamps should burn in the hall known as the Vikrama Chola Mansion, while a third set of lights was endowed on the same occasion by his queen Tribhuvana Mulududaiyal.[58] Vikrama Chola appears to have taken a deep personal interest in at least one other temple. An inscription at Tiruvenkadu, whose master sculptor we will encounter in chapter 5, informs us that while the monarch was seated on the steps at the south side of the hall named after him as the Vikrama-cholan-tiru-mandapa, the monarch gave land for a *matha* (monastery) in a street known as the Vikrama Chola Sacred Way.[59]

Moving to the later history of Tiruvidaimaradur, we find that royal interest in the temple continued during the reigns of Kulottunga II and III, with at least seven gifts being direct orders from the king (*tirumuka-padi*). Two such gifts from Kulottunga III concern the appointments of dance masters, one of whom was a specialist in facial emoting, or *abhinaya*, and they specify the allocation of special rights to these dance masters.[60] Kulottunga III also issued an order to the effect that the procession of the god, which used to start from the south entrance to the temple, would in future start from the eastern entrance. A new road was to be laid for this purpose, and the main gateway to the palace was to be constructed along this new road. The plot occupied by residential buildings along the old south road was to be acquired for conversion to an orchard and flower garden to serve the temple's needs. The record concludes with the signatures of six prominent officials, headed by the royal secretary Minavan Muvendavelan.[61] Two other inscriptions speak of the royal gift of land for the worship of images in the temple, one of goddess Kali that appears to have been set up by the monarch, and the other of Ganesha commissioned by a Bana chieftain.[62]

The final set of inscriptions at Tiruvidaimaradur dates from the period of the dissolution of the Chola kingdom. One such, dated in the reign of the Pandya king Maravarman Vikrama Pandya, belongs to the year 1286 and specifies that the monarch is a friend of Kerala, but enemy to the Cholas, Sri Lanka, king Gopaladeva, and the Kakatiya rulers. Its purpose is to gift tax-free land to cover the daily expenses of worship that was instituted in the name of the Pandya king, as well as for worship on festival days.[63] Chola rule had come to an end.

Royal Copper-Plate Inscriptions

It was customary for Chola monarchs to issue copper-plate inscriptions that served a dual objective. The first was to record a dynastic "history," a eulogy that started with a mythological background for the dynasty from the sun, either directly through Manu, the first mythical king, or indirectly through Vishnu, Brahma, and sage Kasyapa to Manu,[64] thus providing a Chola descent from an important legendary ancestor. The dynastic lineage in these copper plates is then brought into historical times, where we need to discount the hyperbole that was a necessary mode adopted by court poets who composed these eulogies. The second purpose of these charters was a practical one—to record major donations of lands to brahmins or to temples, together with details of the boundaries of such lands, the taxes that the king now forfeited and allocated instead to the temple or the brahmins, together with a host of administrative details regarding such a gift. The donation had already been recorded on palymra leaf in the official court records, and in customary fashion the individual palm leaves carried holes through which a cord was threaded to hold them together as a single document. These charters or orders (*sasanam*) were then inscribed onto sheets of copper and sent out as the personal mandate of the king (*tirumukam* or sacred face) to the temple concerned. As Daud Ali has pointed out in his study of the Tiruvalankadu copper plates of Rajendra I, the king's orders, at this stage probably written on palm leaves prior to being inscribed on copper plates, were received at the site with deep respect as representing the king himself (*tirumukam*), read out to a wider audience, placed on the back of an elephant, and paraded around the lands concerned to announce the acceptance of the conditions of the gift.[65] The copper-plate inscriptions conclude with the name of the poet who composed the eulogy, the name of the scribe who wrote out the text on the copper plates, and the name of the inscriber who chiseled the text into the sheets of copper. Once this process was complete, with all the plates numbered consecutively, a copper ring was threaded through a hole made in each plate, in imitation of the cord threaded through the palm-leaf manuscripts. It was then finalized with a copper seal that carried the Chola dynastic emblems together with the inscribed title of the monarch. The importance given to copper-plate charters as the face/word of the monarch (*tirumukam*) is seen also from the fact that these charters were housed in the temples that benefited from its provisions. In chapter 9, we will see that when temple bronzes were buried for safekeeping from hostile armies, copper plates too were buried with the sacred images.[66] Here, we will consider briefly three sets of Chola copper-plate inscriptions to gain an idea of their intent and their contents.

The Anbil copper plates, a set of eleven sheets of copper, dated in the year 4 of Sundara Chola (960), carry a seal with the inscribed proclamation: "The irrevocable edict of the glorious Rajakesari-varman, the Eye of the earth and the Victorious lotus-seat of Lakshmi."[67] Similarly constructed phrases describing the king are found on seals of other Chola monarchs. As was customary, the genealogical portion of the grant, as well as the fact of the king's gift, in this case of a village given tax-free to his brahmin minister, Aniruddha Brahmadhirayan, was composed in Sanskrit and written in the southern *grantha* script that allowed scribes writing in Tamil to accommodate the expanded alphabet of the Sanskrit language. The charter then shifts to the Tamil language and Tamil script for the larger portion of the grant that provides details of the land given and the privileges granted, and it concludes with the names of thirteen signatories who witnessed the king's orders, starting with the arbitrator (*madhyastha*) Brahmamangalam, who wrote the charter, and ending with Virachola, the metal-smith who cut the inscription. The copper plate of Sundara Chola lists the contents of the village, all of which were to go to the donee—trees, wells, gardens, public places, pasture grounds for calves, the village site, land occupied by ant-hills, platforms around trees, ponds, inundated rivers, river beds, sand banks, mansions, water ponds with fish, fissures in rocks where bees construct their hives for honey. It then lays out the privileges granted to the donee: He may construct houses of more than one story and may tile or terrace them; may dig wells and tanks; may grow specified aromatic plants; may cut water channels for irrigation; may dam the river and other water sources within his property; and no one may construct water lifts in his property. The key role that irrigation and agriculture occupied in the Chola system is evident from the repetition of such items in the many royal copper-plate charters, which frequently tend to be connected with the donation of parcels of land that included villages.

The Tiruvalankadu copper plates of emperor Rajendra, dated in the year 1018, consist of thirty-one sheets of copper that weigh 203 pounds together with its seal-ring that is inscribed to read: "Svasti Sri. This order of Parakesarivarman Rajendra Chola is to rest on the jewels in rows on the crests of [other] kings." As is customary, the Sanskrit portion of the text occupies the first ten plates, while the subsequent twenty-one plates are written in the Tamil script and Tamil language. The final ninety-eight lines of the grant are devoted to the conditions of the grant of the village and its surrounding property as a tax-free sacred gift (*devadana*) to the temple; the privileges pertaining to the land granted to the temple reads like an expanded version of what we encountered with the Anbil plates. Instructions about the proclamation of the gift are entered as early as line 16: "We ordered that it may thus be entered in the registers, engraved on copper, and written in stone."[68] The inscription is specific in its documentation of procedural details, informing us that the oral order of the king was issued on the eighty-eighth day of his sixth year, with the written order released on the ninetieth day of his sixth year. However, the execution of the grant at the site followed a whole year and sixty-five days later when two officers, accompanied by a female elephant, supervised the process of going around the granted property and planting boundary stones. It is of interest to note that four artists, *chitra-karinis*, from the town of Kanchipuram, each one named individually and then described collectively as "ornaments of their race," are mentioned in the last verse as having engraved the eulogy in clear letters.[69]

The largest and most impressive copper-plate charter issued by a Chola monarch consists of eighty-five copper plates, each measuring 17 inches by 8 inches, and weighing an astounding 330 pounds together with its copper ring and seal (fig. 3.11). It was unearthed in the Shiva temple in the village of Tiruvindalur during renovation of the *mandapa* in the year 2010, and was found buried 12 feet below the present floor and beneath a group of buried sacred bronzes. The plates are inscribed on both faces, and the first nine plates are in the Sanskrit language written in the southern *grantha* script, while the remaining seventy-six plates are in the Tamil language and the Tamil script. Each individual plate weighs close to 4 pounds, and Dr. Marxia Gandhi, the translator of the Tamil plates that constitute the bulk of the material, speaks of the difficulty of working with them and manipulating the plates when turning back to check earlier wording or repetition of names and titles.[70] The length of the text at 3,442 lines is extraordinary, with the first 272 lines in Sanskrit and the following 3,170 lines in Tamil. The inadvertent omission of the very first plate, when the copper ring and seal are absolutely intact, is surprising; even more so since the ring itself is inscribed to specify that it holds eighty-six plates (*intha valayattilkotta edu enpatharu*).[71] The charter is unusual in more ways than one. First, it focuses on valor in battle and is composed as a battle-poem, or *yuddha-kavya*, a classical Sanskrit form that, in this instance, makes use of forty-three different poetic metrical modes.[72] Second, it consists of three grants issued within a twelve-year period: the first is a gift of eleven villages to 130 brahmins by the emperor Rajadhiraja in the year 1052/53; the second gift is an additional donation of thirty-four villages to 750 brahmins by his successor Rajendra II in the year 1058; the final grant of Virarajendra in the year 1065 speaks of the remuneration given to the poet, the name of the scribe who wrote the text on the copper plates, and the name of the engraver who cut the letters into the copper surfaces. When the plates were secured with the copper ring and seal in the year 1065, the inexplicable omission of the first plate occurred; apparently, it was never noticed and remained revered by those who received the order (*sasanam*), placed it on the back of an elephant, and took it ceremonially around the boundaries of the villages that made up the gifted brahmin settlement (*agrahara*). The copper plates list fourteen rights and privileges pertaining to the gifted land, similar to those in previous royal charters.

While it is accurate to say that by and large inscriptions on the stone walls of temples and those on copper plates are two different entities, these categories occasionally overlap. Royal gifts are sometimes recorded on both stone and copper, as well as on palm leaf, as we saw in line 16 of the Tiruvalankadu charter. An example of a stone inscription, of which the copper-plate version does not survive, comes from the Konerirajapuram temple, and is dated in the year 1053 during the reign of Rajadhiraja. It tells us that the brahmin *sabha* of Pavaikkudi assembled beneath the tamarind tree on the bank of the channel named Suttamalli, after Rajendra's queen, and decided to give lands tax free for the worship of the temple deity. The brahmin *sabha* agreed to bear all the expenses connected with the land and gave permission to the temple administrators to have the record engraved on the stone of the temple and also on copper sheets.[73]

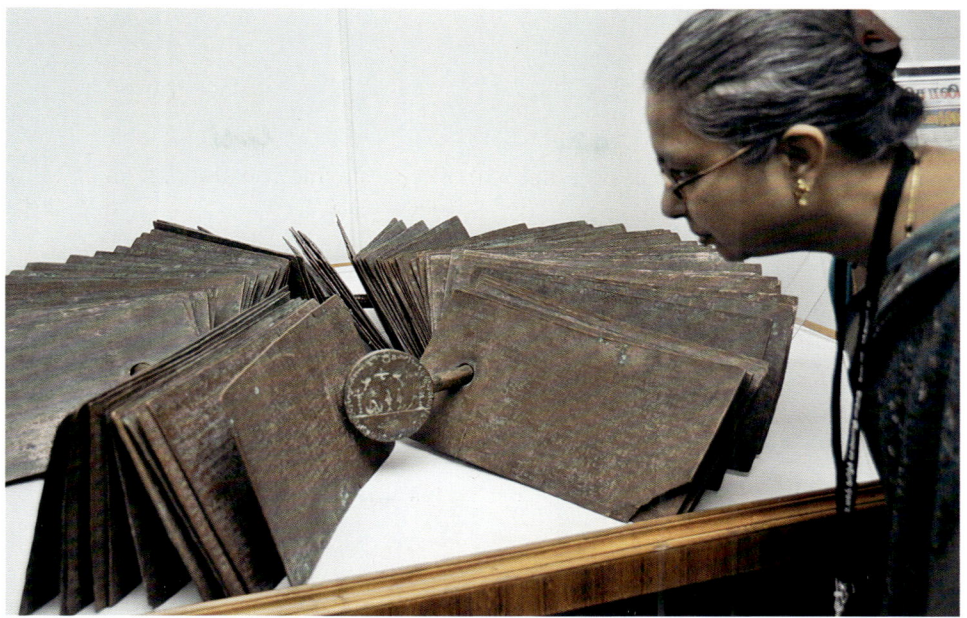

Figure 3.11. Copper plates of emperor Rajadhiraja (continued by Rajendra II and completed by Virarajendra), Tiruvindalur temple, Nagapattinam district, 1065, Government Museum, Chennai, *The Hindu* Archives.

It remains to point out that the extensive Chola inscriptional archive has hardly been touched by scholars and that over half the material remains unprinted and unpublished. It is certain that further research will provide insight into raw history, anthropology, womens' studies, political science, economics, social conditions, and religion. For the field of art history, the historical connection to Sri Lanka and its copper, obvious already in the inscriptions I have uncovered, is of critical importance to understanding the transfer of portable imagery from wood to bronze. Information on the patronage, and the exact role of the patron, the priest, and the artist in designing the bronzes, might perhaps be uncovered. Possibly, we might be enabled to discuss the identities of artists and assistants, workshops and founders, which will enhance knowledge and appreciation of stylistic developments. It is true, however, as Leslie Orr has so aptly put it: "Those who composed the inscriptions are not talking to us and they have not anticipated the kinds of questions we bring to our reading of these texts."[74] This chapter is meant, above all, as a plea to the government of Tamil Nadu, to a range of educational foundations and computer centers, and to scholars of epigraphy to make an urgent push for the digitization of the over 13,000 Chola inscriptions, and thereby preserve and open up this treasure-house of information that will enable us to better understand the Cholas, their art, and their place in history.

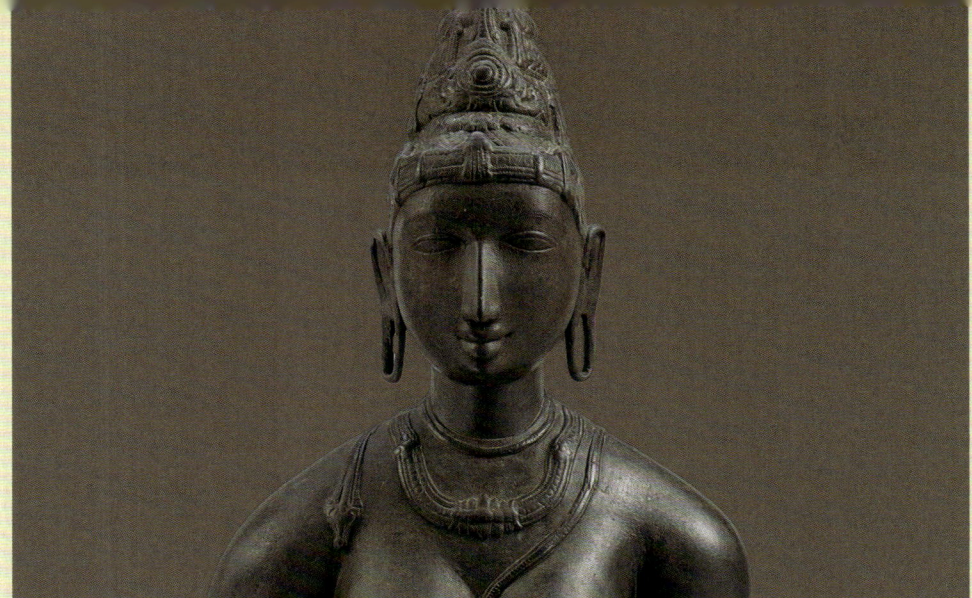

Portrait of a Queen and Her Patronage of Dancing Shiva
941–1002

4

This temple [sri-koyil], together with the snapana mandapa *(bathing hall for the deities), go-*
puram *gateway, enclosing walls, and shrines for the subsidiary deities was constructed by Sembiyan Mahadevi, mother of Uttama Chola, daughter of chief Malapuraman-adigal, queen of Gandaraditya-deva, son of the great Chola Sri Parantakadevar.*
She presented to the temple five copper lamps,
a gold diadem for the bronze image of lord Shiva,
a silver plate and a silver jar [for ritual worship],
two gold flowers,
a gold diadem for [the bronze of] the Great Lord of Dance [kutta-perumal]
a gold marriage necklace for the [bronze of] lady Uma,
a five-string pearl necklace with three gold dividers,
a necklace with a gold pendant and silver dividers,
and a gold flower for the Dancing Lord.

VRIDDHACHALAM TEMPLE, YEAR 12 OF UTTAMA CHOLA (983)[1]

This statuesque bronze image of queen Sembiyan Mahadevi stands in dignity, regally poised, with an elegant stance (fig. 4.1a, b). Resting her weight on her left foot, with her right leg lightly bent, she holds her head high, and her oval face with its straight nose is serene, calm, and relaxed. Her sharply sloping shoulders are held back admirably, as her left hand rests elegantly downward and the right is bent to hold a now-missing lotus or water lily. Her low-slung long skirt hugs her thighs and legs and is held in place with a simple belt (fig. 4.1c). Her jewelry is restrained in its simple sophistication: two necklaces, a sacred thread that snakes it way between her smoothly rounded full breasts, two armlets, bangles, anklets, and rings on her fingers and toes. Her hips are exceptionally narrow, making us wonder if this was the sculptor's subtle way of suggesting that she was a woman who would bear no more than the one child she had borne before she became queen.

She is serious and inward-looking, with full lips that are barely parted; yet she invites us to engage with her. Her hair is held back with a diadem, above which rises a tall conical crown, while at the rear a series of controlled ringlet curls rest along the nape of her neck (fig. 4.1d). Her exaggeratedly elongated earlobes do not carry an earring of any type, dangling or otherwise. Elongated earlobes, as I have shown elsewhere, are a mark of spirituality in Indian imagery; every god and goddess in the Hindu pantheon has such earlobes, and so too do bronzes of the saints.[2] Yet, that never did away with the necessity for ear ornaments. Perhaps the artist was party to the fact that the donor had already ordered an entire set of jewels for this beloved queen. Knowing that she would be adorned right away with gold earrings, he may have dispensed with them in his original wax model. In a ritual context, Chola bronzes were never seen without appropriate adornment that always included added jewelry, and we will see in the next chapter that all temple bronzes were routinely gifted complete sets of jewelry to adorn them from head to toe.

I had the pleasure of communing with this queen during my eight years at the Freer and Sackler Galleries of the Smithsonian Institution, and she became my touchstone and inspiration for asking ever more questions about Chola art and society. I had many queries for her. What do we know about her mother and her father? What was her childhood like? How old was she when given in marriage to a Chola prince? Did he cherish her? How did it happen that her bronze image was carried in procession through the town on her birthday? Why was she modeled on the image of Uma, consort of god Shiva?

This chapter will explore the story of this remarkable woman who, as dowager queen, was given the title "Ruby of the dynasty, Our lady, Great Queen Sembiyan" (*sembiyanmadeviyarana kulamanikkam nam pirattiyar*).[3] Entering her seventies at the end of the tenth century, the queen had created a brahmin township named after her as Sembiyan Mahadevi Chaturvedi-mangalam,[4] a town that bears her name to this day. There, she built a Shiva temple and named it Kailasa-natha, or Lord of Kailasa, after Shiva's Himalayan mountain home. Her name was attached to several institutions: one temple had a "Great Sembiyan Mahadevi plumeria flower garden,"[5] an irrigation channel took her name,[6] a water tank was named Sembiyan Mahadevi great reservoir,[7] a liquid measure took her name.[8] She built new stone temples and converted older brick temples to stone; she sponsored a bronze workshop that produced outstanding images; and she introduced in stone, and popularized in bronze, the image of dancing Shiva.

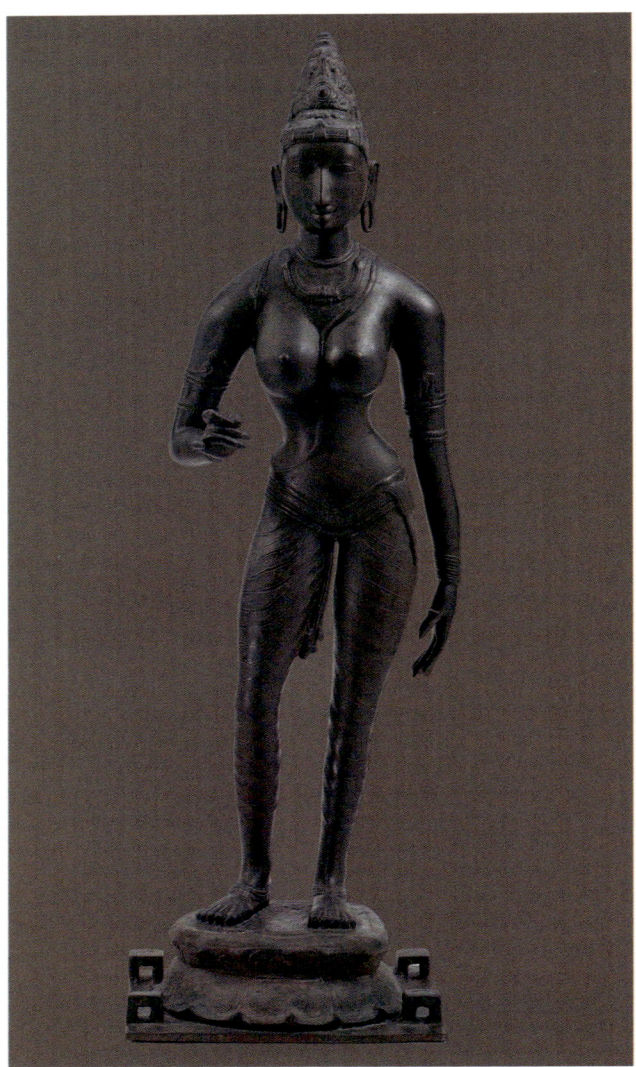
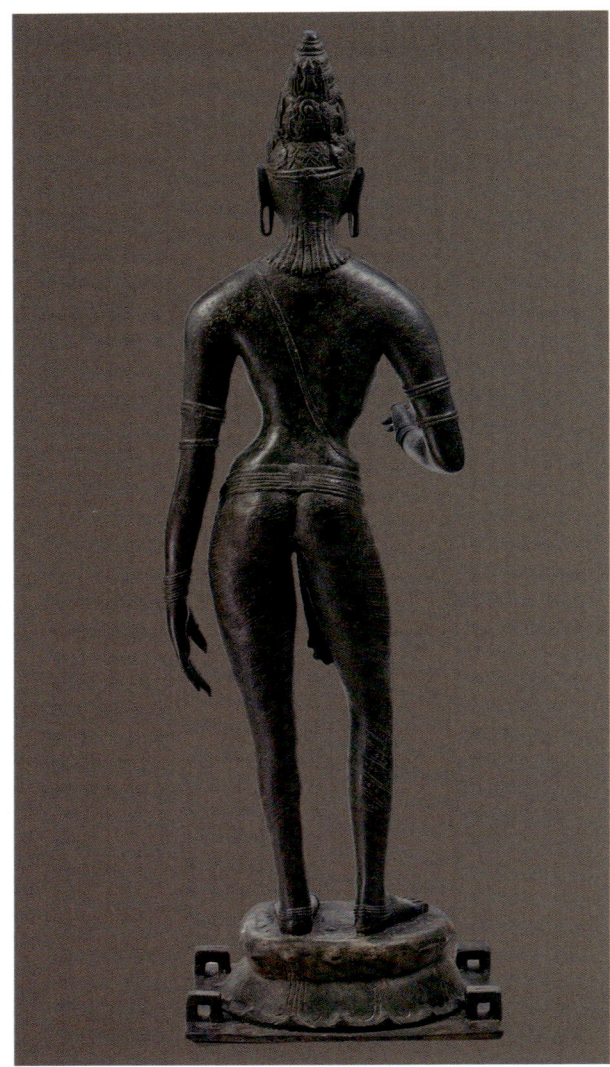

Figure 4.1. (a and b) Sembiyan Mahadevi, ca. 990, Freer Galley of Art, Smithsonian Institution, Washington, DC, Purchase—Charles Lang Freer Endowment. (c, d, e) Details of Sembiyan Mahadevi (fig. 4.1a), ca. 990, Freer Gallery of Art, Washington, DC, Purchase—Charles Lang Freer Endowment.

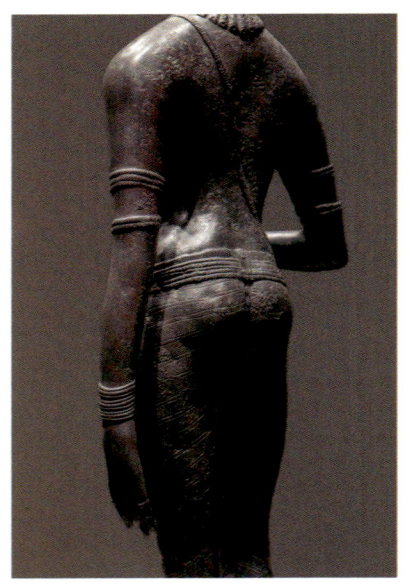
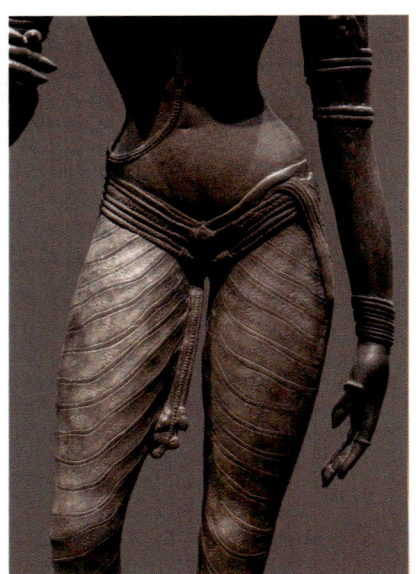
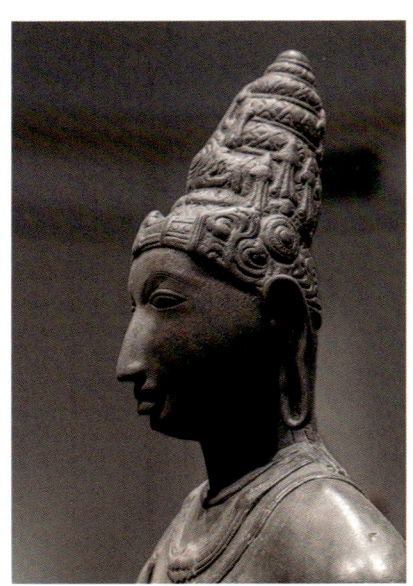

Let me, however, start by anticipating a question that may arise in the minds of many readers: Why am I convinced that the svelte image in the Freer Gallery of Art, that comes from the hands of a talented artist from a coastal workshop, is a portrait of queen Sembiyan? Let me lay out a number of reasons that, I believe, are highly persuasive when considered together. I start with the fact, attested to by no less than seven separate inscriptions, that the queen's birthday was celebrated in more than one temple during Sembiyan's lifetime. A lengthy record of Uttama Chola dated to the year 979 in the Konerirajapuram temple, to which we will return later in this chapter, made provisions for the monthly celebration of his mother's birth-star, Kettai. Since the astronomical phenomenon of a star recurs monthly, there would have been twelve celebrations each year devoted to queen Sembiyan's birth.[9] Additionally, Uttama Chola gives instructions that his mother's desire to feed forty brahmins every single day of the year should be fulfilled.[10] A series of other records, all in the temple at the town of Sembiyan Mahadevi, confirm the prominence given to this celebration. An inscription of the year 982 names five queens of Uttama Chola who jointly made a gift of gold that was to be used for offerings to the deity on the Kettai birth-star of queen Sembiyan.[11] A second inscription, of the year 985, names Uttama's queen Sonna Mahadeviyar, who gave gold for offerings to the deity on the birth-star of Sembiyan.[12] A third record, dated to 986, speaks of Uttama's chief queen Urattayan Sorabbai, and a second queen Aruran Ambalattadigal, who donated gold for offerings to the deity to celebrate their mother-in-law's birth-star.[13] A fourth inscription, dating from the seventh year of Rajaraja or 992, is yet another gift of gold by Urattayan Sorabbai to the brahmins for celebrating queen Sembiyan's natal-star.[14] In the year 992, Rajaraja's sister Kundavaiyar, and his cousin, Arinjikai Pirattiyar, jointly gifted gold for offerings on Sembiyan's birth-star.[15] We encounter an additional gift of gold from a resident of Pangalanadu, who stipulated that the interest accruing from his gift was to be used to feed certain persons on the celebration of the star Kettai in the month of Chittirai that marked Sembiyan's birthday.[16] The inscription that adds the final touch to this story is emperor Rajendra's gift of gold in the year 1019 to the temple in the town of Sembiyan Mahadevi. Its purpose was to provide additional funding for a procession focused on the bronze of queen Sembiyan that was carried through town to celebrate her birthday in the month of April–May (*Markali*).[17] This inscription of 1019 clarifies that it is not a new initiative on the part of Rajendra; rather, his gift is made to enlarge the funding for such a birthday celebration. With the wealth of temple inscriptions that make reference to Sembiyan's birth-star celebrations, we might have hoped for information regarding the commissioning of the bronze image of the queen, but we are out of luck on this issue. On stylistic grounds, however, I would suggest that the bronze in question in the Freer Gallery of Art was created at the very end of the tenth century, perhaps in the year 992, when Rajaraja's own sister and cousin actively entered Sembiyan's celebratory birthday cycle.[18]

Why would the queen be modeled on goddess Uma, consort of god Shiva? The answer lies in the premodern concept of the portrait in India, where portraiture involving verisimilitude, in the sense of warts and all, was unknown. On the contrary, literary evidence confirms that it was commonplace for royal portraits to be based on the imagery of the gods. In act III of *The Statue Play* (*Pratima Nataka*), based on India's *Ramayana* epic, and written in Sanskrit by dramatist Bhasa in pre-Chola times, we find prince Bharata returning to Ayodhya from an extended trip, unaware that his father, king Dasharatha, has died. Requested by the city elders to wait half an hour to enter the city, at which time the stars would be in a better alignment, he decides to while away the time by visiting what he thinks is a temple. He admires the four standing figures carved within.

> *Bharata: What exquisite carving in these sculptures! How lifelike they are. Though these statues represent deities they look just like men. . . . If they be deities it is right to bow the head, . . .*
> *Keeper: No, no, do not worship them.*[19]

The Keeper then explains to Bharata that the statues are not of gods but of *kshatriyas* of the warrior caste, the sons of Ikshvaku and the current rulers of Ayodhya. He names Dilipa, Raghu, and Aja, whom Bharata knows as his great-great-grandfather, his great-grandfather, and his grandfather. Bharata breaks down when he realizes that the fourth statue can be none other than his own father, Dasharatha, who must therefore be dead. If the audience of the play did not mock or ridicule the prince for failing to recognize his father, it was because it was routine practice to create royal portraits that were more or less indistinguishable from the gods.

The poised figure from the Freer Gallery of Art is indeed in the mold of goddess Uma, who always holds a flower in her upraised right hand and allows the left hand to rest gracefully by her side. Yet this is not Uma. To start with, she is a dramatic 40 inches in height, making her substantially taller than the tallest image of Uma as consort of any Shiva bronze; we will see in the next chapter that the statuesque Uma created by the Tiruvenkadu Master to accompany his major commission of Shiva with the bull is 37 inches tall. An interesting detail of the Freer image is the banded drapery of her skirt, which carries a minimalist pattern of dots rather than the three rows of geometric motifs seen on many of the images created by her workshop; it would appear that the artist opted to make the simplicity of her patterned fabric stand distinctly apart. The same may be said for the relative austerity of her ornaments. But there is even more that sets her apart. An undeniable gravitas, a composed, inward-looking absorption, a solemn preoccupation, a rapt concentration, a powerful intensity, and a quiet authority all combine decisively to distinguish her from typical images of a beautiful and gentle Uma. The bronze exudes a personalized charisma of a sort that seems to make a clear statement of difference, of being out of the standard mold, of being her own individual. I see her as the creation of a superb artist who set out to subtly convey the queen's distinctive personality—and he did so with great success. To me, she is Chola queen Sembiyan.

Where did this amazing, highly respected woman come from? How did she function so successfully in what was certainly a male-dominated society? Her great-nephew, emperor Rajaraja, admired her so much that he gave her the authority to issue orders that carried the same weight as his own. One such order of the year 998, during Rajaraja's reign, recorded in the Shiva temple at Tirukodikaval, tells us that the brahmin assembly (*sabha*) and the temple priests (*maheshvaras*) received a royal directive (*tirumukam*) from queen Sembiyan, with instructions on how certain temple lands should be irrigated.[20] The directive commands that water from the new channel (*pudu vaykal*) should go south across temple lands to reach its south boundary, so that lands situated along its southern boundaries would be suitably irrigated. The temple authorities agreed to be responsible for ensuring that the *manis* appointed to manage irrigation of temple lands carried out these instructions.[21] It appears that the queen was clued in to practical issues of irrigation and agriculture; but why would a queen take an interest in such a subject?

If ever there was a monarchy that rose to power on the basis of irrigation and agriculture, it is the Cholas. The irrigation system they put into place remains to this day the mainstay of the prosperity of Tamil Nadu, which is one of the richest agricultural areas of India. The topography of the region through which the river Kaveri winds its way, the two monsoons that affect different parts of the lengthy Kaveri, the slope of the land in the deltaic area, and the texture of the soil, made all this possible; the Chola genius lay in recognizing how to harness what seem to be disparate and unrelated items, and make them work together in harmony.[22]

Close to 500 miles in total length, the river Kaveri rises in the hills of the Western Ghats, enters Tamil Nadu through dramatic waterfalls at Hoganakal along the Karnataka border, and flows through the Tamil plains for a distance of 300 miles before it empties into the Bay of Bengal. Some 7 miles before it reaches the town of Trichy in the plains, the river divides into a northern stream known as the Kollidam and a southern stream that retains the name Kaveri; the two rejoin some 10 miles downstream, thus creating the island of Srirangam, which was to become a major sacred center dedicated to Vishnu. At this joining point, the bed level of the Kollidam is roughly 10 feet lower than that of the Kaveri; left thus, all water would flow into the Kollidam and be lost directly into the ocean, totally depriving the Kaveri delta of water. It was at this strategic point that the Grand Anicut dam was constructed. The exact date of this structure remains uncertain, but it has been attributed to an early king Karikala Chola of the second century, an ancient ancestor of our Cholas who came to power in the ninth century; in fact, the dam alone would have been good reason for Vijayalaya to appropriate the name Chola! Built of large boulders of granite brought and sunk into the riverbed, the dam extends over 1,000 feet across the river. It was first repaired by the British in 1804, and subsequently modernized with the addition of automatic sluices. Today, the Kaveri river helps irrigate 1.2 million acres of paddy fields that entitles Tamil Nadu to the moniker of India's rice bowl; the estimate for the Chola period is 70,000 acres under cultivation.[23] The Kollidam, which flows in a northerly direction from the Grand Anicut, is not used at all for irrigation. It is dry during much of the year (ironically it is colored blue on all maps), and it stands by merely to receive the Kaveri's flood waters, which it then discharges into the ocean, enabling the Kaveri delta to successfully produce its two annual rice crops.

The genius of the Chola irrigation system extends far beyond the fact of the Grand Anicut. Once the Kaveri enters its delta, the river splits into several smaller rivers that further split into streams, each controlled by multiple sluice points until they enter the ocean.[24] The creativity of the Cholas lay in building numerous canals across the deltaic region that decrease in width and hence in the area they irrigate. Today, they are numbered from "A" for the broadest canals, over 30 feet wide, that are the first to split from the river, down to "F" for those no more than 5 feet wide that run between fields. Map 6

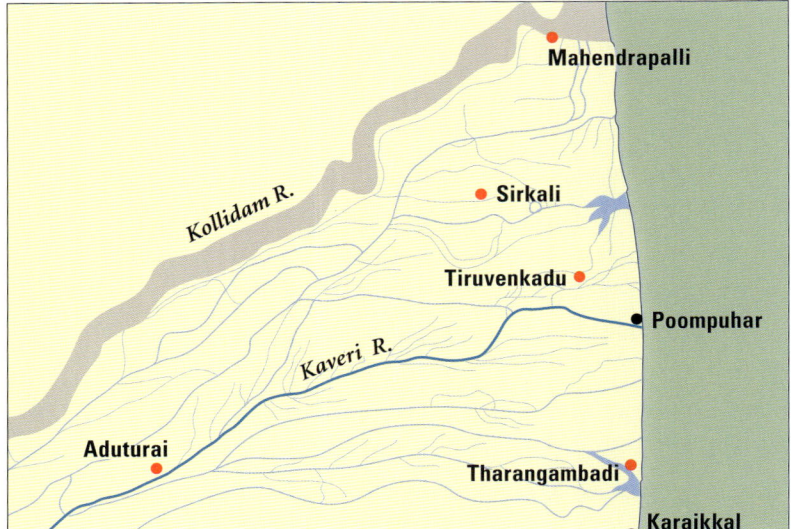

Map 6 Canal system along end of the Kaveri delta, from Aduturai to the ocean.

Figure 4.2. (a) Natural sandbank off Kaveri river creating a canal, location. (b) Pathways across a small canal.

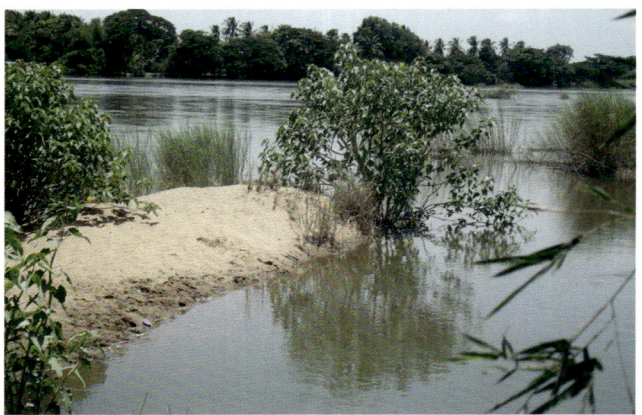
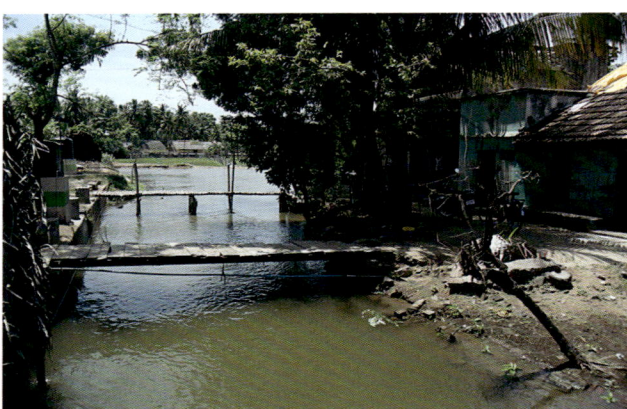

sketches a mini-section of the delta, from the town of Aduturai to the ocean, and shows only the rivers and the A canals. Putting in canals B to F resulted in a diagram akin to a spider's web that was impossible to read. An interesting statistic speaks to the importance of the area's many canals (*kalvays*) and smaller channels (*vaykals*). While the rivers themselves extend a total of 1,000 miles, the A-class canals extend 3,420 miles, while channels B to F jointly extend 11,430 miles.[25] These numerous canals and channels were created by diverting the waters of the Kaveri's many streams at numerous strategic and naturally viable points; one such is a modest natural sandbank (fig. 4.2a) that results in a major B-class canal, the Manniyar, which irrigates over 33,000 acres of rice fields.[26] Smaller channels, running today alongside the metaled roads of the area, are a routine and accepted part of everyday living conditions, as is evident from the casual acceptance by local villagers of the many bamboo bridges across such waters (fig. 4.2b).

Rice is a crop that requires flooded fields, and the Cholas put in place an ingenious Chola system of canals and channels that enabled such flooding and allowed the rice paddy to thrive. A copper-plate inscription of the year 1019, in which we may ignore the hyperbole, speaks of Parantaka Chola, who *caused to be excavated hundreds and thousands of deep channels with clear water in order to make the earth extremely fertile.*[27]

A double rice crop was made possible by the Kaveri river receiving rain from both the monsoons that hit India. Since the Kaveri river rises in the Western Ghats, it is enriched by the summer rains of the southwest monsoon that approaches from the Arabian Sea in early June and drenches the west coast of India. This early water flow into the Kaveri enables the first rice crop of short duration that is harvested in September. The winter northeast monsoon rains, arriving from across the Bay of Bengal to the east coast of India, directly nourishes the Kaveri delta, and enables a second rice crop of longer duration.[28] In the Tamil region, the Kaveri is known affectionately as "Ponni" or "Golden One," since she enables the golden grain in the fields, a name given to her in early Sangam poetry where she is the consort of the early Chola kings, and rival of the Ganges.

> *Even if Venus, star of bright splendor,*
> *were to stray from its course and move south,*
> *even if the skies failed to shower rain, . . .*
> *yet ocean-like Kaveri, born in the mountains,*
> *pours forth its waters, ripening gold*
> *in fields that never stop yielding.*
> *Here buffalo-calves sleep, sated with feeding on*
> *golden grain. Here coconut and plantain trees heavy with fruit,*
> *sweet mangoes, clustered palmyra, root vegetables,*
> *fragrant turmeric, and tender ginger abound. . . .*
>
> —INDIRA PETERSON, FROM *PATTINAPPALAI* 1–20[29]

Rice is indeed a curious and demanding crop. It starts life densely planted in a wet nursery; twenty-five days later, the seedlings must be transplanted, a couple of stems at a time, into flooded fields. The soil along the Kaveri river is a dense alluvial clay known as *kali mun* that is viscous and sticky and uniquely suited to rice cultivation. It maintains aeration but disallows percolation, retaining water in the fields and facilitating the flooding that is necessary for rice. Rice paddy demands alternating weeklong periods of wet and dry soil even after it flowers; it is only in the last fifteen days that the soil is allowed to dry out.[30] Rice, I might emphasize, is a crop that demands a cooperative state of mind. While a wheat farmer may happily tend his field and his alone, ignoring other farmers around him, it is not feasible to do so with rice. A farmer cannot flood his field alone; he is, per se, allowing that same water to flood his neighbor's field as well. Rice growers develop an accommodating and supportive attitude to life that can be very different from that of farmers of other crops.

The multiple channels that criss-cross the Kaveri delta to irrigate the rice fields sustained the prosperity of the towns and villages of the region during the Chola period. Sluices, known as *toombu* or *kumizhi*, that control the flow of water from canals to smaller channels, and from both into reservoirs, or *eris*, find frequent mention in inscriptions. Such records are generally cut into the stone of the sluice itself, or on a slab set up beside the village lake and, on occasion, on the pillars and stones of a bridge across the canal, and I cite a few of these here. For instance, in the year 19 of king Rajakesarivarman (890 if Aditya), the chief goldsmith (*perun tattan*) of the village of Gundur constructed a stone sluice and engraved his record on it.[31] In the year 928 (twenty-first regnal year of Parantaka), a chieftain created a sluice to a reservoir in Olugaiyur in North Arcot district and the inscription, on a slab of stone beside the lake, informs us that the local residents (*nattar*) contributed measures of rice to ensure maintenance of the sluice.[32] In the year 978, a resident of Nallur constructed a sluice at Parindai in South Arcot district "for the merit of his daughter," cutting the record on a slab of stone beside the lake.[33] Interest in irrigation and agriculture was demonstrated by a range of devotees. One such was a woman dancer (*kuttu pillai*) at the temple of Melaipalavur, named Nakkan Aiyaradigal, who, in the year 945, purchased 4 *ma* of wasteland (*abhohana kidanta bhumi*) and then reclaimed it, converting it to cultivable wetland that she donated to the temple, where its produce was sufficient to ensure the burning of a perpetual lamp.[34] It was the resulting agricultural prosperity that enabled the temple culture to thrive even when political circumstances seemed less than ideal. It is important to reiterate a point made by Kenneth Hall regarding the brahmin community: a ritually skilled priestly class who were masters of the ritual calendar, they were also experts who could apply the calendar to the agricultural cycle and who possessed knowledge of irrigation technology.[35] Villages and towns had efficient administrative controls, and we read in an inscription of the year 929, during the twenty-third year of Parantaka's reign, of the tank committee (*erivariya perumakkal*), garden committee (*tottavariya perumakkal*), priests (*bhatta perumakkal*), and eminent persons (*visishtha perumakkal*) who met in the great hall (*per ambalam*) to pass resolutions for the welfare of the village. Members who were entrusted with writing minutes and recording resolutions passed in the meetings were elected by ballot chits after ensuring that they satisfied the required norms; these included being congenial to the brahmin *sabha*, not having themselves served for the past five years, nor having relatives who had served for the past two years.[36]

During the early phase of Chola rule between the founding of the dynasty in 855 and the accession of Rajaraja in 985, Chola kings found it advantageous to share power with a range of chieftains who each controlled specific tracts of land. Chola kings depended on the active support and goodwill of these chieftains who collected taxes and tolls on their behalf in measures of rice, and who provided them with troops to aid in their warfare with rivals to the south and north. The chieftains, in turn, pleased to retain direct control over their territories, recognized the overlordship of the Cholas and dated all their temple inscriptions in the regnal years of the Chola monarchs. For acknowledging Chola supremacy, the chieftains were appointed to important positions in the royal court and given elaborate titles. The most popular among these were "Muvendavelan" and "Brahmadirayar," both indicating persons well-versed in the complexities of administration, the first belonging to the vellala agricultural community and the second to the brahmin caste. The "royal secretary" or *tirumandira olai* of several kings were titled, for instance, Sundarachola Muvendavelan,[37] Uttamachola Muvendavelan,[38] or Rajendrachola Muvendavelan.[39] *Srikaryam* officers appointed to supervise temple affairs were also given these titles, as in Chola Sikhamani Muvendavelan[40] or Rajaraja Brahmarayar.[41] One additional and guaranteed way for the Cholas to ensure the support of the chieftains, these *araiyars* or "little kings" of varying ranks and fluctuating power, was through marriage alliances, and the early Chola kings entered into strategic alliances of this nature with a wide range of chieftain families.

It is in this context that we come across our amazing woman patron, Sembiyan, daughter of a chieftain of the interior region of Kongu, who married Parantaka's second son, Gandaraditya. She appears quietly on the Chola temple scene in the year 941 with a donation of ninety sheep for a perpetually burning lamp in the temple at Tirukkarkuti (today's Uyyakondan Tirumalai just outside the town of Trichy). It was a discrete and appropriate beginning for a young princess who may have been little more than twelve years of age.[42] The inscription does not provide her given name; it identifies her only as daughter of the Kongu chieftain (*Malaperumanadigal*), and wife of Gandaraditya, son of the ruling Chola king Parantaka.[43] We never get to know the name that her parents gave her. Later records identify her as daughter-in-law of Parantaka, queen of Gandaraditya, one who bore Uttama Chola in her sacred womb, and they refer to her solely by the name Sembiyan given to her by her Chola in-laws. Sembiyan is a title associated with the Cholas from the days of the earlier Cholas known to Sangam literature, while Mahadevi merely means "great queen/great goddess."[44] Within eight years, the young princess's life was transformed. Parantaka's heir apparent—his eldest son, Rajaditya—was killed on the Takkolam battlefield, and, in the very next year of 950, her husband, Gandaraditya, became king and she the wife of a ruling monarch.

But things did not move smoothly for her. Within seven years, Gandaraditya was no longer king; we are not given any clear information about his abdication except that an inscription speaks of him as "the lord who rose and went to the west."[45] Whether this phrase is intended to suggest that he died, since the west is the direction of death, or perhaps that he moved to Kerala (which lies to the west of Chola territory) as a religious recluse remains a debatable point.[46] Sembiyan's one and only son was not yet of an age to assume the throne, an age that appears to have been sixteen.[47] And so her husband's younger brother assumed the throne as Sundara Chola. The young queen, likely to have been no more than twenty-eight years of age, was in the difficult situation of an abandoned queen alone with a young son. Clearly, she had political and diplomatic skills, and was an astute judge of character. She laid low for an extended period of time, and things finally worked her way. Before her brother-in-law Sundara Chola died, his own son was assassinated, enabling Sembiyan's son Uttama Chola to become king with minimal opposition.[48] Sembiyan would have been in her early forties then, and she came completely into her own during her son's reign of sixteen years from 971–987, and, one might note, she continued to hold a position of high respect and power during the reign of her grand-nephew Rajaraja. Sembiyan built new stone temples and rebuilt earlier brick temples in stone (fig. 4.3). She sponsored an outstanding bronze workshop that produced inspired and superbly crafted images for her temples, and she made rich donations of jewelry to adorn the bronzes. She gave endowments of cash and land to ensure that her temples were well staffed and well managed and that festivals were celebrated with appropriate splendor.

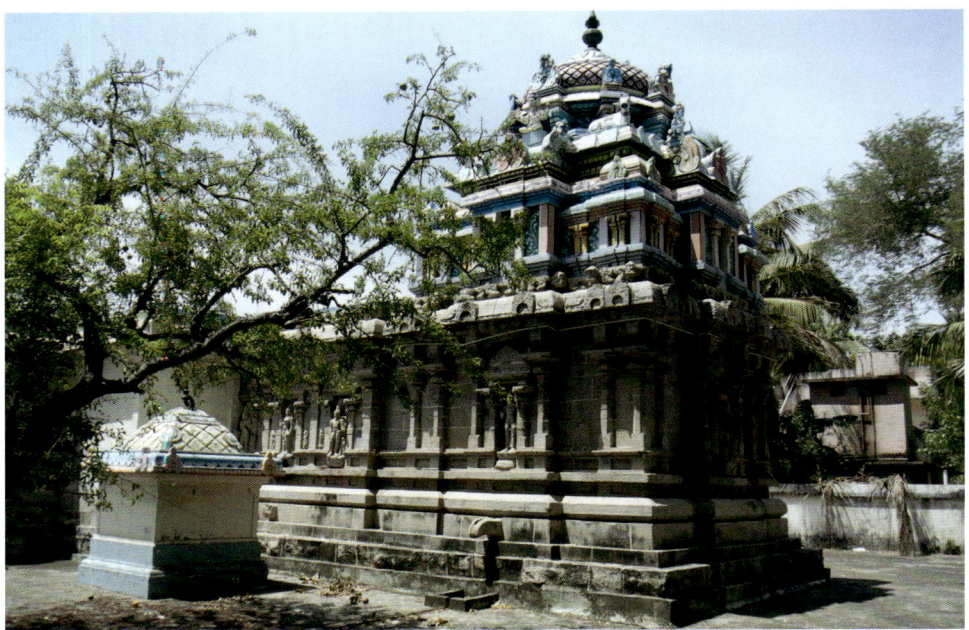

Figure 4.3. Anangur temple, rebuilt by Sembiyan Mahadevi, Tiruvarur, ca. 992.

The manner in which she rebuilt in stone a set of earlier brick temples of ancient renown, celebrated in song by the Tamil saints, is remarkable. It is not just that she rebuilt brick temples in stone—that was being done by others too. Rather, she recognized the role of those who had made gifts to the earlier brick temples and ordered that their contributions be reengraved on her newly completed stone temple. An inscription on the walls of the Aduturai temple reads:

> *In this sacred stone temple which the glorious Sembiyan-Madeviyar caused to be built to Shiva, there were engraved on stone, in the year 987, all such gifts as were made to this god in former times (intended to last) as long as the moon and the sun.*[49]

In the Tirukodikaval temple that queen Sembiyan similarly converted to stone, we find that over half of the inscriptions on the temple walls—twenty-seven of a total of forty-nine—are copies of earlier records.[50] A lengthy record engraved on the wall of the central shrine informs us that the original brick temple (*mun ittigai padayal*) has been completely removed, and a stone *vimana* constructed (*kallale srivimanam amaipittu*) in its place, and that all previous donations were ordered to be inscribed on the stone *vimana*. The record proceeds to inform us that according to Sembiyan's order, such inscriptions have been reengraved and that the gift recorded in the following is one among such earlier records. It then gives us the earlier record, which states that in the fourth year of his reign, Ko Maran Sadaiyan (Jatavarman Pandya, early ninth century) gifted 20 *kalanju* of gold for ghee to keep a perpetual lamp burning in the temple. The Sembiyan record concludes by informing us that the earlier record, on a single stone, being of no use (*ubhayokam illamaiyil*), is now being abandoned.[51] At least twenty recopied inscriptions announce, at both their start and end, that they are copies of an earlier record. Here is one such record:

> *Svasti. This too according to an old stone* [idivum oru parankarpadi].
> *In the year 3 of Parakesarivarman a gift of 90 sheep for the service of Pichcha-devar [Shiva as Begging Lord] and for burning a perpetual lamp in the Mahadeva temple at Tirukkodikaval on the north bank [of the Kaveri] in Nallarrur-nadu, by Vemban Kaliyoti of Padur in Ingalappadi. This, according to the old stone, was engraved on the srivimana.*
> *Now that this has been engraved on the temple, the previously inscribed separate stone, being of no use, it is discarded. In the protection of the Shiva temple Brahmins.*[52]

Sembiyan's actions in this respect are quite extraordinary. They speak to her spirit of generosity and munificence, of correctness and honesty, of shrewdness and acumen, of a desire to give each person his or her due. They also speak of her unusual sense of historicity. It was perhaps the example set by the queen that caused the authorities at the temple of Tiruppaturai to reengrave two land gifts made during the reign of Parantaka; we are told that in the year 978, a mere fifty years later, the inscribed gifts had been engraved along the doorsill of the old temple and were hence badly weathered.[53]

Temples built in the Kaveri basin prior to Sembiyan's involvement reveal an emerging "Chola" style very much in flux. Sembiyan's temples are as often west-facing as east-facing, causing us to pause to consider whether this was an intentional decision.[54] After all, if the precise positioning of the sanctum of a hallowed shrine was retained intact when it was rebuilt in stone, as is very likely, the directionality of her temples may merely reflect the original layout at a time when *agamic* texts laying out details of temple building had not yet been consolidated.[55] Queen Sembiyan introduced a consistent iconographic program that is strikingly apparent in the imagery that adorns the hall in front of the sanctum. Her most important contribution to the iconography of south India was her introduction of the typical Tamil image of Dancing Shiva, known thus far largely from the hymns of Sambandar and Appar. The stone image of Dancing Shiva was placed in a major niche on the south wall of each of her temples, whether newly built or rebuilt in stone. In this Tamil image, Shiva stands on his right leg with the left leg raised high, poised in a dance that appears to have been termed *deshi*, or local,[56] and that much later on came to be known by the Sanskrit term of *ananda tandava*, or dance of bliss. To these images we will turn shortly.

But first, let us explore the highly accomplished workmanship of a coastal workshop of the mid-tenth century from which Sembiyan commissioned several bronzes for a temple at Tirunallam, a hallowed site sung of by the saints. Known today as Konerirajapuram, this temple was rebuilt in stone by Sembiyan to honor her husband Gandaraditya after her son Uttama Chola became the ruling monarch. Two stunning bronzes in the temple, both featuring Shiva with Uma, are mentioned in a temple inscription of the year 979, and they remain in the temple to this day.[57] The first portrays four-armed Shiva standing in elegant splendor with his left front elbow poised to rest against his bull mount, while his right front hand is lowered in a gesture of relaxed elegance; his two rear hands hold his battle-ax and pet antelope (fig. 4.4a, b). His richly caparisoned bull, ornamented

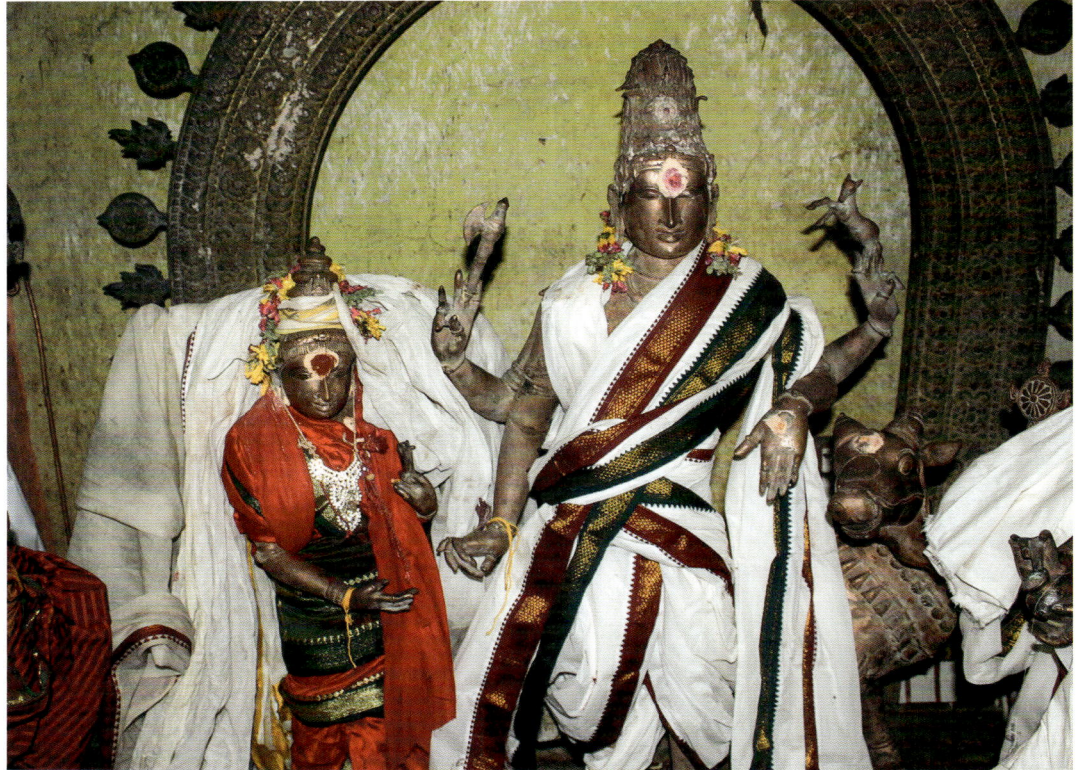

Figure 4.4. (a, b) Shiva as Lord with the Bull, Konerirajapuram temple, Thanjavur district, ca. 979.

in bronze with a necklace of bells, turns his head joyfully toward Shiva to lick his master's hand (fig. 4.4c). A diadem frames Shiva's oval face, above which his matted locks are piled high and adorned with the trumpet flower, crescent moon, serpent, and a central circular medallion, while escaping dreadlocks rest along his shoulders. We see here a continuation of the established iconography of Shiva that we encountered in images created during the first hundred years of Chola rule. Shiva is richly ornamented with two necklaces, a sacred thread of two strands, armlets, elbow band, bangles, anklets, and with rings on eight of ten fingers and toes. A waistband encircles his slender torso, while two belts, one with a lion-head clasp, hold in place his short dhoti. It is instructive to compare the bronze with a stone image of Shiva leaning against his bull from the walls of a Sembiyan temple at Tiruvarur. Though the latter is partly damaged, and portrays Shiva in his form as *Ardhanari*, or Half Woman, a striking similarity in evident in the treatment and adornment of the lithe slender bodies, whether in stone or in bronze (fig. 4.5). During the first century of creating bronze images, craft specialization had not yet arisen, and it is likely that all sculptors learned their trade in stone-carving workshops; this was also the time when stone temples were of modest size so that stone sculptures and bronze images were often of comparable dimensions. The bronze Uma who stands today beside Shiva with the bull is not his original consort; she has her right hand extended toward Shiva and is clearly part of a marriage couple like one we looked at in the introduction and in chapter 1. The original consort for Shiva with the bull may, in fact, be a glorious image from the Calico Museum of Textiles, standing a little under 3 feet high, a suggestion first proposed by

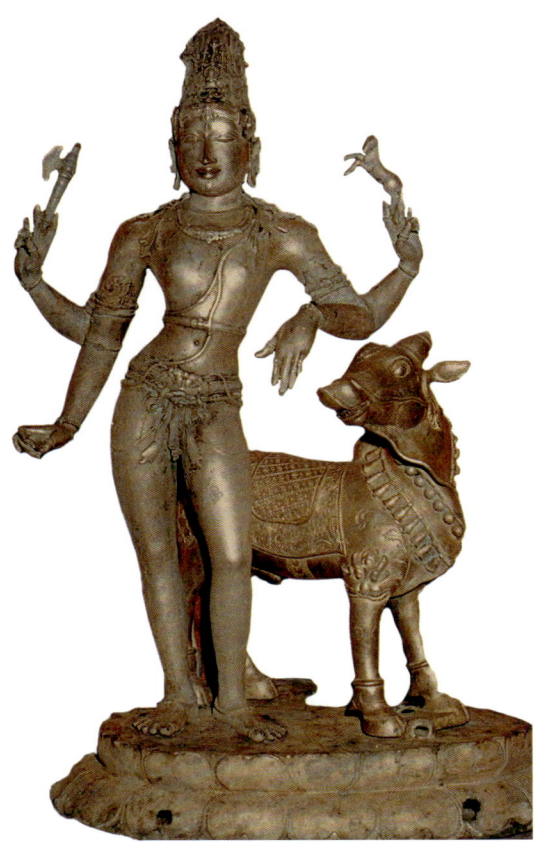

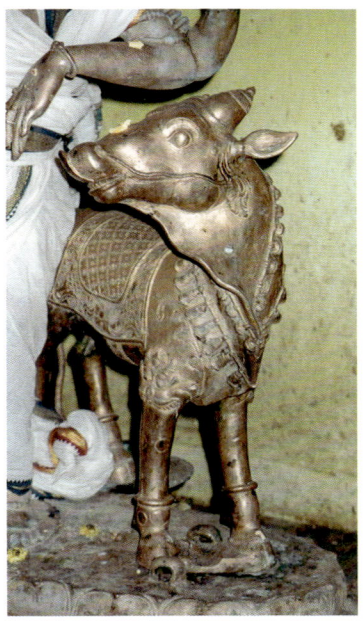

(c) Detail of Shiva's bull in Shiva as Lord with the Bull (fig. 4.4a), Konerirajapuram temple, Thanjavur district, ca. 979.

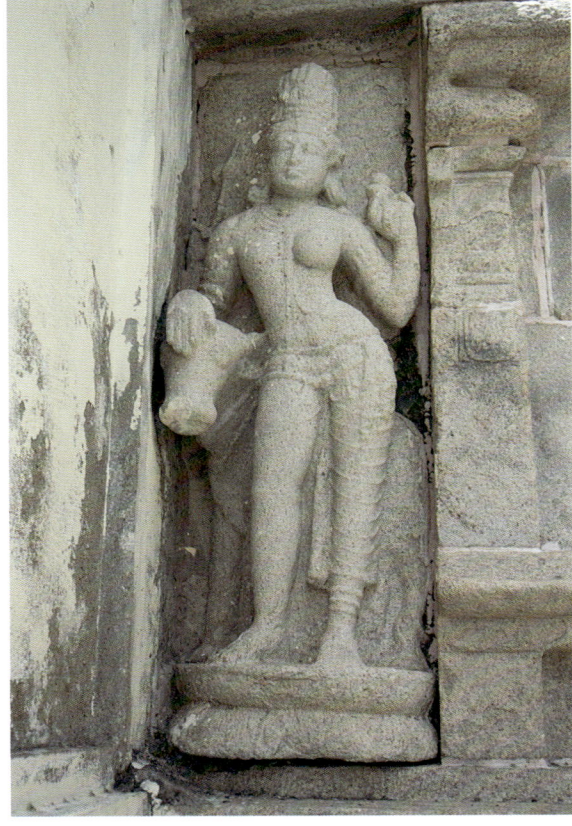

Figure 4.5. *Ardhanari* with Bull in stone, Tiru-araneri temple, Tiruvarur, Thanjavur district, ca. 992.

PORTRAIT OF A QUEEN

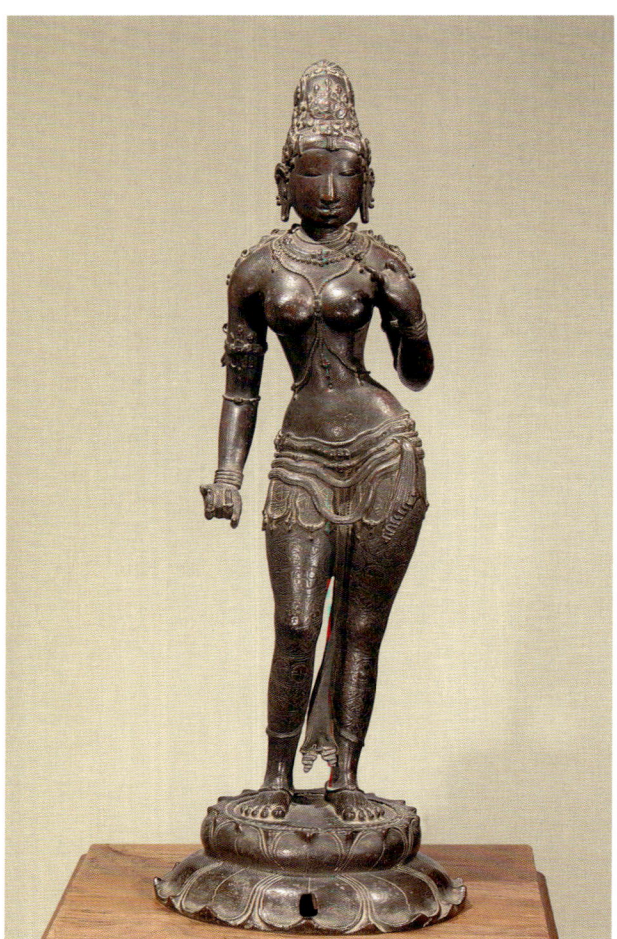 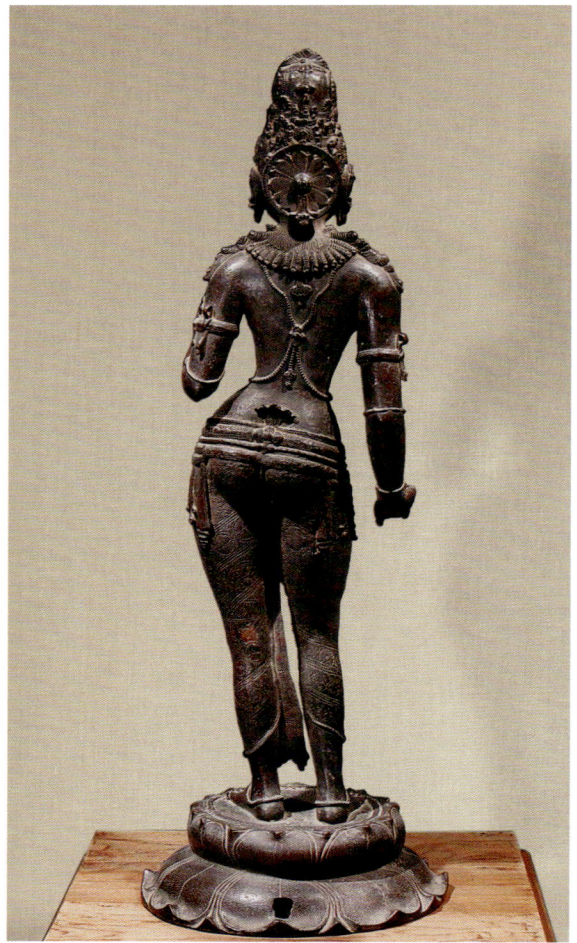

Figure 4.6. (a and b) Uma, ca. 979, The Calico Museum of Textiles and The Sarabhai Foundation Collections, Ahmedabad.

Douglas Barrett over fifty years ago.[58] This sensuously poised Uma is certainly an accomplished piece from the Sembiyan workshop (fig. 4.6).

The second Koneri Shiva mentioned in the inscription of 979 and also in the temple today features Shiva as Victor of Three Forts; the similarity of the sensuously poised form, and the oval face with a gentle smile are so close to Shiva with the bull that there is little doubt that the two images are the work of the same artist. Differences are minor (fig. 4.7): Victor Shiva's proper left hand is raised to hold the bow, while his right hand would have grasped an arrow as his iconography demands, and he sports a triple-strand sacred thread. Otherwise, both images are adorned in almost identical fashion, while the belts that hold the dhoti in place, and the treatment of its pleated bands, are identical. A third image of Ganesha, mentioned in the inscription, is also in the temple today; one might point out the identical manner of arranging the central pleated fold of the dhoti on the Ganesha image as well as on the two Shivas.

Standing beside Shiva as Victor is his willowy consort Uma, tall and slender, with softly rounded breasts (fig. 4.8a, b). She is richly ornamented in typical fashion with three necklaces, the longest of which is a coin necklace, while her torso is encircled by a

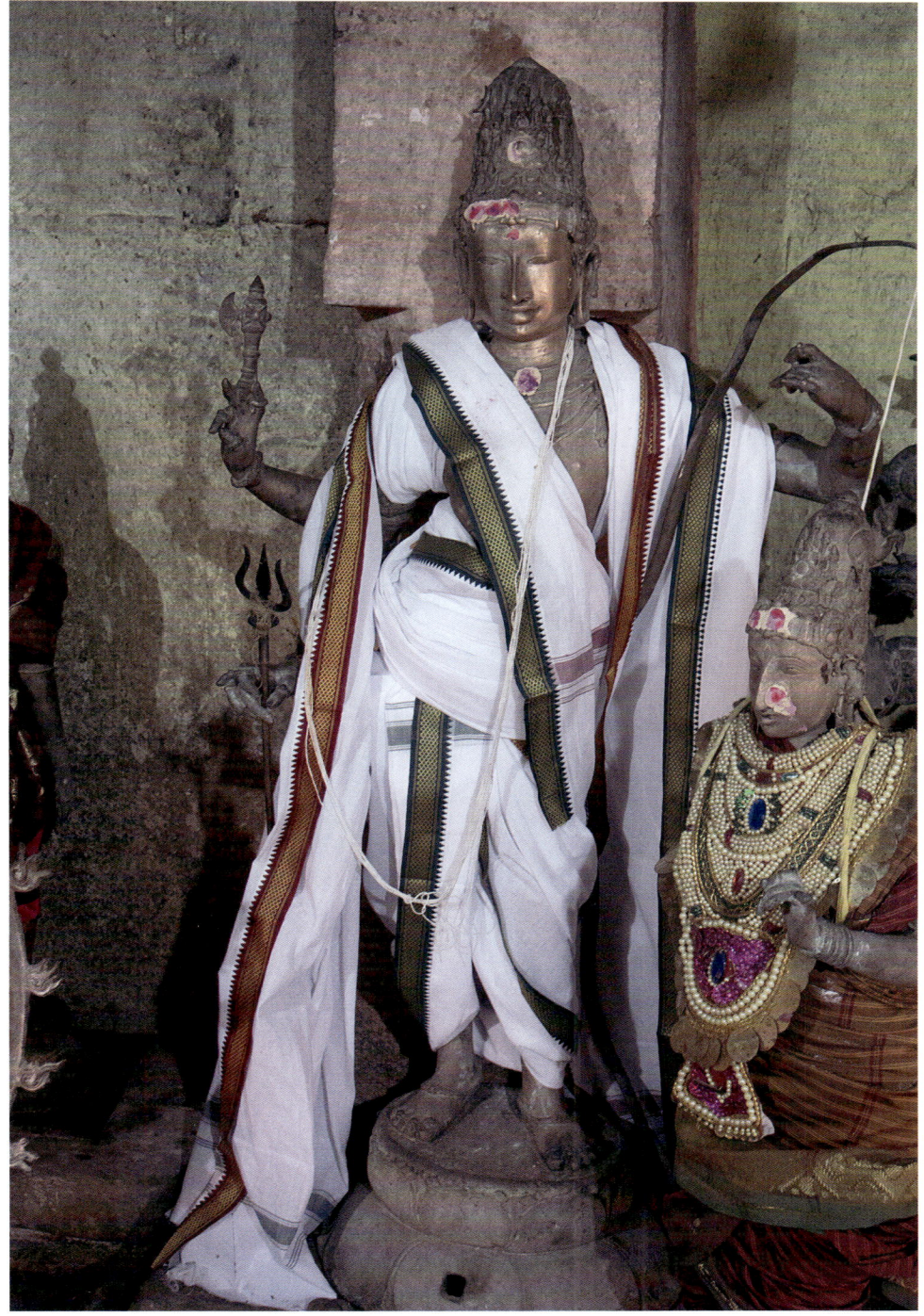

Figure 4.7. Shiva as Victor of Three Forts, Konerirajapuram temple, Thanjavur district, ca. 979.

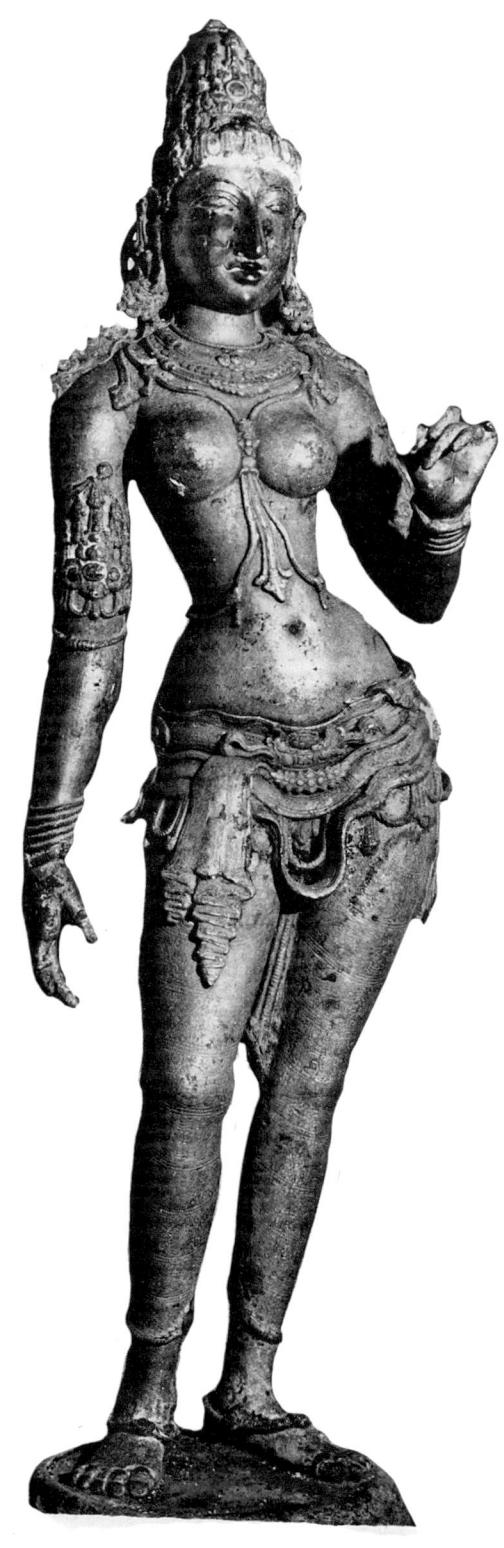

Figure 4.8. (a) Uma as Consort of Shiva as Victor of Three Forts, Konerirajapuram temple, Thanjavur district, ca. 979.

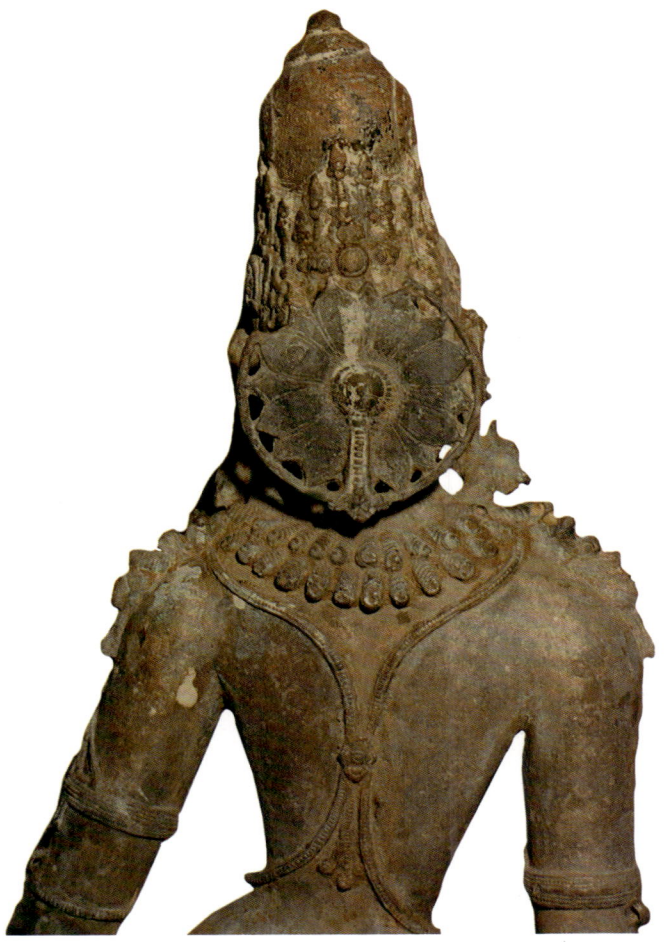

(b) Detail, rear view of Uma as Consort of Shiva as Victor of Three Forts (fig. 4.8a), Konerirajapuram temple, ca. 979.

body-chain (*channavira*) that comes together between her breasts and then meets again along her spinal column. These Koneri bronzes display an unmistakable gravitas, combined with sensuous elegance, that is characteristic of the Sembiyan artist and his skilled workshop. The works represent the mellow maturity achieved by the coastal tradition close to a hundred years after its splendid unforeseen beginnings with the first images that we examined in chapter 2. Certain distinctive decorative details seen in the Koneri Uma as consort of the Victor, the Calico Museum image, and also in a bronze Uma from the nearby Nallur temple, reveal the signature of the Sembiyan workshop. Two small decorative details of the treatment of the outer side of the crown are seen on all three images—a circle encloses a full-blown petaled flower along the upper part of the crown, while a similar circle at the crown's base encloses a tassel (fig. 4.9). The artist of the workshop that Sembiyan commissioned to create her images did not need to think too deeply of how exactly he would decorate the crown; he had a successful formula that he merely reused. As Berenson remarked in the context of drapery in Renaissance paintings, it was just not important enough to come up with a different unique handling of such details.[59]

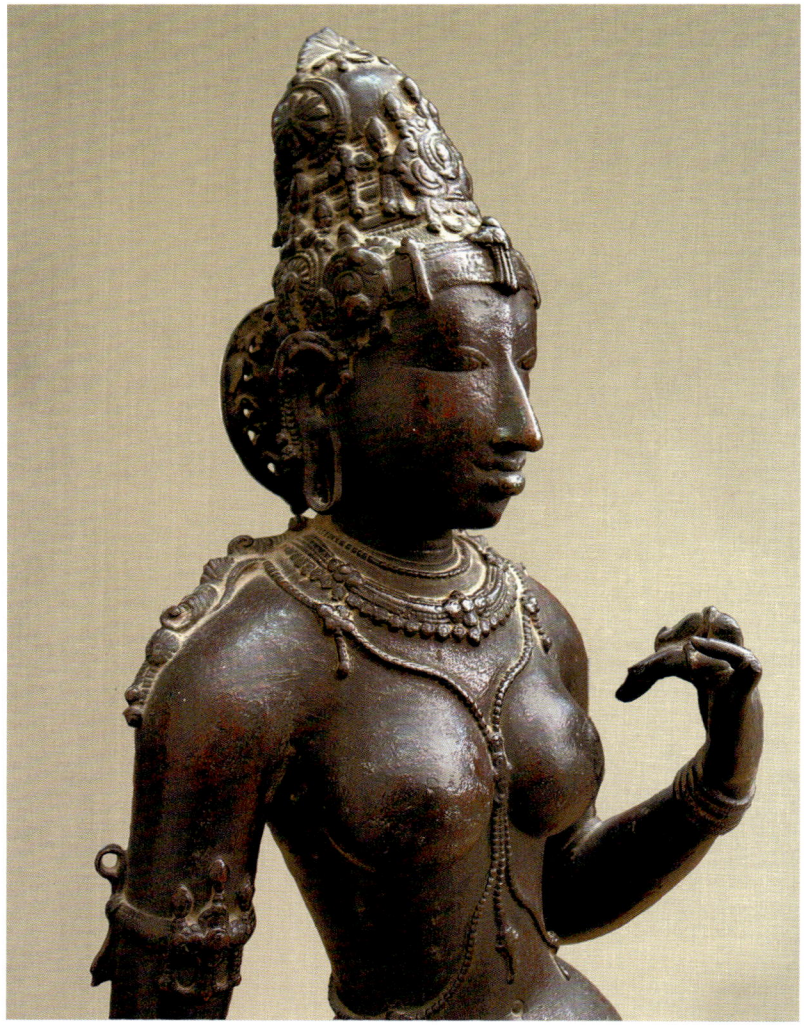

Figure 4.9. Detail of Uma (see fig. 4.6), The Calico Museum of Textiles, The Sarabhai Foundation Collections, Ahmedabad.

Another little detail is the idiosyncratic manner of treating the pleated double ends of the skirt folds as they rest upon the upper thigh, which constitutes a second recognizable workshop "signature" (fig. 4.10a, b, c). A superbly crafted marriage couple, created for the Tiruvilakudi temple, today in an Icon Center, comes from the hands of this same workshop and reveals all the characteristics we have remarked upon.[60] A willowy Uma from the Norton Simon collection that bears comparison with the Koneri images may also be assigned to the Sembiyan workshop, as well as an enchanting image of Shiva, Uma, and their infant Skanda from the same museum collection (figs. 4.11 and 4.12). They display a similar sensuous gravitas that speaks of the Master's touch, while several details of decoration and the pleated folds characteristic of the workshop draw them together as a group.

From the hands of a distinctive workshop that differed stylistically from the Sembiyan workshop is a richly ornamented standing image of Shiva as Victor from the collection of the Cleveland Museum of Art, positioned together with his consort Uma on a

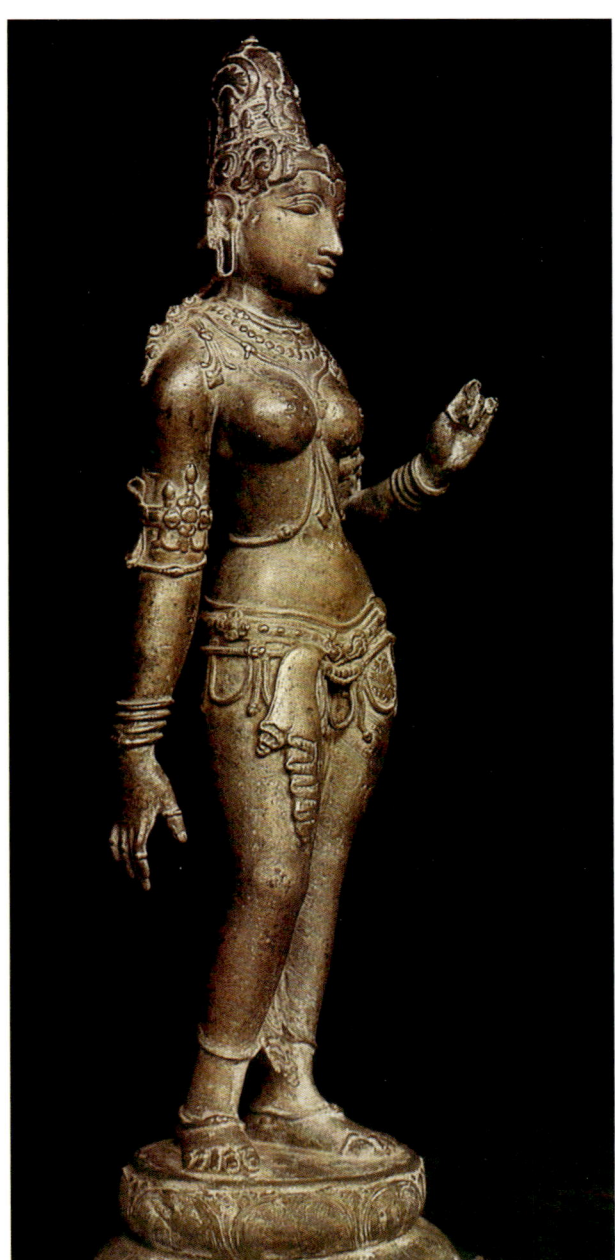
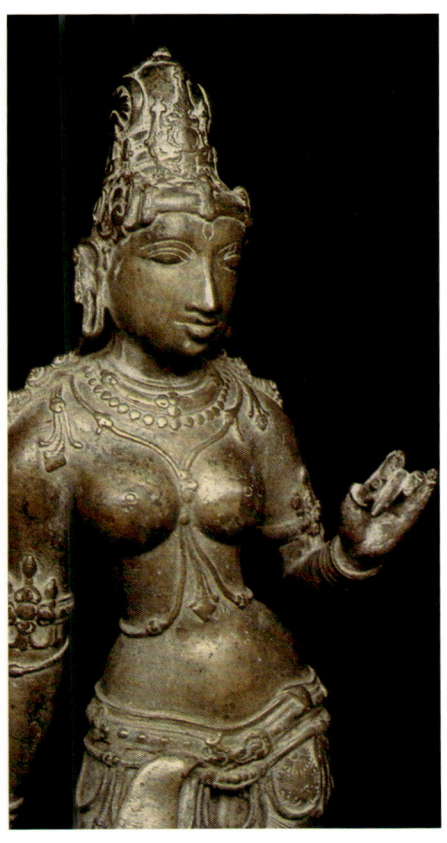
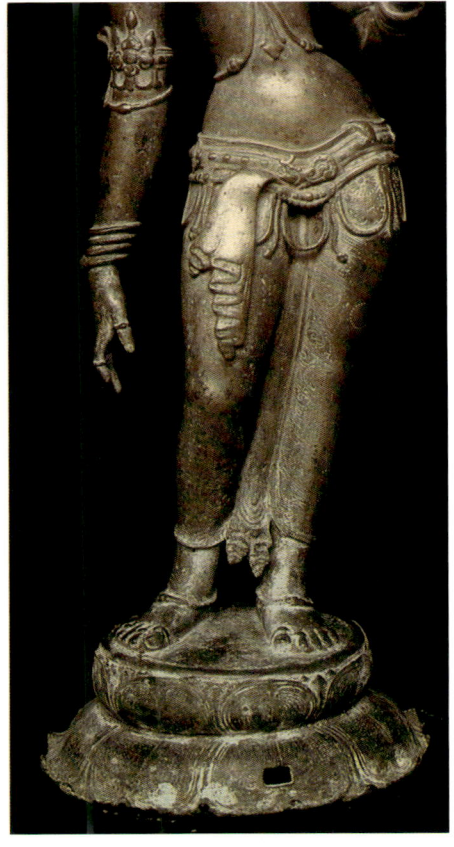

Figure 4.10. (a) Uma, Nallur temple, ca. 979. (b) Detail of Uma (fig. 4.10a), Nallur temple, ca. 979. (c) Detail of Uma (fig. 4.10a), Nallur temple, ca. 979.

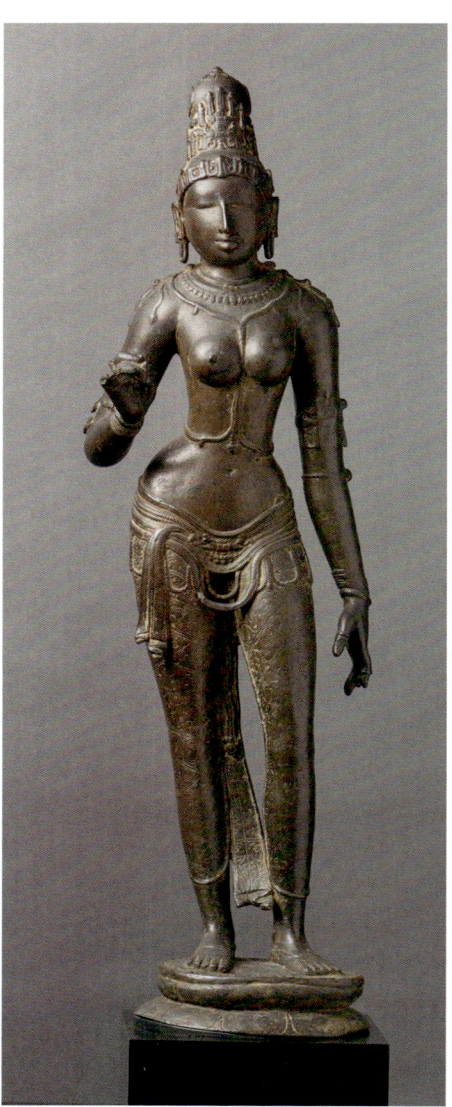

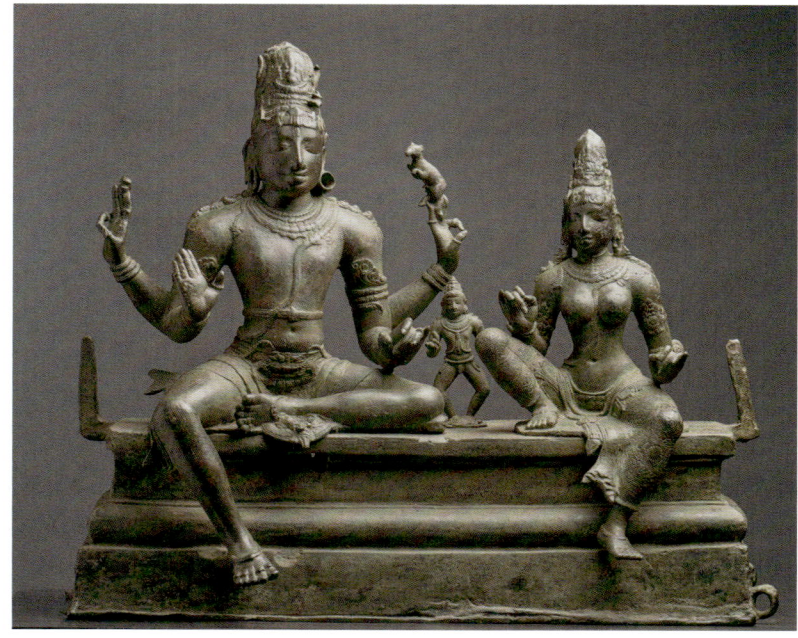

Figure 4.11. Uma, ca. 979, Norton Simon Museum, Pasadena.

Figure 4.12. Shiva with Uma and Infant Skanda (*Somaskanda*), ca. 979, Norton Simon Museum, Pasadena.

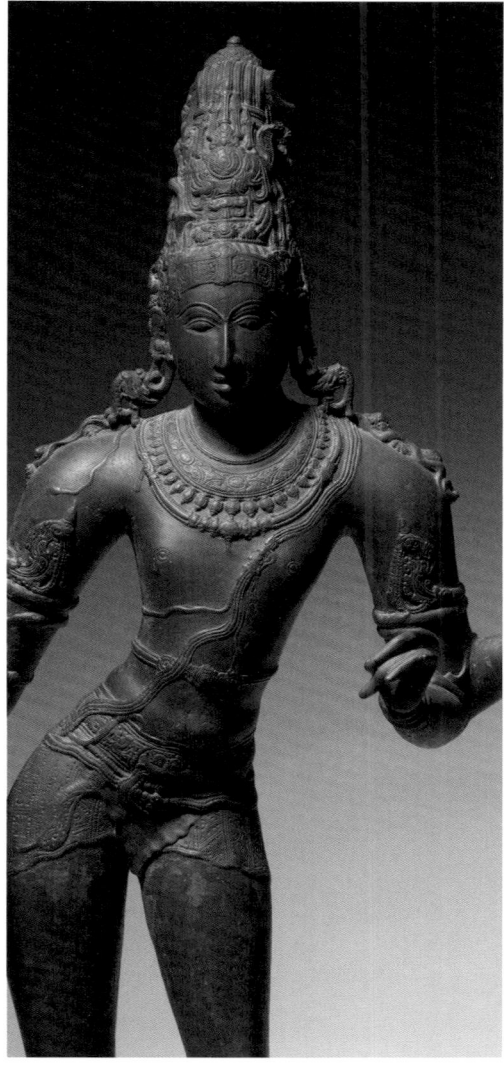

Figure 4.13. Detail of Shiva as Victor of Three Forts (see fig. 1.5), ca. 960, The Cleveland Museum of Art, John L. Severance Fund.

common pedestal (fig. 4.13). His overly slender torso and slightly off-balance stance is a pointer to the image coming from the workshop of the "Master of the off-kilter substyle" to whom we ascribed an early bronze that we examined in chapter 2 (see fig. 2.6). Making the point even more strongly is the rear view of the two Shivas, one created by the original Master in ca. 875 and the second created some eighty-five years later in ca. 960 (fig. 4.14a, b). The Master of the original coastal workshop created idiosyncratic images marked by the tendency to push the limits of what appears to be an unbalanced stance. It is likely that the tenth-century Victor in the Cleveland Museum of Art was created by a grandson or grand-nephew of the original Master who, like his ancestor, enjoyed the challenge of pushing the limits of a seemingly off-balance pose.

It is relevant to consider in some detail the Koneri temple inscription of the year 979, which refers to the bronze images we examined and consists of 100 lines of Tamil prose

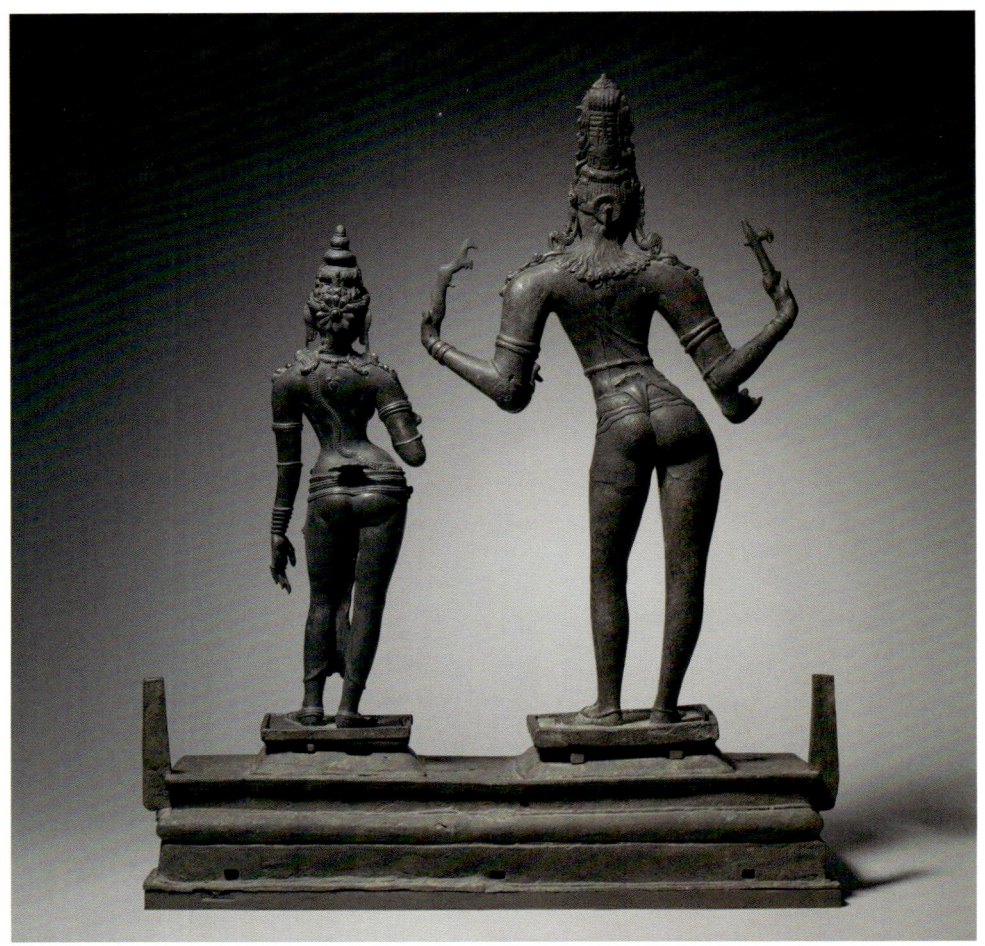

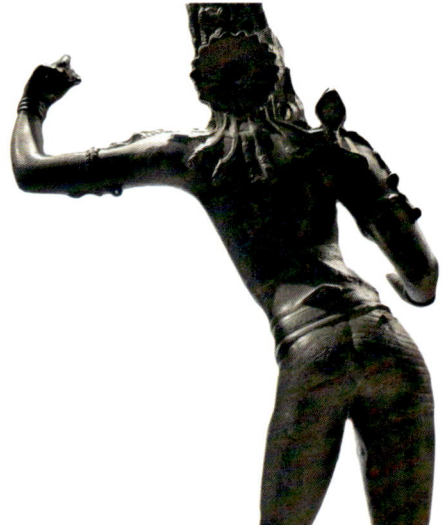

Figure 4.14. (a) Detail of rear view of Shiva as Victor of Three Forts (see fig. 4.13), ca. 960, The Cleveland Museum of Art. (b) Detail of rear view of Shiva as Victor of Three Forts (*Tripura Vijaya*) (see fig. 1.16), ca. 875, Norton Simon Museum, Pasadena.

engraved on the east and north walls of the central shrine. It commences with the order of Uttama Chola, who provided further funds and lands to ensure that the wishes of his mother, queen Sembiyan, regarding worship in the temple were fulfilled with the grandeur she desired. The first part of the inscription gives the details of the king's dedication of newly gifted land, its exact boundaries, and the various rights and privileges it carried. The second part provides details that partake of the quality of an accounts book. It specifies the payment, to be made in measures of rice, to various temple employees, together with details of temple administration, and it only incidentally provides a number of details regarding bronzes and temple ritual relating to the bronze images. Its set of individualized instructions commences with ensuring the celebration of queen Sembiyan's birth-star Kettai that we mentioned earlier. It then speaks of the payment made to the chief priest of the temple,[61] and specifies details of funds to celebrate two major festivals in the month of *Markali* (December–January) and *Vaikhashi* (May–June).[62] The rest of the inscription provides us with a comprehensive picture of all that was involved in the successful running of a small royal temple in Tamil Nadu during the third quarter of the tenth century.

I start with the payments made to three men whose sole duty was to guard the sacred bronzes,[63] a wise precaution that the temples might do well to reinstitute in the twenty-first century in the context of the international art market and smuggling. The record speaks of payments made to temple employees engaged to lustrate the bronzes with milk, curds, ghee, sugar, and honey;[64] to a brahmin who brought water from the river Kaveri to further bathe them;[65] to brahmins who crushed the sandalwood to make the fragrant paste applied to the bronzes;[66] for the purchase of cloth used to drape the images;[67] to those who watered the temple's flower gardens;[68] to those who picked and strung flowers into garlands;[69] to five brahmins whose job was to hold a canopy over the bronzes when they were taken in procession;[70] and to servants who swept the temple floors.[71] The inscription's provisions clarify that the drapery and adornment we see on the images today is not a newly instituted practice, but dates back over a thousand years in the case of bronze images and, as we know from the saints' hymns, to the even earlier wooden precursors of the bronzes. This Koneri inscription speaks too of payments made to those who sounded eight varieties of musical instruments including cymbals and drums;[72] to those who blew conch shells;[73] to two singers of the hymns of the saints;[74] to the astrologer who carried the sacred calendar;[75] and to the official *srikaryam*, or Sacred Works officer, who checked the temple's financial transactions.[76] Additionally, a variety of payments were made to ensure the everyday smooth running of the temple and for maintenance that included renewal of screens and canopies and various other repairs.[77]

The importance of flowers in temple ritual, whether loose or strung into garlands, led temples to routinely establish gardens to supply their daily needs. At Koneri, there were three flower gardens, one named after queen Sembiyan and tended by four gardeners, a second named after her husband, Gandaraditya, and a third that took the name of her son and ruling monarch, Uttama Chola.[78] It is not often that inscriptions give us specific information about the yield of temple gardens; one such record from Tiruvidaimaradur, in the year 985 when Battan Kannan was the temple officer, informs us that the sale of a year's supply of areca nuts from the temple garden yielded 110 3/4 *kalanju* of gold, which was used to make a gold crown for the deity.[79] The three temple gardens at Konerirajapuram were not equipped, it seems, to supply the large number of lilies that seem to have become a temple favorite. In the thirteenth century, during the reign of Rajaraja III, we read that the right of supplying lily garlands for worship in the Konerirajapuram temple was bought from a defaulter and given to two brothers, Selvan and Sendapillai, who became the temple's official suppliers of lilies. They contracted to supply 18,250 garlands yearly for regular daily worship, at the rate of 50 garlands a day; they also agreed to provide 44,000 garlands each year for the December–January (*Markali*) festival and 77,660 garlands for the May–June (*Vaikhashi*) festival. To enable the brothers to supply this yearly total of 139,910 lily garlands, the temple authorities allotted to them lands appropriate for this purpose as well as a house for each brother. The inscription ends with a dispensatory clause to the effect that in the case of floods or drought, the temple and town authorities would jointly decide on the reduced number of garlands to be supplied by the brothers.[80]

In addition to flowers that exuded fragrance and provided vivid color to the ritual proceedings, artificial gold flowers, *por-pu*, were a popular item of donation to temple images. Sembiyan herself presented two gold flowers to the Shiva image in the Vriddhachalam temple that she rebuilt in stone, a single gold flower to adorn the bronze of Dancing Shiva, and twenty-six gold flowers to images in her Shiva temple in the town of Sembiyan Mahadevi.[81] One daughter-in-law, Sorabbiyar Tribhuvanamadevi, presented a gold flower to the Tiruvenkadu temple, while another daughter-in-law, Vanavan Madevi, presented twelve gold flowers to an image of Shiva as Kshetrapala in the temple of Tiruvalanjuli.[82] Her son Uttama converted a number of small gifts of gold coins to a series of impressive ornaments that included a dedication of twenty-three gold flowers.[83] Kundavai, Rajaraja's sister, gifted thirty-five gold flowers to the bronze image of Uma as the consort of the Dancing Lord in the Thanjavur temple, and 130 gold flowers to Uma as consort of Victor of Three Forts; the inscription specifies that each flower weighed 4 3/4 *kalanju*.[84] In the year 1015, queen Dantishakti Vilangi, a queen of Rajaraja, presented 164 gold flowers, weighing a total of 193 *kalanju*, to the Tiruvaiyaru temple.[85] Gold flowers appear to have been popular gift items throughout the Chola period.

The *Suksmagama*, a ritual text published recently for the first time, devotes one chapter to worship with gold flowers indicating that was an accepted mode of honoring both the sanctum deity and the temple's many bronzes.[86] While the text was composed during the thirteenth century, at the very end of Chola rule, it appears to codify preexisting modes of worship. It lists thirteen varieties of flowers and six types of leaves that were suitable for offering in the medium of gold and ranks such gifts as best, middling, or lowest (*uttama*, *madhyama*, *adhama*), depending on their weight.[87] We read that the ritual procedure depended on the caste of the devotee. A brahmin may himself place his gold flower offerings directly on the sanctum linga in the morning hours; a *kshatriya* devotee may place the *por-pu* on the linga pedestal at midday; and a *vaishya* may place it beside the linga pedestal in the evening. While a devotee of lower caste may make his offerings at any time of day, he may stand only in the temple porch and place the gold flower on a *yantra*, or sacred diagram, drawn to align directly with the Shiva linga. The *Suksmagama* text lists the benefits that accrue from regular worship with specified numbers of golden flowers. For instance, one who worships for a full year with 25 flowers acquires knowledge and a male heir, while one who offers 100 flowers will acquire

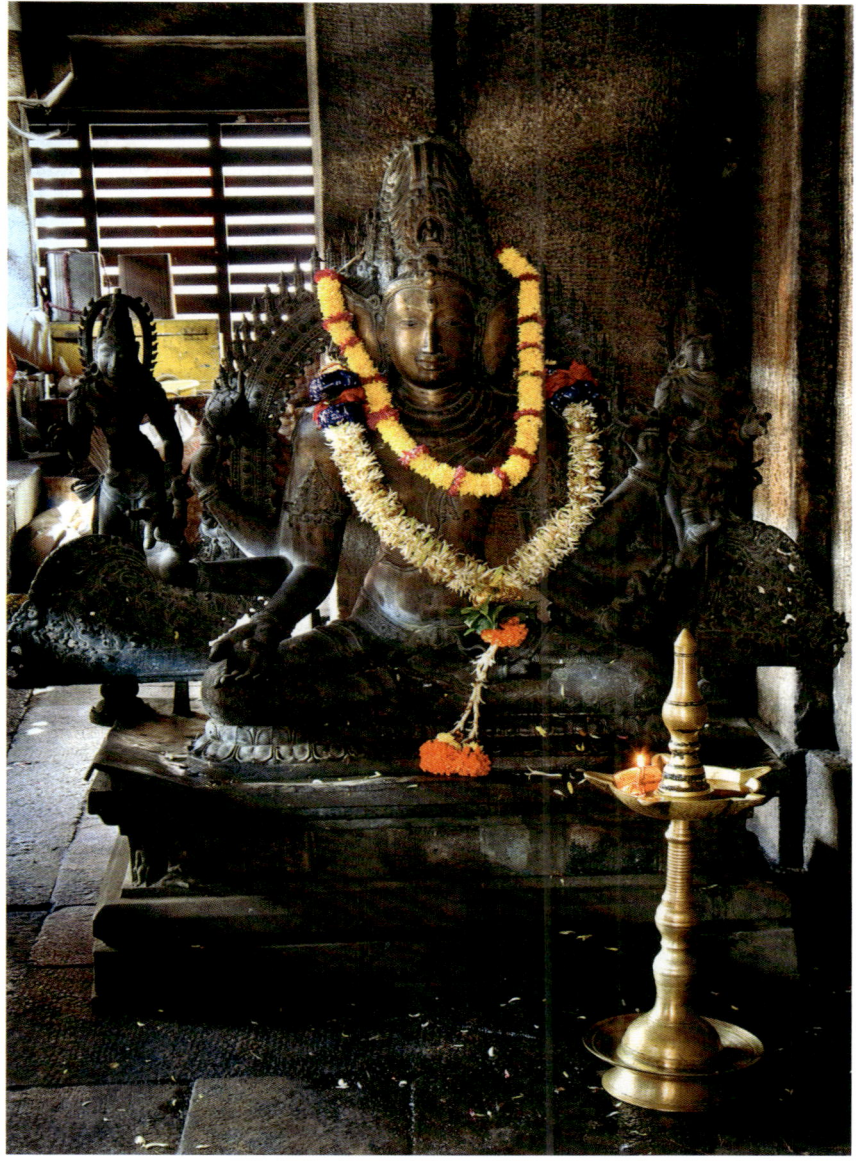

Figure 4.15. Inscribed Lokeshvara, Kadiri Manjunath temple, Mangalore, 968.

abundant riches and great glory. Those who offer 81 flowers over a period of five years will be free from all sickness, while an offering of 108 flowers for a full ten years will bestow one's worldly desires and even liberation.[88]

Returning to the Sembiyan workshop, it is appropriate to consider two impressive bronzes of a Buddhist deity, a *bodhisattva* known as Lokeshvara, or Lord of the World, currently placed within the Kadiri Shiva temple in Mangalore along the Kerala coastline, a good 500 miles to the west (fig. 4.15).[89] Commissioned by king Kundavarman of the local Alupa dynasty, these Buddhist bronzes bear a close resemblance to images from the Kaveri delta, and to the Koneri bronzes in particular; local Kerala bronzes are a world apart in character. I will focus here on the larger of the two bronzes, a three-headed image that carries an inscription on its pedestal; the companion image of the same deity

PORTRAIT OF A QUEEN   113

has a single head. For this Buddhist image (and for its companion), the artist created a towering hairstyle that is exceedingly close to Shiva's matted locks (*jatas*) piled high; in rear view, Lokeshvara's locks are arranged along the nape of the neck just as is done with images of Shiva. A similarly placed third eye adorns the forehead of all three heads of this Buddhist deity too. With the two Koneri Shivas, the double-*makara* clasp that holds back the dreadlocks carries a central tasseled medallion; with the two Lokeshvara images, the artist adhered to Buddhist iconography by adding a tiny seated Buddha image within that central medallion. Additionally, the artist carved an antelope head along the sacred thread of the smaller Buddhist image to identify him as a specific form of Lokeshvara.[90] One might note too that the fabric of the dhoti on the inscribed Kadiri image carries three repetitive bands of a geometric pattern that closely resembles the pattern on the long skirts and the short dhotis worn by Sembiyan's Konerirajapuram images. While Kaveri delta workshops were indeed known for their specialty in creating images of Shiva, it is clear that artists and workshops were not divided along religious lines. Rather, they worked for any patron who requisitioned their services—in this instance, a patron who requested images of a Buddhist deity. Not surprisingly, Kaveri delta artists carved all images according to their traditional models of bodily beauty and followed their own customary decorative techniques. In the case of sacred bronzes in general, it is unlikely that the aesthetics of the image was controlled by the patron; rather, it was left to the skill of the artist.

    A lengthy inscription against the pedestal of the large seated image uses the most lavish of terms to praise its donor, the monarch Kundavarman of the Alupendra dynasty, describing him as a sun to the lotus of the Lunar race, and equating him to god Vishnu in calling him one whose chest is rubbed with saffron from the breasts of Lakshmi. He is equal to Karna in generosity, to Arjuna in valor, to Indra in wealth, to Brihaspati in wisdom, and it was this apparently Hindu monarch who installed the image of Lokeshvara in the beautiful Kadiriki *vihara* in a Kali era date that corresponds to the year 968.[91] Thus, these two Buddhist images predate by ten years the Koneri bronzes we examined. The pedestal inscription is inscribed in the Sanskrit language and *grantha* script that was not that common in the Kaveri basin, rather than in the Tamil language and script of the Chola region, making it likely that the record was inscribed after the image arrived in its new home. The fact that a king from the Kerala coast commissioned an image from a Kaveri delta workshop is testimony to the fame acquired by the Chola coastal bronze workshops. The issue of transporting heavy solid images from a workshop near the port of Nagapattinam on the east coast to Mangalore on the west coast is of interest. I would estimate that the large seated Lokeshvara, close to 4 feet in height inclusive of its pedestal, weighs around 250 pounds.[92] It appears most likely that the images were shipped in one of the trading vessels that regularly plied the route from China to Aden, stopping at both Chola Nagapattinam on the east coast of India and Mangalore on the west coast, and also at Sri Lankan ports, to offload select goods and take on other merchandise. While we may have underestimated the efficacy of the Palghat gap, a pass through the Western Ghats, as an effective overland trade route between the east and west coasts of peninsular India, it seems unlikely that major sacred bronzes would have been consigned to a rough journey on overland carts.

As we contextualize Sembiyan's contribution to the artistic, religious, and cultural life of the Kaveri delta during the second half of the tenth century, I would like to point to her apparently unique status as the only queen of Gandaraditya.[93] She did not have to compete with others for the right to make major donations, to rebuild entire temples in stone, to commission bronzes for these temples, to give money for festivals or lands for conversion to flower gardens. She was indeed the exalted "Ruby of the Dynasty." By contrast, her father-in-law Parantaka had at least eleven queens. We know of them entirely through inscriptions that speak of their donations to various temples. Parantaka's very first wife and thus his senior queen or *agra mahishi* was Kokkilanadigal, mother of crown prince Rajaditya who was killed in battle in 949.[94] Scrutinizing inscribed gifts to temples during the reign of Parantaka yields the names of another nine queens of Parantaka, several specifying the chieftain family from which they hailed:

Tribhuvanamahadevi

Chola Sikhamaniyar, daughter of Nanguri Nangaiyar of Mayilappil

Arinjikai, daughter of Iladaraiyar

Tennavan Mahadeviyar, alias Narayana Nangri Nangaiyar

Trailokyamahadevi

Cheyabhuvana Chinatamaniyar of Kaveripumpattinam

Vallavan Mahadeviyar

Arulmoli Nanagaiyar, daughter of Paluvettaraiyar

Cholamahadeviyar.[95]

Marital alliances, as we stressed, were a crucial and strategic way of strengthening the kingdom and were especially important in an emerging kingship such as that of the Cholas during the tenth century.

It is instructive to note that despite Sembiyan's own privileged queenly position, she clearly subscribed to the need for alliances with chieftains on behalf of the still small, and definitely precarious Chola kingdom. She arranged for her one and only son, Uttama Chola, to marry no less than thirteen young princesses, daughters of several different chieftains. His chief queen was Orattanan Solabbaiyar, also known as Tribhuvanamahadevi (alternately Urattayan Sorabbai),[96] while his remaining twelve queens, named in various inscriptions as donors of temple gifts, are as follows:

Battan Danatongiyar

Malapadi Tennavan Mahadeviyar

Kilandigal, daughter of Vilupparaiyar

Vanavan Mahadeviyar, daughter of Irungolar

——, daughter of Paluvettaraiyar

Viranaraniyar, daughter of Ilamukkaraiyar

Gopan Sakkapu

Aruran Amabalattadigalar, aka Ponamballattu-adigalar

Minavan Madeviyar

Siddhavadavan Chuttiyar, daughter of Miladu-udaiyar

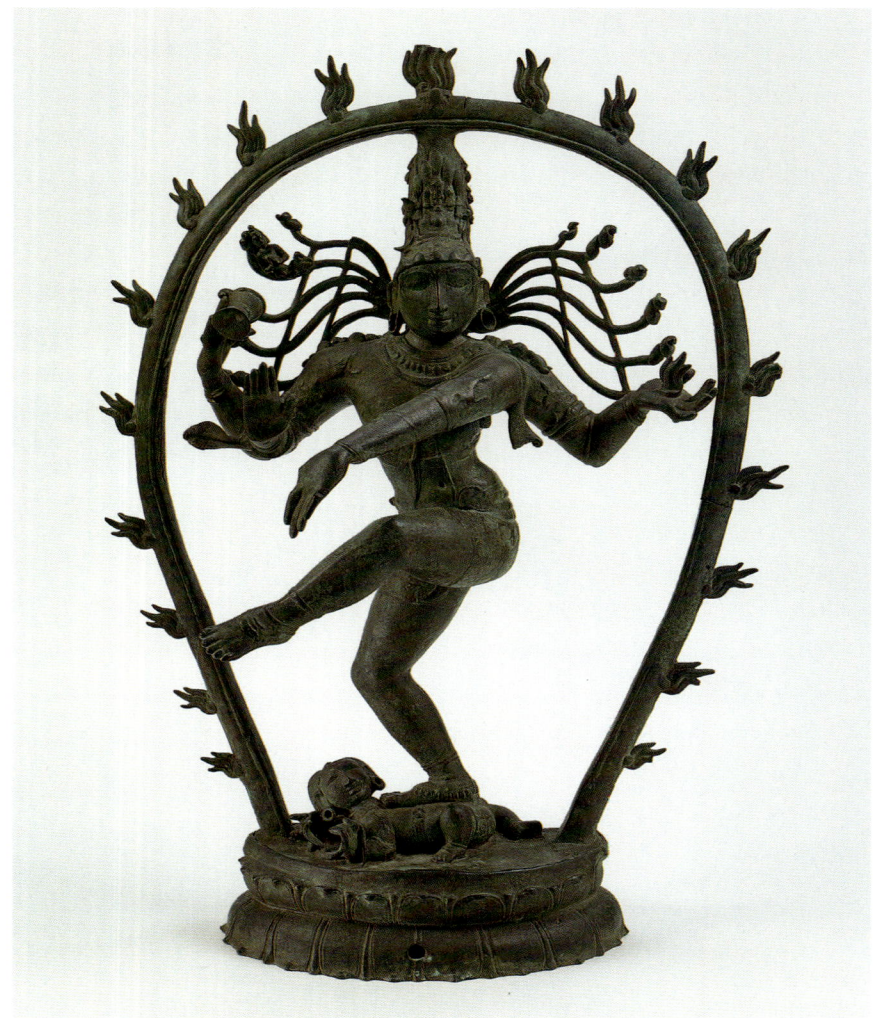

Figure 4.16. (a and b) Shiva as Wondrous Dancer, ca. 970, Freer Gallery of Art, Washington, DC, Purchase—Charles Lang Freer Endowment and funds provided by Margaret and George Haldeman.

Panchavan Madeviyar
Nakkan Tillai Alagiyar[97]

In speaking of the patronage of royal women, it would be well to keep in mind the intense competition that must have existed between the queens for the favors and attention of the monarch, and perhaps the tension between the queens and his senior advisors.

Shiva as "Wondrous Dancer"

Shiva's most widely admired and most popular manifestation is as Lord of Dance, referred to popularly by the term Nataraja, literally Dance-King (fig. 4.16a, b). I will avoid the use of the term in this book, not merely because Nataraja is a Sanskrit word, but because the term itself was introduced into the Tamil country only during the thirteenth century, in an inscription of a Pandya ruler, at a time when Chola rule was ending.[98]

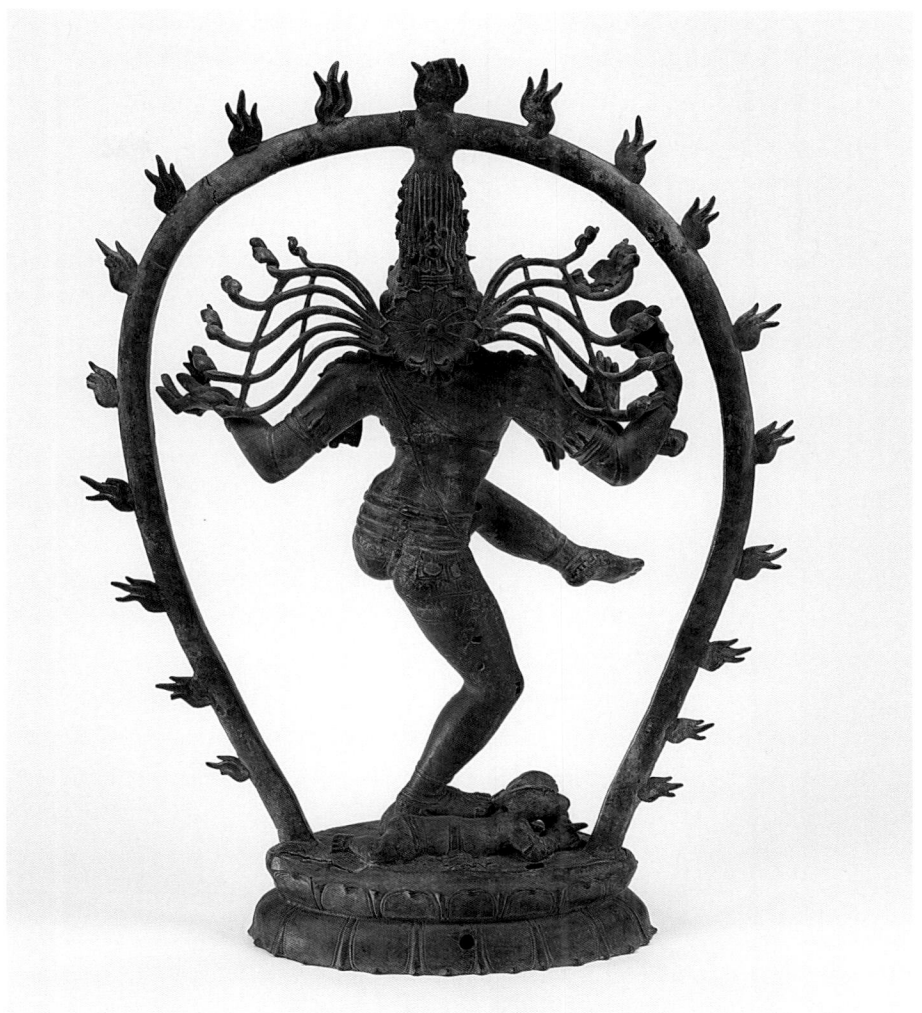

Throughout Chola rule, Dancing Shiva was addressed by a number of expressive Tamil names: Wondrous Dancer (*Arbuda Kuttar*),[99] Ruby Dancer (*Manikka Kuttar*),[100] Beauteous Dancer (*Alagiya Kuttar*),[101] Dancing Lord (*Kuttadum Devar*),[102] Dancing Processional Lord (A*adal Vidanga Devar*),[103] Dancing Leader (*Kuttu Nayakar*), Great Lord of Dance (*Kuttu Perumal*), Expert Dancer (*Adavallan*). It is indeed an amazing concept to think of one's supreme deity as a Master of Dance, and it was queen Sembiyan who popularized this form of Shiva, making his image an indispensable icon for the Tamil country.[104]

In the context of Dancing Shiva, it is intriguing to try and envision the complicated circumstances of Sembiyan's life until the year 971, when her son Uttama Chola ascended the throne. She was probably no more than twelve years of age when she entered the Chola family as a young princess, and just twenty-one when catapulted into the role of queen. And then, when she was around twenty-eight, her husband abdicated the throne and abandoned her, leaving her with their young son to survive palace intrigue as well as she could. Yet, Sembiyan does not appear to have been bitter. Rather, she appears to have

PORTRAIT OF A QUEEN

focused on the hymn that Gandaraditya composed before he handed over the throne to his younger brother, in which he sang of his great longing to see the Expert Dancer at Chidambaram, the only temple at the time to enshrine an image of Dancing Shiva. Perhaps it was the hymn that prompted Sembiyan to ensure that the longing of others to see the Expert Dancer would be more easily fulfilled.

Sembiyan featured a stone image of Dancing Shiva within a niche on the south wall of the *mandapa* of every one of the new stone temples she built, as well as those she rebuilt in stone, with Ganesha and sage Agastya in flanking niches (fig. 4.17). It appears that chiefs and officials who built temples during this same period added niches to accommodate Dancing Shiva. At Tiruvelvikudi, for instance, the stone image of the Expert Dancer, as well as the flanking figures of Agastya and Ganesha, are all placed within roughly cut niches that appear to be the result of updating during this period.[105] By this move, Sembiyan ensured that devotees could view the beauty of the Dancing Lord as often as they wished in temples of the Kaveri delta without the necessity of travel to Chidambaram. Sembiyan also sponsored the widespread introduction of portable bronze images of the Expert Dancer, setting an example followed by temple after temple; now donors commissioned such bronzes to be carried through the town in festival processions where young and old, healthy and infirm, curious and devout, could view his beauty. Whether the form was first created in stone, where it was supported by the backdrop of a stone slab, or as a fully three-dimensional bronze image is a debatable issue though, to my mind, not of crucial significance. After all, we know that wooden three-dimensional images of the Dancing Lord were taken in procession in the seventh century, when the saints sang of the Lord who "goes in procession in his dancing form."[106] Certainly, the dramatic impact of Shiva's dreadlocks splayed out around him with the movement of his dance is lost in stone reliefs where his locks blend with the background of the slab on which he is carved. A well-known verse on the Dancing Lord, written by saint Appar in the second half of the seventh century, some 300 years before these stone and bronze images of the dancing form began to be created in queen Sembiyan's time, highlights the beauty of Dancing Shiva:

> *The arch of his brow,*
> *the budding smile*
> *on lips red as kovvai fruit,*
> *cool matted hair,*
> *the milk-white ash on coral skin,*
> *and the sweet golden foot*
> *raised in dance,*
> *If you could see these*
> *then even human birth on this wide earth*
> *would become a thing worth having.*[107]

For those unfamiliar with this quintessential Chola icon, I should point out that this particular form of Dancing Shiva, with one foot raised high in dance, became a form imbued with deep cosmic significance.[108] To oversimplify a complex set of beliefs, one might say that Shiva dances the world into extinction only to re-create it again through

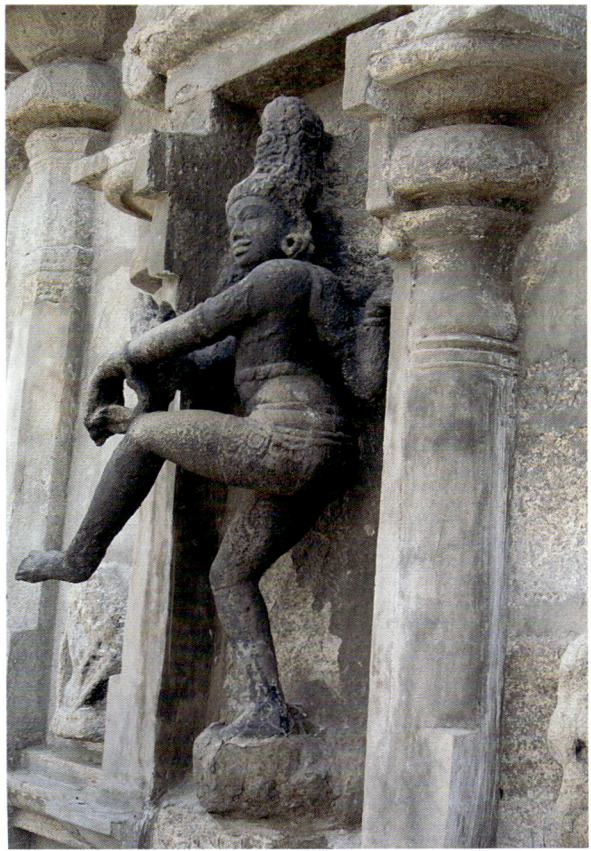

Figure 4.17. Dancing Shiva in *mandapa* niche, Konerirajapuram temple, Thanjavur district, ca. 969; note that the foot of the raised leg from the knee down is a replacement.

dance. His golden raised foot signifies Shiva's grace and acceptance of the devotee. The Tamil saints left the philosophical explication of the form to teachers, gurus, and *acharyas*; they themselves focused on the average lay devotees who thronged to the temple, emphasizing for them only the beauty of the Wondrous Dancer, *Arbuda Kuttar*.

While the hymns of the *nayanmar* appear to lay down the basic iconography for this form, it is interesting to observe the experimentation that took place between 950 and 1000, when the first large-scale images of Dancing Shiva began to be created in both stone and bronze. For instance, early images carry oval aureoles that are replaced by the end of the eleventh century by aureoles that are almost totally circular and became standard thereafter for Dancing Shiva (fig. 4.18a, b). Why this transition? All bronze images were framed by aureoles, even though few bronzes seen today in museum collections retain such framing; inscriptions of emperor Rajaraja specify, for instance, that aureoles enclosing a standing image were cast in three pieces, as two pillars and a crescent-shaped top that resembled an inverted U (fig. 4.18c).[109] When a dancing figure, with one leg raised in dance, was introduced, the aureole needed some adjustment for the lifted leg as also for the outstretched hands of the dancer; so the aureole took on an oval shape. Gradually, as the outstretched hand holding the drum was extended farther, the oval needed to be opened up farther, until it resulted in its final fully circular form (see fig. 1.6).

PORTRAIT OF A QUEEN

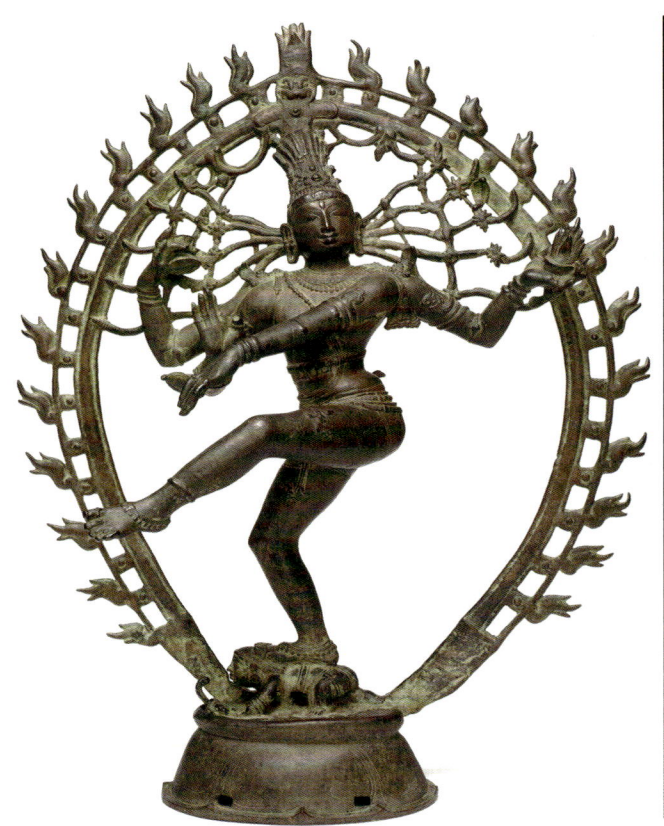
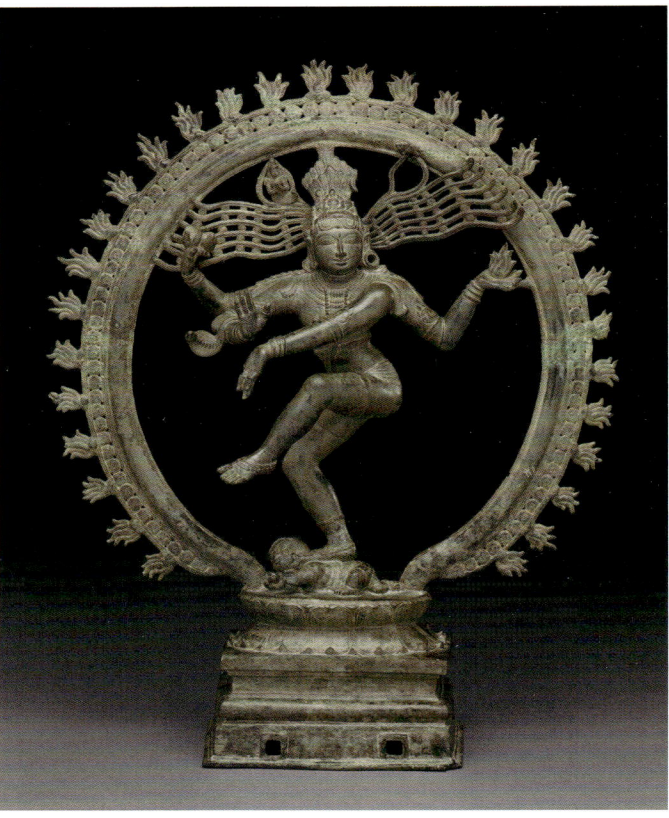
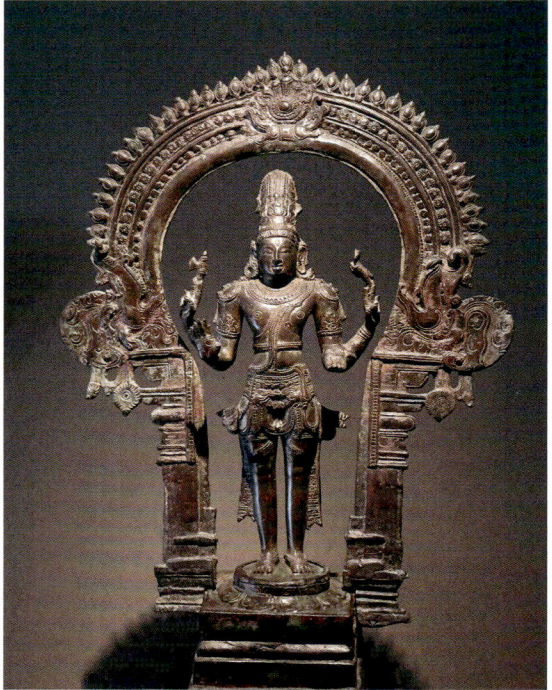

Figure 4.18. (a) Dancing Shiva, ca. 970, Asia Society Museum, New York, Mr. and Mrs. John D. Rockefeller 3rd Collection. (b) Dancing Shiva, eleventh century, Dallas Museum of Art, gift of Mrs. Eugene McDermott, the Hamon Charitable Foundation, and an anonymous donor in honor of David T. Owsley, with additional funding from The Cecil and Ida Green Foundation and the Cecil and Ida Green Acquisition Fund. (c) Typical three-piece aureole surrounding Chola standing bronze Shiva, twelfth century, private collection.

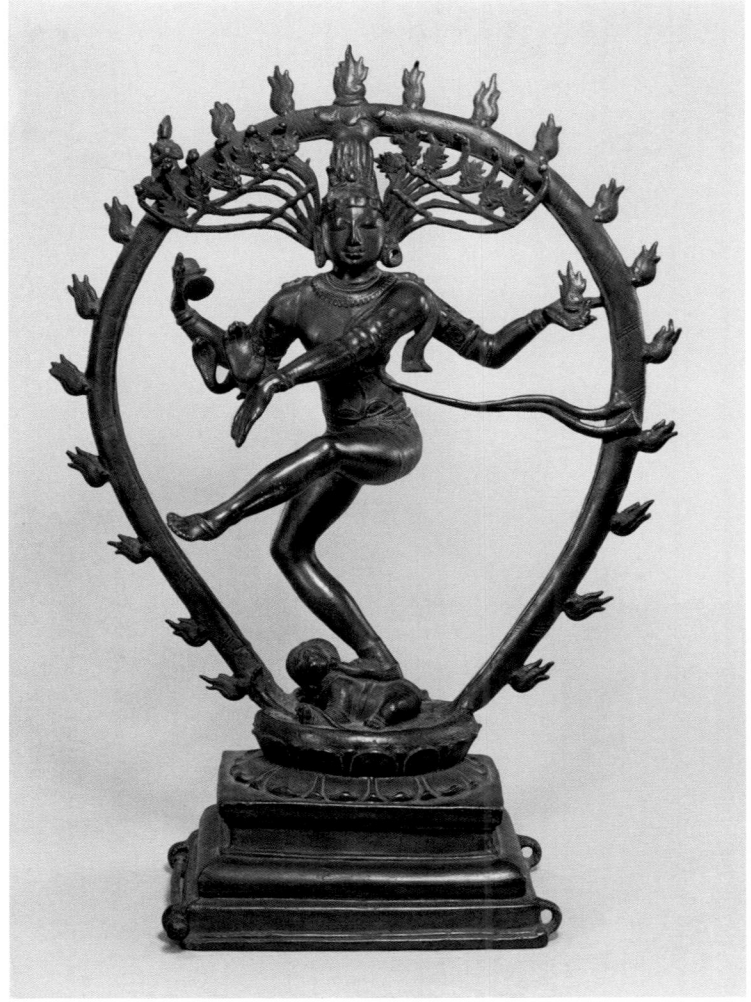

Figure 4.19. Dancing Shiva, ca. 980, Victoria and Albert Museum, London, Bequeathed by Mrs. L. S. Bradley.

Another distinction is the presence or absence of the river goddess Ganges in Shiva's dreadlocks. When the heavenly river Ganges agreed to descend to earth, she asked Shiva to break the force of her flow by receiving her in his dreadlocks and then gently allowing her to flow down to earth. Two early bronzes of the Expert Dancer, one from Shivapuram and the other from Vedikudi, omit the river goddess Ganges despite the fact that child saint Sambandar sang of Ganga's murmuring stream flowing over the cool crescent moon in the locks of dancing Shiva.[110] With the small image of Dancing Shiva in the Victoria and Albert Museum, the wax modeler decided to use one of the flames along the aureole as a support for his river goddess (fig. 4.19). An image once in the temple at Palanam, one of the Sacred Seven that we considered in chapter 2, places the personified goddess Ganga along the band of the aureole.[111] The early artists clearly played with the exact positioning of Ganga. In an image from the Norton Simon Museum, the river goddess seems to need the support of Shiva's head and one of his dreadlocks (fig. 4.20a, b); in the image in the Freer Gallery of Art (see fig. 4.16) and the bronze from

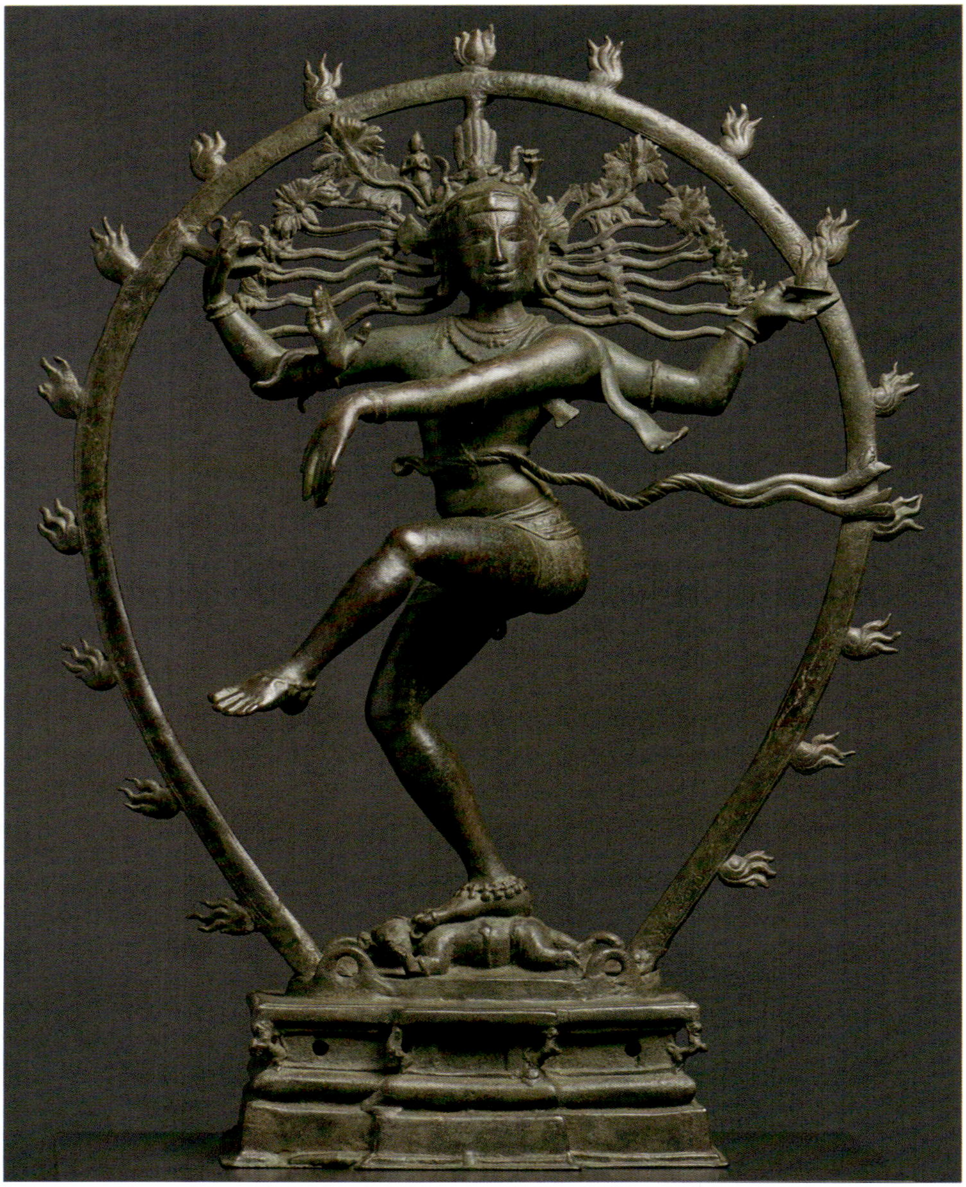

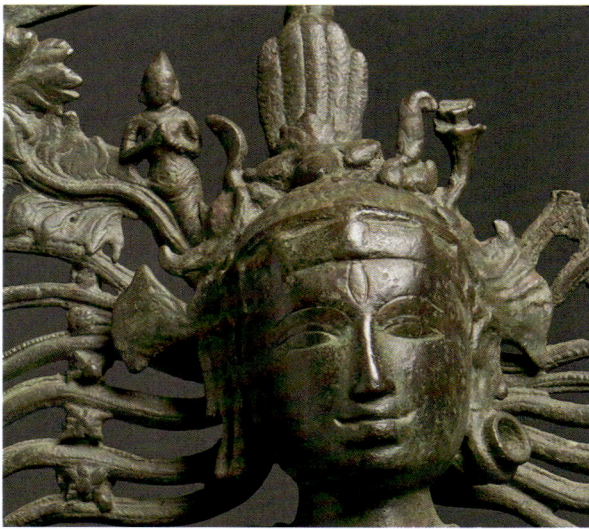

Figure 4.20. (a) Dancing Shiva, ca. 980–990, Norton Simon Museum, Pasadena. (b) Detail of Dancing Shiva (fig. 4.20a), showing the river Ganges in Shiva's dreadlocks.

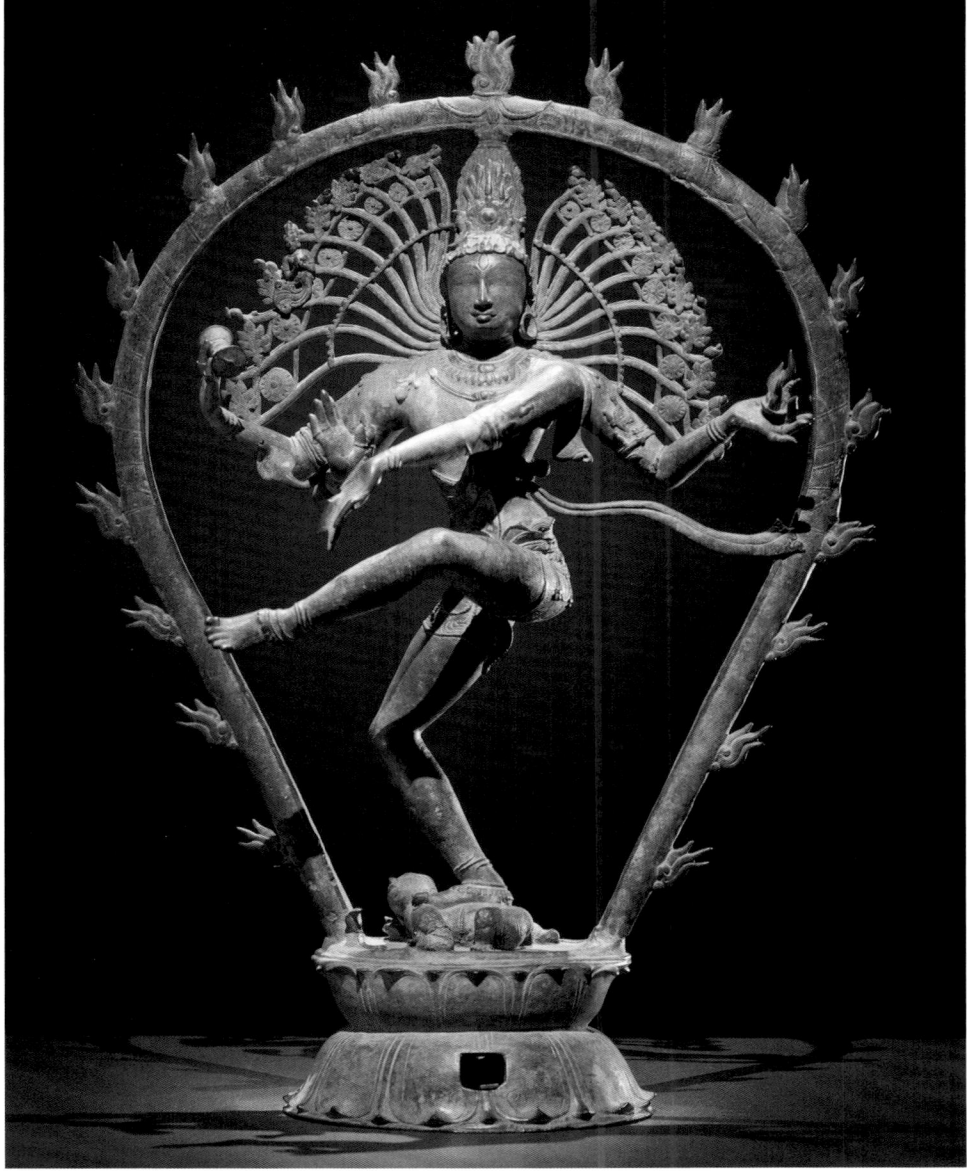

Figure 4.21. Dancing Shiva, ca. 990, Los Angeles County Museum of Art.

the Los Angeles County Museum of Art, the artist has confidently placed her along the ringlet-like curled ends of one of Shiva's dreadlocks (fig. 4.21). The experimentation continued for quite a while, since we find that the artist of the bronze image in worship in a shrine within the Thanjavur temple grounds, a dedication of emperor Rajaraja of circa 1012, still used the band of the aureole as a support for the goddess Ganges.[112]

Another variation occurs with the fiery flame that Shiva holds in his outstretched left hand. Saint Sambandar speaks of Shiva "holding blazing fire in the hollow of his hand." But the first artists modeling the image of dancing Shiva felt it necessary to shield Shiva's palm from the flames, so they placed the flames within a mini-bowl that rests on his palm, as seen in the earliest bronzes (fig. 4.22a), as also in the stone image from the

PORTRAIT OF A QUEEN

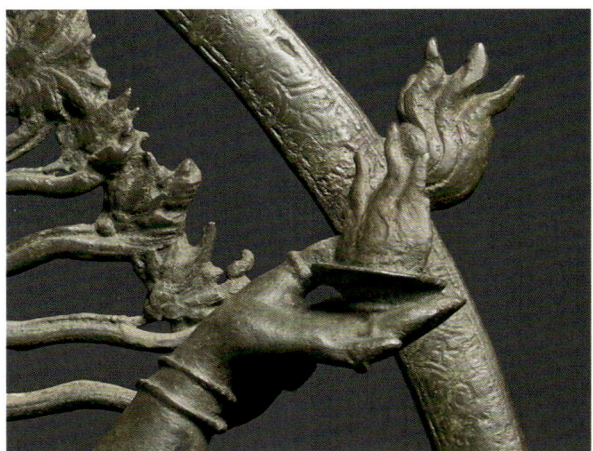 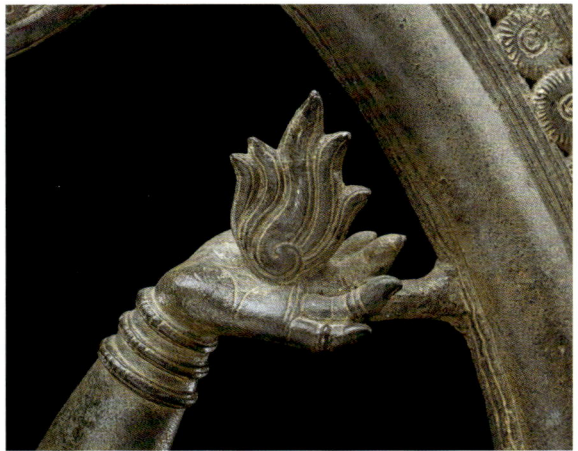

Figure 4.22. (a) Flames emerging from mini bowl in palm, detail of Dancing Shiva of ca. 980/990 (see fig. 4.20a). (b) Flames emerging from palm, detail of Dancing Shiva of eleventh century (see fig. 4.18b).

Sembiyan Mahadevi temple. Later on, this morphs into the original concept of flames emerging from Shiva's very palm (fig. 4.22b). The phase of early experimentation with several details pertaining to images of Dancing Shiva—and I have by no means given you a comprehensive listing—is seen for about seventy-five years after its introduction in the mid-tenth century.

In the context of the first images of Dancing Shiva, I would like to draw attention to an intriguing and largely ignored inscription brought to light by K. Damodaran of the Tamil Nadu State Department of Archaeology. Inscribed along the rectangular pedestal of a relatively small Dancing Shiva commissioned for the Tiruvenkadu temple where it may be seen to this day, it is in the nature of a label, not readable in the image shown here (fig. 4.23). It reads: "Treasure of Protection, the Auspicious, Ornamented lord of *deshi* [dance]" (*Svasti sri deshi abhaya nidhi abharana nayakar sri*).[113] It seems to refer to the dance of Shiva as *deshi*, meaning local and presumably Tamil; the pose of the Wondrous Dancer that we have been considering is indeed unique to the Tamil region of south India, and is not to be found anywhere in northern India, where other forms of Dancing Shiva are popular. This Tiruvenkadu inscription suggests that this particular dance pose may have been described early on in Tamil Nadu as *deshi*, or local, and much later acquired the Sanskrit name of Dance of Bliss (*ananda tandava*). We have seen already that inscriptions in the temple at Tiruvidaimaradur speak also of *deshi* songs and dances, presumably local, vernacular forms of dance and drama that were in Tamil, as distinct from *ariya* songs and dances that were possibly in Sanskrit.[114] Do we know precisely when bronze images of the Dancing Lord were introduced? An extensive survey of inscriptions that is far from comprehensive, since over half of Chola inscriptions are still unpublished, yields one reference to Dancing Shiva in the reign of Parantaka. In the thirty-eighth year of Parantaka, or 944, a trader (*vyapari*) gave a gift of a lamp and of goats to provide ghee to keep the lamp burning day and night in front of an image of *Kuttu Perumal* (Lord of Dance) in the temple at Tirunavalur.[115] Be that as it may, it was Sembiyan who transformed Dancing Shiva into

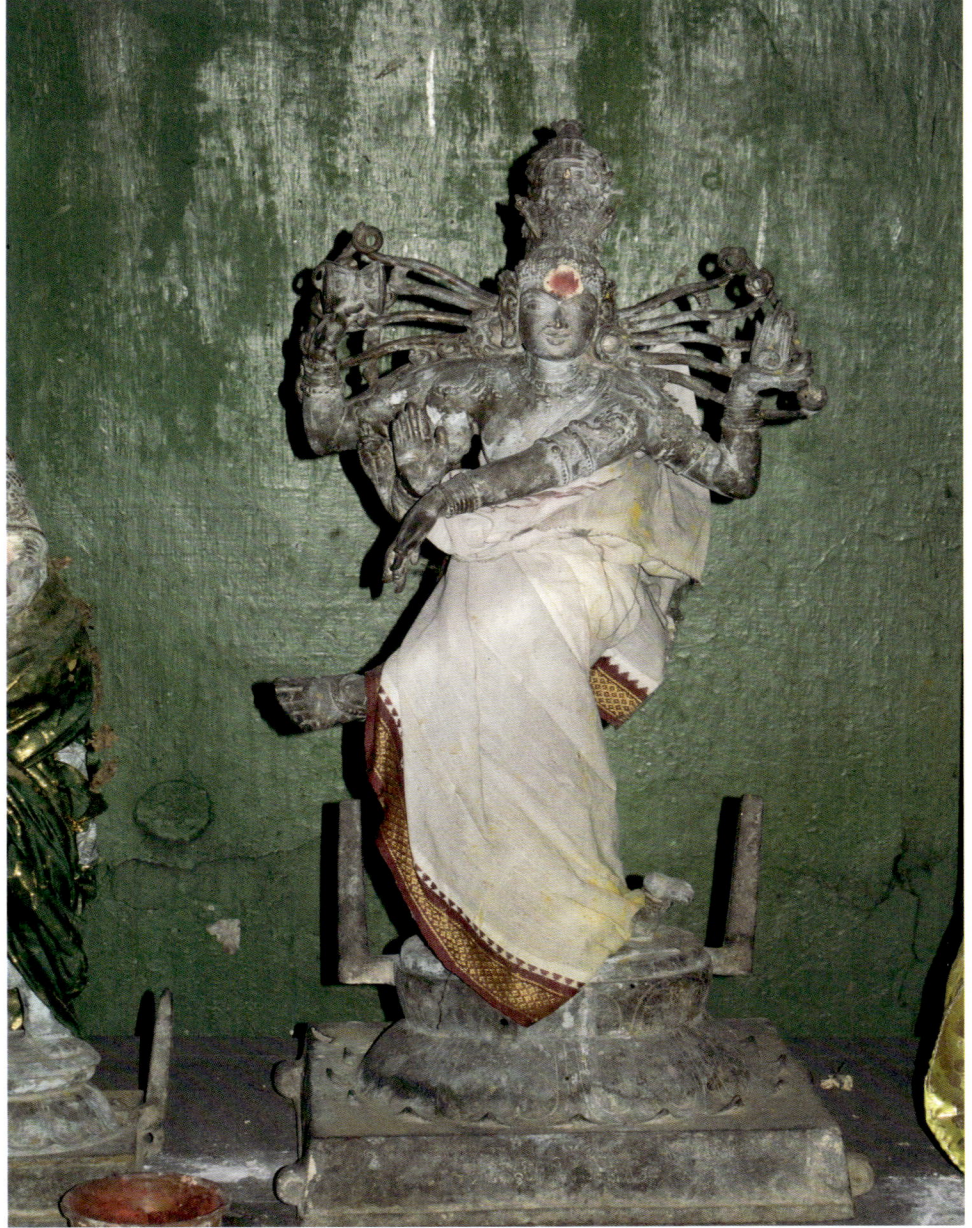

Figure 4.23. Dancing Shiva, with pedestal inscription, Tiruvenkadu temple, Nagapattinam district, ca. 980.

the hugely popular icon it was to become so that one may consider her both an arbiter of artistic taste and a leader in sacred iconography.

Let us return to the possible incentive, the impetus, the passion that motivated Sembiyan to feature large stone images of Dancing Shiva in her temples, and to encourage the creation of bronzes of the Wondrous Dancer to be placed, facing south, in the *mandapa* of temple after temple. Have we perhaps underestimated the role played in her decision by her husband Gandaraditya's intense devotion to Dancing Shiva? That queen Sembiyan was intensely aware of the hymns of the *Muvar*, saints Sambandar, Appar, and Sundarar, is seen from the very fact that she chose the ancient site of Tirunallam sung of by the saints, today's Konerirajapuram, as the site at which to rebuild in stone a temple that she dedicated to Gandaraditya. She then made specific provisions for the recitation of the saints' hymns in the temple, allocating land to be used to support two singers of these hymns (*Tirupadiyam*).[116] Already, in the reign of her father-in-law Parantaka, we hear of three women dedicated to the stone temple (*kattrali*) at Vayalur for the express purpose of serving as *chauri*-bearers and also for singing the *Tirupadiyam* songs.[117] That particular gift was made by the temple arbitrator (*madhyastha*) Nalayirattu Munurruvan, who tells us he "poured water" (*nirodu atti*) and thereby sealed the gift of the women who had thus far been in his service (*adiyal*).[118] We do not know how well known Gandaraditya's poem on Dancing Shiva was in his day, though we may surmise that his abdication would certainly have drawn attention to his devotional hymn. What we do know is that it became so highly regarded that it was added to the *Tirumurai*, the corpus of Tamil sacred hymns, whose first seven books contain the poems of the Revered Three, Sambandar, Appar, and Sundarar. Gandaraditya's hymn is featured in the ninth of a total of twelve books that comprise the *Tirumurai*, which concludes with the *Periya Puranam*, the official hagiography of the saints, written by Sekkilar during the reign of Kulottunga II. It seems possible that Sembiyan's determined espousal of the form of the Expert Dancer, in stone and bronze, may have been inspired by Gandaraditya's hymn on Dancing Shiva at Tillai, the Tamil name for Chidambaram. In the refrain of every verse, of which a few excerpts are quoted here, thanks to Indira Peterson's very first English translation of this hymn made specifically at my request, Gandaraditya asks repeatedly when he will be able to see his beloved Dancing Lord:

> *Our king, sweet ambrosia to me,*
> *abides in the dancing hall of southern Tillai*
> *humming with tuneful bees,*
> *shrine radiating light like a blaze of lightning,*
> *circled by towers with fluttering white flags,*
> *a golden mountain rising before us—*
> *When shall I attain him?* v. 1
>
> *King, you dance on the stage*
> *before the three thousand brahmin priests*
> *When shall I get to see your dance?* v. 2
>
> *Father, in the shrine of southern Tillai*
> *where bees humming tunes*
> *sing the four Vedas chanted by your three thousand priests,*
> *. . . who serve you in utter devotion—*
> *When shall I get to see your dance in the Ampalam Hall?* v. 3
>
> *The immortal crowned with the moon,*
> *. . .*
> *the king of the golden Ampalam hall in Tillai,*

Sprout of wisdom—
When shall I join him? v. 4

When the whole world beseeched him,
he graced Patañjali with the vision of his dance,
dances in the splendid Golden Ampalam Hall
in Tillai, and the gods worship him there—
When shall I see him? v. 6

He wears a garland of fragrant cassia blooms
and dwells in the resplendent hall at Tillai,
When shall I see him? v. 9

In the final signature verse, the poet identifies himself as Gandaradittan, king of Thanjavur (*tanjaiyar kon*), telling devotees that those who sing this song will attain the highest bliss in the everlasting world. Was Sembiyan herself devout? Possibly, although she may have astutely realized that devotion was a widowed queen's chief avenue to power and prominence. Hers must have been a lonely existence, but she triumphed against the odds.

Bronzes of the Expert Dancer are seen in every single temple in Tamil Nadu from the late tenth century onward, and the probability that some 3,000 bronzes of Dancing Shiva were created for temple worship during the Chola period is indicated by officials in charge of the process of registration of temple bronzes that commenced in the year 1972.[119] Inscriptions, of which I give a small sample here, frequently speak of gifts of gem-studded gold jewelry to adorn the Dancing Lord during a range of temple rituals in his honor. At Tiruvidaimaradur, the *srikaryam* officer, Inganattu Pallavaraiyan, set up an image of the Bronze Dancing Lord (*Adal Vitanka Devar*) and presented several gold ornaments to the image.[120] A local merchant (*vyapari*), Kanari Tonri, presented to this same image a golden hand-covering embedded with gems.[121] At the temple in Kovilvenni, we read of the town's residents giving tax-free land to the temple to meet the expenses of the festival of the Dancing Lord (*Kuttadum Nayanar*).[122] At the Tirupattur temple, we read of a gift of land to create a gold garment for the Dancing Lord (*Kuttadum Devar*).[123] A record from Tiruvisalur, dated to 985, stipulates that the donation of 100 *kalam* of paddy was to be used to meet the expenditure involved in beating the drums every day during the early morning ceremony of waking up the Dancing Lord, and also to provide items needed for his ritual bath.[124] In yet another inscription, a musician gave an endowment of 40 *kasu* to Rajaraja's Great Temple at Thanjavur. The interest accruing from the loan of the money to members of the village assembly of Sri-Viranar was to be used to pay five drummers during a three-day annual festival centered on the Expert Dancer. On the first day, as the flag was raised to announce the commencement of the festival, the drummers were to sound the drums and repeatedly proclaim: "The Expert Dancer will be carried in procession for three days starting today."[125] Dancing Shiva was set to become the quintessential Chola icon.

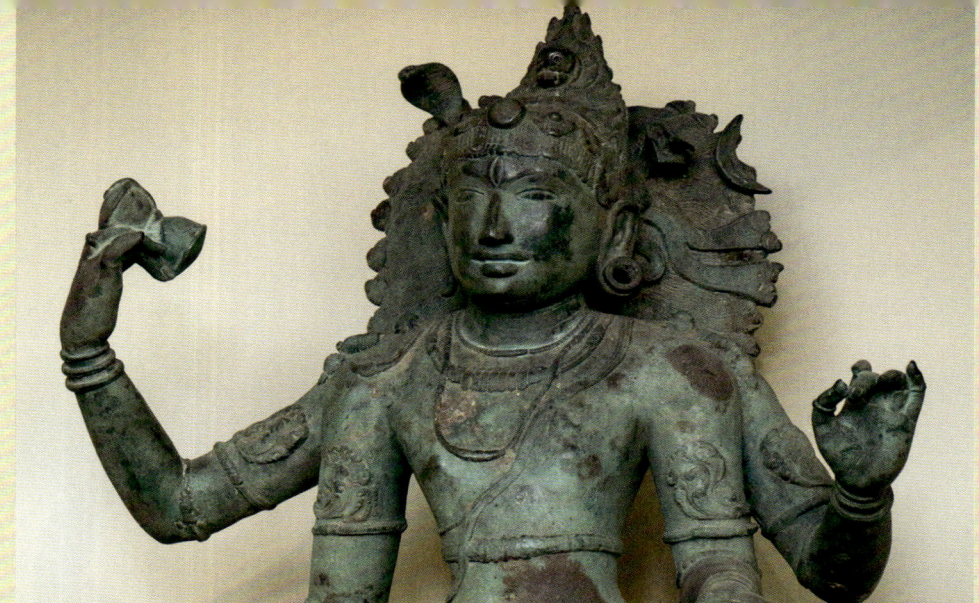

The Tiruvenkadu Master and Ten Thousand Pearls Adorn a Bronze

Eleventh Century

5 | *In the 26th year of Rajaraja [1011 CE] Kadamban Kolakkavan, from the town of Kazhamulam, member of the select military regiment of Sri Rajaraja Jananatha* [Sri rajarajadevar jananatha terinda parivarattu], *who had established* [elundarulivitta] *the Lord whose vehicle is the bull, made for that lord the [following] ornaments* [avarkku sheyvitta tiruvabharangalikku] . . .

TIRUVENKADU TEMPLE, YEAR 1011[1]

The inscription cited earlier invites us to imagine the small coastal village of Tiruvenkadu, 4 miles from where the river Kaveri enters the Bay of Bengal, in the year 1010. One can picture a master sculptor stirring bubbling wax and resin in a large pot, in the cool of dawn, as he prepares the mixture for the image he is going to model. A few days back, the commander of a select military regiment of the Chola monarch Rajaraja had sought him out to ask him to create a majestic bronze image of Shiva leaning against his bull mount. The Master had readily agreed, but since he could not forget child saint Sambandar's hymn that addressed Shiva as the "thief who stole my heart,"[2] he resolved to make his Shiva the ultimate heart-stealer who would captivate one and all.

The Master's bronze Shiva, 3 1/2 feet tall, is bewitching in his beauty, gracefully poised to rest his weight on his left foot, his right foot bent at the knee and crossed in front, with toes resting lightly on the ground (fig. 5.1a). Shiva's left hand is placed elegantly on his hip, while his right arm is bent to rest his elbow upon his now-missing bull. The firm tone of his lithe body gives him a commanding presence; the barest hint of a smile about his lush lips transforms him into an accessible figure whom the devotee may confidently approach. Our Master abandoned the usual mode of portraying Shiva with his matted locks piled high on his head, as we have encountered thus far. Instead, he created a piece that is uniquely charismatic. Taking the length of Shiva's matted locks, the Master wound them around his head to create the effect of an elegant turban; emerging just above the locks to the right is his serpent's hood, while to the left is the blossom of the trumpet flower. While modeling in wax, the Master deftly positioned the crescent moon so that it weaves under and over one of Shiva's dreadlocks (fig. 5.1b). His face, framed by the usual diadem, carries a serene contemplative look, his third eye adorns his forehead, and he wears a large circular ring in one ear, while the other ear remains unadorned (fig. 5.1c). It reminds us that saint Sambandar's hymn describes the thief who stole his heart as wearing an earring in one ear only. Firm-shouldered Shiva wears three necklaces and a brahmanical sacred thread, and his narrow torso is emphasized by a high waistband. His short dhoti, slung well below his navel, is held in place by an elaborate jeweled belt with a lion-head clasp, while fabric bands rest as looped curves below the clasp. Completing his adornment is an elbow band, a wristband, anklet, and rings on eight fingers and eight toes with only the middle finger and middle toe left ringless. Seen from the rear, the image is, if anything, even more enchanting in its sensuous elegance and reveals the artist's masterful touch. It is unfortunate that we have no information at all about this artist, not even his name; we must refer to him only as the Master of Tiruvenkadu, the town whose Shiva temple housed several of his masterpieces.

It is rare for Chola bronzes to be securely dated, but at Tiruvenkadu we are fortunate in having several inscriptions on temple walls and base moldings that provide information about donors and their gifts. While none of these inscriptions has been translated into English in its entirety, and even a complete Tamil version is not available in print or online, Job Thomas's slim 1986 publication affords important clues to locate some of the records.[3] A trip to the offices of the Epigraphical Survey of India in the town of Mysore is necessary to put together the entire series of Tiruvenkadu inscriptions, either in the form of original rubbings taken from the temple walls, or as hand-transcribed copies. In the case of our glorious Shiva, a partly damaged inscription along the base moldings of

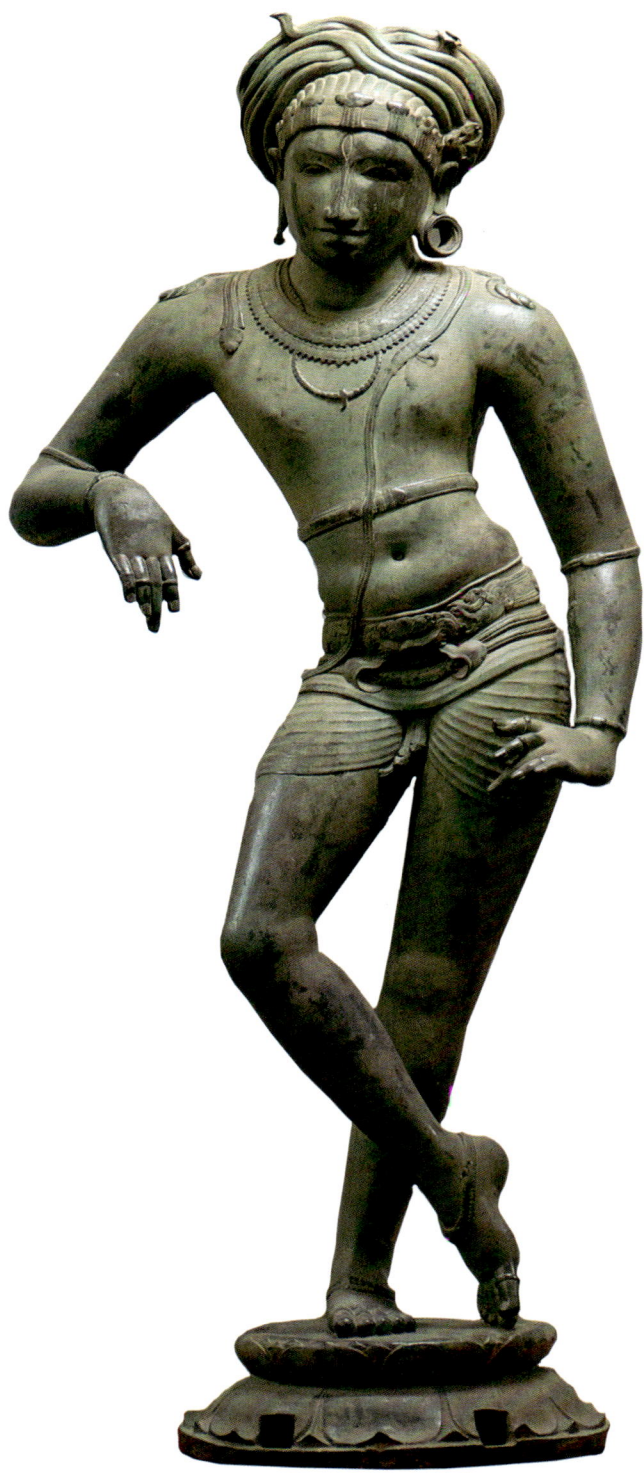
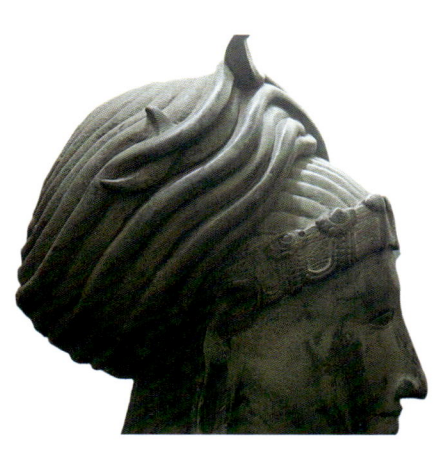

Figure 5.1. (a) Shiva with Bull (bull now missing), Tiruvenkadu temple, Nagapattinam district, 1011, Art Gallery, Thanjavur. (b) Detail of crescent moon in Shiva's locks, Shiva with Bull (fig. 5.1a). (c) Detail of Shiva with Bull (fig. 5.1a).

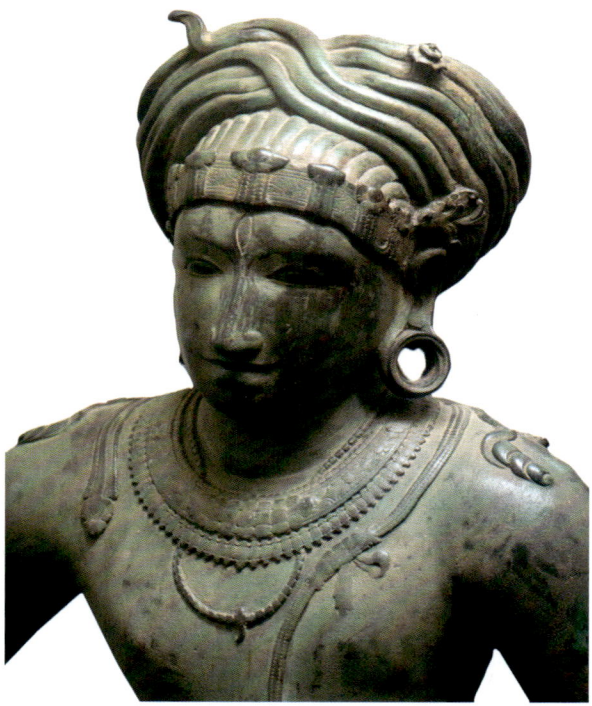

130   CHAPTER 5

the south wall of the central shrine, dated to the year 1011, informs us that this bronze was set up by a military chief (*nayaka*) who belonged to a select military regiment known by the name of emperor Rajaraja, who was also called Jananatha (people's leader) and who ruled from 985–1014. The donor, Kadamban Kolakkavan, came from the town of Kazhamulam, 8 miles from Tiruvenkadu.[4] The inscription further informs us that this military chief was now making a gift of jeweled ornaments to adorn his bronze, and it specifies that these ornaments were made with money from taxes collected by officials under the leadership of Kadamban Kolakkavan. Damage to the stone of the inscription deprives us of details about these jewels, but we may be sure they were sumptuous. This we will see when we turn, in the second half of this chapter, to the lavish gold jewelry set with gems that was given to adorn bronzes that are already richly adorned in the medium of bronze. Let me emphasize that this bronze masterpiece is not a royal commission, but a gift from an official of high stature who had the wherewithal to commission an image from the Tiruvenkadu Master. Why did he choose to dedicate an image of Shiva with the bull? We know from several finely crafted surviving images that this form of Shiva appears to have been popular during early Chola rule. An inscription in the Punjai temple, dated in the year 1026 during the reign of Rajendra, provides information that suggests that worship of Shiva with the bull was believed to confer victory on the king's army. The Punjai record speaks of an agreement made by the local assembly to pay taxes on lands owned by the temple, so that they could celebrate the daily worship of Shiva as Lord with the bull (*Rishabhavahana Devar*), as well as a special annual festival dedicated to Shiva with the bull that was held in order to secure the monarch's victory (*sribhujangal varddhitarula vendum enru*).[5]

The companion image of Uma, who always accompanies Lord Shiva, stands in serene elegance just over 3 feet tall (fig. 5.2). Gracefully poised in a triple-bend contrapposto, her oval face with its diadem is topped with a tall conical crown, while at the rear is a small "circle of glory." Her long skirt clings to her legs and is slung way below the navel and held in place with belts ending in a decorative clasp. Part of the fabric of the wrap skirt is pulled into a pleated fold that rests along her left hip, while the other end of the fabric forms loops closely similar to those on Shiva's dhoti. Her slender torso, with its gently rounded breasts, is adorned with three necklaces, while a sacred thread snakes its way between her breasts. She wears elaborate armlets whose design resembles the decorative motif on her crown, a simple elbow band, a cluster of bangles, and rings on eight fingers. The distinctive treatment of the hands, the ringed fingers, and the gently rounded fingernails are among the signature touches of our Master (fig. 5.2).

Intriguing information about the joint donation of this copper image of goddess Uma to accompany Shiva as Lord with the bull is contained in an inscription dated to the year 1012 engraved along the north wall of the central shrine. The gift was coordinated by a certain lord Sarpan, headman of Andanur, who was also accountant and chief supervisor and, like the donor of the Shiva bronze, belonged to the select military regiment of Rajaraja Jananatha. Lord Sarpan ensured that eleven other individuals contributed their share toward the expenses involved in commissioning the image of Uma, and also an image of the bull, to accompany the Shiva bronze created the previous year. The inscription is damaged along its central segment; yet, with its repetitive use of an ending

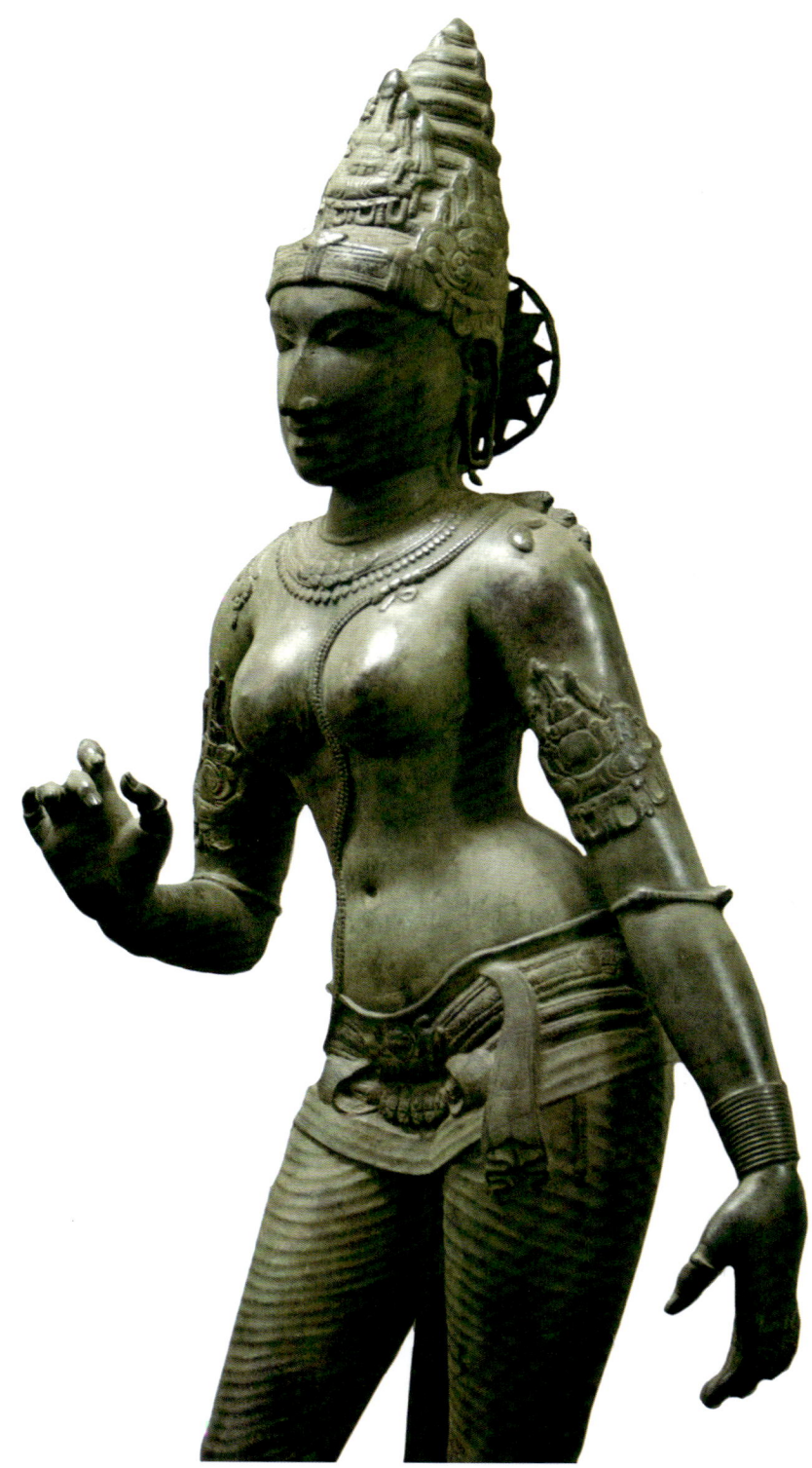

Figure 5.2. Uma as Consort of Shiva with Bull, Tiruvenkadu temple, Nagapattinam district, 1012, Art Gallery, Thanjavur.

to each name that corresponds to "also," it clearly indicates that a varied group of eleven individuals pooled their money to commission the bronze of the goddess, and the bull for Shiva, thus completing this important commission.[6] Immediately thereafter, in the same year of 1012, chieftain Sundara Cholan from the Vel family of Kodumbalur donated a three-stringed gold chain for this image of Uma, as well as a gold flower to be placed on the knotted locks of Shiva when the bronze lord "took pleasure in his sacred bath," a reference to the ritual bathing of the bronze. This chieftain donor, whose inscription is placed on the same north wall of the shrine, informs us that he is the son of Siriya Velan, who lost his life in a battle against Sri Lanka in the year 960.[7]

There has been a tendency to assume that the finest works of art owe their origin to royal sponsorship—an all too easy assumption.[8] But frequently, as with the evocative bronzes we are examining, this proves not to be the case. Equally, we find that the size of a bronze had little to do with the stature of its donor. A bronze of Shiva with the bull commissioned by Rajaraja's queen Cholamahadevi for the royal temple at Thanjavur was only half the size of this Tiruvenkadu masterpiece from a military commander.[9] Widely acknowledged as representing the very finest of Chola bronzes, this Tiruvenkadu image was among the works of art displayed at the National Gallery in the 1985 *Sculpture of India* exhibition, and the catalogue featured the enchanting form of god Shiva, in front and rear views as its front and rear covers.[10] Commissioned over one thousand years ago for a Shiva temple in coastal Tiruvenkadu, these bronzes are part of a treasure trove unearthed from erstwhile temple land. Their striking green patina testifies to their long-time burial underground, a mystery that we will set aside to unravel in chapter 9.

The superb artistry of our master sculptor is seen also in the sensitive four-piece bronze group representing the divine marriage of Shiva and Uma that we considered in our introduction to the art of the Chola bronze.[11] Standing to the far right is god Vishnu, present here in his role as Uma's brother, a unique relationship celebrated only in south India and unknown in the north of the subcontinent; Vishnu's consort, Lakshmi, positioned to the far left, acts as Uma's friend and confidante. A couple of comments from that introduction bear repetition in the context of the Tiruvenkadu Master. Notice the sensitive manner in which the Master has positioned the shy bride Uma to stand hesitantly with shoulders curving inward, a few steps behind the confident bridegroom (fig. 5.3). Bride Uma presents a noticeable contrast to the confident consort Uma who accompanies Shiva with the bull. And consider the empathy displayed by the Master in his portrayal of the confidante's understanding of the bride's diffidence, as she uses both her hands to gently urge Uma to move closer to Shiva. Together with the lotus base and lower pedestal, bridegroom Shiva and Uma (*Kalyanasundarar*) would have been the same size as Shiva with the bull (*Rishabhavahana Devar*) and his consort. Both sets of images created by the Master would have stood over 4 feet tall together with their now missing lower rectangular pedestal and, when carried in procession through temple and town, their imposing size and grandeur would indeed have struck wondrous reverence into devotees.

From the hands of our Master Sculptor come three more images of god Shiva that, together with lotus base and pedestal, would also have stood around 4 feet high. Shiva as Enchanting Mendicant is a form truly beloved of Shiva devotees in Tamil Nadu, and the

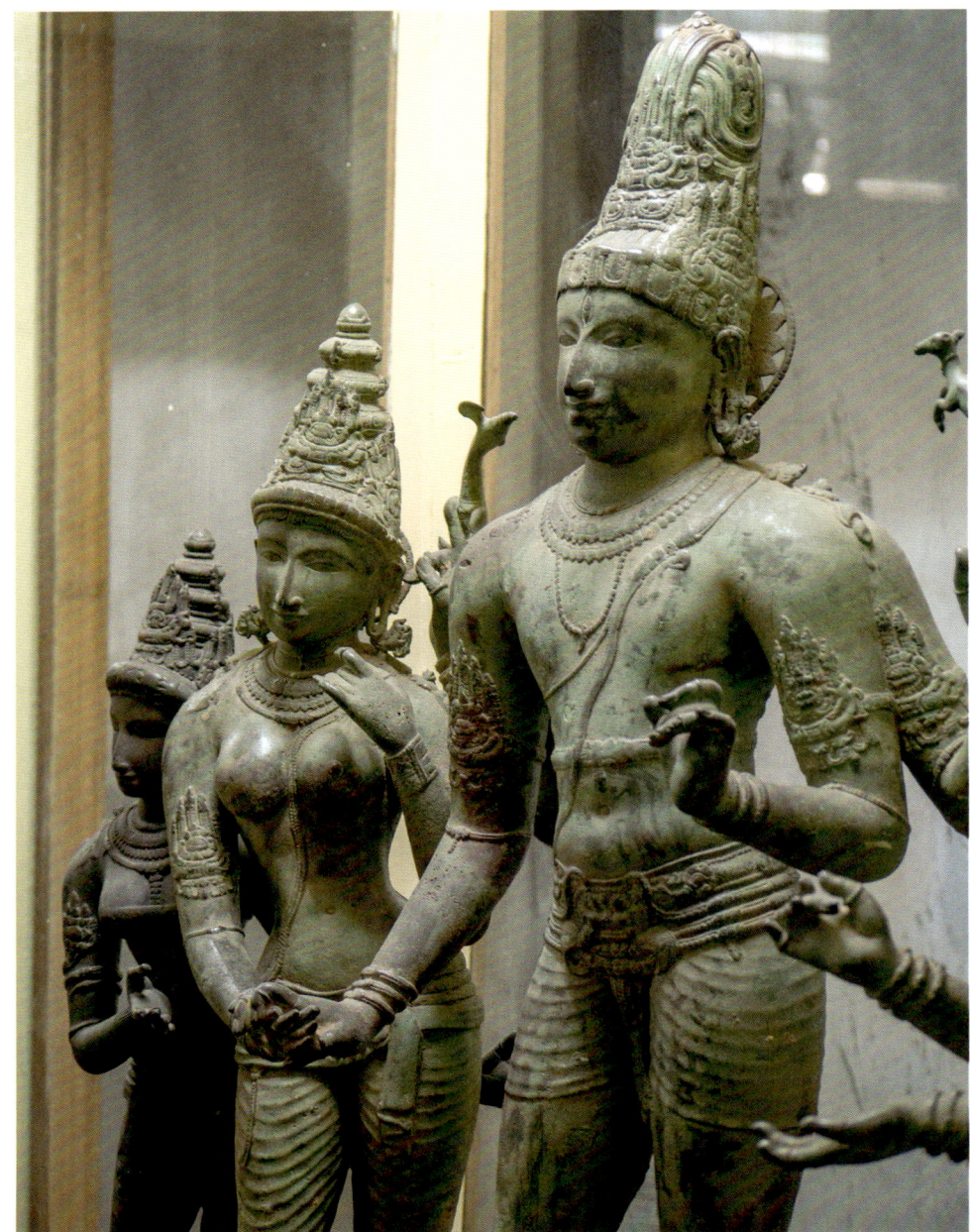

Figure 5.3. Detail of Marriage of Shiva and Uma (*Kalyanasundarar*) (see fig. 0.1).

Tiruvenkadu Master's exhilarating yet subtle treatment of the naked beggar is profoundly haunting (fig. 5.4a). In this manifestation, Shiva wandered the Tamil country, walking in wooden clogs from village to village and home to home, accompanied by his pet antelope, and seeking food in the alms bowl he holds in his left hand. The Tamil saints sang of the inexpressible radiance of this form of Shiva, whom they addressed simply as Begging Lord, or *Pichcha Devar*, and they described how the women of every household were hopelessly enamored of him. Saint Sundarar sang eloquently of this paradoxical, even eccentric form of Shiva, placing each verse on the lips of a different woman who came to give him alms. One such verse reads:

> *What strange attire is this of yours?*
> *The music of the Tamil tongue adorns your speech*
> *meanwhile, the serpent dances on your hand*
> *we bring you alms—*
> *but how to give it to you when your serpent hisses?*
> *Pray tell us, Handsome One of the Forests*
> *does not the radiance of your form*
> *mock the glory of the setting sun?*[12]

The conversational language used by the saints in a large number of their hymns is both unexpected and disarming. The women address Shiva in common everyday parlance and not in high-flown literary language: the wording they use is simple, "When you come for alms, lord, don't have your serpent on your hand!" (*balikki neer varum podu, un kaiyil pambu vendam piranire!*).

A hymn by saint Appar highlights dramatically the spell cast by the Begging Lord over the women who encounter him. A woman says to her companion:

> *Listen, my friend*
> *yesterday in broad daylight*
> *I'm sure I saw that Holy One.*
> *As he gazed at me, my garments slipped*
> *I stood entranced.*
> *I brought him alms*
> *but nowhere did I see that Cunning One—*
> *If I see him again*
> *I shall press my body against his body*
> *never let him go*
> *that wanderer who lives in Ottriyur.*[13]

In the Tiruvenkadu bronze, Shiva's torso is adorned with three simple necklaces, a sacred thread that divides into two strings, and a waistband, while an armlet, elbow band, bangles, and rings on sixteen fingers adorn his four hands. His pet cobra wraps itself about his hips as if to serve as loin cloth but, as saint Sambandar playfully sang, the serpent has a mind of its own and fully reveals Shiva's naked form (fig. 5.4b).

> *With perfect touch*
> *he tied*
> *upon his waist*
> *the angry hissing serpent,*
> *to serve in place of loincloth*
> *as only he could do.*[14]

A tiny detail we could easily miss, but one that the master sculptor took pains to portray, is the forked tongue of the serpent that is visible when viewed from a slight angle (fig.

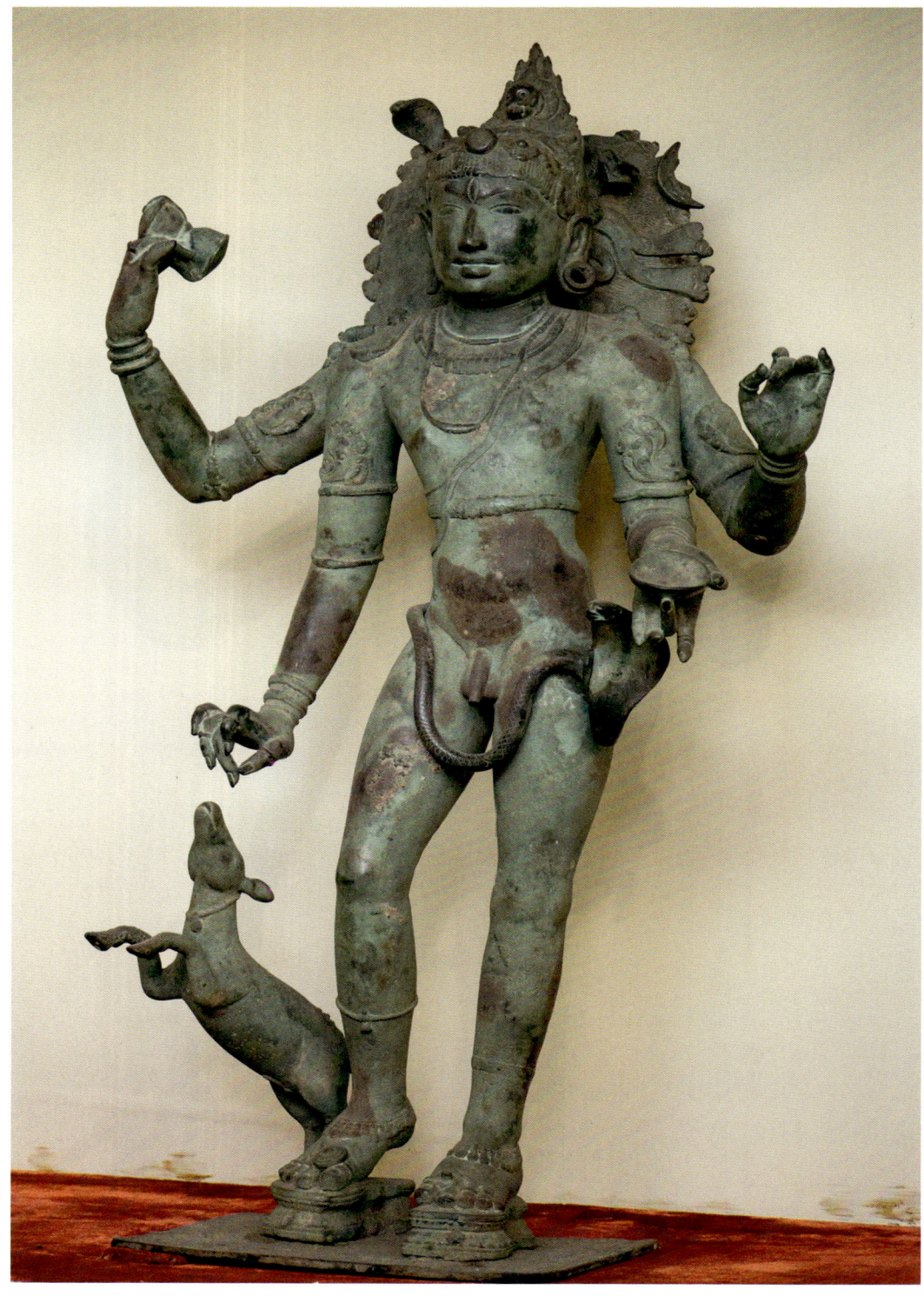

Figure 5.4. (a) Shiva as Begging Lord, Tiruvenkadu temple, Nagapattinam district, eleventh century, Art Gallery, Thanjavur.

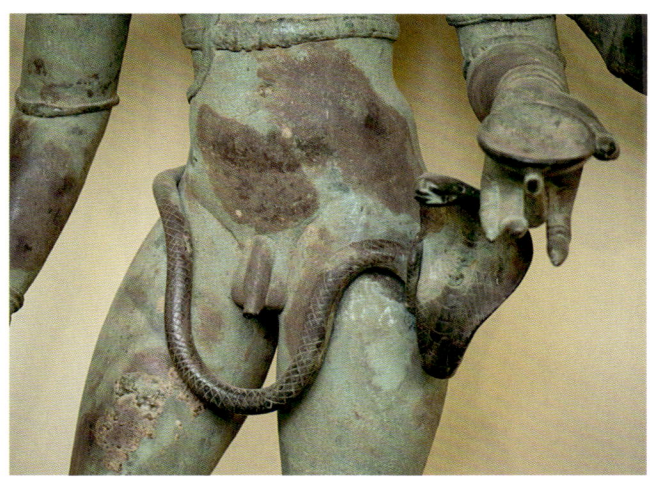
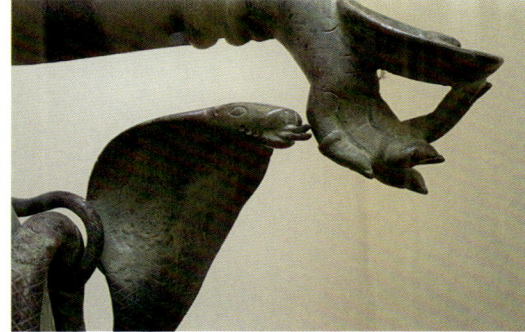

(b–d) Details of Shiva as Begging Lord (fig. 5.4a).

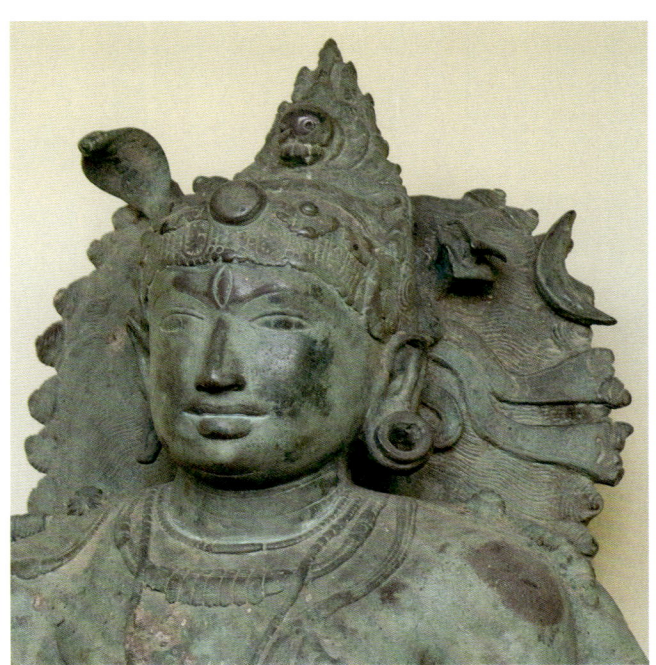
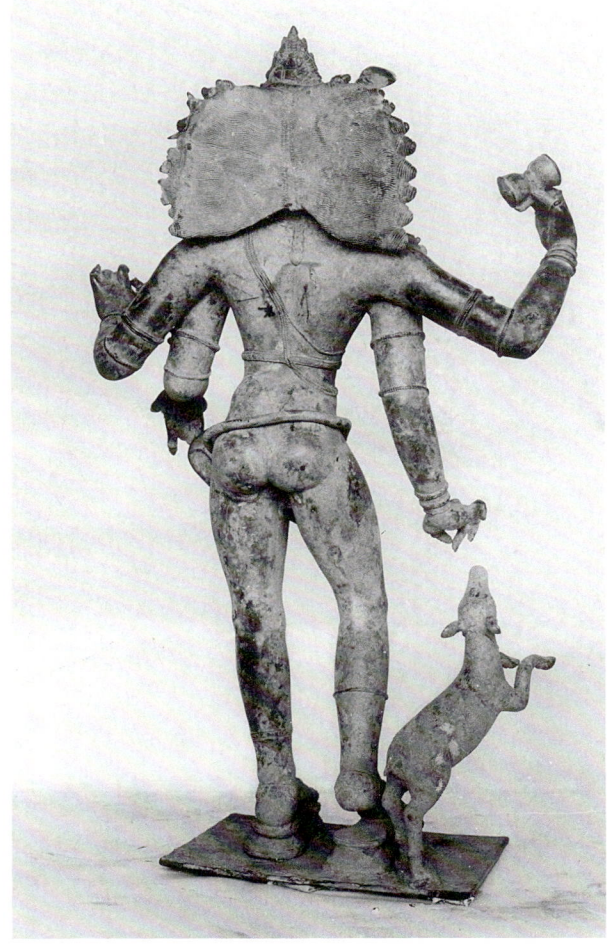

(e) Rear view of Shiva as Begging Lord (fig. 5.4a).

TIRUVENKADU MASTER

5.4c), though only to the close looker! Any biblical associations of the serpent with temptation, or the Western concept of a forked tongue as duplicitous speech, must be set aside. Such connotations are unknown in India, where the cobra is highly revered as Shiva's pet companion, and admired by one and all, and where no one will undertake to kill a cobra. I cite the attention paid to delineating the fork of the cobra's tongue purely as an example of the Master's painstaking attention to detail.

Shiva's matted locks, which splay out in halo-like formation around his head in this manifestation, are partially held back by his diadem, whose knotted bands are seen to the viewers' right. Emerging from the locks are the serpent, the crescent moon, and trumpet flower, while a human skull with inset silver eye sockets adorns the centrally upswept locks (fig. 5.4d). The sensitive and delicate treatment of the fingers that curve in pliant gestures, and the attention to fingernails, are hallmarks of the Tiruvenkadu master. The sensuous nature of the tight, rounded buttocks of the Begging Lord add to the charm of this invigorating and stimulating image created in the years following the Shiva and Uma of 1011 and 1012 (fig. 5.4e).

Two lengthy inscriptions in the temple, carved along the base moldings and running around the south, west, and north sides of the central shrine, both dated to the reign of Rajadhiraja, one to the year 1046 and the other to 1048, speak of several gifts relating to the image of the Begging Lord. The inscription of 1048 explains that Amalan Sheyyavayar, who had previously dedicated the image of the Begging Lord to this temple (*munbu ikkoyilil ezhundarulivitta*), was now donating land to meet the regular expenses for worship of his bronze image,[15] making it clear that the bronze was dedicated some time prior to the date of the inscription. The inscription of 1046 lists jewels given to adorn the Begging Lord. While jewelry to adorn a bronze is normally given soon after a bronze is dedicated to a temple, a close reading of the inscription clarifies that the donor Amalan was now making a series of new donations of jeweled items to ensure and raise the visibility of his earlier dedication.[16] To achieve this, Amalan combined a range of his earlier donations to create a dramatic and more impressive series of ornaments of gold and precious stones for his Begging Lord. The list is extensive and includes gold to increase the size of a previously made gold snake (*munbu sheyda pambu perisheyya pon*), presumably one that would wrap around Shiva's hips like the bronze serpent. Newly made gifts include jeweled covers for Shiva's hands and feet; a gold three-string necklace; a gold sacred thread; a "choker"-style gold neckband; a pearl nose-ring, a pearl sacred thread; a low-hanging waistband; a gold skull cup; a gold pot; a gold pedestal studded with diamonds, rubies, pearls, and corals; and twelve gold flowers.[17] A final gift of an aureole, made with 888 *kalanju* of gold and studded with gemstones, came jointly from Amalan and a lady who supervised the temple's sacred kitchen; their relationship is not specified.[18]

The inscription of 1048 also lists the construction of a hall for feeding brahmins in the name of the Begging Lord; the replating with gold of the roof of the shrine of the Begging Lord; gold and silver plates for offering food to the Begging Lord; a fly-whisk whose handle was studded with pearls and blue stones; and ornaments to adorn the *tiruvatchi* aureole that framed the bronze but is missing today. A few gifts from other donors are also listed in these two inscriptions. They include two rings for the Begging

Lord from two devotees, a gold string of *rudraksha* beads from a chieftain, Vanavan Pallavaraiyan, and the gold plating of the roof of the dance hall and its further adornment by a brahmin general named Karikala Kanna Brahmadhirayan.[19]

Another powerful creation of the Master is a riveting image of Shiva as Half Woman (*Ardhanari*), in which Shiva takes his consort Uma's body as one half of himself (fig. 5.5a, b). India's myths provide various explanations of the manifestation; here, I will say only that this androgynous form may indeed be read as an affirmation that the godhead is both male and female. Divided vertically down the middle into a female half with a single arm to the proper left, and a male half with two arms to the proper right, this bronze adopts a more exaggerated triple bend contrapposto than the Master's other images. If we compare it with the Master's Shiva from the Marriage group, we appreciate how subtly he has here expressed the distinctions between the male and female halves, quite apart from the obvious distinction of the breast and the considerably indented curve of waist and hip on the female side that contrasts with the straighter lines of the male body (fig. 5c). He featured a broader jawline and matted locks for the male half versus the softly curved jawline of the female and her jeweled crown, as well as a broader shoulder on the male side compared to the softer curve on the female side.

Who was responsible for commissioning this spectacular creation by the Tiruvenkadu Master? A lengthy inscription of forty-four lines inscribed on the west wall of the central shrine and dated to the reign of Rajadhiraja in the year 1047 seems devoted entirely to lands donated by the Chola king for various purposes, together with extensive details on the boundaries of each piece of property. Working patiently through the record leads to the woman who donated this bronze to the temple. In line 35, the subject matter changes and we find the king making arrangements for the daily worship of the image of Shiva as Half Woman that had been installed in the temple; it is only in line 42 that we finally encounter the donor, a lady named Tuppayan Uttamacholi.[20] To ensure worship of the image for posterity, the king ceded to the temple all taxes from a specified piece of agricultural land, exempting from the gift those lands occupied by the temple to the goddess Kali, the temple tank, and the tank that provided drinking water. The inscription specifies that from Rajadhiraja's twenty-ninth regnal year onward, and annually for ever after, this tax was to go toward the ritual worship of this bronze, further adding that the gift had been recorded as such in the tax register (*variyilittu koduttadu*). Why would the king take so deep an interest in providing for the image installed by Uttamacholi? It seems that she may have been his *bhogiyar*, or concubine, or more likely his *anukkiyar*, a more intimate relationship as mistress. Uttamacholi certainly commissioned the most accomplished Master of the day, who, doubtless, was suitably rewarded for his stunning bronze.

A final image of Shiva that I'd like to introduce here is the Master's portrayal of the fearsome form of the god as Bhairava. Eight-armed Shiva, 42 1/2 inches tall and thus of the same size as Shiva as lord with the bull, stands bolt upright with both feet planted firmly on the ground in a posture that suggests his forbidding nature as a god whom the devotee should not approach lightly (fig. 5.6). Shiva Bhairava's hair is arranged around his head to create an oval flame-like formation, with two serpents coiled in the hair, which is further adorned with a human skull and Shiva's crescent moon. Ferociously

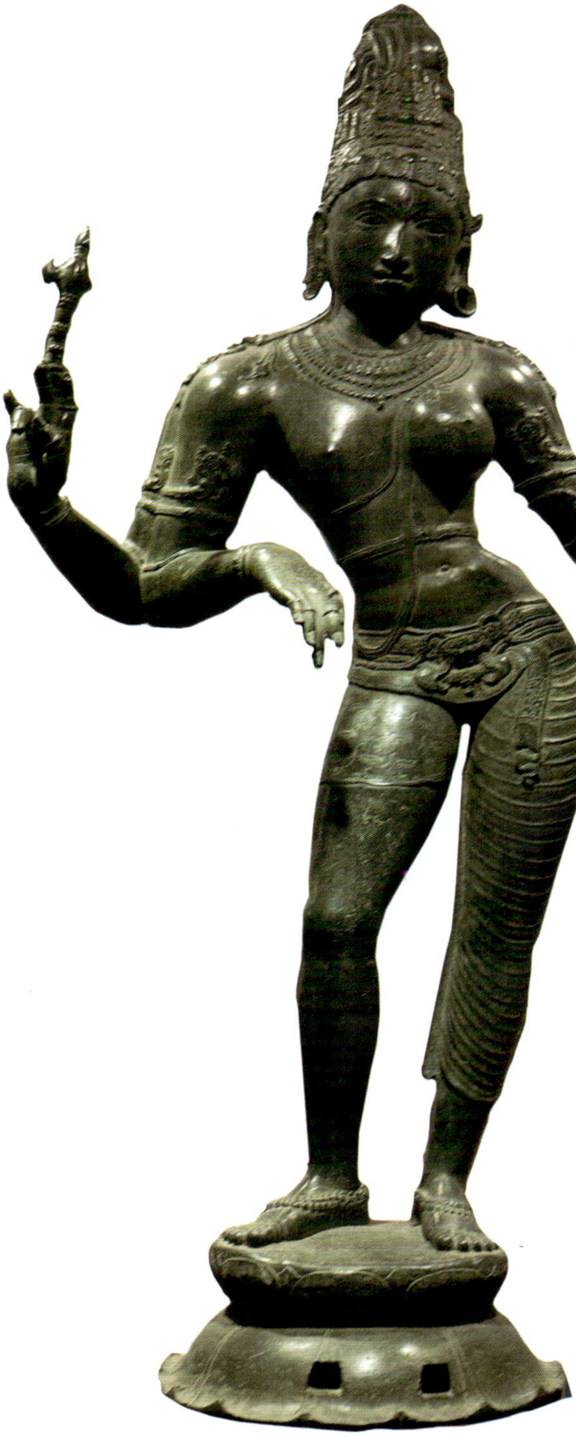

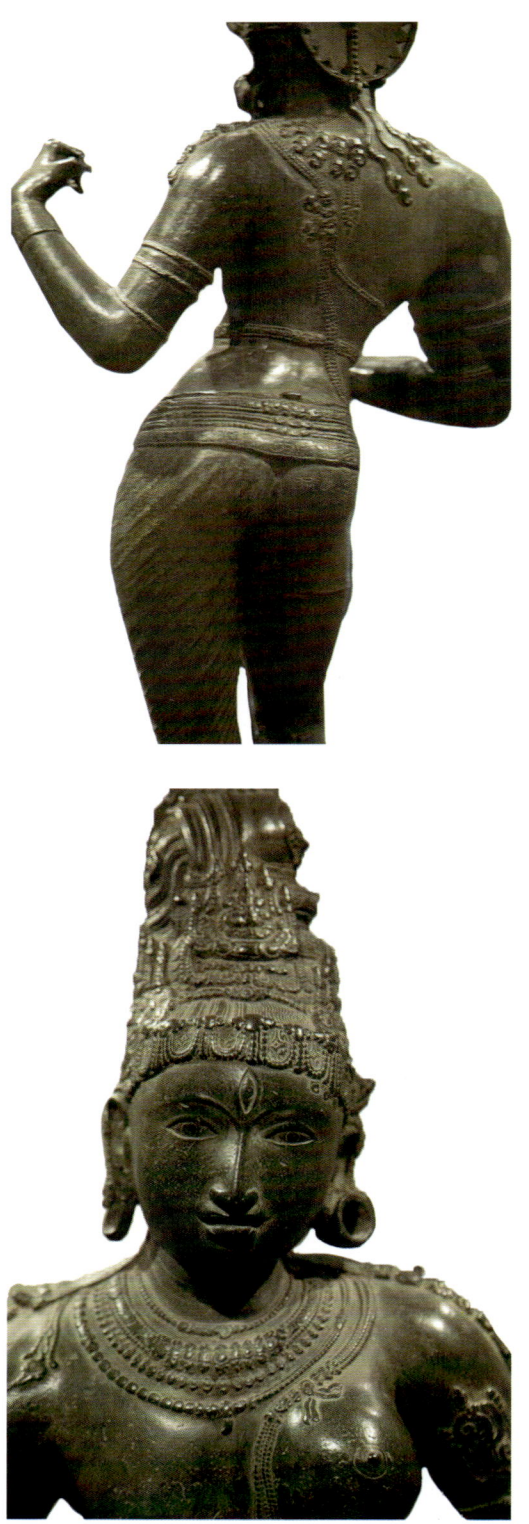

Figure 5.5. (a) Shiva as Half Woman, Tiruvenkadu temple, Nagapattinam district, ca. 1015–1020, Government Museum, Chennai. (b) Rear view of Shiva as Half Woman (fig. 5.5a). (c) Detail of Shiva as Half Woman (fig. 5.5a).

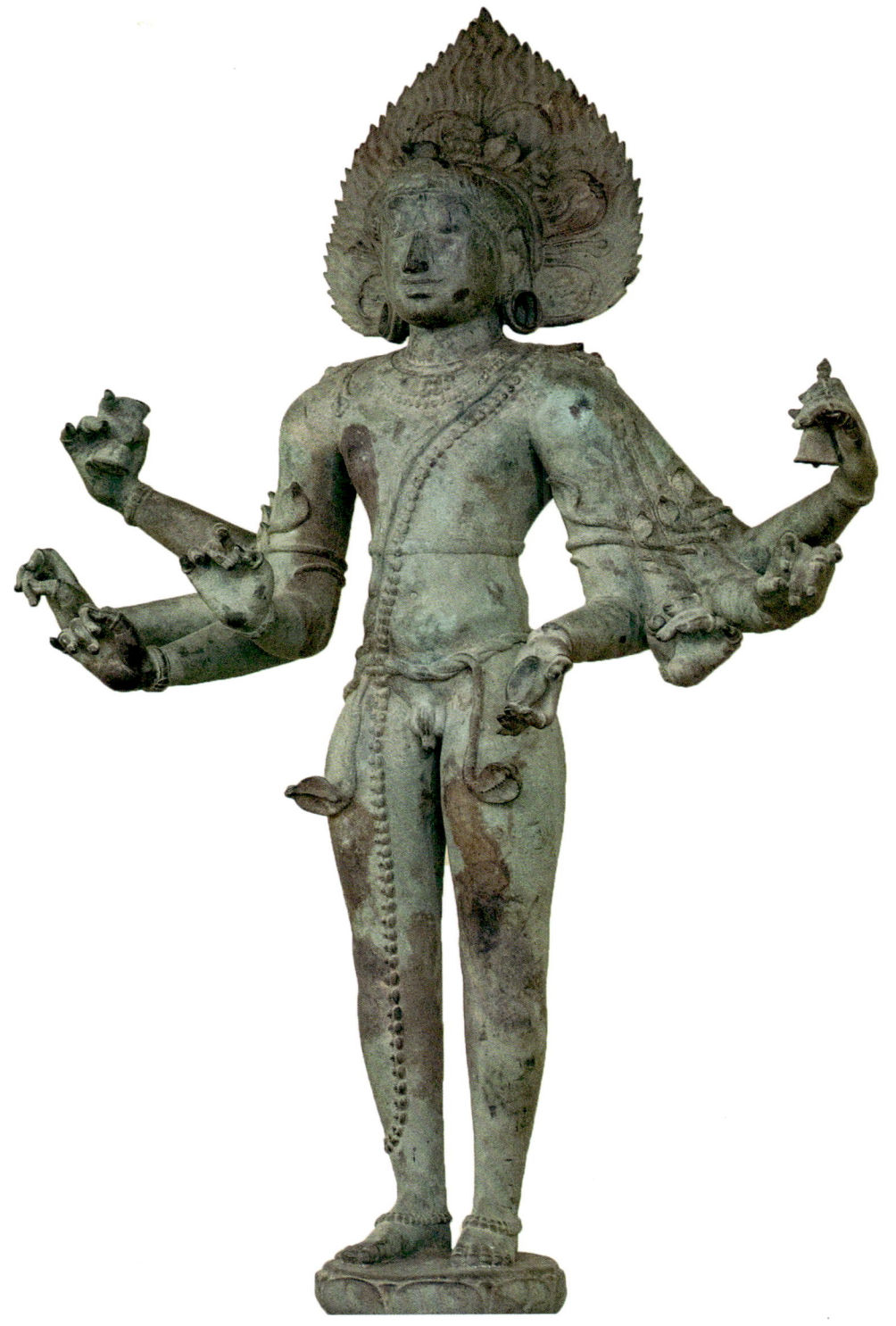

Figure 5.6. Shiva as Bhairava, Tiruvenkadu temple, Nagapattinam district, ca. 1010, Art Gallery, Thanjavur.

curved eyebrows, and fangs at either end of his mouth, emphasize his fierce nature. Each of his eight arms, arranged in perfect balance on both sides, are encircled with snake-armlets, while his hands, some in casual gestures, hold a skull-cup (*kapalam*), a bell, and a drum. Shiva's naked form is adorned with three necklaces, a high waistband, simple bracelets, bone anklets, a serpent knotted around his hips as a loin cloth, entwined serpents as sacred thread, and a long chain of skulls that extends down to his proper right ankle. An inscription of queen Cholamahadevi, wife of Rajaraja, dated to the year 1005 speaks of her gift of a gold skull-cup to the lord of the Tiruvenkadu temple.[21] If the queen's gift was to this bronze of Shiva as Bhairava, it is possible that this image is one of the Master's first creations.[22]

The Tiruvenkadu Master created not just images of the gods but also those of the saints. An unusual creation is the Master's portrayal of saint Kanappan, bearded, mustached, and wearing strapped sandals, a simple hunter who was single-minded in his devotion to god Shiva, and unaware of social taboos (fig. 5.7a). His story tells us that since he felt Shiva would be hungry, Kanappan took him raw pork from the wild boar he had just hunted; since Shiva would be thirsty after the meal, and since his own hands were filled with pork, he carried water for Shiva in his own mouth. And when the eye on the linga emblem of Shiva began to tear—Shiva was testing him—he plucked out his own eye to replace it. Our Master has portrayed the empty eye socket of Kanappan (literally "he of the eyes") and simultaneously shown us the extracted eyeball that the saint offers in his right palm to god Shiva (fig. 5.7b). No other portrayal of this saint has captured so effectively, in a single image, the magnitude of the hunter's gift. The Master abandoned his usual sensitive rendering of elegant fingers and delicate fingernails in favor of gnarled fingers and stubby fingernails that befit a forest dweller and hunter.

Noteworthy too is the Master's portrayal of devotees, whether it be his 20-inch-high bronze of a dedicated young novice, or a slightly taller (26-inch) pot-bellied brahmin general, a Brahmadhirayan (fig. 5.8a, b). The latter would be similar in status to Rajaraja's brahmin general at Thanjavur, whom we will encounter shortly as the donor of a bronze of Shiva as Half Woman, to whom he also gifted several items of jewelry.

The Tiruvenkadu Workshop: The Next Generation, ca. 1050 Onward

The workshop established by the Tiruvenkadu Master undoubtedly attracted donors who were willing to pay steep prices for the very best work; but it also drew wax modelers who wished to benefit from the reputation of the workshop, to watch its accomplished Master model images in wax, and perhaps even have the opportunity to apprentice with him. One such sculptor, undoubtedly aiming to strive for a high level of perfection, created a couple that features saint Sundarar and his wife Paravai that is roughly the same size as the Master's five bronzes of Shiva that we just examined. Sundarar, whose name means "handsome one," stands relaxed, 33 inches high, with his upraised elbow poised to rest gently against the shoulder of his wife, who stands 7 inches shorter (fig. 5.9a, b). Both saint and his wife are richly adorned and stand in elegant contrapposto. Their expertly modeled chignons distinguish them from divine figures, who

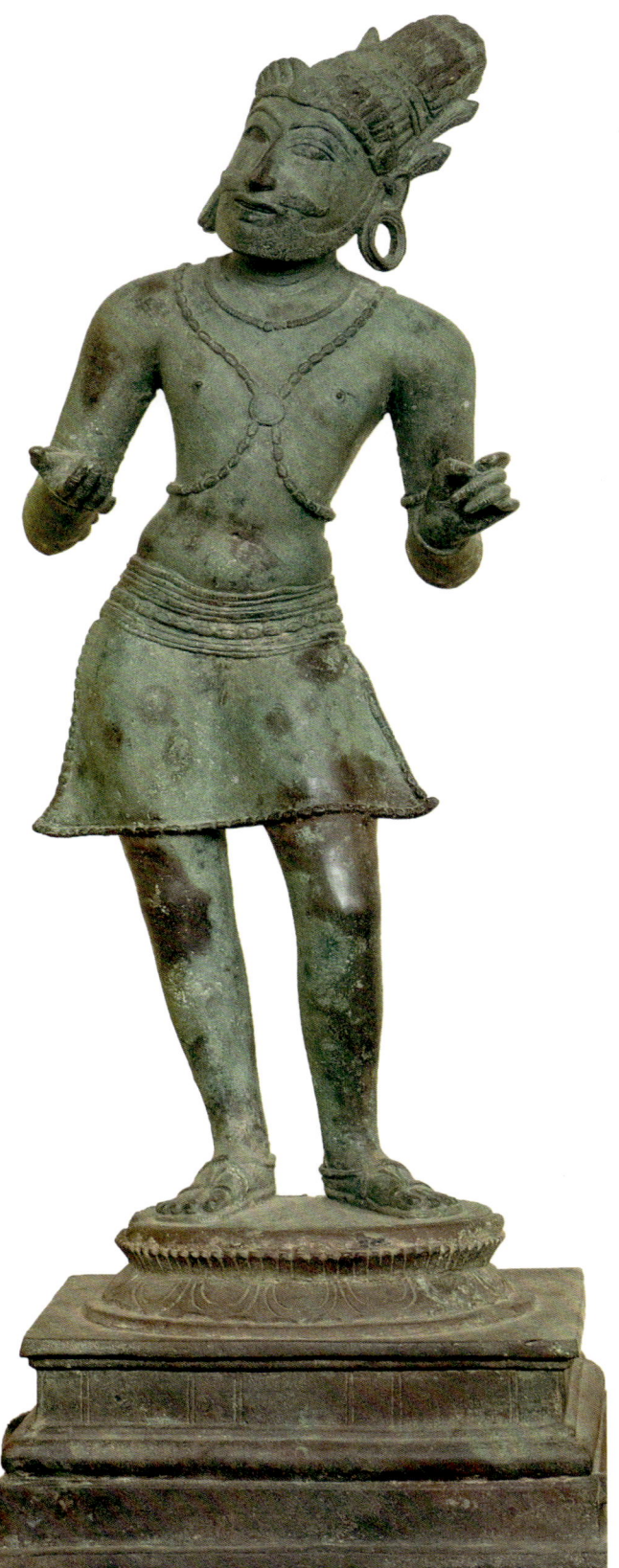
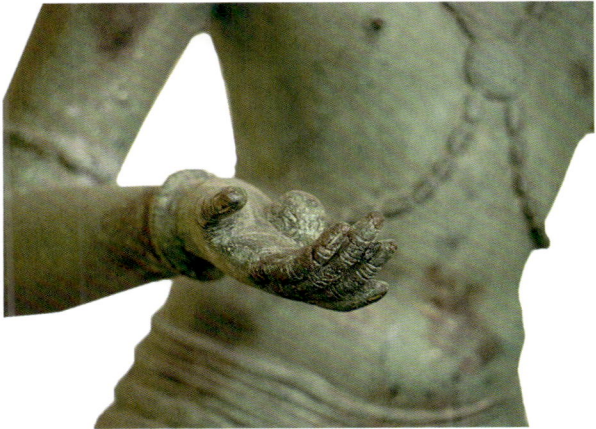

Figure 5.7. (a) Saint Kanappan, Tiruvenkadu temple, Nagapattinam district, ca. 1020, Art Gallery, Thanjavur. (b) Detail of Saint Kanappan (fig. 5.7a).

TIRUVENKADU MASTER

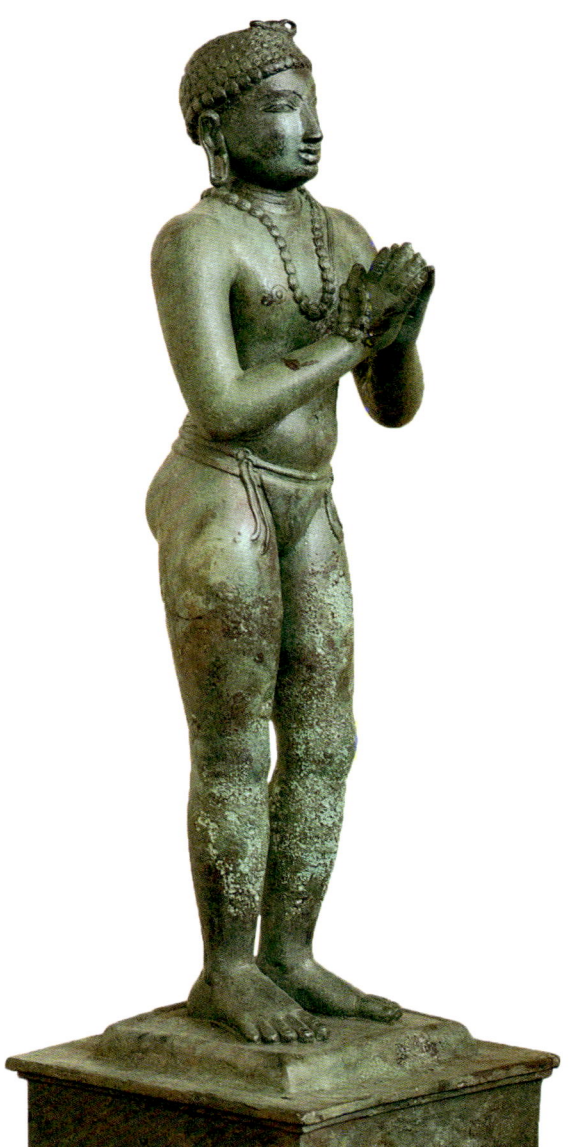
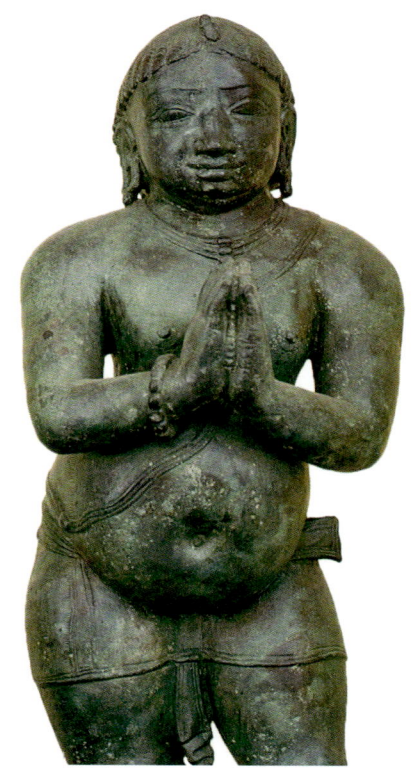

Figure 5.8. (a) Novice Devotee, Tiruvenkadu temple, Nagapattinam district, ca. 1020, Art Gallery, Thanjavur. (b) Devotee Brahmadhirayan, Tiruvenkadu temple, Nagapattinam district, ca. 1020, Art Gallery, Thanjavur.

generally wear crowns; Sundarar's chignon is a large oval twisted knot, while Paravai's is an elaborate circular arrangement with ringlet curls framing her face. Pointing to the inspiration of the Master's work is the poised stance, the treatment of ornamentation, the elegant fingers and fingernails, and the hint of a smile on their lips (fig. 5.9c). But the artist also introduced a new detail of drapery that was to become typical of this workshop well into the twelfth century. As part of the folded and pleated fabric of Paravai's skirt, we now see, against the inner side of both thighs, an upper loop and a lower ornamental strip that become even more stylized in the next century, as we shall see in chapter 7. It seems to be a new introduction of this next generation at Tiruvenkadu.

A second commission from an artist of this next generation is a threesome group featuring god Subrahmanya, younger son of Shiva and Uma, flanked by his two consorts (fig. 5.10). This is superior work in the tradition of the Tiruvenkadu workshop, but it lacks

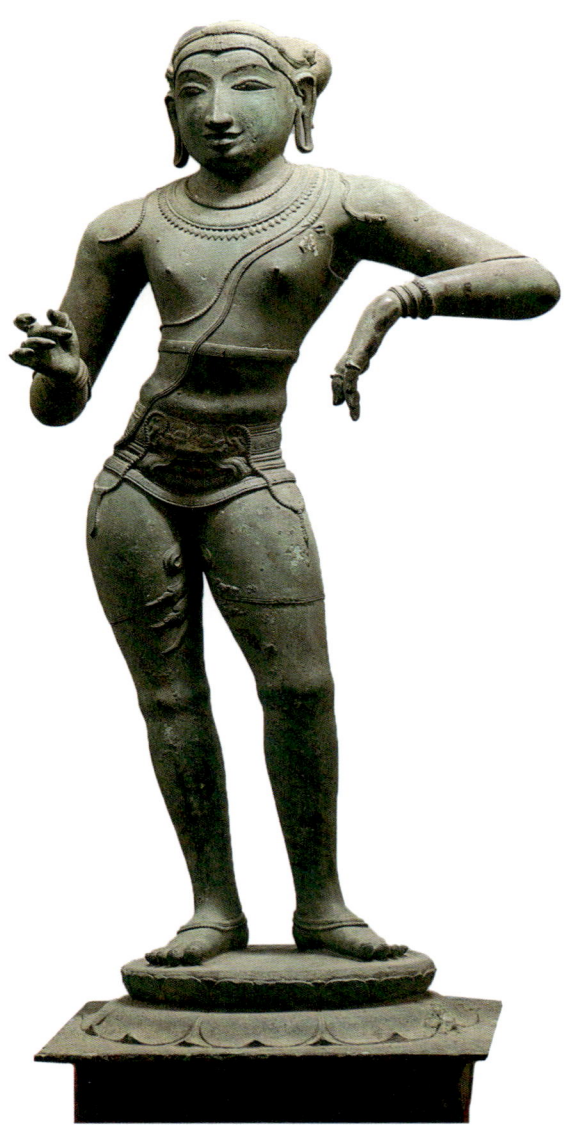
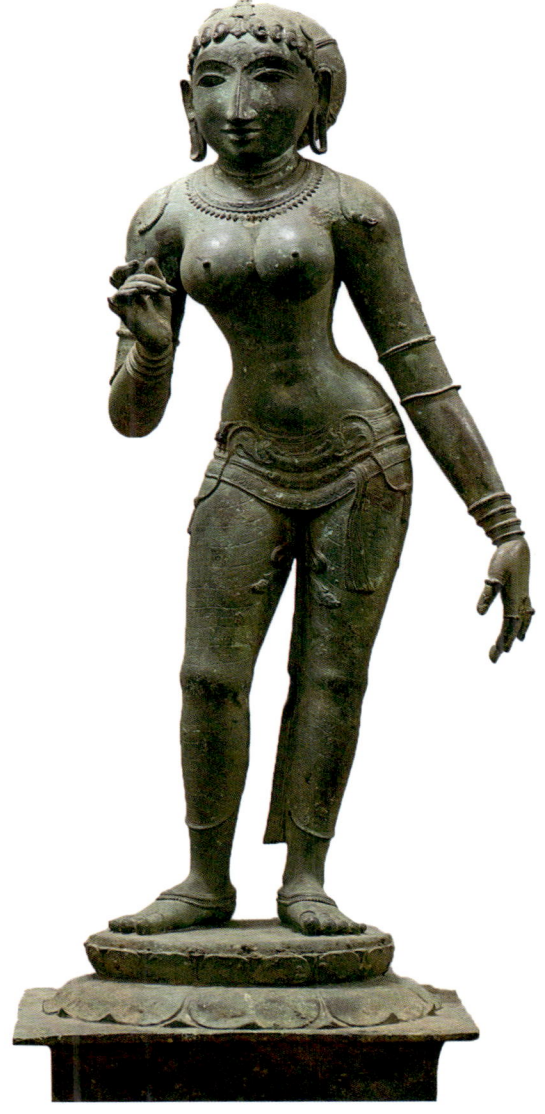
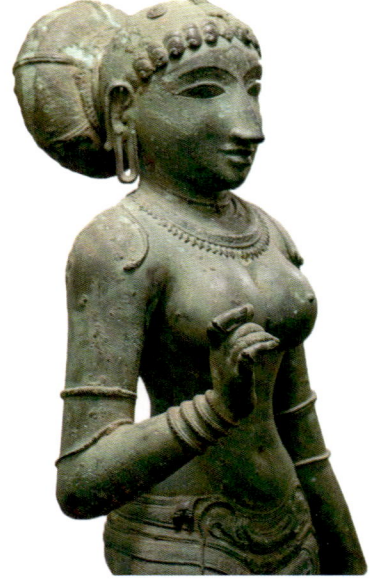

Figure 5.9. (a and b) Saint Sundarar and Wife Paravai, Tiruvenkadu temple, Nagapattinam district, ca. 1050, Art Gallery, Thanjavur. (c) Detail of Paravai, Saint Sundarar and Wife Paravai (fig. 5.9a,b).

TIRUVENKADU MASTER

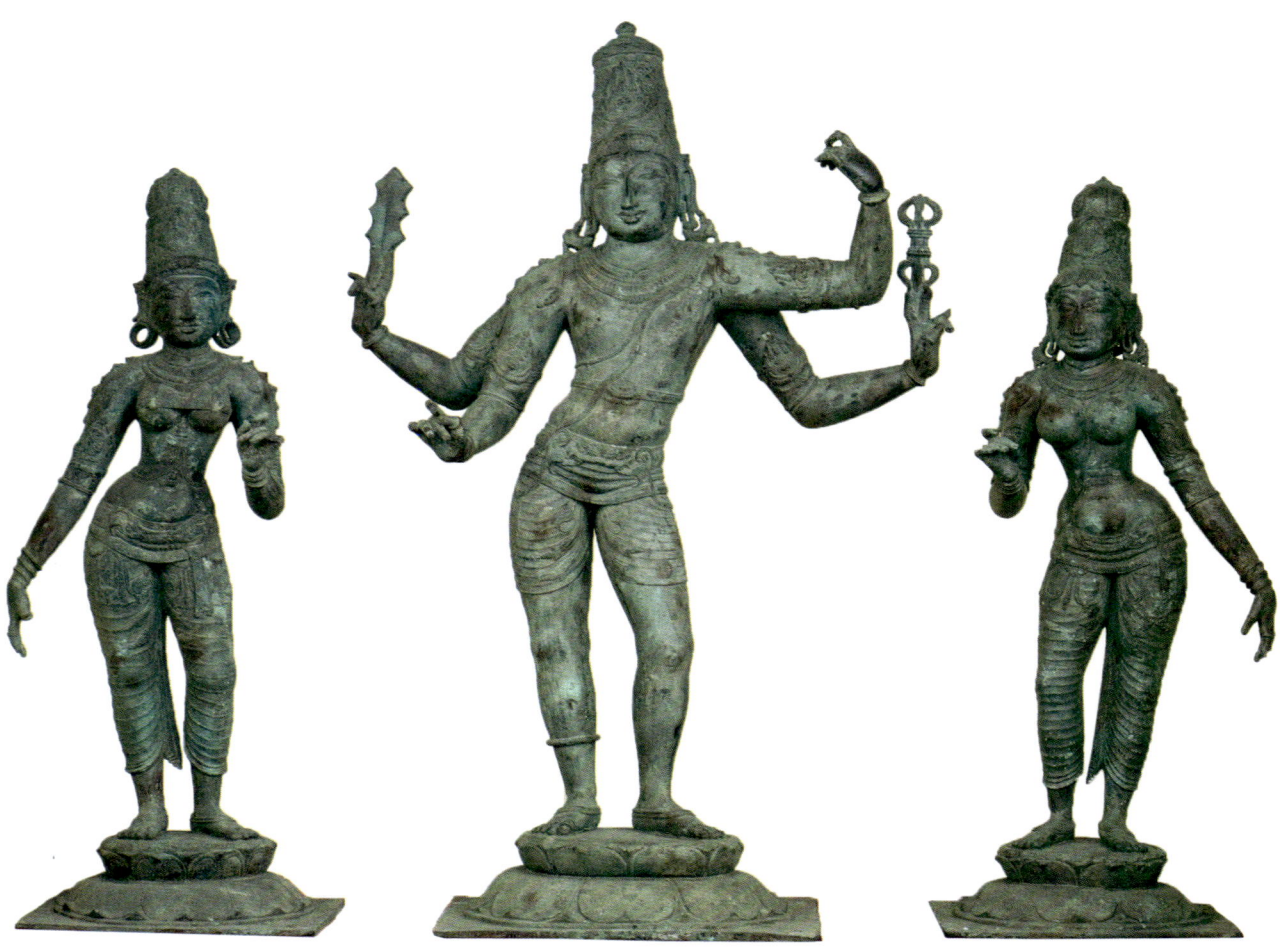

Figure 5.10. Subrahmanya and Consorts, Tiruvenkadu temple, Nagapattinam district, ca. 1050, Art Gallery, Thanjavur.

the vitality, the flair, the spark of our Master. The god stands 36.6 inches high—as imposing in size as the Master's Shiva with the bull—and his two consorts are but 6 inches shorter. Wearing a tall crown, the richly adorned four-armed god stands in graceful contrapposto, with weight resting on his right foot. The elegant flanking goddesses are posed almost as mirror images of each other, although they are distinguished by the fact that one wears a breastband, and that they wear different types of earrings. Note that resting along the inner thighs of both goddesses is an upper fabric loop and two lower stylized fabric bands that are typical of this slightly later phase. These are fine bronzes, following a bodily proportion and a decorative scheme similar to that of the Master. Yet the distinctions are striking. One need only compare the exquisite smile on the oval face of Shiva created by the Master with the somewhat flabby jawline on the Subrahmanya image modeled by the artist of the next generation (see fig. 5.1). A closely similar comment may be made about the images of Subrahmanya's two consorts as compared to the two Umas from the Master's hand (see figs. 0.1 and 5.2). The work of this particular artist is remarkably good, but it cannot match the Master's perfection, nor indeed is it of the caliber of the artist who modeled saint Sundarar and his wife Paravai.

Rajaraja's Great Temple and Its Daily and Festival Administration

The Master of Tiruvenkadu was active during the reign of Chola king Rajaraja who, in the year 985, inherited a small kingdom still centered on the delta of the Kaveri river. Born Arulmoli (He whose speech gives grace), queen Sembiyan's great-nephew was soon to transform the Cholas into a force to be reckoned with. As early as his third year, he adopted the title of Rajaraja, or King among Kings, indicating his future intentions.[23] Rajaraja battled with the Cheras and Pandyas who accepted his overlordship, and he assumed the title *Mummudi* or "Triple-crowned One (Chola, Chera, Pandya)." He then engaged in successful battle against the rulers of Sri Lanka, forcing them to retreat in disarray to the southernmost parts of their island. For a period of over seventy years, the larger part of Sri Lanka became a province of the Chola empire, sending tribute to Rajaraja's treasury and contributing supplies of rice and oil toward the operation of Rajaraja's Thanjavur temple. He also captured the many islands (*pannir ayiram*) of the Maldives that constituted a significant waystation along the silk route of the ocean to China.

Having established himself as a matchless warrior in battle, Rajaraja set out to prove that he was an unequaled devotee of Shiva and the foremost of temple patrons. At his capital of Thanjavur, he conceived and constructed a temple that was six times the size of any temple hitherto built along the river Kaveri, and taller than any temple yet built in any other part of India (see fig. 2.14). Known popularly as the Great Temple (Brihadishvara, literally [temple of] the Great Lord), the immensity of this ambitious venture can scarcely be overstated; his success in getting architects and sculptors to translate his lofty ambitions into a towering granite structure that reached 210 feet high speaks volumes for his determination and his drive. Rajaraja clearly wished to complement his military prowess with his status as an unparalleled leader in times of peace, a trailblazer who would make his subjects proud to be citizens of the Chola empire. He was driven, though we do not know what precisely drove him. Part of it surely relates to the definitive battle losses of the previous fifty years. Part may also be attributed perhaps to the inspiring example of his great-aunt, queen Sembiyan, who never allowed her mortifying personal circumstances, as they must have appeared to some, to limit her considerable achievements.

Like queen Sembiyan, Rajaraja too had this tremendous urge to record in stone, along the walls, base moldings, and pillars of his Great Temple, every detail of temple administration, and every gift made to the temple (fig. 5.11). A lengthy inscription on the walls of the shrine informs us of the king's order in 1011, the twenty-sixth year of his reign:

> *Let the gifts made by us, those made by our elder sister, those made by our wives, and those made by other donors to the lord of the sacred stone temple Sri Rajarajeshvara—which we caused to be built at Tanjavur, in Tanjavur-kurram, a subdivision of Pandyakulasani-valanadu—be engraved on stone of the sacred shrine.*[24]

Following in the footsteps of his great-aunt Sembiyan, Rajaraja too gave orders for at least one set of earlier inscriptions to be copied and reengraved on a newly renovated stone temple. We see this at Tirumalavadi in the Trichy district, where his royal order to reconstruct the *vimana* of the temple in stone is engraved on the south wall of the main

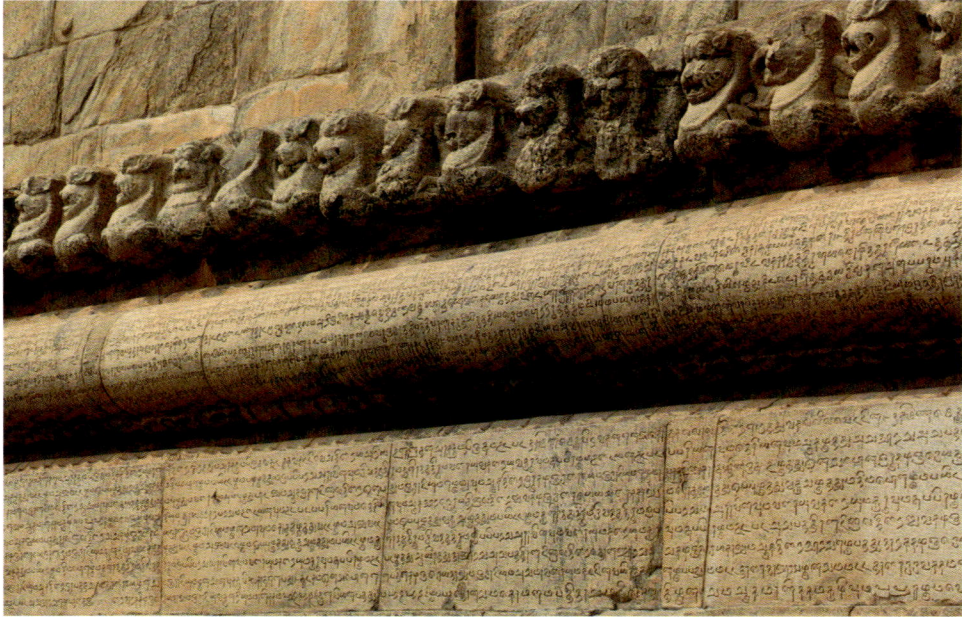

Figure 5.11. Inscriptions along base moldings, Rajaraja Chola's Great Temple, Thanjavur, ca. 1010.

shrine. It contains instructions to his officials to copy the earlier inscriptions on the *vimana* and to have them reengraved on the renovated temple.[25] An inscription of his son Rajendra, dated in his fourteenth year of 1026 and engraved on the same south wall, testifies to the fulfillment of this order. It speaks of work on the newly built *vimana* and records the order of Uttamachola Brahmamarayan, a *dandanayaka* (naval officer), to reengrave the old inscriptions found on the *vimana*.[26] Why this royal reconstruction of the *vimana* in stone should have taken a full thirteen years remains unclear.

The records on Rajaraja's Thanjavur temple provide information of a type unknown from anywhere else in India and, taken in their entirety, give us specifics about every aspect of temple administration. The many details provided by these inscriptions include the amounts of rice that each village within Rajaraja's empire had to contribute to the temple; the name of each village that provided either a temple watchman or a brahmin priest; the villages that had to supply cardamom pods, *champaka* buds, and the aromatic *khus-khus* root to perfume the bathing water of the bronzes; the number of goats or cows given to specific shepherds who contracted to provide ghee each day for burning the temple lamps. One extraordinary inscription lists the names and remuneration of 800 temple employees.[27] These included 400 dancing girls who were called upon to perform for the deity of the temple, with two supervisors appointed solely to oversee matters pertaining to them. There were twelve dance masters, forty-eight singers of the sacred hymns of the saints, three Ariyan (Sanskrit?) singers, four Tamil singers, sixty-six drummers, seven pipers, and several other musicians. Temple employees included four men whose job was to hold parasols over the bronze images when they participated in festivals; four men to keep the temple premises dust-free by sprinkling the grounds with water; eight men to light the temple's 152 lamps every evening; 141 watchmen in charge of temple security; and 174 priests to conduct temple ritual. Further catering to temple needs were eleven potters who supplied the temple kitchen, two washermen, two barbers, several tailors, and three carpenters. Jewel-stitchers contributed toward the adornment of the temple's sixty-six bronzes, and a superintending goldsmith served also as appraiser of jewels. Last, eleven chief accountants, aided by forty-one subaccountants, kept track of temple monies.

An aspect of daily ritual that has aroused little interest, but that I find fascinating, relates to Chola temple food; with the sensorium becoming a subfield of study, this focus on taste may be of interest to many. In temples across Chola territory, endowments were made to provide food offerings to the many bronzes that every temple housed. Sacred food (*tiru amudu*—literally, "sacred nectar") was prepared in the temple's kitchens, ritually offered to the bronzes, and then distributed to the temple's various stakeholders, which included the priests and a range of temple functionaries. And several inscriptions go out of their way to specify that the sacred food was to be allotted in this manner.[28] Rajaraja's inscriptions name specific villages in his empire and the exact quantities of the various ingredients that they were required to provide to the temple to be converted to food offerings to each of the many bronze images in his Thanjavur temple.[29]

A lengthy inscription on the walls of the Tyagaraja temple at Tiruvarur provides a comprehensive list of the food ingredients that the temple kitchen required in order to prepare cooked food for the daily worship of the three major Shaiva saints, Sambandar, Appar, and Sundarar, as well as for annual festivals in their honor.[30] We read that in the year 1145, emperor Kulottunga II created three tax-free villages that were required to provide the ingredients for four daily food offerings to the temple, as well as ingredients for food prepared for an annual range of thirteen festivals, of which three were multiday celebrations that took place outside the temple. Two of these tax-free villages were to provide food for celebrating saint Sundarar accompanied by his wife Paravai, both undoubtedly in the form of bronze images, while the third village was to provide food offerings for festivals focusing on bronzes of the child saint Sambandar and of the older saint Appar. The items listed are rice, a range of vegetables, salt, mustard seed, black pepper, cumin, turmeric, ginger, tamarind, jaggery, dried mango, ghee, curds, cane sugar, areca nuts, betel leaf, oil, honey, and the perfumed roots and bark of *sitari* (?), sandal, and *akil* (?). Special ingredients like jackfruit, bananas, coconut, dal, and milk were added to the list for the two major festivals in March–April and in October–November.[31] The ingredients are strictly indigenous and do not include potatoes, tomatoes, or green chilis, all items that the Portuguese brought to India from Brazil after 1500. India's famous black pepper is there, but not chilis.[32] It bears repeating that all of this food, prepared in temple kitchens and offered ritually to the sacred bronzes, was not a drain on resources but quite the opposite, since it was then distributed to temple employees and devotees. For each festival, the inscription provides a list of the payments to be made to a range of temple servants, starting with four priests for ritual puja, ten attendants to carry the bronzes in procession, the flower garland supplier, the gardeners, and musicians, and concluding with the cleaning staff.

The similarity of the ingredients to what would be required in a standard traditional south Indian kitchen of today speaks of the remarkable persistence of food habits over the past 1,000 years in Tamil Nadu.[33] The standard food, then as now, appears to consist of three courses of rice, all served on a banana leaf. Rice is eaten first with a tamarind-based liquid known as *rasam*; next comes rice with sambhar (in which lentils are added to the tamarind-gravy) accompanied by a variety of vegetable dishes; the third course is rice mixed with yogurt. The sweet was a *payasam*, or rice pudding cooked in milk, with either jaggery or cane sugar, and occasionally with the addition of bananas and coconut. Concluding the meal was the traditional aromatic and digestive offering of betel leaves rolled around areca nuts.

It is of interest to note that when Chola royalty performed two major brahmanic and Vedic rituals that are not of Tamil origin, the royal endowment for their enactment speaks of temple food offerings. A record inscribed on the wall of the Tiruvisalur temple speaks of an endowment of 458 *kasu* by Rajaraja's queen Lokamahadevi to mark Rajaraja's performance of *tulabhara*, a ceremony in which the king weighed himself against gold to be distributed to temple authorities and devotees, and of the queen's performance of the complex rite of *hiranyagarbha* (literally, "golden womb"). Her gift was specifically to ensure adequate food offerings to the deity of the temple, and to the brahmin *sabha*, and the temple agreed that the interest accruing from the loan of the queen's money would be used also to meet the daily expenses of such food offerings. The inscription specifies the items to be delivered each day, together with their exact quantities: rice, tuvar dal, cows' milk, ghee, sugar, plantain fruit, areca nut, betel leaves, an earthen pot, firewood, with a final notation of the amount to be set aside as remuneration for the cook. The transaction was made in the name of Chandeshvara, who, as we shall see shortly, was Shiva's divine financial agent, and the protection of this deed was handed over to the temple's priests, whose role was also to guarantee that all gifts to the temple were adequately secured.[34]

Ten Thousand Pearls Adorn a Bronze

The inscriptions on the walls, base moldings, pillars, and enclosures of the Thanjavur temple, as well as on its mini-temple of saint Chandesha, constitute a remarkable archive on the bronzes commissioned for its temple festivals, with descriptions of each individual bronze and, in most cases, their measurements too. As many as sixty-six bronzes were gifted by royalty and court officials;[35] with the exception of one Dancing Shiva placed today in a later shrine, and one Victor of Three Forts in the Thanjavur Art Gallery, the whereabouts of the rest remain uncertain. Adding to the remarkable nature of this documentation is the extraordinary passion for jewelry reflected in the inscriptions that provide the most astonishing details of the lavish gifts of jewelry to these very same sixty-six bronzes. All jewelry was made of gold and most were further studded with a variety of gems. Every item of jewelry was created to adorn the bronze festival images, and multiple items of jewelry were given to adorn, from head to toe, every single bronze in the Thanjavur temple. It seems clear that temple jewelry was seen to affirm and enhance the power of the divine images and, being themselves the gifts of enthusiastic devotees, served also to emphasize acts of devotion.[36] A few examples will serve to illustrate the magnitude and generosity of such gifts.

Rajaraja's queen Panchavan Mahadevi had presented to the temple, prior to the year 1014, an image of Shiva, known in its inscription as *Thanjai Alaghar*, or Beauteous Lord of Thanjavur. Described as standing with his left leg raised slightly to rest on the back of the dwarf-demon Musalagan, the bronze is clearly Shiva as Victor of the Three

Forts. Its ancient measurements translate into just under 39 inches; an image answering this description and of similar measurement stands today in the Thanjavur Art Gallery (fig. 5.12).[37] The temple inscription tells us that Shiva was accompanied by his consort Uma, and that the two images stood upon individual lotus bases that were then placed upon a common rectangular pedestal. In the year 1014, the queen made a lavish gift of several items of jewelry, strung with over 10,000 pearls, to adorn both Shiva and his consort. The inscription is sufficiently intact to read that the twenty-one items of jewelry given to adorn god Shiva were strung with over 7,771 pearls (an additional number that formed part of a long garland are in a damaged section of the inscription), while Uma's ten ornaments included 1,909 pearls.[38] I give here an abbreviated list of Shiva's ornaments, all made of gold and embellished with gems:

1 garland with——pearls, 94 crystals, 4——-, 2 diamond crystals

1 necklace with 31 pearls, 2 corals, 2 lapis

1 necklace with 28 old pearls, 2 corals, 2 lapis, an eye and a hook

1 necklace with 30 old pearls, 2 corals, 2 lapis, 1 sapphire

1 necklace with 32 old pearls, 2 lapis

1 srichanda ornament (which appears to have been a large and impressive torso ornament) had 2524 pearls with 8 front plates, 2 front-plates, 2 pendants, 8 nails for pearls sewn on. The clasps and pendants had 37 crystals, 27 gold balls, 75 bell metal flowers (tarappu).

1 Telugu earring

1 armlet with 49 crystals, 181 diamond crystals, and 263 pearls

1 elbow-let with 411 pearls, 32 crystals

1 arm ring with 385 pearls and 32 crystals

1 arm ring with 415 pearls and 32 crystals

1 arm ring with 426 pearls and 32 crystals

1 hip ornament with 2349 pearls and a clasp sewn with 9 pearls. It had 24 crystals, 9 "potti," 56 diamond crystals. 12 flowers were embedded with 54 crystals and 4 "potti." 1 bud on top of the main pendant had 1 crystal, 9 diamond crystals, 8 bundles of three strings.

1 anklet with 469 pearls and 42 crystals

1 anklet with 408 pearls and 42 crystals

4 gold armlets

2 gold anklets

The queen gave the accompanying bronze of Uma ten items of jewelry:

1 pair of pearl sidduku *with 18 pearls*

1 pearl bracelet with 70 crystals, 14 strings carrying 481 pearls

1 pearl bracelet with 485 pearls and 79 crystals

1 anklet with 87 crystals and 467 pearls

1 anklet with 81 crystals and 468 pearls

2 choker-style gold necklaces

2 gold armlets

1 gold anklet

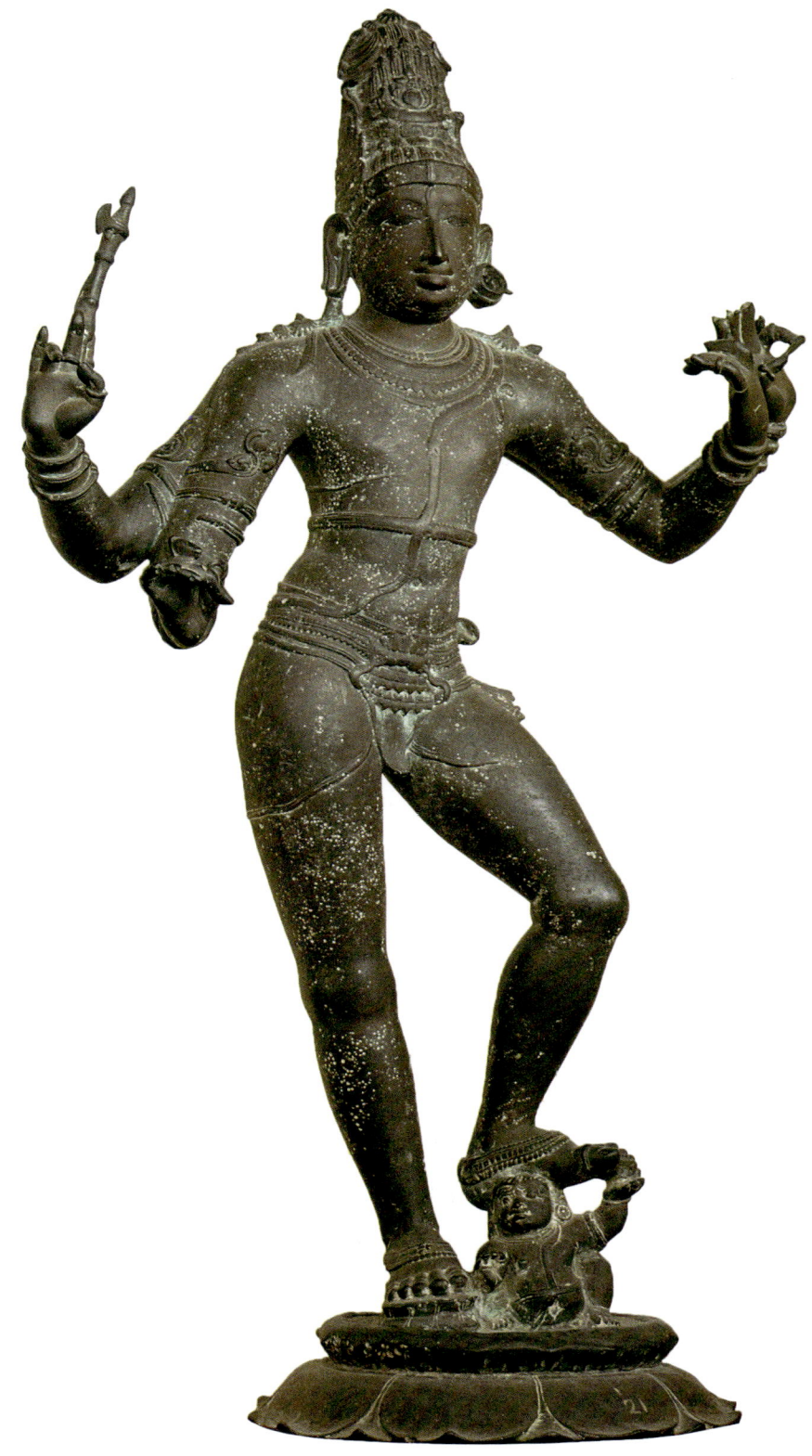

Figure 5.12. Shiva as Victor of Three Forts (*Tripura Vijaya*), ca. 1010, Art Gallery, Thanjavur.

Queen Panchavan's gift is by no means unique in its extravagance and is typical of the ardent devotional fervor of both the emperor's family and of his close circle of trusted officers. Rajaraja's elder sister Kundavai, for instance, made equally lavish gifts of jewelry to the images she had set up in the temple. An instance is a crown that she gifted to Uma as the consort of Shiva in his form of *Dakshina Meru Vitankar* or Lord of southern mountain Meru. It is interesting to note the detailed recording of the quality of the gemstones involved, from those of the highest quality to those marred with spots, cracks, dots, and even fire damage.

*One sacred crown (*makuta*) containing 348* kalanju *and a half . . . of gold.*
859 diamonds set into it namely
    636 diamonds with smooth edges
    169 square diamonds with smooth edges
    32 flat diamonds with smooth edges
    including those that had spots, cracks, red dots, black dots, and marks as of burning
309 large and small rubies
    125 halahalam *of superior quality*
    122 halahalam
    41 smooth rubies
    11 bluish rubies
    10 unpolished rubies including those with cavities, cuts, holes, specks, flaws and such as still adhered to the ore
669 large and small pearls including
    round pearls, roundish pearls, polished pearls, small pearls,
    nimbolam, payittam, *old pearls, such as had been polished while still adhering to their shells, pearls of red water and of brilliant water, and*
    pearls with lines, stains, red dots, specks.
Altogether the crown weighed 407 kalanju *. . . corresponding to a value of*
5000 kasu.[39]

A study of these gifts, and those in other temples, indicates that women, whether queens or laywomen, generally commissioned bronzes of Uma, and gifted jewelry to adorn the goddess; by and large, they left it to male relatives to commission bronzes of Shiva and to gift jewelry to adorn him.

The Thanjavur inscriptions speak of two measures used to weigh the ornaments: for gold, a stone measure known as "Expert Dancer" (*Adavallan*) was used;[40] gemstones were weighed against a stone known as "Lord of sacred mountain Meru," that was probably seated Shiva and Uma with infant Skanda.[41] The earlier mentioned inscription of the twenty-sixth year of Rajaraja's reign, which required all gifts to be engraved on the temple walls, is in itself a consolidated list of Rajaraja's own gifts to his temple until the year 1011. Lines 4 to 32 specify details of each golden bowl, salver, and ritual vessel that Rajaraja gifted to the temple from his own treasury, immediately following the consecration of the temple. His inscriptions often specify that one other of his gifts came from treasures seized in his military campaigns. The gift of gold fly-whisk handles, parasol tops, trumpets, and betel-leaf salvers in lines 35–91 are "out of the treasures which he seized after having defeated the Chera king and the Pandyas in Malainadu." Line 92 tells us that when he returned from his conquest of the Rashtrakutas (Satyasraya), he "poured out at the feet of the Lord" twenty-seven gold flowers of substantial weights including one in the form of a lotus. Lines 100–107 list the various items of jewelry given to the bronze of *Dakshina Meru Vitankar*, including a gold diadem from the treasures secured after battles against the Cheras and Pandyas. Gifts from war booty find occasional mention at other temples too, including Palanam, one of the Sacred Seven that we looked at in chapter 2. Vikriasinga Muvendavelan, headman of Tonur, and one of Rajarajas's officers, gifted an emerald image to the Palanam temple, specifying in his inscription that the emperor had given it to him from the treasures seized in a successful campaign in Kerala.[42] Clearly, Rajaraja shared seized booty with those who helped him secure victory.

A phenomenal amount of gold was involved in the gifts at the Great Temple, and its source was probably the famed Kolar gold mines of Karnataka that would have been part of Rajaraja's expanded south Indian possessions. While the mine is depleted today, we might note that plans were recently announced to use modern equipment to access deeper levels of the mine shafts. The Thanjavur temple's supervisory goldsmith, also an appraiser of jewels, and an important temple employee, weighed the gold separately from the gemstones whenever possible. He also separated the weight of the gold from that of the thread and lac, the resin used in gold jewelry to hold gems in place. Here is one example of the minutiae that is specified in the jewelry inscriptions:

> *Those (jewels) which could be weighed separately, were weighed without the threads, the frames, the copper nails, the lac, and the pinju [thread]. Those jewels, the net weight of which could not be ascertained, as they were united with the lac and thread, were weighed together with the lac and pinju.*[43]

Such details indicate that gold and gemstones were generally weighed independently prior to being strung into the jewelry commissioned by patrons for individual bronzes. Many records speak of the hook-and-eye closures, as in a marriage necklace given to a 12-inch-high image of goddess Durga:

> *One gold marriage tali, with five diamonds and one ruby, with one eye* (padukan) *and one hook* (kokkuvay) *round the collar.*[44]

It is intriguing to note that the minor detail of hook-and-eye closures were specifically delineated by the wax modeler, and emerge clearly in the work of the metal expert, as seen in a rear close-up of a sacred bronze (fig. 5.13).

When we consider the gold contained in Rajaraja's gifted items of ritual usage, and add it to the gold in the jewelry that adorned the sacred bronzes in his temple, we arrive at an amazing estimate of 590 pounds (9,450 ounces) of gold. At current prices for 22-karat gold per ounce ($1,747.20 on October 2, 2020), just the gold in these gifts would cost approximately $16.5 million.[45] To this, we must add the considerable cost of the thousands

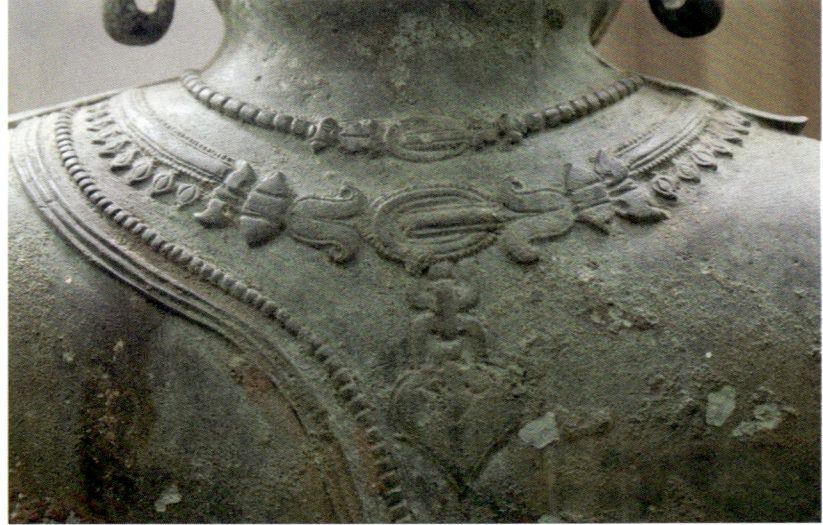

Figure 5.13. Detail of hook-and-eye closures in rear view of Saint Sundarar and Wife Paravai (see fig. 5.9a), Tiruvenkadu temple, Nagapattinam district, ca. 1015–1020, Art Gallery, Thanjavur.

of gemstones with which the gold jewelry was studded. A hint to the extraordinary value of gemstones is contained in an inscription of Rajaraja's sister Kundavai that gives details of the gems contained in a single armlet of a pair that she gave to an image of Uma:

One sacred armlet containing 14 ozs of gold
441 diamonds set into it, namely,
> *20 pure diamonds,*
> *406 diamonds with smooth edges,*
> *5 flat diamonds with smooth edges,*
> *10 square diamonds with smooth edges—*

54 large and small rubies, namely
> *8 halahalam of superior quality,*
> *17 halahalam,*
> *19 smooth rubies,*
> *2 bluish rubies, and*
> *8 unpolished rubies—*

68 strung pearls,
> *including round pearls, roundish pearls,*
> *polished pearls, small pearls,*
> *pearls of brilliant water, pearls of red water,*
> *such as had been polished while still adhering to their shells—*[46]

The inscription informs us that the gold in the armlet cost 180 coins, but that the entire armlet together with the stones cost 1,250 coins. The gold, it appears, was less than a tenth of the total value of the jeweled armlet.

TIRUVENKADU MASTER   155

Court officials joined royalty in giving bronzes as well as jewelry to adorn the bronzes, and while their gifts are of lesser value, they are still substantial. Rajaraja's brahmin general gifted to the temple a bronze of Shiva as Half Woman, 15 inches tall, and he adorned it with eleven items of jewelry:

Gold crown with 128 pearls, 11 diamonds, 34 crystals
Gold garland with 10 pearls, 26 diamonds, 32 crystals
Gold diadem set with 111 pearls
Pair of gold armlets, each set with 3 crystals
Gold waistband set with 1 crystal, 2 diamonds
3 gold bracelets
1 gold girdle
2 gold anklets[47]

The total amount of gold in these gifts was 58 *kalanju*, which cost 100 coins; unfortunately, the inscription says nothing of the additional cost of the pearls and gemstones.

A special favorite to adorn bronzes of the saints were necklaces made by stringing together the sacred *rudraksha* bead, which is the dried fruit of a species of evergreen tree. When Rajaraja's temple officer, Adittan Suryan, commissioned bronze images of the three saints Appar, Sambandar, and Sundarar, he gave each a necklace made of these beads set in gold.[48] Jewelry was so vital a part of the embellishment of festival bronzes that a chieftain who gifted a bronze of the emaciated sage Bhringi felt the need to adorn even this gaunt Shiva devotee with a triple-strand necklace of 150 pearls, a *rudraksha* necklace, three anklets, and three armlets.[49]

Let's pause for a moment to consider the reason for such detailed recording of the exact weight of the gold used minus the lac and thread, the precise quality of gemstones and pearls, and the cost of each item. While these royal records are exceptionally comprehensive, it appears to have been standard practice for large, wealthy temples to carry inscribed lists of the gold and silver ornaments, and the ritual vessels in their possession, often with notations on the weight of each ritual item, and details of each individual item of jewelry. Occasionally, such inventories were also engraved on copper plates, as in the instance of a small set of five plates, measuring 5 1/2 inches by 12 7/8 inches, belonging to the Tirukkalar temple. The fourth and fifth plates, dated in the twenty-ninth year of Kulottunga III (r. 1178–1218), consist exclusively of a list of thirty-six gold and silver ornaments belonging to the temple, with their weight as measured by the "*kudinai kal*" and a notation on the fineness of the gold in each instance. The specifics of gold purity are fascinating; a marriage necklace is made of gold of "9 fineness," a garland is of "8 5/16th fineness," a string of beads of gold of "8 1/2 fineness," a pair of earrings of gold of "8 1/4 fineness."[50] These inscribed records appear to constitute an inventory and, as Josephine Shaya has pointed out in the context of ancient Greek temples, "oversight of the administration of the treasure" was certainly one important reason for inscribing such records on temples. Her point that "In antiquity, the temple's contents were much more precious than the architectural pieces that we admire today"[51] is indeed worth keeping in mind in the context of Chola temples. Temple inscriptions occasionally speak of jewels discovered to be missing on the occasion of regular inspections of temple possessions, suggesting that a concern for accountability played a major role in inscribing inventories on temple walls; on such surfaces, they could be consulted easily during official inspections, when thefts were often detected. A few instances of missing jewelry are cited here. In the year 9 of Rajaraja, or 994, an inscription informs us that 96 *kalanju* of gold was collected as a fine from a temple employee who was found to have stolen temple gold; this was then used to make new ornaments for the deity at the Palanam temple.[52] At the Tirupanandal temple, the embezzlement of jewelry given to adorn the bronzes was discovered during an inspection of the temple treasures by a panel consisting of the Sacred Works officer and two military generals in the year 1099 during the reign of Kulottunga I. This inscription refers to two prior thefts in the reigns of two earlier monarchs. One of the six priests responsible for these thefts was unable to pay back his share, which amounted to 540 coins. Though pardoned by the king, it was necessary for him to sell his right of performing temple worship for 4 1/2 days each month until such time as the amount he owed was recovered;[53] performing temple *puja* was clearly a productive occupation. At a temple in Pandanallur, an order of king Rajaraja II (1152) speaks of the punishment of certain temple priests who had misappropriated gold from the temple treasury that was intended for conversion to ornaments for the sacred bronzes. The culprits were deprived of the right of temple service, and the 300 coins realized from the sale of those rights to others was given to the temple for creating replacement jewelry; additionally, the offenders and their descendants were permanently barred from entry into the temple.[54] An example we cited in chapter 3 relates to the priests at the Shivapuram temple who gave a pearl necklace that adorned the bronze image of Uma to a concubine, and whose defiance and inappropriate response was considered a crime against both Shiva and the king.[55] Like other inscriptions, such crimes and the judgment passed on offenders would have been written first on palm leaf and then on the temple walls, and occasionally also on copper plates.

The Cholas put in place an amazing bureaucracy to effectively manage all aspects of the administration of their kingdom. From the numerous records of such control, I feel it most appropriate here to give you an idea of the checks and balances in place to handle the refashioning of the jewelry that is so intimately connected with our bronzes, and to point out that accountability was required at each level of the process. In 1042, the thirtieth year of emperor Rajendra, an inscription engraved on the north wall of the central shrine of the large and wealthy Shiva temple at Tirunageshvaram near Kumbakonam tells us of the emperor's decision to use gold already accumulated in the temple to create major new items of jewelry to adorn three sets of temple bronzes.[56] The three bronzes in question were Shiva with the bull and consort, Shiva crowned with the moon and consort, and seated Shiva and Uma with child Skanda (*Somaskanda*). The order (*niyoga*) formulated by the emperor's personal secretary, Rajendrachola Muvendavelan, was communicated to four parties: the temple's Sacred Works (*srikaryam*) officer, the district's land revenue officer, the town council, and to the priests, administrators, accountants, and treasurers of the temple itself. It was decided to form a committee of sixteen members, named individually in the inscription, to oversee this important task. The committee consisted of two overseers, the temple's *srikaryam* officer, a military officer, two members of the temple's administrative body, two priests, a singer of sacred hymns, a recordkeeper, two security officers, an accountant, a member of the local council, an arbitrator, and "Lord Shiva's own accountant." A jewel merchant weighed the available gold in the presence of a chieftain, after which the process of creating the new sets of ornaments commenced. The inscription records meticulously the sets of items gifted earlier and exactly how they were converted; I cite here an abbreviated version of the very first item:

> *A gold handle for a fly-whisk, weighing 19 kalanju according to the kudinjjaikal measure, and gifted by Udaiya Pirattiyar [the queen], together with gold collected from local taxes [antarayam] in the year 14 of Rajakesarivarman, were refashioned into 7 gold flowers.*

The final and most major conversion, detailed at the end of this lengthy inscription, tells us of separate gifts from seven different individuals that were combined to make three major items of jewelry for the bronzes.[57]

"Shiva's own accountant" is saint Chandesha, who features prominently in the context of temple monies and especially in transactions in which the temple functioned as a banking institution that loaned cash at a rate of interest approximating to 12 1/2 percent. The original story of Chandesha speaks of his occupation as a cowherd, his intense devotion to Shiva, and his zealous protection of a mud Shiva linga that he built afresh each day and lustrated with milk from the cows in his charge. In objecting to the misuse of milk, his father kicked the linga, causing Chandesha to lash out with his cowherd staff, which turned miraculously into the ax of Shiva, felling the father to the ground. While emperor Rajaraja commissioned a small six-piece group to portray the entire story,[58] Chandesha is generally portrayed as an independent figure who stands holding Shiva's sacred ax in the crook of his arm (fig. 5.14). During the Chola period, Chandesha acquired a new role as divine financial agent in Shiva temples, and it was in his name that a temple's financial transactions were conducted. We see this, for instance, when Rajaraja's sister, Kundavai, gave an endowment of cash to the Thanjavur temple to ensure the regular worship of the four temple bronzes that she had commissioned. The expenses of worship were to be met from the interest that accrued on the loan of her money to the inhabitants of an entire series of villages; interest was to be paid annually to the temple treasury either in the form of rice or as cash. Notice how the inscription, quoted here in abbreviated form, phrases it:

> *We have received from lord Chandesvara, who has been pleased to take up residence in the temple called Rajarajesvara at Thanjavur, and who is the first servant of the supreme lord, 500 kasu coins out of the money that has been deposited ... for this we have to pay, as long as the sun and moon endure, an interest of 64 1/2 kasu to the treasury of the lord.*[59]

The loan was received, not from the temple or from Kundavai, but from Chandeshvara, described here as the first servant of the supreme lord.

Another such record from the Thanjavur temple, also cited here in highly abbreviated form, speaks of money deposited by a temple officer, Kadan Kanavadi, who describes himself as keeper of the small treasury (*siru danam*). The money was loaned to

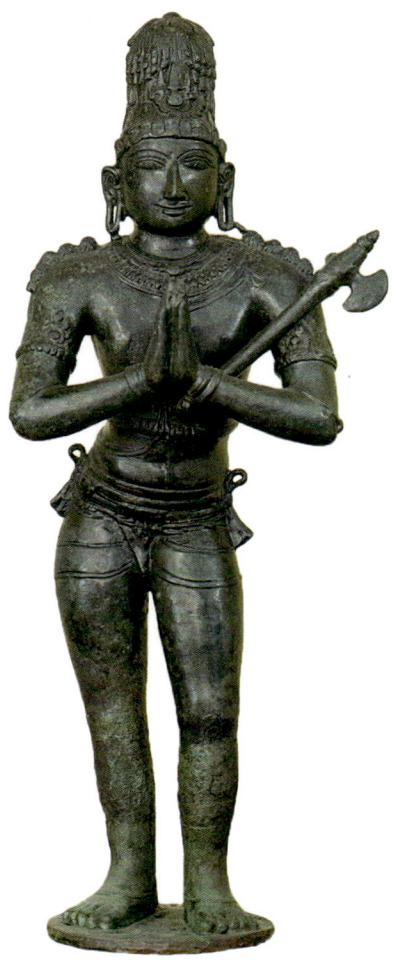

Figure 5.14. Saint Chandesha, Muthupet, Tiruvarur, eleventh century, Art Gallery, Thanjavur.

members of the assembly of Iramanur, and the interest that they paid on the loan was to be used to purchase aromatic items from the great market at Thanjavur, named after Rajaraja's chief queen as the Tribhuvanamahadevi market:

> *big champaka buds, cardamom seeds, and khus-khus roots to be thrown into the bathing water, and onto the surface of the fresh water of the Lord of the temple and the bronze image of Lord of Southern [sacred mountain] Meru. . . .*
>
> *The village and market that has received the money from Chandesvaradeva, who is the first servant of the supreme lord, who has been pleased to take up residence in the temple of Rajarajeshvaradeva in Thanjavur, agree to supply:*
>
> > *five* kuruni *of cardamom seeds per year . . .*
> > *five* kuruni *of big champaka buds per year . . .*
> > *2160* palam *of khus-khus roots per year . . .*[60]

Similar language is used in an entire series of inscriptions in which the temple lent money to a variety of clients at the accepted rate of 12 1/2 percent interest.[61] Chandesha's increased importance during the Chola period resulted in the building of a mini-temple to enshrine

TIRUVENKADU MASTER   159

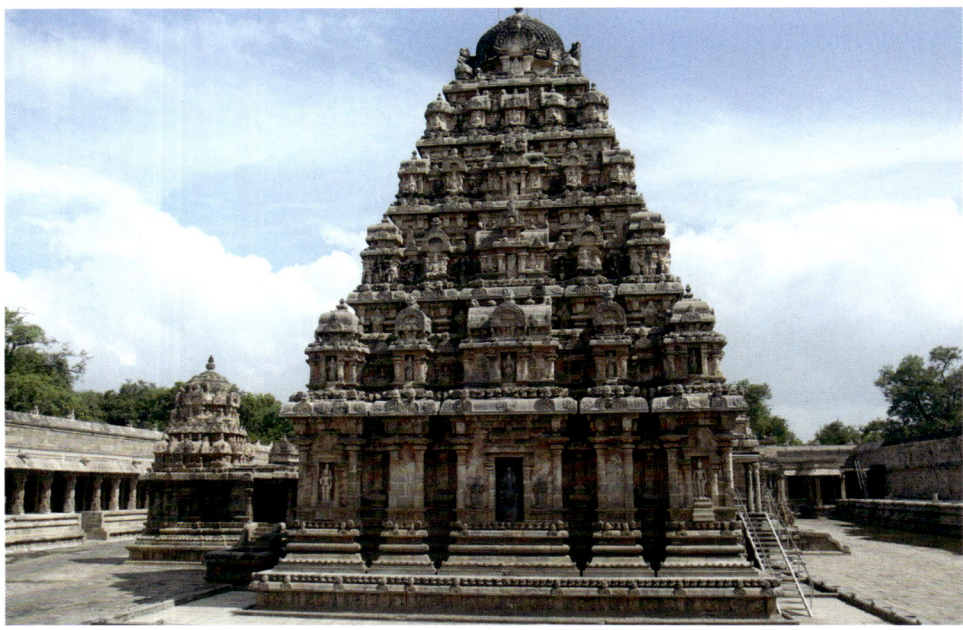

Figure 5.15. Saint Chandesha shrine (left side of main temple as seen from rear), Darasuram, Thanjavur district, ca. 1150.

his image within the compound of all large Shiva temples (fig. 5.15; see also fig. 9.1). To this day, Chandesha continues to be regarded as guardian of a Shiva temple, and devotees leaving the premises of a Shiva temple stop before his shrine and clap their hands above their heads. This is not to applaud the divine financial agent but to demonstrate that their hands are empty and that they are not purloining any temple property.

We have not spent any time looking at the stone sculptures in the niches of the Great Temple at Thanjavur largely because these over-life-size images are somewhat disappointing by comparison with the bronzes created by the Tiruvenkadu Master. How could this be when we are speaking of the Great Temple whose royal patron, Rajaraja, surely employed the finest stone sculptors of the day? A comparison of a few stone and bronze images of identical or similar iconography is instructive. The stone image of Shiva as Begging Lord on the south wall of the shrine seems powerful when seen on its own; but when compared with the Master's bronze, it appears a bit flabby, with thighs and shoulders that are too broad (fig. 5.16; see fig. 5.4a). The stone image of Shiva as Half Woman on the shrine's north wall is graceful, but the stone face is too broad and the body lacks the dynamic contrapposto of the bronze (fig. 5.17; see fig. 5.5). There is a certain stiffness and heaviness about the stone figure of Shiva standing beside Uma on the shrine's north wall, a stolid quality compared to bronze couples (fig. 5.18; see fig. 5.1). The explanation for this appears to reside in the vast enlargement of stone images to fit into niches on the Thanjavur temple, which are close to 9 feet tall. The artists were no longer able to eye their images as a single piece, as they had done in earlier temples that were one-sixth the size of Thanjavur's Great Temple. They now had to work on their stone images in sections, squatting upon the block of stone they were carving as is the customary practice in India. In the process, they appear to have lost out on the overall proportionality; each section might

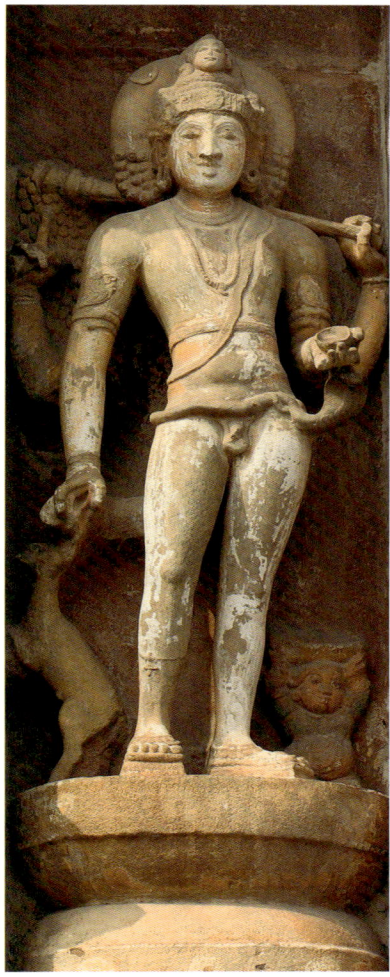 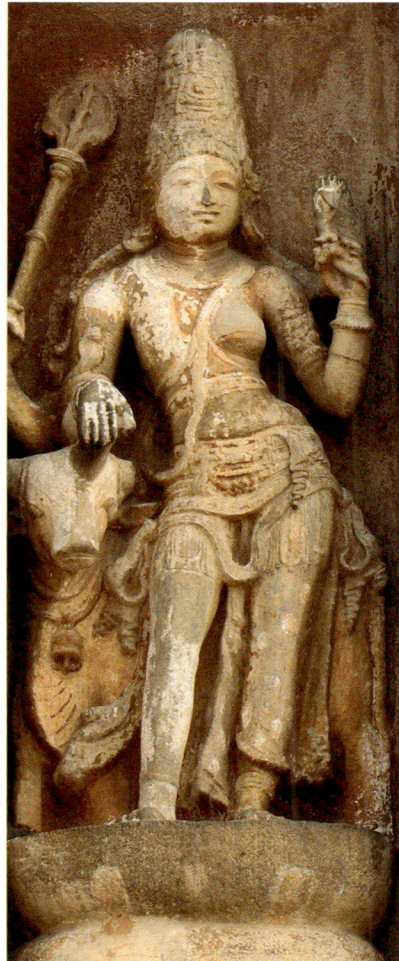 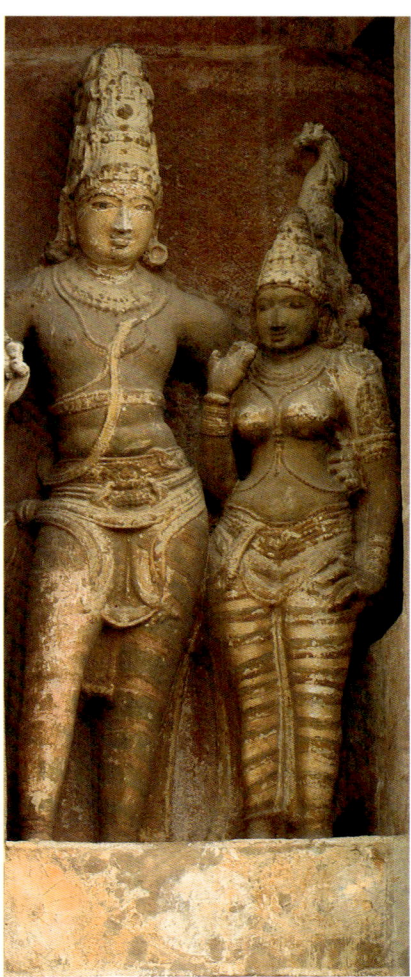

Figure 5.16. Shiva as the Begging Lord, south wall of Rajaraja Chola's Great Temple, Thanjavur, ca. 1010.

Figure 5.17. Shiva as Half Woman, north wall of Rajaraja Chola's Great Temple, Thanjavur, ca. 1010.

Figure 5.18. Shiva with Uma, south wall of Rajaraja Chola's Great Temple, Thanjavur, ca. 1010.

seem fine on its own, but when it all came together, it did not do justice to the stone carvers' art. By contrast, the wax modeler, creating images with bodies no more than 3 feet high, was able to fine-tune his image to a level of perfection.

It is apparent that Rajaraja's achievements, both as one who raised the military profile of the Chola kingdom and as a great devotee of Shiva who built and lavishly endowed the Great Temple at Thanjavur, were widely celebrated in his lifetime. Two inscriptions, one in the Thanjavur temple itself and a second at Poonturutti, one of the temples of the Sacred Seven only 7 miles from the capital, testify to this fact. While the Poonturutti inscription remains as a mere fragment, inscribed on a stone that is today built into the outer *gopuram* gateway, sufficient text remains intact to alert us to an allocation of land made to a *bhattan*, or temple priest, named Suvarnan Narayana Bhattadittan. It was payment for reciting a work titled *Sri Rajaraja Vijayam*, or the "Victory of

Sri Rajaraja," a text that may have been devoted to celebrating the emperor's military prowess.⁶² The inscription in the Thanjavur temple, dated in the sixth year of Rajendra, or 1018, speaks of a royal decree ordering payment to be made to the actor (*santi kuttan*) Vijaya Rajendra Achariyan for acting the *Rajarajesvara Natakam*, or "Rajaraja Play," during the great festival in the month of *Vaikhashi* (December–January).⁶³ The inscription speaks of a subsequent royal order that this dispensation should be inscribed in stone, and concludes with the statement that such an order had now been carried out. The epigraph concludes by informing us that the allowance for the actor and for members of his troop was to last as long as the sun and moon endure. It also specifies that the order itself was signed by the royal secretary on the 160th day of Rajendra's fourth year, and engraved on stone on the 160th day of the sixth year.

In conclusion, I highlight the overlooked role in temple patronage of the *anukkis*, or "intimates," of the Chola emperors, either directly by way of constructing temples and making gifts of jewels, ritual utensils, and lamps, or indirectly by way of ensuring a steady source of income to enable temples to adequately celebrate their major festivals. Inscriptions contain references to these *anukkis*, who cultivated highly charged relationships with one or another Chola king and were accorded a status of high respect by temple priests and court officials. Two examples of such influential women are Rajendra Chola's *anukki*, Paravai Nangaiyar (she adopted the name of saint Sundarar's wife), who was actively involved with the Tiruvarur temple, and Nakkan Pavai, *anukki* of Rajendra II, who was instrumental in establishing a suburb of Chidambaram that was named after what I assume to be her sobriquet.

A lengthy inscription at the Tyagaraja temple in Tiruvarur provides details of Paravai Nangaiyar's various gifts, which commence with her rebuilding the temple in stone, covering with gold its crowning pot-like *kalasha* finial and lotus base, as also its rounded *stupi* and the *kudu* arches adorning it. The temple's bedroom chamber was of special interest to her, and she covered with gold both the door leading into it and its crowning *kalasha*. She gave an extraordinary range of gifts to the temple's linga, and to its processional image named Vidi Vitanker (the portable lord of the avenues), that included pearl strings, gold fly-whisks, a gold choker with a ruby, gold necklaces, gold flowers, and gold belts, bracelets, bangles, anklets, rings, all studded with gems. The climactic event for *anukki* Paravai Nangaiyar occurred in 1032, the twentieth year of Rajendra, when, together with the monarch, she rode on the temple chariot, the *ter*, and was received ceremonially at the temple. To mark the spot at which she stood with Rajendra Chola to receive temple honors, Paravai Nangaiyar donated a large series of lamps, including two *pavai* lamps that invariably take the form of a woman holding a large lamp-bowl in her hands. To these two *pavai* lamps, named Pachchai Pavai Umaialvi and Sariya Mulai Nangai, Rajendra's *anukki* gifted a rich series of ornaments. All gifts from *anukki* Paravai Nangaiyar were recorded in the temple registers soon thereafter during Rajendra's twentieth regnal year of 1032.⁶⁴ Paravai Nangaiyar's largesse to Tiruvarur did not end with Rajendra's reign. An inscription dated in the twenty-seventh year of Rajadhiraja, or 1045, informs us that Rajendra Chola's *anukki* Paravai Nangaiyar extended her patronage to Tiruvarur's Araneri temple, which had been built earlier by Sembiyan Mahadevi. She added a *mandapa* named Rajendra-chola-deva, and she provided paddy for food offerings (*tiru amudu*) to Paravai Nangai and

Rajendra Chola, clearly images in bronze of herself and the king that she had dedicated but that no longer survive.[65]

Equally significant in the context of the economics of temple festivals is the case of the suburb of Gunamenagaipuram established at Chidambaram by Nakkan Pavai, *anukki* of Rajendra II.[66] The name itself is of interest since Menagai or Menaka is the celestial nymph who seduced the great sage Visvamitra, and the qualifying phrase *guna* means virtuous. We encounter here a woman who seems to have been well versed in the economics of town and temple, and able to ensure that the one could be used to support the other, partly by promising major concessions to traders and merchants as an inducement to relocate to her township. Once there, she made it the collective responsibility of all its permanent residents, and of their support staff of craftsmen, to ensure the celebration of three major festivals in the months of *Markali*, *Ani*, and *Masi* at the Chidambaram temple. The inscription contains her detailed calculations of how exactly she ensured that this would be possible for the residents who settled in Gunamenagaipuram.[67] These two *anukkis*, one of Rajendra I and the other of Rajendra II, are not unique in their support of the temple culture of their day. *Anukkis* of various other Chola kings find mention in temple inscriptions, and it is clear that, alongside queens and princesses, these influential women played a significant role in both court and temple.

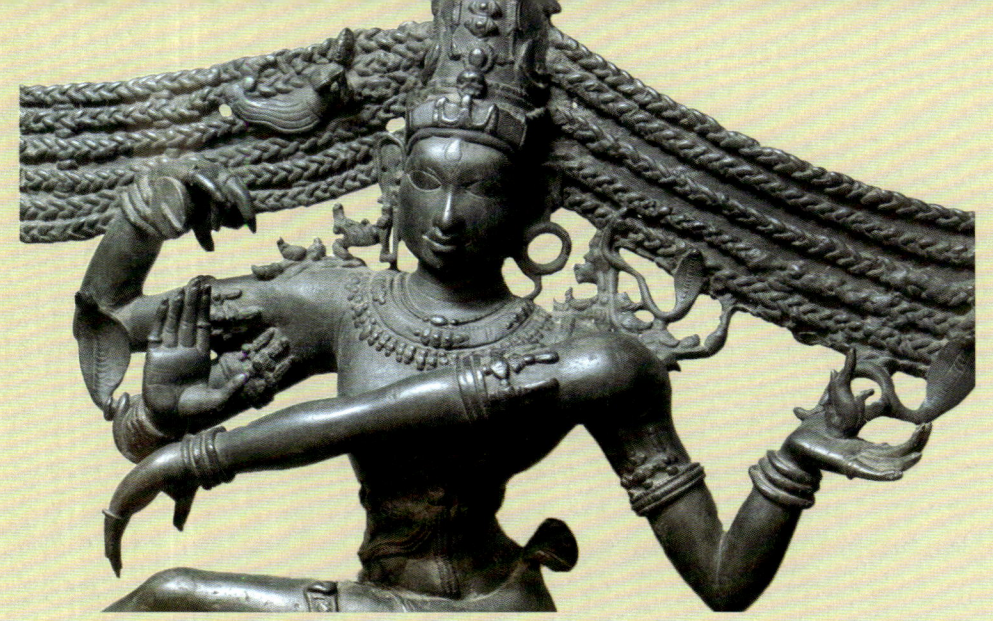

Chola Obsession with Sri Lanka and Hindu Bronzes from the Island
Eleventh Century

6

Success. The customs duties of the port of Goda-pavata, Raja Gamani Abhaya granted to the Buddhist vihara.

Success. Ahalya Bathikamithaya, Queen of King Gamini Abhaya, granted 22 acres of land to the Arabapaya Godapavata vihara. At the same time, another twenty-two acres of land from the rice field of Jawahakavilaka city was granted to the Stupa.

STONE INSCRIPTION OF CA. 113–135 CE[1]

The two inscriptions cited here encourage us to imagine the flurry of activity as trading ships from distant lands arrived and departed at the busy port of Boulder Mountain (Goda-pavata) built along a reef on the southern coast of Sri Lanka. Ships' captains discharged their cargo, reloaded fresh merchandise, and sailed either toward China or toward the Gulf, where goods would ultimately be shipped to towns along the Mediterranean. Boulder Mountain had an efficient bureaucracy in place to ensure that customs duties were paid on goods entering or transiting the port, and terracotta seals emblazoned with a lion were used to stamp cargo on which duty had been paid. A sacred Buddhist relic stupa sat at the top of the low rounded mountain that gave its name to the port and served as a landmark for approaching mariners. The pious king Gajabahu (Gamini Abhaya), ruler of island Sri Lanka, decided to dedicate all customs duties that accrued at this port to the Buddhist temple (*vihara*) atop the hill, and his announcement was carved in finely executed letters varying in height between 2 1/2 to 6 inches on a rock beside the stupa. His queen Ahalaya donated two parcels of land, each 25 acres in extent, for the upkeep of the Buddhist sacred site, and ordered her inscription to be carved on the same rock.[2]

From the centuries BCE, the ports of Sri Lanka and south India offered safe and profitable harbors to traders making the lengthy sea voyage from the Middle East all the way to China and back (map 7). The Kerala port of Muziris on India's western Malabar coast has recently been identified with Pattinam, where excavations have yielded Roman glass, Roman coins, and amphorae for storing wine.[3] The famous Muziris papyrus of the second century CE, written in ancient Greek, gives details of cargo shipped from Kerala to Alexandria, refers to customs duties, and contains an agreement between two traders, one in Muziris, who shipped cargo to Alexandria in Egypt.[4] The value of a single shipload of cargo appears to have been as much as six million drachmas after tax, and may be considered in the context of Pliny's lament that Roman gold was pouring into India. Lionel Casson points out that expatriate traders certainly lived in Muzuris, since a map known as the Tabula Peutingeriana shows a temple to Augustus next to that town, and he surmises that none other than expatriates would build such a temple there.[5] Tamil Sangam poetry, roughly dated between 300 BCE and 300 CE, also speaks of Muciri, where "Yavanas [Ionians] come with their fine ships, bearing gold, and leave with pepper."[6] On the eastern Coromandel (originally Chola-mandalam) coast, the Tamil literary text, *Silappadikaram*, better known as *The Tale of the Anklet*, and written around the fifth century of this era, describes Puhar (today's Poompuhar), where the river Kaveri empties into the ocean, as a wondrous town filled with fine goods from varying parts of the globe, and with an area set aside for expatriate merchants who made it their home.

> *Near the harbor, the passerby was stopped dead*
> *by the homes of Yavanas whose profits never shrunk.*
> *On the edge of the burnished waters lived*
> *and mingled as one traders from distant*
> *lands, come for goods carried*
> *by ships.*
> *. . .*

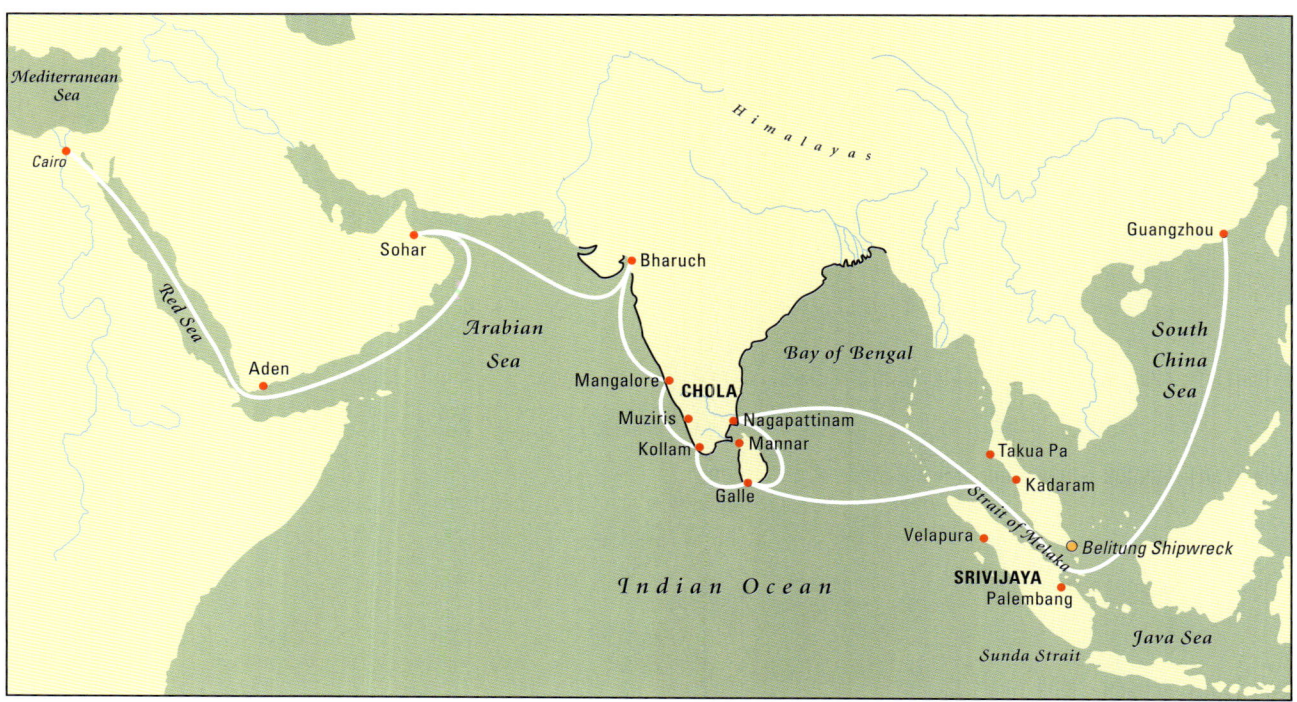

Map 7 Maritime trade routes, first millennium.

Silk, coral

sandalwood, agar, flawless pearls,

gems, gold, and an endless profusion

of rare ornaments were piled high

in the commodious streets.

. . .

Overcrowded shops packed with food;

Braziers; coppersmiths; painters; sculptors;

goldsmiths; jewelers; tailors; cobblers;

a host of artisans making various

flawless objects with cloth and pith.[7]

Two monsoons regulated traffic at these southern ports, the southwest monsoon from the Arabian Sea and the northeast monsoon from the Bay of Bengal. The logbook of an unknown Greek sailor written in the first century CE, known as *The Periplus of the Erythraean Sea*, speaks of navigating the west coast of India according to the monsoon winds. It gives details of exports and imports at the ports of Barygaza, today's Broach north of Mumbai, and of Muziris in Kerala.[8] Arab dhows voyaging to China docked in the harbors along the west and east coasts of India and in the ports of Sri Lanka that lay at the tip of the Indian peninsula, where they refitted their boats, replenished their goods, bartered and traded, before proceeding. They were able to make the journey to China in a single season. But the timing and the direction of the two monsoons was such that on the return journey it became necessary to spend downtime of several months in one or other of these ports, or in the Sumatran kingdom of Srivijaya, in order to sail successfully with the next round of monsoon winds.

An Arab ship that was on its way back from China in the year 862 was shipwrecked off the island of Belitung near Singapore; underwater salvage has revealed that 90 percent of its cargo consisted of Chinese ceramics, which were in high demand in the Middle East. A fascinating exercise to produce a modern replica of the sunken dhow, using materials similar to those of the original ninth-century boat, was undertaken through a recent collaboration between the sultanate of Oman and the government of Singapore. Its planks were made of African hardwoods, while coconut fiber from India was used to sew the planks together; nails, which characterized Chinese boat construction—Chinese junks—were not used at all.[9] Such sewn ships require an enormous amount of rope made from coconut fibers combined with creepers and barks of trees; this modern replica used a full 74 miles of such cord.[10]

From the tenth century onward, when the Cholas were on their way to becoming a major power in south India with ambitions to reach beyond their immediate waters, ships stopped making the entire lengthy voyage. Instead, goods from both the Persian Gulf and Sung China came into the strategically located ports of Sri Lanka, south India, and Sumatra for trans-shipment to the other end of the route. Substantial taxes from ships passing through these ports provided a lucrative source of revenue that could be used to build temples, commission bronzes and jewelry, and sponsor temple festivals. Ships journeying from the West probably found it more convenient to stop along India's west coast or in Sri Lankan harbors rather than sail around the island to reach Chola ports on India's east coast. For the Chola kings, control of the ports of Sri Lanka was a prize worth fighting for since it would provide the opportunity to take over customs duties from Sri Lankan ports and to divert ocean trade to their own major port of Nagapattinam. The Chola preoccupation with Sri Lanka is seen in the royal copper-plate charters issued by each Chola monarch that enumerate the conquests of the ruler; with an exception or two, the list of battles fought and won always commence with Sri Lanka, clearly a highly coveted possession.

A second major reason for the Chola obsession with Sri Lanka was their passion for pearl jewelry to adorn their sacred temple bronzes, and the resulting need to obtain easy access to, or direct control of, the pearl fisheries in the Gulf of Mannar that lay between south India and Sri Lanka (map 8). Since major sand banks have always existed in these shallow waters,[11] ships from the west could not take a shortcut through the gulf to reach Nagapattinam, but had necessarily to detour around island Sri Lanka with its easily accessible ports if they wished to reach the Chola coastline. The waters of the Gulf of Mannar sustained major pearl oyster fisheries that yielded all manner of pearls, from tiny seed pearls to those the size of a green pea. They were known as early as the first century to both Pliny's *Natural History* and to the unknown Greek sailor who authored the logbook known as the *Periplus of the Erythraean Sea*. Pliny tells us that the island of Toprabane (ancient Sri Lanka) is productive of pearls of greater size than even India, and confirms that "the sea that lies between the mainland and the island is full of shallows

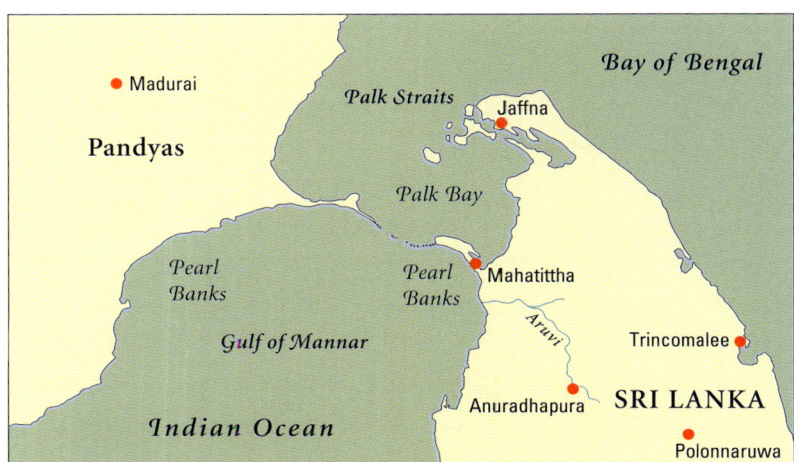

Map 8 Gulf of Mannar between south India and Sri Lanka.

not more than six paces in depth."[12] The author of the *Periplus* reports knowledge of Kolchoi under the Pandyan kings "where diving for pearls goes on," adding that such diving was carried out by convicts.[13] Chinese Buddhist pilgrim Faxian, who traveled to Sri Lanka in the mid-fifth century, also spoke of its pearls:

> The kingdom is on a large island. . . . Left and right from it are as many as 100 small islands, distant from one another ten, twenty, even 200 *le*; but all subject to the large island. Most of them produce pearls; there is one which produces the pure and brilliant pearl. The king employs men to watch and protect it, and requires three out of every ten such pearls, which the collectors find.[14]

When we move to the year 1284 at a time when Chola power was in a state of severe decline, we find Venetian traveler Marco Polo speaking of the Pandyan territory of Mabar and the pearl fisheries located where "the sea forms a gulf between the island of Seilan [Ceylon] and the mainland." He speaks of the many boats that carry pearl divers between the months of April and mid-May, and informs us: "Of all the produce they have first to pay the King, as his royalty, the tenth part."[15]

The southwest monsoon arriving in late May or early June annually swept the oyster beds that lay along the Pandya coast of India toward Sri Lanka, where they settled at the mouth of the Aruvi river at Mannar, free from the dangers of ocean currents. The northeast return monsoon currents of late December or early January partially dislodged the oyster beds, moving some back toward India and the Pandyan coastline. In these shallow waters, divers dived for pearl oysters, "their backs gracefully arched and their heels above their heads, whilst their generally long hair waves gracefully behind them supported by the water." Writing in 1902 in an innocent age free of the burden of political correctness, Captain Legge commented admiringly, "No European diver in a diving dress can compete with a naked native."[16] Diving for the Sri Lankan pearl oyster took place in the fairly narrow period of time between the end of the northeast monsoon and the start of the southwest monsoon, from April to mid-May, at a time when the Gulf of Mannar is not affected by the currents of either monsoon.

The Cholas had a long-standing rivalry with the Pandyas of Madurai, whose territory lay to their immediate south, and also with the rulers of Lanka, who were allies of the Pandyas. It is likely that access to the pearl fisheries that lay strategically between Pandya and Lankan territory was one major reason for the discontent and conflict. In his earliest inscriptions, Parantaka Chola (r. 905–955) assumed the title "He who captured Madurai"; twelve years into his reign, he enlarged that title to "He who captured Madurai and Ilam [Sri Lanka]." In the year 939, his naval general made a gift to the coastal Shiva temple at Maraikkadu as thanksgiving for his successful campaign in Sri Lanka and his defeat of the Sinhala king.[17] Battles with both the Pandyas and the rulers of Sri Lanka were a regular feature of Chola polity and remained so throughout the four centuries of Chola rule. Aditya Karikala (r. 956–969) titled himself "He who took the head of the Pandya";[18] Sundara Chola (r. 956–973) was "He who took Madurai";[19] Rajadhiraja II (r. 1166–1181) assumed the title of "He who was pleased to take Madurai and Ilam";[20] while Kulottunga III (r. 1178–1218) was "He who was pleased to take Madurai, Ilam, Karuvur, and the crowned head of the Pandya."[21] Chola battles with the Pandyas and the rulers of Sri Lanka were recurring events, and victories were fleeting and quickly overturned; the only exception was during the reigns of emperors Rajaraja I and Rajendra I in the eleventh century, when the Chola kingdom was at its most powerful. The myth of uncontested Chola supremacy must be set aside despite the fact that Chola rule as such extended over a period of four centuries.

Chola passion for pearls is amply evident in the many inscriptions on the Thanjavur temple that record numerous gifts of jewelry that consist almost exclusively of pearls. One such ornament is a *srichanda* that appears to have been in the nature of a large ornamental breastplate to adorn the body of a male deity. Each gold *srichanda* ornament gifted to Shiva, of which several are mentioned in the inscriptions, contained on average between 700 to 900 pearls, while dozens of gifted pearl bracelets each contained between 350 and 560 pearls. A lengthy inscription of Rajaraja, engraved in eleven sections in his Thanjavur temple upon the east, north, and west walls of the shrine to saint Chandesha, consists of a consolidated list of ten sumptuous ornaments that the emperor gifted to the images in his temple prior to his twenty-ninth year of 2014.[22] Nine were ornamental gold belts to adorn the hips of bronze images (*pattigai*), each strung with anywhere from 1,541 to 5,611 pearls.[23] The tenth was a gold diadem (*vira-pattam*) given by Rajaraja to an image of Shiva and contained crystals, corals, and

> *13,328 pearls, which the lord Sri Rajarajadeva had poured out as flowers at the sacred feet and with which he had worshipped the feet of the god—round pearls, roundish pearls, polished pearls, small pearls,* nimbolam, payittam, ambumudu, *crude pearls, twin pearls,* sappatti, sakkattu, *pearls of brilliant water and of red water weighed 547* kalanju . . .[24]

The pearls in this one royal inscription of Rajaraja, detailing the gift of one diadem and nine belts, add up to the astounding number of 31,458 pearls.[25]

A second consolidated list of gifts to the Thanjavur temple similarly listing gifts given by Rajaraja up to the year 1014 is contained in an inscription in thirty-eight sections of fifteen lines each that we encountered in the previous chapter as engraved on the north wall of the temple's central shrine. It specifically states that these gifts are in addition to those engraved on the Chandeshvara shrine, and in addition to those inscribed along the temple's base moldings.[26] It speaks of six hip-belts, each with over 1,500 pearls; sixteen pearl bracelets, each with anywhere from 337 to 401 pearls; five pearl-studded *srichandas* to encircle the male torso, of which the grandest contained 998 pearls; a crown, a garland, and a parasol decorated with 1,372 pearls in strings. The total number of pearls in this set of gifts is 19,523.

Pearls in large quantities were also part of the lavish gifts carried by the diplomatic missions sent to the Chinese court by Rajaraja and Rajendra. In her study of Tamil merchant guilds, Meera Abraham points out that the Chinese sources, *Sung Shih* and *Ma Tuan-lin*, inform us that gifts from the Chola envoys to the Chinese emperor included 6,600 ounces of pearls and 3,300 catties (3,625 pounds) of aromatic substances.[27] The gifts carried by the 1033 mission to China included "a pearl hat and coat, 105 ounces of pearls, 100 ivory tusks, and a letter written on gold foil."[28] These pearls surely came from Sri Lanka's Gulf of Mannar. Additionally, we learn that the gifts carried by Kulottunga I's 1077 mission to China consisted of "pearls of various sizes, an opaque glass bowl, 'plum blossom,' camphor, rhinocerous horns, frankincense, rose water, putchuk, asafetida, borax, cloves and textiles."[29] Since few of these items are native to the Chola country, it is clear that the Cholas were seeking to act as carriers. And last, we may justifiably assume that pearls were part of the jewelry that Chola royalty and aristocracy themselves wore. The desire to control the pearl oyster fisheries of the Gulf of Mannar is an overlooked reason, and surely a substantial additional reason, for the Chola fixation with Sri Lanka.

The constant interaction between Chola territory and Sri Lanka is seen in temple inscriptions that speak of gifts of Sri Lankan coins, or *Ilakkasu*, that appear to have been accepted as valid currency in the Chola kingdom. A few examples of such gifts will clarify their widespread nature. In the year 966, during the reign of Sundara Chola, a servant-maid of Kokkilan, Parantaka's queen and mother of slain crown prince Rajaditya, gave a sum of 20 *Ilakkasu* to the temple of Tiruvidaimaradur for burning a perpetual lamp.[30] In 970, during the reign of Sundara Chola, 25 *Ilakkasu* was given to pay for two perpetually burning lamps in a temple at Kalitattai in Kumbakonam district; the donors were the wife and daughter of commander-in-chief Parantaka Siriyavelan.[31] During the same period, another two lamps were gifted to the Kalitattai temple, each for 25 *Ilakkasu*, by two individuals from two separate towns.[32] At Tirumandurai (Kumbakonam district), the brahmin *sabha* of Nalur gave land tax-free to the temple in return for 100 *Ilakkasu*.[33] In the village of Sendalai, a gift of 150 *Ilakkasu* was made by a certain Kanakasena-bhattarar for dredging a tank named Virasikhamani-Pereri.[34] A clue to the exchange rate of *Ilakkasu* to Chola *kasu* is contained in two different inscriptions. The record of the maidservant of queen Kokkilan, encountered earlier, provides the information that 20 *Ilakkasu* was equivalent to 10 *kalanju* of gold. An inscription of the year 992 at Tiruvarur, during the reign of Rajaraja, informs us that 234 *kasu* (Chola *kasu*) was the equivalent of 200 *kalanju* of gold.[35] The implication appears to be that Sri Lankan coins were half the value of Chola coins, thus approximating the situation that exists today between the Sri Lankan rupee and the Indian rupee. The close contacts between Sri Lanka and the Chola kingdom is further evident, for instance, in a gift to the Thanjavur temple of an octagonal brass spittoon, described as made in Sri Lankan fashion, that was given to a bronze of Ganesha by Rajaraja's *srikaryam* officer who was also the supervisor of the temple accountants (*kankani nayakan*).³⁶

A third possible reason for the Chola preoccupation with Sri Lanka lies in my proposal that Sri Lanka's Seruwila belt may have been a source of the copper ore necessary to make sacred bronzes in Chola temples. The transformation of processional festival images from the medium of wood to that of copper, a changeover that occurred at the start of Chola rule in the mid-ninth century, was a major innovation that was both dramatic and revolutionary. It seems warranted to assume that such a radical move would not have been made without confirmed access to a nearby and readily available source of copper. We saw in chapter 1 that Sri Lanka's Seruwila copper belt has yielded evidence of copper extraction on an industrial scale, and that Sri Lankan archaeologists and metallurgists agree that Seruwila copper was definitely exported, most likely from the nearby port of Ilankaturai, south of the port of Trincomalee. It would have been relatively easy to ship the copper directly to the Chola port of Maraikkadu or Nagapattinam; alternatively, the route may have been overland to the town of Mannar and across the gulf to Pandya territory, from where it could go by land to the Chola kingdom. In the Introduction and in chapter 1, I estimated that 153 tons of copper would have been required to fulfill the ritual requirement of twelve festival bronzes for each of the 311 Chola temples in just the three districts of Trichy, Thanjavur, and Nagapattinam, which comprise the southern part of Chola-mandalam on which my study focuses. This estimate does not take into account the northern part of this central district of Chola-mandalam, which includes, for instance, the important site of Chidambaram, nor of districts farther north to Kanchipuram and beyond. Clearly, the total amount of copper required for temples across the entire Chola kingdom would be much greater than 153 tons. Access to a source of copper ore—and this may indeed be the case—would have constituted one further reason for the Chola obsession with Sri Lanka.

Hindu Temples in Sri Lanka

Sri Lanka was a staunchly Buddhist island from the centuries BCE, when a sapling from the *bodhi* tree (pipal or *Ficus religiosa*) at Bodh Gaya, beneath which the Buddha gained enlightenment, was brought to the island and planted in the capital of Anuradhapura. It is interesting then to note that the Tamil *nayanmar* saints sang of two sites on the island, Tirukonamalai and Matottam, as renowned for their Shiva temple. In the second half of the seventh century, child saint Sambandar sang of Shiva at coastal Tirukonamalai, today's Trincomalee. Sambandar devoted the third and fourth line of each verse of this hymn to a description of the seaside location of the site and its Shiva temple:

> *He dwells in great Kōṇamalai,*
> *prosperous place,*
> *where people cry in fear*
> *at the cruel roar of the ocean*
> *as it crashes on the shore.* v. 3

He dwells in great Kōṇamalai,
where surging waves
bring to the shore fine gold and shells
swept up from the angry, roaring sea. v. 4[37]

Saint Sundarar, who lived around the year 800, sang of Shiva at Matottam, today's Mannar; the later hagiographic text, the *Periya Purana*, tells us that Sundarar sang his song from the sacred town of Rameshvaram on the mainland, addressing the lord of Matottam from across the gulf of Mannar.[38]

He shares his body with a woman
on the bank of the Palavi
in the good town of Matottam
by the sea crowded with ships—
Our lord of Tirukketiccuram
circled by coconut groves.[39]

We will see that it was at Matottam that a Chola temple named after emperor Rajaraja was built in the eleventh century.

For a period of seventy years, from approximately 998–1070, the Cholas took over the northern parts of the Buddhist island of Sri Lanka, including its capital of Anuradhapura, and converted it to a province of the Chola empire, naming it Mummudicholamandalam (after Rajaraja's title of Mummudi, or Three-Crowned One), or alternatively referring to it as Ila-mandalam. They established a new capital farther south at Polonnaruwa, that the Sri Lankan text of the *Culavamsa* calls Pulatti-nagara, and that Tamil inscriptions at the site name Jananatha-mangalam (after another of Rajaraja's tiles). At the end of the tenth century, when the Cholas decided that Polonnaruwa was the ideal location for the capital of their Sri Lankan province, it was an empty plain with three large lakes, and this ready source of water supply may have been an important reason for the Chola choice of the site. A hundred and fifty years later, the three lakes were linked to create a vast artificial lake known to this day as King Parakrama's Ocean (*Parakrama Samudra*). The grandeur of the city as we know it today is due to king Parakrama Bahu's (r. 1153–1186) extensive building program, which commenced three-quarters of a century after his ancestor Vijayabahu had ousted the Cholas and regained control of Sri Lanka.

Once Rajaraja Chola took over large areas of northern and central Sri Lanka, forcing its rulers to move to the southernmost parts of the island, as many as sixteen Hindu temples, known in Sri Lanka as *devales*, were built at Polonnaruwa. Only Shiva *devales* 1 and 2 were built of stone; all others were constructed of brick and wood, occasionally with stone pillars, upon stone foundations.[40] The earliest temple at Polonnaruwa, Shiva temple 2, was named after Rajaraja's first queen, Vanavan Mahadevi, and built entirely of stone (fig. 6.1). The close similarities of the treatment of the temple's base moldings, its shrine walls, and its *sikhara* to temples along the Kaveri are striking (see fig. 2.1 a–g), and it is likely that the queen's temple was the work of an architect brought for this specific purpose from the Kaveri delta. The five Tamil inscriptions on its walls and base

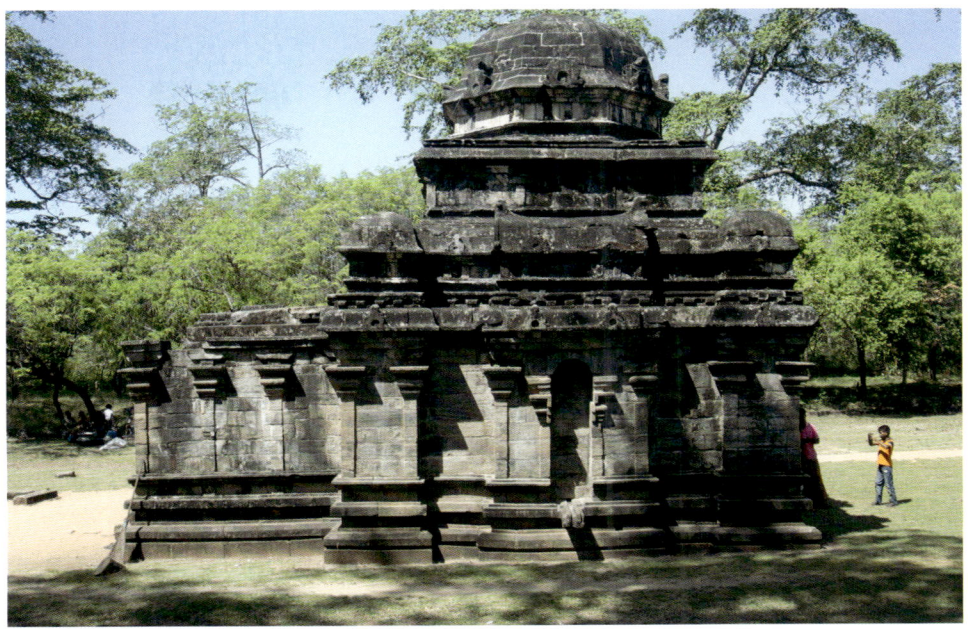

Figure 6.1. Shiva *devale* 2, Polonnaruwa, ca. 1010.

moldings are not coeval with the construction of the temple, but belong to the reign of Adirajendra (r. 1067–1071), just before Sri Lanka was wrested away from Chola control. One intact record speaks of a chieftain named Gangaikondachola Pallavaraiyan, an agricultural lord from Mayilapadi, who made a gift of a lamp of bell metal (*tara*) together with 5 *kasu* for oil to keep the lamp burning night and day.[41] An intriguing but damaged record on this Shiva temple speaks of the reclining lord (*pallikondar*), a phrase that can refer only to reclining Vishnu.[42] Another damaged record makes reference to *Alagiya Manavala*, a term used along the Kaveri river to refer to Shiva as the Lord with the bull,[43] while a fifth record speaks of the donation of another bell metal lamp.[44]

A temple named after Rajaraja was built in coastal Mannar of pearl fisheries fame rather than at Polonnaruwa, the Chola capital of the newly captured island. We have seen that Mannar, ancient Matottam, was a sacred site celebrated in song by saint Sundarar. It would appear that earlier settlers, perhaps from Pallava territories, had focused their worship on a sacred Shiva shrine in Matottam along the northern tip of Sri Lanka. This, presumably, was one important reason for the temple named after Rajaraja to be built at this site. While the Matottam Rajarajishvara temple is no longer standing, it appears likely that it too would have been constructed by an architect from the mainland, so that two temples, one named after the emperor and the other after his chief queen, would have served as "flagships," so to say, of the new administration. A few surviving stone slabs from this temple, now in the Colombo Museum, testify to ritual and festival practices familiar from the mainland.[45] The longest of three inscriptions gives us precise geographical details of the site of the temple as well as the exact home of the patron. It speaks of Talikumaran, headman of the town of Kuttranallur, in the Kshatriyasikhamani-valanadu of Cholamandalam, who made a gift to the Lord of the Rajarajishvaram temple, which he had constructed in Rajarajapuram, also known as

CHOLA OBSESSION WITH SRI LANKA

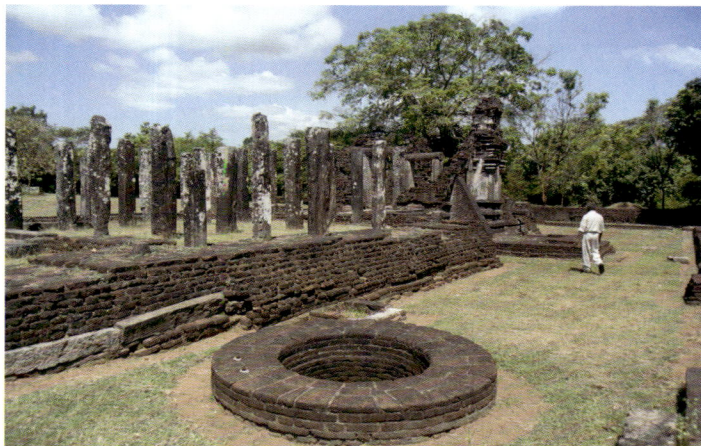
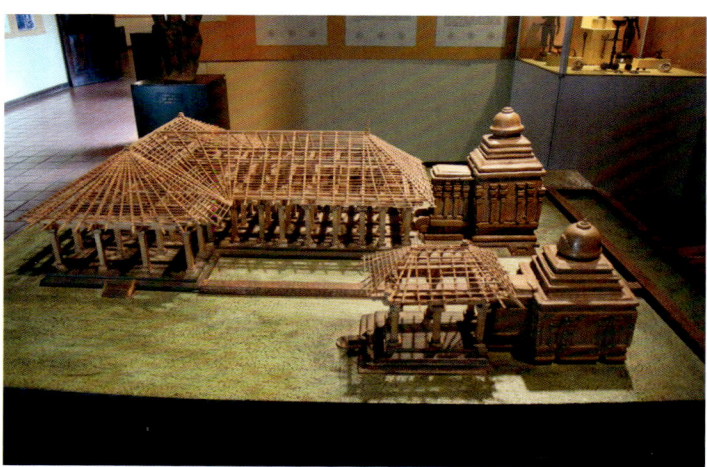

Figure 6.2. (a) Ruins of Shiva *devale* 5, Polonnaruwa, ca. 1010–1050. (b) Conjectural restoration of Shiva *devale* 5, Polonnaruwa Museum.

Matottam in Mummudicholamandalam. His gift of tax-free land specifies its boundaries, including a street named Rajaraja Great Avenue (*rajaraja perum teruvu*). The cash accruing from the land donated, together with his gift of money collected as a toll, was to be used for three purposes: for daily late-night worship (*ardhajama puja*), for the provision of sacred food in the temple three times a day, and for the celebration of a seven-day festival in the month of *Vaikhashi* (May–June).[46] While damage to the first few lines of this inscription has deprived us of the name of the ruler and his regnal year, an inscribed pillar from the same temple site, relocated to the Colombo Museum, commences with the eulogy (*meykirti*) of Rajendra. The pillar inscription speaks of a high official of Rajendrachola who made a gift of four *kasu*; two *kasu* were loaned to the oil merchants guild, and one each to the betel-leaf merchants and the plantain merchants. The interest from this endowment was to be used to burn a twilight lamp at the temple in Rajarajapuram, also known as Matottam, for the deity Ramishvaram Udaiyar, described further in the inscription as Shiva with the bull (*Rishabhavahanam Udaiyar*) and surely a bronze image.[47]

The largest of temples at Polonnaruwa is the sadly ruined Shiva temple 5, of which a miniature conjectural restoration in wood and brick is on display in the Polonnaruwa Museum, providing an idea of its layout, orientation, and the wooden roofing of its many halls (fig. 6.2a, b). Its considerable dimensions, combined with the fact that the largest number of Hindu bronzes was found in clearance and excavations around the temple, suggests that it was the center of Hindu devotional activity in the new capital.[48] One of its stone pillars carries a Tamil notation on each of its four sides that records the name and, in one instance, the hometown in the Kaveri delta of four individuals who appear to have been donors to the temple, and who were most likely Tamil merchants recently settled in Polonnaruwa.[49] The Hindu temples are widely scattered across an area of 2 kilometers, south to north, and the reason for their precise location, as well as their relationship to one another, remains to be investigated. The two stone Shiva temples 1 and 2, and the ruins of four small brick temples, two dedicated to Shiva, one to Vishnu, and one to Ganesha, are within Parakrama's Inner City of Polonnaruwa, which is bisected by a wide north-south road and entered through a northern gateway. Another four Hindu temples are located within the expanded city, which extends a total of almost 5 kilometers from north to south. The most significant temple of Chola days, Shiva *devale 5*, and six other *devales*, are located outside Parakrama's expanded Buddhist city and close to the three large lakes that had attracted Chola attention.

Hindu Bronzes from Sri Lanka

The bronzes recovered from clearance and excavations at Polonnaruwa are an intriguing group that pose challenging stylistic questions revolving around issues of borrowing, citation, and selective adaptation. Several bronzes are distinctive in style and noticeably different from those seen in the Kaveri delta, and were clearly created in a local workshop whose wax modelers had varying success in coming to terms with an unfamiliar Hindu iconography. For over a thousand years, Sri Lanka had been an exclusively Buddhist island. Its artists were accustomed to modeling images of a seated or standing Buddha, two-armed, quiet and serene, wearing a simple monastic robe with no ornaments of any type (fig. 6.3). All of a sudden, these sculptors were faced with the extraordinary concept of a god famed as a Dancer, a god who wore exuberant ornaments, a god whose animated movement through dance was the essence of his imagery, a god whose consort stood poised in elegant contrapposto. Possibly, the new Tamil patrons provided the local artists with models in the form of small bronzes of personal devotion that they had brought with them; perhaps they even presented them with a mini-iconographic manual of drawings, although nothing of the type survives from Chola times.[50]

An eleventh-century Dancing Shiva from Polonnaruwa, found during clearance in and around Shiva temple 5, stands 4 feet 7 1/2 inches high, and is thus even larger than the early eleventh-century image still in worship in Rajaraja's Thanjavur temple (fig. 6.4a).[51] While the Kaveri delta bronze conveys a fluid sense of movement, this Sri Lankan example created by sculptor "A" displays a certain hesitance, even a sense of discomfort, in the treatment of a four-armed deity who raises his leg high at the pelvic joint to stand poised in dance. The shoulders of this Sri Lankan Dancing Lord are excessively broad, and the sculptor's disquiet at having to add two additional arms is noticeably evident in his attachment of Shiva's left front arm. While his problem is evident in a frontal view, it is seen even more dramatically from the rear, especially at a three-quarter angle, which conveys the extent of the challenge faced by the wax modeler in adapting to an

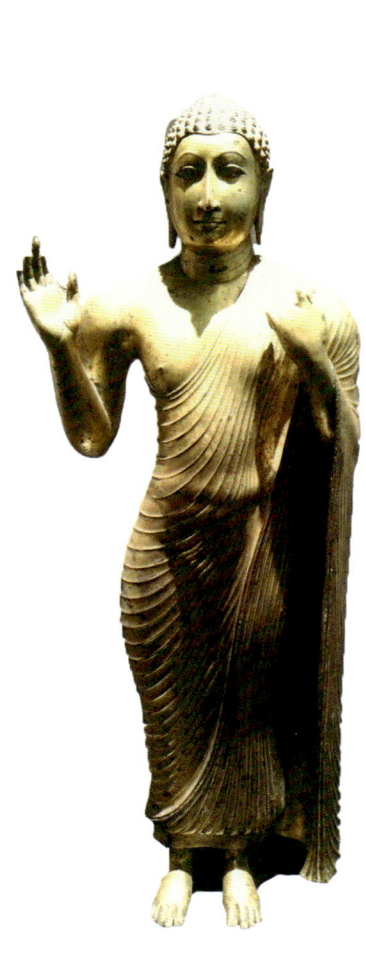

Figure 6.3. Sri Lankan Buddha, Veregala, ninth century, Colombo National Museum.

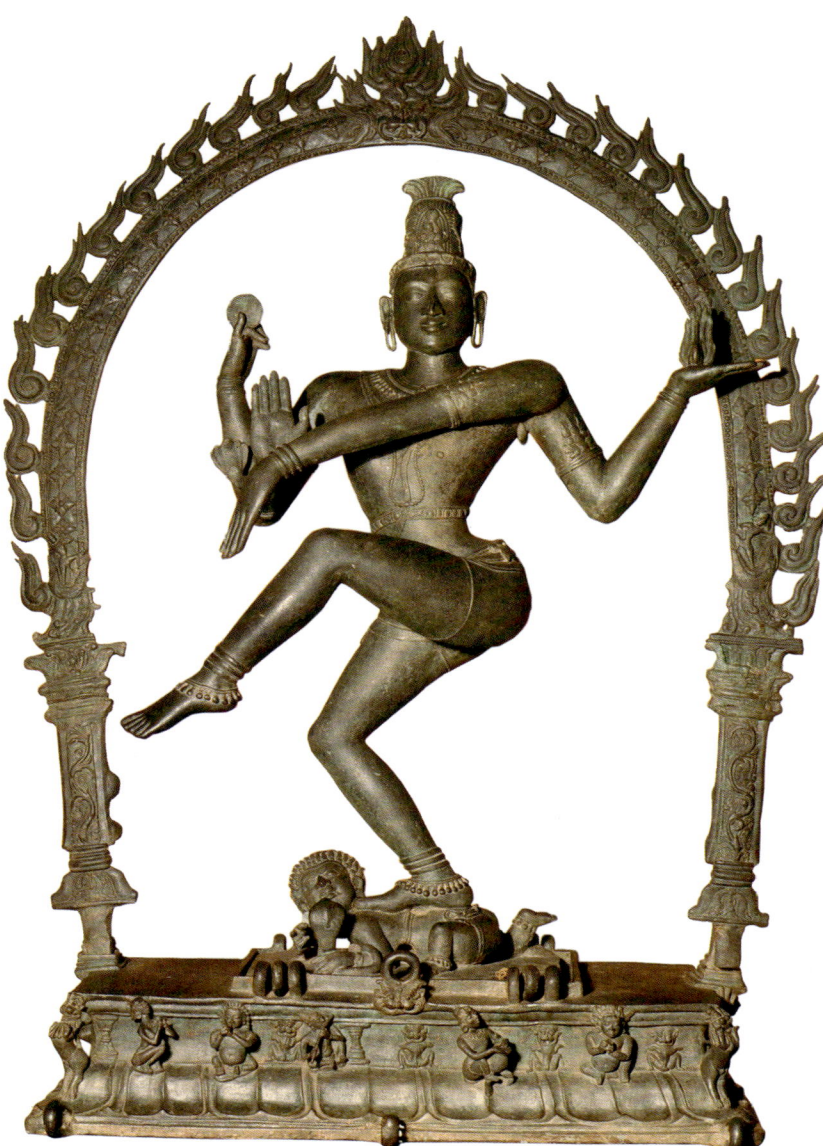

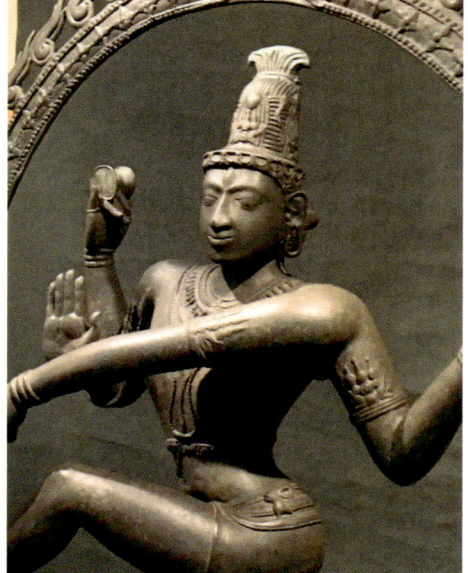

Figure 6.4. (a) Dancing Shiva. Sculptor "A," Shiva *devale* 5, early eleventh century, Polonnaruwa Museum. (b) Detail of Dancing Shiva (fig. 6.4a).

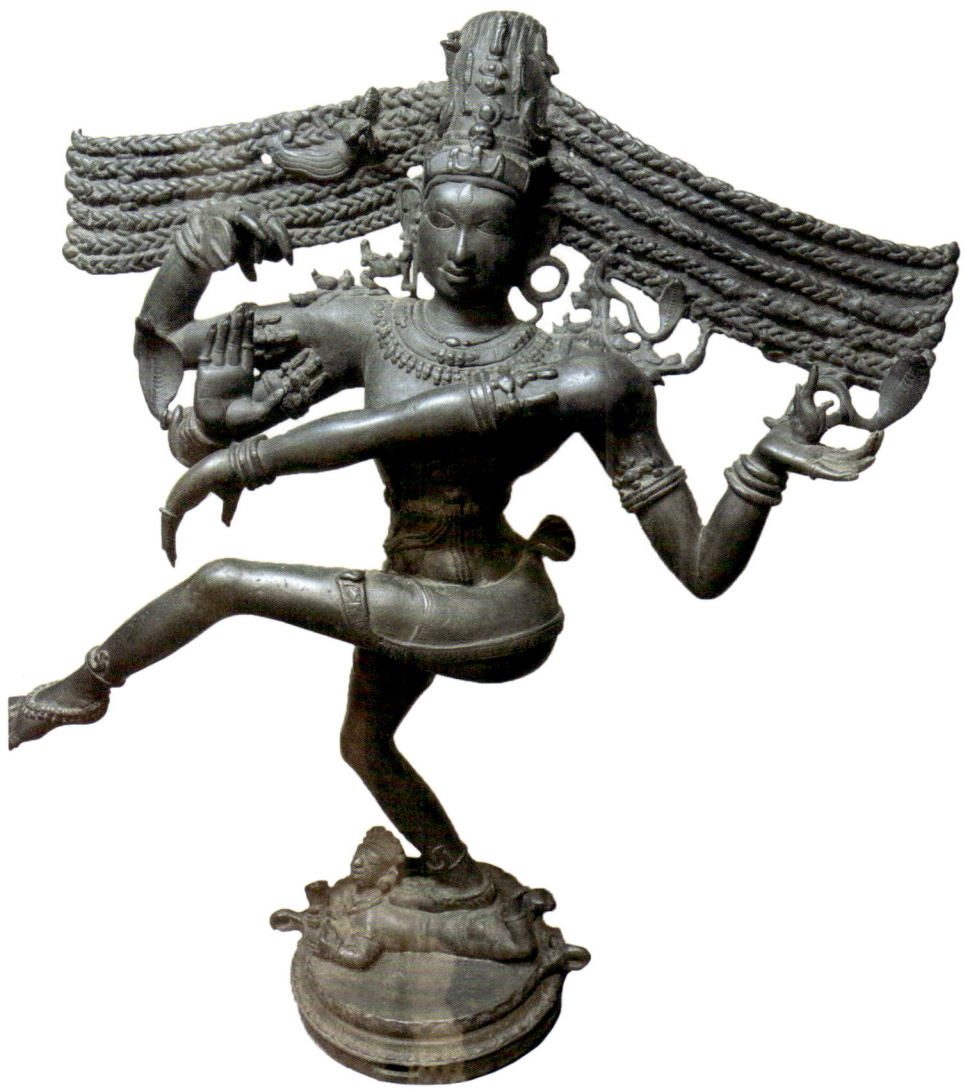

Figure 6.5. Dancing Shiva, Sculptor "B," Shiva *devale* 5, early eleventh century Colombo National Museum.

unfamiliar iconography (fig. 6.4b). The outline of Shiva's proper left torso is markedly exaggerated in its indentation, while the left thigh moves up at an unwieldy angle. Dancing Shiva's squarish face, and the truncated nature of his matted locks that are normally piled high on his head, are quite different from the Kaveri delta mode of presentation.

A second Dancing Shiva, just over 3 feet in height, also from Shiva temple 5, was created by wax modeler "B," who appears to have studied Chola models more closely (fig. 6.5).[52] He gave Shiva a face that would be at home in the Kaveri delta, and almost every detail is close to the Kaveri mode of presentation, including the diadem, the treatment of the towering locks adorned with trumpet flower, crescent moon, and serpent, and the ear ornaments that consist of a ring in one ear and a dangling earring in the other. The matted locks that swing out with the movement of Shiva's dance are unusual but accomplished in their treatment as tight braids, and the river goddess Ganges reclines elegantly against

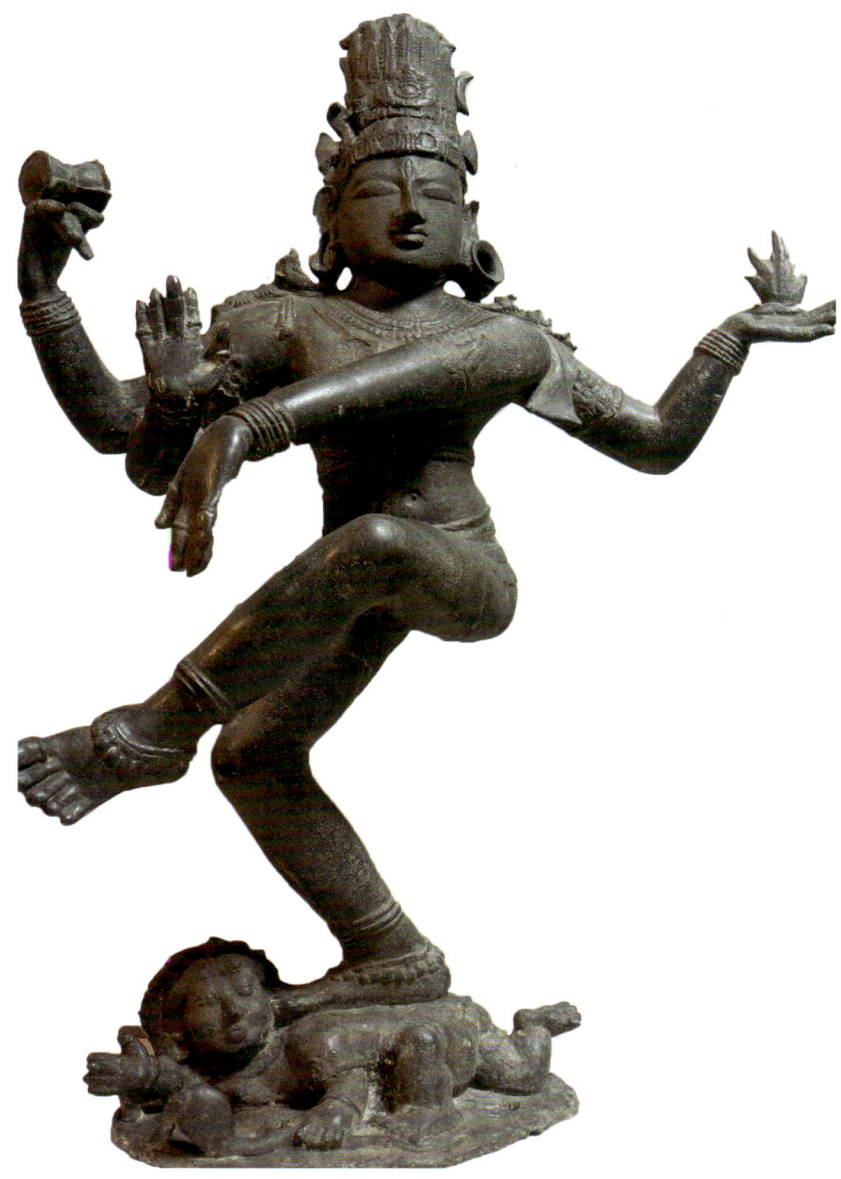

Figure 6.6. (a and b) Dancing Shiva, Sculptor "C," Shiva *devale* 5, Polonnaruwa, early eleventh century, Colombo National Museum.

them. There is a continuing problem with the width of Shiva's shoulders and the attachment of a second set of arms, and here too the outline of Shiva's torso, to his proper left, is sharply indented.

A third Dancing Shiva of smaller dimensions is closer to the more classic examples of the Dancing Lord from the Chola heartland in the Kaveri basin, and was created by sculptor "C" (fig. 6.6a, b). The comfort level of this sculptor is evident in his treatment of the gently sloping shoulders, the positioning of the second set of arms, the smooth curve of the torso, and the angle at which the left thigh is raised in dance. One crucial detail is the addition of a scarf that hides the joint of the two arms along Shiva's proper left. This seemingly minor detail was routinely added in Kaveri delta Dancing Shivas (see figs. 4.16,

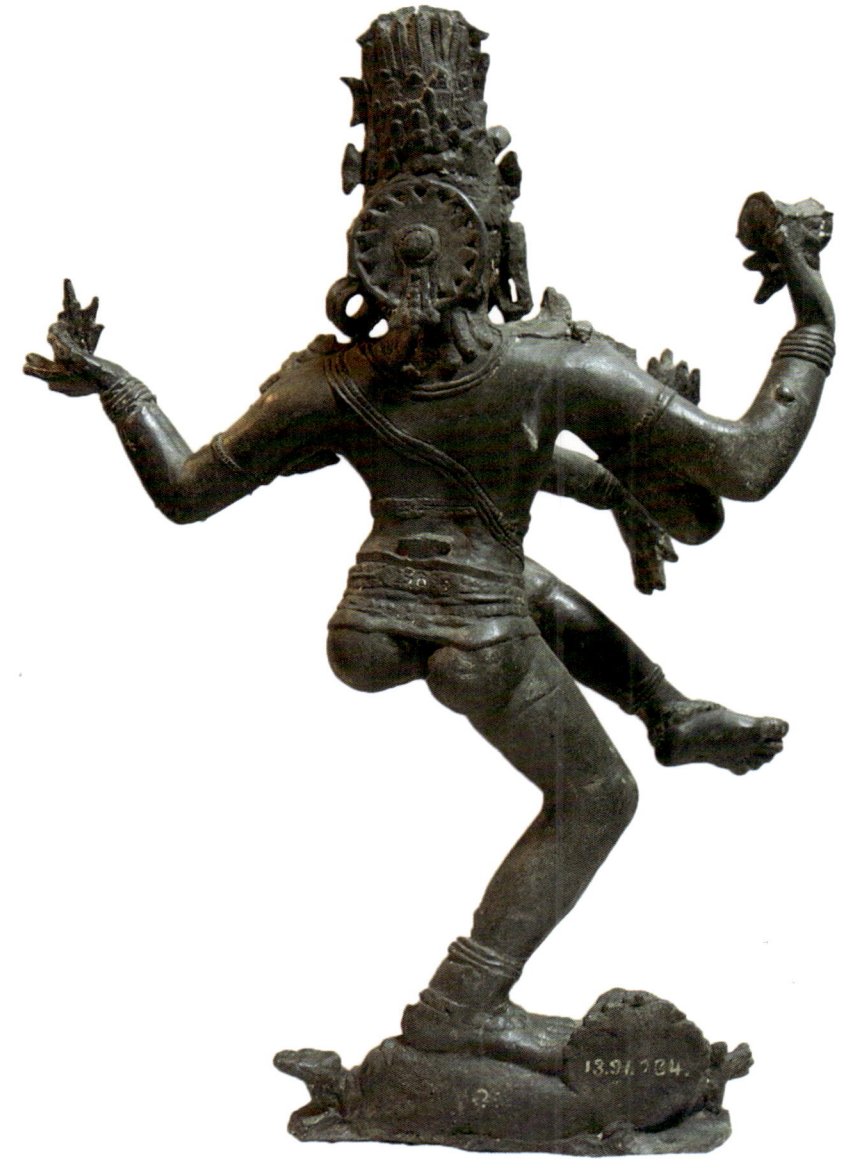

4.18a and b, 4.19, 4.20, 4.21), but was missed by the two different Sri Lankan artists responsible for the two large Dancing Shivas created for Polonnaruwa's temples. The fact that the sculptor of the smaller Dancing Shiva did not miss this detail presents us with an intriguing problem, since this image comes from the very same Shiva temple 5 at Polonnaruwa as the two larger dancing images. One of three possibilities may account for this unusual situation. First, the small Dancing Lord might be an image carried all the way from the Kaveri delta by a merchant who did not wish to be parted from his beloved Dancing Shiva. It is all of 2 feet high and extremely heavy, but it could have been transported to Polonnaruwa. A second possibility is that a Kaveri delta wax modeler traveled with Tamil merchants to Sri Lanka, where he created the Dancing Lord in a bronze workshop that

CHOLA OBSESSION WITH SRI LANKA

welcomed his participation. The third option is that it was created by an accomplished Sri Lankan wax modeler who carefully studied the positioning of Shiva's body in the models to which he had access. He noticed, for instance, the little trick of the scarf over the left shoulder to conceal the difficult joint of the two left arms. The unknown Sri Lankan modeler "C," and I think this is the most plausible solution, created an image that would challenge art historians of the early twenty-first century, making us puzzle over the smooth sculptural quality of this particular Dancing Lord found at Polonnaruwa.

Also from temple 5 comes an exceptional portrayal of the emaciated woman saint known as Mother of Karaikkal, the Chola port town a little north of Nagapattinam (fig. 6.7). She is one of the sixty-three saints of Shiva and lived in the sixth century, prior to the Revered Three of child saint Sambandar, Appar, and Sundarar. Her story is bizarre and centers around the fact that this once-beautiful young woman beseeched Shiva to take away the unnecessary weight of her body, and to permit her forever to watch his wondrous dance. And, a miraculous transformation is believed to have occurred. In place of a young woman, there stood an emaciated hag-like creature, all skin and bones, with spinal column and rib cage clearly visible, as portrayed by the artist of this 11-inch-high bronze. Her hair is in wild disarray around her head, and her depleted pointed breasts swing fiercely outward. A stone portrayal of the Dancing Lord at emperor Rajendra's royal temple at Gangaikondacholapuram on the mainland carries, in shallow bas relief, a similar powerful portrayal of the emaciated saint, playing her cymbals. At that temple, she is seated beneath Shiva's feet and accompanied by Shiva's dwarfish attendants, who sing while playing various instruments (fig. 6.8a, b). The Sri Lankan bronze is so close to the portrayal on Rajendra's temple that it is difficult to avoid the conclusion that it was the work of an artist familiar with this particular mainland imagery. Why did the artists create so bizarre a portrayal, both in Sri Lanka and in Rajendra's mainland temple, north of the Kaveri? The inspiration appears to lie in the poems that the woman saint wrote on Shiva dancing in the company of female ghouls in a fearsome forest environment where cremation fires burn. Here is the verse with which the saint commences one of two poems she wrote in this mode:

> *A female ghoul with withered breasts, bulging veins,*
> *red hair, two fangs,*
> *bony ankles, and elongated shins,*
> *stays in this cemetery, howling angrily.*
> *This place where my Lord dances in the fire with a cool body,*
> *his streaming hair flying in eight directions*
> *is Tiruvalankatu.*[53]

In her final signature verse, she describes herself as a ghoul with unkempt hair:

> *Those who are able to recite the ten verses in classical Tamil*
> *by Karaikkal pey [ghoul] with uncombed hair,*
> *on the feet of the Lord*
> *who is in the auspicious Tiruvalankatu*
> *will attain the bliss of reaching Siva.*[54]

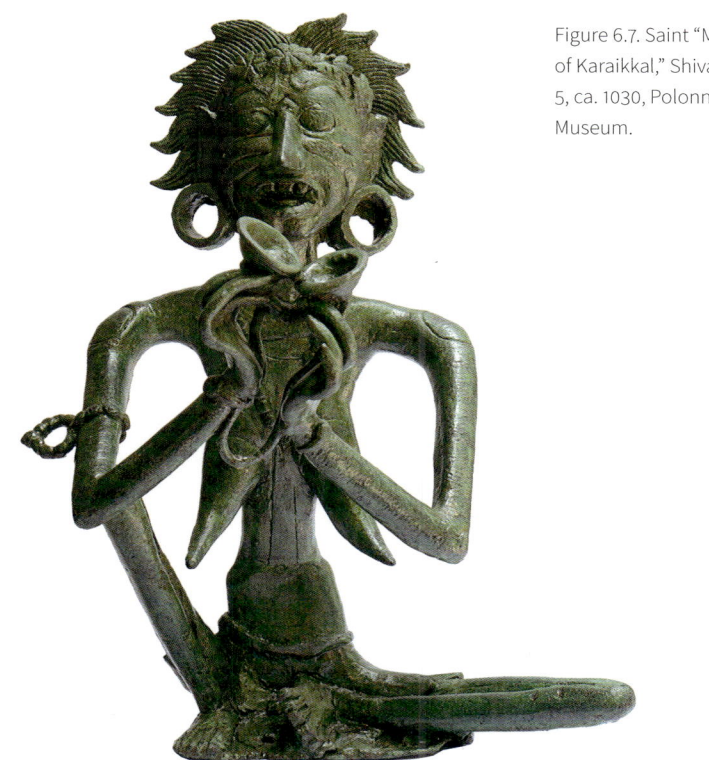

Figure 6.7. Saint "Mother of Karaikkal," Shiva *devale* 5, ca. 1030, Polonnaruwa Museum.

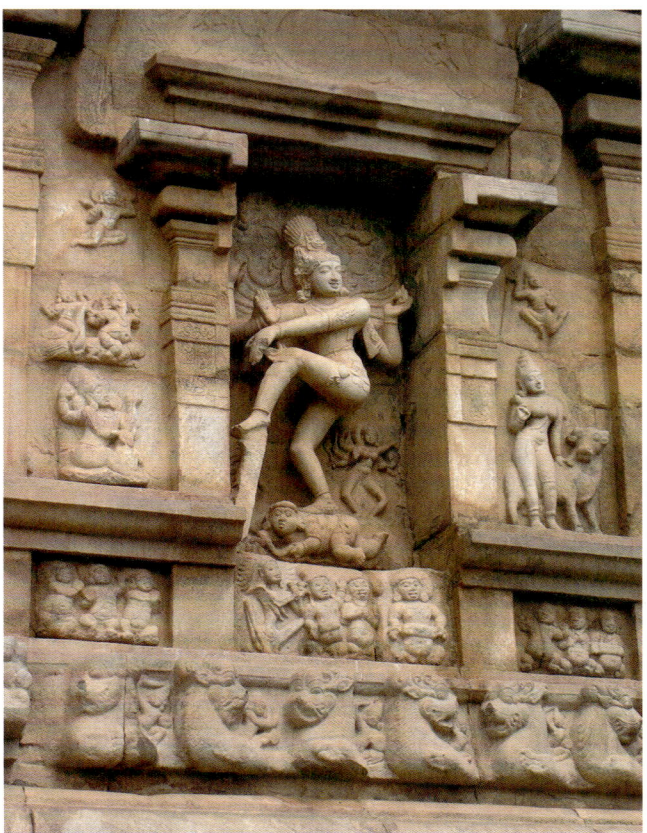

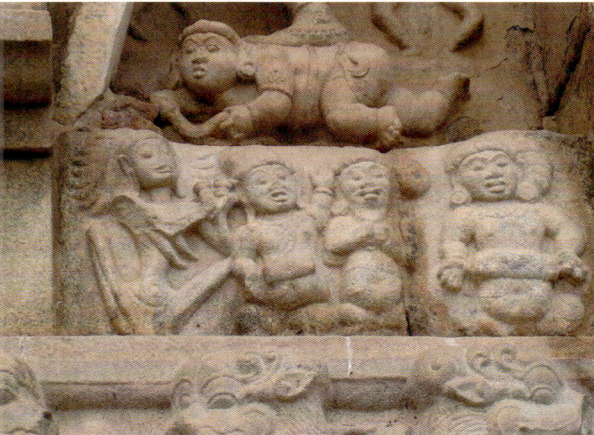

Figure 6.8. (a) Dancing Shiva, Gangaikondacholapuram, Ariyalur district, Tamil Nadu, ca. 1030. (b) Detail of pedestal of Dancing Shiva (fig. 6.8a), depicting woman saint Karaikkal Ammaiyar seated at far left.

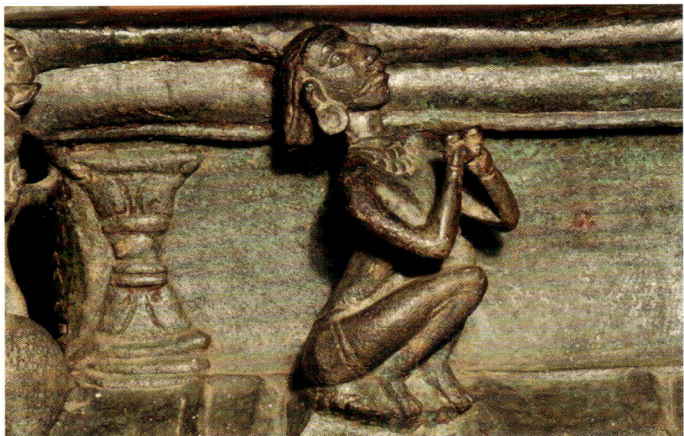
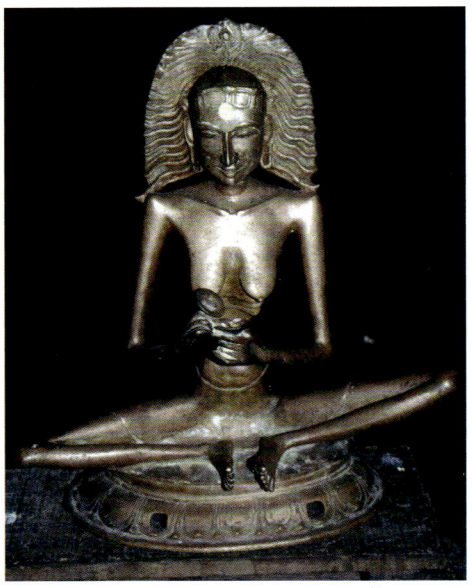

Figure 6.9. Detail of Saint "Mother of Karaikkal" along pedestal of Dancing Shiva, Polonnaruwa Museum (see fig. 6.4).

Figure 6.10. Saint "Mother of Karaikkal," Tiruvalankadu temple, ca. 1030.

In the signature verse of her second poem in this mode, she describes herself as "Karaikkal pey who has sharp teeth and a fiery mouth."[55] Both the stone image on the mainland and the Polonnaruwa bronze capture the essence of the saint's own bizarre verbal portrayal of the forest ghouls who watch Shiva's dance, and of her own ghoulish self.

At Polonnaruwa, Karaikkal Ammaiyar is also portrayed as a less forbidding tiny figure to the far left of the pedestal of the large Dancing Shiva, where she squats sideways, gazing up at her dancing lord and sounding her cymbals (fig. 6.9). Four of Shiva's dwarfish *gana* attendants, who sit facing forward, provide further accompaniment for their master's dance; one blows a conch shell, a second plays the flute, a third sounds the *ghatam* (earthen pot played as a drum), and the fourth sounds the cymbals. This more sympathetic portrayal of the saint is closer to the tone and feel of the bronze in the temple at Tiruvalankadu on the mainland, located beside the forest where Karaikkal Ammaiyar's poetry locates her dancing lord (fig. 6.10). Sitting cross-legged with sharply delineated collarbones, depleted breasts that hug her rib cage, and raised knobbly shoulder joints, her face reflects a peaceful calm as she sounds her cymbals. In this portrayal, her shrunken body accords more closely with the tale of a beautiful young woman deprived of her fleshy contours, rather than a fearsome ghoulish creature.

In their difficulty in portraying the typical *tri-bhanga* or "triple-bent" contrapposto, Sri Lankan bronzes of Uma present us with yet another example of the sculptors' misinterpretation of a major aspect of Kaveri basin imagery. A mere glance at the Tiruvenkadu Uma whom we examined in the previous chapter clarifies that *tribhanga* requires Uma's crowned head and lower limbs to be posed at the same angle, while the torso moves in the opposite direction (see fig. 5.2). The artist of a powerful Polonnaruwa Uma, standing over 3 feet tall together with pedestal, appears to have found this a baffling concept. His Uma's head and torso are at more or less the same angle; for the viewer standing in front of the image, they both slope to the left, while the lower body is more or less vertical (fig. 6.11a, b). The result is an uncoordinated and somewhat ungainly effect that is especially evident

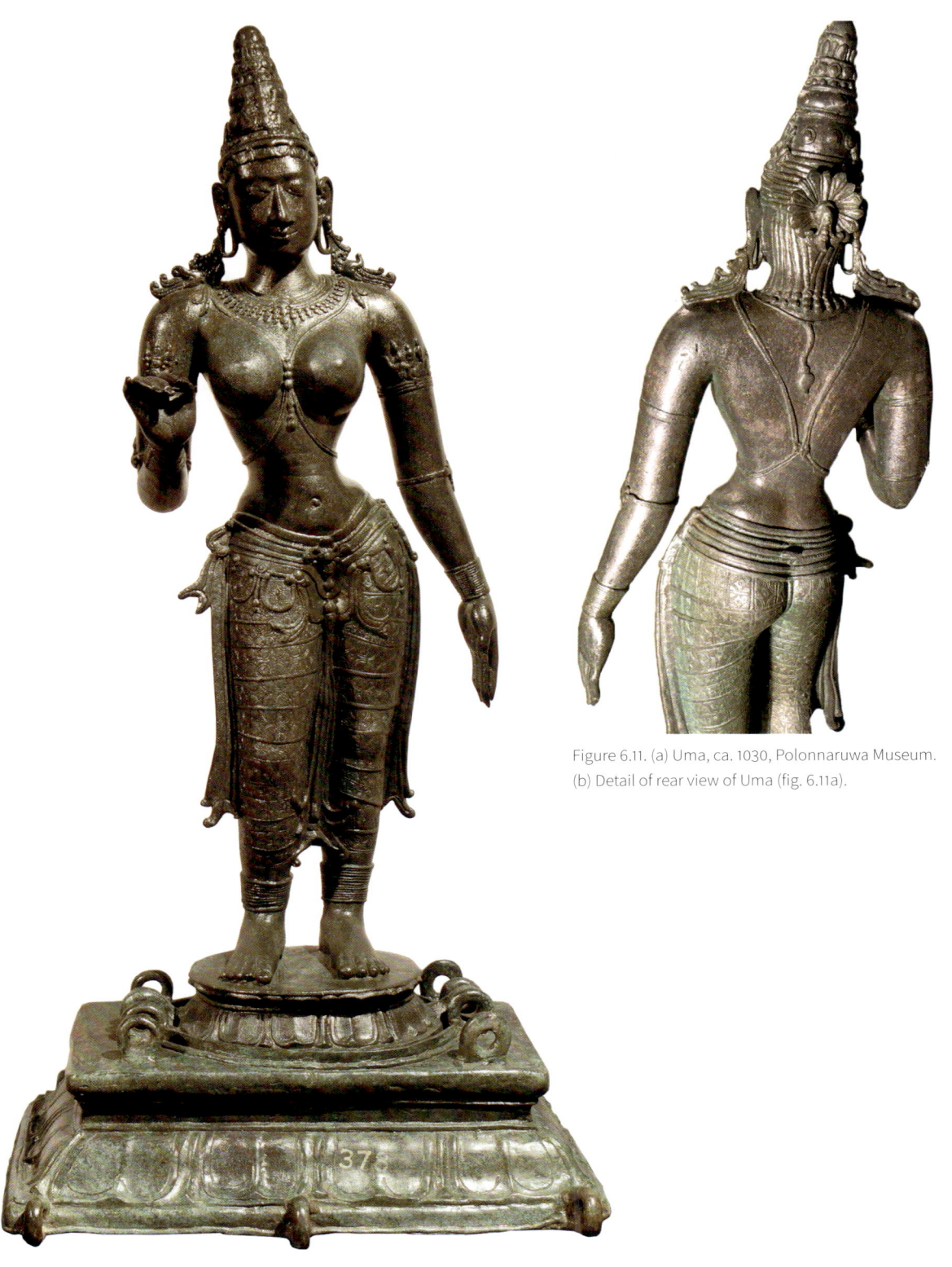

Figure 6.11. (a) Uma, ca. 1030, Polonnaruwa Museum.
(b) Detail of rear view of Uma (fig. 6.11a).

through comparison with Kaveri delta images. It is intriguing though to compare this Polonnaruwa Uma with a second Uma from Polonnaruwa whose sculptor better understood the triple-bent posture and created an image that is more appropriately balanced (fig. 6.12). Images of Uma are to be found in both categories, raising the identical issues revolving around selective adaptation, citation, and successful adoption that we encountered with Dancing Shiva. It would appear that bronzes in both categories were welcomed by the patrons and donors of Shiva temple 5; presumably it was necessary to accept the best of what was available when more experienced sculptors were called away to other more prestigious, probably Buddhist commissions.

Another Sri Lankan stylistic idiosyncrasy is a predilection for totally level and overly broad shoulders that is seen in image after image including the Uma of fig. 6.11. Might this feature be related in any way to the more familiar Buddhist stipulation that one of the thirty-two marks of a *chakravartin*-Buddha is that his shoulders are wide and straight, and that "there is no furrow between his shoulders"?[56] A Polonnaruwa bronze of saint Chandesha, standing 30 inches high, has ruler-straight, level shoulders that create a taut and rigid effect; adding a visual effect of imbalance is the further fact that the image is poised stiffly on both feet (fig. 6.13). More than one Sri Lankan image, including this Chandesha bronze, appears to list slightly as if a mere touch might make it fall forward. By contrast, a second image of Chandesha, 28 inches tall, and now in the Colombo Museum,[57] is quite different in treatment and more closely resembles images from the Chola mainland (fig. 6.14a). The sloping shoulders of the saint, the relaxed stance of the legs with weight resting on his right foot, the treatment of the face itself, and the manner in which his matted hair is piled high on his head, all speak of the hand of a sculptor who was familiar with Kaveri basin imagery. This image has a fragmentary inscription on its pedestal that is not in Tamil, as one might perhaps have anticipated, but in Sinhala and written in a mixed Sinhalese and *grantha* script (fig. 6.14b). With its first letter/s damaged, it reads ". . . *pati rsabha vamse*," which suggests that it might be a donor's name and genealogical title.[58]

The popularity of the poems of the Shaiva *nayanmar* saints, and the significance of the saints themselves in the religious life of Chola settlers in Polonnaruwa, is indicated by the number of bronzes of the saints that the Tamil settlers appear to have commissioned. It is evident that the various sets of images reflect different aesthetic criteria and clearly came from the hands of different craftsmen and even different workshops. For instance, an image of child saint Sambandar playing the cymbals and of the older saint Appar holding a hoe in the crook of his arm, are creations of sculptor "X," who modeled smooth images with an exceedingly narrow waist and trim hips, giving his saints a shaven head with just a small segment of hair pulled into a tiny *kudumi* knot. Both images stand straight, resting their weight stiffly on both feet; a chain of bells is wrapped around child Sambandar's waist and a loin cloth knotted around Appar's, and both wear garlands of *rudraksha* beads (fig. 6.15a, b). Their closely similar broad shoulders, narrow waist, and straight narrow hips point to both Sambandar and Appar being the work of the same craftsman "X," who may originally have created a threesome group of the *Muvar* or Revered Three, of which the image of saint Sundarar is missing today. A second image of saint Appar, wearing a dhoti that stops above the knees and with his hoe secured so as to rest against his left shoulder,

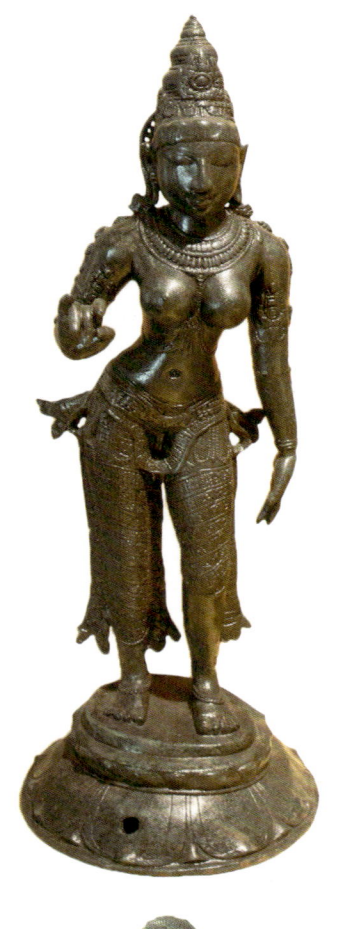

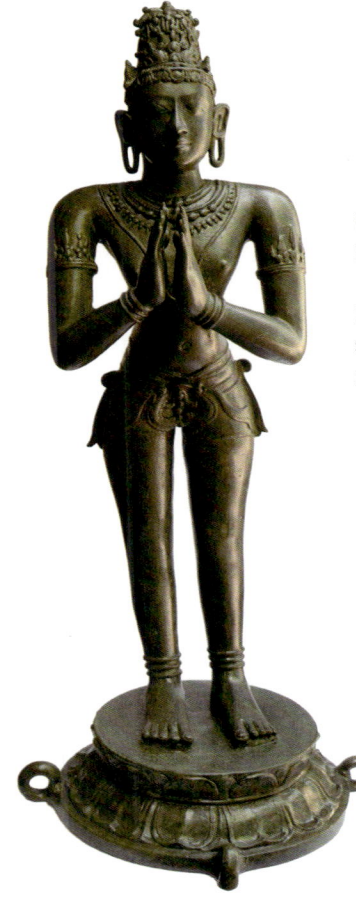

Figure 6.12. Uma, ca. 1050, Polonnaruwa Museum.

Figure 6.13. Saint Chandesha, ca. 1030, Polonnaruwa Museum.

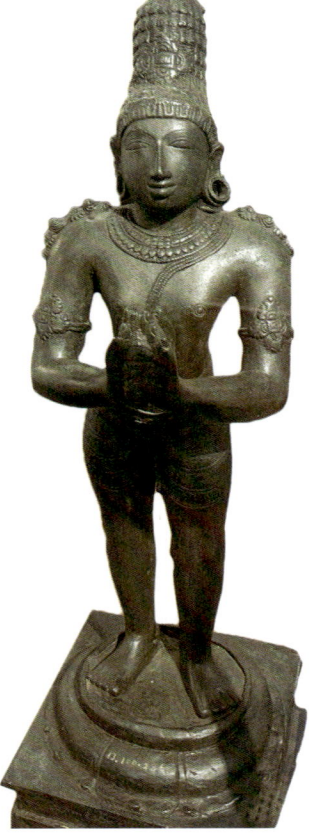

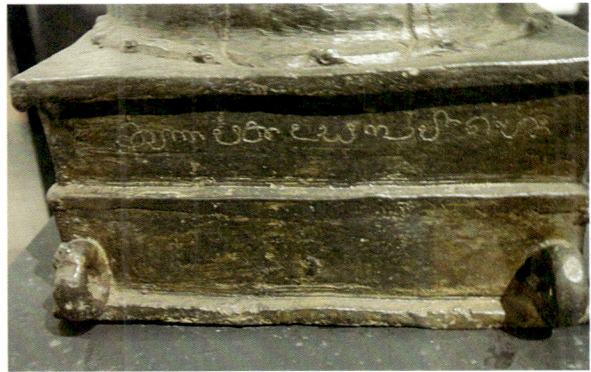

Figure 6.14. (a) Saint Chandesha, Polonnaruwa, ca. 1030, Colombo National Museum. (b) Detail of inscribed pedestal, Saint Chandesha (fig. 6.14a).

CHOLA OBSESSION WITH SRI LANKA 185

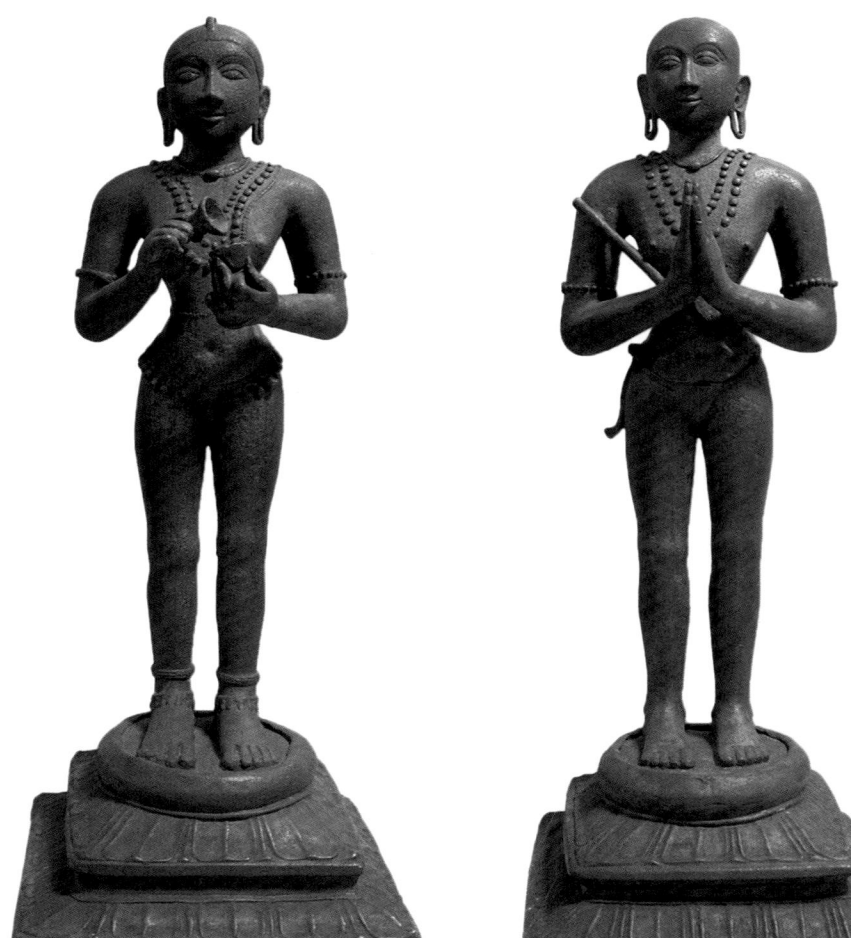

Figure 6.15. (a) Sculptor "X," Saint Sambandar, Polonnaruwa, ca. 1030–1050, Colombo National Museum. (b) Sculptor "X," Saint Appar, Polonnaruwa, ca. 1030–1050, Colombo National Museum.

comes from the hand of artist "Y," who appears to have sought, with limited success, to give the saint a relaxed stance by resting his weight on his left leg (fig. 6.16). However, Appar's torso and shoulders lean markedly toward his proper left, and in rear view the awkward treatment of the waist, hips, and buttocks is pronounced. From the hands of yet another artist "Z" comes an image of saint Sundarar, who stands well balanced in elegant contrapposto with weight resting on his left leg. He is richly adorned as befits his iconography of the bridegroom claimed as servant by Shiva, and his hair is pulled into a small chignon at the rear of his head with the pronounced ends of two ribbons visible in frontal view, giving his face a somewhat pert look (fig. 6.17). A bronze of dancing child saint Sambandar, and an image of saint Manikkavachakar, who lived after the sixty-three *nayanmar*, speak of the importance of the saints to the merchant communities settled on the island.

Also from Polonnaruwa's *devale* 5 is a seated image of Shiva along with Uma and child Skanda (fig. 6.18a). Shiva and his consort are separated today, so Shiva resides in the Polonnaruwa Museum while Uma may be seen in the Colombo Museum; to see them reunited you have to turn to a photograph published in the catalogue accompanying a special exhibition of Sri Lankan bronzes.[59] This bronze, while somewhat different from images of parallel

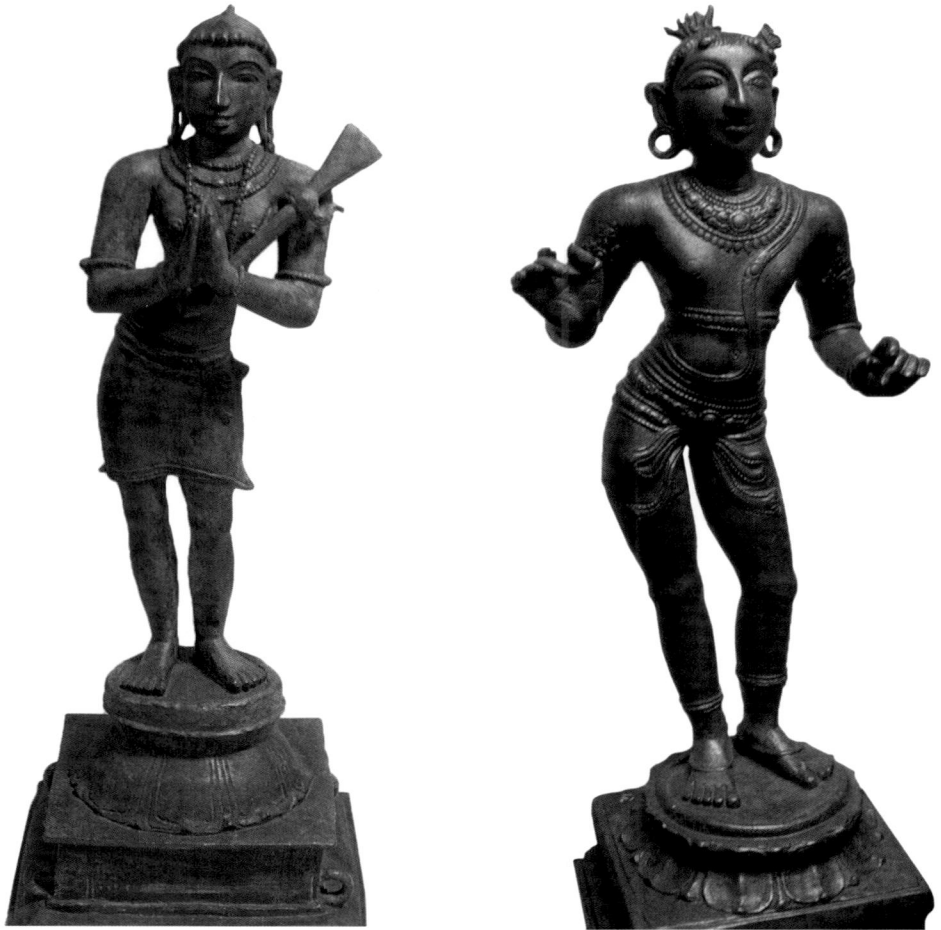

Figure 6.16. Sculptor "Y," Saint Appar, Polonnaruwa, ca. 1030–1050, Colombo National Museum.

Figure 6.17. Sculptor "Z," Saint Sundarar, Polonnaruwa, ca. 1030–1050, Colombo National Museum.

iconography from the Kaveri delta (see fig. 4.12) is a superb example of Sri Lankan workmanship. Challenging as the subject must have been for the wax modeler, he created features that would meet with the approval of his patron, who was most likely a Tamil merchant living in or around Polonnaruwa. Shiva's tall crowning locks, held back with a diadem, accurately feature the trumpet flower, the snake, the crescent moon, and the central skull. Shiva's third eye is featured on his forehead, he wears a ring in one ear and a dangling earring in the other, and holds antelope and battle-ax in his two rear hands. Necklaces, armlets, sacred thread, waistband, dhoti, and anklets are appropriately depicted. And yet, the image comes undoubtedly from the hands of a Sri Lankan artist—the width and straightness of the shoulders, the somewhat tubular handling of the limbs, and the pronounced curve of the lower eye socket that is never seen in (fig. 6.18b) Kaveri basin images are among features that are Sri Lankan giveaways. A gifted Sri Lankan artist selectively embraced a set of features typical of Chola bronzes, and adapted them to create a masterful image of Shiva, but one that reveals its creator's Sri Lankan origins.

A final and unique Sri Lankan masterpiece of stunning proportions, close to 3 feet tall, portrays elephant-headed Ganesha seated with one leg bent at the knee to rest

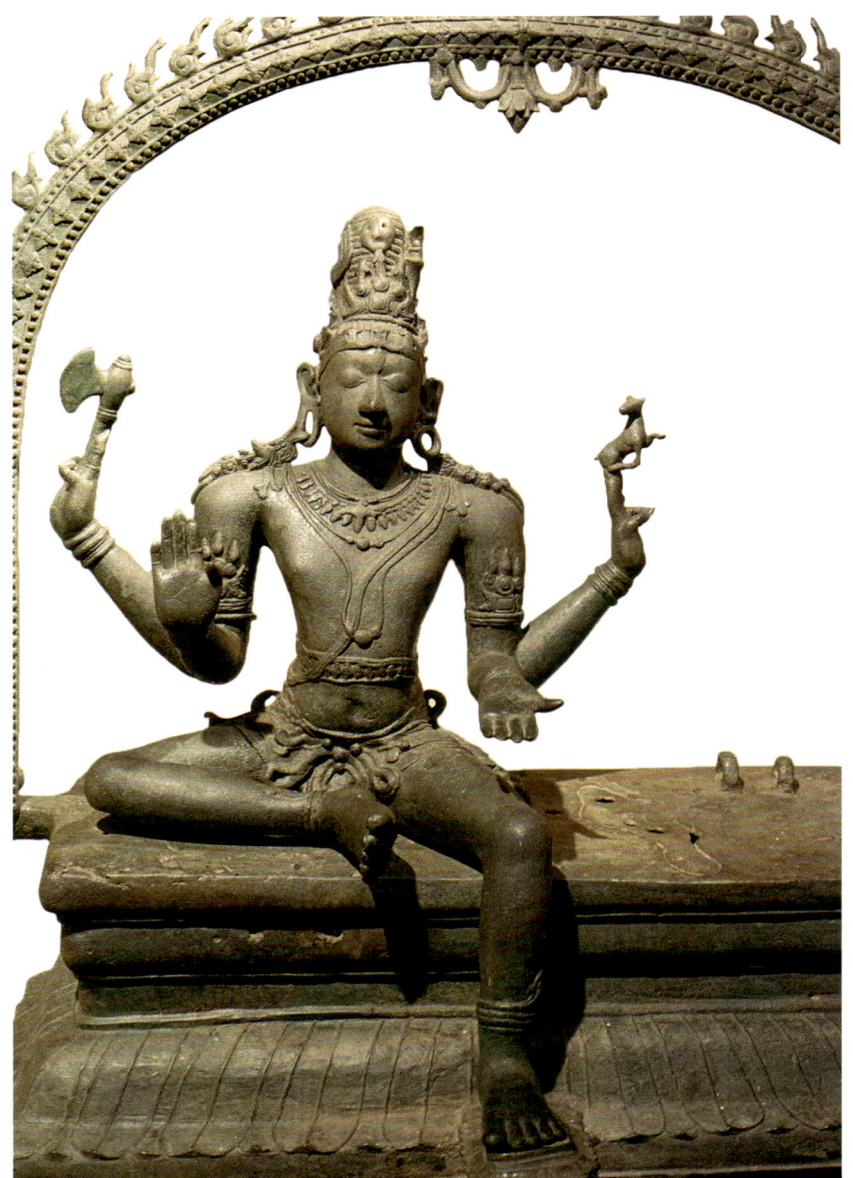 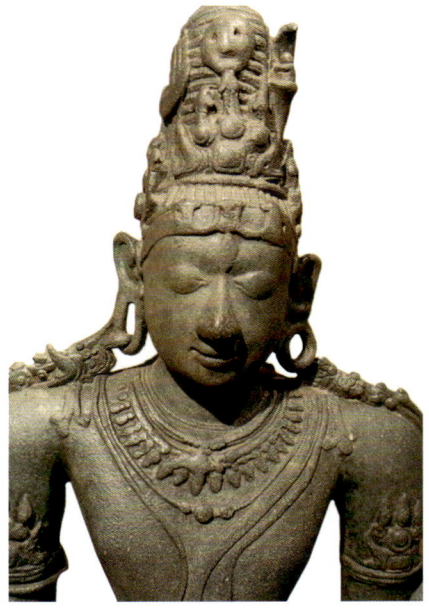

Figure 6.18. (a) *Somaskanda* Shiva, Shiva *devale* 5, ca. 1030, Polonnaruwa, Sri Lanka, Polonnaruwa Museum. (b) Detail of *Somaskanda* Shiva (fig. 6.18a).

the sole of his foot on the ground while the other leg, also bent at the knee, rests flat along his seat. Found at Shiva temple 5, the piece is a superb example of imagery that differs from the many standing Ganeshas found on the mainland (fig. 6.19a). The iconography is the same in that Ganesha holds a sweetmeat and his broken tusk in two front hands, while the rear hands hold the battle-ax and a rosary. He is exuberantly adorned with a small conical crown, sacred thread, armlets, waistband, and anklets. His short dhoti of patterned fabric and the *siraschakra* tied below his crown are seen best in rear view, where we also see the lugs cast in bronze on both the figure and its base plate in order to secure the weighty image appropriately (fig. 6.19b). The strength and power of Ganesha emerges unmistakably from the treatment of his robust and powerful body, which diverts attention from the unusually small size of his face proportionate to his substantial body.

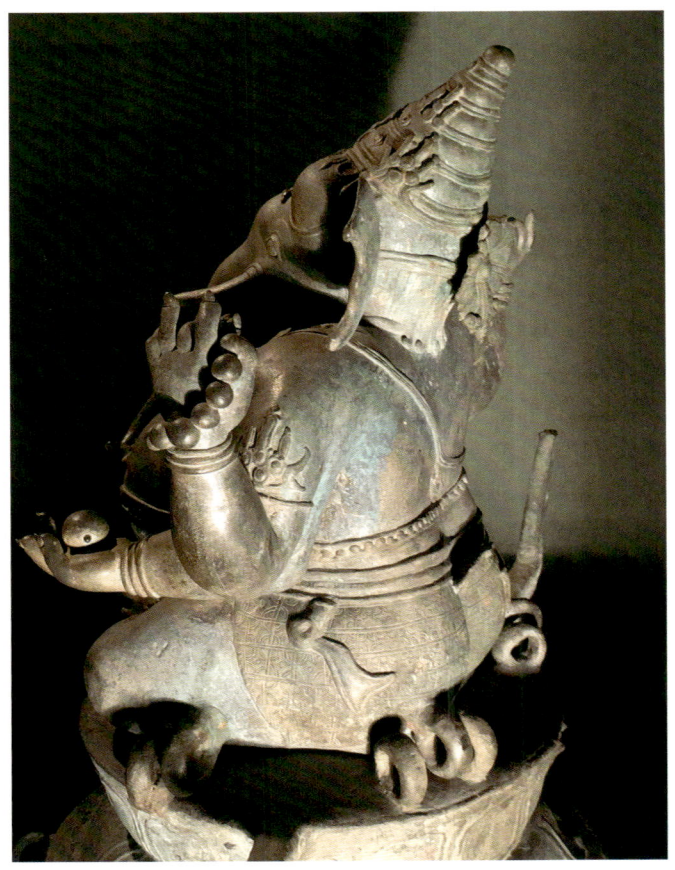

Figure 6.19. (a and b) Ganesha, Shiva *devale* 5, ca. 1030, Polonnaruwa Museum.

CHOLA OBSESSION WITH SRI LANKA

Tamil Patronage of Sri Lankan Buddhist Shrines

The Tamil expatriate community in Sri Lanka, while being of the Hindu faith and building temples and commissioning bronze images for festival worship, were astute enough to realize that it would be in their interest to extend their support to Buddhist temples. At the earlier Sri Lankan capital of Anuradhapura, commissioner H.P.C. Bell's excavations carried out a hundred years ago uncovered the remains of a number of small brick temples to Shiva that he named "Tamil ruins."[60] The northern area near the Thuparama stupa appears to have been occupied by a community of Tamil traders and merchants who also extended their support to Buddhism. A Tamil inscription speaks of a gift of 30 *Ilakkasu* by a merchant, Sekkilan *chetti*, that was deposited with a guild named Kumaraganam whose members undertook to administer the endowment and to provide for a lamp and sacred food. This record is dated in the fifth year of king Sri Sanghabodhimarayar or Vijayabahu, which corresponds to 1075, the very year in which the monarch defeated the Cholas and reclaimed the island.[61] Another inscription at Anuradhapura speaks of a south Indian merchant community, the Nankunattu (Four districts), who ordered the inscription to be engraved in order to ensure that their charity (*dharma*) would continue to be performed at the Buddhist shrine of Makkotai-palli.[62] Other inscriptions in fragmentary condition include the gift of a pillar from a woman named Pichchai, and a second pillar from a military officer (*munrukai velaikkaran*). Among Tamil records engraved on pillars or slabs in the districts or *korales*[63] surrounding Polonnaruwa is a gift for a perpetual lamp by commander-in-chief Jayamuri-nadalvan, dated in the reign of Rajendra.[64]

At Polonnaruwa, the circular Buddhist temple known as Vatadage or "circular relic-house," carries two Tamil inscriptions, badly damaged today, that date to the reign of Rajendra; one clearly records a gift of a lamp, ghee, and thirty cows to this circular Buddhist relic house.[65] The most intriguing Polonnaruwa Tamil record dates to the reign of Vijayabahu and commences with thirteen lines in praise (*meykirti*) of Vijayabahu, all in Tamil, the language of the temporary Chola masters.[66] It speaks of Vijayabahu's newly constructed royal Buddhist monastery within the precincts of the Abhayagiri Great Vihara at Pulanari, also known as Vijayapuram (city of victory), referring to Polonnaruwa. We read that this new shrine was known as the Buddha's perfumed chamber (*gandha kuti*), that it was named Taladaya-perumpalli, and was built to enshrine (*mula sthana*) the Lord (*swamy*) of the bowl relic (*patra dhatu*). The victorious Sri Lankan king Vijayabahu signed a contract for the security of this monastery through his representative, Devasena Viruddhar; somewhat ironically, he placed the welfare of his royal monastery in the hands of Tamil mercenary troops who protected Tamil merchant guilds. The mercenaries, referred to as the threefold warriors (*munrukai velaikkarars*),[67] secured the monastery by appointing servants (*sevakas*) who were each given one *veli* of land for their service. The king performed three *tulabhara* ceremonies in which he weighed himself against gold, and gave that money to those who followed the three Buddhist *nikaya* texts, in order to protect the Buddha's laws (*Buddha sasanam rakshita vendum enru*). Thereafter, the monastery that enshrined the Taladapatra-dhatuswamy was renamed after the protective sentinel body as Munrukai Tiruvelaikkarar Taladaya-perumpalli. The inscription records that all this was done at the request of the highly qualified[68] royal guru, the Vyarinimugalan (?), the Buddhist monks (*maha sthaviras*), and the royal ministers (*Rajamatyar*).

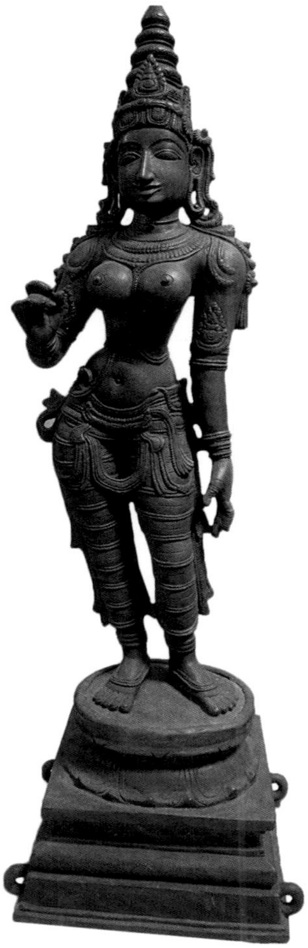

Figure 6.20. Uma, Polonnaruwa, thirteenth century, Colombo National Museum.

Later Bronzes

While Buddhism once again became the official faith of Sri Lanka in the late eleventh century, Tamil merchant communities did not leave the island en masse after the defeat of the Cholas. Temples in Polonnaruwa, and in a few other towns on the island, appear to have continued to commission bronze images of Hindu deities for festival processions, though perhaps on a lesser scale than during the period of Chola occupation. Images of Uma dating from the thirteenth century, currently in the Colombo museum storage, were probably commissioned to accompany later images of Dancing Shiva, one of which is on display in the Colombo Museum. While lacking the smooth grace of images that date to the Chola occupation, these later images of Uma reveal the same trends we will encounter in thirteenth-century images from the Chola kingdom. The sharpness of details in these images, the female breasts raised high with prominent nipples whose areolas are clearly depicted, and the exaggeratedly tall conical crowns, all speak of a date after 1200 (fig. 6.20). These images serve to remind us that thirteenth-century Chola rulers continued to campaign against Sri Lanka, winning battles on occasion but never taking control of Sri Lankan territory. Tamil merchants, whose interest lay in securing lucrative trading rights, remained on the island and these expatriate communities continued to commission portable bronzes for their temple festivals.

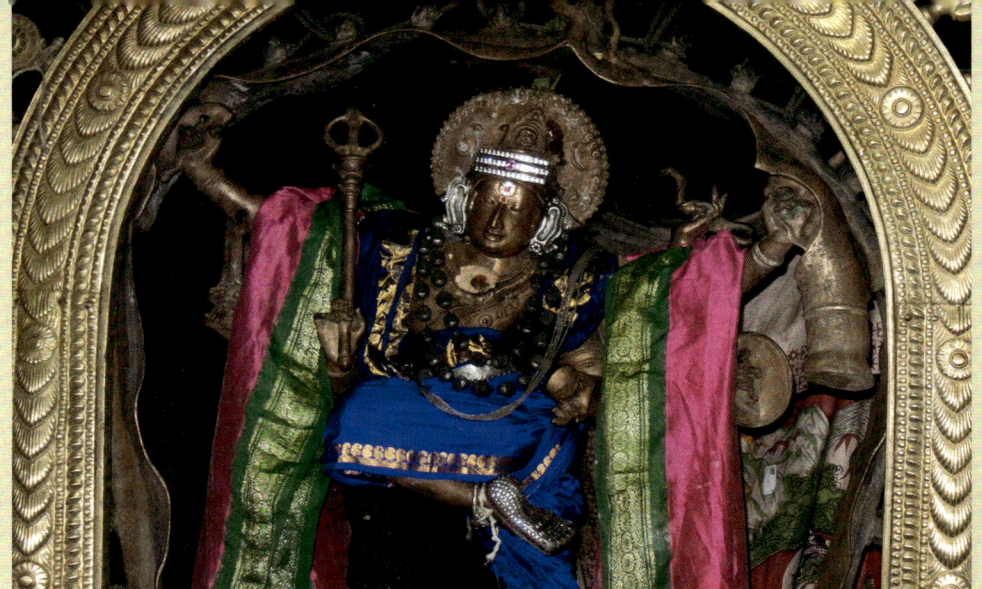

The Silk Route of the Ocean and Temple Art in the Days of Rajaraja II
Twelfth Century

7

In the Saka year 1010, month Masi,
We, the Five Hundred of the Thousand Directions, known in all countries and directions, having met at Velapuram in Varochu alias Matankari-vallava-techi-uyyakkonta-pattinam
decided to grant as follows to "our sons" Nakara-senapati Nattu chettyar, Patinen-bhumi-techi-appar and the mavettus:
[Each of] the ship's . . . , the ship's Captain and the kevis shall pay the fee anchu-tunt-ayam in gold according to the price of kasturi and [then only] shall step on the cloth spread.
Thus we, the Five Hundred of the Thousand Directions, known in every direction in all the Eighteen Lands, got this stone written and planted. Do not forget charity; charity alone is the good companion.

BARUS PILLAR INSCRIPTION[1]

The preceding inscription suggests that in the year 1088 the commercial port of Velapuram, on the northwestern coast of Sumatra, was under the control of a Tamil expatriate merchant community. The leader of the powerful merchant guild, "The Five Hundred of the Thousand Directions," had apparently concluded a profitable deal with a mercantile group that wished to use the facilities of his port, probably en route to China. He had negotiated a deal by which the captain and crew of their cargo ships would pay handsome fees in gold, linked to the price of musk, to enter Velapuram,[2] and the agreement was engraved in Tamil on an octagonal column.[3]

The previous chapter demonstrated how the strategic location of south India and Sri Lanka, roughly at the midpoint of the major ocean trade route connecting Aden with China, was a factor of significance to the economic viability of the Chola kingdom, enabling its vibrant temple culture, focused on sacred bronzes, to thrive. It is of interest then to look closely at the circumstances that enabled the Tamil merchant guild, The Five Hundred of the Thousand Directions, to find itself in so comfortable a position on the west coast of Sumatra, the westernmost and largest of the many islands of Indonesia, which was under the control of the largely Buddhist kingdom of Srivijaya. This guild (*disai ayirattu ainurruvar*), also known as the Ayyavole, from the town of Aihole in the Deccan that is their supposed original home,[4] appears to have been the most powerful of three merchant guilds operating in peninsular and south India. Their active presence in the Chola kingdom during the mid-tenth century is known from several inscriptions dated in the reign of Uttama Chola (r. 969–987). For instance, The Five Hundred of the Thousand Directions took charge of an endowment of land given by a local merchant to the temple at Tiruvilakudi,[5] and also handled an endowment of ninety sheep to provide ghee for a perpetual lamp at the Maraikkadu temple.[6] At Tiruvilakudi, they appear to have been responsible also for the construction of part of the stone temple,[7] while at Tiruvidaimaradur they supervised the funding provided by a military regiment for the construction of the windows, doors, and steps of a *mandapa*.[8] Two other trading entities active in south India were the Anjuvannam, apparently a group of Muslim merchants with strength in Kerala, and the Manigramam, a Hindu group centered in the town of Kodumbalur, home of the Vel chieftains who aided the Chola kings in their wars with Sri Lanka. That Tamil merchant guilds employed their own troops to safeguard their valuable cargoes and protect them in their travels was evident from the Tamil Sri Lankan inscription discussed in the previous chapter, in which king Vijayabahu placed the security of his royal Buddhist monastery in the hands of the mercenaries employed by such guilds.

To appreciate the complexities of the ocean trade scenario, we need to retrace our steps a hundred years to 987, the second year of Rajaraja's reign, when Sung China dispatched four missions to foreign countries with the promise of special facilities and import licenses if their merchants would come more frequently to Chinese ports.[9] China's exports of silks and large quantities of fine ceramics were much in demand in the Gulf states; the Chinese imported a range of luxury goods among which were Arabian frankincense, sandalwood from the Indonesian islands, and black pepper and cloves that were acquired from across the region including India and Sri Lanka, and resold at several-fold profit to traders stopping at Srivijayan ports.[10] Tribute from Srivijaya to China involved large quantities of these much sought after items, and tribute-bearers were given preferential tax rates at Guangzhou and other Chinese ports.[11] When the Cholas showed interest in entering this controlled trading network to try and tap into a lucrative source of income, Srivijaya attempted to keep them out. In fact, a Chinese document quoted by Indian Ocean scholar Tansen Sen indicates that Srivijaya intentionally misled the Sung court by suggesting that the Cholas were mere vassals of Srivijaya.[12] Such a vassal status would result in the Cholas being assigned a lower level of trading rights at Chinese ports. Crucial to this power play was the topographical fact that access to the South China Sea was restricted: ships had to ply either the narrow, 50-mile-long Straits of Melaka, or the tiny Sunda straits, "pinch points" that were both in the hands of the Srivijayan kings of Sumatra, who also controlled Kadaram in peninsular Malaysia.[13]

In light of this tricky relationship, let us reassess the motivation that lay behind the construction of a Buddhist monastery by a Srivijayan ruler at the Chola port of Nagapattinam around the year 1006, and also reconsider Rajaraja's assignment of the village of Anaimangalam for its support. A copper-plate inscription of Rajaraja's son Rajendra informs us:

> *To the Buddha residing in the surpassingly beautiful Culamanivarma-vihara of high loftiness as belittled Kanakagiri (mount Meru) . . .*
> *which had been built in the name of his father, by the glorious Maravijayottungavarman who was born in the Sailendra family, who was the lord of the Sri-vishaya (country), who was conducting the rule of Kataha, who had the makara crest (and) who was the son of Culamanivarman—at Nagipattana . . .*
> *The village of Anaimangalam . . .*
> *This lord of Kataha of great valour, the abode of virtues, thus prays to future kings: "Protect (ye) for ever this my charity."*[14]

We may assume that the Srivijayan construction of the Buddhist monastery at Nagapattinam, and Rajaraja's grant of the village to support the monks of the monastery, was due in large part to a pragmatic desire on both sides to maintain an amicable and peaceful relationship. It says much of Srivijayan diplomatic skills that at the very time that its ruler built a monastery in Nagapattinam, he also built a Buddhist temple in China for the emperor's long life, asking that it be named "Ten thousand years of receiving (blessings) from heaven."[15]

Srivijaya on its part sent several gifts to the Shiva temple in Nagapattinam during Rajendra's reign, aimed presumably at keeping the Chola rulers happy. In 1015,

> *Sri Mulan Agattisvaran, who is an agent of the Srivishayam, arranged to erect a gateway to the compound wall of Tirukkaronmudaiya Mahadevar temple in Nagapattinam . . .*
> *I, Eran Chadaiyan alias Devarkanda Achari, carpenter of this village, have engraved this charity on stone.*[16]

Also in 1015, and engraved on stone by the same Eran Chadaiyan, is a gift by a second agent of the king of Srivijaya, this time "a collection of jewel-stones, like ruby, emerald etc, weighing 14 1/2 *kalanju*" to be used "for the purpose of [decorating] a silver image of *Nagaialagar* [The Beautiful Lord of Nagapattinam, perhaps Shiva as Victor of Three Forts]."[17] Four years later, a total of 236 1/4 *kalanju* of Chinese gold (*chinakkanakam*) was sent by Sri Kuruttan Kesuvan, agent of the king of Kidaram, ear-marked to provide food offerings to the image of Shiva as Half Woman, or *Ardhanari*, that he had set up in the temple, and intended also for consumption by temple officials and brahmins.[18]

The seemingly amicable relationship between the Cholas and Srivijaya went sharply downhill in the year 1023, when the Sung emperor, apparently prompted by the disruption of overland caravan routes, urged Arab envoys to shift their trade from the overland silk route across central Asia to the silk route via the oceans.[19] In 1025, Rajendra Chola undertook naval campaigns against Srivijaya and Kidaram. The motivation for these campaigns was surely not territorial acquisition, as Meera Abraham has pointed out,[20] but the loosening of Srivijaya's dominating hold over sea trade routes with the hope that the Cholas might assume a more active role in the sea silk route to China.

Our information about the Chola naval engagement with Srivijaya, a littoral power with long experience with the forces of the ocean, comes almost entirely from an inscription of the year 1027 inscribed on the south wall of the Great Temple at Thanjavur. It commences by recounting Rajendra's victorious campaigns within India that culminated in his march to the Ganges, that most sacred of India's rivers, and then moves to his naval expedition in which his very first conquest is Srivijaya and the last is Kidaram.[21] The following is a sharply abbreviated version of the naval conquests listed:

> *Having dispatched many ships in the midst of rolling seas, and having caught the king of Kidaram, he [Rajendra] took:*
> *Srivijayam with large heaps of treasures, the "war-gate" of the city, the "jewel gate," and the "gate of large jewels" . . .*
> *Pannai with landing ghats . . .*
> *Great Yirudingam surrounded by the deep sea as a moat . . .*
> *Lankasokam that is undaunted in fierce battles . . .*
> *Great Pappalam having abundant high waters as defence . . .*
> *Valaippanduru with cultivated field and jungle . . .*
> *Takkolam . . .*
> *Great Tamalingam, firm in great and fierce battles . . .*
> *Ilamuridesam of fierce strength and impetuous nature . . .*
> *Great Nakkavaram full of flower gardens with much honey . . .*
> *Kidaram of fierce strength, protected by the deep sea.*[22]

While the inscription seems to suggest a decisive victory, Rajendra's campaign appears to have been little more than a raid with temporary success, since 50 years later, an inscription of the year 1070 refers to Chola king Kulottunga I as "He who conquered Kidaram."[23] Clearly, international holdings were fluid, changing with the fortunes and ambitions of individual Chola rulers who repeatedly attempted to become players of consequence along the silk route of the sea. Returning briefly to the Nagapattinam Buddhist monastery of the Srivijaya kings, an inscription of the year 1090 records that two ambassadors of the king of Kidaram requested Kulottunga to renew the grant of the villages originally gifted by Rajaraja I;[24] obviously, this grant had been allowed to lapse in the interim period of naval raids, conflicting ambitions, and diverging objectives.

As an aside, we might note that Kamboja (Cambodia), witnessing the wealth being amassed through sea trade, decided to enter into negotiations and diplomatic gifting with the main players. A copper-plate inscription of the eighth year of Rajendra, 1020, tells us:

> *The Kamboja king, aspiring for his [Rajendra's] friendship and in order to save his own fortunes sent him a triumphant chariot titled "My soul's fortune," with which he had conquered the armies of the enemy kings in battles.*[25]

Close to a hundred years later, in 1114, the Cambodian monarch presented a gemstone to Chola monarch Kulottunga I, who had it inset into the stone wall facing the shrine of the Chidambaram temple.[26]

The crucial importance of ocean trade, not only for the Cholas but also for their rivals, is seen from a remarkable inscription of the year 1244 at the port of Motupalli in the Krishna river delta, territory directly north of the Cholas that was controlled by rulers of the Kakatiya dynasty. Kakatiya king Ganapati issued a safety edict that appears to have been intended to induce "traders by sea, starting for and arriving from all continents, islands, foreign countries, and cities" to come farther north and dock in ports along the coastline of his kingdom. King Ganapati highlights the fact that shipwrecked traders normally lost all their cargo to the powers that controlled the area where they had been stranded. His edict guarantees the safety of traders and assures them that he will levy only the standard duty on their cargo at the accepted rate of one in thirty. Here is how he phrases it:

> *Formerly kings used to take away by force the whole cargo, viz. gold, elephants, horses, gems etc carried by ships and vessels which, after they had started from one country for another, were attacked by storms, wrecked and thrown on shore.*
> *But we out of mercy for the sake of glory and merit, are granting everything besides the fixed duty to those who have incurred the great risk of sea-voyage with the thought that wealth is more valuable than even life.*
> *The rate of duty is one in thirty on all exports and imports.*[27]

The focus of trading activities in south India was not entirely in the direction of China via southeast Asia, but also westward toward the Gulf that constituted the other end of the ocean trade route. In chapter 1, we encountered the Cairo Geniza's cache of letters between Jewish traders in Aden and their counterparts living in the town of Mangalore along the west coast of India. These indicate that copper items produced in Kerala were sufficiently valued in Aden for merchants to send raw copper to India, and request the finished goods to be shipped back to Aden. Consider the request in this letter written sometime between 1134–1137 by Joseph Ben Abraham, a Jewish client in Aden, to Abraham Ben Yiju, who ran a bronze factory in Mangalore:

In your name, O Merciful

The letter of your excellency, the illustrious elder, my master, has arrived . . .

    All the copper vessels that you sent with Abu Ali arrived, and the "table-jug" also arrived. It was exactly as I wished . . .

I am sending you a broken ewer and a dipper that together weigh seven pounds less a quarter. Please make me a ewer of the same measure from its copper, for its copper is good copper. The weight of the ewer should be five pounds exactly.

    I am sending also eighteen and a quarter pounds of good yellow copper in bars . . .

From the rest of all the copper make me an attractive lamp. Its column should be octagonal and stout; its base should be in the form of a lampstand with strong feet. On its head there should be a copper lamp with two ends for two wicks, which should be set on the end of the column so that it could move up and down. All the three, the column, the stand and the lamp, should be in separate parts. If they could make the feet in spirals, let it be so, for this is more beautiful.

. . .

[From] He that loves you and is proud of your good name, Joseph b. Abraham[28]

The importance that the Cholas placed on the revenue made possible through successful control over ocean trade routes should not be underestimated.

This chapter will focus on emperor Rajaraja II, who built a royal temple at Darasuram and in whose reign eight major bronzes of Shiva's eight heroic forms were first created. We will then turn to the workshop established by the Tiruvenkadu Master in the early eleventh century, and consider the bronzes of outstanding caliber that the Master's descendants continued to create for a period of over a century and a half. In conclusion, we will examine the central role played by the priests in the increasingly complex and vibrant festival cycle, and consider the growing importance of the *nayanmar*, the recital of their hymns, and the presence of their bronze images within temple premises.

Rajaraja II and Shiva's Eight Heroic Forms (*Attha virattanam*)

Holding the trident
its prongs flashing like the rays of the sun
with resounding drum in hand
he came in the guise of Kala-Bhairava
he ripped apart the elephant's skin—
Seeing Uma shrink in fear
his beautiful mouth widened into laughter . . .
thus did he shower his grace . . .

—APPAR, HYMN 73[29]

When Rajaraja II came to the throne in 1146, the relationship between the Chola monarchs and Srivijaya was at best distrustful. Rajaraja assumed a series of martial titles, among them being Flow of Heroism (*Viradhara*), Sunrise of Heroism (*Virodaya*), Lion of the Cholas (*Cholendrasimha*), and Pride of Kingship (*Rajagambhira*). Is it possible that he harbored an ambition to reestablish a foothold in the ports of the Kidaram region, fully aware that a Chola presence there would be downright offensive? In the context of Chola bronzes, I wonder if it was perhaps this aspiration that led to the commission of striking bronze tableaux of the eight heroic forms of Shiva. Each of Shiva's eight heroic forms (*attha virattanam*) represents his defeat of a powerful demonic force, and as a group these heroic forms were known and celebrated from early times in the hymns of the Tamil *nayanmar* saints. Victor of Three Forts, our focus in chapter 2, in which Shiva let loose only a single arrow to destroy the forts of three demons, is one of the eight manifestations. Another popular form centers around Shiva's victory over the elephant-demon Gajasura, celebrated in the verse of saint Appar quoted earlier. The remaining six heroic forms include Shiva's dominance over Yama, god of death; Andhaka, demon of darkness; Manmatha, god of love; and the powerful and threatening forces of Daksha, Brahma, and Jalandhara. While known earlier through the songs of the saints, it was only in the twelfth century that a temple was constructed at each of the eight sites associated with one of Shiva's eight heroic forms, with each temple housing a dramatic bronze image of its special form of heroic Shiva. This twelfth-century appearance of eight dynamic bronzes, one in each of eight newly built twelfth-century temples, suggests a level of controlled planning not seen previously. Worth consideration is the possibility that we are witnessing here a centralized, perhaps royal, decision to project these eight heroic bronzes as exemplary dynastic prototypes while contemplating a venture into exceedingly troubled international waters.

In a south-facing shrine within the *mandapa* of the temple at Valuvur in the coastal belt is an impressive bronze tableau in which Shiva's triumphant dance is partly obscured by the brilliant silks and sparkling jewels that adorn him; an archival photograph permits a clearer view of the image (figs. 7.1 and 7.2). Shiva is poised in a dramatic yogic twist with one foot planted firmly on the head of the elephant-demon he has defeated and skinned, and the other foot raised in joyful triumph. The edges of the flayed elephant skin appear around Shiva, who turns in jubilant movement to display his effortless prowess, holding in his eight hands a variety of weapons including a sword, shield, cleavers, trident, as well as a skull bowl and a serpent. The elephant's tail is positioned almost directly above Shiva's head, and its two hind legs are seen alongside Shiva's outstretched hands holding cleavers. With the clash of cymbals and the beat of drums, two of Shiva's dwarfish *gana* minions standing on the pedestal on either side of the elephant head, provide the musical accompaniment for Shiva's triumphant dance (fig. 7.3). Standing apparently serene beside Shiva is his consort Uma, with infant Skanda held against her hip; however, the subtle angle of her feet clues us in to the fact that she is moving away, alarmed by the battle, although not quite "shrinking in fear," as Appar phrased it in the verse with which we commenced this section (figs. 7.4 and 7.5). Meanwhile Skanda, who is intently watching the fierce encounter, leans toward his victorious father and points at him with outstretched hand. This processional bronze group of Shiva's victorious dance upon the head of the vanquished elephant-demon is the work of a twelfth-century artist who hesitated not the slightest in modeling a wax image with exaggerated torsion. Shiva is close to 4 feet tall, with accompanying Uma around 3 feet in height. Cast in the direct lost-wax process, they are solid images like all Chola bronzes; I would estimate that the Shiva image, together with its base and lower pedestal, weighs

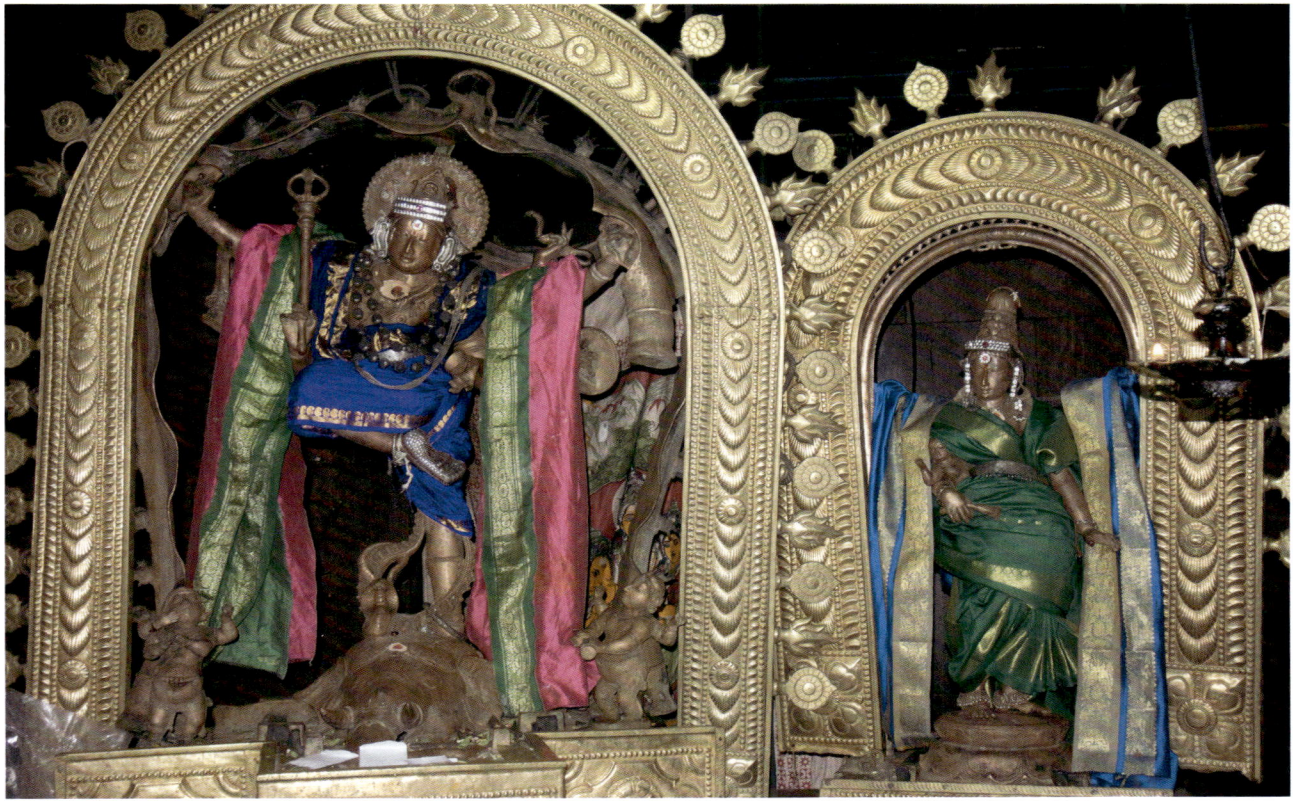

Figure 7.1. Shiva as Victor over Elephant Demon and Consort Uma, Valuvur temple, Nagapattinam district, ca. 1150.

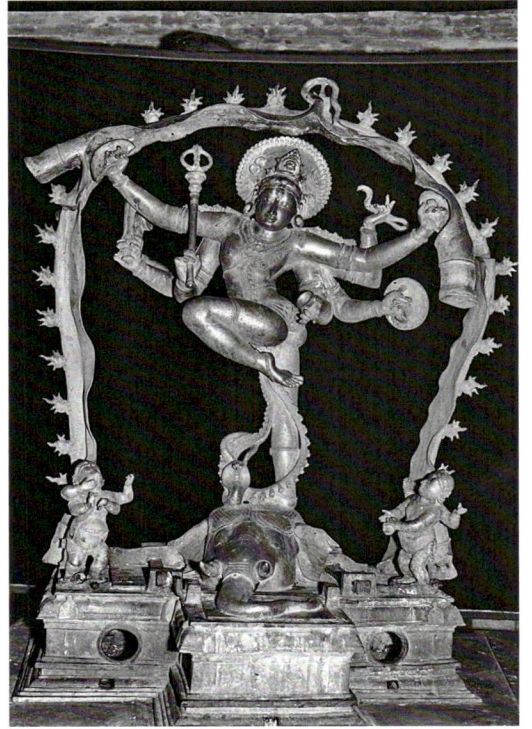

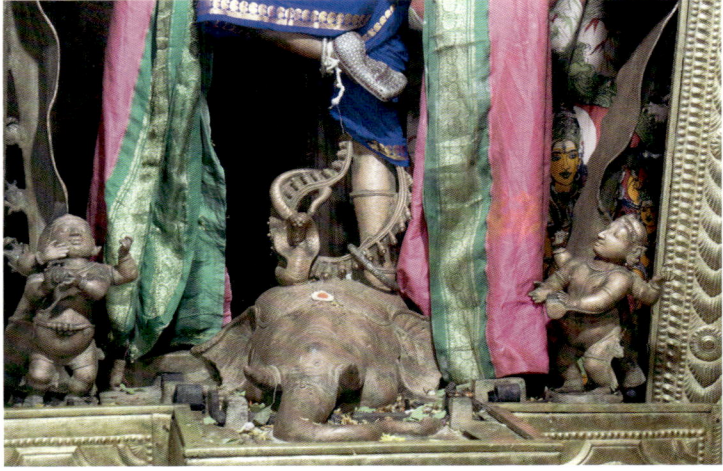

Figure 7.2. Archival photograph of Shiva as Victor over Elephant Demon, French Institute of Pondicherry.

Figure 7.3. Detail of *ganas* at Shiva's feet in Shiva as Victor over Elephant Demon (see fig. 7.1); note gem-studded cover over Shiva's foot that confers grace.

SILK ROUTE OF THE OCEAN

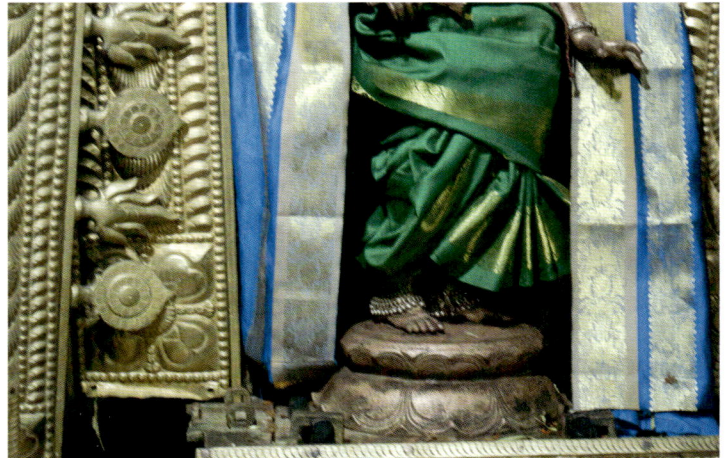

Figure 7.4. Detail of Uma as Consort of Shiva as Victor over Elephant Demon (see fig. 7.1), Valuvur temple, Nagapattinam district, ca. 1150.

Figure 7.5. Archival photograph of Uma as Consort of Shiva as Victor over Elephant Demon, French Institute of Pondicherry.

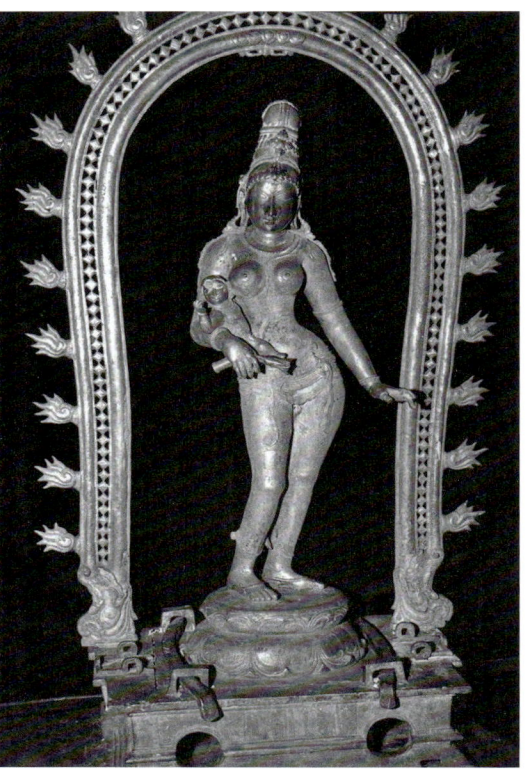

around 250 pounds,[30] while Uma and child probably weigh in the vicinity of 100 pounds.[31] In order to stabilize this weighty image and facilitate carrying it in procession, the bronze casters provided two substantial lugs on either side of the elephant head to contain rods to secure the bronze to its pedestal; smaller lugs are provided between the feet of the dwarf musicians to hold them securely in place. The modern brass repoussé fronting blocks our view of the sizable rectangular pedestals of both Shiva and Uma, where two massive slots are intended to hold large poles that would be threaded through them, while two smaller slots were provided lower down to further secure the bronze during processions.

It is useful to compare the bronze with a stone rendering of the same theme from Rajaraja II's newly built royal temple at Darasuram, 25 miles away. Cut in deep relief into a granite slab, the stone image portrays Shiva dancing with a torsion similar to that of the bronze as he holds aloft the skin of the elephant demon (fig. 7.6). In both the bronze and the stone, Shiva twists fluently to present the onlooker with a view of his behind as well as a frontal view of his torso. In both bronze and stone versions, we see smoothly rounded, tight buttocks, and in both, the sculptor emphasized the softly curved insole of Shiva's foot raised in dance. The importance of this raised foot is highlighted in the temple bronze by the addition of a diamond-studded foot cover; priests remove this cover to permit favored devotees to glimpse the perfection of Shiva's foot (fig. 7.7). The curved insole of Shiva's raised foot is of special significance in that it is the vision of this foot that confers grace on devotees. The repeated phrase *kuncitanghrim* to describe Shiva's insole is celebrated in Umapati Sivacharya's poem written around the year 1300 to

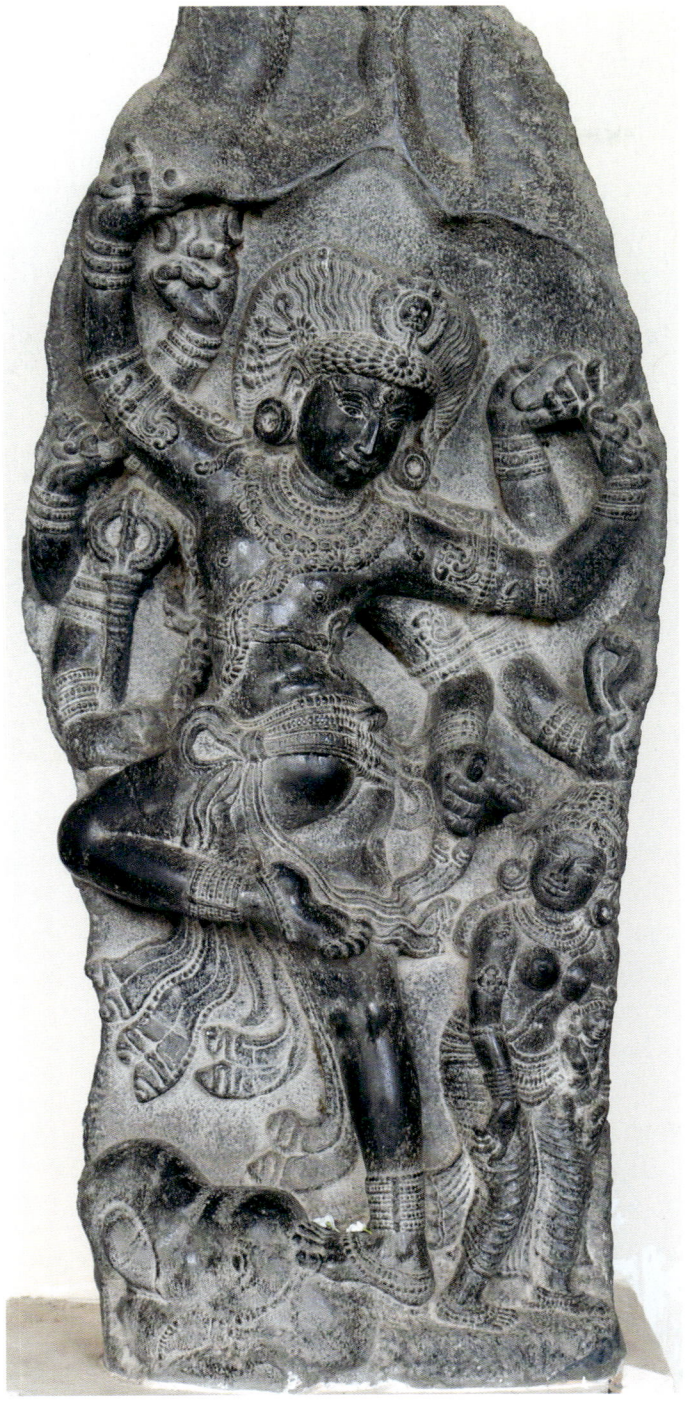

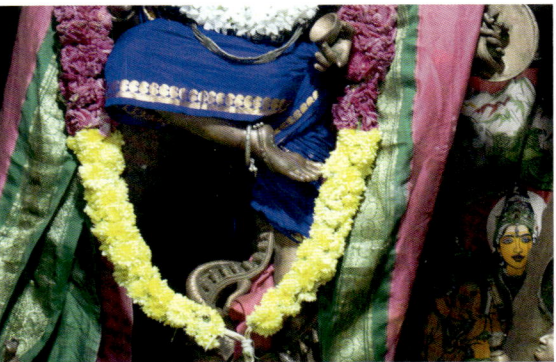

Figure 7.6. Shiva as Victor over Elephant Demon, granite, Darasuram temple, Thanjavur district, ca. 1150.

Figure 7.7. Detail of foot of Shiva revealed without diamond-studded foot cover, in Shiva as Victor over Elephant Demon (see figs. 7.1 and 7.3).

SILK ROUTE OF THE OCEAN

applaud Shiva's manifestation as the Expert Dancer in which, too, it is this curved insole that transfers grace to the devotee.³²

The Valuvur temple dedicated to Shiva as Destroyer of the elephant-demon appears to have been constructed in stone during the time of Rajaraja II and the earliest inscriptions on the temple walls, dating to 1157 and 1160, speak of gifts of lamps to an already functioning temple.³³ Valuvur is also the hometown of the influential saint Manikkavachakar (literally, "He whose words are like rubies"), who lived around the year 900, almost a century after the group of sixty-three Shaiva saints was finalized in song by Sundarar, the latest of the *nayanmar* saints. The poems of Manikkavachakar became so popular that he was added to the established threesome *Muvar* grouping of Sambandar, Appar, and Sundarar to create a new group, the *Nalvar* or Sacred Four; additionally, Manikkavachakar is often referred to as the sixty-fourth Shaiva saint or *nayanar*. Inscriptions at Valuvur indicate that the temple once housed two bronzes of Manikkavachakar. The first was a gift made in the year 1167, during the reign of Rajadhiraja II, to ensure the recitation of Manikkavachakar's important sacred poem, *Tiruvempavai*, in front of the bronze of this saint during two major multiday festivals, one in *Markali* (December–January) and the other in *Panguni* (March–April).³⁴ The second image was gifted in 1181, during the reign of Kulottunga III, presumably to ensure the saint's celebrity.³⁵ It is unfortunate that both bronzes of this saint are missing from the Valuvur temple, which still houses a striking bronze of Shiva as the Begging Lord and a rare bronze of Vishnu's manifestation as the stunning Mohini who entranced Shiva. Inscriptions at Valuvur also emphasize the importance of goddess worship that became a priority for temples during the twelfth century. In 1183, a Bana chieftain constructed an independent shrine to the goddess in the northwest corner of the temple, and a second inscription speaks of a further gift to maintain active worship in that goddess shrine.³⁶ The latest record at Valuvur is of the year 1276 and is dated in the reign of Jatavarman Sundara Pandya, when Chola power was all but gone.³⁷

A second twelfth-century bronze from the group of eight heroic forms of Shiva depicts his victory over Yama, god of death; it is in worship in the temple at Kadaiyur, some 14 miles northeast of Valuvur, where throngs of devotees gather regularly at the temple to pay homage to the image, which I was unable to photograph. The piece is roughly the same size as the Valuvur bronze and depicts four-armed Shiva, holding noose and battle-ax in two rear hands, and accompanied by a bronze Uma. Shiva stands on his right foot with left leg raised slightly off the ground after having kicked the arrogant god of death, Yama, who lies senseless at his feet. On the pedestal to the viewers' left is Shiva's devout teenage devotee, Markandeya; it was to save him from an untimely death that Shiva assumed this manifestation known either as Destroyer of Time (*Kalantaka*) or Destroyer of Yama (*Yamantaka*).

It was a total anticlimax to discover that the remaining six temples honoring Heroic Shiva do not house the original twelfth-century images but contain later bronze replacements of post-Chola date. Six of the eight temples of Heroic Shiva are located along the coastal belt in close proximity to each other, with one farther north and one to the west near Thanjavur (map 9). The positioning of most of these temples along the coast may possibly have been motivated by the idea that they could serve either as the

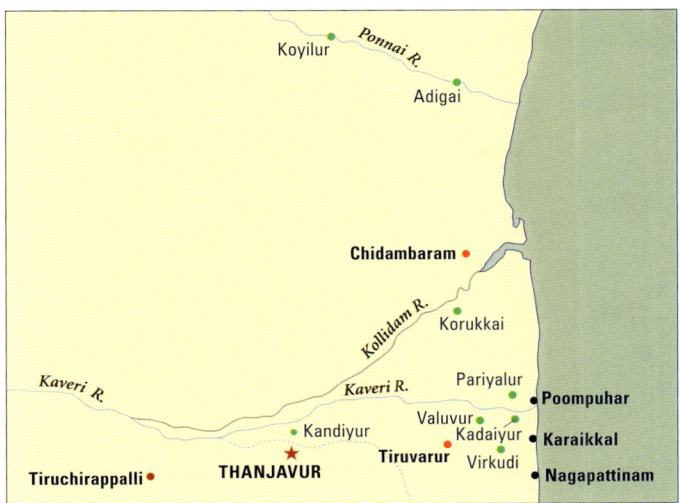

Map 9 Temples of Shiva's Heroic Forms (*attha virattanam*) (marked in green).

jumping off point for attack or the place of first defense in case the decision was taken to send the Chola navy to seek access to the China Sea.

Rajaraja II built his own monumental royal temple at Darasuram, a site with no sacred ancestry and with connections to him alone, in imitation of his ancestors Rajaraja I and Rajendra I (fig. 7.8a). The *sikhara* of his temple rises to a relatively modest height of 83 feet, and the broad pillared hall in front is carved to resemble a chariot with large wheels flanking the southern stairway. Darasuram is the very first temple to carry a complete series of relief carvings of each of the sixty-three saints of Shiva, identified by an inscribed label; they are placed in a narrow band that runs around the entire temple between the uppermost level of base moldings and the wall niches carrying images of deities.[38] The relief pictured here portrays saint Naminandi, who, when taunted by the Jains to use water to burn lamps in the Shiva temple, successfully did so (fig. 7.8b).Rajaraja II's special interest in saints was perhaps due to the recent composition of the lives of the saints by court poet Sekkilar during the reign of his father, Kulottunga II. The resulting work, known as *Periya Purana* or "Great Ancient Text," became the official hagiography of the sixty-three *nayanmar*, and was added to the Tamil "sacred canon," the *Tirumurai*, as its twelfth and final book. The reliefs at Darasuram portray seventy-eight rather than sixty-three images; in this, it follows the narrative of the *Periya Purana*. It commences with a relief of the brahmins of Chidambaram, then portrays an additional grouping of saints between *nayanmar* numbered 59 and 64, and it concludes with seven reliefs of Sundarar, who was responsible for the song that brought the set of sixty-three *nayanmar* together.

Rajaraja II also appears to have sponsored the creation of a bronze set of all sixty-three saints. Two bronzes that emerged some thirty-five years ago in clearance at the site are of saints who are not generally sculpted on their own; their presence suggests that they formed part of a complete set of sixty-three. Inclusive of the pedestal that carries their inscribed names, both stand 50 centimeters tall. One bronze portrays a sedate image, hair pulled back in a chignon, with simple ornaments of strung beads including earrings, a necklace, armband, and wristband; wearing a short dhoti, he stands with hands joined in adoration. An inscription on the pedestal identifies him as the chieftain Narasinga

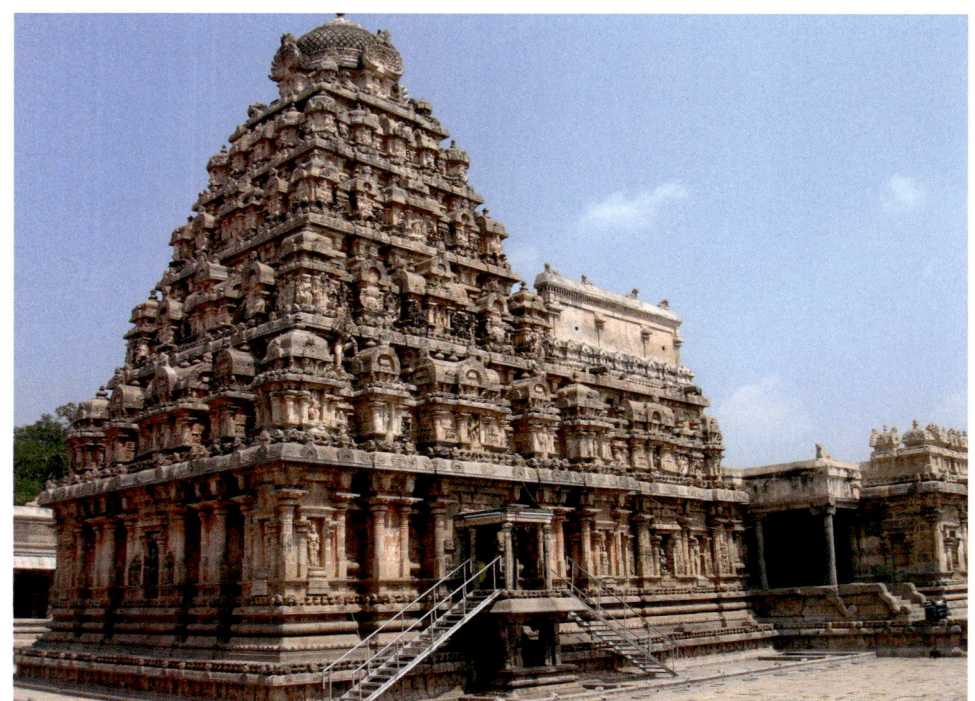

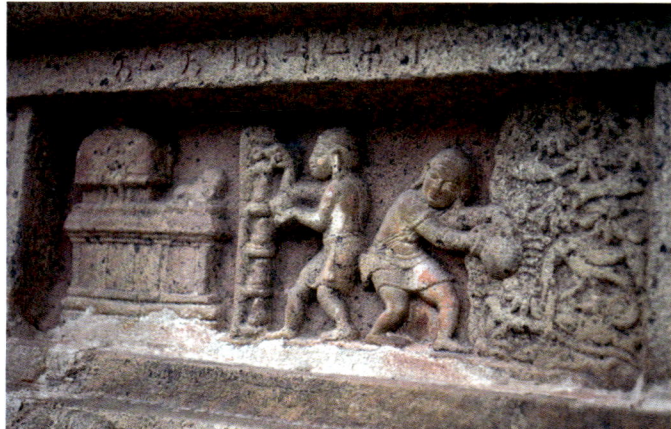

Figure 7.8. (a) Darasuram temple of Rajaraja Chola II, Thanjavur district, ca. 1150. (b) Detail of panel, Story of Saint Naminandi, Who Caused Water to Burn as Oil, Darasuram temple, Thanjavur district.

Munaiyaraiyar who "adopted" saint Sundarar and served as his foster-father. The second bronze, also inscribed, is a threesome composition cast to stand together on a single pedestal and portrays saint Siruttondar, his wife, and their infant son Sirala who was resurrected by god Shiva after an extraordinary sacrifice (fig. 7.9). Wearing a short dhoti, Siruttondar stands bare-chested, with two strings of *rudraksha* beads around his neck, and simple beaded armlets and wristbands. His hair is pulled into a topknot, while his palms, joined together in the gesture of adoration, enclose an offering of blossoms to Shiva. To his proper right stands his elegant and elaborately adorned wife. Ringlet curls frame her face and her hair is swept into an elaborate chignon adorned with a band of flowers. With her left hand, she reaches out to grasp the arm of their young son Sirala, a naked boy with his hair swept up into a crown of sorts. The modeling skill and sensitive rendering of these two saints, numbered 35 and 40 in the official listing of the 63, makes one regret deeply the loss of the other bronzes of this set commissioned for Rajaraja II's temple at Darasuram.

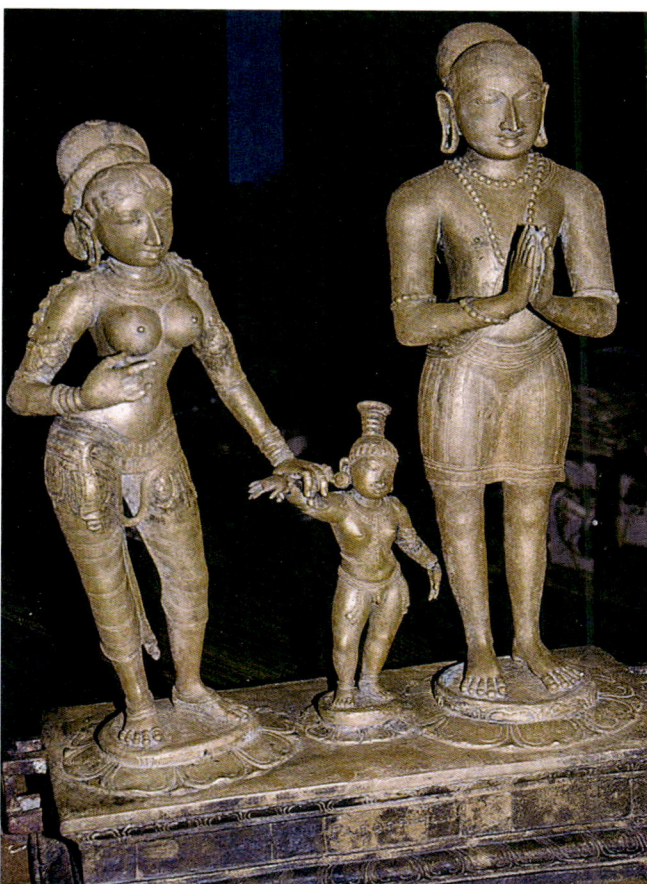

Figure 7.9. Saint Siruttondar, Wife, and Infant Son Sirala, Darasuram temple, Thanjavur district, ca. 1150.

The story of Siruttondar is dramatic, with shades of Abraham and Isaac though more gory, and tells us how the saint proved himself up to the sacrifice that Shiva demanded of him. According to hagiography, Siruttondar, whose given name was Paranjoti, was commander-in-chief of the Pallava armies that won a famous battle at Badami, generally identified with the Pallava victory over the Chalukyas in the year 642, after which he renounced military service and became an ardent devotee of Shiva. The story goes that Shiva decided to test the strength of his devotion and appeared at his home in the guise of a wild Shaiva mendicant, asking for a meal of *pashu*, a term that usually means a cow. When Paranjoti agreed and asked his "guest" to choose a cow from his herd, the mendicant responded that for him *pashu* meant a child, five years of age, who must be cut up and cooked by his parents. Paranjoti acquiesced to this hideous demand and proceeded to sacrifice his child. When the meal was ready, the mendicant insisted that Paranjoti join him; as they sat down, he instructed Paranjoti to call out to his son to join them. And lo and behold, miraculously five-year-old Sirala came running in response to his father's call, while the mendicant, Shiva in disguise, was nowhere to be seen. A set of friezes on the wall of a structure adjoining the main gopuram leading into the Darasuram temple enclosure tells the entire bizarre story;[39] the bronze, inscribed as Siruttondar, reflects the happily reunited family.

Not surprisingly, the temple in Siruttondar's hometown of Tiruchengatankudi in the Nagapattinam area, some 45 kilometers from Darasuram, houses a shrine for the saint

SILK ROUTE OF THE OCEAN 205

where festivals in his honor were celebrated. In 988, during the reign of Rajaraja, an officer titled Muvendavelan made a gift of land to keep two lamps burning in the shrine of child Sirala.[40] The inscription does not refer to the donation of the bronze image itself though we may assume that it was a recent dedication. A record of the year 1004 speaks of a festival in April–May (*Chittirai*) during which the bronze of Sirala was taken in procession to the *mandapa* of Siruttondar in the temple; it speaks of the donation of land to feed the devotees who attended the festival.[41] An inscription dated in the year 1197, during the reign of Kulottunga III, speaks of the gift of land for laying out a special road along which the image of child Sirala (*sirala pillaiyar*) would be taken in procession from the Siruttondar hall in the temple at Tiruchengatankudi to the village of Tirumarugal, less than 2 miles away, for a special celebration.[42] While we find that in Europe saints became increasingly important at times of crises like the onset of plagues, it seems a stretch to attribute the increasing importance of the saints in the twelfth century to the Cholas being under stress militarily.

The Tiruvenkadu Master's Workshop during the Twelfth Century

The high level of excellence in the creation of bronze images seen in the workshop headed by the Tiruvenkadu Master at the start of the eleventh century, and the work of the next generation, was our subject in chapter 5. Here, we will follow the continuing distinction of this workshop, both in the refinement of wax modeling and in the technique of bronze casting, into the third quarter of the twelfth century. This sustained quality of workmanship is seen in bronzes created for the coastal temple of Valampuram (today's Melaperumpallam), a mere 5 miles from Tiruvenkadu and 3 miles from the port of Poompuhar, and a site sanctified in song by saint Sundarar:

> *This is his place*
> *crowded with carp*
> *tall palmyras*
> *and* atumpu *vines on every side,*
> *where the dark sea drives*
> *newly wedded conches*
> *to the shore*
> *in Valampuram.* v. 6[43]

An outstanding bronze from Valampuram portrays a tall and slender Shiva, poised in the perfect equilibrium of contrapposto; the light tilt of his head aligns perfectly with the positioning of his lower limbs, while his torso slopes gently in the opposite direction (fig. 7.10). He wears wooden clogs on his feet, and his walking posture is indicated by the fact that heel of his right foot is lightly raised, while the toes press into the ground. Shiva is accompanied by his pet antelope, which prances up toward him, and by his dwarfish *gana* attendant, who holds an offering tray upon his head. The bronze is a variation on a form that the original Tiruvenkadu Master created as *Pichcha Devar*, the Begging Lord who walked from house to house seeking alms, only to capture the hearts of the women who came to fill his alms bowl with food. At Tiruvenkadu, we encountered a nude Begging Lord;

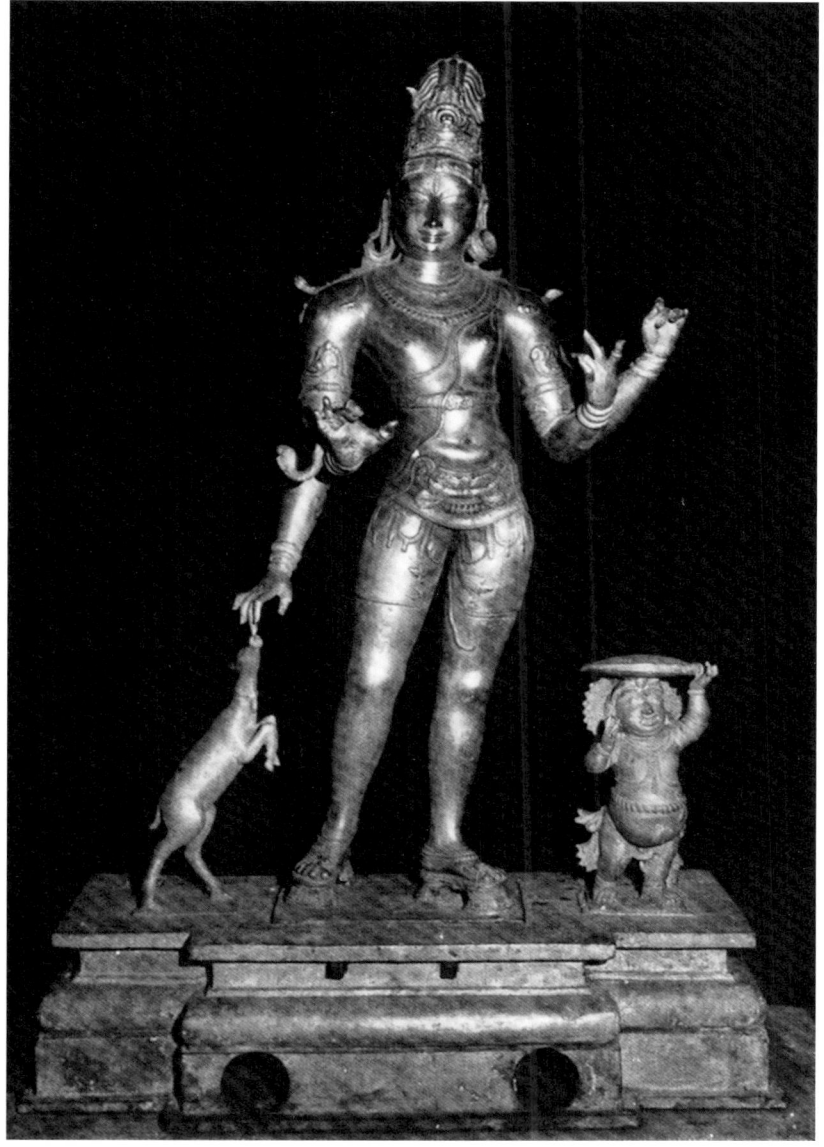

Figure 7.10. Shiva as "Lord Who Walked with Swaying Gait," Valampuram temple, Nagapattinam district, 1178.

at Valampuram, Shiva is portrayed wearing a short dhoti held in place with jeweled belts while his two front hands are poised to hold the lute-like vina. When I first entered the temple in the 1980s and saw a shining copper image with a mirror hanging behind it, I walked by, assuming it to be a modern piece. I then did a double-take as I realized that it had to be the very bronze I had traveled a great distance to see. Since I knew that it had been found buried near the now dry temple tank, it was clear that the temple authorities had cleaned it. Luckily, they had followed an age-old tradition of using the "olive" of a local palm tree; the soapy olive, when soaked briefly in water, suds up, and it is this palm olive that gave Colgate-Palmolive its brand name, and added sheen to the bronze.

The image is described in an inscription on the south wall of its central shrine as *Vattanaigal padanadanda nayakar*, or "the Lord who walked with swaying gait," and was dedicated in the eighth regnal year of Rajadhiraja II, or 1178.[44] Since the phrase "Lord with swaying gait" does not refer to any standard iconographic form, the implication of the words remained unclear until R. Nagaswamy identified the phrase in a hymn composed by Appar to describe mendicant Shiva.[45] Appar's poem describes Shiva, not as a naked mendicant, but as a silk-clad, lute-playing mendicant "who walked with swaying gait." We may assume that the donor who commissioned this image requested the wax modeler to create an image based on this specific poem. It is exceedingly rare to find a direct correlation between a well-read patron, a specific line in a poem, and a bronze, but we have it in this instance. Here is my translation of the relevant section of Appar's hymn, placed in the lips of a woman who came to give Shiva alms:

> *He came, holding the vina*
> *the smile upon his lips swept my heart away*
> *he did not turn back to look at me*
> *he spoke enchantingly*
> *he came to Valampuram; here he abides.*
>
> *Clad in silk,*
> *fresh sandal paste upon his form of coral hue,*
> *heel to toe, he placed his feet in dancing steps*
> *I asked "my lord, which town is yours?"*
> *The piercing eyes that gazed cast a spell upon me*
> *as if to go elsewhere*
> *he walked with swaying gait [vattanaigal padanadanda nayakar]*
> *spoke enchantingly*
> *he came to Valampuram; here he abides.*[46]

Saint Appar's lord who walked with swaying gait and favored Valampuram was immortalized in this bronze commissioned for the Valampuram temple by a devotee who describes himself as Tiruvidhi Tiruvalampuram Nambi.[47] We should note that Shiva as "lord with swaying gait" (*vattanaigal udaiyar*) seems to have acquired increasing popularity by the year 1200, and we see this abbreviated reference to such images in several temples after this date. For instance, during the reign of Rajaraja III, the temple at Tiruvaymur carries a number of inscriptions dated in the years 1236–1246 that speak of gifts for expenses incurred during the procession of *Vattanaiadal Udaiyar* in *Puratasi* (September–October) and in *Chittirai* (April–May), and also for saffron, camphor, and other select items required for his worship.[48] One epigraph speaks also of a donation of cash for arrangements made for the early morning awakening ceremony of the "lord with swaying gait."[49]

The Valampuram bronze is an eloquent testimony to the impeccable standard maintained by the artists of the remarkable Tiruvenkadu workshop, who were clearly responsible for this stylistically assured image. It is apparent that descendants of the original Tiruvenkadu Master continued to produce bronzes that maintained the reputation of the workshop for expertise in wax modeling, while its foundry workers retained their technical perfection in metal casting. This coastal workshop upheld an exceptionally high standard for the better part of two hundred years, starting around the year 1000 and extending

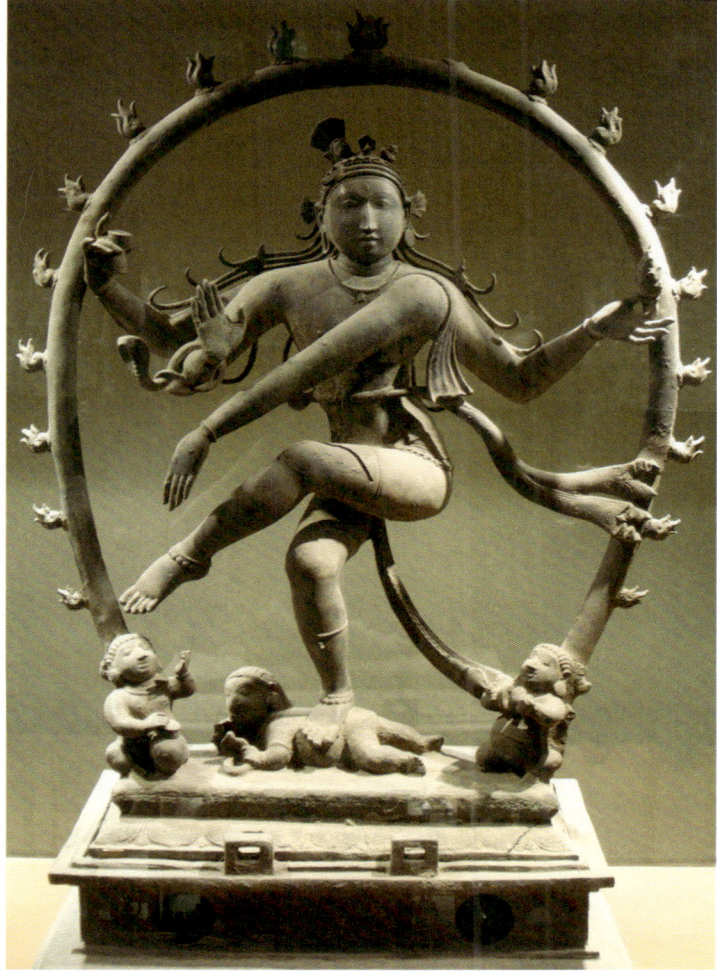

Figure 7.11. Dancing Shiva, Valampuram temple, Nagapattinam district, ca. 1126, Government Museum, Chennai.

to at least the year 1180. The Valampuram "lord who walked with swaying gait" was created by an artist living some three generations after the Tiruvenkadu Master.

The Valampuram temple appears to have been built at the start of the twelfth century, at which time a number of bronzes were commissioned to fulfill the temple's festival requirements. The earliest inscriptions on the temple walls are those of the reign of Vikrama Chola (r. 1118–1135), when we read, for instance, that a chieftain set up a bronze of Dancing Shiva in the year 1126 and gave land to the temple to ensure its regular worship.[50] The broad, rounded face of the Dancing Lord from the temple, displayed today in the Madras Government Museum, is indicative of a twelfth-century date, as is the addition of Shiva's dwarfish *gana* attendants along the base who provide the musical accompaniment for Shiva's dance (fig. 7.11). There is a noticeable similarity in the placement and treatment of these figures with the *ganas* placed at the feet of the bronze depicting heroic Shiva's triumphant dance on the head of the elephant-demon in the Valuvur temple.

The Valampuram temple also contains an unusual bronze of Shiva as *Kirata*, the hunter form he assumed in order to test and challenge Arjuna, hero of the *Mahabharata* epic. Hunter Shiva is a bearded and mustached figure with hands poised to hold the now

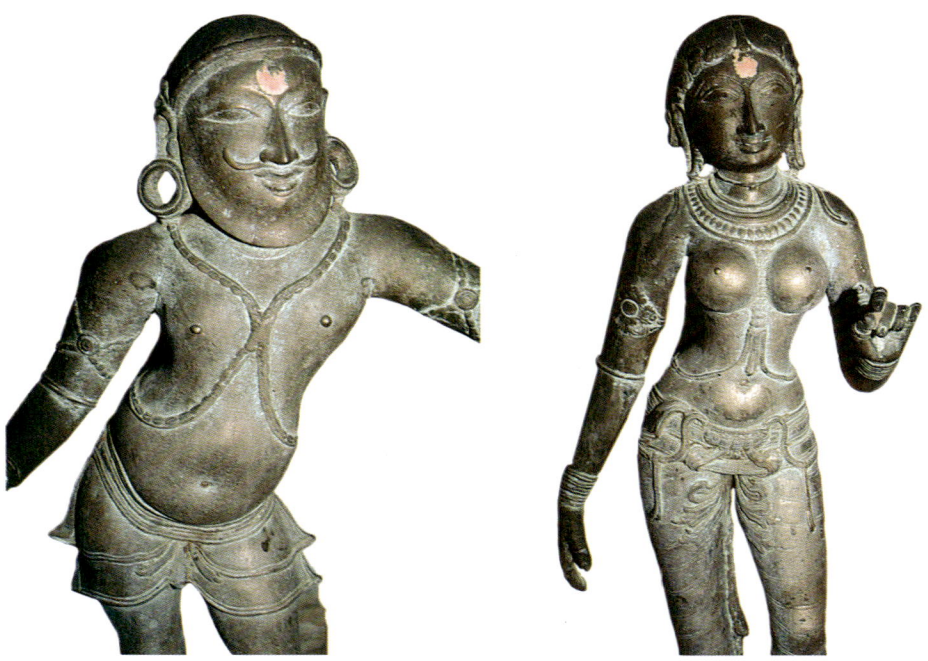

Figure 7.12. Shiva as *Kirata* or Hunter, Valampuram temple, Nagapattinam district, ca. 1150.

Figure 7.13. Consort of Shiva as Hunter, Valampuram temple, Nagapattinam district, ca. 1150.

missing bow and arrow; an ornamental chain crosses and encloses his torso above his short dhoti, while his adornment consists of large rings in both ears, simple armlets, elbow bands, bracelets, and anklets (fig. 7.12). His accompanying consort is an enchanting image with curls framing her face, and with hair coiffed at the rear in an elaborate chignon (fig. 7.13). She is closely similar in the modeling of the body, in the details of adornment, and in the elegant knotted chignon to two other images, the first an image of Paravai, wife of saint Sundarar, now in storage in the Madras Museum,[51] and the second, an image in the Calico Museum in Ahmedabad, identified as a queen (fig. 7.14a, b). All three have perfectly rounded breasts placed high on the torso, with narrow waist, and slender hips. All three wear a *pottu* gem on a string tied high around the neck, and a further set of three necklaces of which the lowest consists of a string of mini-medallions. A body chain, or *channavira*, comes together to lie between the breasts and then separates to encircle the torso, meeting again at the middle back. Their low-slung long skirts dip in a rounded curve below the navel, and ornamental chains hang from the belts of two of the bronzes. Closely similar is the manner in which narrow ribbon-like folds of the skirt's drapery run along the inner side of both thighs to form an upper loop and two stylized lower strips, a feature we saw in chapter 5 to have been introduced at Tiruvenkadu by artists of the generation following its famed Master. The hair of all three is arranged so as to frame the face with curls, an escaping strand of hair lies along their shoulder joints, and in rear view we see that all three have their hair arranged in an elaborate chignon shaped as an elongated oval with a horizontal band of hair crossing the chignon to hold it all in place. The consort of Arjuna belongs to ca. 1125, while the other two images may be a decade or two later, to around 1140.

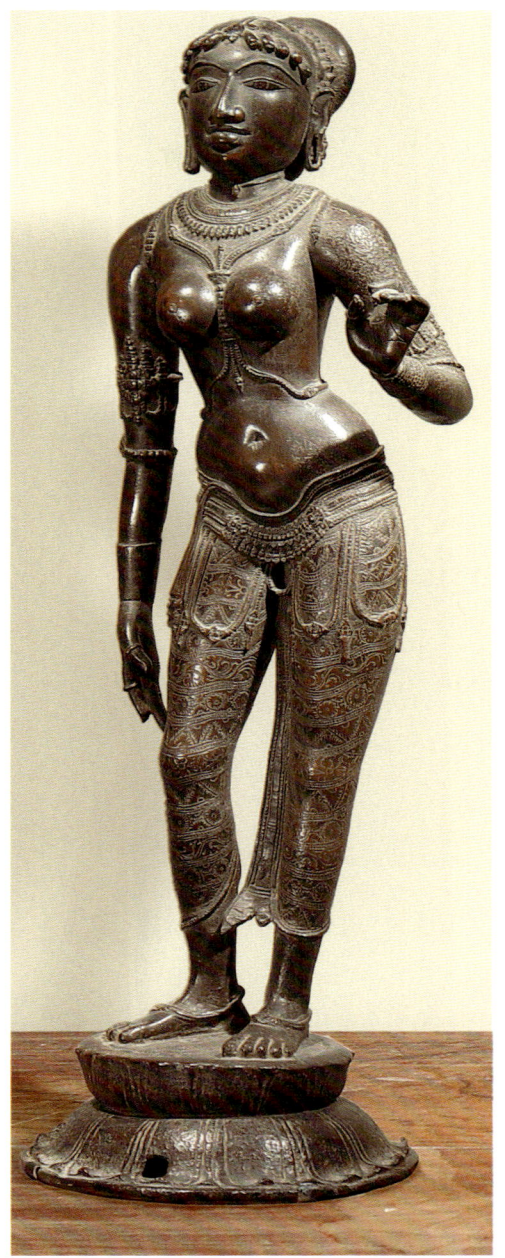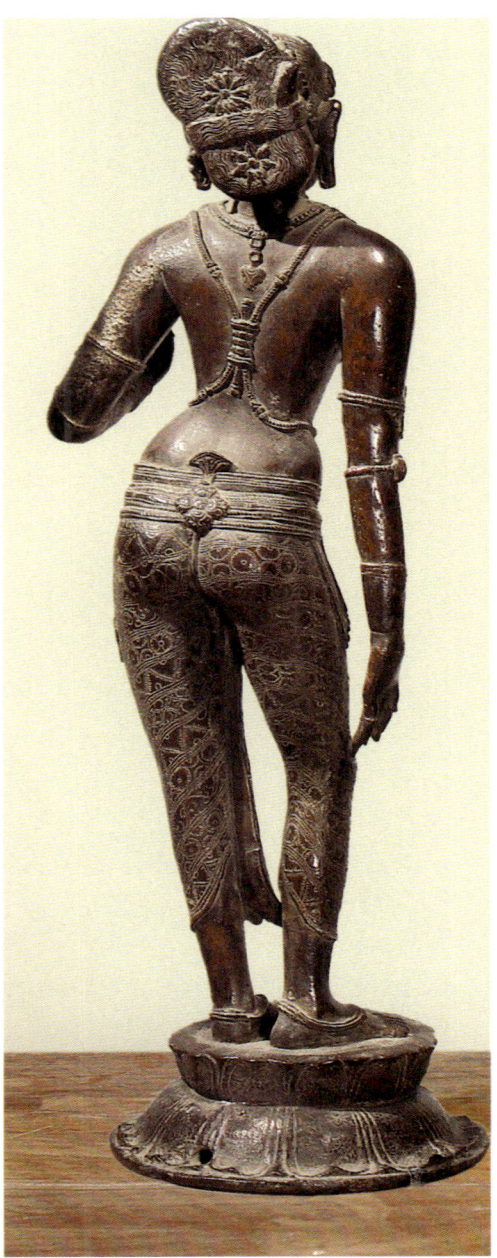

Figure 7.14. (a) Queen, ca. 1150, The Calico Museum of Textiles and The Sarabhai Foundation Collections, Ahmedabad.
(b) Rear view of Queen (fig. 7.14a).

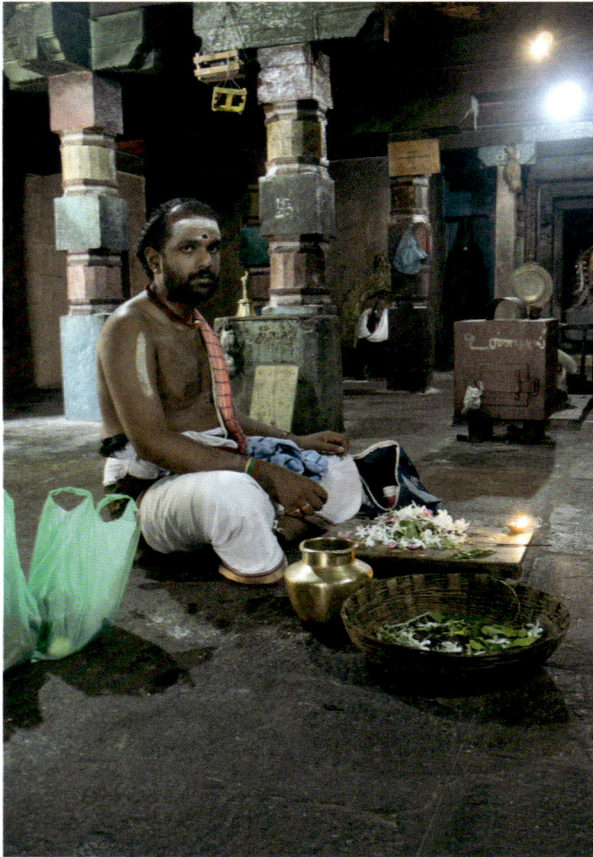

Figure 7.15. Temple priest.

The Role of Temple Priests and the Prominence of the Saints

Let us turn in conclusion to the temple priests, and to the saints who lived several centuries before them, both of whom played a ritual role central to temple ceremonial and to processional festival worship. The priests, in addition, are the formulaic enforcers and protectors of all gifts made to a temple. Each and every inscribed gift, whether of cash, land, a perpetual lamp, goats and cows given to provide ghee to keep lamps burning, a bronze image, or jewelry to adorn a bronze, ends with the phrase "in the protection of the Shiva priests [of that particular temple]" (*pan maheshvara rakshai*).[52] With this concluding formulaic phrase, each devotee entrusts his gift into the safekeeping of the priests of the temple who thereby ensure that they will honor the conditions of the gift. Additionally, the priests are also the custodians of temple bronzes; they dress and adorn them daily, weekly, monthly, and annually for the various rituals and festivals celebrated in the temple (fig. 7.15). They are thereby also the privileged handlers of temple jewels.

A ritual text, "Procedures for the Great Festival" (*Mahotsava vidhi*), written in Sanskrit by Aghora-Shivacharya, a respected brahmin teacher, in the year 1157, during the reign of Rajaraja II, was recently published in English translation.[53] The text addresses the chief priest, who conducts this annual nine-day festival in a Shiva temple, which commences and concludes with a flag-raising and flag-lowering ceremony. The text specifies that the principal icon for this celebration is a threesome group of seated Shiva and Uma with their infant son Skanda between them, known by the term *Somaskanda* (*sa-uma-skanda*, or with Uma and Skanda; see fig. 4.12).[54] The festival procession commences once

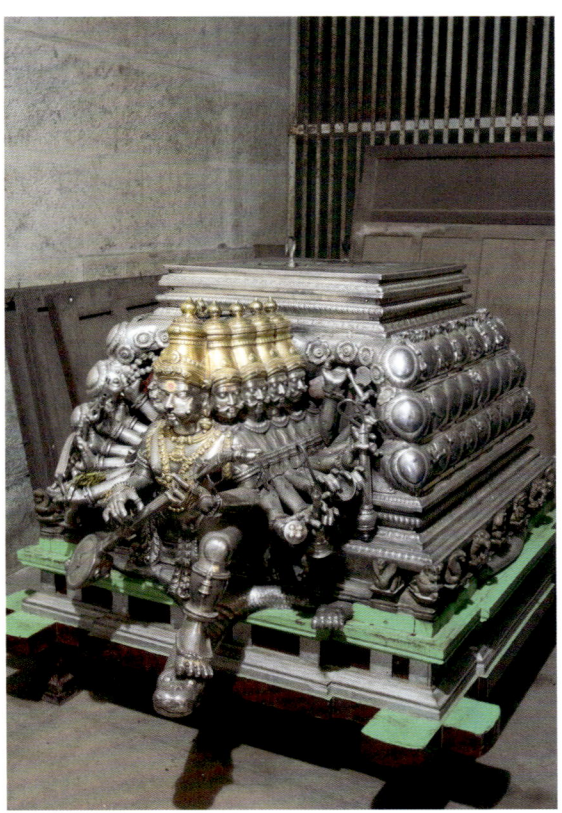 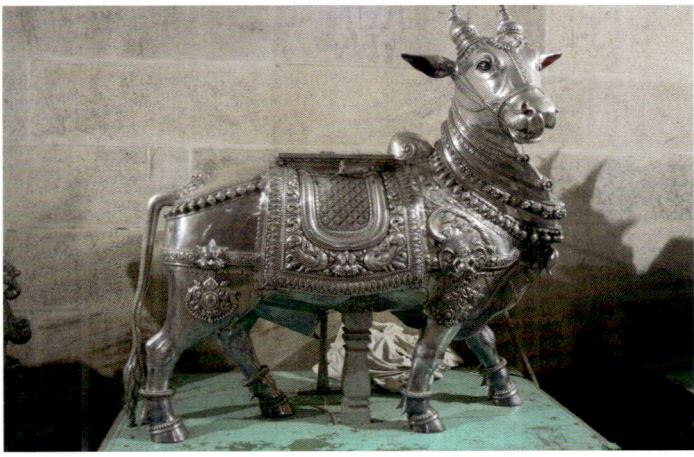

Figure 7.16. (a and b) Vehicles that carry divine images at festivals, Periya Koil, Kanadukathan, eighteenth century.

this bronze group is fully adorned; it is preceded by bronzes of Shiva's bull Nandi and elephant-headed Ganesha, and followed by images of devotees with saint Chandesha bringing up the rear.[55] The bronze group is paraded on a different vehicle on each day and each night of the festival. For instance, on the fourth night, they ride the bull; on the fifth night, they ride on a vehicle depicting multiheaded, multiarmed demon Ravana, who attempted to shake mount Kailasa, the Himalayan home of Shiva and Uma; on the sixth night, the group rides an elephant; on the eighth night, they ride a horse.[56] The vehicles seen here give an idea of the grandeur of the scene but are not of Chola date, being silver-plated wooden images dedicated during the eighteenth century (fig. 7.16a, b).

The twelfth-century *Mahotsava vidhi* speaks of four other major sets of bronzes as part of the celebrations during the nine days of this Great Festival. Dancing Shiva and his consort are to be worshipped on the eighth night, when their bronzes are taken in procession around the temple and then placed in the assembly hall to "spend the rest of the night watching the entertainments."[57] The reference is to the music, dance, and drama that are part of such festivals, and that draw vast numbers of devotees to the temple. On the fifth, seventh, or tenth day, an image of bridegroom Shiva taking Uma's hand in marriage is required, since the text informs us that the priests should perform the marriage ceremony with due pomp and splendor, and with all the necessary services.[58] The text speaks of two other festival rituals to be conducted during the nine days of the Great Festival; one is a celebration of the goddess that may be conducted for a single day or for three, seven, or nine days,[59] while the other is a festival of the sixty-three saints.[60]

SILK ROUTE OF THE OCEAN

The concluding ceremony on the final day of the Great Festival consists of a series of ritual baths to remove the pollution that the deities have encountered while being paraded through the streets of the town. This ritual bathing is conducted in a pavilion constructed for the purpose near a chosen water source, where the priests bathe each image using pots of water brought for this purpose. The final bath is reserved for Shiva's ritual weapon, the trident, and for this the priest must himself enter the water holding the trident; devotees attending the festival are also encouraged to enter the water.[61] The concluding rite, after lowering the flag, is the patron honoring the priest and presenting him with his honorarium, after which the priest is taken in formal procession to his home.[62]

It should be noted that throughout the twelfth century and well into the thirteenth century, devotees continued to commission a range of bronzes that are not specifically mentioned as part of Aghorasiva's Great Festival. One such was Shiva with the bull, an image that we saw to be of importance in ensuring victory for the monarch. In 1117, during the reign of Kulottunga I, for instance, a devotee set up an image of Shiva with the bull, together with his consort, in the Trichy district.[63] In the year 1150, an official under Rajaraja II arranged for offerings of red lilies to adorn the image of Shiva with the bull that he set up in the temple at Tirupugalur.[64] In 1183, a private individual made a gift of money toward an oil bath and offerings to the image of Shiva with the bull that he set up in the Tiruvidavayil temple.[65]

What do we know about the status, the ritual role, the emoluments, and the personal living conditions of these temple priests between the ninth and thirteenth centuries? Did they always have a hereditary status that gave them an apparently privileged position? How were they supported monetarily? We have encountered inscriptions that speak of infractions by temple priests who stole temple jewels or ritual items, or maintained false accounts of temple monies. These records tell us that those who were unable to repay the money equivalent to the stolen items as a single lump sum agreed to forfeit their right to temple *puja* for a certain number of days of each month until the temple collected the amount due to it.[66] Such inscriptions suggest that the priests lived on the money they received as cash emoluments, either from the temple or from devotees, in return for their regular performance of temple rites and rituals on behalf of those devotees.

Do we have any information on where the priests lived? In seeking an answer to this question, it is useful to turn to the increasing number of epigraphic references to *guhais* and *mathas*, both terms used generically for "monasteries" that occur from the mid-twelfth century onward. The *guhai* (literally, "cave") seems generally to have been located within the temple premises, as we see, for instance, from an inscription at the Tirupugalur temple, where a *guhai* was built in the northeast corner of the temple premises in the year 1150, during the reign of Rajaraja II.[67] By contrast, *mathas* were usually located outside the temple walls, as in the case of the "*Matha* of the Sacred Way" at Tiruvaduturai, presumably located along the main sacred street outside the temple.[68] But neither the *guhai* nor the *matha* were institutions intended as residential quarters for temple priests.

Several inscriptions indicate that the *guhai* was connected with those who recited the *Tevaram* hymns of the saints Sambandar, Appar, and Sundarar, or with those who recited the complete expanded Shiva canon known as *Tirumurai* (sacred path), which commences with the *Tevaram* and ends with the official hagiography, the *Periya Puranam*. One might note that hymn singers, known today as *oduvars*, are of a lower ritual status than the temple priests, the *maheshvaras*. An inscription engraved on the south wall of the central shrine of the Tiruvidavayil temple speaks of a shrine for the *Tirumurai* within the temple's *Tiruttondattogaiyan guhai* (*guhai* of the sacred servants, or the sixty-three saints). This inscription suggests that the object enshrined within this *guhai* was a manuscript version of the complete Shiva canon, the *Tirumurai*, that was completed when Sekkilar wrote his *Periya Puranam* around the year 1140. The inscription dates to 1249, during the reign of Rajendra II, a hundred years after the completion of the text, and speaks of a gift of land to meet the expenses of those who looked after the *Tirumurai* shrine, and those who sang the sacred songs (*tiruppattu*).[69] This same inscription incidentally gives us information about a second *guhai*, while speaking of its donor who resided in the "Beloved *Tevaram* and *Tirumurai guhai*" (*tirumurai tevara chelvan guhai*) in the temple of Kazhamulam. In this reference, the first seven books of the canon, the *Tevaram*, is referred to as separate from the entire corpus of the *Tirumurai*, presumably because the hymns of the *Muvar* that comprise the *Tevaram* were especially popular and known independent of the complete canon. The temple and *guhai* at Tiruvidavayil appear to have harbored a special relationship with the saints and their songs. Inscribed upon the south wall of the temple's *mandapa* is a hymn by child saint Sambandar that is unknown from any manuscript version of his corpus of hymns, and has recently been included by François Gros in his Pondicherry edition of the *Tevaram*.[70] Its ancient cutting into stone "in characters of the 12th century AD" is noteworthy, since no other hymn of any other saint appears to have been thus engraved in stone.[71] We do know however, that Naralokaviran, minister to both Kulottunga I and Vikrama Chola, had the *Tevaram* hymns engraved on copper plates for the Chidambaram temple; since these comprise 700 hymns, usually of ten or eleven verses, the copper plates must have been a substantial set.[72]

By contrast with the *guhai*, the chief purpose of the *matha* appears to have been to provide meals for visiting brahmins, holy men, and devotees, and perhaps accommodation too for such visitors. An endowment of land, given to the "*Matha* of the Sacred Way" at Tiruvaduturai in the year 1084, was for the specific purpose of feeding devotees.[73] In the year 1122, during the reign of Vikrama Chola, a *matha* at Tiruvenkadu received a gift of tax-free land from a chieftain to enable them to feed the *maheshvaras*, presumably visiting priests, who attended a festival at the Tiruvenkadu temple.[74] In 1123, a minister built a *matha* and presented land to it in order to ensure meals for fifty brahmins of Sayavanam, a suburb of the port town of Poompuhar.[75] More than one *matha* seems to have been constructed through the generosity of merchant guilds. Like the guild named "The Five Hundred of the Thousand Directions" with which we commenced this chapter, these merchant groups often took their name from the number of its members, more formulaic than actual. In the year 1109, a merchant made a gift of land to the "*matha* of the Seven Hundred" (*elunuttruvan matam*) that was located south of the west gate of the temple at Ratnagiri in the Trichy district; the gift was to be used by the *matha* for feeding temple staff (*devaradiyar*), Shiva yogis, and penance-performing renunciants (*tapasvins*).[76] Whether such yogis and renunciants were permanently attached to the temple or were wandering holy men is not clear. An inscription in the Sankaracharya *matha* at Tiruvannaika refers to the rebuilding of the "*matha* of the Forty-eight Thousand" (*nar-pattennayiram matam*), located to the north of the temple, and indicates that its purpose was to feed ascetics.[77]

While the *guhai* and the *matha* indirectly "supported ritual activity within the temple," in Tamil Nadu they did not house "the holy practitioners who officiated over daily services to the gods," as they did in, say, central India.[78] *Guhais* and *mathas* were not intended as residential quarters for the temple's priests who, in Tamil Nadu, have always lived a married life, occupying individual houses in the streets immediately surrounding the temple. Tamil priests were not part of any organized celibate monastic system. Celibacy was not a commended model; in fact, at the famous Chidambaram temple, only married priests were and still are qualified to conduct temple ritual. Chidambaram *dikshitars* (the term applied to Chidambaram temple priests) explain that their young priests need to be able to focus solely on the deity; this they can do only when they are fulfilled and happy in their personal lives and have fully experienced the joys of marriage. One might recall a verse of saint Appar in his hymn "We may lead a good life on earth" (*mannil nalla vannam varalam*) in which Appar cites the example of lord Shiva who is always accompanied by his consort Uma:

> *Do not scorn the joys and delights of life*
> *they are not hostile to a life beyond,*
> *Look at our Lord, ascetic of ascetics*
> *who dwells in our midst with his spouse*
> *of wondrous virtues, goodness, grace, and charm.*[79]

It is interesting to ponder over the role played by the priests in commissioning bronzes. These householder priests, dutifully executing the instructions of sacred manuals, would have need for a series of key images; the priests probably played a significant role in finding patrons who would commission images that were missing in a temple's collection, as also of ornaments to adorn specific bronzes.

In conclusion, it is pertinent to examine bronze images of the saints who were transformed from holy men and women who lived between 550 to 800 CE into sacred beings who merited devotional worship akin to that accorded to Shiva in his various manifestations. Some of them were historical figures who, through their composition of sacred hymns, played a major role in defining the liturgy of temple worship and in linking devotees to the temple. While we have made frequent reference to the hymns of these saints, and have examined their images when they have been part of our continuing story, they merit further discussion here. The *Muvar*, or Revered Three of Sambandar, Appar, and Sundarar, became a favored temple grouping, and threesome images of the group were cast in bronze as early as the mid-tenth century. Enchanting images of child saint Sambandar, depicting him as a three-year-old child, recall the hagiographic legend that speaks of him being left on the steps of the temple tank at Sirkali while his brahmin father went in for a ritual dip (fig. 7.17a, b). The hungry child began to cry; when his father emerged from his ritual bath, he found the contented child, holding an empty

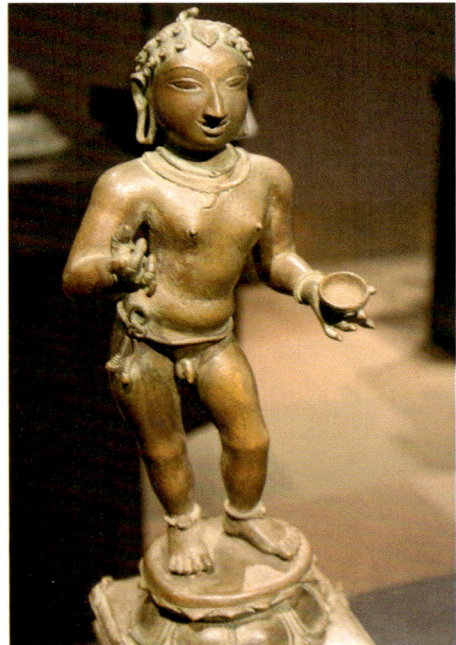 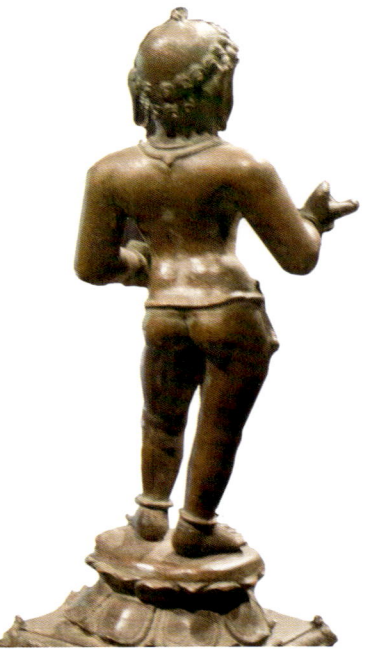

Figure 7.17. (a and b) Child Saint Sambandar, ca. 1100, Norton Simon Museum, Pasadena.

cup in one hand and playing happily while trickles of milk ran down his chin. When questioned as to the source of the milk, the child pointed up to the temple tower, where there was a sculpted image of goddess Uma seated beside Shiva. Hagiography tells us that the three-year-old child then burst into song speaking of Shiva as the thief who stole his heart. Images of the child depict him as an enchanting curly-haired standing infant, naked except for ornaments, holding an empty cup in his left palm and pointing up toward the temple tower with the fingers of his right hand. Such images are generally 18–20 inches high and intended to be portable images carried in temple festival processions, although we also find bronzes barely 3 inches tall that were clearly intended as objects of personal devotion (fig. 7.18). A variation on the iconography of the saint depicts Sambandar as a dancing child, standing on his right leg with the left raised high in dance (fig. 7.19). While I have suggested that this is an iconography that may have been modeled on images of dancing child Krishna, we can firmly set aside suggestions that such images represent child Skanda, son of Shiva and Uma.[80] An inscription in the Nageshvara temple at Kumbakonam, which speaks specifically of a bronze of dancing child saint Sambandar, is definitive on this issue.[81] The second of the *Muvar*, saint Appar (Tirunavukkarasar), elder contemporary of child Sambandar, acquired his popular name of Appar, or Father, from Sambandar. Images of Appar invariably depict him carrying a hoe with which he cleared the weeds within early sacred sites, which, as we emphasized in chapter 1, were open-air sites with the sacred linga beneath a hallowed tree (fig. 7.20).[82] A superb image of the third saint, Sundarar, from the site of Keelaiyur, depicts him standing in elegant contrapposto with a slender, almost sinuous body; his left arm is raised and bent at the elbow to rest upon the shoulder of his beloved wife Paravai, missing in this case (fig. 7.21). An independent image of Paravai, found in a secret room

SILK ROUTE OF THE OCEAN

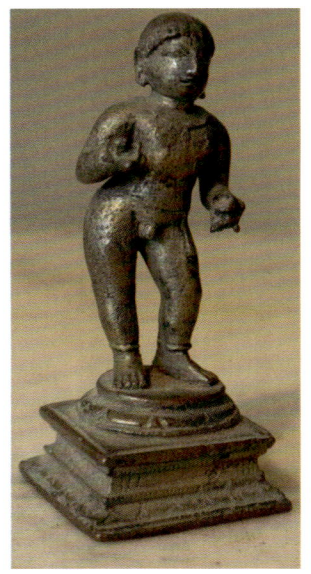
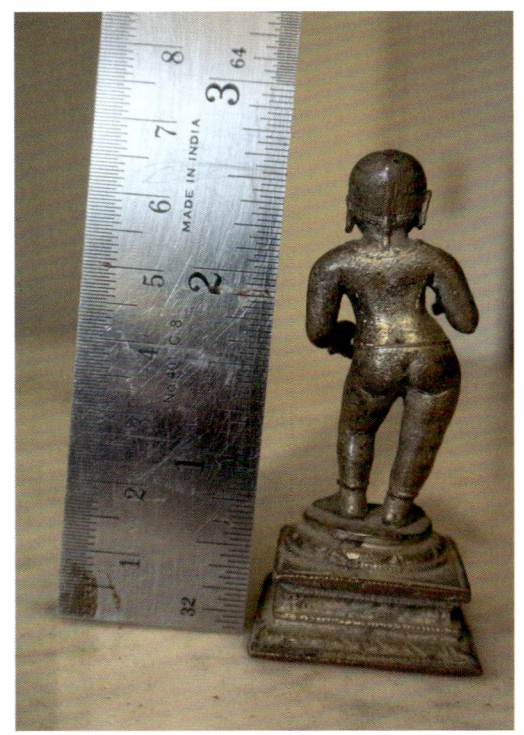
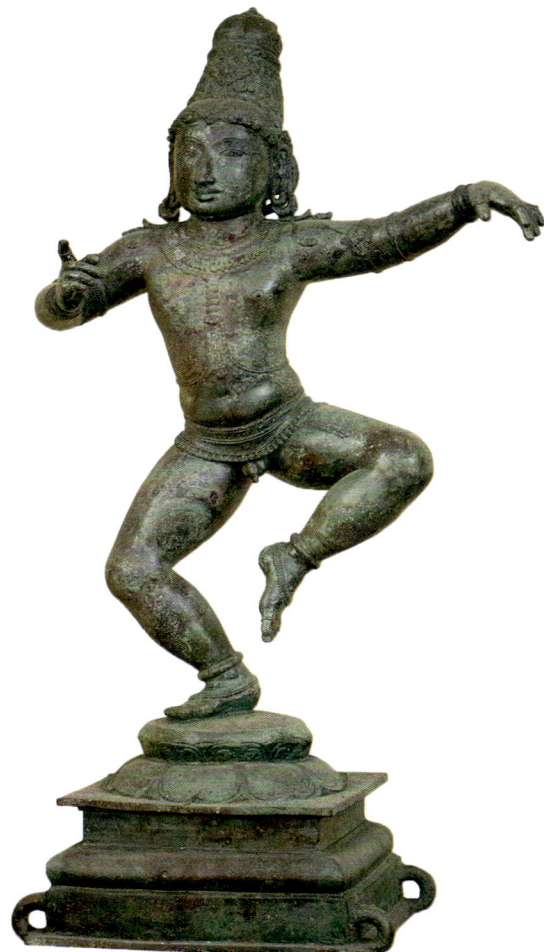

Figure 7.18 (a and b). Child Saint Sambandar, image of personal worship, ca. 1100, private collection.

Figure 7.19. Dancing Child Saint Sambandar, Tiruvenkadu temple, Nagapattinam district, ca. 1030, Art Gallery, Thanjavur.

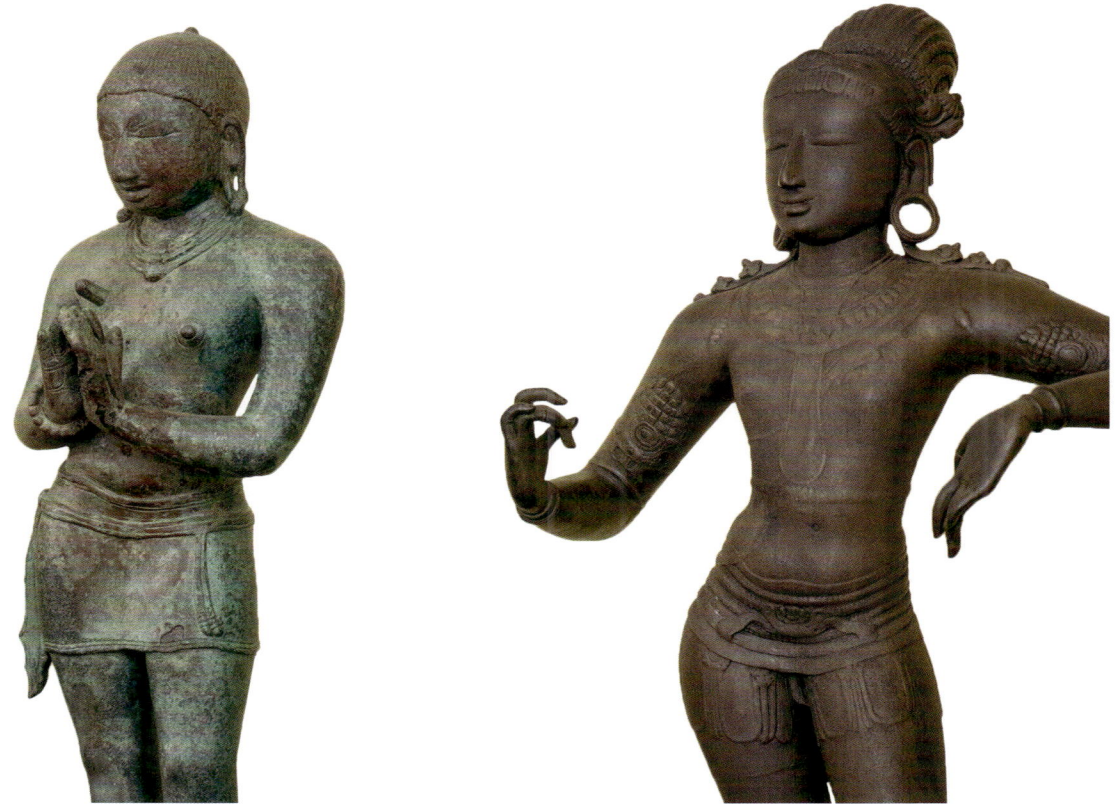

Figure 7.20. Saint Appar, Tiruvenkadu temple, Nagapattinam district, ca. 1030, Art Gallery, Thanjavur.

Figure 7.21. Saint Sundarar, Keelaiyur temple, Nagapattinam district, ca. 950, Art Gallery, Thanjavur.

within the Chidambaram temple, while not the consort of this particular image, is an accomplished early work of the Sembiyan workshop and also belongs to the mid-tenth century.[83] The group of sixty-three *nayanmar*, established in song by saint Sundarar around the year 800, acquired so high a status that images of the key figures began to be created in the mid-tenth century, a mere 150 years later. Within another 100 years, judging from the image of saint Kanappan created by the Tiruvenkadu Master that we examined in chapter 5, images of the complete set of sixty-three *nayanmar* began to be created. Today, saints' days are specifically marked in the ritual calendar of Tamil temples so that devotees may congregate to listen to the day-long recitation of the hymns of a particular saint. The continuing relevance of the *nayanmar* saints in the ritual cycle of the temples of Tamil Nadu is a remarkable and striking phenomenon.

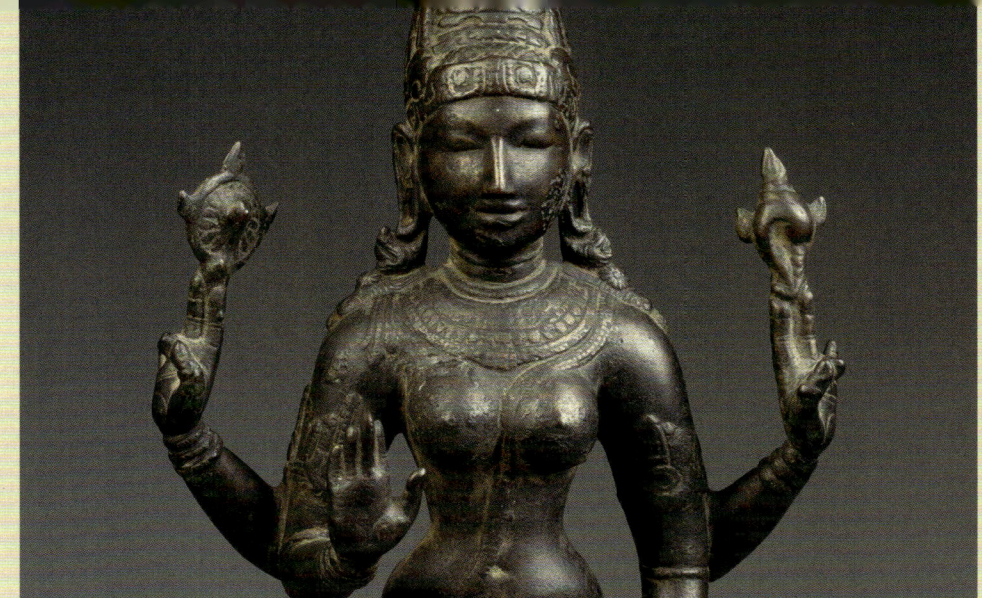

Evolving Manifestations of the Goddess, the God Vishnu, and the Buddha

8

Svasti Sri. In the 15th year of Ko-Parakesari, I Sendan Kari of Vayalur . . . established Uma Bhattaraki in the stone temple of the lord . . . and taking her as my daughter, I celebrated her marriage to the god.

For the sacred food offerings at noon to Uma, I endowed land that I had obtained as stridhanam from my brothers. From the paddy yielded by this land, I arranged that Uma Bhattaraki should be offered rice, ghee, vegetables, curds, and adaikay.[1]

KUMARAVAYALUR SHIVA TEMPLE, *MANDAPA* DOORJAMB, YEAR 986

In discussing Shiva's many manifestations, whether peaceable or in a role in which he destroys forces of cosmic evil, we have seen that he is invariably accompanied by his consort Uma, who watches his feats as a supportive admirer. We have learned too that, more often than not, female donors chose to dedicate bronzes of Uma as consort to one or another form of Shiva, and also to commission rich jewelry to adorn such images. Women donors frequently referred to Uma in affectionate terms as "my daughter," as in the record cited earlier from the Kumaravayalur temple in Trichy district, where Sendan Kari consecrated a bronze of Uma, whom, she tells us, she took as her daughter (*enmakalarkkondu*). Accordingly, she celebrated Uma's marriage with Shiva (*vivaham sheyvittu*) and also provided daily food offerings for the bronze couple by endowing land that she had received at her own wedding, as *stridhanam* or woman's wealth.² At the Karuttangudi temple, in the thirty-eighth year of Parantaka, or 943, a woman donor endowed a piece of land to be used for the worship of Uma-bhattaraki, referred to as her daughter (*tam makalar*), and received from the townsfolk of Manalokkur a written confirmation of this gift.³ At Tirukolambiyur, Uttama Chola's queen Aruran Ponnambalattadigal donated land for the worship of Uma, who is referred to in the inscription as the queen's daughter (*ivar makalar*).⁴

While Uma does indeed play the role of a devoted consort, she is a dominant force in her own right and the powerful deity of *Devi Mahatmyam*, or "Glory of the Goddess," a text composed during the sixth century. Defying stereotypes, she is unaccompanied by any male, and destroys powerful forces of evil in fierce battle; she is addressed variously as *Mahisha Mardini* or Killer of the buffalo-demon Mahisha, as *Nishumbha Sudani* or destroyer of demon Nishumbha, and as Kali or Dark One. In the year 855, when Vijayalaya Chola captured the town of Thanjavur and made it his capital, his first major act was to give thanks to the goddess for his victory. A royal charter tells us: "He consecrated there the image of the goddess who is the destroyer of demon Nishumbha. By the grace of that goddess, Vijayalaya bore the whole earth as lightly as if it were a garland."⁵ Vijayalaya's original commission appears to have been a stone image that has been identified as one currently reinstalled in Thanjavur in a temple of late date, though there is some disagreement on this issue.⁶ We turn, instead, to an early eleventh-century bronze that portrays a slender and sensuous though clearly formidable goddess as *Nishumbha Sudani*. Seated with one leg bent to rest upon her seat, her other foot is placed upon the figure of demon Nishumbha, who lies crumpled at her feet (fig. 8.1a, b). She wears a serpent as breastband, and holds a skull bowl in her left front palm, while her other seven hands brandish various weapons. The third eye in her forehead, fangs at either end of her mouth, and hair standing up in fearsome disarray and adorned with a skull contrast with the beauty of her bodily form, making us aware of the implicit continuum between the auspicious, the formidable, and the fearsome. The *Devi Mahatmyam* makes it clear that the goddess who destroys demon Nishumbha is none other than Shiva's consort Uma in her fierce aspect. As an independent warring goddess who took on ferocious male opponents representing various forces of evil and triumphed over them with ease, she is also frequently addressed as Durga, or Invincible One, and is of pivotal importance in the context of Indian kingship. Whichever deity a monarch normally worshipped, whether Shiva, Vishnu, or other aspect of godhead, it was the goddess to whom he needed to turn

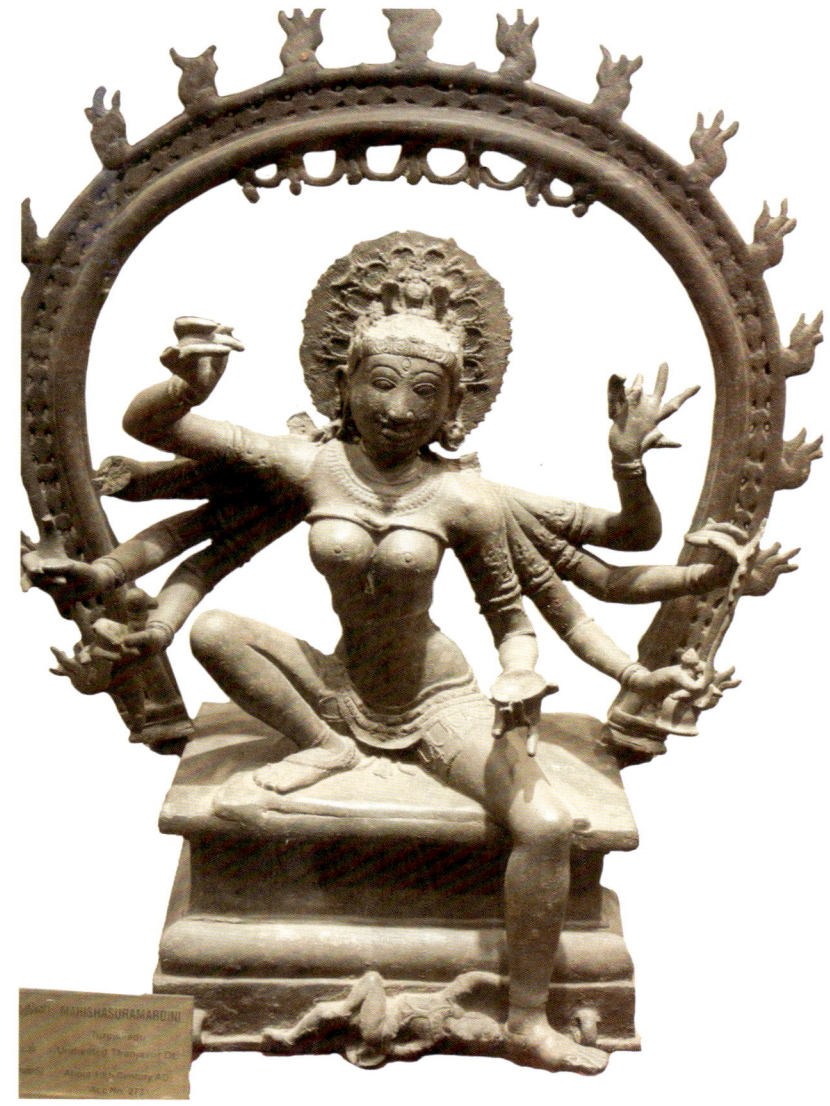

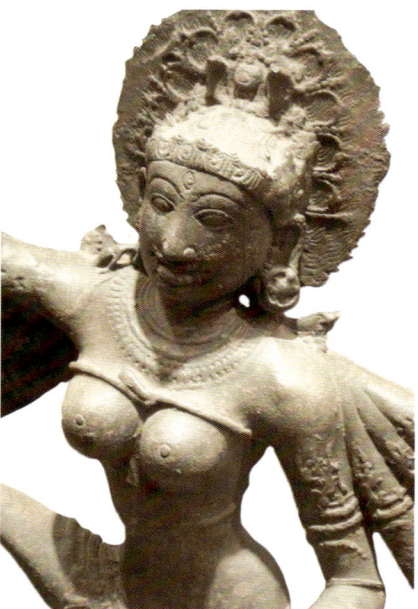

Figure 8.1. (a and b) *Goddess as Destroyer of Nishumbha*, early eleventh century, Government Museum, Chennai.

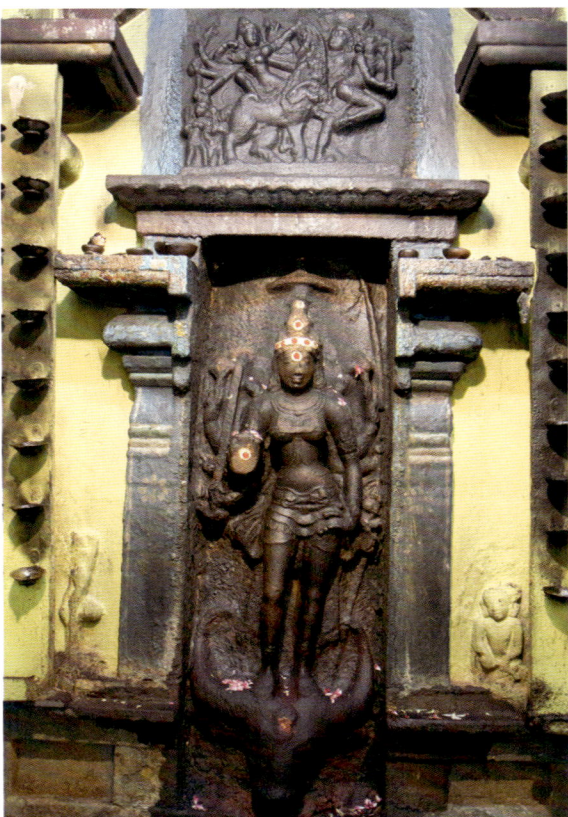
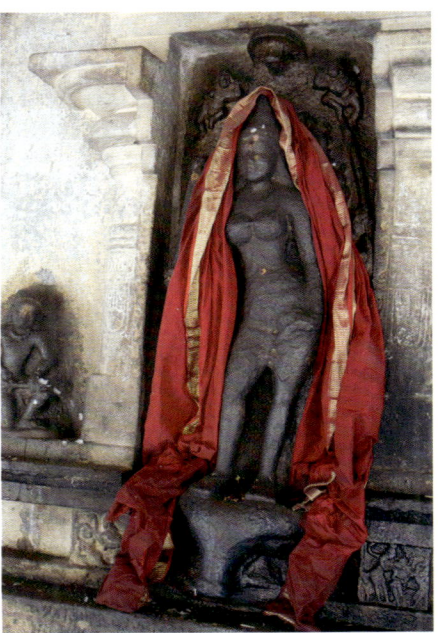

Figure 8.2. *Durga Conquers Buffalo-Demon Mahisha*, Korangaduturai temple, Thanjavur, ca. 981.

Figure 8.3. *Durga Victorious over Buffalo-Demon Mahisha*, Konerirajapuram temple, Nagapattinam district, ca. 969.

for triumph in battle. This belief finds expression in both of India's great epics in which its heroes, Rama in the Ramayana and Arjuna in the Mahabharata, worshipped the goddess before facing enemies on the battlefield. And with Vijayalaya Chola, we may assume that it was as thanksgiving for his victory at Thanjavur that he commissioned a stone image of the goddess victorious over demon Nishumbha.

Durga-Uma's most applauded feat across the length and breadth of India is her destruction of the buffalo-demon Mahisha, who took the brutish form of a wild black water buffalo. In stone temples in Chola territory, it became customary to portray Durga within a niche on the north wall of the *mandapa*, depicting her standing victorious on the severed head of the buffalo. It is exceedingly rare to see a portrayal of the battle itself. In an unusual portrayal at the temple at Korangaduturai built by queen Sembiyan, a small rectangular panel above the niche carrying the standing goddess features the battle in relief sculpture, with the retreating demon shown as a human with a buffalo head (fig. 8.2). From the time of queen Sembiyan in the mid-tenth century, the victorious goddess appears regularly in a niche of Chola temples dedicated to Shiva. The ghastly deed of destruction is over, and the beautiful goddess stands serenely confident upon the severed buffalo head; the darkened stone of such images indicates the regular lustration with oil that Durga receives during ritual puja (fig. 8.3).

Among the earliest bronzes of this form is a badly damaged, partly mutilated image that nevertheless makes a powerful statement (fig. 8.4a). The individual who discovered and retrieved the bronze in the early twentieth century clearly did not

EVOLVING MANIFESTATIONS

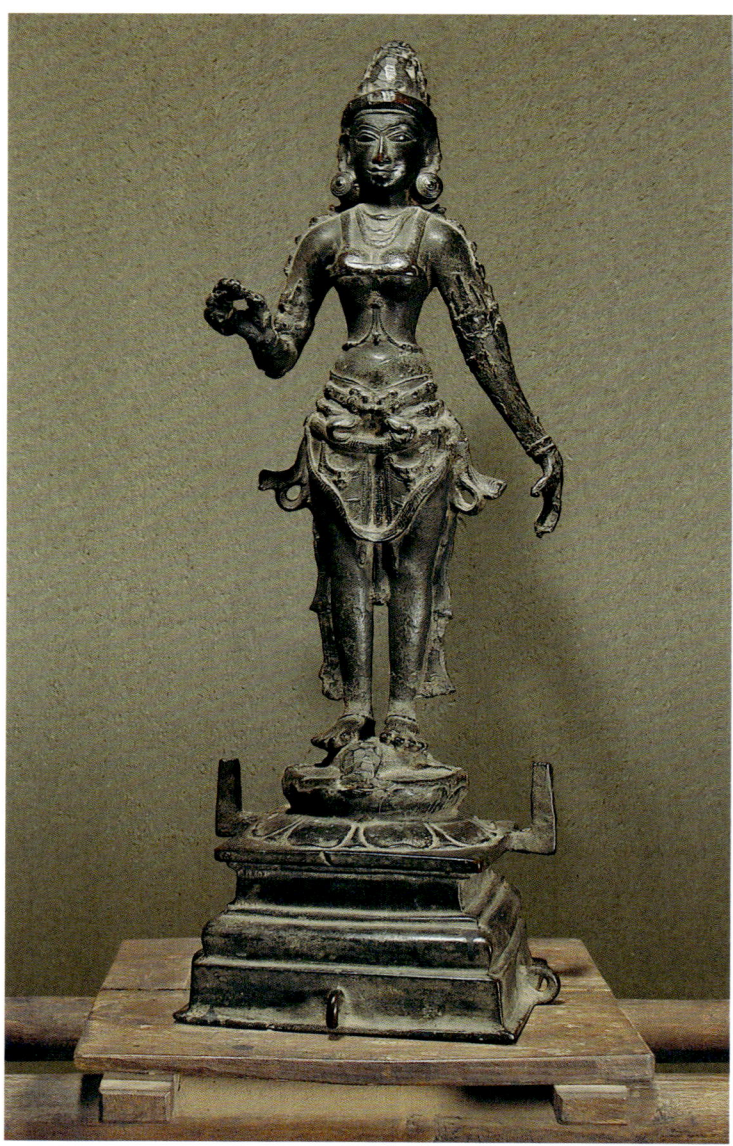
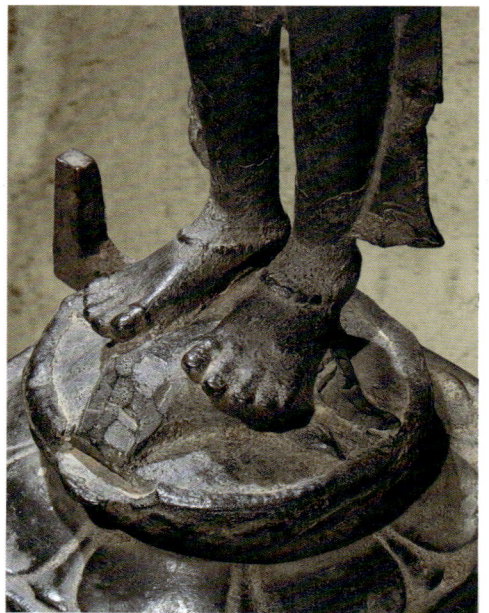
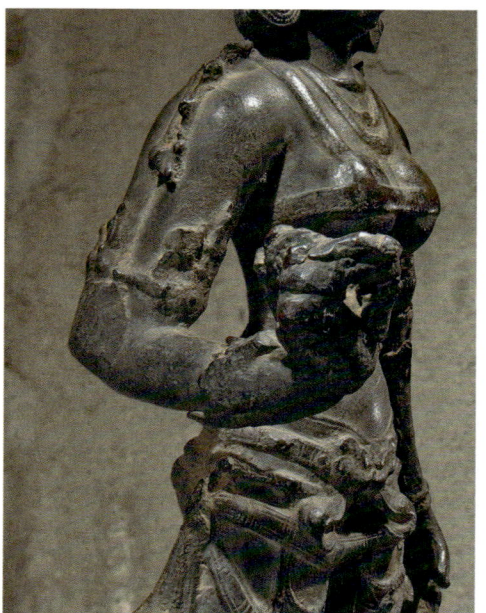

Figure 8.4. (a) *Durga Conquers Buffalo-Demon Mahisha*, ca. 860, The Calico Museum of Textiles and The Sarabhai Foundation Collections, Ahmedabad. (b, c) Details of *Durga Conquers Buffalo-Demon Mahisha* (fig. 8.4a) showing alterations to base and arms.

understand the significance of the buffalo head on which the goddess stands and attempted to chisel it away (fig. 8.4b). He also chiseled away Durga's second pair of arms (fig. 8.4c). In the course of his ham-fisted attempt to remove the encrustations and accretions resulting from burial underground, he caused further damage to the form of the exceedingly slender, lithe, and youthful goddess. Created in a coastal workshop, this bronze was commissioned soon after the Cholas came on the scene in 855. An image of this goddess created a hundred years later, also in a coastal workshop, dispenses with the buffalo head beneath her feet (fig. 8.5a, b). Here, she holds conch shell and discus, both symbols of god Vishnu, since in the Tamil country, Durga is visualized as sister of Vishnu.[7] Making Shiva's consort into the sister of his rival deity, Vishnu, was a neat

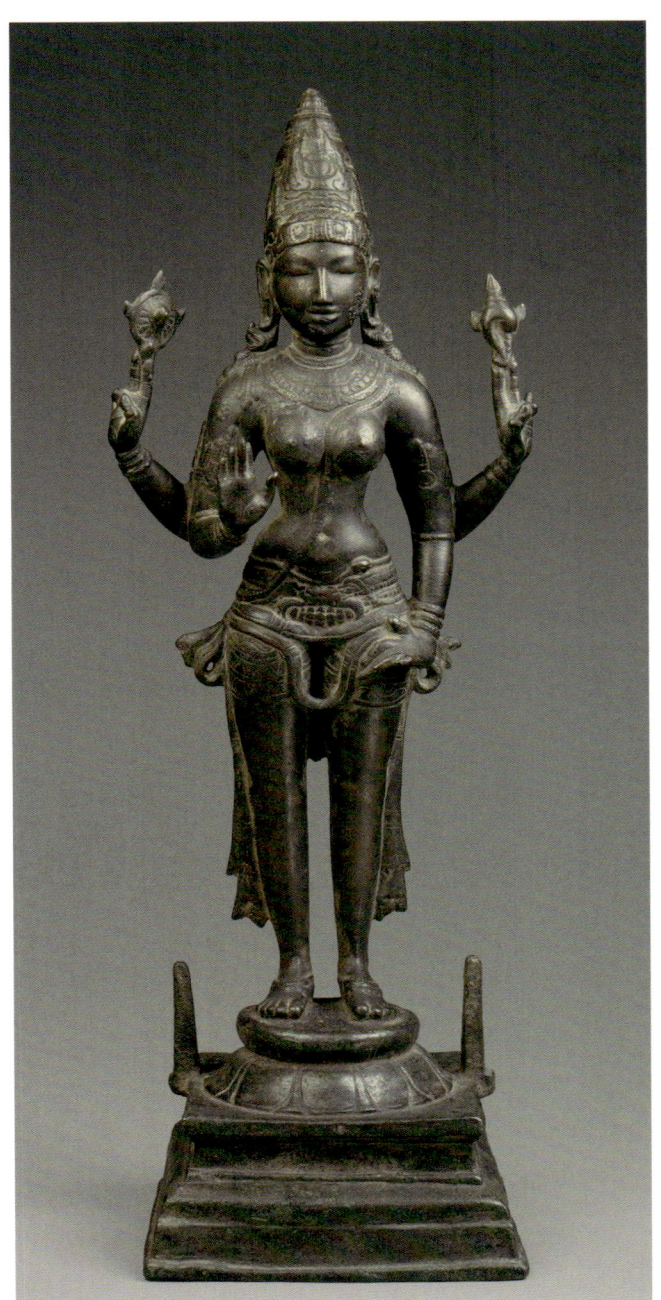 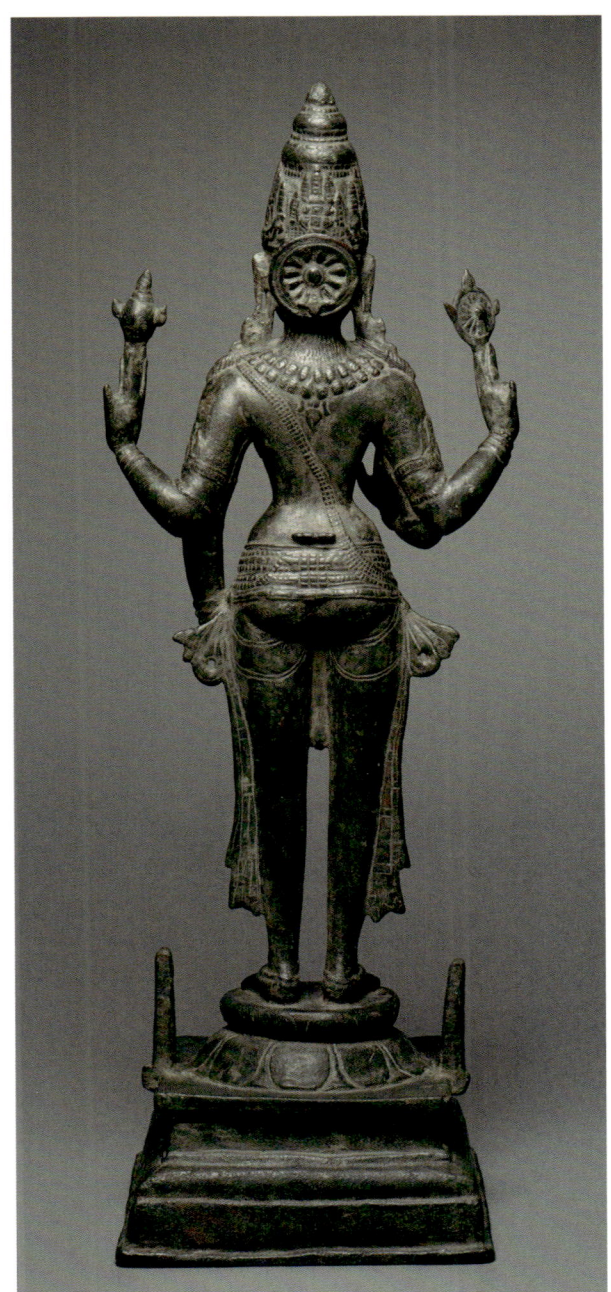

Figure 8.5. (a and b) *Durga*, ca. 970, Brooklyn Museum, Gift of Georgia and Michael de Havenon.

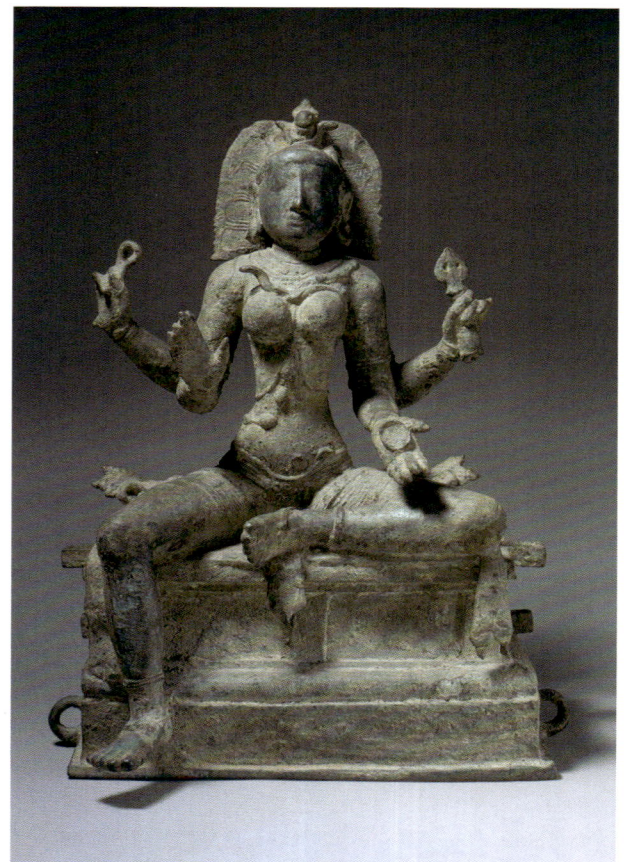 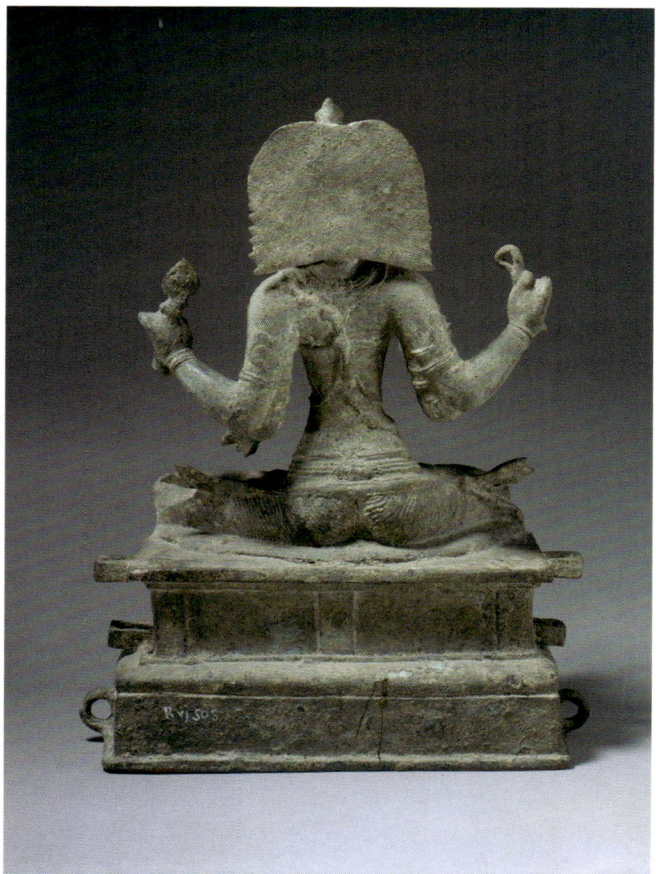

Figure 8.6. (a and b) *Kali*, ca. 900, Museum Rietberg, Zurich, Gift of Eduard von der Heydt. From the repository: *Goddess Kali*, first half of the tenth century, 40.5 × 32 cm, Museum Rietberg, Zurich, Gift of Eduard von der Heydt, RVI 505.

strategy, unheard of in north India, that may have been aimed at bringing closer together two different strands of sectarian worship.

It would not do to underestimate the persuasive and compelling appeal of the goddess whose worship was widespread among large sections of the Tamil population. Shrines to Kala Pidari, the goddess as the power of time and of darkness (*kala* means both), existed across the Kaveri delta, and she was venerated by large sections of the population. In a donative record of the year 965, during the reign of Chola king Aditya II Karikala, an officer named Mummudi Chola Kadupatti of Timisur lists among his gifts the construction (*edupitta*) of a temple (*koyil*) to Pidari in which he consecrated her image. His inscription contains a curse on anyone who interferes with his endowment, stating that such individuals would be banished, alone and abandoned, to a hell beneath the seven traditional hells.[8] A powerful bronze from the collection of the Rietberg Museum in Zurich, and created in a coastal workshop around the turn of the tenth century, portrays an exceedingly lean goddess sitting at ease with one leg bent to rest on her seat and the other pendant (fig. 8.6a, b). Her open hair is arranged in halo-like formation, with a cobra hood and a human skull crowning the arrangement. Entwined serpents are knotted together to form her breastband and she wears a sacred cord threaded with human skulls. In two rear hands, she holds a noose and a trident-headed bell, a skull cup rests in her front left palm, while her front right hand is in the gesture of blessing and reassurance. The lugs along the pedestal confirm that this powerful bronze of the goddess is a portable festival image.

Once the tenth-century Chola kings got into their stride, we have seen that they turned the Kaveri delta into the land par excellence of god Shiva, rebuilding in stone the many earlier shrines that were the focus of the saints' hymns. Goddess temples that already existed across the area remained in worship, but they were rarely converted to stone or given major support. That such a pattern was the norm across the Chola kingdom is confirmed by numerous land grants to Shiva temples; in outlining the boundaries of gifted land, these inscriptions specify an exemption of the land occupied by the local temple to goddess Kali.[9] One interesting and rare record of emperor Rajaraja's support of a temple to Durga comes from an inscription of 991 in which he orders his minister Villavan Muvendavelan to donate to the Durga temple in Little Kanchipuram all 900 sheep captured in attacks on certain local territories; a group of chosen shepherds were instructed to convert the resulting milk to the ghee needed to burn ten perpetual lamps in the Durga temple in the emperor's name of Rajaraja.[10]

Uma's role as consort of Shiva intensified and strengthened with the passage of time. In addition to being a constant presence in all of Shiva's manifestations, the belief now arose that Shiva in his aniconic form of the *linga*, hitherto positioned to stand in compelling isolation within the sanctum, also required the critical presence of Uma. By the twelfth century, bronzes of Uma as *Bhoga Shakti*, or "pleasure force," were routinely commissioned to stand on the threshold of temple sanctums that enshrined the *linga*. Since the iconography of Uma remained the same, the identification of an image as *Bhoga Shakti* rests almost exclusively on the fact that such images are substantially larger than the Uma bronzes that accompany Shiva's various anthropomorphic manifestations.

From the twelfth century onward, Shiva temples testify to the ever-mounting popularity of the concept of *kamakottam*, or "fortress of love," in which Uma plays a key role. This is the same time when bronzes of Shiva's eight great heroic forms (*attha virattanam*) were immensely popular. It would appear almost as if twelfth-century Chola India introduced the concept of the love fortress to counteract the formidable and frenzied aspect of Shiva evident in the heroic bronzes. This intensifying emphasis on the goddess manifested itself in two parallel streams. In newly built temples like Rajaraja II's royal temple at Darasuram, a separate self-contained temple to Uma with its own enclosing courtyard and entrance gateway was built to stand beside the Shiva temple (fig. 8.7a). The schematic plan helps to clarify the alignment of the two temples at Darasuram and demonstrate that the goddess temple, while of slightly smaller proportions than the temple to Shiva, is nevertheless monumental in its own right (fig. 8.7b, c). The many smaller, preexisting Shiva temples already built across Chola territory found a different and unique way to handle this concept of a sacred love fortress. Donors now commissioned seated bronzes of Uma as "Consort of the Bedroom Chamber" (*Palliarai Nachchiyar*), and constructed a "bedroom" within the premises of existing temples. To this day, such bedroom chambers, with the identifying Tamil label of "*palli arai*" painted above the doorway, are seen adjoining the Shiva shrine. Within this

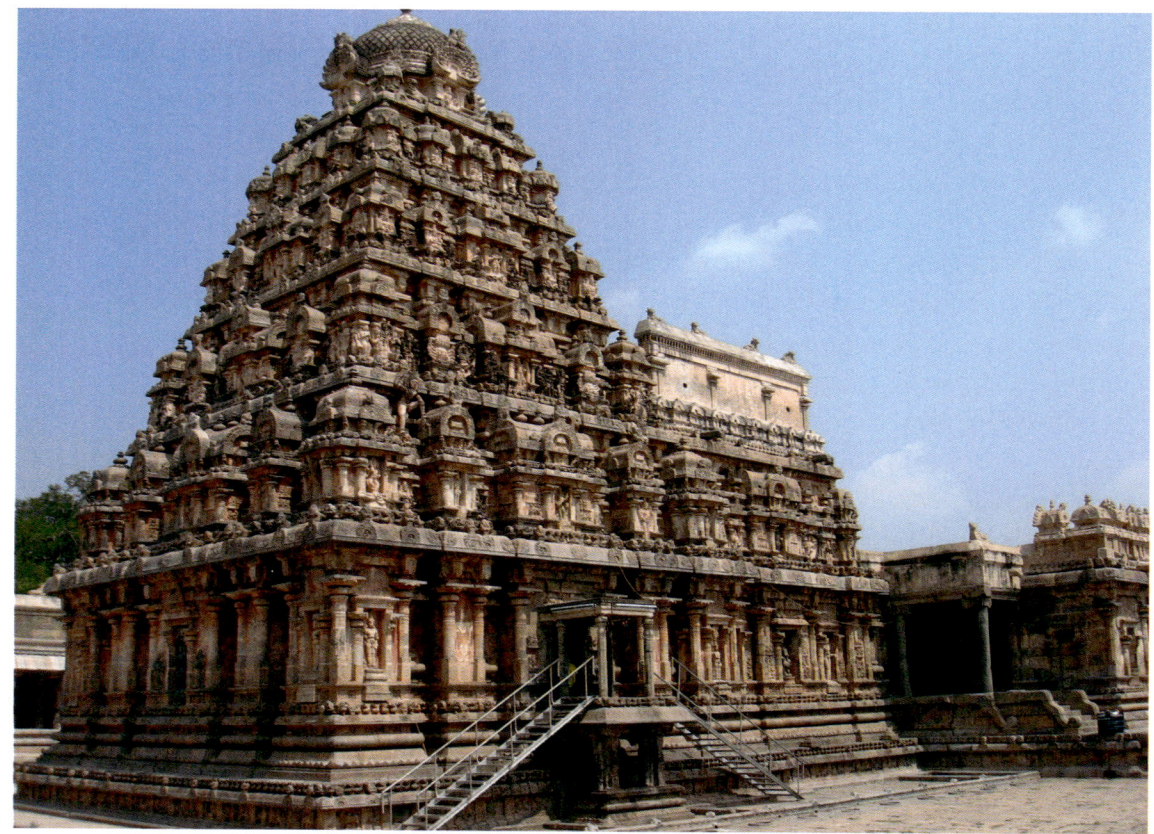

Figure 8.7. (a) Rajaraja II's royal temple at Darasuram, ca. 1150. (b) Rajaraja II's goddess temple at Darasuram, ca. 1150. (c) Schematic plan of the two shrines at Darasuram.

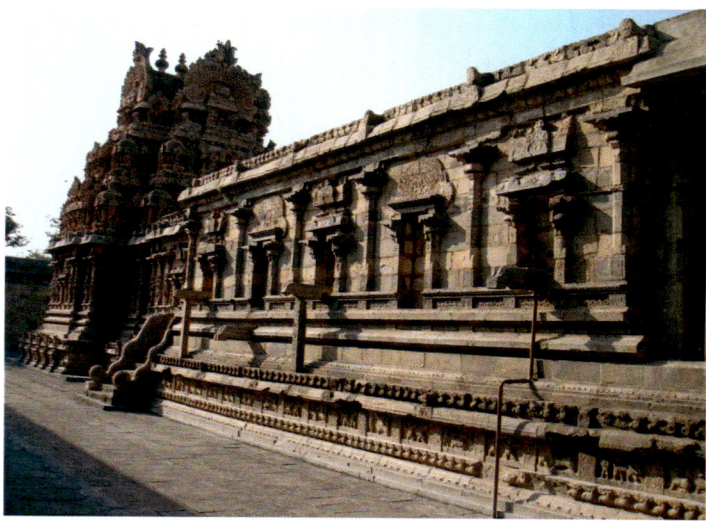
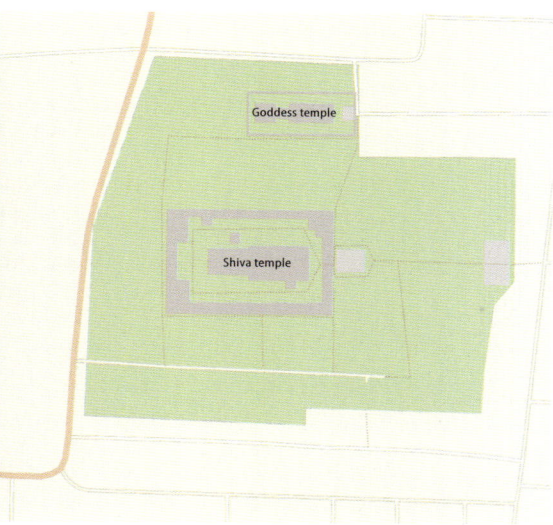

bedroom, a canopied throne-bed carries a bronze seated image of Uma as "Consort of the Bedroom Chamber."

It is at the bedroom chamber that a temple's first, early morning service is conducted by priests who perform a sacred awakening of god and goddess (*tiru palli elichi*). The final late-night *puja* concludes at the bedroom chamber, after which the temple doors close for the night. The thirteenth-century ritual text of the *Suksmagama*, encountered earlier in the context of worship with gold flowers, devotes an entire chapter to this late-night service. It speaks of Shiva's footprints, in bronze or silver, which should be placed on a tray and carried in a palanquin to the bedroom chamber with appropriate ceremonial pomp.[11] In today's worship, it is often a bronze image of Shiva that is taken to the *palli arai*. One cannot but experience a sense of wonder at the phenomenon of man thus visualizing god in his own image. Inscriptions dedicating bronzes of the Consort of the Bedroom Chamber appear with increasing frequency during the twelfth and thirteenth century, and a few examples are given here. In the year 1124, during the reign of Vikrama Chola, an official named Velan Gandaradittan made a gift of land for the worship of the Consort of the Bedroom Chamber (*Tirupalliarai Pirattiyar*), and also for the worship of Dancing Shiva (*Kuttadum Devar*) and consort that he had set up in the temple at Valampuram.[12] In 1176, during the reign of Rajadhiraja II, a female donor Ariyan Umaiyalvi dedicated an image of *Palliarai Nachchiyar* and her consort Atkondar in the temple at Panaiyur (today's Korukkai), and provided money for offerings to the images.[13] The thirteenth century saw the continuing importance of this form of the goddess. In the year 1226, during the reign of Rajaraja II, a local merchant (*vyapari*) commissioned a set of seven bronzes that included an image of the Consort of the Bedroom Chamber for a temple at Avalivanallur.[14] In 1229, a chieftain named Araiyan Tiruvegamanudaiyar from the town of Porosaikkudi established an image of the Consort of the Bedroom Chamber in the Mayuram temple. He also gave the temple an endowment of land, exempt from taxes, to ensure a rice offering to the Consort of the Bedroom Chamber during the early morning service in the temple. The inscription specifies that after the rice was ritually offered to the goddess, it was to be distributed among the members of the temple establishment. The donor demanded that he be accorded temple honors during this rice offering service with the repeated announcement of his presence: "the lord from Porosaikkudi has arrived."[15] In one role or another, the concept of the divine female retained its prominence, reputation, and prestige throughout the Chola period.

Bronzes of Vishnu

Our Lord of marvels
with eyes beautiful as red lotuses,
Mouth red as a berry
Body dark as blue sapphire,
He dwells in Venkatam hill
with its springs full and clear . . .

—SAINT NAMMALVAR[16]

Only 16 of the 211 temples constructed during Chola rule in the two districts that form the heart of the Kaveri delta—coastal Nagapattinam and the more interior Thanjavur—were dedicated to Vishnu.[17] Shiva was indeed the god par excellence during Chola times. Yet, Vishnu and his bronze images held a place of their own from an early date, as did those of two of Vishnu's avatars, the first as Rama, prince of Ayodhya, and the second as Krishna, the enchanting cowherd youth and his later life as the gracious king of Dwarka. While Shiva largely dominated the Chola scene during the ninth through eleventh century, followers of Vishnu increased in number toward the end of the Chola period. In the year 1160, the brahmin *sabha* of the coastal town of Kadaiyur, whose temple houses a monumental bronze of Shiva as Victor over Yama, god of death, thought fit to issue a warning to its priests. As custodians of a Shiva temple, they risked having their property confiscated by the temple if they mingled freely with Vishnu devotees, and if they either sold the lotuses intended to adorn Shiva or themselves wore such blossoms.[18] The increasing popularity of the worship of Vishnu is seen in a temple at Kannapuram that carries an inscription dated to 1230 during the reign of Rajaraja III, and also alerts us to the importance of the hymns of the Vishnu *alvar* saint Satakopa, better known as Nammalvar. We read that the king granted various rights and privileges to local merchants while seated with his queens on a seat named Nambi Kaliyan, beneath a canopy of pearls known as Ravanantakan (He who destroyed Ravana), listening to the hymns of saint Nammalvar on the fifth day of the marriage festival celebrated at Kannapuram in the month of *Chittirai* (April–May).[19]

Three images of Vishnu, one in worship today in a temple at Velacheri near Madras,[20] its close counterpart from the Paruthiyur temple (not pictured here),[21] and a Vishnu in the Metropolitan Museum of Art, belong to the first half of the tenth century and were commissioned during the reign of Parantaka (fig. 8.8a, b). All three four-armed Vishnus stand holding a flame-tipped conch shell and a discus in two rear hands, with proper right front hand in the gesture of protection and the front left hand resting casually on the hip. The conch faces forward and its end rests between the index and middle fingers, while the discus is shown end-on in the Velacheri and Paruthiyur Vishnus, and is angled slightly in the Metropolitan Museum Vishnu. The forehead of all three bronze Vishnus is framed by a diadem, above which is a tall crown with a double-*makara* ornament, while large dangling *makara* earrings rest on the shoulders. Each Vishnu bronze wears three broad necklaces forming a circular loop, and a sacred thread that separates into three different strands below a large knot that rests at the center in the Paruthiyur image, and above the proper left nipple in the Velacheri and Metropolitan bronzes. Armlets and waistbands display varying patterns, but the similarity in the manner in which the long dhoti is knotted, secured, and held in place is almost identical. Their broad faces, and the breadth of the lightly curved shoulders of both images indicate their creation in the Capital style of the central area. The eyes, lips, and nose of the Vishnu in the Metropolitan Museum, and of the Paruthiyur bronze, have been smoothed and partially blurred by years of ritual worship in which the priest lustrated and bathed the image regularly. By contrast, the Velacheri Vishnu's eyes, eyebrows, nose, and lips have been recut after the image was recovered from a tank near the temple early in the twentieth century. Since the temple decided to reconsecrate the image and return it to active worship, it was deemed necessary to restore and reactivate it in a manner considered appropriate for ritual worship.

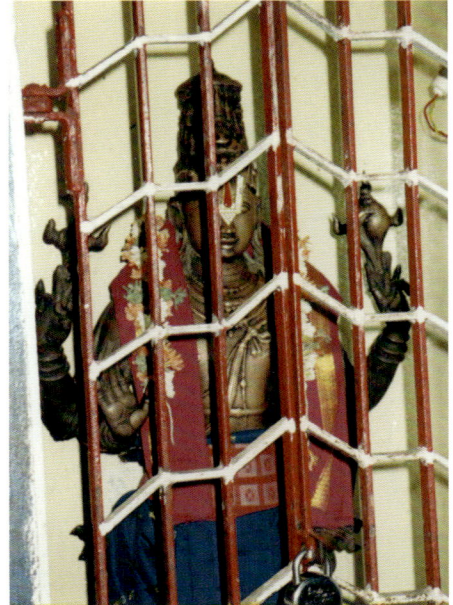

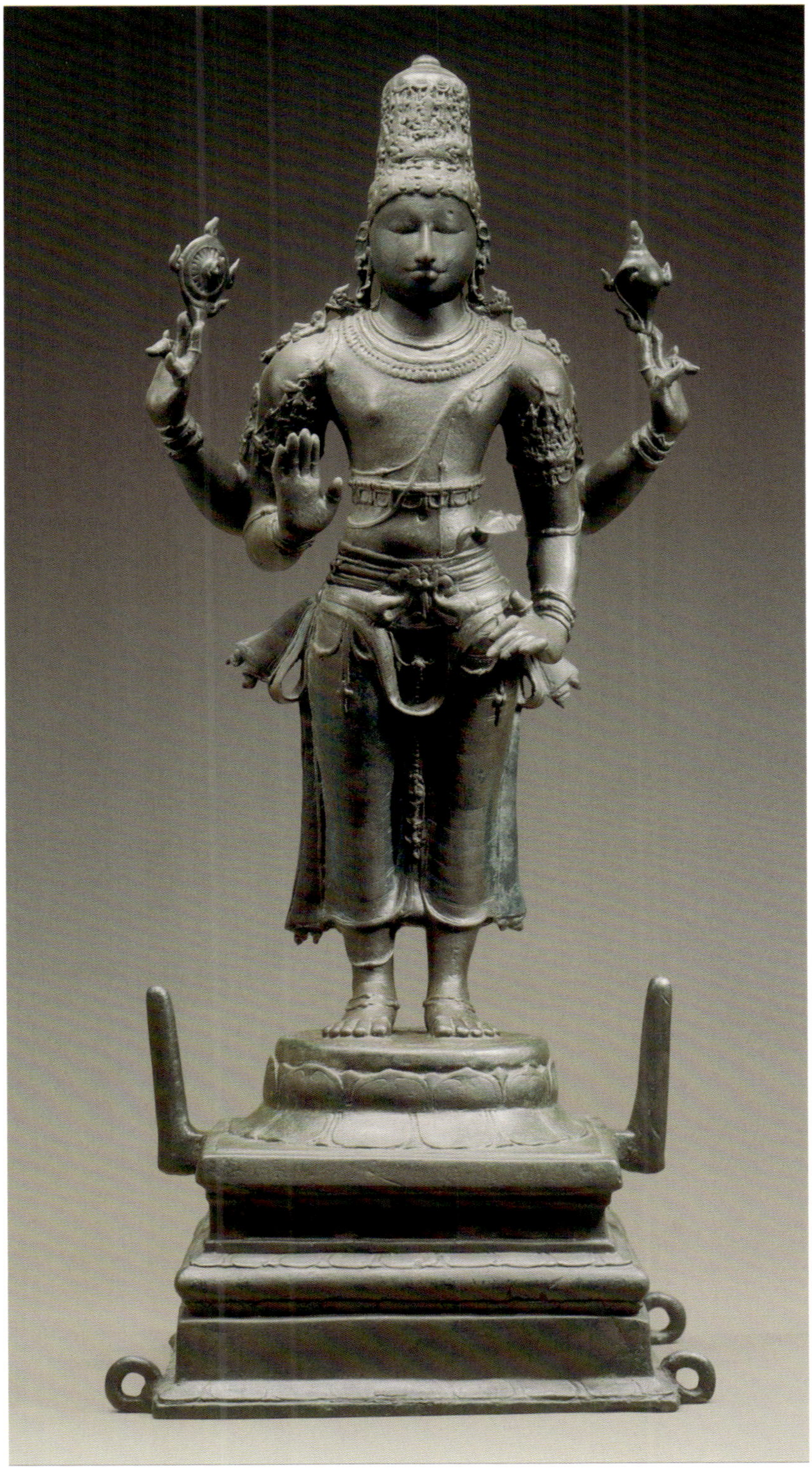

Figure 8.8. (a) *Vishnu*, Velacheri temple (sculpture behind protective grille), ca. first half of tenth century. (b) *Vishnu*, ca. 920, The Metropolitan Museum of Art, New York, Purchase, John D. Rockefeller 3rd Gift.

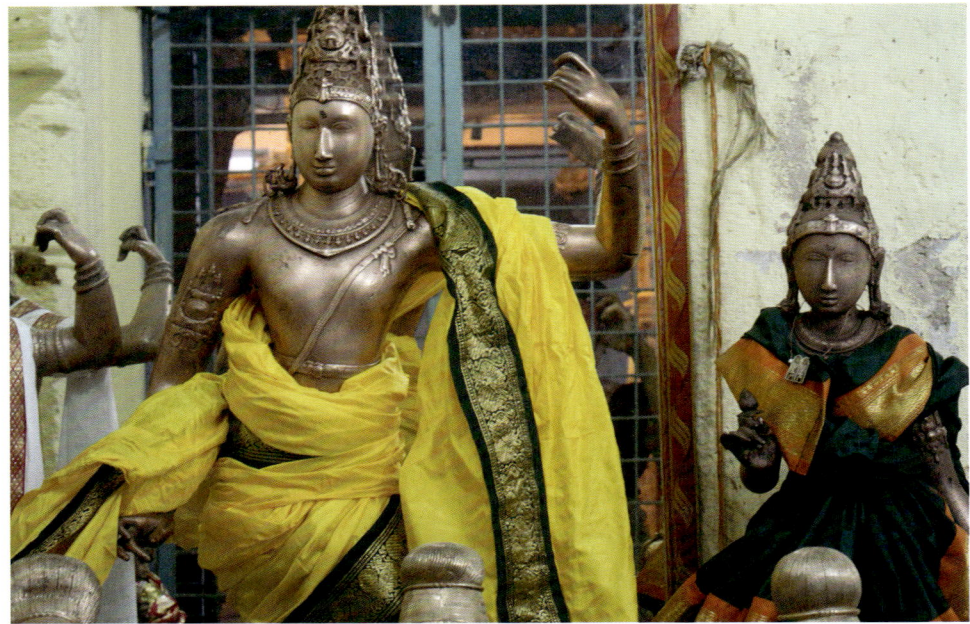

Figure 8.9. *Rama and Sita*, Tirucherai temple, early tenth century.

More than one threesome group of Rama with his wife Sita and his brother Lakshmana, of comparable tenth-century date, has survived, one from Vadakuppanayyar,[22] and a second from Paruthiyur,[23] both today in the Government Museum at Chennai. While Vishnu is invariably clad in a long dhoti, bronzes of Rama and Lakshmana are portrayed wearing a short tight dhoti with a triangular flap at the center. The Paruthiyur Rama wears the same triple-strand knotted sacred thread as the Paruthiyur Vishnu, with the same necklaces and dangling earrings, and is clearly the work of the same workshop if not the same artist. Setting Rama apart from Vishnu is only Rama's short garment, his conical rather than oval crown, and his hands positioned to hold bow and arrow. Lakshmana is more simply adorned, and in place of the sacred thread an ornamental chain envelops his torso. Sita's face is framed with light curls and her hair is swept back up in a large chignon, while a chain ornament encircles her torso, resting in front between her softly modeled breasts. An equally fine set of Rama with Sita of early tenth-century date is still in worship in the temple at Tirucherai (fig. 8.9); also created in the same milieu is a Rama image in the collection of the Philadelphia Museum of Art (fig. 8.10a). The Tirucherai Sita is unusual in that she wears a diadem and a conical crown rather than the more usual curls pulled back into a chignon; additionally, the lotus bud that is usually cast separately and placed in the hands of bronzes is here part of the original casting and survives intact. Several points of resemblance not visible in the clothed image, including the tall conical crown, the treatment of the casual almost untidy folds of the skirt as they rest on the proper left hip, and the knotted bow that secures the armlets link the Tirucherai Sita to the bronze Uma in the Metropolitan Museum of Art (see fig. 2.11).[24] Belonging to around the year 1012 is the Vishnu image from the Tiruvenkadu *Marriage of Shiva and Uma*, with the identifying Vaishnava *srivatsa* emblem clearly depicted on his right chest (fig. 8.10b; see also fig. 0.1).

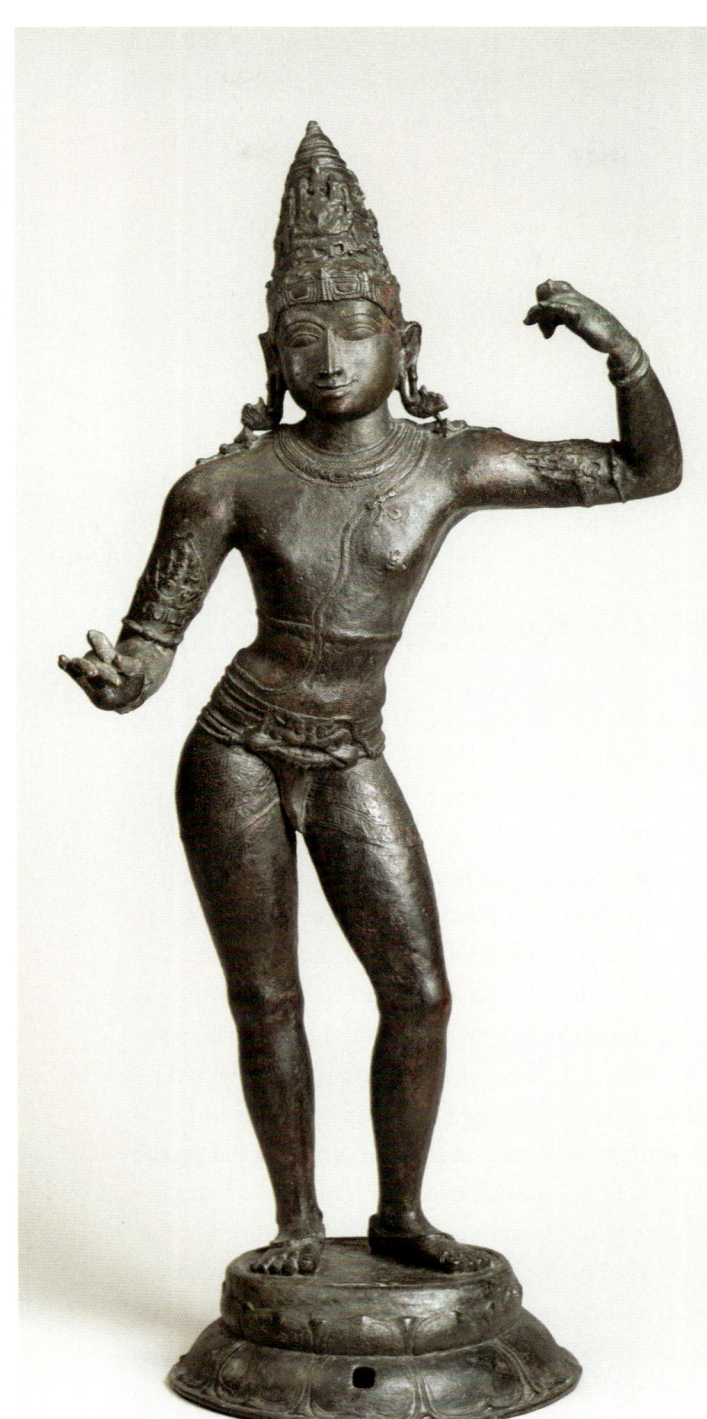
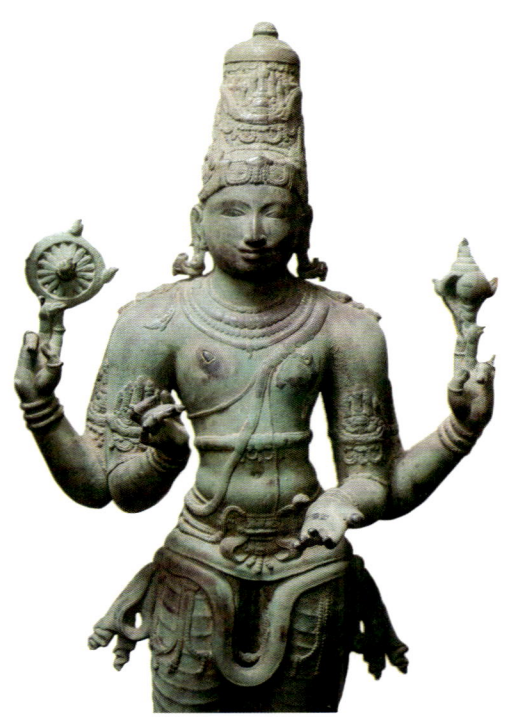

Figure 8.10. (a) *Rama*, ca. 920, Philadelphia Museum of Art, Purchased with the W. P. Wilstach Fund, the John D. McIlhenny Fund, and with funds contributed by the Women's Committee of the Philadelphia Museum of Art in honor of their 100th anniversary. (b) Detail of Vishnu from *Marriage of Shiva and Uma (Kalyanasundarar)* Tiruvenkadu temple, ca. 1012 (see fig. 0.1a).

Vishnu's avatar as Krishna, the enchanting royal infant brought up in the safety of a cowherd village, caught at the heart-strings of Vishnu devotees. The Vishnu saint Periyalvar, who lived around the year 800, sang enchanting verses in *pillai Tamil*, a genre in celebration of the child (*pillai*), whether god or king. Several of the saint's verses are placed on the lips of Yashoda, Krishna's foster-mother:

> *You played in the dirt–*
> *it's all over you*
> *the dabs of butter on your face*
> *are caked with mud—*
> *How can I allow you thus*
> *to sleep by my side tonight?*
> *I have been waiting with oil and soap*
> *for your bath*
> *O Narana, so difficult of approach*
> *O please come and dip in the waters!*[25]

In 930, during the fifteenth year of Parantaka Chola, we hear of a temple dedicated to Vishnu as the reclining lord (*pallikonda alvar*) in the town of Erode, whose residents agreed to a voluntary fee in order to provide food offerings, ritual worship, and other ceremonies to honor their "Lord as butter dancer," or *Vennaikutta Nayanar*.[26] The use of the word "our" (*engal*) as a preface to the butter dancer indicates an affectionate reference to an image of the much-loved child Krishna, who was inordinately fond of fresh churned butter. The proverbial story tells us that upon completing her butter-churning in her simple village home, foster-mother Yashoda tied the pot of butter high on the rafters to place it out of Krishna's reach. Aided by a comrade, Krishna climbed up to reach the pot, ate the butter, and then danced in gleeful abandon. The image in the Erode temple may have resembled a tenth-century bronze in a private collection, some 20 inches high, that captures the charm of the joyful child, naked yet richly ornamented, who stands on his left foot with the right leg raised and bent at the knee in dance. His outstretched left hand is poised in a graceful gesture of dance, while his right hand is in the gesture of protection. Another early bronze of the dancing naked child Krishna, of larger proportions, is in the collection of the Walters Art Gallery. Visible in rear view is a hallmark of all Krishna bronzes in south India—the manner in which his hair is styled as row upon row of ringlet-like curls, neatly stacked upon his head in towering glory (fig. 8.11a, b).

Artists visualized Krishna adopting a similar dancing pose when, as a young lad, he defeated the serpent Kaliya, whose home was the Jumna river and who posed a serious threat to villagers living along its banks. Legend speaks of Krishna diving into the depths of the waters, vanquishing powerful Kaliya, and then dancing a victorious dance upon the multihooded serpent head. A tenth-century bronze from the collection of the National Museum in New Delhi depicts this climactic feat in which Krishna, clad in a short dhoti with a central triangular flap, raises his right hand in the gesture of protection while his left hand casually holds aloft Kaliya's serpent tail (fig. 8.12a, b). Krishna's right leg is poised in dance and the left planted firmly on the five-hooded serpent while Kaliya, in part

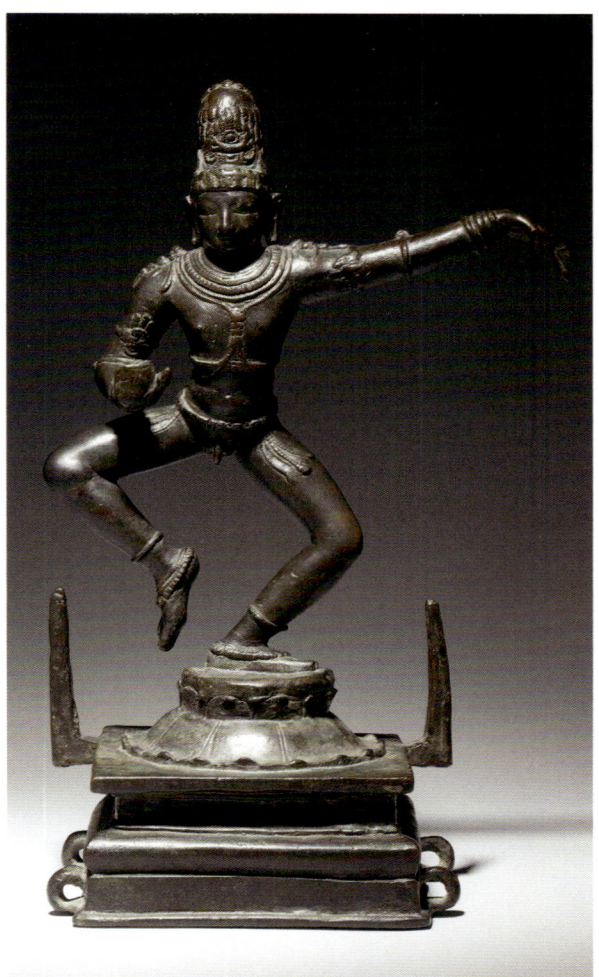 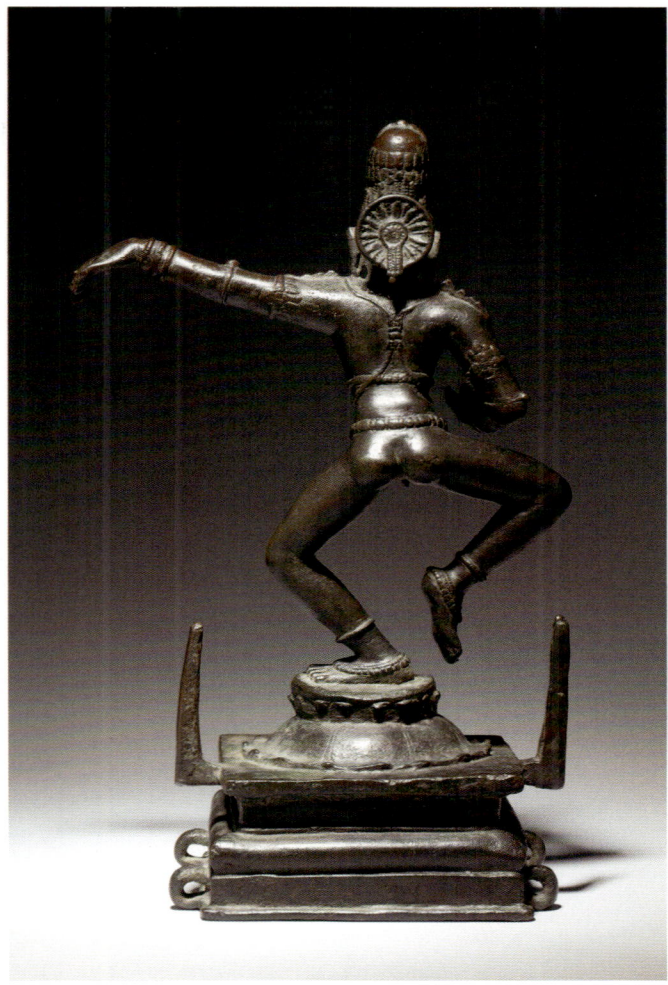

Figure 8.11. (a and b) *Dancing Child Krishna*, ca. 950, Walters Art Museum, Baltimore.

human form, docilely joins his palms in adoration of his conqueror. A magnificent portrayal of the Krishna-Kaliya theme from the collection of the Asia Society in New York is a superbly crafted piece of the eleventh century in which Krishna's towering coiffure of ringlet curls, crowned with an open lotus blossom, is precisely rendered (fig. 8.13a, b, c).

In chapter 2, we saw that when Parantaka's queen Kokkilan built a Shiva temple at Navalur in the early tenth century to honor her son Rajaditya, all those in the close circle of the prince, including his wife Irayiravan Devi, daughter of chieftain Iladarayar, contributed toward its functioning with a range of gifts.[27] The queen was, however, inclusive and all-embracing in her devotion, and set up a bronze of Krishna and his consort Rukmini at a temple at Tiruvellarai, 12 miles north of Trichy, and made arrangements for their ritual worship. This gift of Iraiyiran Devi is dated in the eighth year of king Parakesari, who must be Uttama Chola, so that her gift of a bronze of Krishna as king of Dwarka, together with his queen Rukmini, dates to the year 978, a good thirty-eight years after her gift of perpetual lamps to Rajaditya's Shiva temple.[28] Few early images exist of Krishna as king of Dwarka, and so I briefly refer here to such an image of Krishna from a foursome bronze group of ca. 1200 that I will discuss at length in the next

EVOLVING MANIFESTATIONS   235

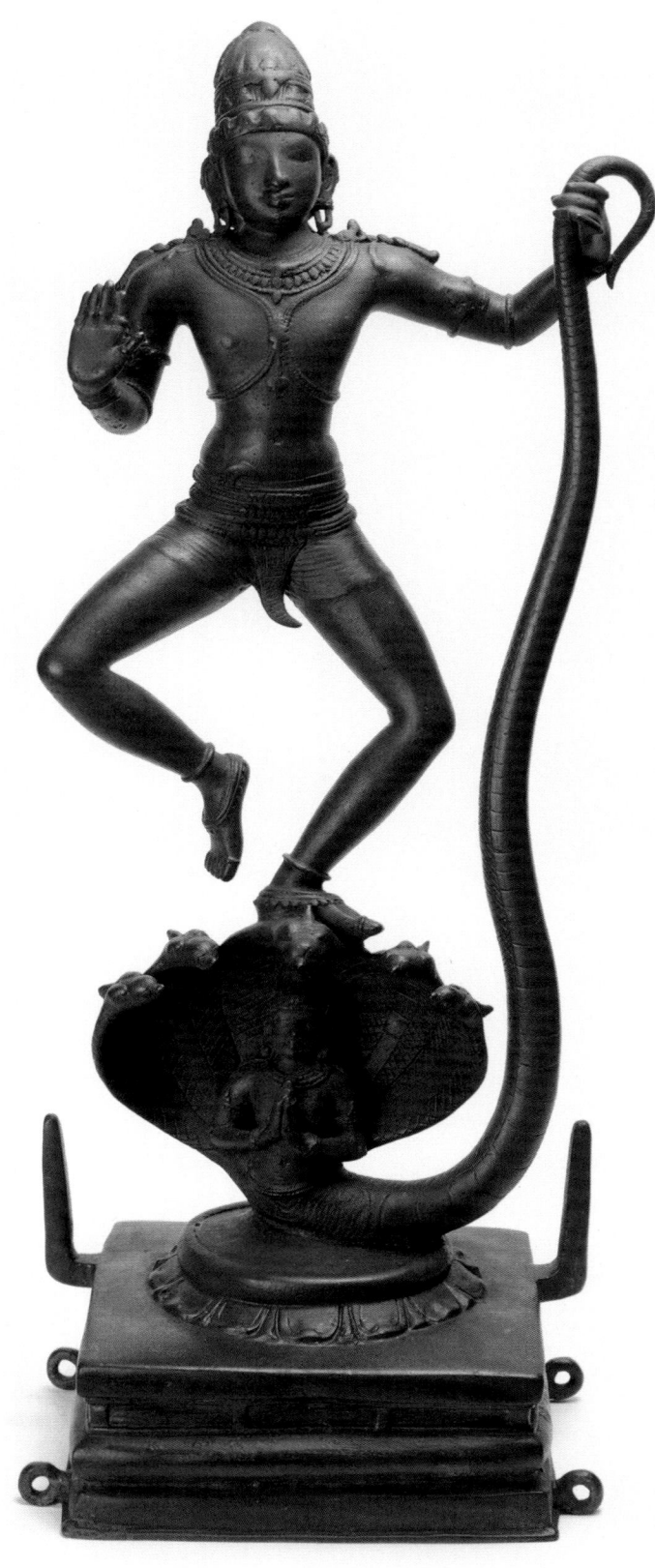

Figure 8.12. (a and b) *Krishna Vanquishes Kaliya*, ca. 950, National Museum, New Delhi.

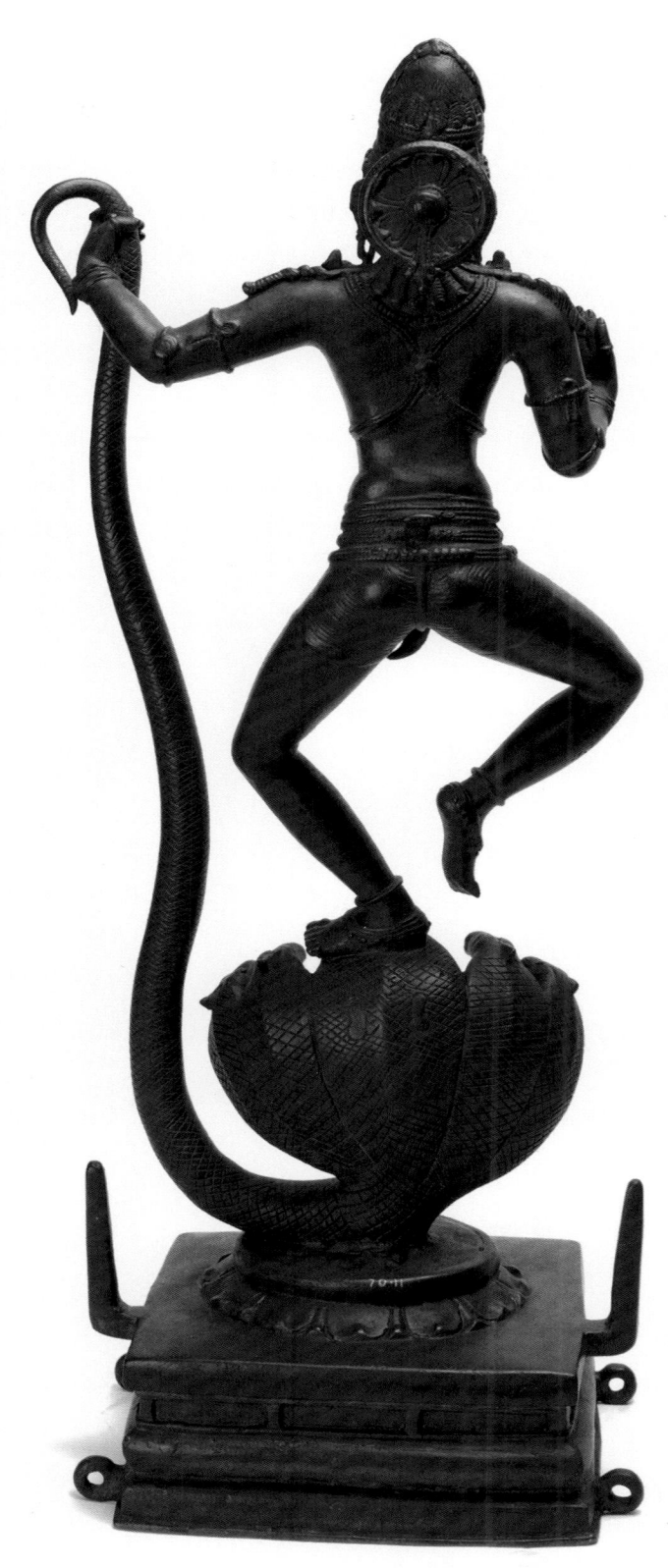

EVOLVING MANIFESTATIONS

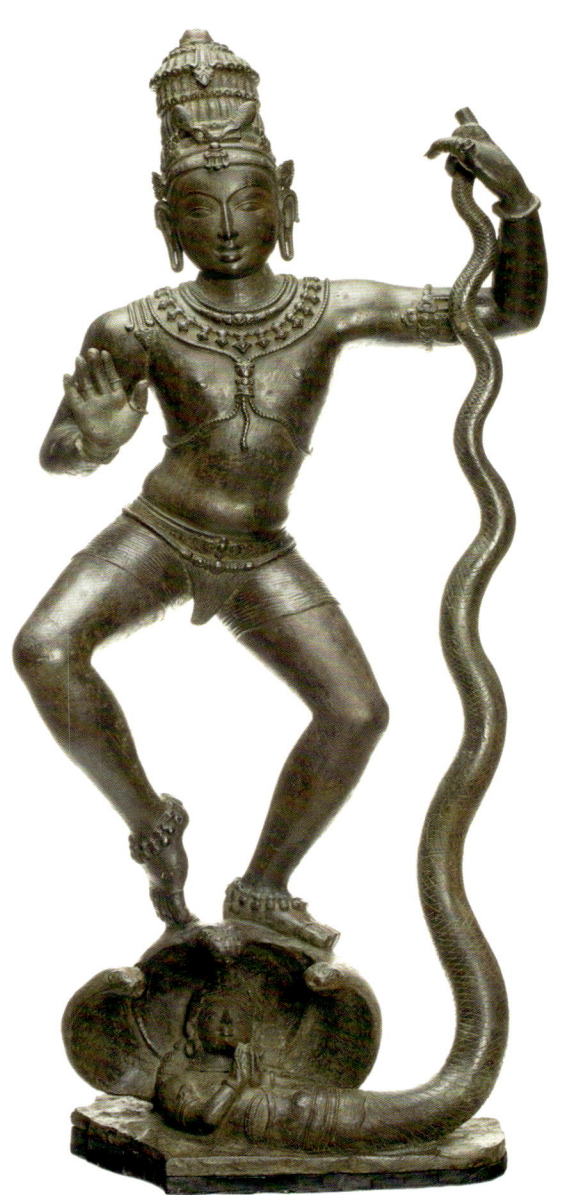
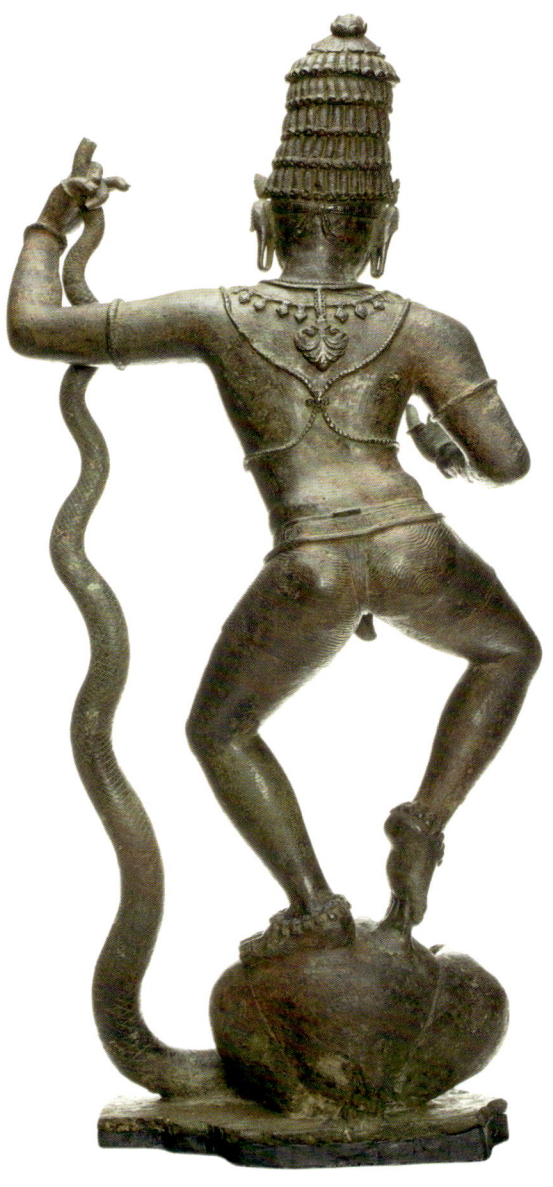
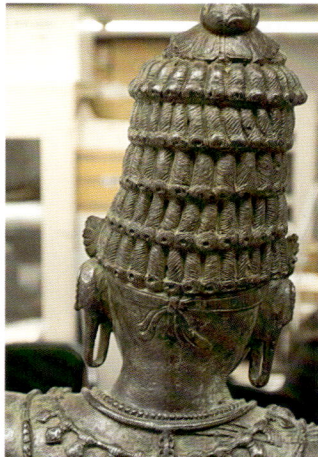

Figure 8.13. (a) *Krishna Vanquishes Kaliya*, ca. 1070, Asia Society Museum, New York, Mr. and Mrs. John D. Rockefeller 3rd Collection. (b) Rear view of *Krishna Vanquishes Kaliya* (fig. 8.13a). (c) Detail of rear view of *Krishna Vanquishes Kaliya* (fig. 8.13a).

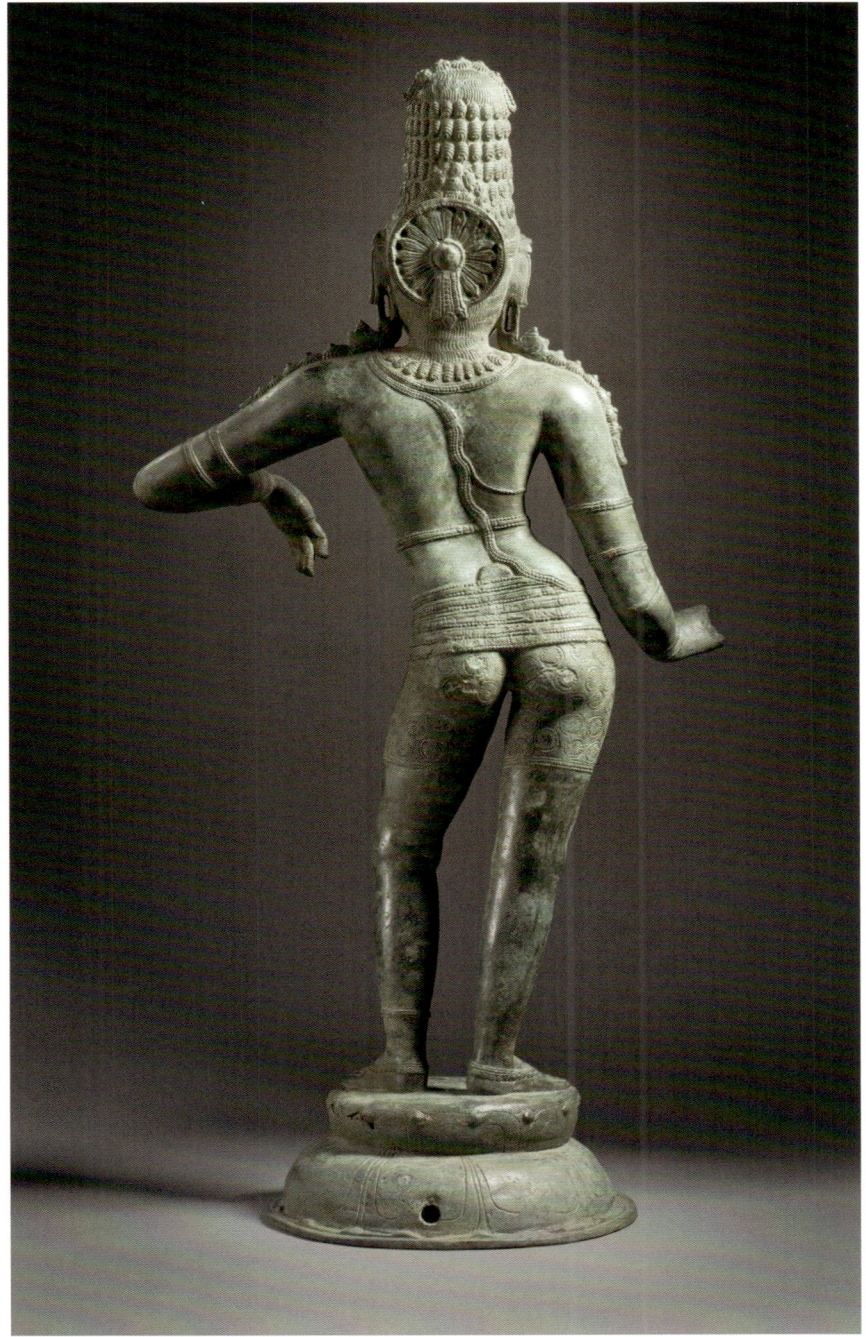

Figure 8.14. Rear view of *Krishna as King of Dwarka*, ca. 1200 (detail of fig. 9.3), Los Angeles County Museum of Art, Gift of Mr. and Mrs. Hal B. Wallis.

chapter. My intention here is solely to emphasize that iconography demands that Krishna's hair be piled on his head in a series of ringlet curls whether he is portrayed as child Krishna, as youth Krishna who defeats serpent Kaliya, or as king of Dwarka (fig. 8.14). In this context, an image in the National Museum in New Delhi with this recognizable arrangement of ringlet curls and identified as Shiva as Victor of the Three Forts poses a conundrum (fig. 8.15a, b). Shiva is the god with dreadlocks piled elegantly upon his head,

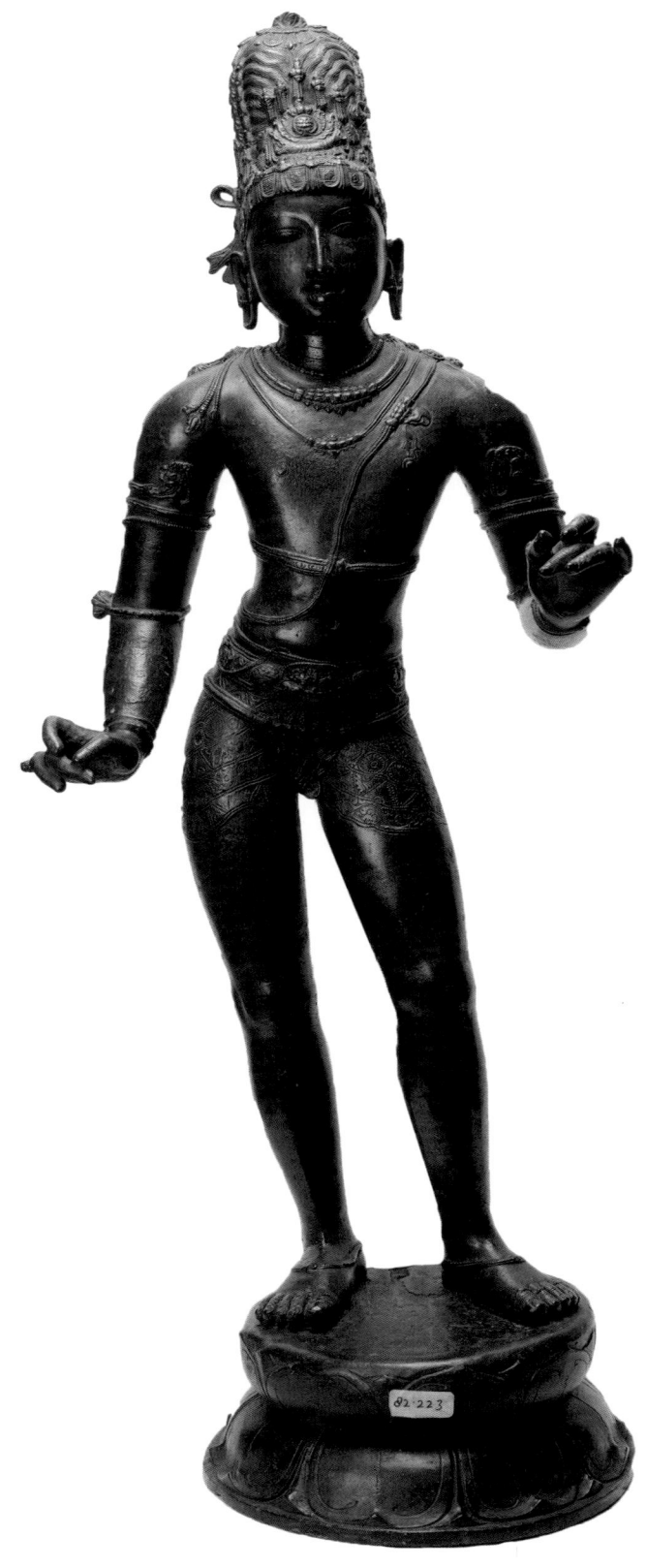

Figure 8.15. (a) *Shiva as Tripura Vijaya* (?), ca. 975, National Museum, New Delhi. (b) Rear view of *Shiva as Tripura Vijaya* (?) (fig. 8.15a); note Krishna's hairdo.

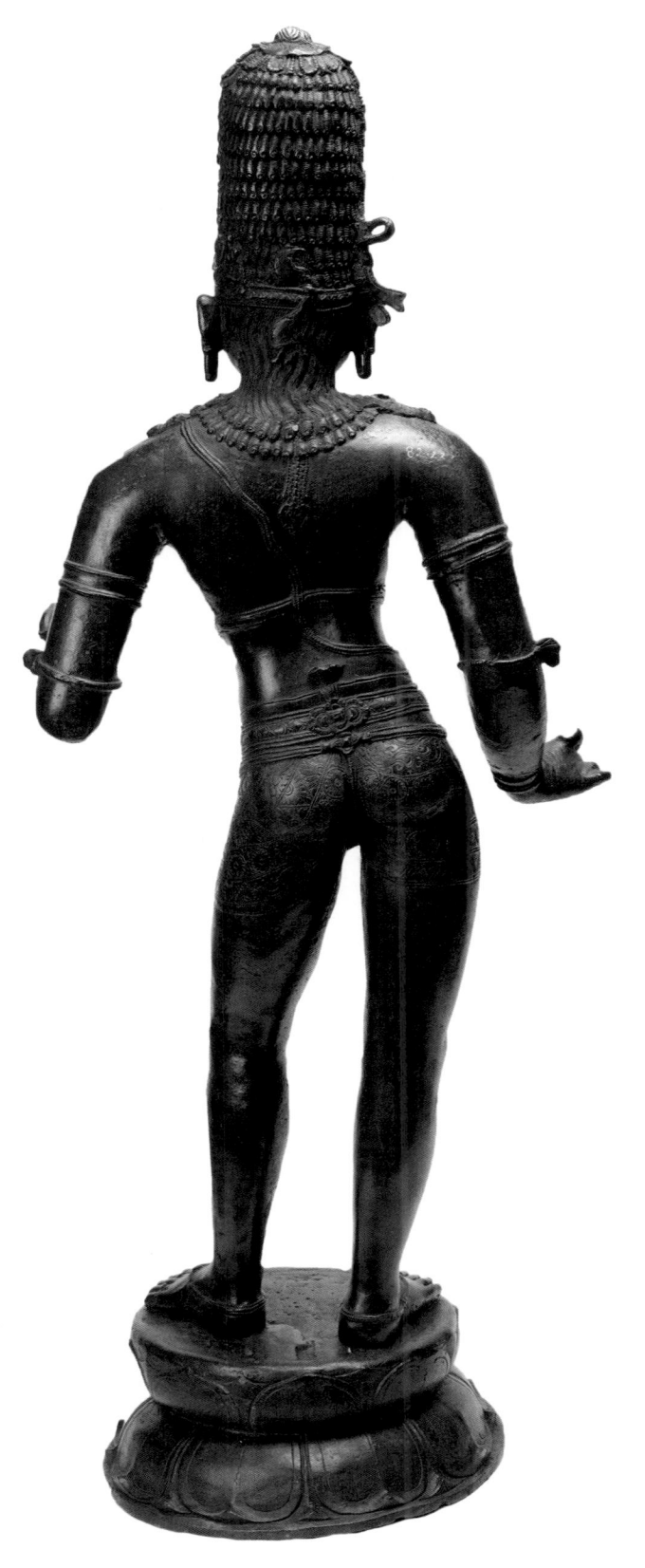

EVOLVING MANIFESTATIONS

and nestling within these locks are the crescent moon, the trumpet flower, and often a serpent and a skull; by contrast, Krishna is the god of the neatly arranged ringlet curls.[29] A careful scrutiny of the front and sides of the coiffure of this particular bronze reveals neither trumpet flower, crescent moon, snake, or skull, while the rear view reveals these typical ringlet curls. Should we assume that the artist who created the image had recently created several images of Krishna, and that he erred, if we may call it that, in using ringlet curls on a Shiva bronze? Or are we mistakenly labeling as Shiva a bronze of Krishna as king of Dwarka? This seeming flexibility of artistic adaptation reaches new heights with Buddhist imagery, to which we turn now.

Buddhist Imagery

They call him beggar, they speak ill of him
they have fallen from the path
those Buddhists and those erring Jains—
But the divine one who came to earth
and begged for alms
He is the thief who stole my heart.

—SAMBANDAR, HYMN 1, VERSE 10[30]

This is the alvar [lord] for a festival procession [tiru-utsavam] of the temple of Akkasalai-perumpalli in Rajendrachola-perumpalli. This alvar [lord] was set up by Nalan-gunakara-udaiyar of Chirutuvur. Svasti sri. Akkasalaikal-nayakar is for all padinen-vishaiyam [eleven districts].

—INSCRIPTION ALONG BASE OF BUDDHA IMAGE[31]

The Buddhist faith established an early stronghold in south India in the area of Andhra, along Tamil Nadu's northern borders, which is dotted with Buddhist monastic establishments dating from the first century BCE onward, including the famous sites of Amaravati and Nagarjunakonda. Tamil Nadu itself also housed Buddhist monasteries, and several literary sources speak of Kanchipuram as a Buddhist center. The Tamil epic *Manimekhalai*, written around the year 550, speaks of the thriving condition of the Buddhist monasteries of Kanchipuram that were permanent residences for the monks, and "in their splendor rivaled the seven temples built by Indra at Puhar."[32] Corroboration comes from the travel accounts of Xuanxang, the Chinese pilgrim who visited Kanchipuram around the year 630; he speaks of the city housing "some hundred *sangharamas* (monasteries) and 10,000 priests. They all study the teachings of the Sthavira school belonging to the Great Vehicle."[33] A rare survival from the seventh century, which speaks to the prevalence of the Buddhist faith, is a farcical play titled *Mattavilasa* (Drunken Sport) written by Pallava king Mahendravarman, who ruled ca. 580–630. It is set in Kanchipuram and ridicules a Buddhist priest who reminiscences about the comfort, and the splendid food and drink, he gets in his monastery, complaining only that he needed to get hold of the unexpurgated version of the Buddha's teachings that must surely allow access to women![34] To add further to the widespread acceptance and popularity of the Buddhist faith is the perhaps unexpected addition of the Buddha, as the ninth avatar of

Vishnu, in a seventh-century inscription in a Pallava cave at Mamallapuram that lists the ten avatars.³⁵

Additional confirmation of the popularity of Buddhism and Jainism in Tamil India comes from the hymns of the *nayanmar*, in particular those of child saint Sambandar, who often reserved the last, usually tenth, verse of his songs to denounce the Buddhists and the Jains. His famous first hymn, which praises Shiva as the thief who stole his heart, also carries his criticism of the Buddhists and Jains, as evidenced in the citation at the start of this section. The very fact of the need for such verses speaks to the power of Buddhism (and Jainism) in Tamil Nadu, faiths that the sixty-three *nayanmar* of Shiva and the twelve *alvar* saints of Vishnu had to overcome in order to establish Shiva and Vishnu as the dominant figures in the sacred world of the Tamils. While the hold of Buddhism was certainly diminished in Tamil Nadu by the Hindu saints, the faith never died out in south India. Instead, bronze images of the Buddha, of *bodhisattva* Avalokiteshvara, future Buddha Maitreya, and small models of stupas were created throughout the Chola period and all the way into the seventeenth century, testifying to the persisting power of the faith. The port town of Nagapattinam, in particular, appears to have been an especially active Buddhist center where devotees commissioned bronzes that appear to have been largely for personal worship. The majority of these Buddhist bronzes are between 4 and 9 inches in height, and frequently carry inscriptions along their base naming the donor.³⁶ Only some 6 of the 186 bronzes in T. N. Ramachandran's 1954 catalogue of these bronzes are sizable, measuring 29 inches or over in height.³⁷ An idiosyncratic feature of these Tamil Nadu Buddha images, whether small or large, is the universal appearance of a flame-tipped *ushnisha* atop his head, a feature that may owe its inspiration to the Buddhist text of the *Lalitavistara* that states that when the Buddha is in *samadhi* (the enlightened Buddha), a flame of omniscience hovers above his head.³⁸

A majestic Buddhist bronze in the Nagapattinam style, a little over 27 inches tall, and today in the collection of the Asia Society in New York, is a portable image with holes in its base for threading poles with which to facilitate carrying the bronze in procession (fig. 8.16). Inscribed along its base is the second record cited at the start of this section, in which the image is described as a festival (*utsava*) image, as a donation of the goldsmiths' guild, and intended for a shrine within the great monastery named after Rajendra Chola.³⁹ While the Buddhists had a processional tradition of their own, it would appear that when they found themselves surrounded by the daily, weekly, monthly, and annual Hindu festival cycle, with its exuberance and vibrancy, they further embraced the idea of parading the Buddha as a strategy to attract devotees. Another imposing Buddha bronze, with its gilding partially intact, comes from the collection of the Victoria and Albert Museum in London, and was likewise a processional image (fig. 8.17).

In chapter 4 devoted to the bronze workshop of queen Sembiyan Mahadevi, we examined two monumental Buddhist images, produced in the mid-tenth century in a coastal workshop in today's district of Nagapattinam, that were then exported to a Buddhist monastery at Mangalore on India's west coast. The larger of the two bronzes of Lokeshvara, a form of *bodhisattva* Avalokiteshvara, carries a consecration date of 959. We saw that these two Buddhist bronzes bore a striking resemblance to images of Shiva in any number of ways, from the treatment of the body to the third eye in the forehead, and

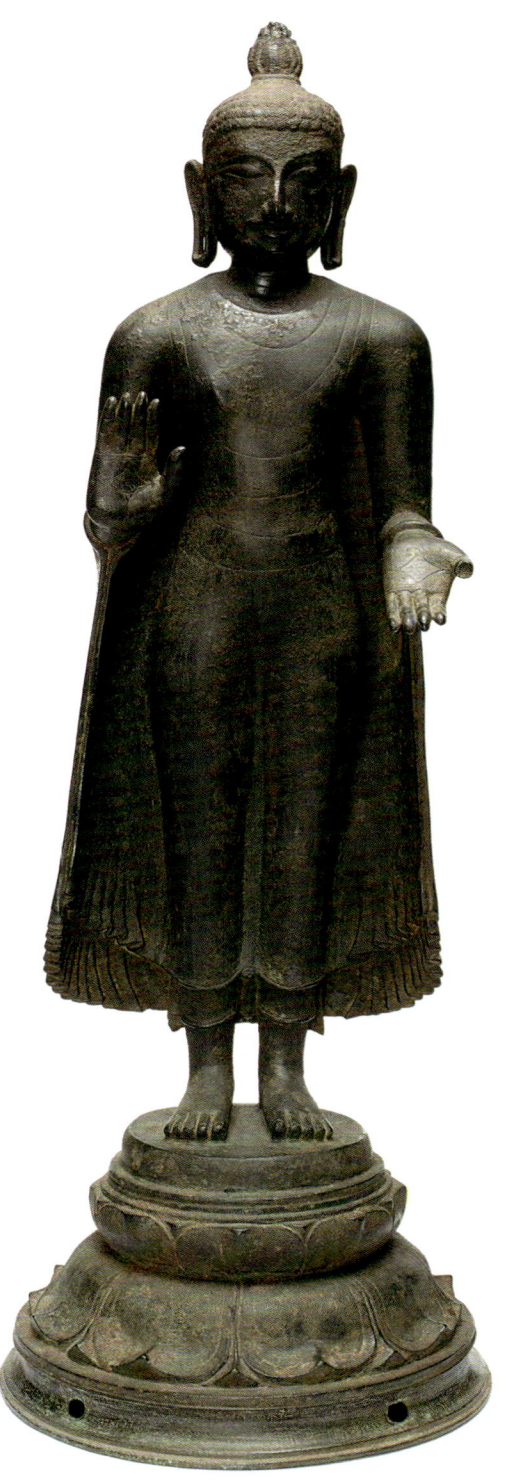
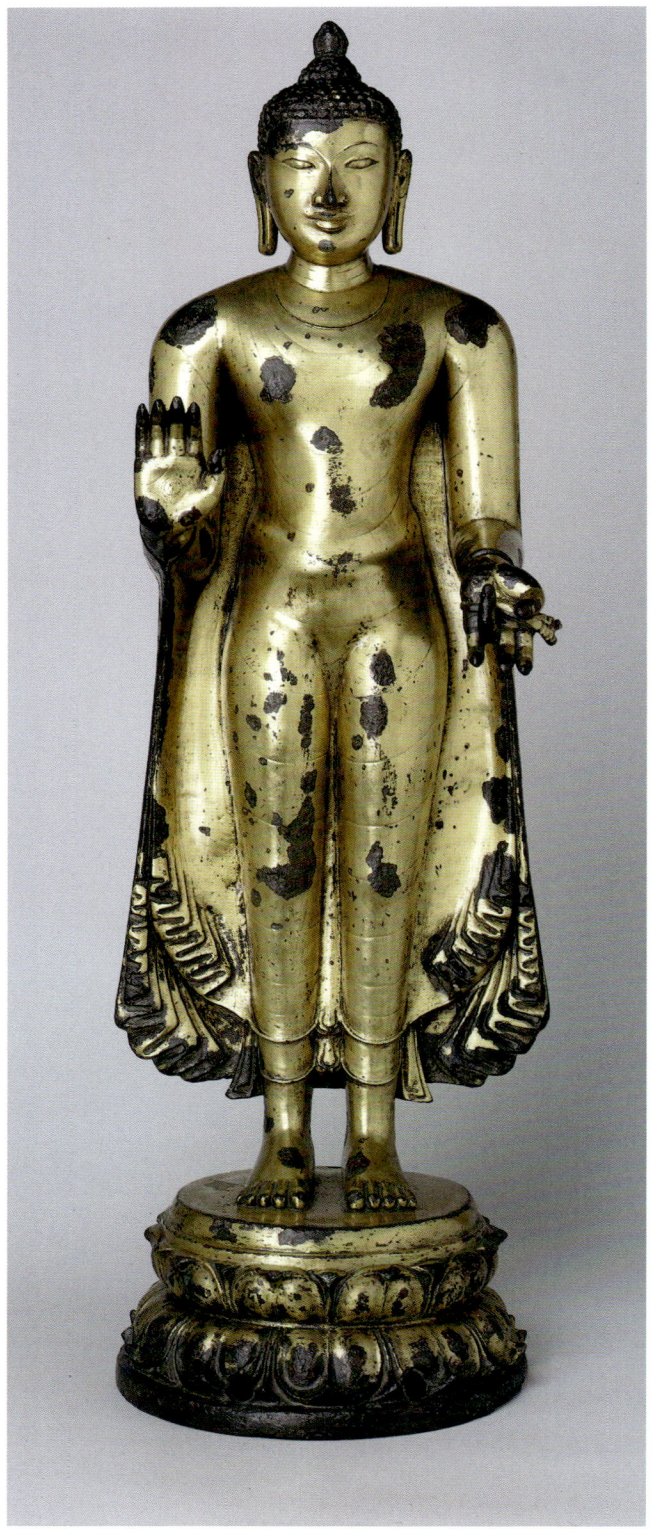

Figure 8.16. *Buddha*, ca. 1030, Asia Society Museum, New York, Mr. and Mrs. John D. Rockefeller 3rd Collection.

Figure 8.17. *Buddha*, ca. 1200, Victoria and Albert Museum, London.

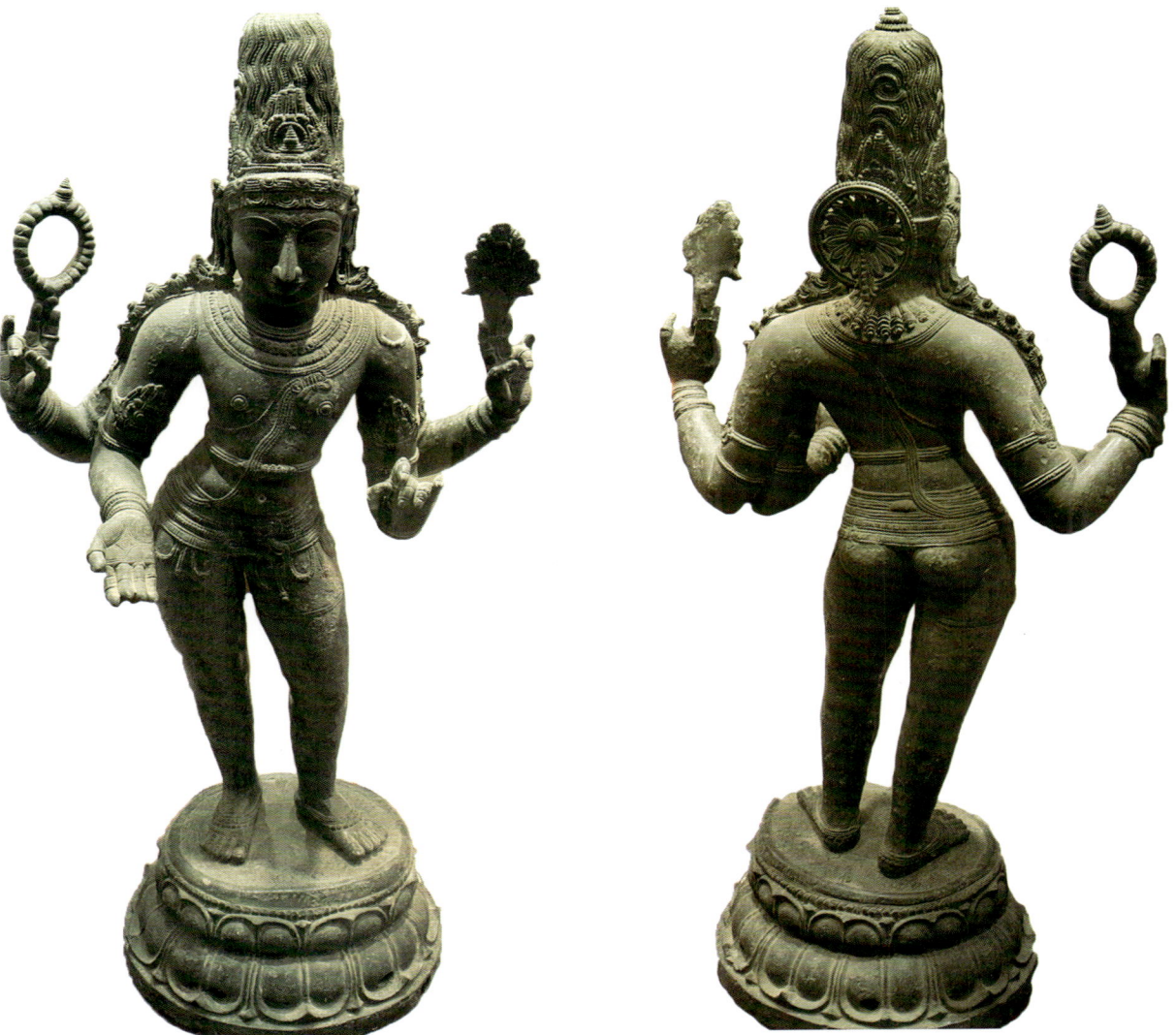

Figure 8.18. (a and b) *Future Buddha Maitreya*, twelfth century, Government Museum, Chennai.

from the hair piled high in the fashion of Shiva's matted locks, to the arrangement of long curls along the nape of the neck. It is clear that wax modelers and bronze casters were not sharply divided on religious lines, but would work for any patron who requisitioned their services. Another example of such cross-fertilization is seen in a bronze of future Buddha Maitreya, some 29 inches tall, that may be seen today in the Government Museum in Chennai (fig. 8.18a, b). A comparison with an image of Shiva as Victor of Three Forts of the same period is instructive in this regard. At first glance, the Maitreya of twelfth-century date, who stands in graceful contrapposto with two rear hands holding a rosary and a bunch of flowers, and two front hands in the gesture of wish-granting and protection, could easily be mistaken for an image of Shiva. Maitreya too wears a multistrand sacred thread, a high waistband, several necklaces, impressive armlets, bangles, anklets, and dangling *makara* earrings. A diadem frames his face, and his hair rises in a towering hairdo. The single clear clue to his identity as a Buddhist deity, and as future Buddha Maitreya in particular, is the mini-stupa enclosed within the medallion

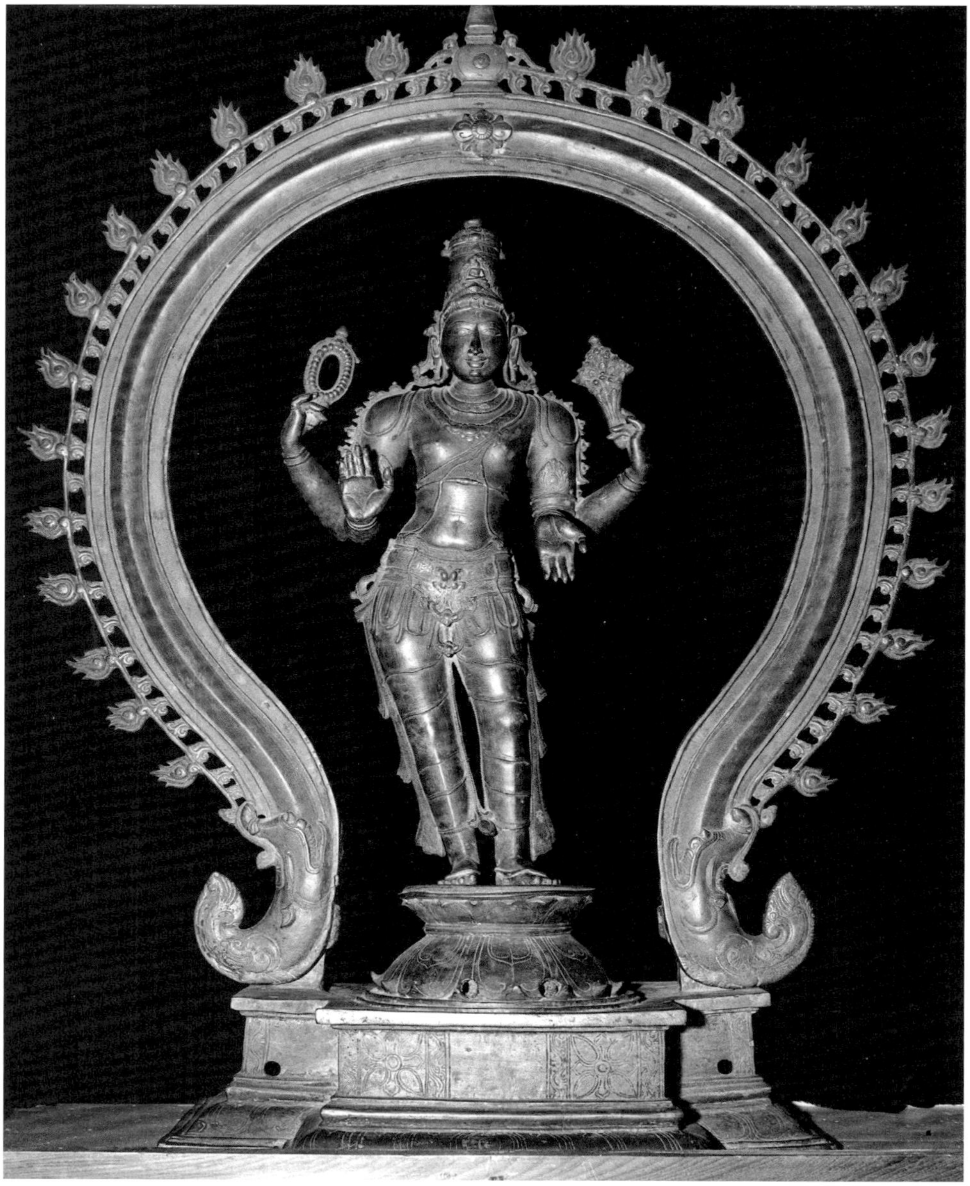

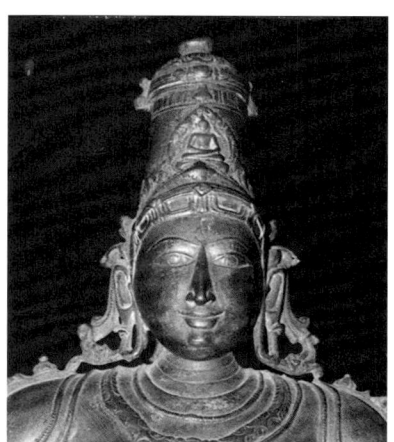

Figure 8.19. (a and b) *Buddhist Bodhisattva Avalokiteshvara*, seventeenth century, Government Museum, Chennai.

of the double-*makara* ornament above his diadem. Similarly crossing artistic boundaries is a crowned image of the seventeenth century, wearing a long dhoti, a multistrand sacred thread, and rich ornaments, and standing within a flame-tipped aureole that rises from the mouths of *makaras*. It would be easy to mistake the bronze, at first glance, as a portrayal of god Vishnu. But a closer look at the medallion on his crown reveals within it a seated figure of the Buddha, alerting us to the identity of the bronze as *bodhisattva* Avalokiteshvara (fig. 8.19). Buddhist bronzes were made by the same artists who created images of Shiva and of Vishnu.

This chapter suggests then that workshops with wax modelers and bronze founders worked for a range of patrons, using the same aesthetic standards and similar details of hairdo, clothing, and ornamentation, regardless of whether the bronze was created for a Shaiva, Vaishnava, or Buddhist patron. Artists adjusted their work to reflect required iconographic prerequisites, but the standards of beauty remained the same.

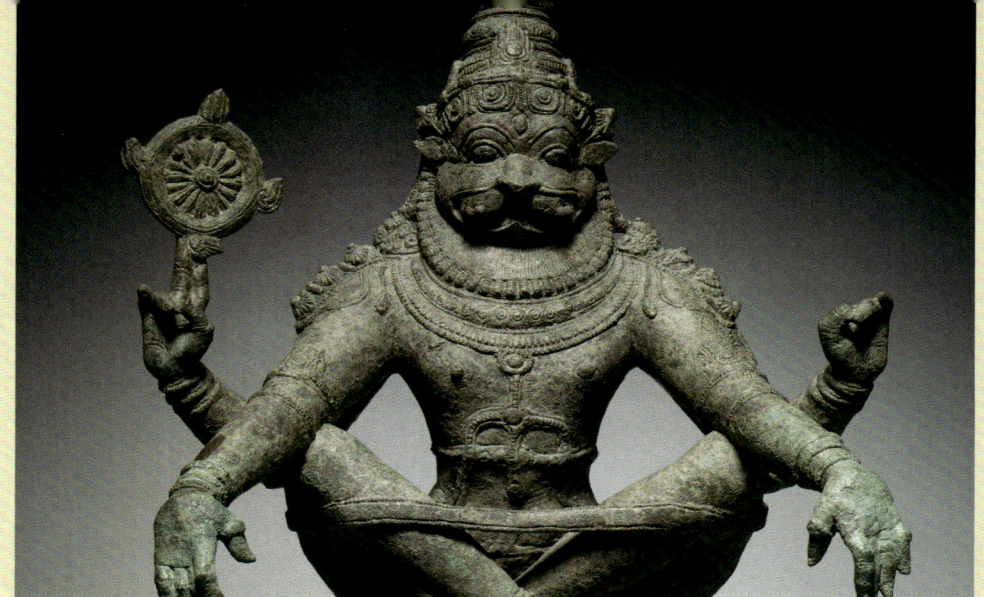

Worship in Uncertain Times and the Secret Burial of Bronzes
Thirteenth Century

9

In the 25th year of Rajaraja III, following the invasion of the Chola country by Singana Dandanayaka that disrupted worship in the temple, and resulted in an increase in costs and a shortage of funds in the temple treasury, the temple trustees of Kodikulagar contacted Uttaman Nambi for financial assistance. He made a cash donation of 50,000 kasu for repairs to the temple; he undertook to reconsecrate the bronzes of the temple and made provisions for their regular worship as well as during temple festivals. The temple trustees bestowed on Uttaman Nambi a deed of the temple by which he would be hailed by the title "parichinam of Pulavar-talaivar" during the various pujas and processions of the deities.

MARAIKKADU TEMPLE, YEAR 1246 [1]

At the start of the thirteenth century, emperor Kulottunga III completed the construction of the fourth and last royal temple of the Cholas in the town of Tribhuvanam on the south bank of the Kaveri, a mere 6 miles from the Darasuram temple built by Rajaraja II. Rising to a height of 126 feet, it takes to a culmination the trend started two centuries earlier by Rajaraja I of building monumental temples at sites with little sacred history and linked exclusively with royalty and personal power (fig. 9.1). Undoubtedly, the temple once possessed a stunning array of bronzes commissioned around the year 1212. Of the few that remain, one is a powerful bronze of the Begging Lord that carries on the distinguished tradition of workmanship that we witnessed in the late twelfth-century bronzes at the Valampuram temple that were created by the Tiruvenkadu coastal workshop (fig. 9.2). The high level of artistry was sustained despite the many calamities, natural and manmade, that struck the coastal belt around the turn of the thirteenth century.

The temple at Tiruvenkadu, home of the superb bronzes created by the Tiruvenkadu Master whose work we examined in chapter 5, is located mere miles from the oceanfront, and its inscriptions reveal just how badly it was affected by natural disasters. In the twenty-fourth year of Kulottunga III (1204), a resident of Kunrattur gifted a piece of land to the Tiruvenkadu temple, with the intention that the income accruing from it would be used for lamps in the temple. Since that piece of land had been lying fallow for many years, he also made a gift of money to bring it into cultivation.[2] In the same year, a devotee from Alampakkam gifted land to the temple, speaking of the extra money he donated for the reclamation of the land.[3] In the year 1219, during the reign of Rajaraja III, a donor purchased a piece of land at Tiruppanangadu to provide lamps for the Tiruvenkadu temple. He lamented the inundation in the area that had submerged fields and silted them up so extensively that they needed serious reclamation. He speaks of his donation of a plot of land, 6 *mas* in extent, that had cost 2,000 *kasu* coins to purchase and that now required an additional 3,000 *kasu* to make the land usable.[4] It seems possible that this situation was the result of a thirteenth-century tsunami; studies conducted after the 2004 tsunami hit this coastal belt have found evidence of a "medieval tsunami" that dates roughly from this period.[5] Such an event, unforeseen as it always is, would have had disastrous consequences for the thriving towns and temples along the coastal belt.

The natural calamities of the thirteenth century were accompanied by chieftains making raids that resulted in major losses. The lengthy reign of Rajaraja III (r. 1216–1260) seems to have witnessed considerable instability, and several inscriptions including one dated in 1235 mention the disturbed state of the country (*duridangal*) in the fifth, eleventh, and fifteenth years of his reign, when many temples lost their documents and registers.[6] An inscription from the Tiruvilakudi temple on the south bank of the Kaveri river is an example of the troubled times of the fifth year of Rajaraja III. We read that with the approval of the temple authorities, the followers of a Bana chieftain carried away four important bronzes from Tiruvilakudi for safekeeping—Shiva as Manavala Nambi and consort, Vinayaka or Ganesha, and the Consort of the Bedroom Chamber. Eleven years later, a lay devotee, Mavulavan Malayan, instituted a search for the bronzes, located and redeemed the images, reconsecrated them, and made further provisions for their ritual worship. The lengthy and somewhat damaged inscription speaks

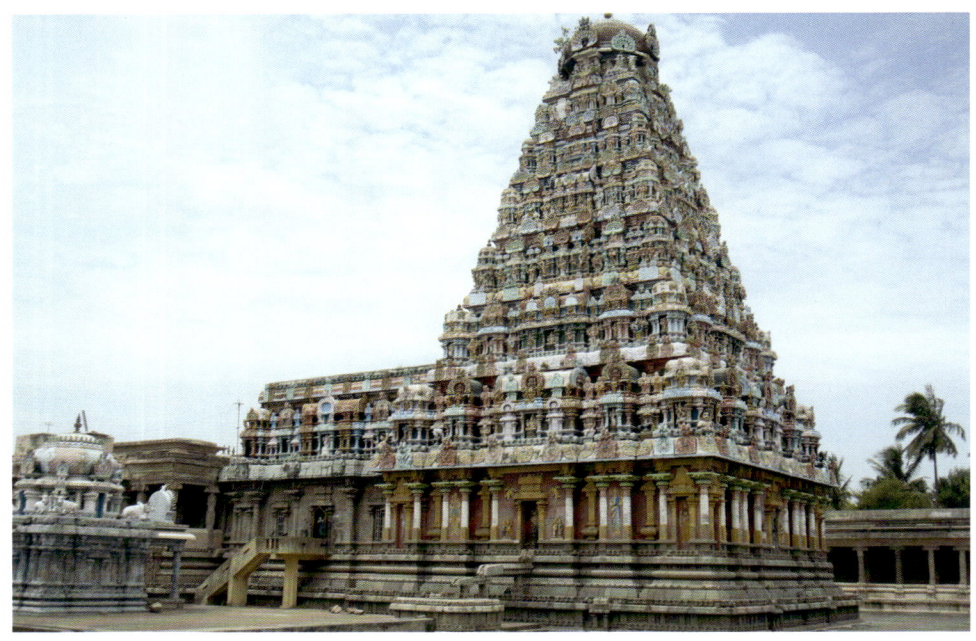

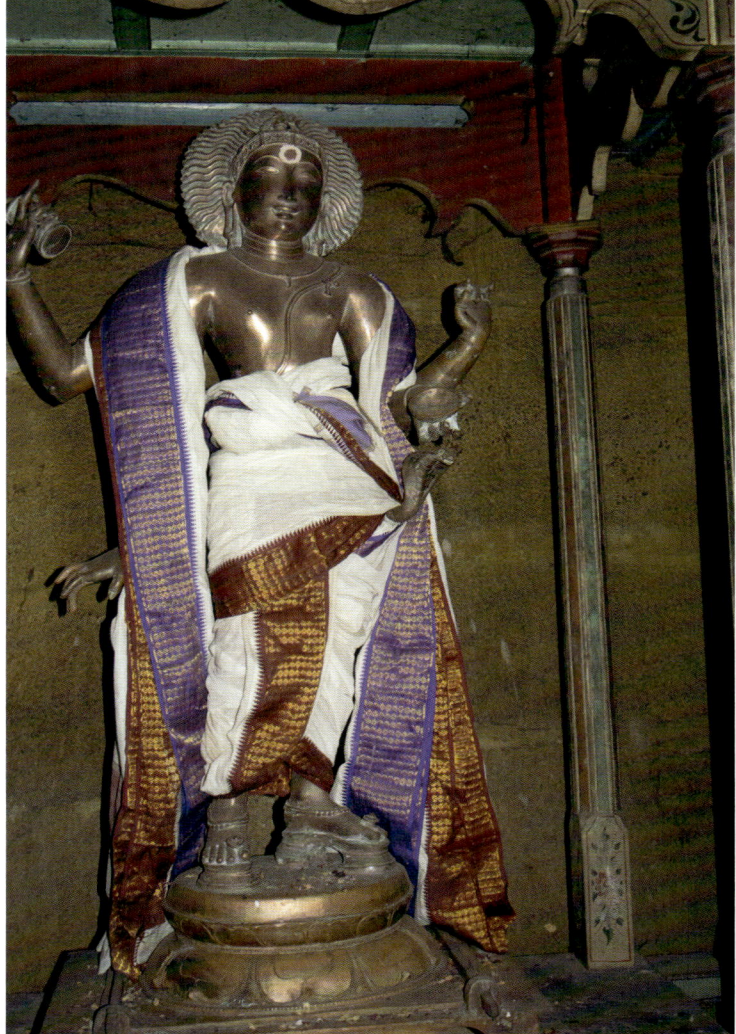

Figure 9.1. Emperor Kulottunga III's Tribhuvanam temple, Thanjavur district, ca. 1212.

Figure 9.2. *Shiva as the Begging Lord*, Tribhuvanam temple, Thanjavur district, ca. 1212.

of a total of eighteen bronzes at Tiruvilakudi that include four forms of Shiva accompanied by Uma, Lord Who Gives Grace through Dance (*Kuttadi Arulakinra Devar*), Consort of the Bedroom Chamber, Lady of the Sacred Love Fort, Ganesha, and four saints Chandesha, Sambandar, Appar, and Sundarar, the last accompanied by his wife Paravai.[7] A second example of disturbances during the fifth year of Rajaraja III comes from the Udaiyalur temple, where an inscription speaks of images, ornaments, ritual utensils, and fly-whisk fans being stolen by two individuals; action was taken against them and the money from the sale of their property was put into the treasury.[8]

With conditions as bad as they were, it appears that wealthy individual donors stepped in to bolster the temples in their town or village and to receive temple honors in return. Apart from Mavulavan Malayan's intervention at Tiruvilakudi, the inscription at Maraikkadu cited at the start of this chapter speaks at length of the generosity of a wealthy merchant. Uttaman Nambi made a major cash donation to enable repairs of the temple, he undertook the reconsecration of the temple bronzes to restore them to worship, and he funded their celebration both on a regular basis and during the temple's main festivals. In return, he was accorded major temple honors whereby the trustees gave him a deed of the temple as well as an honorific title, and acceded to his desire to be ceremonially announced on his visits to the temple. A third example of individual generosity is recorded in an inscription in the temple at Ukkachi, dated in the year 1239 during the reign of Rajaraja III.[9] Realizing that the temple's income was insufficient to carry out adequate ritual worship, due largely to defaulting landowners, Sirandan Munaiadaraiyan, an official appointed to lease lands and collect assessments (*kaval kaniyalar*), decided to intervene. His first intervention prevented defaulting tenants from leaving the area and ministered to the needs of both brahmins and agriculturalists in the village. He followed this up by commissioning bronze images to be paraded in temple procession, personally supplementing temple funds to meet ritual expenses, and nominating brahmins to perform rituals. The inscription speaks of his managerial acumen in transforming temple lands from their status as abandoned, uncultivated tracts into rich fields that produced an annual yield of 2,000 *kalams* of rice. In return, Munaiadaraiyan requested, and received, a range of coveted temple privileges and honors. These included the right to enter the temple holding a bow, a house on temple premises that he could rent to whomsoever he wished, one-half of the payments made to those who carry the bronzes in procession, and the right to have the terms of his generosity and his involvement engraved on the temple walls.

The impoverished conditions of the time are reflected even in the royal temple built by queen Sembiyan Mahadevi in the town that took her name. An inscription of the year 1233 in the reign of Rajaraja III informs us that the village assembly made the decision to hold their meetings for the conduct of village business and tax matters only during daytime hours. The reason stated is that nighttime meetings consumed lamp oil in excess of the quantity sanctioned for lighting the temple in the evenings.[10]

In chapter 4, we saw that strong administrative control was maintained of the various committees in villages, towns, and temples.[11] During the thirteenth century, we find a substantial increase in the number of temple inscriptions that lay down rules regarding the persons who may and may not serve on such committees, suggesting that corruption was on the rise and that checks and balances needed to be strictly enforced. One such instance is seen at the Senganur temple in the year 1245, when the temple authorities laid down a set of ten stringent stipulations regarding those eligible to serve as village administrators, informing us of their decision to have the rules engraved on stone in the temple itself. Members of such committees were to stand down for five years before reelection, and restrictions regarding the eligibility of their sons and brothers were added to the five-year rule. Only those under forty years of age were deemed eligible to serve, and all decisions were to be ratified by the citizens in a town-hall assembly. Those who violated these rules would be declared traitors and their property confiscated, while those who tried surreptitiously to extend their tenure would be liable to punishment as *gramadrohins*, or enemies of the village. Elected members were to refrain from collecting more than the legitimate rates of taxes. Items of expenditure exceeding 2,000 *kasu* needed the approval of the brahmin *sabha*, and those who did not abide by this rule were liable to specific fines. The final tenth clause restricts the service of members of the crucially important Accounts Committee to a single year.[12] All in all, such decisions laid down term limits, restricted nepotism, and prevented discrimination.

It is in this context that we best understand a lengthy resolution by the 4,000 members of the brahmin *sabha* in a temple at Mannargudi in the year of 1239, in response to complaints by the local *vellala* agriculturalists that were directed at the agricultural officers. The *vellalas* maintained that all their cash and rice paddy had been forcibly taken from them through taxes, and that they could no longer continue to live in the area. A royal order was issued to reassess tax rates, and to provide relief from the obligatory repair of the Kaveri river banks (*kaveri karai . . .*) and the removal of islands of obstruction (*kurai varuppu*) in the water flow. The agreement was engraved on the walls of both the Shiva and Vishnu temples at Mannargudi, with the stipulation that those who did not abide by its rules would be treated as traitors to both the village (*gramadrohi*) and the district (*nadudrohi*). The agreement was witnessed and attested by the village accountant and a range of other officials.[13]

The regrettable state of affairs in the mid-thirteenth century is further evident in a series of inscriptions from coastal temples that have largely escaped attention; these speak of individuals unable to make ends meet who resorted to selling themselves and members of their family as "temple servants," or *devar adiyar*. It would appear that in return for food and lodging, they would devote themselves, for the rest of their lives, to serving the temple; in other words, the status of such individuals is perhaps best described as permanent indentured servitude. At the coastal temple of Valampuram, whose striking twelfth-century bronzes we encountered in chapter 7, an entire series of inscriptions of this nature are all written in the first person. A woman agriculturalist (*vellati*), Araiyan Perungadi, tells us she sold herself (*ennaiyum*) to the temple, together with her three sons, a daughter-in-law, and her younger brother and younger sister. The sale of these seven persons to the temple, for a sum of 30 *kasu*, was signed on behalf of Araiyan by a male representative (*mudukan*).[14] A second record speaks of six male and female members of the family of *vellala* Soman Tattan who sold themselves (*vitru koduttu*) to the temple for 13 *kasu*;[15] the lower rate may perhaps reflect the fact that members of this family were too old to command a higher price. A third sale names eight members of the *vellala* family of

Kalaiyan Kumaran.[16] A fourth record speaks of fifteen persons sold by *vellati* Namba Nambi Kadukkal Nangai; she sold herself, her daughter, son, granddaughter, her two brothers, sisters, and other relatives to obtain 30 *kasu* from the sale.[17] Several other temples contain similar inscriptions that testify to the dire state of affairs in the thirteenth-century Chola kingdom. For instance, at the Seshapurishvara temple at Tirupamburam, during the reign of Kulottunga III, we read of a *vellala* who sold himself and his two daughters to the temple. He states in the inscription that the cost of living was so high, with three *nali* of paddy selling for one *kasu*, that they could not afford to eat; as a result, he sold himself and his two daughters into temple service for 32 *kasu*.[18]

A somewhat different category of sale involves individuals who were already *adiyars*, or servants in private homes. At Maraikkadu, in 1219 during the reign of Rajaraja III, a security officer (*kaval adhikari*) named Ariyan Pichchan reaffirmed his father's previous gift of five personal servants to be temple servants; he now sold another five persons, together with their descendants, into temple servitude (*adimai*), for the sum of 1,000 *kasu*.[19] In the year 1240, the same Ariyan Pichchan sold another two of his servant girls (*en adiyaril*), Kalani and Kudiyal, to the temple as slaves of god after receiving money from the temple treasury, and after recording the sale in stone (*udaiyarku adimayaka kalvetti koduten*).[20] At Sulamangalam, in the year 1218 during the reign of Kulottunga III, two brothers recorded "a sale deed of persons" (*al-vilai pramanam*), and sold five maidservants who were already among their personal *adiyars* to be temple servants.[21] At the coastal temple in Tiruchengatankudi, home of saint Siruttondar, a lady named Lakshmi sold four women to the Shiva temple of Tiruvalankadu as *devar adiyar* (servants of the lord) for the sum of 700 *kasu*; she informs us that these women were already in her service as part of her *stridhanam*, or a father's gift to a bride at her marriage.[22] One last inscription of relevance here, dated in 1231, the nineteenth year of Rajaraja III, comes from Korukkai in the coastal strip. This extraordinary record consists of a consolidated list of the names, and the relationship to each other, of a number of clusters of temple servants amounting to close to one hundred men and women. The inscription specifies that the temple received these individuals either from the king himself (*tirumukapadi petra adimaikum*), through purchase (*velar kondu*), or through donations (*danattal petra*).[23]

Despite the apparently unstable economy and the skyrocketing cost of living, magnificent bronzes were produced even during this troubled period. A striking foursome group depicts god Krishna in his role as Royal Lord (Rajamannar), King of Dwarka, flanked by his two consorts, Rukmini and Satyabhama. Standing by is his vehicle, the divine eagle Garuda, portrayed as a winged human with a beaked nose, and who is as "swift as the wind itself"; his speed and infallibility, one assumes, were factors that influenced Indonesia to name its national airline after Vishnu's divine eagle. The bronzes of this commanding group reflect the peak of the Chola artists' achievements during the thirteenth century (fig. 9.3). We see a predilection for sharp definition, whether of the nose or the nipples, and a closer than ever attention to details of jewelry and ornamentation (figs. 9.4 and 9.5). The imagery is admirable for its precise execution. It is far distant, however, from the beginnings of bronze imagery in the ninth century. Some may infinitely prefer the crisp, detailed, and precise execution of the later images. And why not? Is it Bernini's exuberance or

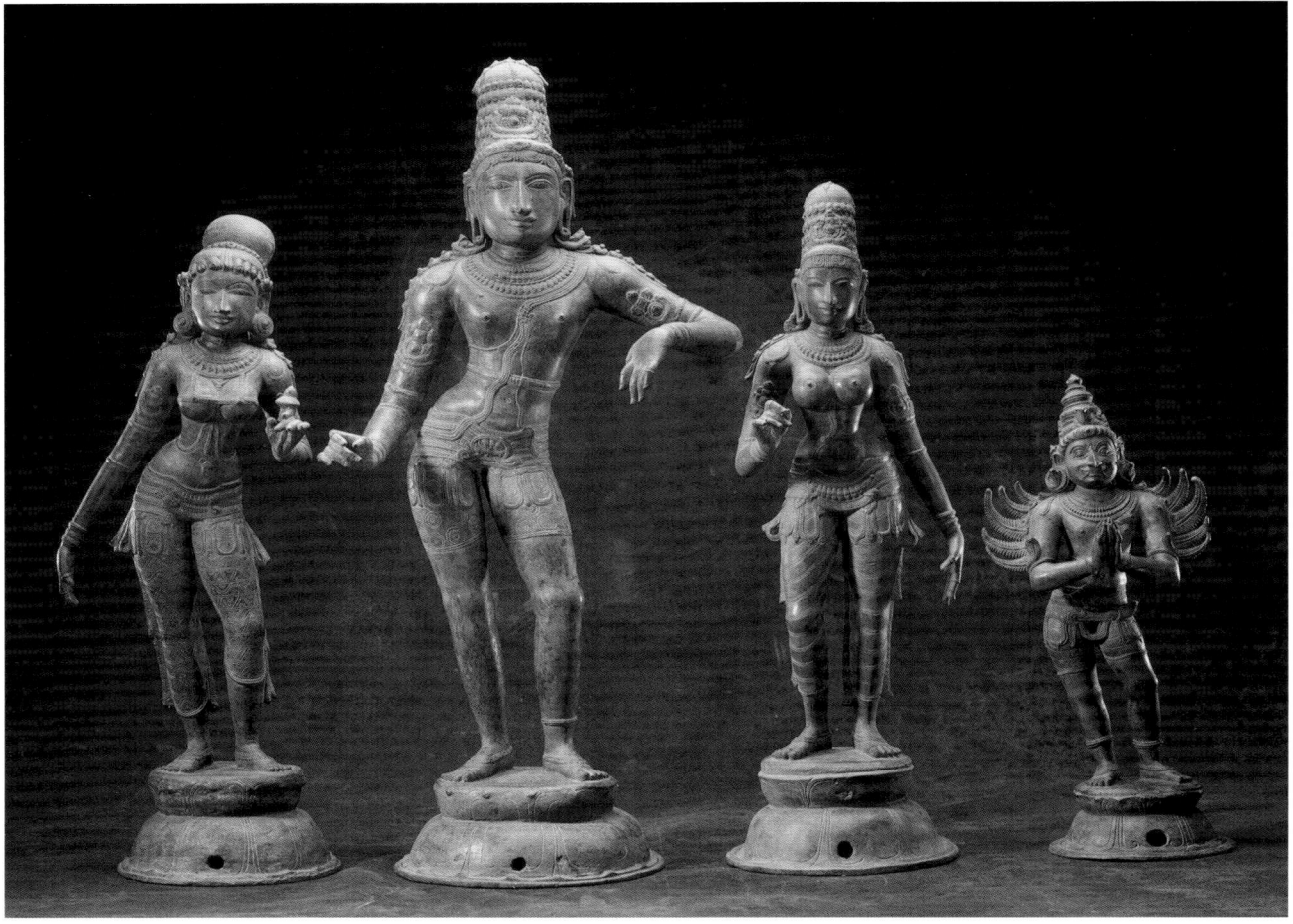

Figure 9.3. *Krishna as King with Two Consorts and Garuda*, ca. 1225, Los Angeles County Museum of Art, Gift of Mr. and Mrs. Hal B. Wallis.

Michelangelo's restrained power that the reader finds more appealing? Meticulously executed images of Vishnu's other avatars too were created during the thirteenth century, when the prevalence of Vishnu images went hand in hand with declining Chola control. Vishnu, after all, is the god with messianic appeal; while Shiva manifests himself in varying forms, it is Vishnu who is associated with ten avatars, of which the final, tenth avatar is yet to come. A favored bronze image was Vishnu's third avatar as the gigantic snouted boar, Varaha, in which form Vishnu prevented the earth from drowning in the waters of the cosmic ocean. He dived into its depths and rescued the earth, whom you see as a personified goddess seated on Varaha-Vishnu's bent left knee (fig. 9.6). Also popular was Vishnu's fourth incarnation as man-lion, Narasimha (fig. 9.7).

By the late thirteenth century, artists created bronzes that are solemn, dignified, regal, and stately, such as a fine seated Shiva and Uma couple (fig. 9.8). A comparison with a tenth-century group from the Shivapuram temple reveals a loss of intimacy, a lessening of interaction between the two figures, and a distancing from the viewer-devotee (see fig. 4.12). This should not be viewed as a diminishing of artistic talent, nor a weakening of interest on the part of patrons. Rather, it is a change in taste, and a corresponding intentionality of response on the part of the artist. A single feature of the torso of goddess Uma—the

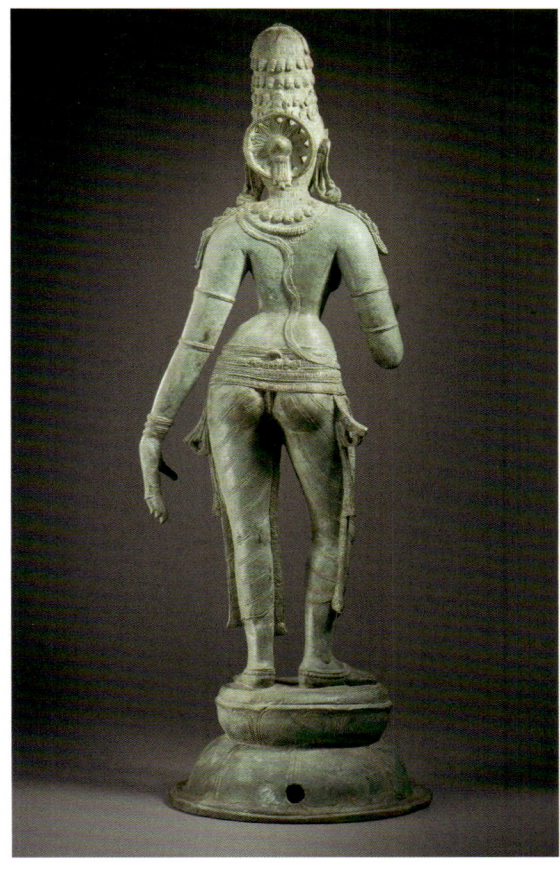

Figure 9.4. Rear view of Rukmini, detail of *Krishna as King with Two Consorts and Garuda* (see fig. 9.3).

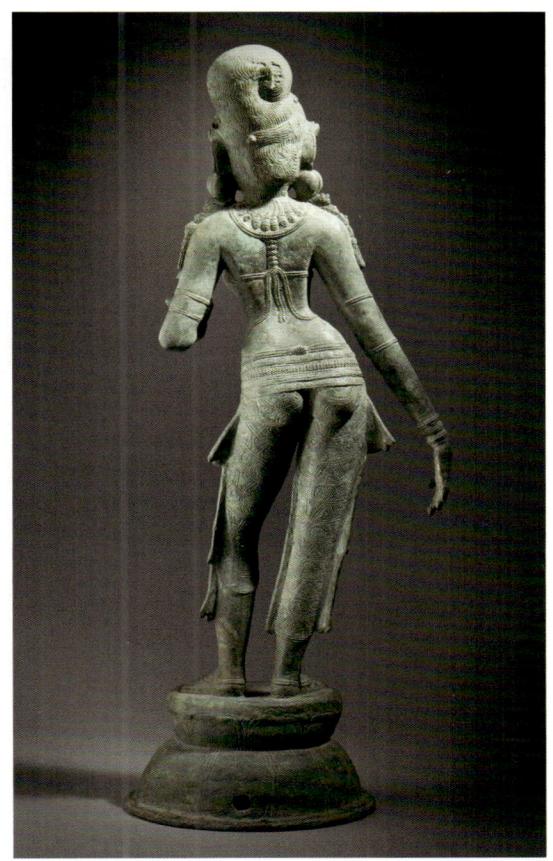

Figure 9.5. Rear view of Satyabhama, detail of *Krishna as King with Two Consorts and Garuda* (see fig. 9.3).

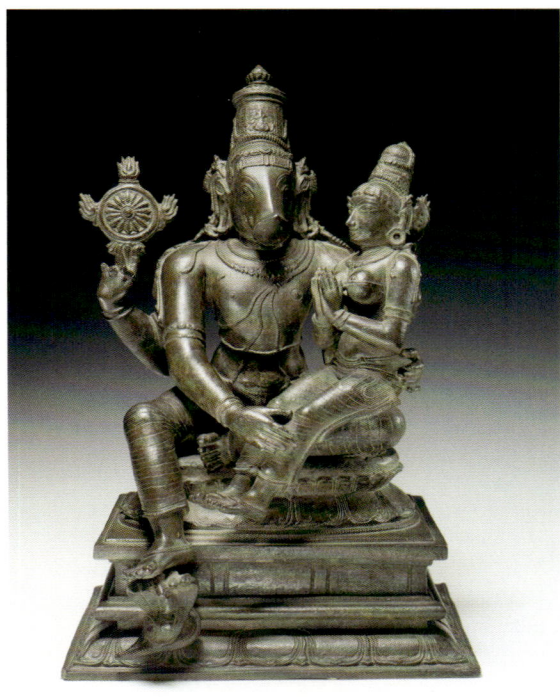

Figure 9.6. *Vishnu as Varaha*, thirteenth century, Victoria and Albert Museum, London.

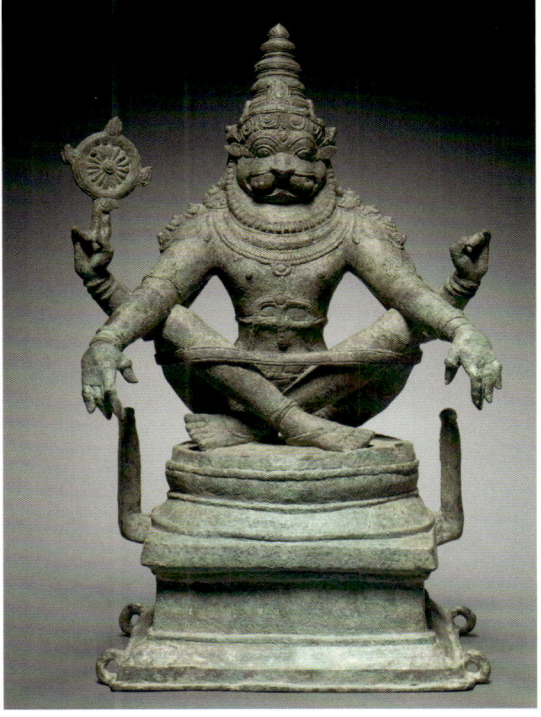

Figure 9.7. *Vishnu as Narasimha*, thirteenth century, The Cleveland Museum of Art, Gift of Dr. Norman Zaworski.

WORSHIP IN UNCERTAIN TIMES

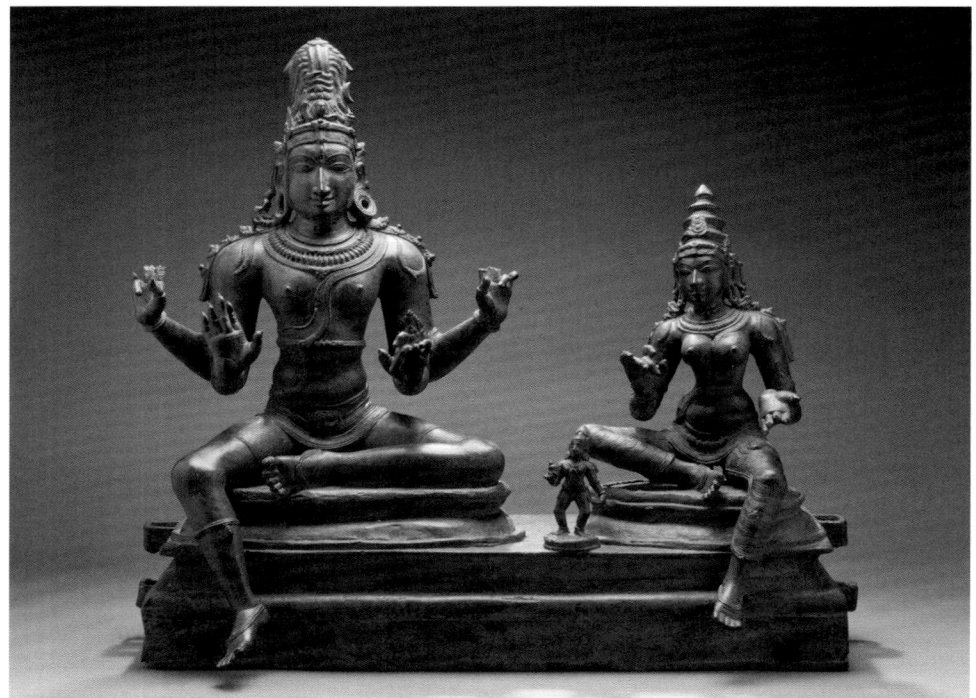

Figure 9.8. *Shiva with Uma and Skanda*, late thirteenth century, Norton Simon Museum, Pasadena.

contour and placement of her breasts—will allow us to demonstrate this change. Consider the smooth flow of the breasts on the Tiruvenkadu masterpiece of the year 1012; descending gently from her sloping shoulders, the breasts curve under softly, with nipples barely indicated (fig. 9.9a; see also fig. 5.2 and fig. 0.1). By 1100, the urge is seen to pull up those absent bra straps so that the breasts are uplifted, though still softly rounded (fig. 9.9b). We move into the 1200s, and the breasts are placed about as high as they can go, nipples stand out prominently, and the encircling areola is accentuated (fig. 9.9c, d). We are witnessing a change in aesthetic taste accompanied by a precision of technique that clearly held greater appeal for many artists and their patrons.

By 1275, Chola power was severely weakened, and rivals to both south and north began taking over portions of Chola territories and sponsoring festivals in their temples. At Tiruvenkadu, the temple of our Master bronze sculptor, this may have happened somewhat earlier, since the latest Chola inscription in the temple appears to date to 1238, in the twenty-second year of Rajaraja III.[24] This record is followed by an entire series of gifts of land and coins dated in the regnal years of a range of Pandya kings whose genealogy, precise names, and dates are still far from settled. Thus, the dates given here may be treated as approximations. An inscription on the inner *prakara* wall of the Tiruvenkadu temple, dated in the sixth year of Maravarman Sundara Pandya I, or 1222, speaks of a special service instituted in the name of that king for bathing the gods and the *nayanmar* at the mouth of the Kaveri river.[25] A record of Jatavarman Sundara Pandya, dating to the year 1256, records offerings to the god of the temple in the name of the Pandya king.[26] An inscription of the reign of Maravarman Vikrama Pandya refers to the outer eastern gateway of the temple as the Vikrama Pandya sacred gateway (*tiruvasal*),

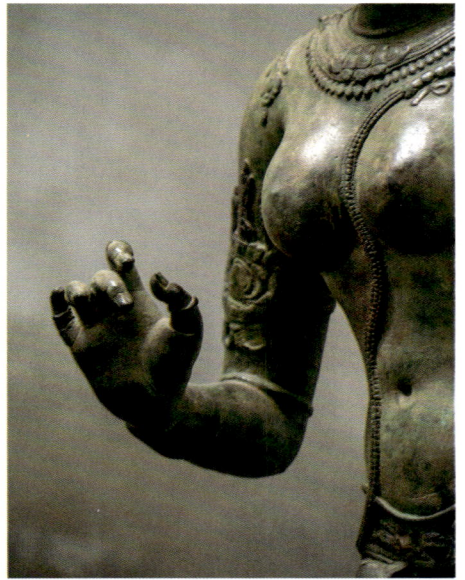
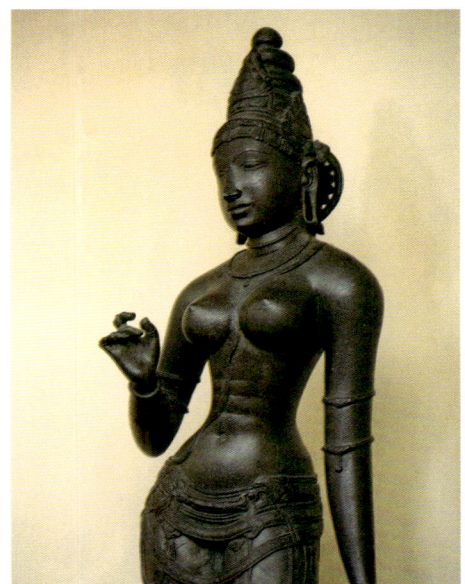
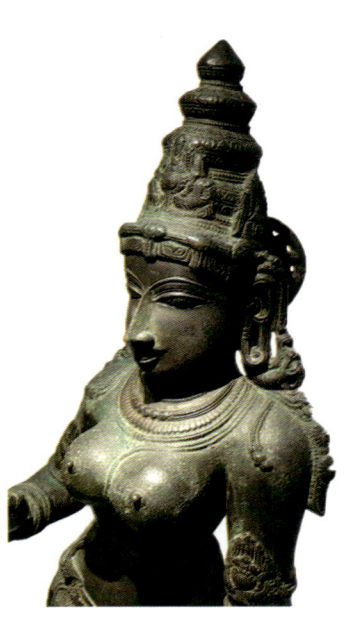
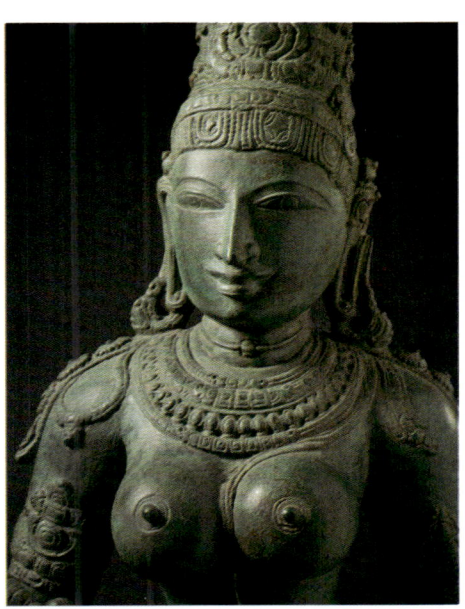

Figure 9.9. (a, top left) Detail of *Uma*, Tiruvenkadu temple, Nagapattinam district, ca. 1012, Art Gallery, Thanjavur. (b, top right) *Uma*, ca. 1100, Art Gallery, Thanjavur. (c, above left) *Uma*, ca. 1200, National Museum, New Delhi. (d, above right) *Rukmini*, ca. 1225, Los Angeles County Museum of Art.

suggesting that it was a late addition by the Pandya king.[27] Two final inscriptions may be noted here. The first, dated in the thirty-third year of the reign of Srivallabha Pandya (1280?), informs us that festivals had not been celebrated at the temple for several years prior.[28] Three years later, during the reign of Jatavarman Sundara Pandya, we are told that a gift of land enabled the restart of rituals and festivals in the name of the Pandya king.[29] The Chola dynasty was a thing of the past.

It is somewhat ironic then that at the precise time that Chola power ended in India, a Chola-style Shiva temple was built in Quanzhou in south China by an expatriate Tamil merchant community. The temple is celebrated in a bilingual inscription of just over five lines of Tamil script that proclaims that it was built in the year 1281 by a Tamil merchant named Sambanda-perumal,[30] and that it received the sanction and blessing of the Mongol ruler Chekachai Khan. The sixth line of the inscription, written in Chinese characters that run horizontally like the Tamil script rather than the usual vertical format, does not reveal a clear meaning.[31] While the temple itself was destroyed early on, a few stone pillars that carry bas reliefs of Krishna, Shiva, and other deities, and are modeled on the lines of the *mandapa* pillars in Rajaraja II's royal temple at Darasuram, were incorporated into a later Chinese Buddhist temple to Kaiyuan. The base moldings of this Kaiyuan temple also incorporate over 140 carved stones from the base moldings of the original Chola-style temple. Additionally, the Quanzhou Maritime Museum houses some 117 stone pieces from various portions of the destroyed temple, while a few more such stones are scattered in the environs of the city.[32] The importance of the ocean silk route to China, and the role played in the patronage of art by diasporic Tamil merchant communities, whether they were based in Takua-pa, Barus, Quanzhou, or elsewhere, clearly merits further exploration.

Buried Bronzes Reemerge

In the course of these chapters, I have made reference to buried bronzes with the green patina they acquire from the wet soil that has surrounded them over the centuries, and contrasted them with the dark hue that develops on bronzes that remain exposed to air within temple premises. The question to be addressed here is the prevalence of the phenomenon of buried bronzes and the reasons for their burial. The superb eleventh-century Tiruvenkadu bronzes that were our focus in chapter 5 were discovered during the twentieth century as four different buried hoards. The first, which included a modest-size Dancing Lord, emerged in 1925 and the group was deposited in the temple itself.[33] In 1951, farmers plowing a field adjoining the temple discovered three sets of images that we examined as the outstanding work of the Tiruvenkadu Master—Shiva as Rider of the bull and consort, the dramatic Marriage group of Shiva, Uma, Vishnu, and Lakshmi, and Shiva as Begging Lord.[34] The district revenue collector had just established the local Tanjore Art Gallery, and he acquired these bronzes for display in the new premises. In 1960, construction workers unearthed another twelve images while digging foundations for a new shrine; two of these images, Shiva as Half Woman and a seated image of saint Chandesha, went to the Government Museum in Chennai, while ten were deposited in the temple.[35] Last, in the year 1972, sixteen more images were found, all of which are now in the Thanjavur Art Gallery.[36] The patrons of the Tiruvenkadu temple commissioned over thirty-five bronzes (I do not include in this count the 1925 group, for which I have been unable to locate clear statistics) to fulfill the requirements of what was surely an expanded and elaborate ritual festival cycle. The images that participate today in the Tiruvenkadu festival cycle belong to post-Chola times, and were created during the period of Vijayanagara rule to enable continuation of worship in the temple.

The Shiva temple in the village of Tandantottam, part of the extended coastal belt, yielded bronzes belonging to two sets of burials. In the 1950s, a group of bronze images together with a copper plate of the previous Pallava rulers of the Chennai area, was uncovered. Ten years later, a further burial containing images of stunning size and beauty came to light, and include the late ninth-century image of Shiva as Victor of the Three Forts that we have ascribed to the Master of the off-kilter substyle (see fig. 2.6).[37] Equally exquisite from this same find-spot is a three-piece group of Shiva, his bull, and his consort Uma.[38] Nothing in these various buried hoards dates after 1300.

In 1987, a small temple at Esalam in the coastal belt yielded a smaller and differently constituted group of buried bronzes while laborers were trying to level the granite paving stones of the courtyard. Slowed down by a protruding object that turned out to be the metal leg of a tripod, the laborers removed the adjoining paving stones to find three bronze bells and a few other ritual objects. Beneath these, they found a second layer of the same burial; placed upside down in river sand and arranged radially were two levels of bronze images, with smaller images placed at a higher level upon the larger bronzes that could withstand the weight of the smaller pieces. Beneath all the images, none of which are of the large proportions we have seen thus far, was a copper-plate charter of Rajendra that contains the information that the Esalam temple was built in the year 1027 by Ishana Shiva Pandita, the guru of emperor Rajendra.[39] The largest image, measuring 27 inches, is of Uma, while next in size are an image of an *acharya*, perhaps the patron guru himself (25 inches), saint Chandesha (25 inches), dancing Sambandar (20 inches), and two forms of Shiva that measure 16 and 13 inches. The other bronzes, roughly 8 inches high, probably served as objects of personal adoration for the guru. Of the twenty-three metal objects unearthed, eight appear to be processional ritual bronzes of modest size, four the guru's objects of personal devotion, while the rest are ritual objects.

In the year 2010, at a small temple at Tiruvindalur in the coastal belt, temple authorities dug a trench 12 feet deep into the floor of the hall in front of the sanctum as part of a program of renovation and expansion. They discovered twelve bronzes[40] that include a stunning image of the emaciated woman saint known as the Mother of Karaikkal, whom we encountered both in the Kaveri delta and in Sri Lanka. The excavated image carried the accretion acquired over several centuries; it was then cleaned and restored with its patina intact (fig. 9.10a, b). This burial at the Tiruvindalur temple included the largest set of royal copper-plate charters yet recovered, carrying intact the ring and the seal of the ruling Chola king Rajadhiraja.[41] Dating to the year 1065, the eighty-five copper plates, each a little larger than legal pad size, weigh 330 pounds. The plates' layer of accretion and patina were removed to restore the original coppery sheen in order to enable clear reading of the entire 3,442 lines of writing (see fig. 3.11).

A temple at Nallur revealed a different modus operandi in that its priests did not bury their bronzes but hid them away in a complex secret underground cellar. R. Nagaswamy recounts how a brick wall was broken down in the year 1980 to reveal two strong wooden doors, locked and sealed. These were broken open and led to an empty room filled with sand. The wall caved in almost immediately to reveal granite slabs at one corner that opened up like a trap door. Steps led to an empty underground chamber that led to yet another room that contained sixteen bronzes of exceptional quality, together with ornamental lamps and temple vessels.[42] Among the bronzes discovered is the striking image of Uma discussed in chapter 4 as a creation of the workshop of queen Sembiyan Mahadevi (see fig. 4.10a, b, c).[43] Suggesting royal interest in this temple is an

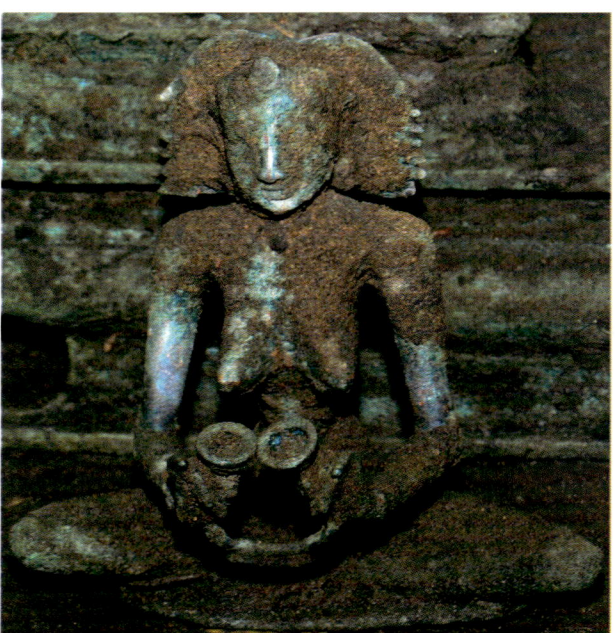 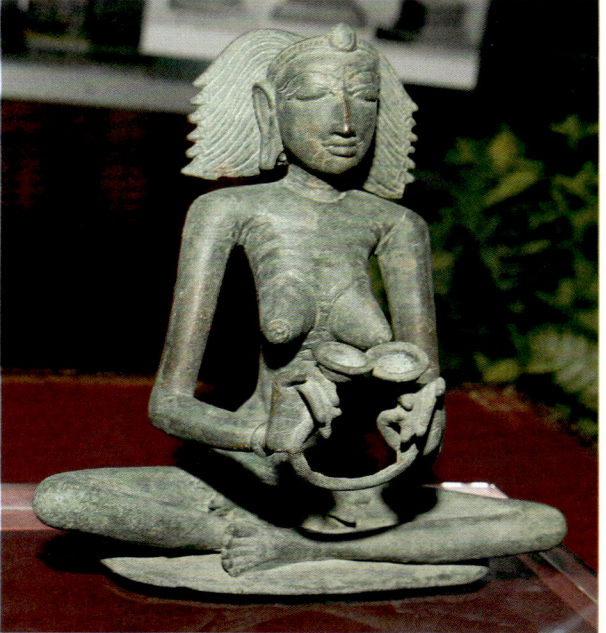

Figure 9.10. *Saint "Mother of Karaikkal,"* Tiruvindalur temple, Nagapattinam district, ca. 1040, *The Hindu* Archives. (a) Immediately after excavation. (b) After cleaning.

inscription dated in the tenth regnal year of Sembiyan's son Uttama Chola (981) that speaks of an investigation into the finances of the Nallur temple by the *srikaryam* officer on the direct order of the king (*tirumukam*).[44] The Nallur cache includes three bronzes dating between the sixteenth and eighteenth/nineteenth centuries that were probably added to this hidden chamber after the Portuguese became an active colonial power in south India during the sixteenth century.

A similar tactical course is seen at the Chidambaram temple, whose sanctum roof monarch after monarch claimed to have gold-plated. A secret hidden chamber yielded over eighty bronzes, dating from the tenth century to the seventeenth century, with the bulk of the images belonging to the period of mature Chola bronze art from the twelfth and thirteenth centuries. Two images that predate the era of queen Sembiyan Mahadevi's workshop are an exquisite image of Paravai, wife of Sundarar, as well as an image of saint Manikkavachakar, both created in the mid-tenth century. An unusual image of sage Patanjali in part-human and part-serpentine form, as well as more than one image of seated Shiva and Uma with child Skanda, belong to the twelfth and thirteenth centuries. This hidden storeroom at Chidambaram, like the one at Nallur, appears to have been opened up in later times to accommodate further bronzes including a seventeenth-century Dancing Shiva.[45] One assumes that the existence of this hidden treasure-house was an open secret among the high-ranking *dikshitar* priests of Chidambaram.

The town of Konulampallam (Tiruvidaimaradur district), whose Shiva temple no longer stands, yielded a group of twelve buried bronzes. These include Shiva as *Chandrashekhara* with his consort, the Dancing Lord with his consort, *Somaskanda*, and three images of Uma, of which one of considerably larger size represents her form as *Bhoga Shakti* or "Pleasure Force," and a second as the seated Consort of the Bedroom Chamber

(*Palliarai Nachchiyar*). Completing the set are an image of Ganesha, two images of Dancing Sambandar, and one of saint Chandesha. A series of ritual vessels, as well as pieces of aureoles, were part of the finds. A metal tripod inscribed "Edirilichola," a title assumed by Kulottunga II (r. 1133–1150), was also part of this buried hoard.[46]

Every few months, the Tamil Nadu newspapers carry an item about yet another temple restoration or road expansion that results in the find of early buried bronzes. Most such finds do not make their way into the media. It is close to impossible to obtain any reliable figures on the number of bronzes that have been unearthed as "treasure troves" in the last fifty years; my estimate, a pure guesstimate, and probably a woeful underestimate, is 2,000 bronzes. The fate of buried bronzes that are recovered as treasure troves is diverse. Some are placed in barred (see fig. 8.8a) and often in double-barred temple safe-rooms, others in the government of Tamil Nadu's "Icon Centers," and some find their way into museum storerooms in Tamil Nadu. All are highly susceptible to "bronze disease" and require special conservation approaches. Ground water contains chloride salts, and the chloride ions react with copper and adhere to it, forming a copper chloride layer on the metal surface upon which other corrosion builds. Such corrosion is highly reactive to humidity, producing something akin to hydrochloric acid that keeps corroding the bronze and can break it down so that its surface becomes pitted and may finally even consume the image.[47] It requires only two simple elements—water and air—to minimize the expansion and spread of such sites of corrosion. The pristine condition of Chola sacred bronzes in Tamil Nadu temples is simply the result of exposure to a variety of liquids including water that is part of ritual bathing and lustrating of temple bronzes, combined with exposure to air that occurs when the bronzes are taken in procession as part of the festival cycle.[48] Icon Centers, by contrast, are concrete blocks with no windows and a single door; they are sealed, not air conditioned, and have no provision for humidity control. Many of their bronzes have been taken from temples in which they were regularly worshipped, but the centers also contain bronzes from buried hoards. Tamil Nadu's Icon Centers today house exemplary items of Indic and world heritage in the form of Chola sacred bronzes; these centers need to be receptive to conservation requirements that will help maintain, for future generations, this invaluable and irreplaceable heritage.

In addition to the mystery of buried bronzes, there is the additional enigma of missing bronzes. We know from inscriptions that Rajaraja's royal temple possessed sixty-six bronzes (see appendix B, I); only two of these appear to survive, a Dancing Lord in a small shrine within the temple premises, and perhaps Shiva as Victor of Three Forts in the Art Gallery, Thanjavur (see fig. 5.12). Where are the remaining sixty-four bronzes that the temple inscriptions describe, giving us measurements for the majority?[49] They were certainly not melted down to create new images, as might happen in the West, since sacred bronzes retain their sacrality in India over the ages. If temple authorities felt that the facial features of a bronze had lost their definition as a result of centuries of ritual worship, then they would recut eyes, eyebrows, and lips in order to reactivate the image for worship. At the modestly sized Tiruvaduturai temple, an inscription of the year 1018 records the gift of jewelry and ritual vessels by emperor Rajendra's mother-in-law, his guru, and two court ladies, and records the temple's twenty-five sacred bronzes (see appendix B, II). We are given the size of each bronze, and realize, for instance, that Shiva with the bull was a full 3 1/2 feet high, making it the same stature as its counterpart at Tiruvenkadu.[50] None of these eleventh-century images survive in the temple; all images seen today date from the post-Chola period. Where did the early Aduturai bronzes go? What happened to them? A similar situation exists across much of Tamil Nadu. For instance, an inscription records the gift of seven sacred bronzes commissioned in the year 1226 for the temple at Avalivanallur by a merchant named Amarakon (see appendix B, III).[51] The Tiruvilakudi temple, briefly referenced earlier in this chapter, once possessed eighteen sacred bronzes (see appendix B, IV). The whereabouts of only two bronzes from Tiruvilakudi are known today, raising the issue of the fate of the remaining images. Or we could turn to Kulottunga III's royal temple of the year 1212 at Tribhuvanam, whose bronze Begging Lord we glimpsed earlier in this chapter, and inquire into the whereabouts of the remaining images that were undoubtedly commissioned for this temple. A parallel situation exists with the hundreds of smaller temples in the Kaveri basin. In fact, during my first research trip into Tamil Nadu, a good thirty-five years ago, I remember my sharp disappointment at seeing everywhere bronze images that date largely from the fifteenth century, during the post-Chola period of Vijayanagara rule. What happened to the many Chola bronzes of the inscriptions?

The explanation for the mystery of the buried bronzes, and the enigma of the missing bronzes, lies largely in the events of 1310, when Malik Kafur, general of the armies of the Delhi Sultanate, marched south to tap into the wealth of the temples of south India. The sultanate was in need of money to fund its activities in north India, and the fabled temple jewels of south India provided the perfect answer. News of the approach of the army of Malik Kafur spread fast, especially after the Hoysala temples were damaged in the quest for gold and jewels, and many temples in the Tamil country began to take precautions. Fearing desecration of their sacred bronzes, temple authorities secretly buried them in carefully prepared pits upon a bed of sand, covering them with *darbha* sacrificial grass, following ceremonies prescribed by ritual texts.[52] One such Sanskrit Vishnu text, *Vimanarcanakalpa*, carries instructions for burying images in times of danger from thieves and enemies in its chapter 70 titled "Manner of Securing Safety from Danger." I quote here Richard Davis's translation of a key part of the text:

> *In a clean and hidden place the temple priest or worshipper should dig a pit, sprinkle sand in it and strew sacrificial grass over the sand. He worships the Earth Goddess in the pit, reciting the mantra "Apohistha." Together with the patron and devotees, he enters the sanctum of the god, bows to the deity, and makes a request: "As long as there is danger, O Visnu, please lie down in a bed with the goddess Earth." He transfers the divine energy (sakti) located in the image into a fixed image, or in lieu of the fixed image he may transfer the energy into his own heart.*[53]

One might note that the Esalam temple bronzes were found on *darbha* grass strewn upon a bed of sand as prescribed.

Malik Kafur's southern campaign lasted an entire year; he left Delhi on October 13, 1310, and returned on October 18, 1311, with tremendous wealth that included 312 elephants, 20,000 horses, and gold equivalent to 100 million coins.[54] Here's what Amir

Khusrau, fourteenth-century poet-scholar, wrote about the Delhi Sultanate army's determined raids for treasure. "At every corner, conquest opened a door to them, and in all that devastated land, wherever treasure remained hidden in the earth, it was sifted, searched through, and carted away so that nothing remained to the infidels of their gold but an echo, and of their gems, a flaming fire."[55] The description of the gemstones in Khusrau's *Khazain ul Futuh* (Treasures of Victory) is worth repeating in its entirety:

> *The diamonds were of such a colour that the sun will have to stare hard for ages before the like of them is made in the factories of the rocks. The pearls glistened so brilliantly that the brow of the clouds will have to perspire for years before such pearls again reach the treasury of the sea. For generations the mines will have to drink blood in the stream of the sun before rubies such as these are produced. The emeralds were of a water so fine, that if the blue sky broke itself into fragments, none of its fragments would equal them. Every diamond sparkled brightly; it seemed as if it was a drop fallen from the sun.*[56]

Sacred bronzes are not mentioned, and we assume they were of little interest to Amir Khusrau and Malik Kafur.[57] While the army's interest was indeed in the valuable gold and gems that would help the sultanate in its northern campaigns, it is likely that temple bronzes suffered incidental damage; how many were destroyed as a by-product of the sultanate's mission is difficult to say.

The intention of the temple custodians who buried their beloved bronzes was, of course, to retrieve them for worship once the threat from the north had receded. But things did not go according to their plans. The amazing success of Malik Kafur's yearlong mission induced the Delhi Sultanate to send a second army under Khusrau Khan; the sultanate also established its own governor in Madurai, the erstwhile Pandya capital, to the south of the recently defunct Chola kingdom. The Delhi-appointed governor soon declared himself as the independent sultan of a new sultanate named Ma'bar that lasted in the Madurai region under a series of sultans between 1334–1378. The intention of Chola temple priests to restore buried bronzes had to be reevaluated and postponed. The secret burial spots, and hidden storage areas of the bronzes, would have been known only to a trusted few in each temple. Sixty-eight years intervened from 1310, the year of burial, to 1378, when the last sultan of Madurai was defeated and killed by the army of the newly formed Vijayanagara empire. During this interim period, the trusted senior priests who knew the location of the secret burial spots died without passing on what must have been highly classified information.

In the fifteenth century, the Hindu rulers of the new Vijayanagara dynasty took over Chola territory and all its sacred temples. To replace the many missing bronzes, they commissioned fresh bronzes that now took pride of place in the newly vibrant and continuing temple festival cycle. An occasional inscription speaks specifically to such a situation. For instance, a Vishnu temple at Tirupputkuli carries a record dated to the year 1573 that speaks of making new images of nine *alvar* saints because the earlier images had been destroyed by the Muhammadans, and of repairing three images to make up the entire series of twelve saints.[58] Vijayanagara bronzes lack the panache, the graceful stance, and the gentle poise of their earlier Chola counterparts; limbs tend to be

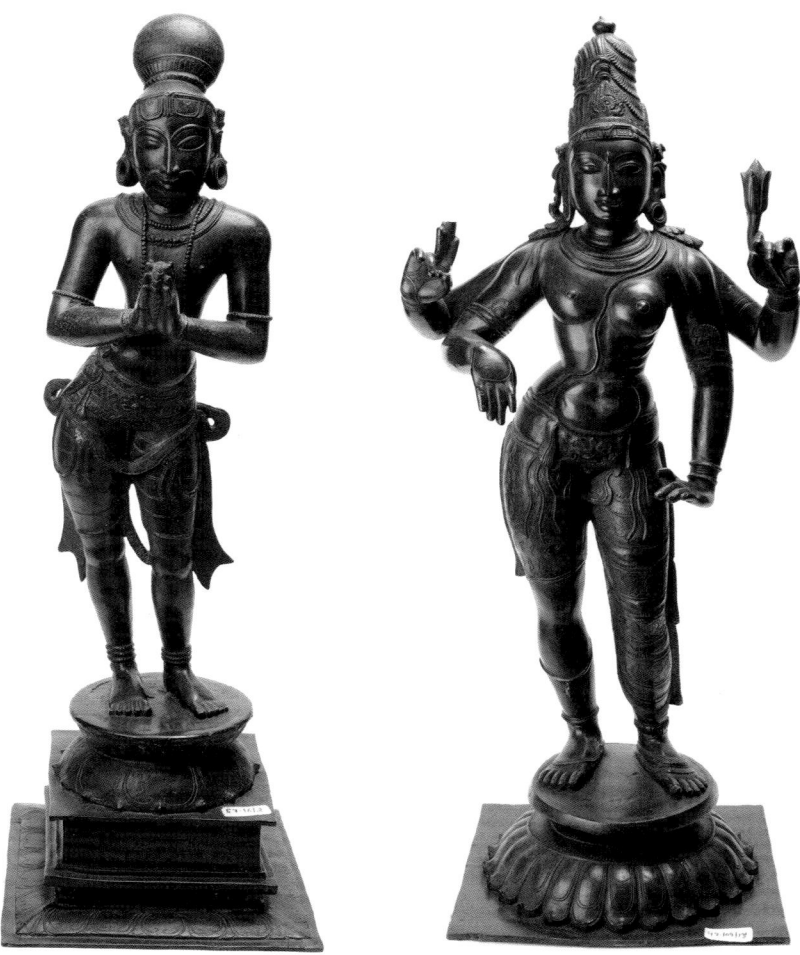

Figure 9.11. *Hunter Saint Kanappan*, Vijayanagara period, ca. 1550, National Museum, New Delhi.

Figure 9.12. *Shiva as Half Woman (Ardhanari)*, Vijayanagara period, ca. 1550, National Museum, New Delhi.

tubular, bodies elongated, and stances stiff. We need but compare hunter-saint Kanappan from the hands of a Chola artist with one from a Vijayanagara artist (fig. 9.11; see fig. 5.7a, b), or make a similar comparison between Chola and Vijayanagara images of Shiva as Half Woman (fig. 9.12; see fig. 5.5a, b, c). In the 150 years that had intervened, the lack of demand for temple bronzes apparently caused expert wax modelers to move away from the Kaveri delta. Yet the best of Vijayanagara bronzes, like the portraits of the early sixteenth-century emperor Krishnadevaraya with his two queens, embody a quiet authority and display a commanding presence (fig. 9.13).

Once the power of the Vijayanagara empire was established, the few temples that retained memory and specific information of the burial spots of their Chola bronzes were able to unearth them. For instance, a Vishnu temple at Kannanur, northeast of Trichy, informs us in an inscription of the fifteenth century that the image of Vishnu, who had "retreated to a safe-house" due to the invasion of the Turushkas (Turks, and a generic term for Muslims), was now reconsecrated and restored to its original place of worship.[59] However, large numbers of images, both of Shiva and Vishnu, stayed buried, while an

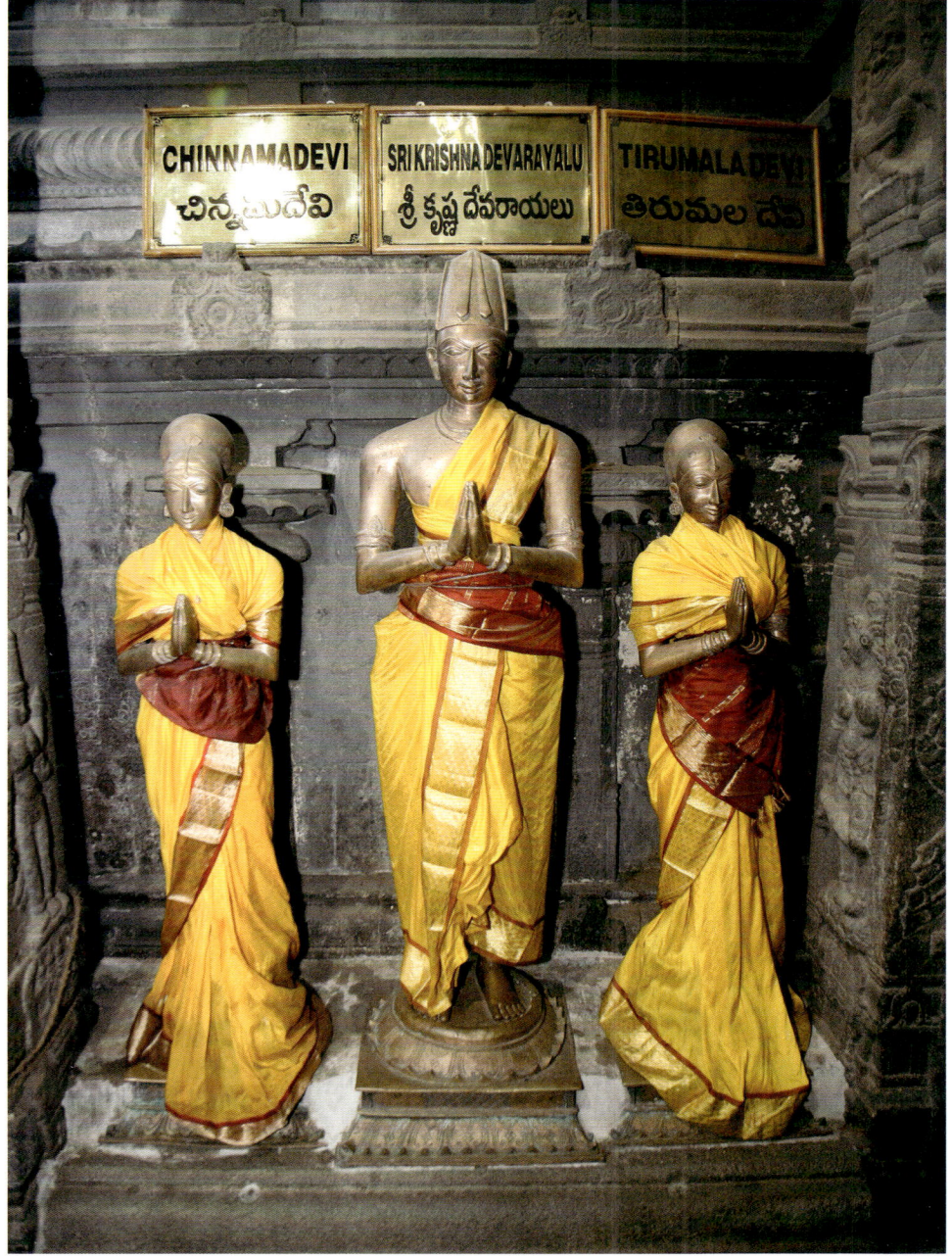

Figure 9.13. *Vijayanagar King Krishnadevaraya and His Two Queens*, Tirumala temple, Tirupati, Vijayanagara period, ca. 1530.

equally large number were probably damaged by the sultanate army's quest for jewels. Buried bronzes began to reemerge in the twentieth century, as temples in Tamil Nadu embarked on a process of expansion to accommodate growing numbers of devotees. As temple after temple dug down to lay new foundations for additional shrines, halls, kitchens, and other buildings, they came across buried bronzes. Those ancient Chola bronzes, buried in 1310, had, in fact, survived in sufficiently large numbers to testify eloquently to the talent of Chola wax modelers and bronze casters.

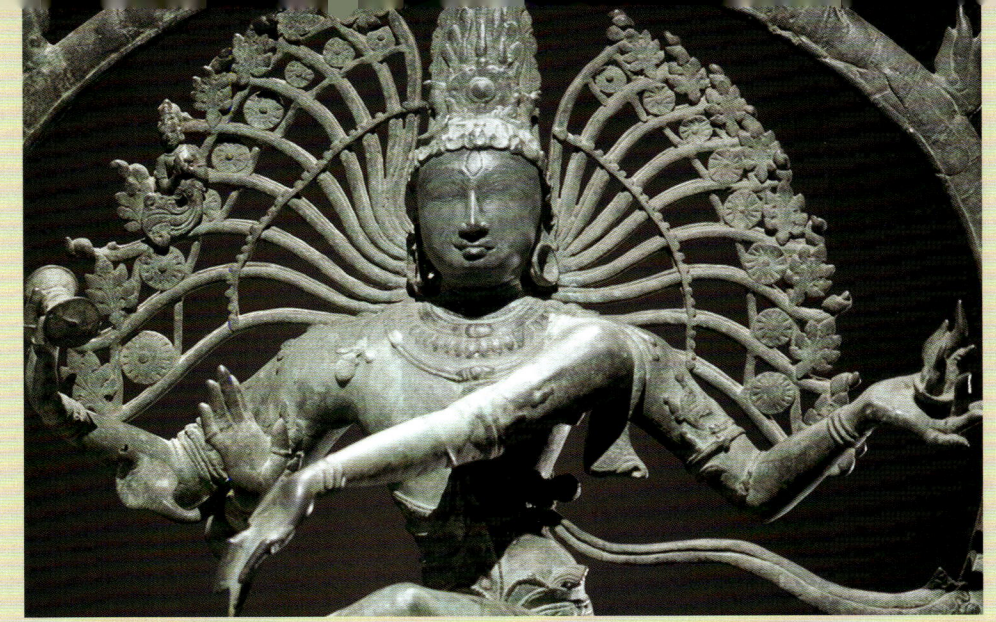

Reviewing the Chola Achievement a Millennium Later

10

In the middle of the ninth century, a dramatic sea change occurred in the creation of the sacred images that partook in festival celebrations in the temples of Tamil Nadu. Abandoning the medium of wood in which images needed renewal on a regular basis due to ritual lustration with a range of unguents and liquids, artists began to create their sacred images in copper. Temple inscriptions refer to them as *sheppu tirumeni*, or sacred forms of copper, and as *vitanka*, or minus chisel—in other words, not carved of either wood or stone but rather cast in metal. The conditions leading up to this major shift in material have been lightly bypassed and scholars have assumed that it merely involved using locally available copper. However, with each temple requiring a minimum of ten to twelve bronzes in order to fulfill the requirements of the ritual festival cycle, workshops with foundries would have had to be set up on a very large scale. Additionally, as I have stressed in chapter 1, there is no ore in Tamil Nadu with a sufficiently high concentration of copper to make copper extraction a feasible venture or a profitable undertaking. While a large group of metallurgists believe it may never be possible to pinpoint the specific source of metal used in creating images anywhere in the world, there is strong circumstantial evidence to suggest that one source of copper for Chola bronzes was Sri Lanka's Seruwila belt. Apart from the details provided in chapter 1, the sudden shift from wood to copper that occurred in the ninth century was surely made on the basis of a readily available, reliable, and preferably nearby source of copper.

Sri Lanka, as I have shown, was a Chola obsession for other reasons too. The first was the quest for pearls from the oyster beds in the shallow Gulf of Mannar that lay between Sri Lanka and the southernmost areas of Tamil Nadu and that was largely controlled by the Pandya rulers of Madurai. Vast numbers of pearls are attested to in temple inscriptions as having formed a vital part of the sets of temple jewels gifted to adorn each of the many sacred bronzes. Access to, and preferably control of, the Mannar pearl fisheries was thus a priority for the Cholas. Another equally important reason for Chola preoccupation with Sri Lanka was the fact that the island lay at the center of the ocean trade route between Aden and China. While Chola ports too occupy the same general region, it was easier for ships coming from the Arabian Sea to dock at Sri Lankan ports rather than make the circuit around the island to reach Chola harbors. Navigating the shortcut through the Gulf of Mannar was not feasible, since the sandbanks in the region make it impossible for large ships to traverse these waters. Control over Sri Lankan ports was thus a desirable goal for Chola monarchs.

The earliest temple bronzes were created in the coastal belt that extends some 65 miles south of the Kaveri river and constitutes territory under the control of the early Chola kings. The inscriptions in the temples that carry such bronzes record gifts from a wide range of lay devotees and not from the Chola monarchs themselves; however, these inscriptions invariably commence by establishing the precise date of the gift by specifying the regnal year of the Chola monarch in power. The first portable bronzes, close to 3 feet high together with their pedestals, are surprisingly assured in form and in casting. This seems remarkable considering that sacred bronzes of the previous rulers, the Pallavas, were small objects of personal devotion standing no more than 9 inches high. However, bronze casting as such was known in the neighboring Andhra region of south India, where small Buddhist bronzes had been made since the third or fourth centuries CE.

The almost total lack of dedicatory inscriptions in Tamil temples is a curious phenomenon. Of the 211 stone temples in the Chola heartland comprising the districts of Thanjavur and Nagapattinam in the Kaveri deltaic region, a mere 25 contain information about their builders. Why was there this reticence about claiming construction of temples? While this has led to the suggestion that the early Chola monarchs followed a regressive form of kingship that did not include temple building as one of its characteristics, it is important to review the role played in this surprising absence of dedicatory inscriptions by the fact that so many early stone temples were built at ancient hallowed sites where a shrine of brick and wood already existed. Those who replaced and rebuilt such structures in stone may have considered it inappropriate and even dishonest to claim construction of a temple that they had merely rebuilt. In using the phrase "Chola temples," I am not suggesting that these shrines were built by the Chola monarchs; I use the phrase to indicate that the temples were built in territory controlled by the Chola monarchs. The same applies to the phrase "Chola bronzes," which are rarely royal commissions. As I have pointed out in chapter 2, an inscription along the pedestal of a bronze Uma commences by establishing the date as the eleventh year of Parantaka Chola (917), and then proceeds to inform us that the image was a gift of a local chieftain. We saw too in chapter 5 that a group of eleven diverse individuals pooled their money together to commission the Tiruvenkadu Master to create a bronze Uma and a bronze bull for the Tiruvenkadu temple.

The role of women in building temples, and in dedicating bronzes and jewelry to adorn such bronzes, is of consequence. Queens such as Kokkilan, who built a temple at Tirunamanallur to honor her son, crown prince Rajaditya, and Sembiyan Mahadevi, who built a range of temples that include one in honor of her husband and another in honor of her son, are relatively well-known figures. But the large number of smaller dedications from queens, mothers of queens, attendants of queens; from *tatis* or foster-mothers of princes; and from the intimates or *anukkis* of Rajendra and other monarchs has not been adequately documented or sufficiently recognized. Rajendra's *anukki* Paravai made major donations to the temple at Tiruvarur where she and Rajendra were received by the temple priests with special honors. Nakkan Pavai, the influential *anukki* of Rajendra II, had sufficient authority to create an area of Chidambaram named Gunamenagaipuram after one of her sobriquets, and to provide special inducements to merchants and traders to relocate to this suburb. Equally interesting is the fact that many women, including a few princesses and queens, were major donors of bronze images of Uma; inscriptions often speak of women as having "adopted" Uma as their daughter and having thereby acquired the right to sponsor the celebration of the ritual marriage of their (bronze) "daughter" to (bronze) god Shiva.

The role of irrigation in harnessing the notoriously unreliable waters of the Kaveri, and thereby turning the Chola delta into the rice bowl of the south, may have been understated. I have highlighted it largely to emphasize that agricultural wealth lay at the heart of the ability of Chola chieftains, princes and princesses, women and men from varying walks of life to contribute toward the building of vast numbers of stone temples that they then endowed with sacred bronzes, lavish jewelry to adorn the bronzes, and endowments to ensure regular daily worship as well as the celebration of the many temple festivals held around the year. We saw in chapter 1 that fifty-four days of the year were festival days at the temple at Tiruvarur. Also significant is the role of temple food, referred to by the term *tiru-amudu*, or sacred nectar, created in temple kitchens to be offered ritually to the bronze images and to the immovable stone sanctum image, and then distributed to the temples' various stakeholders. In the last few years, as I visited temples that date back to the Chola period, I too was a recipient of this largesse and was given a leaf-sewn "bowl" of *pongal*, a risotto-like rice dish that I happily accepted and invariably finished. The effect of a range of musical instruments sounded to announce the opening of the shrine or the start of a parade of the bronze deities around the temple, the smell of incense and flowers, and the vision of the richly decorated bronze images, work together today as in Chola times to create an overwhelming sensory experience that animates and inspires an atmosphere of ardent and dedicated worship.

The bronze festival cycle initiated by the Cholas, and sustained by the succeeding Vijayanagara and Nayak dynasties, continued to thrive during British rule, and to this day dominates the religious life of the large towns and major temples of Tamil Nadu. I give just one example. A few years back, I arrived in the port town of Nagapattinam only to discover that the government authorities had announced, the day before, that its schools and public institutions would remain closed on June 30, 2015, so that everyone could partake in a major temple festival. The English-language newspaper, *The Hindu*, carried the following report on the day after:

> Devotees pulled the cars with religious fervor at 7 am through main streets in the town and brought them to rest at about 6 pm. . . . It was a local holiday for schools in Nagapattinam taluk on Tuesday. S. Palanisamy, Collector, was among those who pulled a car in the morning. Vehicular traffic on the Nagapattinam-Nagore highway was diverted through East Coast Road to facilitate smooth flow of traffic.[1]

Today, many small Chola-era temples, including Vadakkalathur, Tandantottam, and Tiruvilakudi, have no bronzes at all. In the light of the smuggling that, unfortunately, has accompanied the thriving art market both in India and overseas, all bronzes from many temples have been removed to safe-houses, referred to as "Icon Centers." Such incarceration to ensure security has had the unforeseen side effect of depriving temples of their ability to conduct festivals. A "loaner" bronze that is not from their own collections is given to these temples for a single day so that they may condense into that one day the celebration of the major annual festival, the *brahmotsavam*, which normally extends over ten days. Many smaller temples and towns have lost the cohesive mechanism that brought the residents together for at least two days in every month and for three multiday festivals in a year. Such gatherings in joyous celebration of the sacred fostered togetherness, mutual understanding, and a tranquil confidence that also provided socioeconomic benefits. When sequestered in Icon Centers, these exquisite bronzes with deep religious significance and aesthetic reputation are not available to priests, to devotees, or to art lovers, thereby depriving the bronzes of their many consequential levels of meaning.

As we take leave of the remarkable bronzes created during the period of Chola rule, several overarching ideas resonate in meaningful ways. We have seen

master artists capable of touching an emotional and aesthetic chord in our hearts,
a depth of devotion that manifests as superb imagery,
zeal to participate in festivals of a celebratory nature,
priestly support to fulfill donors' wishes,
temple obligations to safeguard images, and
a strong female donor base that included princesses and queens.

And what were the circumstances that enabled the accumulation of wealth that translated into this unprecedented creativity in which political turmoil rarely interfered with the production of superb imagery? The key factors were an innovative irrigation system that led to exceptional agricultural prosperity, powerful merchant guilds engaged in lucrative overseas trade, and a quest, via both war and trade, for pearls, coral, rubies, gold, and copper. Certain singular moments in time do indeed generate unprecedented creativity and originality in the arts, and the Chola period was one such exceptional chapter in the artistic history of India. Technology, trade contacts, agricultural prosperity, the socioeconomic milieu, merged and bonded with religious intensity and aesthetic intentionality to result in the creation of superb works of sacred art.

Let me conclude this immersion in the world of the Cholas by indulging in some meditations on the title of this book, and ponder the powerful hold that a supreme deity, visualized as "the thief who stole my heart," exerted over the emotions of devotees. This entrancing being, this Shiva, was conjured up in compelling verbal pictures by the saints, and translated into bronzes of enchanting beauty by Chola artists. India visualizes its divinities as youthful, captivating beings whose bodily beauty is a pointer to their spiritual grandeur; it is an ethos in which physical beauty is viewed as an invariable accompaniment of divine spiritual glory. The saints sang ecstatically of a beauty that enters the heart, and captures the body and soul. Here is how saint Appar invoked Lord Shiva in three consecutive verses of one of his sacred hymns, using words like sugar and honey that just about every language uses for a dearly beloved:

> *Honey, milk, moon, and sun*
> *youth crowned with the celestial white moon,*
> *wisdom incarnate as the fire*
> *that consumed the god of spring—*
> *How should I forget him?*
>
> *Sugar, sweet syrup of sugarcane,*
> *bright one, brilliant as a lightning flash,*
> *golden one, my lord who glitters*
> *like a hill of gems—*
> *How should I forget him?*

Sugarcane, lump of sweet sugar candy (shakkara katti),
bee in the fragrant flower,
light that dwells in the light of every flame
our Lord who loves flower buds gathered at dawn—
How should I forget him?[2]

Mesmerized and enthralled by his beautiful lord, saint Appar expressed his total surrender to Shiva as seen in the joyous and triumphant final lines of three verses from one of his hymns:

I have placed him in my heart

I have encircled him in love's embrace

I have devoured him in desire.[3]

To a multitude of Tamil devotees, their chosen deity Shiva, embodied in bronze, is child saint Sambandar's "thief who stole my heart."

Appendix A
Main Rulers of the Chola Dynasty
A Tentative Genealogy

Note: Regnal years routinely overlap, since it was the Chola custom for the crown prince to rule together with his father for a few years. Rajaraja I and Rajendra I are set in bold type to highlight that it was during their reigns that the Chola empire was at the height of its power and territorial expanse.

Vijayalaya	855–871
Aditya	871–905/6
Parantaka	905/6–955
Gandaraditya	949/50–957
Queen Sembiyan Mahadevi	active 941–1001
Sundara Chola	956–973
Aditya Karikala (jointly with his father)	956–969
Uttama Chola	969–987
Rajaraja I	**985–1014**
Rajendra I	**1012–1044**
Rajadhiraja	1018–1054
Rajendra II	1052–1064
Vira Rajendra	1062–1069
Adirajendra	1067–1071
Kulottunga I	1070–1120
Vikrama Chola	1118–1135
Kulottunga II	1133–1150
Rajaraja II	1146–1173
Rajadhiraja II	1166–1181
Kulottunga III	1178–1218
Rajaraja III	1216–1260
Rajendra III	1246–1279

Appendix B
Assemblages of Sacred Bronzes

Inscriptional Evidence

Throughout this book, we have seen that the exteriors of Chola temples—their walls, base moldings, pillars, and even grille windows—are covered with inscriptions that relate in one way or another to the temple in question. We read of gifts of gold to conduct rituals pertaining to sacred bronzes, of bronzes themselves and of jewels to adorn them, of cattle and goats whose milk was converted to ghee to light temple lamps, of inspections of temple premises, and a host of administrative details. Occasionally, such records yield information about the complete set of bronzes, or a substantial group of bronzes, that an individual temple possesses. This appendix provides information regarding the bronzes housed in four temples. In the case of Rajaraja's Great Temple at Thanjavur, the information is collected from an entire series of inscriptions, each recording a gift from a different royal or aristocratic donor. With the other three temples, the information comes from a single inscription.

I. Rajaraja's Great Temple at Thanjavur

This section provides a consolidated list of sixty bronzes (sixty-six if bronzes in a group are counted individually) gleaned from a range of records contained in *South Indian Inscriptions*, volume II, numbers 1, 6, 9, 11, 29, 30, 32, 34, 35, 38, 39, 40, 42, 44, 46, 47, 49, 50, 51, 53, 55, 56, 79, 80, 81, 83, 84, 91, and 95. These records are inscribed largely on the pillars and the side walls of the pillared enclosure surrounding the temple that was constructed by the general of Rajaraja's army, Krishna Raman. The bronzes are variously gifted by the emperor himself; his elder sister Kundavai; his queens Lokamahadevi, Panchavan Mahadevi, Chola Mahadevi, and four other consorts; the temple *srikaryam* officer Adittan Suriyan; Chola general Krishna Raman; a group of court officials; a highly placed musician; and Rajaraja's guru Ishana Shiva Pandita. In most cases, the size of the bronze is given, while occasionally its weight is also provided.

The conversion into modern measurements is made on the basis of 1 *muram* = 34.58 centimeters; 1 *shan* = 17.28 centimeters; 1 *viral* = 1.44 centimeters; 1 *torai* = 18 millimeters. It should be noted here that the equivalent measurements for the Chola period, as provided in Jan Gyllenbok's recent *Encyclopedia of Historical Metrology, Weights and Measures*, volume I (Cambridge: Birkhauser Boston, 2018), vary from these. If we wish to follow Gyllenbok, we should round up the actual measurements, making the images somewhat larger, both at Thanjavur and in the following section II at Tiruvaduturai.

With the exception of two images of gold, four Vishnu images in silver, and a brass Shiva as "Lord of Tevaram," all other images are bronze.

1. Gold linga set with five gems to represent the five aspects of Shiva (*Golakai Devar*)
    Size not available; weight approximately 4.4 kilograms
2. Gold Shiva as Guardian of the Sacred Site (*Kshetrapala*)
    5.9 centimeters; weight = 1/3 kilogram
3. Dancing Shiva (*Adavallar Dakshina Meru Vitankar*)
    Not available
4. His consort Uma
    Not available
5. Dancing Shiva (*Adavallar*)
    41.5 centimeters
6. His consort Uma
    33.4 centimeters
7. Victor of Three Cities (*Tanjai Alagar*) with Mushalagan at his feet, together with consort Uma, on a common pedestal
    97.9 centimeters and 86.4 centimeters
8. Victor of Three Cities (*Tanjai Vitankar*)
    Not available
9. His consort Uma
    Not available
10. Shiva and Uma on Mount Meru with Ganesha, Skanda, and others (*Mahameru Vitankar*)
    Shiva: not available; Uma =19.44 centimeters from mountain base to top of her head
11. Begging Lord (*Pichcha Devar*)
    74.1 centimeters
12. Group of seven images celebrating story of saint Chandesha
    Tallest image, of standing Chandesha, is 33.4 centimeters

13. Five-bodied Shiva (*Panchadehamurti*)
    Central image = 37.4 centimeters
14. Four-armed Shiva as Teacher resting one foot on Mushalagan, seated on a mountain with sages (*Dakshinamurti*)
    Mountain = 17.2 centimeters; Shiva rises 25.9 centimeters above mountain
15. Shiva as Rider of the Bull (*Rishabhavahana*)
    68.5 centimeters; bull = 58.14 centimeters
16. His consort
    59.9 centimeters
17. Shiva as Drinker of Poison (*Srikantha*)
    46.7 centimeters
18. Marriage group of Shiva, Uma, Vishnu, and Brahma (*Kalyanasundarar*)
    Shiva = 70.5 centimeters; Uma = 57.6 centimeters; common pedestal = 12.9 centimeters
19. Shiva manifesting within the *linga*, with Vishnu and Brahma (*Lingodbhava*)
    42.4 centimeters
20. Shiva as Lord of Beasts (*Pasupata*)
    Not available
21. Shiva as Half Woman (*Ardhanari*), with the Uma half-plated with brass
    38.1 centimeters
22. Eight-armed Shiva as Guardian of the Site (*Kshetrapala*)
    43 centimeters
23. Two-armed fierce Shiva dancing (*Bhairava*)
    38.8 centimeters
24. Shiva as Divine Hunter Confronting Arjuna (*Kirata-arjuniya*)
    Not available
25. Seated Shiva and Uma with Skanda and Ganesha
    From top of pedestal to top of head: Shiva = 20.8 centimeters; Uma = 16.5 centimeters; Skanda = 7.9 centimeters; Ganesha = 7.2 centimeters
26. Durga Parameshvari
    48.9 centimeters
27. Seated Kali (*Kala Pidari*)
    34.9 centimeters
28–31. Vasudeva (four Vishnu images in silver)
    Sizes not available; largest weight = 1 kilogram; next = 1/2 kilogram; others much smaller
32. Maha Vishnu
    40.3 centimeters
33. Surya, the solar deity
    37.4 centimeters
34. Four-armed Subrahmanya (son of Shiva and Uma)
    34.7 centimeters
35. Ganesha standing
    25.9 centimeters
36. Ganesha standing
    14.4 centimeters
37. Ganesha standing
    26.9 centimeters
38. Ganesha standing (four-armed)
    40.86 centimeters
39. Ganesha seated with shrub
    12.9 centimeters; shrub 0.9 centimeter
40. Ganesha seated
    5 centimeters
41. Ganesha seated
    2.8 centimeters
42. Ganesha dancing
    6.4 centimeters
43. Ganesha dancing
    27.7 centimeters
44. Sundara Chola, Rajaraja's father
    Not available
45. Vanavan Mahadevi, Rajaraja's mother
    Not available
46. King Rajaraja (*Periya Perumal*)
    56.8 centimeters
47. Queen Lokamahadevi
    46.8 centimeters
48. Saint Patanjali (half man, half snake)
    78.3 centimeters
49. Three-legged, emaciated sage Bhringi
    58.1 centimeters
50. Four-armed *Chandrashekhara* as Lord of the Tevaram (*Tevara Devar*), in brass
    11.1 centimeters
51. Saint Chandesha
    59 centimeters; ax = 18.7 centimeters
52. Saint Sundarar
    31.6 centimeters
53. His wife Paravai
    30.6 centimeters
54. Saint Appar
    41.7 centimeters
55. Child Saint Sambandar
    41 centimeters
56. Saint Miladu-Udaiyar
    40.3 centimeters

57–59. Saint Siruttondar, his wife, and son Sirala
    36 centimeters; 33.1 centimeters; 28.8 centimeters
60. Rajaraja's guru, Ishana Shiva Pandita
    Not available

II. Tiruvaduturai Temple

An inscription at the Tiruvaduturai Temple, dated to the year 1018 during the reign of Rajendra, gives us a list of jewels given by Rajendra's mother-in-law, his guru, and two ladies on the court to a set of twenty-five bronzes that already existed in the temple. The inscription comes from the *Annual Report on Indian Epigraphy, 1925*; the transcript was made available to us courtesy of Dr. M. D. Sampath of the Epigraphical Survey of India, Mysuru. If we follow Gyllenbok and round up the measurements, Shiva as Rider of the Bull would be larger than any known bronze of this form.

1. Dancing Shiva (*Adiyarulumudaiyar*, Lord Who Gives Grace by Dancing)
    103.6 centimeters
2. His consort (*Nampirattiyar*, our lady)
    36 centimeters
3. Shiva as Lord Who Sports a Crescent Moon (*Chandrashekhara*)
    69.1 centimeters
4. His consort (*Tampirattiyar*, his lady)
    34.5 centimeters
5. *Chandrashekhara*, or Lord Crowned with the Moon
    18.7 centimeters
6. Uma as Beauty of the Three Worlds (*Tribhuvanasundari*)
    103.6 centimeters
7. Ganesha
    34.5 centimeters
8. Shiva as Guardian of the Site (*Kshetrapala*)
    34.5 centimeters
9. A second Shiva as Guardian of the Site (*Kshetrapala*)
    23 centimeters
10–12. Shiva as Rider of the Bull (*Rishabhavahana*), with consort and bull
    103.6 centimeters
13. Shiva as Enchanting Mendicant (*Bhikshatana*), with deer and dwarf
    73.4 centimeters
14. Shiva as Half Woman (*Ardhanari*)
    34.5 centimeters
15. Shiva as Teacher seated beneath tree (*Dakshinamurti*)
    34.5 centimeters
16. Uma as Consort of the Bedroom Chamber (*Palliarai Devi*)
    69.1 centimeters
17. Uma with Skanda
    69.1 centimeters
18. Trident (*Astra Devar*)
    Not available
19. Bull
    Not available
20. Seated saint Chandesha
    34.5 centimeters
21. Saint Appar
    40.3 centimeters
22. Child Saint Sambandar
    43.2 centimeters
23. Saint Sundarar
    43.2 centimeters
24. Portrait of mother (*tammaiyaka varta*) of Kalahastipichar (madman of Kalahasti)
    34.5 centimeters
25. Portrait lamp (*tanaku varta vilakku*) of Kaviniyan Mahendra Neelan
    not available

III. Avalivanallur Temple

The complete group of bronzes commissioned by this temple is not available to us. Inscription no. 201 from *South Indian Inscriptions*, volume VIII, reflects the donation in the year 1226, during the reign of Rajaraja III, of a single major merchant donor, Tamparisudaiyan Adichchadevan, known as Amarakon. He may have built the temple, since it is named after him as the Tamparisudaiya-nayanar temple (today known as Sakshinathasvamin).

1. Ganesha (*Vinayaka*)
2. Subrahmanya and consort (*Amberinda Perumal* and *Nachchiyar*)
3. Shiva and Uma (*Atkondanayakar* and *Nachchiyar*)
4. Consort of the Bedroom Chamber (*Tirupalliarai Nachchiyar*)
5. Child Saint Sambandar (*Aludaiya Pillaiyar*)

IV. Tiruvilakudi Temple

This list of thirteen bronzes (eighteen if bronzes in a group are counted individually) comes from inscription no. 141 in the *Annual Report on Epigraphy, 1926*, courtesy of Mr. Karuppiah of the Epigraphical Survey of India, Mysuru. Dated to the year 1232, during the reign of Rajaraja III, the images are those reconsecrated by a wealthy devotee, Mavulavan Malayan, after retrieving bronzes that earlier went missing from the temple.

1. Shiva and Uma (*Manavalanambi* and *Nachchiyar*)
2. Vinayaka or Ganesha
3. Consort of the Bedroom Chamber (*Palliarai Nachchiyar*)
4. Dancing Shiva (*Kuttadi Arulakinra Devar*)
5. Shiva and Uma (*Tampiranar* and *Nachchiyar*)
6. Shiva and Uma (*Vedavana Nayakar* and *Nachchiyar*)
7. The Lady of the Love Fort (*Kamakottamudaiya Periya Nachchiyar*)
8. Shiva and Uma (*Atkondanayakar* and *Nachchiyar*)
9. Saint Chandesha (*Adichandesvara Pillaiyar*)
10. Shiva as Lord with the Bull (*Rishabhadevar*)
11. Child Saint Sambandar (*Aludaiya Pillaiyar*)
12. Saint Appar
13. Saint Sundarar and wife Paravai (*Sundara Perumal* and *Paravai*)

Appendix C
Tenth-Century Chola Yoginis in Context

While this volume is devoted to an exploration of the milieu of bronze portable images and their crucial role in mainstream worship in Tamil Nadu, I turn briefly to a seemingly sinister aspect of the sacred feminine that existed alongside the bronze festival tradition. This unusual stream of worship focused on the divine feminine revolves around a group of female goddesses known as yoginis, generally sixty-four in number, worshipped within circular temples that remained open to the sky, through a series of esoteric rites outside of brahmanic temple ritual.[1] That a Chola yogini temple once existed in the vicinity of Kanchipuram is known from a set of seated yoginis carved on granite slabs measuring roughly 4 feet in height, and seen today in museums around the world, courtesy of collector-scholar Jouveau-Dubreuil and an intrepid early twentieth-century dealer, C. T. Loo, based in Paris.[2] My decision to briefly reference the yoginis here is based on two considerations. The first is the remarkably close stylistic relationship they bear to early Chola temple images in both stone and bronze. The second is the fact that a text describing the yoginis was composed in 959 in the town of Melpadi, a mere 65 kilometers from Kanchipuram, the likely find spot of the yoginis and hence the possible location of the yogini temple.[3] The Chola yoginis, all four-armed, have fangs at the corners of their mouth, wickedly curved eyebrows, loose hair that stands up around their heads in fearsome halo-like formation or is held under control with a crown, snakes and skulls in their adornment, and a skull-cup that rests in their left front palms. Each goddess sits cross-legged on the ground with her vehicle, or *vahana*, lightly incised on the narrow band below her feet.

Three ferocious yoginis with a commanding presence are housed today in the Musée Guimet in Paris (fig. C.1a, b, c). One yogini has a withered neck[4] and a lean torso with loose, hanging breasts and a stern face with hollow cheeks, bulging eyes, dangerously curved eyebrows, and sharp curved fangs descending below her lower lips, with deep furrows around her mouth. A human skull is placed centrally above her diadem, which can barely hold back her unkempt hair spread out to create a halo-like effect, and dangling *makara* earrings rest on her shoulders. A rearing snake is knotted around each arm to serve as an armlet, and a medallion necklace and a sacred thread adorn her torso. Her short skirt is held in place by a modest ornamental belt, and she wears simple anklets, with an iguana as her vehicle. Of the two other yoginis, both with fuller bodies, one holds a trident and has a pecking goose as vehicle, while the second wears a sacred thread studded with skulls and has a serpent as vehicle.

A truly formidable yogini seen today in the British Museum wears a severed human hand as adornment in one ear and a serpent in the other (fig. C.2), while a stunningly beautiful yogini holding a hammer and nasty-looking pincers or tongs, in the collection of the Royal Ontario Museum, has a serpent mount (fig. C.3). A yogini surviving only as a damaged torso enveloped with snakes bears a striking resemblance to the bronze image of Kali that we just considered (fig. C.4; see fig. 8.6a, b).

Reflecting the potent ferocity of these heady images is a Sanskrit literary text, *Yasastilaka*, or "Mark of Fame," composed for the Rashtrakuta king Krishnadeva, the arch enemy of the Cholas, in Saka year 881, which corresponds to 959. Ten years prior, Krishnadeva had defeated Parantaka Chola in the disastrous battle of Takkolam at which the Rashtrakuta ally, the Ganga king, had killed Parantaka's son and crown prince Rajaditya. Inscribed gifts to temples in the northern parts of Chola territory are dated in the regnal years of the Rashtrakuta king in place of the Chola monarchs, indicating that Krishnadeva's authority was accepted in Chola territory for almost twenty years[5] after the 949 Takkolam battle. Krishnadeva was camped in the Chola kingdom, celebrating the battle's victorious aftermath, when his poet, who had accompanied him on his mission south, composed this text.[6] Considering his graphic description of the yoginis, one cannot but wonder if poet Somadevasuri actually visited this Chola period yogini temple.

As abruptly as darkness descends at nightfall, even so, without warning did the Mahayoginis appear out of the sky, the earth, the depths of the nether regions, and the four corners of space. They traversed the skies at tremendous speed, causing their locks of hair to come undone, and these flowing tresses swept across the sky, obscuring the Sun, Moon, and planets, who in their boisterous protest angered the other denizens of the aerial regions. In their

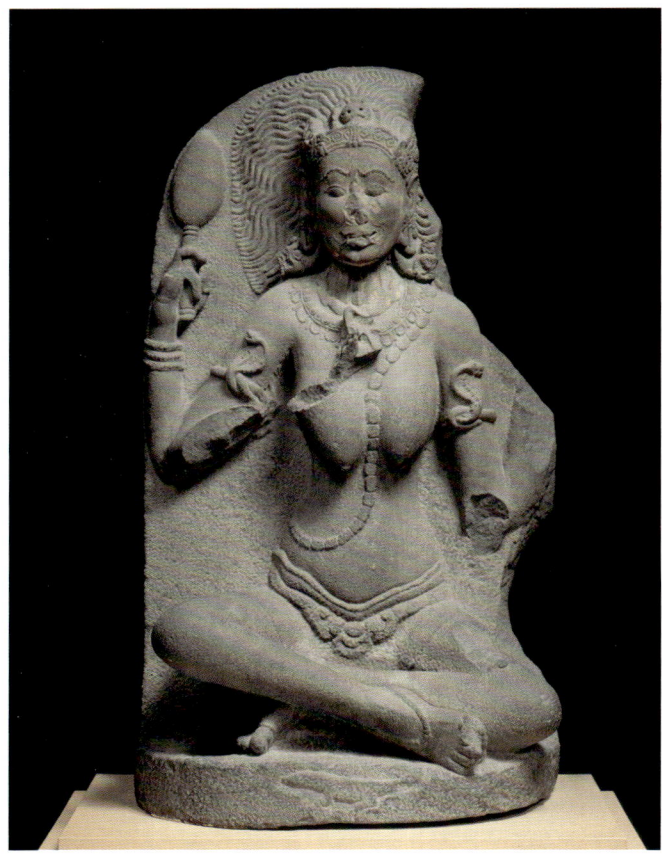

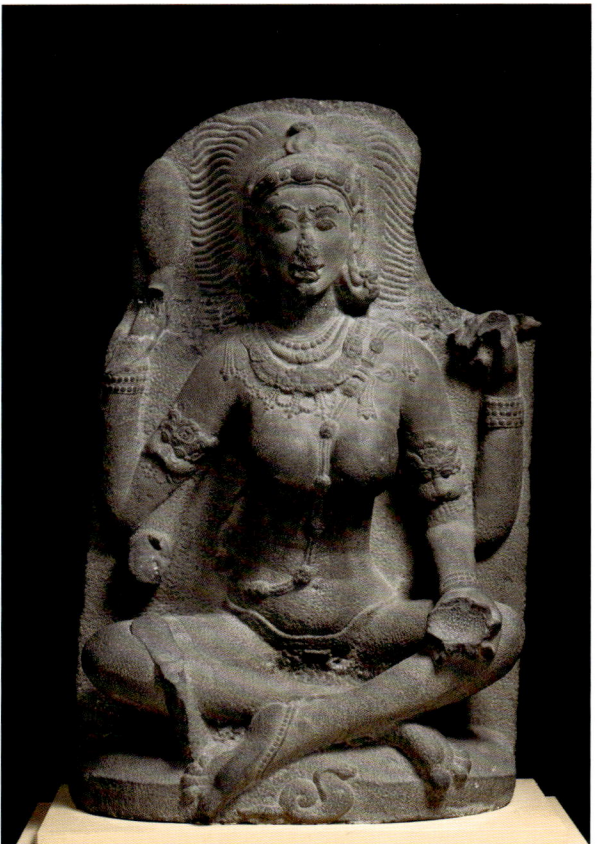

Figure C.1. (a, b, c). Yoginis, first quarter of tenth century, Musée National des Arts Asiatiques—Guimet, Paris.

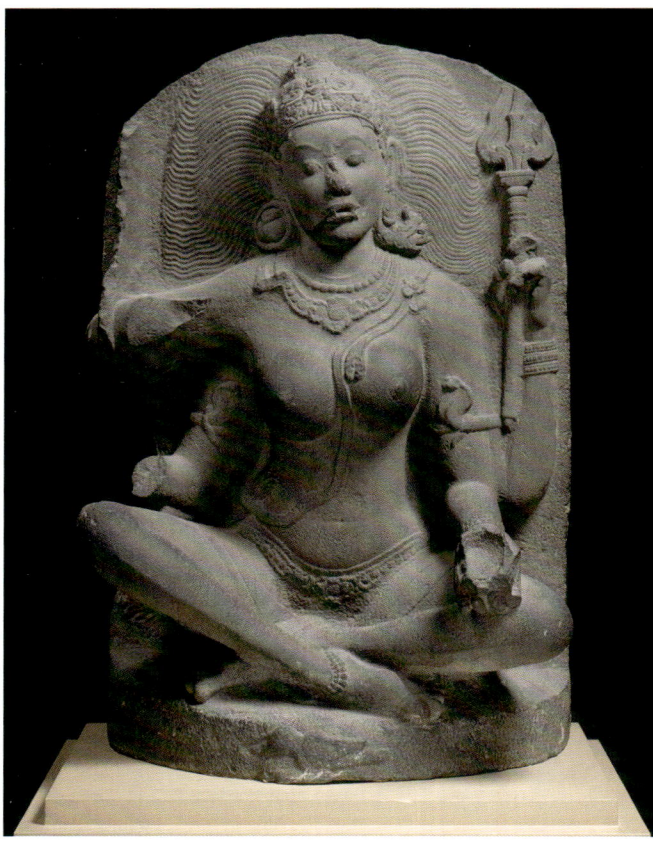

hands they held staffs topped with skulls and decorated with myriads of little bells which jingled furiously with the speed of their flight and sometimes shattered into hundreds of fragments. Their approach was heralded by this chiming, tinkling, pealing reverberation which caused dancing Narada to appear on the scene, much to the confusion and embarrassment of the Yoginis.

Sparks issuing from the third eye on their foreheads were fanned into flames by the gasping of the helpless serpents ruthlessly enmeshed in the tangled masses of their hair; and these flames leapt forth so high as to singe the banners of the Sun's aerial chariot. The ornamented designs on their cheeks were painted with blood which was being lapped up by the many snakes adorning their ears. Hovering over the gruesome human skulls decorating their heads were vast numbers of giant vultures who obstructed the rays of the Sun. Tripping over one another in their haste, the Yoginis glowered repulsively and unleashed a host of tremendous and terrifying howls. Startled by the uproar, the Moon's deer bolted off, trailing behind it scrambling constellations of stars entrusted with its care.

Tired by their great journey across the sky, the Mahayoginis stretched out their great tongues to drink the waters of the celes-

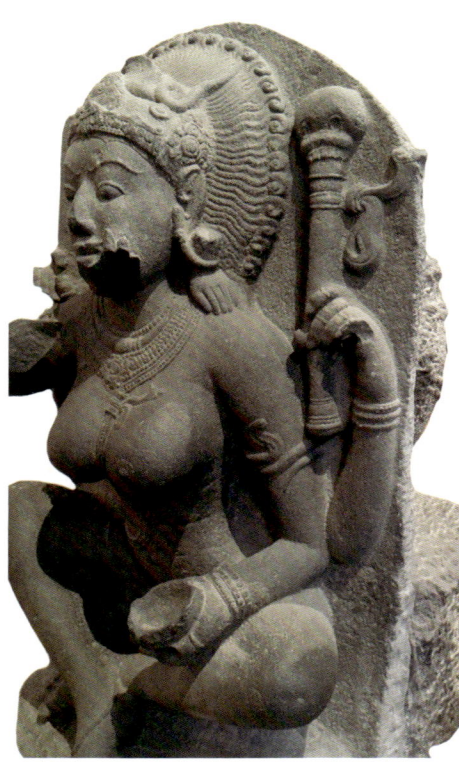

Figure C.2. Yogini with Human Hand as Ear Ornament, first quarter of tenth century, British Museum, London.

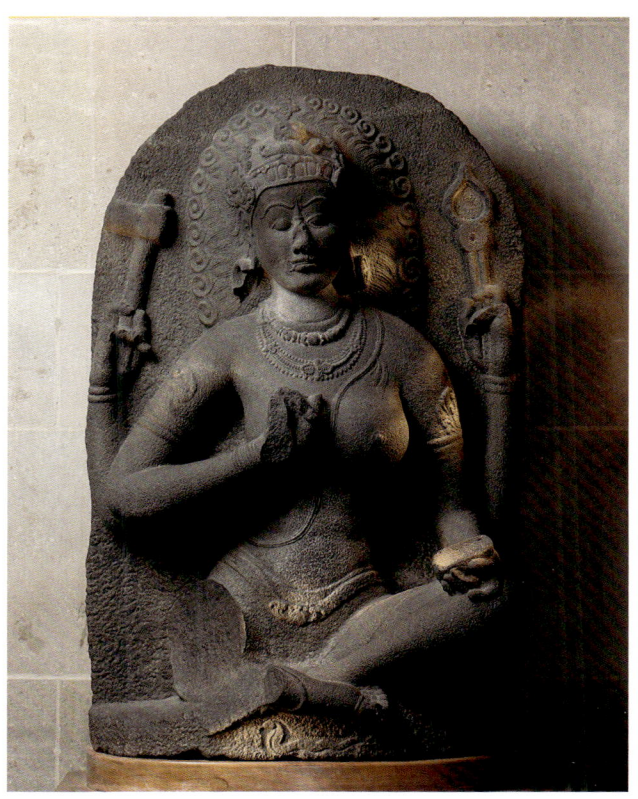

Figure C.3. Yogini Holding Hammer and Pincers, first quarter of tenth century, Royal Ontario Museum, Toronto, purchase made possible with the support of The Reuben Wells Leonard Bequest Fund.

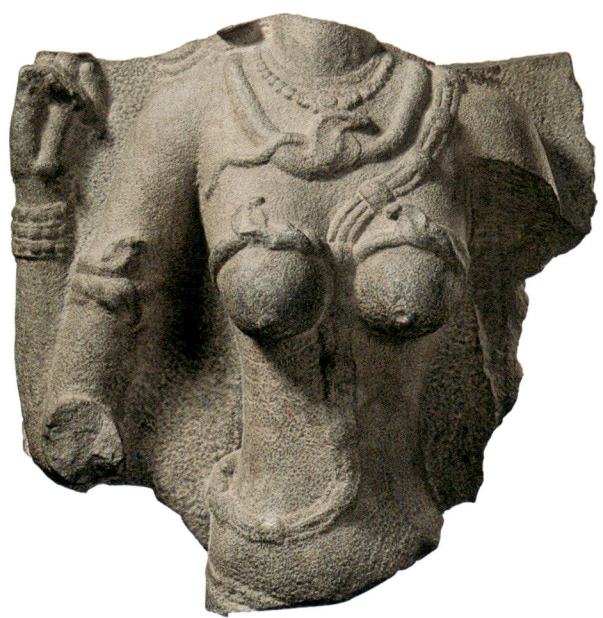

Figure C.4. Snake-Wrapped Yogini Torso, first quarter of tenth century, Museum Rietberg, Zurich, Gift of Eduard von der Heydt.

tial Ganges and by this action angered the seven great sages (the stars of the Great Bear). Between the edges of the long teeth protruding from their mouths, the Yoginis held the clouds, thus outclassing Varaha who held but the earth in his tusks. The companions of the gods were alarmed by the vibrating resonance of their anklet bells as the Yoginis danced the distance between the sky and the earth. Their dark loose tresses splaying out across the daytime sky, darkened it, and their terrible yet glowing skull crowns stood out among the black tresses like stars at night. Just as the night of destruction will appear intolerable and long to the world, so these Mahayoginis appeared intolerably ferocious and long-limbed, as they occupied the space within the temple of their Great Goddess, Caṇḍamari.[7]

Slightly less ferocious yoginis wear a conical crown that holds their tresses in control, and they carry a less fearsome group of attributes; the largest of the group, 52½ inches high, is a bell-ringing yogini with a pecking goose as mount (fig. C.5).[8] An imperious yogini, holding a jar that probably has medicinal-cum-magical associations, has circular tattoos or face paint on both cheeks and between her eyebrows,

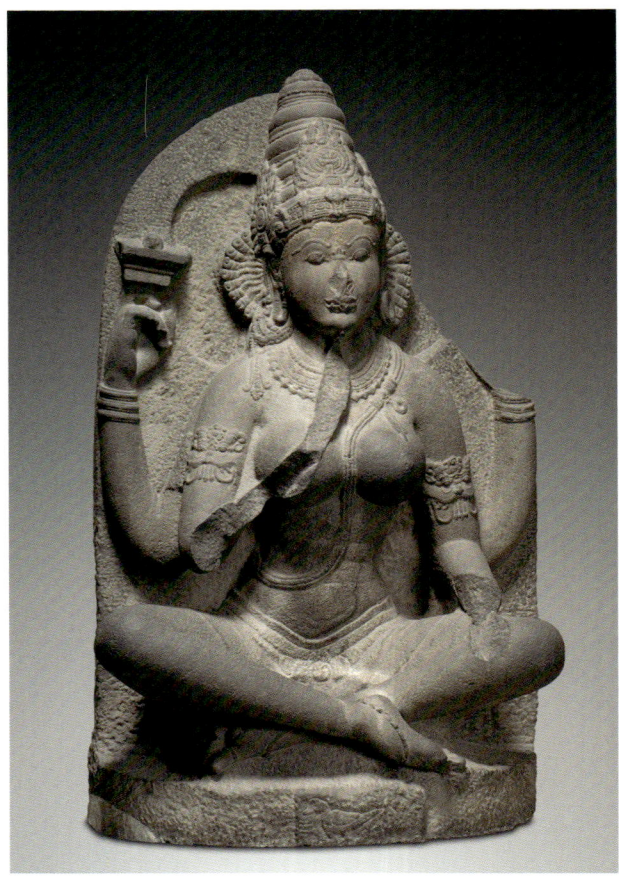

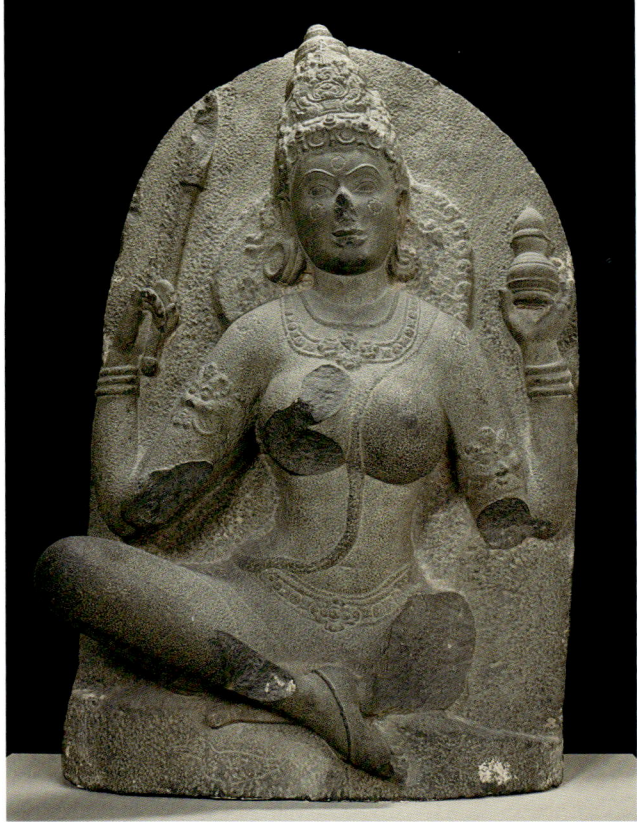

Figure C.5. Bell-Ringing Yogini, first quarter of tenth century, The Nelson-Atkins Museum of Art, Kansas City, Purchase: William Rockhill Nelson Trust.

Figure C.6. Medicine Jar Yogini, first quarter of tenth century, Minneapolis Institute of Art, The Christina N. and Swan J. Turnblad Memorial Fund.

Figure C.7. Shield-Bearing Yogini, first quarter of tenth century, Detroit Institute of Arts, USA Founders Society Purchase.

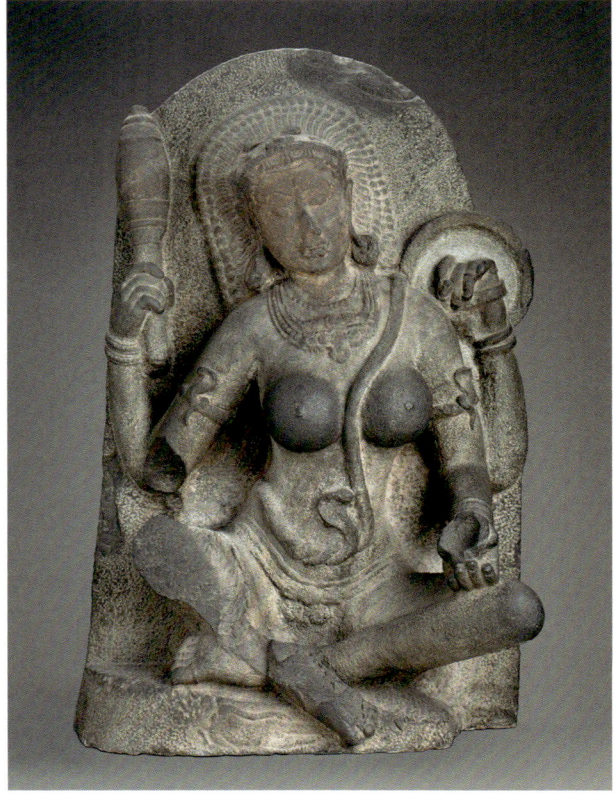

and a goose mount, while a shield-bearing yogini has a headless human corpse as her mount (figs. C.6 and C.7). Perhaps the least fearsome, yet most solemn and intense yogini holds a broom of sacred *darbha* grass and a "dust-pan";[9] these are not mundane everyday objects of household use but rather indispensable tools to be used to prepare sacred space for sacrificial ritual and speak to her elevated status, her authority, and her sanctity (fig. C.8). She too has a goose mount. A vajra-bearing yogini in the Madras Museum, badly damaged and today missing her head, wears a snake knotted as a necklace and has a goose as vehicle. The popularity of the goose mount may lie in the fact that Indian lore credits the pecking goose, or *hamsa*, with the ability to distinguish the genuine from the false; the *hamsa* is featured in literary texts, for instance, as able to distinguish milk from water.[10]

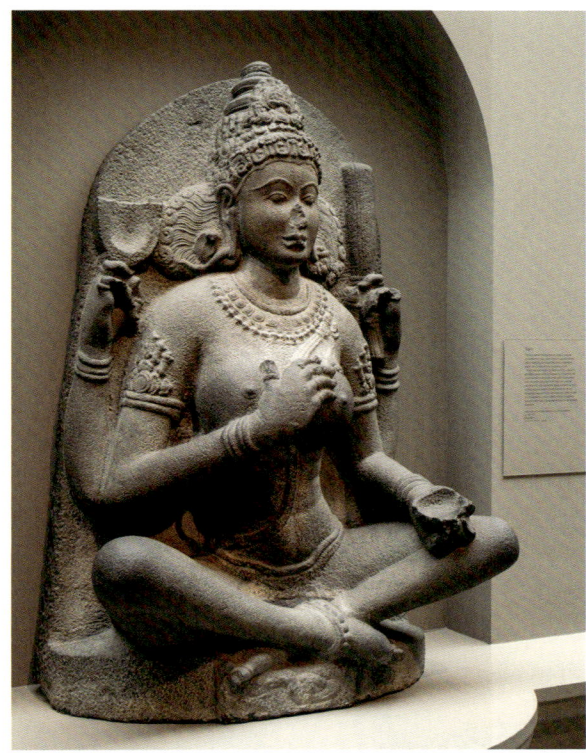

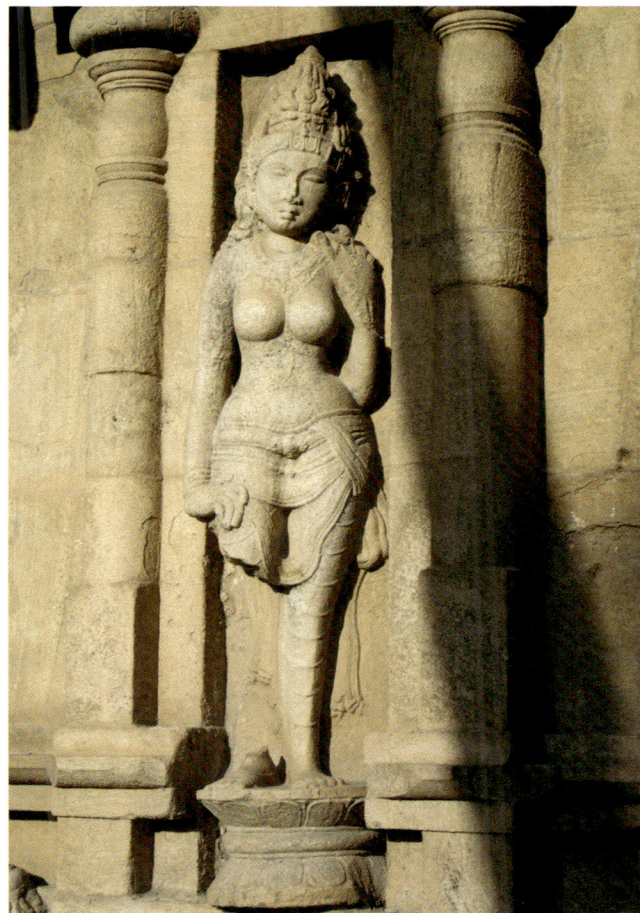

Figure C.8. Yogini with Sacrificial Accessories, first quarter of tenth century, Arthur M. Sackler Gallery, Smithsonian Institution, Washington, DC.

Figure C.9. Attendant on wall of Srinivasanallur temple, "Capital style," early tenth century.

Figure C.10. Detail of Uma (see fig. 2.11), "Capital style," ca. 900, The Metropolitan Museum of Art, New York.

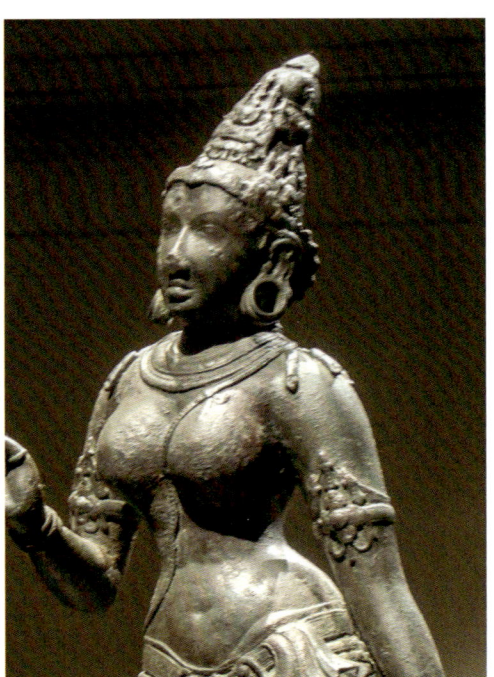

The yogini images bear striking similarities in the handling of form and bodily proportions and in their broad faces to Chola stone sculptures and temple bronzes of the "Capital style." A close relationship exists, for instance, between the medicine jar yogini or the bell-ringing yogini, and the female chowri-bearers of the early tenth century on the walls of a Chola temple at Srinivasanallur west of Trichy. Despite the fearsome aspect of the yoginis as compared to peaceable female attendants holding a fly-whisk, the treatment of the figures is strikingly similar (fig. C.9). One may also compare the yoginis with a bronze Uma whom we assigned in chapter 2 to the Capital style in the early tenth century. In spite of the seeming difficulties of a comparison between a seated yogini and a standing Uma, it is easy to discern similar bodily proportions, a broad face, and a parallel treatment of ornamentation (fig. C.10). The Chola yoginis were carved early in the tenth century by artists working in the stylistic mode of the central, capital area.

TENTH-CENTURY CHOLA YOGINIS

Appendix D
Trace Metal Analysis on Five Chola Bronzes

MATTHEW L. CLARKE,* NICOLE C. LITTLE,**
AND DONNA K. STRAHAN***

The composition of bronze objects can provide clues as to the methods employed in their manufacture and potential sources of raw materials. Indeed, several studies of Indian and Sri Lankan bronzes have been performed using techniques to examine the chemical or elemental components, with examination by trace metal and lead isotope analyses being frequently utilized.[1] Such research typically faces the challenges of examining a limited number of objects and related materials (ores, slags), and working with very small sample sizes that may include heterogeneities in the composition. In these conditions, it is often daunting to quantify the variability found using a given measurement, as it may pertain to the object heterogeneity, processing methods, and source materials. Here, only a small number of objects were examined and analyzed for their trace metal composition. For this reason, the analytical methods and data are reported, yet definitive sourcing is not pursued. It is the aim of this work to share the data in order to fit within continued studies of similar objects.

Experimental Methods

Five objects were examined: three from the Freer Gallery of Art, one from the Asia Society, and one from the Norton Simon Museum (Table D.1). One brass and two bronze certified reference materials were chosen to span concentration ranges for the trace elements of interest, particularly cobalt and nickel (MBH Analytical Limited 31X7835.9A, 32XLB14G, 32XLB17A). For each object or reference material, a small sample was taken from the bottom of the objects using a carbide drill. The surface layer was discarded and the drill bit cleaned before further drilling of the object. A small amount of material (10–50 milligrams [mg]) was removed in the form of small filings and stored in plastic centrifuge tubes.

Metal composition analysis was done by two methods. First, x-ray fluorescence (XRF) analysis was performed. XRF primarily reports the composition of the elements residing at the surface of a material and cannot distinguish chemical structure, oxidation states, or isotopes. The bronze filings were placed on thin Mylar films over analysis cups. A collimated XRF beam was aligned over the pile of filings, and triplicate measurements were performed over different areas of the pile. The filings were kept for further analysis. XRF was performed on a Bruker Artax XRF (at the National Gallery of Art, Washington, DC) using a tungsten anode operating at 50 kilovolts (kV) and 700 microamps (μA) with a 25 micron nickel excitation filter and a 1 millimeter (mm) collimator for an analysis time of 200 seconds (s) with a silicon drift detector. The analysis was carried out in ambient air. Quantitation was performed using Bruker MQuant software based on a fundamental parameters calibration of the instrument.

The samples were then prepared for analysis by mass spectrometry using a GBC 9500 time-of-flight inductively coupled plasma-mass spectrometer (TOF-ICP-MS). The bronze filings were weighed into trace metal free vials before digestion with 5 milliliters (mL) of concentrated nitric acid. Samples were heated at 100°C for 3 hours to fully digest the metals. Aliquots of 100 milligrams (mg) for each sample and reference material were diluted into 50 grams (g) of 2% nitric acid (in 10 megaohm deionized [DI] water) for analysis by TOF-ICP-MS. Solutions were ionized in an 8,000–10,000 Kelvin (K) plasma torch before passing through a three-stage interface (sampler and skimmer cones) into the high-vacuum time-of-flight detector. The resulting ions were then quantified by comparing the results to a range of elemental solution standards.

Prior to data acquisition, the TOF-ICP-MS was turned on and allowed to warm up for a minimum of 40 minutes, allowing the instrument's components to reach their optimum operating temperature and vacuum pressure, greatly reducing background noise and drift. Once the instrument had stabilized, a 10 parts per billion (ppb) multielement solution standard was used to optimize the instrument settings to maximize sensitivity while minimizing noise. Then data were generated for blank and multielement solution

---
* Freer Gallery of Art and Arthur M. Sackler Gallery, Smithsonian Institution, Washington, DC.
** Museum Conservation Institute, Smithsonian Institution, Suitland, Maryland.
*** Freer Gallery of Art and Arthur M. Sackler Gallery, Smithsonian Institution, Washington, DC.

Table D.1 Bronze Objects Analyzed

Freer Gallery of Art

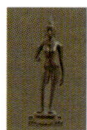

F1929.84
Queen Sembiyan Mahadevi as the Goddess Parvati (fig. 4.1a)

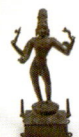

F1997.28
Shiva Vinadhara (Holder of the Lute)
(fig. request Has this come in from the Freer?)

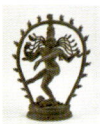

F2003.2
Shiva Nataraja (fig. 4.16a)

Asia Society

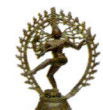

AS 1979.020
Shiva as Lord of the Dance (Nataraja)
(fig. 4.18a)

Norton Simon Museum

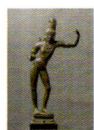

NS F.1972.45.07.S
Shiva as Destroyer of Three Cities (fig. 1.16)

---

standards at the following concentrations: 1 ppb, 5 ppb, 10 ppb, 20 ppb, and 30 ppb. Following measurement of the blank and elemental standards, each sample was analyzed for five replicates after a 60 s delay, thereby allowing the solution to reach the plasma torch. Each sample was analyzed for the following isotopes: silver (Ag), aluminum (Al), arsenic (As), bismuth (Bi), cadmium (Cd), chromium (Cr), cobalt (Co), manganese (Mn), nickel (Ni), lead (Pb), antimony (Sb), selenium (Se), tin (Sn), and zinc (Zn). Four-point calibration curves based on the measurement of the standard solutions and blanks were used to calibrate the count rates in the unknown solutions. Final numbers (expressed as percent mass) for each sample were obtained by multiplying the standard-calibrated data by the final dilution factor. Due to very low concentrations in the samples (most below detection limits), the values for Al, Cd, Cr, Mn, and Se will not be discussed. Additionally, due to the poor stability of Sn under these digestion conditions, the Sn value will not be reported for TOF-ICP-MS.[2]

Discussion

Results for the analysis of the reference materials are presented in Table D.2. When comparing the concentrations obtained by ICP-MS to the Certificate of Analysis (COA), the values of the former were consistently lower than those reported by the COA (sometimes in excess of 2× less). This is expected due to the elemental inhomogeneity of bronzes, particularly when comparing different techniques with varying sensitivities. The XRF results have more variability. This is also expected due to the small sample analysis area and surface sensitivity, leading to greater deviations due to sample heterogeneity. The presence of lead inclusions in bronzes has been reported, leading to changes in lead content distribution, with notable differences in the lead concentrations between corroded and noncorroded areas.[3] These effects of surface enrichment and nonhomogeneity can be lessened by sampling the bronzes via drilling and discarding the surface area, and by performing the analysis using solution-based ICP-MS-TOF, as was done in this study.[4] However, some variability will remain.

With these challenges in mind, there are trends that can be observed in the Chola bronzes (Table D.3). For instance, the iron concentration falls in the range of 0.5–1.5%. F1929.84 stands out with its very high copper content (95%), while the other four range from 82–85%. Three of the bronzes have similar profiles: F1997.28, F2003.2, and AS 1979.020. The remaining bronze, NS F.1972.45.07.S, is somewhat similar, but the zinc concentration is noticeably

Table D.2 Elemental Composition in Mass Percentage for the Bronze Reference Materials

Name	Result	Ag	As	Bi	Co	Cu	Fe	Ni	Pb	Sb	Sn	Zn	Co/Ni
31X7835.9A	Certified	2.12	0.107	0.810	0.081	78.48	0.408	0.1	1.024	0.445	1.48	14.34	0.813
	XRF	1.396	0.105	n.m.	0.086	79.839	0.399	0.228	1.533	0.235	0.783	14.426	0.378
	ICP	1.262	0.063	0.437	0.047	n.m.	n.m.	0.067	0.632	0.266	n.m.	10.785	0.704
32XLB14G	Certified	0.12	0.05	0.720	0.089	77.01	0.009	0.254	15.42	0.075	5.63	0.586	0.35
	XRF	0.091	0.056	n.m.	0.112	77.059	0.04	0.478	17.718	0.047	3.222	0.417	0.234
	ICP	0.076	0.039	0.512	0.05	n.m.	n.m.	0.177	19.665	0.102	n.m.	0.386	0.281
32XLB17A	Certified	0.911	1.51	0.220	0.008	74.83	0.488	0.465	9.83	4.1	5.97	0.634	0.018
	XRF	0.743	1.448	n.m.	0.023	76.051	0.561	0.652	12.487	2.986	4.163	0.492	0.036
	ICP	0.608	0.984	0.164	0.005	n.m.	n.m.	0.318	12.668	3.784	n.m.	0.377	0.015

Note: The certified values are supplied by the manufacturer. The abbreviation n.m. indicates that the element was not measured or reported.

greater. The concentration of lead varies significantly among the group, and also demonstrates a large discrepancy between the XRF and ICP-MS results. Again, this may result from the poor alloying characteristics of Pb in bronzes, leading to heterogeneities.

The ratio of cobalt and nickel has been noted as of interest in similar bronze objects.[5] In comparing the cobalt-to-nickel (Co/Ni) ratio, it is observed that F1929.84 has the highest ratio (as well as the highest overall cobalt and nickel content), followed by F2003.2 and AS 1979.020, and the lowest values belong to F1997.28 and NS F.1972.45.07.S. As noted, the composition calculated from the standard solutions (for ICP-MS) or the calibrated fundamental parameters (XRF) were found to differ from the reference materials. Ideally, a set of standards of similar composition to the analyzed bronzes would be used to refine the calibration. For the reference materials, the response for both techniques was found to be quite linear for Co and Ni. To account for the differences between the certified and calculated values, an adjusted metal concentration may be calculated for both XRF and ICP-MS techniques using the fitted linear regression equation. Such calculations should not be performed outside the range of concentrations present in the reference materials. Due to the small number of reference materials employed in this study, the adjusted concentrations were calculated only for Co and Ni (see Table D.4). This method brings the ICP-MS and XRF results for the bronzes in closer agreement. For pertinent Co/Ni ratio, there is less deviation between the techniques. The Co/Ni values range from about 0.2–0.5 for the initial calculation and 0.3–0.6 for the adjusted values.

Conclusion

The challenges of assigning provenance based on trace metals of copper materials employed in bronzes are well summarized by Reedy,[6] including the variability of those elements within an ore deposit, the intentional or unintentional changes to concentration that may occur during smelting and alloying, the introduction of trace elements present in noncopper sources (e.g., lead and tin) or reused materials (or mixed source materials). In the case of southern Indian bronzes, possibly copper sources from India and Sri Lanka have been discussed previously by Craddock and Srinivasan;[7] however, very few slag samples have been investigated, nor have details of their variability.

Further research using trace element or isotope analysis on bronze objects along with related mineralogical sources can inform the working methods and potential trading routes within a region. To that end, it is vital to pay sufficient attention to the potential conflicts that arise from readily available scientific instrumentation. Comparison of these analytical methodologies allows for a better understanding of the limitations of each technique and the heterogeneities that may exist not just among objects, but also within drilled areas of a single object. With the use of standard reference materials, we can continue to validate and adapt our working methods while evaluating data collected from different institutions. This will help determine which variances observed in the data are relevant to the sample or to the analytical methods themselves. This study adds to the increasing knowledge of southern Indian bronzes analysis, particularly in regard to the potential sourcing of bronze

Table D.3 Elemental Composition in Mass Percentage for the Samples

Name	Result	Ag	As	Bi	Co	Cu	Fe	Ni	Pb	Sb	Sn	Zn	Co/Ni
F1929.84	XRF	0.035	0.496	n.m.	0.193	95.308	1.45	0.521	1.085	b.d.	0.761	0.123	0.371
	ICP	0.007	0.078	0.003	0.134	n.m.	n.m.	0.261	0.572	0.013	0.781	0.01	0.515
F1997.28	XRF	0.078	0.328	n.m.	0.071	85.489	0.48	0.378	6.709	0.148	6.061	0.226	0.189
	ICP	0.026	0.029	0.013	0.036	n.m.	n.m.	0.142	3.253	0.021	0.683	0.121	0.253
F2003.2	XRF	0.059	0.457	n.m.	0.106	82.366	0.623	0.439	9.51	0.103	6.185	0.103	0.242
	ICP	0.006	0.021	0.018	0.057	n.m.	n.m.	0.164	5.533	0.02	0.852	0.239	0.351
AS 1979.020	XRF	0.058	0.286	n.m.	0.072	84.202	0.492	0.316	8.103	0.148	6.227	0.049	0.228
	ICP	0.007	0.009	0.013	0.034	n.m.	n.m.	0.105	3.397	0.012	0.177	0.21	0.322
NS F.1972.45.07.S	XRF	0.087	0.3	n.m.	0.057	83.105	0.616	0.307	10.304	0.127	3.524	1.514	0.188
	ICP	0.023	0.015	0.017	0.027	n.m.	n.m.	0.101	5.346	0.014	0.23	1.009	0.267

Note: n.m. indicates that the element was not measured or reported; b.d. indicates below the detection limit.

Table D.4 Elemental Composition in Mass Percentage for the Samples for Cobalt and Nickel Calibrated Using the Reference Materials

Name	Result	Co	Ni	Co/Ni
F1929.84	XRF	0.178	0.333	0.536
	ICP	0.237	0.38	0.623
F1997.28	XRF	0.057	0.207	0.276
	ICP	0.063	0.207	0.305
F2003.2	XRF	0.092	0.261	0.352
	ICP	0.101	0.238	0.424
AS 1979.020	XRF	0.058	0.153	0.378
	ICP	0.059	0.153	0.388
NS F.1972.45.07.S	XRF	0.043	0.145	0.299
	ICP	0.047	0.148	0.321

alloys. Although the sample size is too limited to make deductions regarding potential copper sources, this project builds upon the existing analytical works to assist in the construction of historic trading pathways in India.

Acknowledgments

Vidya Dehejia (Columbia University) provided the impetus for this investigation. John Griswold (Norton Simon Museum) and Clare McGowan and Adriana Proser (Asia Society Museum) generously provided samples. The authors thank Lisha Glinsman (National Gallery of Art) and Bruce Kaiser for assistance and discussions of the XRF analysis.

Glossary

abhisheka—ritual anointing of sacred image; also of a human monarch, especially at coronation

Adavallar—master of dance; Tamil term for Dancing Shiva

Aditya—another name for Surya, the sun god

Agastya—a Vedic sage

alvar—saint of Vishnu

ananda tandava—Shiva's dance of bliss

anukki—literally, "intimate"; the prime mistress of a monarch

Appar—Shaiva Tamil poet-saint

Ardharnari—Shiva as half woman, half man

Arjuna—central heroic character in the Mahabharata epic

Avalokiteshvara—a Buddhist bodhisattva

avatar—descent; divine incarnation, especially of Vishnu

Bhairava—fierce (*ugra*) or destructive (*samhara*) form of Shiva

bhakti—deep devotion to a personal godhead

Bhikshatana—enchanting mendicant form of Shiva

bhogiyar—mistress, concubine

Bhringi—ancient sage; devotee of Shiva

Bhu—"earth," the goddess earth

Bhu Lakshmi—earth Lakshmi, consort of Vishnu

Brahma—a major god in Hinduism, responsible for the creation of the earth

Brahmi—early script from which all Indian scripts, northern and southern, are derived

Brahmotsavam—major annual festival in a Shiva temple that extends over a period of ten days

Chandesha—Shaivite Tamil poet-saint identifiable by an ax held in the crook of his arm

Chandrashekhara—Shiva with the Moon in his crown

channavira—a chain-like ornament that encloses the torso, meeting at the center of the body, both at front and back

Chittirai—mid-April to mid-May in the Tamil calendar

Dakshinameru—world mountain of the south; world axis

Dakshinamurti—Shiva as Great Teacher

darshan—ritual "seeing" of the enshrined temple deity that involves a dynamic act of awareness

devadana—gift to the gods; gifted temple lands

Durga—"Impassable One"; the great goddess as warrior; she is the same deity who is also consort of Shiva

dvarapala—door guardian

Ganesha—elephant-headed god; elder son of Shiva and Uma; remover of obstacles

Ganga—the river Ganga (Ganges) personified as a goddess

garbhagriha—literally, "womb house"; the temple sanctum

grantha—script used in south India for Sanskrit letters that are not part of the Tamil alphabet

gunas—qualities

hiranyagarbha—golden womb; source of all creation according to the Rig Veda; name given to a Vedic ritual

Indra—Vedic deity; god of war, rain

jagati—lowest level of a temple's base moldings

kalanju—ancient weight measure

Kali—power of time; the black one; name of the great goddess in her fearsome aspect

Kalyanasundarar—Shiva as bridegroom with bride Uma

Kanappan—Shaiva Tamil poet-saint who was a hunter

Karna—major character in the Mahabharata epic

Kasyapa—Vedic sage

kirtimukha—literally, "face of glory"; a decorative motif with a lion-like head from whose mouth emerge strands of pearls

kodanda—name of the bow held by Rama

koyil—temple, palace; literally, "abode of the lord/king"

kshatriya—one of four castes in Hindu society, kshatriyas are the military and ruling classes

kudinai-kal—a measure of weight (unknown today) referred to in Chola inscriptions

kumuda—the rounded or angular base molding of a temple, above the *jagati*

kuttu—dance

Lakshmi—goddess of wealth and good fortune; consort of Vishnu

Lalitavistara—Buddhist sutra that narrates the story of the Buddha, starting with his descent from the Tushita heavens and ending with the First Sermon

linga—literally, "sign"; aniconic, pillar-like form of Shiva; phallic emblem, often placed in a yoni-shaped base

Lokeshvara—"lord of the world"

Mahadevar—"great god"

Maitreya—the future Buddha

makara—mythical crocodile-like creature

mandalam, as in Chola-mandalam—territorial division within a kingdom

mandapa—temple hall; place of assembly

Manigramam—influential guild of medieval merchants in South India

Manikkavachakar—Shaiva Tamil poet-saint who lived after the sixty-three *nayanmar*

Minakshi—goddess enshrined at Madurai; literally, the "fish-eyed one"

mula vigraha—deity enshrined in the temple sanctum

Musalagan—dwarf-like demonic figure in Shiva mythology

Muttaraiyar—chieftains and landowners in pre-Chola Tamil Nadu who became Chola feudatories

Muvar—"Revered Three"; the three great Shaivite poet-saints: Appar, Sambandar, and Sundarar

nagaram—merchant township

nagarattar—merchants

nataka-salai—dance hall

nayanmar—saints of Shiva; in the singular, the term is "*nayanar*"

padal petra sthalam—literally, "temple sung of" (in the saints' poems); sacred sites of hallowed antiquity

Palavettaraiyar—chieftains and landowners in pre-Chola Tamil Nadu who became Chola feudatories

Periya Puranam—"Great Sacred Text" compiled by Sekkilar; the hagiographic account of the lives of the sixty-three *nayanmar*, or the Shaiva poet-saints

Pichcha Devar—literally, the "begging god" (Shiva); also known as Bhikshatana in Sanskrit

prabha—aureole

pradakshina—act of circumambulating a deity or place of reverence

prakara—enclosure surrounding the Hindu temple

Rishabhavahana—Shiva with his bull vehicle

Sambandar—Shaiva Tamil child poet-saint who lived toward the end of the seventh century

sapta sthala—seven holy places

Sekkilar—compiler of the *Periya Puranam*

Shiva—major Hindu deity, who holds battle ax and trident, carries the crescent moon in his locks, and whose vehicle is the bull

Skanda—younger son of Uma and Shiva; known by various other names, including Kumara and Subrahmanya

Somaskanda—Shiva with Uma and infant Skanda (sa-uma-skanda)

Sri—goddess of wealth and fortune; consort of Vishnu; also known as Sri Lakshmi

sthapati—master builder/sculptor

Sundarar—last of the sixty-three Shaiva Tamil poet-saints

Tevaram—first seven volumes of the Shaivite canon of devotional poetry, the *Tirumurai*, consisting of the hymns of Sambandar, Appar, and Sundarar

Tirumurai—name of the Shaiva sacred canon that includes the *Tevaram*, and has an additional five books that concludes with the *Periya Puranam*

tribhanga—literally "triple-bent"; exaggerated contrapposto

Tripura Vijaya—Shiva as Destroyer of the Three Forts

Tripurasundari—Uma as Beauty of the Three Forts, as consort of Tripura Vijaya

Uma—consort of Shiva; known in north India as Parvati

utsava murti—portable festival image

vahana—vehicle; mount on which a deity rides

vimana—term given to the temple shrine and its tower

Vishnu—major Hindu god who holds conch shell and discus and whose vehicle is the divine eagle Garuda

Notes

ACKNOWLEDGMENTS

1. The Tamil Nadu state government department that today oversees all aspects of temple administration, known as the Hindu Religious and Charitable Endowments (HR&CE), handles the affairs of no less than 36,680 temples of all periods.

2. S. R. Balasubrahmanyam, *Early Cola Art* (London: Asia Publishing House, 1966); *Early Chola Temples: Parantaka I to Rajaraja I (A.D. 907–985)* (Bombay, Orient Longman, 1971); *Middle Chola Temples: Rajaraja I to Kulottunga I (A.D. 985–1070)* (Faridabad: Thomson Press [India], Publication Division, 1975); *Later Chola Temples: Kulottunga I to Rajendra III (A.D. 1070–1280)* (Madras: Mudgala Trust, 1979).

3. Françoise L'Hernault avec des collaborations de P. R. Srinivasan et de Jacques Dumarçay, *Darasuram: Epigraphical Study: Etude Architecturale: Etude Iconographique* (Paris: École Française d'Extrême-Orient, 1987). Françoise L'Hernault, *The Iconography of the Brhadisvara Temple*, ed. Lalit M. Gujral (New Delhi: Indira Gandhi National Centre for Arts; Pondicherry: École Française d'Extrême-Orient, 2002). Pierre Pichard, *Vingt Ans après Tanjavur, Gangaikondacholapuram*, 2 vols. (Paris: École Française d'Extrême-Orient, 1994). Pierre Pichard, *Tanjavur Brhadisvara: An Architectural Study* (New Delhi: Indira Gandhi National Centre for the Arts; Pondicherry: École Française d'Extrême-Orient, 1995). See also B. Venkataraman, *Rajarajesvaram, the Pinnacle of Chola Art* (Madras, India: Mudgala Trust, 1985).

4. Padma Kaimal, "Early Cola Kings and 'Early Cola Temples': Art and the Evolution of Kingship," *Artibus Asiae* 56, nos. 1/2 (1996): 33–66; "A Man's World? Gender, Family, and Architectural Patronage, in Medieval India," *Archives of Asian Art*, LIII/ (2002–2003): 26–53; "The Problem of Portraiture in South India, 970–1000 CE," *Artibus Asiae* 59, nos. 3/4 (2000): 139–179; "The Problem of Portraiture in South India, 870–970 CE," *Artibus Asiae* 59, nos. 1/2 (1999): 59–133; "Shiva Nataraja: Shifting Meanings of an Icon," *Art Bulletin* 81, no. 3 (1999): 390–419. See also Michael W. Meister and M. A. Dhaky, eds., *Encyclopaedia of Indian Temple Architecture: South India, Lower Dravidadesa, 200 B.C.–A.D. 1324*, 2 vols. (New Delhi: American Institute of Indian Studies and Oxford University Press, 1983): chapter 7, "Muttaraiyars of Nemam and Sendalai"; chapter 8, "Colas of Tanjavur: Phase I"; chapter 9, "Irrukuvels of Kodumbalur"; chapter 10, "Paluvettaraiyars of Paluvur"; and chapter 12, "Colas of Tanjavur: Phase II."

5. Douglas E. Barrett, *Early Cola Bronzes* (Bombay: Bhulabhai Memorial Institute, 1965). P. R. Srinivasan, *Bronzes of South India* (Madras: Printed at India Press for the Controller of Stationery and Printing, 1963). C. Sivaramamurti, *South Indian Bronzes* (New Delhi: Lalit Kalā Akademi, 1963). R. Nagaswamy has written a number of articles, generally devoted to finds at a particular site. See his "New Bronze Finds from Tiruvenkadu," in *Transactions of the Archaeological Society of South India, 1959–1960*, pp. 108–122; "Some Adavallan and Other Bronzes of the Early Chola Period," *Lalit Kala* 10 (1961): 34–40; "Pallava Bronzes from Vadakkalathur," *Oriental Art* 17, no. 1 (1971): 55–59; "Dancing Kali and Other Early Chola Bronzes," *Lalit Kala* 18 (1977): 9–13; "Chidambaram Bronzes," *Lalit Kala* 19 (1979): 9–16; "Archaeological Finds in South India: Esalam Bronzes and Copperplates," *Bulletin de l'École Française d'Extrême-Orient* 76 (1987): 1–68; "On Dating South Indian Bronzes," in *Indian Art & Connoisseurship: Essays in Honor of Douglas Barrett*, ed. John Guy (Chidambaram; Ahmedabad, India: Indira Gandhi National Centre for the Arts in association with Mapin Publishing, 1995); *Masterpieces of Early South Indian Bronzes* (New Delhi: National Museum, 1983); and most recently his *Masterpieces of Chola Art* (Chennai: Tamil Arts Academy, 2011).

6. Nilakanta Sastri, *The Cōlas* (Madras: University of Madras, 1935).

7. Noboru Karashima, "South Indian Temple Inscriptions: A New Approach to Their Study," *South Asia* XIX, no. 1 (1996): 1–12. Y. Subbarayulu, *South India under the Cholas* (New Delhi: Oxford University Press, 2012).

8. In particular, see Tansen Sen, "The Military Campaigns of Rajendra Chola and the Chola-Srivijaya-China Triangle," pp. 61–75, and Tansen Sen with Noburo Karashima, "Appendix II: Chinese Texts Describing or Referring to the Chola Kingdom as Zhu-nian," pp. 292–315, in *Nagapattinam to Suvarnadwipa: Reflections on the Chola Naval Expeditions to Southeast Asia*, ed. Hermann Kulke, K. Kesavapany, and Vijay Sakhuja (Singapore: Institute of Southeast Asian Studies, 2009).

9. Kenneth Hall, *Networks of Trade, Polity, and Societal Integration in Chola-Era South India, c. 875–1279* (Delhi: Primus Books, 2014). George Spencer, *The Politics of Expansion: The Chola Conquest of Sri Lanka and Sri Vijaya* (Madras: New Era, 1983). R. Champakalakshmi, *Trade, Ideology, and Urbanization: South India 300 B.C. to A.D. 1300* (Delhi: Oxford University Press, 1996). Kanakalatha Mukund, *The Trading World of the Tamil Merchant: Evolution of Merchant Capitalism in the Coromandel* (Chennai: Orient Longman, 1999). Leslie Orr,

Donors, Devotees, and Daughters of God: Temple Women in Medieval Tamilnadu (New York: Oxford University Press, 2000).

10. Richard Davis, *Lives of Indian Images* (Princeton, NJ: Princeton University Press, 1997); trans., *A Priest's Guide for the Great Festival: Aghorasiva's Mahotsavavidhi* (New York: Oxford University Press, 2010).

11. Indira Peterson, *Poems to Śiva: The Hymns of the Tamil Saints* (Princeton, NJ: Princeton University Press, 1989). David Dean Shulman, *Songs of the Harsh Devotee: The Tevaram of Cuntaramurttinayanar* (Philadelphia: University of Pennsylvania Press, 1990). John Carman and Vasudha Narayanan, *The Tamil Veda: Pillan's Interpretation of the Tiruvaymoli* (Chicago: University of Chicago Press, 1989).

12. Vidya Dehejia, *Slaves of the Lord: The Path of the Tamil Saints* (New Delhi: Mushiram Manoharlal, 1988).

13. Vidya Dehejia, ed. *Āṇṭāḷ and Her Path of Love: Poems of a Woman Saint from South India* (Albany: State University of New York Press, 1990).

14. Vidya Dehejia, *Art of the Imperial Cholas* (New York: Columbia University Press, 1990).

15. Vidya Dehejia, ed., *The Sensuous and the Sacred: Chola Bronzes from South India* (New York: American Federation of Arts; Seattle: University of Washington Press, 2002).

16. Vidya Dehejia, ed., *Chola* (London: Royal Academy in London, 2006).

17. Arjuna Thantilage, "An Archaeo-Metallurgical Investigation of Sri Lankan Bronzes," Colombo, Postgraduate Institute of Archaeology, unpublished PhD thesis, 2008.

INTRODUCTION

1. Indira Peterson, *Poems to Śiva: The Hymns of the Tamil Saints* (Princeton, NJ: Princeton University Press, 1989), p. 270f.

2. Ibid., p. 210.

3. Ibid., p. 213.

4. Vidya Dehejia, *Slaves of the Lord: The Path of the Tamil Saints* (New Delhi: Mushiram Manoharlal, 1988), pp. 44–45.

5. This is most clearly enunciated in the case of the Buddha, born as an Indian "prince" before he became a deity of significance across south Asia, east Asia, and southeast Asia. A sacred text known as the *Lakkhana Sutra*, or Text on Signs, clearly links bodily beauty and pious sacrality. It describes each element of the bodily beauty of the Buddha, and attributes each to a particular set of praiseworthy actions that he performed in a previous life. For details, see Vidya Dehejia, *The Body Adorned: Dissolving Boundaries between Sacred and Profane in India's Art* (New York: Columbia University Press, 2009), pp. 60–66.

6. T. V. Mahalingam, *A Topographical List of Inscriptions in Tamil Nadu and Kerala States*, 8 vols. (New Delhi: Indian Council of Historical Research, 1985–1992).

7. This count, taken from Mahalingam's volumes 7 and 8 only, does not include temples treated in his first six volumes devoted to the districts of South Arcot, North Arcot, Chinglepet, Coimbatore/Dharmapuri, Nilgiris, Pudukottai, Ramanathapuram, and Salem.

8. Scholarship in the burgeoning field of Indian Ocean studies is highly aware of such issues.

9. Ben B. Johnson, "Krishna Rajamannar Bronzes: An Examination and a Treatment Report," in Pratapaditya Pal, *Krishna: The Cowherd King* (Los Angeles: Los Angeles County Museum of Art, 1972), p. 56.

10. The starting point for this calculation was a selection of twelve bronzes that each temple would have acquired to fulfill its ritual festival cycle. For the starting phase, I chose the following as probably the ones of utmost importance: Astra Devar, *Chandrashekhara* and Uma, *Somaskanda*, Shiva as Victor of Three Forts and Uma, Kalyanasundarar Shiva with Uma, Ganesha, Chandesha, and Adavallan or Expert Dancer, and Uma. I then assumed that each of the 311 temples in the districts of Trichy, Thanjavur, and Nagapattinam would have commissioned twelve bronzes each (ignoring the fact that temples like Tiruvaduturai had twenty-four images and Tiruvenkadu had over thirty-five), leading to a total of 3,732 bronzes. I estimated the weight of these bronzes based on three factors. The first was the given size of the twenty-four bronzes listed in the Tiruvaduturai inscription (see appendix B, II). I then compared and double-checked this against the weights of similarly sized bronzes provided to me by the Cleveland Museum of Art and the Asia Society, New York. The combined weight of nine bronzes from the Cleveland collection with three from the Asia Society (of a size comparable to those at Tiruvaduturai)—a total of twelve bronzes—adds up to a total of 985 pounds per temple, or close to half a ton for each of 311 temples.

11. David Howes and Constance Classen, *Ways of Sensing: Understanding the Senses in Society* (New York: Routledge, 2014), a collection of essays that is an introduction to sensory experience, makes reference only in passing to the sense of taste.

12. "Art and Affect" is another relatively new focus in recent scholarship.

13. Sascha Ebeling, "The Digital Archive of South Indian Inscriptions (DASI)—A First Report," in *South-Indian Horizons: Felicitation Volume for François Gros on the Occasion of His 70th Birthday*, ed. Chevillard Jean-Luc (Pondicherry: Institut Français de Pondichéry [and] École Française d'Extrême-Orient, 2004), pp. 495–503. I have been unable to find an update on this project.

14. Mahalingam, *A Topographical List of Inscriptions in Tamil Nadu and Kerala States*.

15. See chapter 3, later.

16. See Carlo Ginzberg, "Vetoes and Compatibilities," *Art*

Bulletin 77, no. 4 (December 1995): 534–536. The word "connoisseurship" probably holds different connotations for each of us. Is it the art of appreciation? Intuitive appreciation? A refinement of perception? Maybe we think of a connoisseur as an expert in matters of taste? A critical judge in matters of art? How about defining connoisseurship as the "silent language of the eye"?

Critic and scholar Bernard Berenson, writing in 1903, described the process of connoisseurship as "the isolation of the characteristics of the known, and their confrontation with the unknown." See his *The Rudiments of Connoisseurship: Study and Criticism of Italian Art* (New York: Schocken Books, 1962) and "The Rudiments of Connoisseurship (A Fragment)," in *The Study and Criticism of Italian Art*, second series (London: George Bell, 1902), pp. 111–148; esp. p. 123.

17. As quoted in Edgar Wind, "Connoisseurship," in *Art and Anarchy* (New York: A. A. Knopf, 1965).

18. Sydney J. Freedberg, "Some Thoughts on Berenson, Connoisseurship, and the History of Art," in *I Tatti Studies in the Italian Renaissance* 3 (1989): 11–26.

19. David Freedberg, "Why Connoisseurship Matters," in *Munuscula Amicorum: Contributions on Rubens and His Colleagues*, ed. Katlijne van der Stighelen (Turnhout: Brepols, 2006). Freedberg also cites Malcolm Gladwell, the author of the popular little book titled *Blink: The Power of Thinking without Thinking* (New York: Little, Brown, 2005), who commenced his book with a piece on the now infamous Getty kouros in which he stressed the importance of "intuitive" judgement.

20. Vidya Dehejia and Peter Rockwell, "Epilogue: The Animal Master of Mamallapuram," in *The Unfinished: Stone Carvers at Work on the Indian Subcontinent* (New Delhi: Lustre Press, Roli Books, 2017), pp. 240–249.

CHAPTER 1: GODS ON PARADE

1. H. Krishna Sastri, ed., "The Tiruvalangadu Copper-Plates of the Sixth Year of Rajendra-Chola I," in *South Indian Inscriptions*, vol. III, part III (Madras: Superintendent, Government Press, 1920), no. 205, p. 418. I have taken the liberty of lightly paraphrasing the text to make it easier to understand.

2. T. A. Gopinatha Rao, "Anbil Plates of Sundara-Chola: The 4th Year," in *Epigraphia Indica*, vol. XV, 1919–20, ed. F. W. Thomas (Calcutta: Government of India, 1925), no. 5, p. 68.

3. For instance, the temple at Esalam carried twelve bronzes, while the Tiruvenkadu temple possessed some forty-five images. See chapter 9, later.

4. For Karrali Picchan, see T. V. Mahalingam, *A Topographical List of Inscriptions in Tamil Nadu and Kerala States*, vol. 7: *Thanjavur District* (New Delhi: Indian Council of Historical Research, 1992), no. TJ 1350, p. 315. For Parantaka Chola, see Mahalingam, *A Topographical List: Thanjavur*, no. TJ 1354, p. 316.

5. See Vidya Dehejia, "Assemblages of Sacred Bronzes," in *The Sensuous and the Sacred: Chola Bronzes from South India*, ed. Vidya Dehejia (New York: American Federation of the Arts, 2002), p. 82f. The measurements given in the inscription use the ancient measures of *muram* (elbow to fingertips), *shan* (span), *viral* (finger), and *torai* (rice grain) that Dr. Marxia Gandhi and I converted to inches and centimeters. See also appendix B, I.

6. See Vidya Dehejia, "Assemblages of Sacred Bronzes," p. 83ff. The bronzes in the Thanjavur temple are not from a single inscription, as at Tiruvaduturai, but taken from an entire series of inscriptions of the royal and aristocratic donors of the temple's bronzes. B. Venkataraman, *Rajarajesvaram: The Pinnacle of Chola Art* (Madras: Mudgala Trust, 1985), in his chapter 5, pp. 148–162, has a preliminary listing of these images, although without measurements. See appendix B, I, for discussion of the conversion of ancient to modern measurements.

7. E. Hultzsch, ed., *South Indian Inscriptions*, vol. II, part I, no. 2, section 2 (Madras: Superintendent, Government Press, 1891), refers to Adavallan Dakshina Meru Vitankar.

8. Paul Younger, *The Home of Dancing Śivan: The Traditions of the Hindu Temple in Citamparam* (New York: Oxford University Press, 1995), p. 52. See also H. Krishna Sastri, ed., *South Indian Inscriptions*, vol. IV (Madras: Superintendent, Government Press, 1923), no. 225, pp. 31–34.

9. Mahalingam, *A Topographical List: Thanjavur*, no. TJ 1484, p. 346; see also *Annual Report on Indian Epigraphy* 1925, no. 269.

10. K. V. Subrahmanya Aiyer, ed., *South Indian Inscriptions*, vol. VII (Madras: Superintendent, Government Press, 1932), no. 485, pp. 298–301. See also Mahalingam, *A Topographical List: Thanjavur*, no. TJ 1653, p. 386. The three festivals outside the temple were (1) a processional festival on the star *Sadayam* in the month of *Aipashi* (October–November) that extended over six days; (2) a festival on the star *Uttiram* in the month of *Panguni* (March–April) that included hoisting of the flag and that lasted ten days; (3) the spring festival in the month of *Adi* (July–August), in which the deity took a sacred bath. The *Panguni* festival lasted a full ten days and appears to have been the equivalent of what is today a temple's most important festival known as *Brahmotsavam*. For these three festivals that involve processions outside the temple, the inscriptions list the various persons required for its performance and the payment to be made to them. Eight persons carried the deity in procession (*sripadam tanguvar*), while twenty-six persons served as *nivantakaras* who ensured the appropriate performance of the festival. The section on sacred food to honor the images of child saint Sambandar and saint Appar concludes with a list of persons involved in the festivals and it speaks of ten persons to lift the images, three to perform puja, a washerman to wash sacred clothes, an accountant, a potter, and a person to perfume and water the bed chamber.

11. *Tiruveedhi parka ezhundarulum tirunal.*

12. Indira Peterson, "Singing of a Place: Pilgrimage as Metaphor and Motif in the Tevaram Songs of the Tamil Saivite Saints," *Journal of the American Oriental Society*, 102, no. 1 (1982): 69–90; esp. p. 73.

13. Mahalingam, *A Topographical List: Thanjavur*, no. TJ 417, p. 96. The temple itself was constructed in the reign of king Parantaka, prior to 935; the road named *Raja-gambhira-vidi* (road of royal pride) was built 250 years after the temple was constructed according to the inscription engraved on the enclosing *prakara* wall.

14. Mahalingam, *A Topographical List: Thanjavur*, no. TJ 1685, p. 394.

15. T. V. Mahalingam, *A Topographical List of Inscriptions in Tamil Nadu and Kerala States*, vol. 8: *Tiruchchirappalli District* (New Delhi: Indian Council of Historical Research, 1991), no. Tp 1616, p. 357. See also G. V. Srinivasa Rao, ed., *South Indian Inscriptions*, vol. XIX (Madras: Superintendent, Government Press, 1967), no. 171, p. 87.

16. Mahalingam, *A Topographical List: Thanjavur*, no. TJ 579, p. 132. See also H. Krishna Sastri, ed., "On the North Wall of the Central Shrine in the Mahalingasvamin Temple at Tiruvidaimarudur," in *South Indian Inscriptions*, vol. III, part III (Madras: Superintendent, Government Press, 1920), no. 202, p. 378, and Sastri, ed., *South Indian Inscriptions*, vol. V (Madras: Superintendent, Government Press, 1925), no. 718, p. 302. The inscriptions are dated in the eighteenth year of Kulottunga.

17. Mahalingam, *A Topographical List: Thanjavur*, no. TJ 184, p. 41. The performer was a certain Virudaraja-bhayankara Achariyan.

18. S. Swaminathan, ed., *South Indian Inscriptions*, vol. XXXII (New Delhi: Director General, Archaeological Survey of India, 2012), part II, no. 198, p. 332. The inscription belongs to the reign of Uttama Chola. The ancient measure of the *palam* has not been translated into modern measures; the *Tamil Lexicon*, vol. IV, p. 2534 (Madras: University of Madras, 1982 reprint) defines *palam* as "a standard weight."

19. Leslie Orr doubts whether they actually traveled themselves or merely incorporated information received from travelers and composed their hymns around such received information. In view of the hometown of Sambandar at Sirkali and that of Appar at Pugalur, all within the immediate vicinity of the temple cluster, it seems quite possible that they visited several of these shrines. Clearly, their singing of a few sites in northern India and two in Sri Lanka may have been from travelers' tales. Leslie Orr, "Processions in the Medieval South Indian Temple: Sociology, Sovereignty and Soteriology," in *South Indian Horizons: Felicitation Volume for Francois Gros on the Occasion of His 70th Birthday*, ed. Jean-Luc Chevillard and Eva Wilden (Pondicherry: Institut Français de Pondichéry; École Française d'Extrême-Orient, 2004), pp. 437–470.

20. Indira Peterson, *Poems to Śiva: The Hymns of the Tamil Saints* (Princeton, NJ: Princeton University Press, 1989), p. 184, cites Appar IV. 21.1.

21. Ibid., p. 183, cites Sambandar I.71.5.

22. H. Sarkar, *Nagarjunakonda* (New Delhi: Archaeological Survey of India, 1966), p. 25. We may turn also to a variety of texts that speak of a priest accompanying an artist to the forest to choose a suitable tree for an image; before they cut it down, they make offerings to it and request any spirits that might inhabit it to depart. See Richard Davis, *Lives of Indian Images* (Princeton, NJ: Princeton University Press, 1999), pp. 34–35. For continuing current practice with the Vishvakarma craftsmen, see Vijaya Ramaswamy, "Vishwakarma Craftsmen in Early Medieval Peninsular India," *Journal of the Economic and Social History of the Orient* 47, no. 4 (2004): 548–582.

23. Ben B. Johnson, "Krishna Rajamannar Bronzes: An Examination and a Treatment Report," in Pratapaditya Pal, *Krishna: The Cowherd King* (Los Angeles: Los Angeles County Museum of Art, 1972), pp. 45–58; esp. table V, p. 56. The copper content varies from 89.65 percent to 94.46 percent.

24. I am grateful to the Cleveland Museum of Art for having weighed their bronzes and supplied me with the weight and measurements of each. The *Dancing Shiva* is 113 centimeters, or 44 1/2 inches, high.

25. Robert Raymond, *Out of the Fiery Furnace: The Impact of Metals on the History of Mankind* (University Park: Pennsylvania State University Press, 1986), p. 26.

26. Ibid., p. 35: "However unlikely it may seem . . . we must consider the possibility that tin from southeast Asia was carried thousands of kilometers to the Near East as long ago as the fourth millennium BC."

27. Sastri, "Tiruvalangadu Copper-Plates," p. 205. The charter was issued in Rajendra's sixth regnal year. S. Sankaranarayana, Marxia Gandhi, A. Padmavathy, and R. Sivanantham, *Thiruvindalur Copper Plate* (Chennai: State Dept. of Archaeology, 2011), p. 5.

28. S. Krishnaswamy, *India's Mineral Resources*, 2nd edition (New Delhi: Oxford and IBH, 1979), p. 177.

29. Panchanan Neogi, *Copper in Ancient India* (Patna: Janaki Prakashan, 1979), p. 21f.

30. B. P. Radhakrishna, *Mineral Resources of Karnataka* (Bangalore: Geological Society of India, 1996), p. 162.

31. See introduction, note 10, for details. I profited immensely from meeting Professor Srinivas, together with Professor S. Srinivasalu, at Madras University. Srinivas emphasizes, and I agree, that wars have never been a deterrent to trade, so north India may indeed have been the source of copper for the Cholas and ships of the first millennium could easily carry one to two tons of cargo.

32. Lionel Casson, *The Periplus Maris Erythraei* (Princeton, NJ: Princeton University Press, 1989), pp. 27–29.

33. Neogi, *Copper*, p. 64. See Krishnaji Govind Oka, *Srimad-*

amarasimhavirichita (Poona: Law Printing Press, 1913), chapter 2, verse 97, p. 155: *tamrakam mlechchamukha* in a discussion on *Nama-linganushasanam*.

34. Neogi, *Copper*, p. 65. See Ashok T. Satpute, trans., *Rasaratna Samuchchaya* (Mysore: Chetan Prakashana, n.d.), chapter 5, "Loha (Metals)," verse 22, p. 45, speaks of *tamra* or copper and tells us it is of two types, *Mlechcha* and *Nepalika*, of which Nepali copper is superior.

35. S. D. Goitein and Mordechai A. Friedman, *India Traders of the Middle Ages: Documents from the Cairo Geniza "India Book"* (Leiden: Brill, 2011), part 2: letter III, 2: pp. 564–566.

36. Ibid., letter III, 19: Accounts of Abraham Ben Yiju's Workshop for Bronze Vessels, pp. 644–646.

37. Arjuna Thantilage, "An Archaeo-Metallurgical Investigation of Sri Lankan Bronzes," Colombo, Postgraduate Institute of Archaeology, unpublished PhD thesis, 2007.

38. In conversation. To be published in forthcoming *Memoirs of the Post Graduate Institute of Archaeology, Colombo, Sri Lanka*.

39. Senarat Paranivatana, *Inscriptions of Ceylon*, vol. 1 (Colombo: Department of Archaeology Ceylon, 1970). See nos. 350 and 351, p. 28.

40. Sudarshan Seneviratne, "The Ecology and Archaeology of the Seruwila Copper-Magnetite Prospect, Northeast Sri Lanka," *Sri Lanka Journal of the Humanities* 21, nos. 1–2 (1995): 113–145. This speaks of the inscription as dating to 350 AD. He refers us to Paranavitana Senarat, "Two Rock-Inscriptions from Labuatabandigala," *Epigraphia Zeylanica* III (1928–1933): 247–253. Seneviratane's article is also published in Vibha Tripathi, ed., *Archaeometallurgy in India* (Delhi: Sharada Publishing House, 1998), pp. 156–175. Information on copper minister in conversation with Arjuna Thantilage to be included in a forthcoming *Memoirs of the Post Graduate Institute of Archaeology, Colombo, Sri Lanka*.

41. Arjuna Thantilage, Indika Vithanage, T.D.C. Pushpakumara, Jayampath Senanayake, and Pathmakumara Jayasinghe, *Ilankaturai International Port Site, Memoirs of the Postgraduate Institute of Archaeology*, 2013, no. 2 (Colombo: Postgraduate Institute of Archaeology, University of Kelaniya, 2013).

42. Arjuna Thantilage, "An Archaeo-Metallurgical Investigation of Sri Lankan Bronzes."

43. I am indebted to Paul Jett, ex-head of the Freer Gallery of Art's laboratory, for lengthy conversations about copper, its conservation, and related issues.

44. Noboru Karashima and Y. Subbarayalu, appendix I, "Ancient and Medieval Tamil and Sanskrit Inscriptions Relating to Southeast Asia and China," in *Nagapattinam to Suvarnadwipa: Reflections on the Chola Naval Expeditions to Southeast Asia*, ed. Hermann Kulke, K. Kesavapany, and Vijay Sakhuja (Singapore: Institute of Southeast Asian Studies, 2009), no. 12, p. 284. The inscription is currently in the Nakhon Si Thammarat Museum.

45. Vidya Dehejia, *The Body Adorned* (New York: Columbia University Press, 2009).

46. Blake Tucker Wentworth, *Yearning for a Dreamed Real: The Procession of the Lord in the Tamil Ulas* (Chicago: University of Chicago, Divinity School, 2011), pp. 343–344.

47. See chapter 5, later.

48. Joanne Waghorne, "Dressing the Body of God: South Indian Bronze Sculpture in Its Temple Setting," *Asian Art* (Summer 1992): 9–23.

49. At the same time, it would not do to downplay the finishing touches that are crucial to the finished product whether in Chola times or in current practice. See also Levy Thomas & Alina Levy, *Masters of Fire: Hereditary Bronze Casters of South India* (Bochum: Deutsches Bergbau Museum, 2008).

50. Carol C. Mattusch, *Classical Bronzes: The Art and Craft of Greek and Roman Statuary* (Ithaca and London: Cornell University Press, 1996), p. ix. Her work contains a clear and succinct account of the indirect lost-wax process used for ancient bronzes.

51. Ibid., p. 33f.

52. Shiva is 32 1/4 inches tall, while Uma is 25 5/8 inches.

53. R. Nagaswamy, "On Dating South Indian Bronzes," in *Indian Art & Connoisseurship: Essays in Honor of Douglas Barrett*, ed. John Guy (Chidambaram; Ahmedabad: Indira Gandhi National Centre for the Arts in association with Mapin Publishing, 1995), p. 107f.

54. One of the reasons that there are over a hundred words in the Sanskrit language to describe beauty is this very concept of beauty in motion. To give just one example, the Sanskrit verb *lasati* indicates grace at rest that arouses desire; with the prefix *vi* added, *vilasati* indicates beauty added through movement. Vidya Dehejia, *The Body Adorned*, p. 12, and for further details, see H. Ingalls, "Words for Beauty in Classical Sanskrit Poetry," in *Indological Studies in Honor of W. Norman Brown*, ed. Ernest Bender (New Haven, CT: American Oriental Society, 1962), p. 63.

55. Peterson, "Singing of a Place," p. 30.

56. Malashri, "Translating Rabindranath Tagore's Poems," *Indian Literature* 56, no. 3 (May–June 2012): 122–125.

57. Martin Kampchen, "Translating Rabindranath," *Sunday Statesman*, March 27, 2016 (www.martin-kaempchen.de, accessed December 24, 2017).

CHAPTER 2: BATTLING FOR EMPIRE AND SHIVA AS VICTOR OF THREE FORTS

1. Marxia Gandhi, ed., *Thanjavur Vattak Kalvattigal*, vol. II [also known as *Tamilnattuk Kalvettukal Vol. VIII*] (Chennai: State Dept of Archeology, 2015–2016), no. 82/2014, p. 127. *Annual Report on Indian Epigraphy* 1911, no. 286.

2. S. Swaminathan, ed., *South Indian Inscriptions*, vol. XXXII (New Delhi: Director General, Archaeological Survey of India,

2012), part I, no. 1, p. 1 (Inscriptions of the Early Chola Kings up to Uttama Chola). It commences with the words "*Thanjai kotta Koparakesari panmarku yandu avadu . . .*," which confirms that it refers to Vijayalaya. The hero-stone is now in the Government Museum, Chennai.

3. H. Krishna Sastri, ed., "The Tiruvalangadu Copper-Plates of the Sixth Year of Rajendra-Chola I," in *South Indian Inscriptions*, vol. III, part III (Madras: Superintendent, Government Press, 1920), no. 205, verse 45, p. 418.

4. T. A. Gopinatha Rao, "Anbil Plates of Sundara-Chola: The 4th Year," in *Epigraphia Indica*, vol. XV, 1919–20, ed. F. W. Thomas (New Delhi: Director General, Archaeological Survey of India, 1925), no. 5, p. 44–72. In particular, see verse 18, p. 68, also quoted as the second epigraph at the start of chapter 1 in this volume.

5. Padma Kaimal, "Early Cola Kings and 'Early Cola Temples': Art and the Evolution of Kingship," *Artibus Asiae* 56, nos. 1/2 (1996): 33–56. Kaimal speaks of "an unusually regressive style of kingship being practised by the early Cola kings," as an explanation for their lack of temple-building. See pp. 34, 64. It seems to me that there is a circular argument here that needs to be resolved: the fact of a "regressive form of kingship" is based largely on the lack of temple building; in turn, the lack of temple building is attributed to a regressive form of kingship.

While I myself have been seen by some as overemphasizing the role of the Chola monarchs, I should specify that my use of the term "Chola" or "Chola temples" refers to the period and geographic location of such monuments. The patrons of some of these temples were indeed chieftains, but they openly acknowledged Chola overlordship, as is evident in their use of the regnal years of Chola monarchs to secure the date of their gifts recorded through inscriptions. My additional problem is with calling these temples "Palavettaraiyar temples" simply because their patron was a Palavettaraiyar chieftain. I do not see anything specific about their temples that merits giving them a title that implies a substyle.

6. Padma Kaimal, "Early Cola Kings and Early Cola Temples,'" pp. 33–56. "Possibly Aditya did not build any temples," p. 54.

7. These numbers are based upon T. V. Mahalingam's volumes of inscriptions, *A Topographical List of Inscriptions in Tamil Nadu and Kerala states*, 8 vols. (New Delhi: Indian Council of Historical Research, 1985–1992).

8. G. V. Srinivasa Rao, ed., *South Indian Inscriptions*, vol. XIX (Madras: Superintendent, Government Press, 1967), no. 329, p. 166; see also S. Swaminathan, ed., *South Indian Inscriptions*, vol. XXXII, part II, no. 127, p. 242f.

9. Two temples in and around Palavur carry multiple inscriptions detailing gifts to the temples, and orders passed regarding temple administration from the Palavettaraiyar chiefs, Maravan Kandanar and Kandan Maravanar, and from their immediate circle. See T. V. Mahalingam, *A Topographical List of Inscriptions in the Tamil Nadu and Kerala States*, vol. 7: *Thanjavur District* (New Delhi: Indian Council of Historical Research, 1992), nos. TJ 1558–1670, pp. 362–391. Inscription no. 1574, p. 366, in the temple at Melaipalavur, also known as Chirupalavur, the ancient Alandurai Mahadevar, speaks of the temple having been constructed by Palavettaraiyar Maravan Kandanaradigal.

10. G. V. Srinivasa Rao, ed., *South Indian Inscriptions*, vol. XIX, no. 329, p. 166.

11. H. Krishna Sastri, ed., *South Indian Inscriptions*, vol. V (Madras: Superintendent, Government Press,1925), no. 621, p. 246, dated in the fifteenth year of Rajaraja, identified by his unmistakable "tirumagalpola," and hence belonging to the year 1000.

12. Padma Kaimal, "A Man's World? Gender, Family, and Architectural Patronage in Medieval India," *Archives of Asian Art*, LIII/2002–2003, pp. 26–53.

13. Indira Viswanathan Peterson, *Poems to Śiva: The Hymns of the Tamil Saints* (Princeton, NJ: Princeton University Press, 1989), p. 126.

14. Peterson, *Poems to Śiva*, p. 216.

15. I should explain that in citing the Tamil names of many temple sites, I have adopted the option presented by the *nayanmar* themselves to drop the term *tiru*, or sacred, before these names. Thus, with the Sacred Seven, in place of Tiru-neyttanam, Tiru-palanam, Tiru-chottruturai, I have opted to use Neyttanam, Palanam, and Chottruturai.

I cite here two verses from a Sambandar hymn on Aiyaru (Peterson, *Poems to Śiva*, p. 165, verses 6 and 7). In the first, the description of the site is beautiful but formulaic, while the second seems to incorporate an incident that the poet actually witnessed.

> The temple of the mountain's lord,
> The bowman who shot the great arrow
> which shattered the three fortresses
> that oppressed great heaven,
> is Tiruvaiyaru,
> where the cuckoo sings on every hill,
> and the lush sugar cane slumbers in the fields
> caressed by the soft breeze that bears the scent
> of flowers full of rich honey.

> The temple of the lord
> who first crushed the ten heads
> and mighty shoulders of the demon-king
> when he dared to lift Kailasa hill,
> and then blessed him
> is Tiruvaiyaru
> where the young buffalo runs,
> scared by a coconut falling from a shady young palm,
> and blunders into a bed of waterlilies,
> scattering the ripe grain in a paddyfield.

16. Only Vedikudi is taller, though not a fully double-story structure—it is more a story-and-a-half.

17. For Nandivarman, see Sastri, ed., *South Indian Inscriptions*, vol. V, no. 608, p. 242. For Maranjadaiyan, see Mahalingam, *A Topographical List: Thanjavur*, no. TJ 2724, p. 619.

18. For instance, the inscriptions of Nripatunga and of Nandivarman may be found on the stone doorjambs of the temple at Tiruvadigai Veeratanam. See Marxia Gandhi, *Tiruvadigai Virattanam* (Chennai: Amuthan Patippakam, 1994). A second example of this phenomenon comes from the temple at Tirumukkudal, where an inscription of Nripatunga is engraved on a doorjamb that is today fixed into the wall of the inner *prakara*. See *ARE 1915*, no. 179. Information on its current location comes from Marxia Gandhi, who visited the temple in 2017.

19. Charlotte Schmid, *La Bhakti d'une reine: Siva a Tiruccennampunti* (Pondicherry: Institut Français de Pondichéry; Paris: École Française d'Extrême-Orient, 2014), Annexe 4, inscriptions 1 and 2, pp. 297–317, where, at the temple of Tiruccenampundi, we find early inscriptions on the doorjambs and on stone pillars.

20. For Varaguna, see Mahalingam, *A Topographical List: Thanjavur*, no. TJ 2767, p. 629. For Nripatunga, see Sastri, ed., *South Indian Inscriptions*, vol. V, no. 572, pp. 226–227.

21. Marxia Gandhi, ed. *Thanjavur Vattak Kalvattigal*, vol. II [also known as *Tamilnattuk Kalvettukal Vol. VIII*] (Chennai: State Dept of Archeology, 2015–2016), no. 110/2014, p. 171.

22. An inscription from Tirumalavadi informs us that Ilangon Pichchi, daughter (*magalar*) of Vallavaraiyar or Krishnadeva II was Aditya's senior queen (*muttadeviyar*); it seems that she named her son Kannaradeva after her father. A. S. Ramanatha Ayyar, "Two Records of Parantaka I from Takkolam," in *Epigraphia Indica*, vol. XXVI, 1941–42, ed. N. P. Chakravarti (Delhi: Manager of Publications, 1952), no. 29, p. 233. For those who might look at the paleography and consider it late, we should recall that the temple was renovated by Rajaraja and the inscriptions reinscribed during the reign of Rajendra I. See Sastri, ed., *South Indian Inscriptions*, vol. V, no. 652, pp. 273–275. Also discussed in chapter 5, later.

23. It seems likely that the *tati* was a relative or close friend of a bride from a chieftain's family who would accompany the bride into her new home to keep her company and help her transition into her new family. As a confidante, she also became the godmother to the child born of this union.

24. Sastri, ed., *South Indian Inscriptions*, vol. V, no. 693, p. 289.

25. Gandhi, *Thanjavur Vattak Kalvattigal*, vol. II, 73/2014, p. 114.

26. Ibid., vol. II, p. 143.

27. Clearly identified in these inscriptions as *Madirai konda koparakesari*.

28. Here again, the prefix Parantaka before the name Arikulakesari is the typical Tamil mode of identifying the father of the prince (*makanar*), while the term Cholaperumanadigal is the way of referring to the ruling monarch. See Sastri, ed., *South Indian Inscriptions*, vol. V, no. 550, pp. 221–222. Also Mahalingam, *A Topographical List: Thanjavur*, no. TJ 3011, p. 677. Dated in the year 30 of Rajakesari.

29. Sastri, ed., *South Indian Inscriptions*, vol. V, no. 575, p. 229. Uttamasili also dedicated a lamp to the temple at Tiruvidaimaradur: Rao, ed., *South Indian Inscriptions*, vol. XIX, no. 448, p. 230. Also in G. V. Srinivasa Rao, ed., *South Indian Inscriptions*, vol. XXIII (Madras: Superintendent, Government Press, 1979), no. 196, p. 150. Uttamasili was an ill-fated Chola prince who died early; it is interesting that a village along the Kaveri, near Trichy, retains to this day the name Uttamasili.

30. Rao, ed., *South Indian Inscriptions*, vol. XIX, no. 462, p. 236. The record is damaged at the point where the year is specified. Arinjaya appears to have ruled jointly with his brother Gandaraditya and, upon his brother's death, with his own son Sundara Chola.

31. Sastri, ed., *South Indian Inscriptions*, vol. V, no. 693, p. 289.

32. Padma Kaimal, "A Man's World? Gender, Family, and Architectural Patronage in Medieval India," *Archives of Asian Art* 53 (2002/2003): 26–53. See also Kaimal, "Early Cola Kings and 'Early Cola Temples,'" p. 64.

33. Mahalingam, *A Topographical List: Thanjavur*, no. TJ 3003, p. 675.

34. G. V. Srinivasa Rao, ed., *South Indian Inscriptions*, vol. XIII (Madras: Superintendent, Government Press, 1952), no. 304, p. 162.

35. Rao, ed., *South Indian Inscriptions*, vol. XIII, no. 351, p. 186. Also Gandhi, *Thanjavur Vattak Kalvattigal*, vol. II, part II (hereafter *Marxia Gandhi Part II*), no. 148/2014, p. 221.

36. Sastri, ed., *South Indian Inscriptions*, vol. V, no. 599, p. 239.

37. Ibid., vol. V, no. 684, p. 287.

38. Ibid., vol. V, no. 685, p. 287; Rao, ed., *South Indian Inscriptions*, vol. XIX, no. 269, p. 135.

39. For Neyttanam, see Sastri, ed., *South Indian Inscriptions*, vol. V, no. 602, p. 240. Chottruturai: Rao, ed., *South Indian Inscriptions*, vol. XIX, no. 77, p. 40. Also *Marxia Gandhi Part II*, 170/2014, p. 248. Palanam: Sastri, ed., *South Indian Inscriptions*, vol. V, no. 689, p. 288. Poonturutti: Rao, ed., *South Indian Inscriptions*, vol. XIX, no. 74, p. 39.

40. Parantaka queen: Sastri, ed., *South Indian Inscriptions*, vol. V, no. 525, p. 214. Also *Marxia Gandhi Part II*, 166/2014, p. 244. Queen's mother: Mahalingam, *A Topographical List: Thanjavur*, no. TJ 2791, p. 633. Also *Marxia Gandhi Part II*, no. 57/2014, p. 91.

41. Rao, ed., *South Indian Inscriptions*, vol. XIII, no. 219, p. 118–119. Also *Marxia Gandhi Part II*, no. 43/2014, p. 69.

42. New reading in *Marxia Gandhi Part II*, 108/2014, p. 168f. See Rao, ed., *South Indian Inscriptions*, vol. XIII, no. 247, p. 131; also Sastri, ed., *South Indian Inscriptions*, vol. V, no. 593, p. 237–238.

43. Sastri, ed., *South Indian Inscriptions*, vol. V, no. 543, p. 219–220.

44. Ibid., vol. V, no. 588, p. 236.

45. Mahalingam, *A Topographical List: Thanjavur*, no. TJ 2744, pp. 623–624.

46. Ibid., no. TJ 2747, p. 624. See Sastri, ed., *South Indian Inscriptions*, vol. V, no. 597, p. 238.

47. Sastri, ed., *South Indian Inscriptions*, vol. V, no. 625, p. 248.

48. Ibid., vol. V, nos. 610 and 612, pp. 243–244.

49. Names include—and I provide an extensive sampling—Parantaka Ilangovelan (Mahalingam, *A Topographical List: Thanjavur*, no. TJ 2745, p. 624); Tennavan Malanattu Velan alias Korran Maran (Mahalingam, *A Topographical List: Thanjavur*, no. TJ 2777, pp. 230–231); Tennavan Ilango Muttaraiyan (K. V. Subrahmanya Aiyer, ed., *South Indian Inscriptions*, vol. V [Madras: Superintendent, Government Press, 1925], no. 618, p. 246); Velan Tiruvenkadadigal alias Muvenda Pidur Velan (Mahalingam, *A Topographical List: Thanjavur*, no. TJ 2804, pp. 635–636); Sembiyan Arkattu Velan alias Maravan Nakkan (Rao, ed., *South Indian Inscriptions*, vol. XIII, no. 315, p. 162); Palavettaraiyan Kandan Amudan (Sastri, ed., *South Indian Inscriptions*, vol. V, no. 551, p. 222); Palavettaraiyar Kumaran Maravan (Rao, ed., *South Indian Inscriptions*, vol. XIX, no. 172, p. 88); Adittan Viman of Kumarapadi, *araiyar* of Andurai (Rao, ed., *South Indian Inscriptions*, vol. XIX, nos. 30 and 31, pp. 14–15); Nakkan Arinjikai alias Parantaka Pallavaraiyan (Rao, ed., *South Indian Inscriptions*, vol. XIX, no. 70, p. 37).

50. Marxia Gandhi, ed., *Thanjavur Taluk Inscriptions*, vol. 1 (Chennai: State Department of Archaeology, 1979): Inscription nos. 23/1979, 26/79, 27/79, 30/79, 31/79.

51. This last inscription (Gandhi, ed., *Thanjavur Taluk Inscriptions*, vol. 1, no. 31/1979, p. 38; also *ARE* 1911, no. 278) speaks of the *nagarattar* of Parakesaripuram, who had given the *mukattodu*, or crowning stone, and who were now gifting gold for a fly-whisk or *chamara*.

52. Gandhi, ed., *Thanjavur Taluk Inscriptions*, vol. 1, no. 29/1979, p. 36. This particular inscription that had intrigued us is one that Marxia double-checked in situ when we made a second trip to the temple.

53. Sastri, ed., *South Indian Inscriptions*, vol. V, no. 652, pp. 274–275.

54. Mahalingam, *A Topographical List: Thanjavur*, no. TJ 2352, pp. 536–537. The Bana chieftain (Vanadaraiyar) Pundi-udaiyan Suriyan Pavalakunranar petitioned the king in his thirty-second year for permission to rebuild the Vaigavur temple; the inscription is dated in his fortieth year, suggesting that the rebuilding took only eight years. *Annual Report on Indian Epigraphy*, 1914, no. 51.

55. I am indebted to Professor S. Srinivasalu of the Geology Department of Annamalai University in Chennai for this observation.

56. Mahalingam, *A Topographical List: Thanjavur*.

57. Mahalingam, *A Topographical List: Thanjavur*, no. TJ 1350, pp. 315–316.

58. Tirumananjeri: Mahalingam, *A Topographical List: Thanjavur*, no. TJ 1313, p. 308. Tirukkalitattai: Mahalingam, *A Topographical List: Thanjavur*, no. TJ 247, p. 59; also Sten Konow, ed., *Epigraphia Indica*, vol. XII (Calcutta: Government of India, Archaeological Department, 1913–1914), no. 15, p. 126. Tiruvelvikudi: Mahalingam, *A Topographical List*, no. TJ 1485, p. 346.

59. I am grateful to Dr. Muniratnam of the Epigraphical Survey of India for access to the transcript of *Annual Report on Indian Epigraphy*, 1926, no. 131. This record clearly states that a fourth part of the temple (*nalopadi*) came from the two guilds, and that the rest was from Tiruvaiyaru Yogiar and his son Srika, known as Tirukattrali pichchan. In a slight diversion, it bears mention that two inscriptions at the Nageshvara temple at Kumbakonam speak of the Thanjavur lady of the stone temple (*thanjavur tirukattrali piratti*) named Amitravalli; however, both epigraphs merely record gifts to a functioning temple.

60. Members of military regiment: Mahalingam, *A Topographical List: Thanjavur*, no. TJ 1497, p. 348. Scribe: Mahalingam, *A Topographical List: Thanjavur*, no. TJ 1498, p. 348. Single stones: Mahalingam, *A Topographical List: Thanjavur*, nos. TJ 1486, 1488, 1493, pp. 347–348.

61. One such example at Tiruvilakudi is *ARE* 1926, no. 126, where an inscribed stone was given by Velan Solai. At Tirumananjeri, a woman employed by the palace at Thanjavur gave ninety-six sheep as well as the stone on which the gift was inscribed (Mahalingam, *A Topographical List: Thanjavur*, no. TJ 1339, p. 313). Another gift of a range of ritual vessels to be used for the Sribali puja, plus the stone on which it was inscribed, was the gift to Tirumananjeri by a merchant named Mundan Arangan. Mahalingam, *A Topographical List: Thanjavur*, no. TJ 1340, p. 313; G. V. Srinivasa Rao, ed., *South Indian Inscriptions*, vol. XIX (Madras: Superintendent, Government Press, 1967), no. 99, p. 51.

62. As inscriptions are subject to further scrutiny, it is likely that a few more names will emerge.

63. The fourth royal temple, that of Rajendra at Gangai-konda-chola-puram, is in the South Arcot district.

64. Kaimal, "Early Cola Kings and 'Early Cola Temples,'" p. 54: "Possibly, Aditya did not build any temples."

65. Phyllis Granoff, "Halayudha's Prism: The Experience of Religion in Medieval Hymns and Stories," in *Gods, Guardians, and Lovers: Temple Sculptures from North India, AD 700–1200*, ed. Vishakha N. Desai and Darielle Mason (New York; Ahmedabad: Asia Society Galleries, in association with Mapin Publishing, 1993), p. 69.

66. The number may be slightly higher, since seven records are too fragmentary to include in the count.

67. I am using for this mini-survey the inscriptions as recorded in Mahalingam, fully aware that his list has since been expanded by those among us studying the inscriptional records on temples.

68. Mahalingam, *A Topographical List: Thanjavur*, no. 2043, p. 473; or Sivali Kamudaiyan, Tiruvegam Udaiyan, chief of Thanjavur, no. 2044, p. 473; Ambalattadi Ponnambalakuttan, chief of Kottur, no. 2047, p. 474.

69. Sastri, ed., *South Indian Inscriptions*, vol. V, no. 625, p. 248; Gandhi, *Thanjavur Taluk Inscriptions*, vol. I, 25/1979, p. 31.

70. Gandhi, *Thanjavur Vattak Kalvattigal*, vol. II [also known as *Tamilnattuk Kalvettukal Vol. VIII*] (Chennai: State Department of Archaeology, 2015–2016), no. 187/2014, p. 269.

71. Peterson, *Poems to Śiva*, p. 134.

72. Marxia Gandhi, ed., *Thanjavur Vattak Kalvattigal*, part II (Chennai: State Department of Archaeology, 2015–2016), no. 33/2014, p. 59.

73. It is intriguing that the form was celebrated in bronze portable images rather than in the medium of stone sculptures inserted into the niches of temples. Bruno Dagens, *The Mayamata*, ch. 36, verses 65–67a, p. 348, tells us that the worship of the Victor of Three Forts brings about the death of enemies.

74. N. Marxia Gandhi, ed., *Thanjavur Vattak Kalvattigal*, part II: inscription no. 33/2014, p. 59.

75. An inscription of the year 939 of Parantaka records a gift of sheep for a perpetual lamp to the temple of Maraikkadu by Gunavan, resident of Indaiyur, on the occasion of his return from a successful campaign in Sri Lanka that resulted in the defeat of the Singhala king. See Mahalingam, *A Topographical List: Thanjavur*, no. TJ 3204, p. 719; also K. G. Krishnan, ed., *South Indian Inscriptions*, vol. XVII (Madras: Superintendent, Government Press, 1957), no. 501, p. 207.

76. An attractive flower associated with Shiva, and sometimes called the thorn-apple, all parts of the plant are poisonous and cause delirium.

77. The middle toes and fingers always lack rings.

78. An instance of this is provided by an image of child saint Sambandar holding an empty cup in his left hand and with a finger of his right hand pointing upward (wrongly identified as bala-Krishna) that was "discarded because of a miscast; the mold was not completely filled with molten metal." See Ben B. Johnson, "Krishna Rajamannar Bronzes: An Examination and Treatment Report," in Pratapaditya Pal, *Krishna: The Cowherd King* (Los Angeles: LA County Museum of Art, 1972), pp. 46ff and plates 18, 19, 20, 22, 23, 26.

79. It is worth noting that to this day, villages in this area still retain their ancient names, many reflecting royal or sacred figures of bygone days. Thus, the town of Sembiyan Mahadevi, somewhat northwest of Nagapattinam, takes the name of a queen whose influential patronage we will examine in chapter 4, while the same area houses the village of Vanavan Mahadevi, named after another Chola queen, and the village of Paravai is named for the dancing girl who was saint Sundarar's wife, and whose name was later adopted by various women, including Rajendra Chola's *bhogiyar*, or concubine.

80. R. Nagaswamy, "A Nataraja Bronze and an Inscribed Uma from Karaiviram Village," *Lalit Kala* 19 (1979): 17. The inscription starts with the identifying phrase "*madiraiyum ilamum konda ko Parakesari*," a clear reference to Parantaka I, whose reign commenced in 906. The inscription specifies that the image was established in the eleventh year of the monarch, which corresponds to the year 917. This should not delude us into thinking of the bronze as a royal commission. The inscription specifies that the image was established, set up (*elundarulivitta*), by Katanagan Nagattaraiyan of Sellur in Indalanadu, and the inscription further specifies that he did this *srikaryam* or "sacred task" at the behest of a certain Brahma Sri Tongarasar.

81. Those pleats appear to be an early stylistic trait that is seen also in the Ardha-nari, or Half Woman image of Shiva, from the Nageshvara temple.

82. John Mosteller's book, *The Measure of Form: A New Approach for the Study of Indian Sculpture* (New Delhi: Abhinav Publications, 1991), seemed to provide a step in a new direction. While his collection of plates, in which each image is accompanied by a modular grid, seemed to hold great promise, the work did not carry us forward in any meaningful way. It might be time for a renewed look at modular systems, since in a direct and purely visual sense one can discern differences in proportional systems. For instance, one need but compare a stone image on a Chola temple with one from the adjoining Hoysala kingdom to be sure that the method *must* produce interesting insights.

83. See Françoise L'Hernault, *The Iconography of the Brhadisvara Temple*, ed. Lalit M. Gujral (New Delhi: Indira Gandhi National Centre for Arts; Pondichery: École Française d'Extrême-Orient, 2002), plates 5–6, pp. 12–14.

CHAPTER 3: WRIT IN STONE

1. Marxia Gandhi, ed., *Thanjavur Vattak Kalvattigal*, vol. II [also known as *Tamilnattuk Kalvettukal Vol. VIII*] (Chennai: State Department of Archeology, 2015–2016), no. 104/2014, p. 163f.

2. The reader would do well to refer to Leslie Orr, "Preface," in *Putuccēri Māṇilakkalveṭṭukkaḷ* (*Pondicherry Inscriptions*), 2 vols., ed. Bahour S. Kuppusamy and G. Vijayavenugopal (Pondicherry: Institut Français de Pondichéry/École Française d'Extrême-Orient, 2006), pp. i–xxviii. See also Kathleeen D. Morrison and Mark T. Lycett, "Inscriptions as Artefacts: Precolonial South India and the Analysis of Texts," *Journal of Archaeological Method and Theory* 4, nos. 3/4 (September 1997): 215–237.

3. Historian Romila Thapar has suggested ways of reading texts like the Puranas, mythological texts interspersed with kernels of factual political information, to extract history.

4. To get some idea of the vast number of inscriptions involved, see James Heitzmann, "Appendix: Sites of Chola-Period Inscriptions in Five Study Areas," in *Gifts of Power: Lordship in an Early Indian State* (New Delhi: Oxford University Press, 1997), pp. 238–244, which lists 2,391 inscriptions in five talukas. On the immense task of producing a usable archive of these inscriptions, see Sascha Ebeling, "The Digital Archive of South Indian Inscriptions (DASI)—A Preliminary Report," in *South-Indian Horizons: Felicitation Volume for François Gros*, ed. Jean-Luc Chevillard (Pondicherry: Institut Français de Pondichéry/École Française d'Extrême-Orient, 2006).

5. E. Hultzsch, V. Venkayya, and H. Krishna Sastri, eds., *South Indian Inscriptions*, vol. 2 (Madras: Superintendent, Government Press, 1891–1916).

6. T. V. Mahalingam, *A Topographical List of Inscriptions in Tamil Nadu and Kerala States*, 8 vols. (New Delhi: Indian Council of Historical Research, 1985–1992), covers inscriptions discovered and recorded until the year 1972, when the project commenced. The numbers of inscriptions are marginally greater than recorded by Mahalingam—for instance, only four inscriptions are recorded for the Tiruvedikudi temple (nos. 3072–3075 on p. 690), while Marxia Gandhi, ed., *Thanjavur Taluk Inscriptions*, vol. 1 (Chennai: State Department of Archaeology, 1979) lists over twenty (with more to be added after our field visit).

7. For instance, the volumes on the three royal temples of Thanjavur, Gangaikondacholapuram, and Darasuram published by the Institut Français de Pondichéry. Françoise L'Hernault, with P. R. Srinivasan et Jacques Dumarçay, *Darasuram: Epigraphical Study: Etude Architecturale: Etude Iconographique* (Paris: École Française d'Extrême-Orient, 1987); Françoise L'Hernault, *The Iconography of the Brhadisvara Temple*, ed. Lalit M. Gujral (New Delhi: Indira Gandhi National Centre for Arts; Pondicherry: École Française d'Extrême-Orient, 2002); Pierre Pichard, *Vingt Ans après Tanjavur, Gangaikondacholapuram*, 2 vols. (Paris: École Française d'Extrême-Orient, 1994); Pierre Pichard, *Tanjavur Brhadisvara: An Architectural Study* (New Delhi: Indira Gandhi National Centre for the Arts; Pondicherry: École Française d'Extrême-Orient, 1995).

8. I spent days working with this material together with my epigraphy colleague; we unrolled such rubbings across the floor of an open corridor—and tried not to transfer soot patches from our fingers onto our face and clothes!

9. The head count is taken from T. V. Mahalingam, *A Topographical List of Inscriptions in Tamil Nadu and Kerala States*, vol. 7: *Thanjavur District*, and vol. 8: *Tiruchchirapalli District* (New Delhi: Indian Council of Historical Research, 1991–1992).

10. Mahalingam, *A Topographical List: Thanjavur*, no. TJ 228, p. 54. Reign of Rajaraja III, 1239.

11. Ibid., no. TJ 1746, p. 407. Reign of Kulottunga III.

12. G. V. Srinivasa Rao, ed., *South Indian Inscriptions*, vol. XIX (Madras: Superintendent, Government Press, 1967), no. 431.

13. The only temple for which such a record exists is Pullamangai: Charlotte Schmid, "Au seuil du monde divin: reflets et passages du dieu d'Alanturai a Pullamankai," *Bulletin de l'École Française d'Extrême-Orient*, 92 (2005): 39–157, 747–748, 753. The inscriptional record is on pp. 112–143.

14. Gandhi, *Thanjavur Taluk Inscriptions*, vol. I, no. 49/1979, no page numbering.

15. Ibid., vol. I, no. 39/1979, no page numbering.

16. Ibid., vol. I, no. 35/1979, no page numbering.

17. One Gandaraditya record only: Gandhi, *Thanjavur Taluk Inscriptions*, vol. I, no. 59a/1979, but missing today; Aditya Karikala (seven/eight records): nos. 15, 16, 17, 18, and 32 of 1979, plus three missing today; Gandhi, nos. 47, 60, and 61 of 1979; and four records of Uttama Chola: Gandhi, nos. 19, 20, 21, and 28 of 1979, no page numbering.

18. Gandhi, *Thanjavur Taluk Inscriptions*, vol. I, no. 43/1979, no page numbering.

19. Ibid., nos. 30, 37, 38, 40, 41, 41(I), 41(II), and 50 of 1979, no page numbering.

20. Ibid., no. 28/1979, no page numbering, dated in the sixth year of a Parakesarivarman. Since it is specified that she is the queen of Uttama Chola, it appears that this might be an inscription in the reign of Arinjaya and thus dating to 958.

21. Ibid., no. 20/1979, no page numbering, dated in the eighth year of Parakesarivarman.

22. Vasudevan Mahadevi specifies that she is wife of Korran Damodaran of the Gautama gotra. Marxia Gandhi, *Thanjavur Taluk Inscriptions*, vol. I, no. 36/1979.

23. The enclosing *prakara* walls carry inscriptions of Kulottunga III and Rajaraja III, while a late inscription of Saka era 1467 = CE 1545 is engraved on the *gopuram* gateway. See Gandhi, *Thanjavur Taluk Inscriptions*, vol. I, nos. 11, 12, 13, 14 of 1979, no page numbering.

24. Gandhi, *Thanjavur Taluk Inscriptions*, vol. I, nos. 15, 16, 17, 18 of 1979, no page numbering.

25. In Goa, which follows the old Portuguese system, all legal documents (even today in the digital era) are hand-copied with pen and ink, often from computer-printed records into large ledgers. Requisitioning one's own copy of such a record took nearly two months in the year 2015. I have no idea of how long it would take a lawyer or an adjudicator to requisition access to the original record, which would be necessary for legal recourse.

26. I am indebted to one of the readers of my manuscript for pointing out the importance of legitimacy and protection.

27. T. V. Mahalingam, *A Topographical List of Inscriptions in the Tamil Nadu and Kerala States*, vol. 2: *South Arcot District* (New Delhi: Indian Council of Historical Research, 1988), no. SA 1660, p. 387; also K. V. Subrahmanya Aiyer, ed., *South Indian Inscriptions*, vol. VII (Madras: Superintendent, Government Press, 1932), no. 1009, p. 480.

28. Mahalingam, *A Topographical List: South Arcot*, no. SA 1664, p. 388; see also E. Hultzsch, ed., *Epigraphia Indica*, vol. VIII, 1905–1906 (Calcutta: Government of India, Department of Archaeology, 1981), no. 18A, p. 180.

29. Mahalingam, *A Topographical List: South Arcot*, no. SA 1668, p. 389; also Aiyer, *South Indian Inscriptions*, vol. VII, no. 963, p. 468.

30. Mahalingam, *A Topographical List: South Arcot*, nos. SA 1693–SA 1696, pp. 394–395.

31. S. Swaminathan, ed., *South Indian Inscriptions*, vol. XXXII (New Delhi: Director General, Archaeological Survey of India, 2012) Appendix, nos. 5–9, pp. 390–395.

32. Mahalingam, *A Topographical List: South Arcot*, nos. SA 1696–SA 1701, pp. 395–396.

33. Ibid., no. SA 1707, p. 397.

34. Ibid., no. SA 1715, pp. 399–400.

35. Ibid., no. SA 1745, p. 406; also no. SA 1746, pp. 406–407. For the complete set of records at Tirunamanallur, see Mahalingam, *A Topographical List: South Arcot*, nos. SA 1659–SA 1751, pp. 387–408. See also Aiyer, *South Indian Inscriptions*, vol. VII, no. 954, p. 466.

36. David Dean Shulman, *Songs of the Harsh Devotee: The Tevaram of Cuntaramurttinayanar* (Philadelphia: University of Philadelphia Press, 1990), p. 457.

37. T. V. Mahalingam, *A Topographical List of Inscriptions in the Tamil Nadu and Kerala States*, vol. 7: *Thanjavur District* (New Delhi: Indian Council of Historical Research, 1992), nos. TJ 3173–3259, pp. 712–733 covers Maraikkadu inscriptions.

38. Ibid., no. TJ 3204, p. 719.

39. Ibid., no. TJ 3198, p. 718.

40. Ibid., no. TJ 3210, p. 721.

41. Ibid., no. TJ 3212, p. 721.

42. Ibid., no. TJ 565, p. 129. See also *Annual Report on Indian Epigraphy* 1907, no. 227.

43. Mahalingam, *A Topographical List: Thanjavur*, no. TJ 554, p. 126. See also *ARE* 1907, no. 251.

44. Mahalingam, *A Topographical List: Thanjavur*, no. TJ 574, p. 131.

45. Ibid., no. TJ 576, p. 131.

46. Ibid., no. TJ 589, p. 135; also Rao, ed., *South Indian Inscriptions*, vol. XIX, no. 346, p. 177.

47. Mahalingam, *A Topographical List: Thanjavur*, no. TJ 612, p. 141.

48. Ibid., no. TJ 595, p. 137.

49. Ibid., no. TJ 607, p. 140.

50. Ibid., no. TJ 579, p. 132. See also H. Krishna Sastri, ed., "On the North Wall of the Central Shrine in the Mahalingasvamin Temple at Tiruvidaimarudur," in *South Indian Inscriptions*, vol. III, part III (Madras: Superintendent, Government Press, 1920), no. 202, p. 378f. One part was to be performed on *Tai pusam*; parts 2, 3, and 4 were to be performed on consecutive days after the tank festival; and the remaining three parts were to commence on the days following *Vaikhashi Tiruvadirai*. The dancer was Kirti Maraikandan, alias Tiruvellarai chakkai kootan.

51. Mahalingam, *A Topographical List: Thanjavur*, no. TJ 586, p. 135.

52. Ibid., no. TJ 615, pp. 141–142.

53. Ibid., no. TJ 617, p. 142.

54. Ibid., no. TJ 614, p. 141.

55. Ibid., no. TJ 620, p. 143. Also Rao, ed., *South Indian Inscriptions*, vol. XIX, no. 4, p. 2.

56. Mahalingam, *A Topographical List: Thanjavur*, no. TJ 656, pp. 152–153.

57. Ibid., no. TJ 657, p. 153.

58. Ibid., no. TJ 662, p. 154.

59. Ibid., no. TJ 2505, pp. 567–568.

60. Ibid., no. TJ 666, 667, pp. 155–156. See G. V. Srinivasa Rao, ed., *South Indian Inscriptions*, vol. XXIII (Madras: Superintendent, Government Press, 1979), no. 306, p. 216.

61. Mahalingam, *A Topographical List: Thanjavur*, no. TJ 668, p. 156.

62. Ibid., no. TJ 671–672, pp. 157–158.

63. Ibid., no. TJ 679, pp. 159–160.

64. For the descent direct to Manu, see K. V. Subrahmanya Aiyer, "The Larger Leiden Plates (of Rajaraja I)," in *Epigraphia Indica*, vol. XXII, 1933–1934, ed. N. P. Chakravarti (Delhi: Manager of Publications, 1938), no. 34, pp. 213–266. The descent through Vishnu, Brahma, and Kasyapa to Manu is given in Sastri, "The Tiruvalangadu Copper-Plates of the Sixth Year of Rajendra-Chola I," *South Indian Inscriptions*, vol. III, part III, no. 205, pp. 383–439.

65. These plates have been the subject of a penetrating article by Daud Ali, a must-read for thinking about dynastic eulogies and the use of hyperbole, as indicated by its title: "Royal Eulogy as World History: Rethinking Copper-Plate Inscriptions in Cola India," in *Querying the Medieval: The History of Practice in South Asia*, ed. Ronald B. Inden (New York: Oxford University Press, 2000), pp. 165–229.

66. See chapter 9, later.

67. T. A. Gopinatha Rao, "Anbil Plates of Sundara-Chola: The 4th Year," in *Epigraphia Indica*, vol. XV, 1919–20, ed. F. W. Thomas (New Delhi: Director General, Archaeological Survey of India, 1925), no. 5, pp. 44–72. I have marginally changed the phraseology.

68. Sastri, "The Tiruvalangadu Copper-Plates of the Sixth Year of Rajendra-Chola I," *South Indian Inscriptions*, vol. III, part III, no. 205, p. 426.

69. Ibid., p. 439.

70. Personal communication from Marxia Gandhi. The Karandai copper plates of Rajendra I, fifty-seven in number, weigh 246 pounds, while the thirty-one Tiruvalankadu plates, also of Rajendra, weigh 203 pounds.

71. Marxia Gandhi, "Thiru Indalur Copper Plate—A Critical

Study," *Bulletin of the Department of Museums*, Tourism Endowment Lecture, October 2016: 2–18.

72. S. Sankaranarayana, Marxia Gandhi, A. Padmavathy, and R. Sivanantham, *Thiruvindalur Copper Plate* (Chennai: State Department of Archaeology, 2011), p. 9.

73. P. R. Srinivasan, ed., *South Indian Inscriptions*, vol. XXVI (Madras: Superintendent, Government Press, 1942), no. 665, p. 449, and no. 685, p. 469.

74. Leslie Orr, "Preface," in *Putuccēri Mānilakkalveṭṭukkaḷ* (*Pondicherry Inscriptions*), 2 vols., ed. Bahour S. Kuppusamy and G. Vijayavenugopal (Pondicherry: Institut Français de Pondichéry; École Française d'Extrême-Orient, 2006), pp. xiii.

CHAPTER 4: PORTRAIT OF A QUEEN AND HER PATRONAGE OF DANCING SHIVA

1. G. V. Srinivasa Rao, ed., *South Indian Inscriptions*, vol. XIX (Madras: Superintendent, Government Press, 1967), no. 302, p. 149.

2. Vidya Dehejia, *The Body Adorned* (New York: Columbia University Press, 2009).

3. H. Krishna Sastri, ed., *South Indian Inscriptions*, vol. V (Madras: Superintendent, Government Press, 1925), no. 549, p. 221. Tiruvaiyaru: "Cholaperuman pattakal deviyar, sembiyan-madeviyarana kulamanikkam nam pirattiyar."

4. G. V. Srinivasa Rao, ed., *South Indian Inscriptions*, vol. XIII (Madras: Superintendent, Government Press, 1952), no. 72, p. 33–34.

5. Temple at Tiruvidaimaradur. T. V. Mahalingam, *A Topographical List of Inscriptions in Tamil Nadu and Kerala States*, vol. 7: *Thanjavur District* (New Delhi: Indian Council of Historical Research, 1991), no. TJ 614, p. 141. See also Rao, ed., *South Indian Inscriptions*, vol. XIII, no. 133, p. 68, and G. V. Srinivasa Rao, ed., *South Indian Inscriptions*, vol. XXIII (Madras: Superintendent, Government Press, 1979), no. 215, pp. 156–157.

6. Rao, ed., *South Indian Inscriptions*, vol. XIII, no. 151, pp. 79–80. In the year 961, during the reign of Sundara Chola, speaks of the *Sembiyan Mahadevi vaykkal*.

7. T. V. Mahalingam, *A Topographical List of Inscriptions in the Tamil Nadu and Kerala States*, vol. 8: *Tiruchchirappalli District* (New Delhi: Indian Council of Historical Research, 1992), no. 1686, p. 372. See H. Krishna Sastri, ed., *South Indian Inscriptions*, vol. V (Madras: Superintendent, Government Press, 1925), no. 638, p. 258. Reference to *Sembiyan-mahadevi-per-eri* in 1008 in temple at Tirumalavadi.

8. Mahalingam, *A Topographical List: Tiruchchirappalli*, no. Tp 1757, p. 389, in the reign of Rajaraja III—that is, 1247.

9. Sastri, ed., *South Indian Inscriptions*, vol. III, part III, no. 151A, p. 318: line 28.

10. Ibid., line 31.

11. Swaminathan, ed., *South Indian Inscriptions*, vol. XXXII, part II, no. 100, p. 215f; also *Annual Report on Indian Epigraphy*, 1925, no. 494; also Mahalingam, *A Topographical List: Thanjavur*, no. TJ 1563, p. 363.

12. *ARE* 1925, no. 492; also Mahalingam, *A Topographical List: Thanjavur*, no. TJ 1568, p. 364.

13. Swaminathan, ed., *South Indian Inscriptions*, vol. XXXII, part II, no. 213, p. 355; also Mahalingam, *A Topographical List: Thanjavur*, no. TJ 1569, pp. 364–365.

14. Swaminathan, ed., *South Indian Inscriptions*, vol. XXXII, part II, no. 235, p. 379f; also Mahalingam, *A Topographical List: Thanjavur*, no. TJ 1574, p. 366; also *ARE* 1925, no. 480.

15. *ARE* 1925, no. 482; also Mahalingam, *A Topographical List: Thanjavur*, no. TJ 1575, p. 366.

16. Mahalingam, *A Topographical List: Thanjavur*, no. TJ 1570, p. 365.

17. Ibid., no. TJ 1577, pp. 366–367. For details, see *ARE* 1925, no. 481. The two images to which additional funds were given for food offerings are Shiva with the bull and the bronze of Sembiyan Mahadevi. Additionally, provisions were made for the first time for food offerings to Atkondar (probably *Chandrashekhara*), Uma of Adavallar, Uma-sahita, Uma of Shiva with the bull, and Uma of the Begging Lord.

18. Personal communication from Samuel Eilenberg, obtained from a source he did not divulge and dating well before the time I began investigating the bronze, was to the effect that the bronze was recovered from a well in or near the town of Sembiyan Mahadevi.

19. A. C. Woolner and Lakshman Sarup, trans., *Thirteen Plays of Bhasa* (Delhi: Motilal Banarsidass, reprint, 1985), p. 174f.

20. Nicholas Cane, "Queen Cempiyan Mahadevi's Religious Patronage in Tenth-Century South India: The 'Missing Link' between Local and Royal Bhakti?" in *The Archaeology of Bhakti: Royal Bhakti, Local Bhakti*, ed. Emmanuel Francis and Charlotte Schmid (Pondicherry: Sri Aurobindo Ashram Press, 2016), pp. 372–375, mentions two other inscriptions, one at Tenneri near Kanchipuram and the other at Konerirajapuram, that are *tirumukams* or royal orders issued by Sembiyan Mahadevi.

21. *Manis* are usually brahmacharins. Inscription is at Tirukodikaval: *Annual Report on Indian Epigraphy* 1930–31, no. 19: the royal order was known as *tirumukam*, or "sacred face."

22. I have drawn extensively on the excellent analysis of S. Y. Krishnaswamy, "Major Irrigation Systems of Ancient Tamil Nadu," in *Proceedings of the First International Conference Seminar of Tamil Studies, Kuala Lumpur*, ed. Xavier S. Thani Nayagam (Kuala Lumpur: International Association of Tamil Research, 1968), pp. 451–461.

23. Ibid.

24. Each has backwaters that extend roughly 6 kilometers inland, where major sluice points disallow the saltwater of the ocean to flow farther inland.

25. These statistics come from a PowerPoint presentation by the Public Works Department (PWD) that is in charge of Tamil Nadu's Kaveri waters.

26. Statistics of this type are posted on boards at each canal's branching off point from the river.

27. K. G. Krishnan, *Karandai Tamil Sangam Plates of Rajendrachola I* (New Delhi: Archaeological Survey of India, 1984), p. 196.

28. In years when the southwest monsoon rains fail, a single long duration crop (150–160 days) known as *samba* is planted.

29. Indira Peterson, "Kaveri in Legend and Literature," in *Eternal Kaveri: Historical Sites along South India's Greatest River*, ed. George Michell (Mumbai: Marg Publications, 1999), pp. 35–48, citation on p. 40.

30. I must thank my *athimber*, M. S. Swaminathan, who put me in touch with the Rice Research Institute, based in Aduturai, and to its staff, especially to Dr. Rajendran and Mrs. Saraswati, for taking the time to educate me on the complexities and niceties of rice-growing.

31. S. Swaminathan, ed., *South Indian Inscriptions*, vol. XXXII (New Delhi: Director General, Archaeological Survey of India, 2012), part I, no. 6, p. 6. Only two Rajakesarivarmans had reigns that long—Aditya and Rajaraja. Dr. S. Swaminathan is of the opinion that the paleography is early and that the record must hence belong to Aditya.

32. Swaminathan, ed., *South Indian Inscriptions*, vol. XXXII, part I, no. 27, p. 35.

33. Ibid., part II, no. 44, p. 141. A record of the time of Rajaraja III that refers to the construction of a stone sluice to the Karikala Chola *Per aru* (Great River) at Musiri is cut into the stone of the head-sluice of what is known today as the *Periya vaykal* (Great Canal) at Musiri. Inscriptions of the time of Kulottunga III, referring to the construction of sluices, are found on a pillar and a stone on the bridge over the Uyyakondan canal at Vettuvaytalai in Trichy district.

34. Swaminathan, ed., *South Indian Inscriptions*, vol. XXXII, part I, no. 51, p. 65f.

35. Kenneth R. Hall, ed., *Structure and Society in Early South India: Essays in Honour of Noboru Karashima* (New Delhi; New York: Oxford University Press, 2001), pp. 1–27.

36. Swaminathan, ed., *South Indian Inscriptions*, vol. XXXII, part I, no. 28, pp. 36–39. The inscription is engraved on a pillar and a loose stone at Tiruninravur in Chinglepet district.

37. G. V. Srinivasa Rao, ed., *South Indian Inscriptions*, vol. XIII (Madras: Superintendent, Government Press, 1952), no. 151, pp. 79–80.

38. Rao, ed., *South Indian Inscriptions*, vol. XIX, no. 359, pp. 187–188.

39. Mahalingam, *A Topographical List: Tiruchchirappalli*, nos. Tp 2, p. 1, and Tp 1304, pp. 287–288.

40. Ibid., no. Tp 857, p. 184.

41. Ibid., no. Tp 1146, p. 255.

42. This suggestion is based on the *Yasastilaka*, a text written in the tenth century by the court poet of Rashtrakuta king Krishnadeva while that king was camping in Chola territory after his victory in the battle of Takkolam. The text speaks of the perfect match as that between a girl, twelve years of age, and a young man of sixteen.

43. The temple of Uyyakondan Tirumalai. Mahalingam, *A Topographical List: Tiruchchirappalli*, no. Tp 1400, p. 309.

44. Similarly, from Sangam days, Tennavan and Panchavan are references to Pandya connections.

45. Rao, ed., *South Indian Inscriptions*, vol. XIX, no. 11, pp. 5–6; also Swaminathan, ed., *South Indian Inscriptions*, vol. XXXII, part II, no. 218, p. 359.

46. See Nicholas Cane, "Queen Cempiyan Mahadevi's Religious Patronage," pp. 353–356, for a discussion of this issue.

47. See note 42, earlier.

48. For an order issued by Rajaraja regarding punishment for the assassination of Aditya Karikala Chola, see Swaminathan, ed., *South Indian Inscriptions*, vol. XXXII, part II, no. 230, p. 369f. The punishment is seemingly lenient in that only the property of the two brothers and all members of their immediate families were confiscated, sold, and the proceeds deposited in the royal treasury. See also Nicholas Cane, "Queen Cempiyan Mahadevi's Religious Patronage," pp. 365–369, for an extensive discussion of a small bas relief panel on the walls of the Koneri temple that features Gandaraditya and Uttama Chola; Cane convincingly argues that the panel demonstrates Sembiyan Mahadevi's attempt to "legitimate the rule of her son."

49. H. Krishna Sastri, ed., *South Indian Inscriptions*, vol. III, part III (Madras: Superintendent, Government Press, 1929), no. 144, p. 294. The full text follows:

Hail! Prosperity! In this sacred stone temple which Udaiyapirattiyar Madevadigalar *alias* the glorious Sembiyan-Madeviyar who had obtained in her sacred womb the glorious Madhurantakadeva *alias* the glorious Uttama-Chola—had graciously caused to be built to the god (*alvar*) at Tirukkurangaduturai in Tiraimur-nadu, were engraved on stone, in the sixteenth year of (*the reign*) the glorious Uttama-Choladeva *alias* king Parakesarivarman (*such*) *lakshanas* (*i.e., inscriptions?*) as were made to this god in former times (*to last*) as long as the moon and the sun, and which *lakshanas* on examination were found to have become old.

50. T. V. Mahalingam, *A Topographical List of Inscriptions in the Tamil Nadu and Kerala States*, vol. 7: *Thanjavur District* (New Delhi: Indian Council of Historical Research, 1992), nos. TJ 259–308, pp. 62–73, deals with this temple of Tirukodikaval. No. TJ 274 speaks of Sembiyan having rebuilt the temple. See also Rao, ed., *South Indian Inscriptions*, vol. XIX, no. 292, p. 144f. The reengraved records commence with gifts of Pandya ruler Maranjadaiyan and Pallava king Nripatunga during the late 800s, and extend through the reigns of Chola king Parantaka and Rajakesarivarman, between 905–969. It is only with inscriptions of Rajaraja that this formula of reengraving

comes to an end, since Sembiyan's stone temple was already built and any new records could now be engraved directly on its stone walls and base moldings.

51. Rao, ed., *South Indian Inscriptions*, vol. XIX, no. 292, pp. 144–145.

52. Ibid., vol. XIX, no. 72, p. 38.

53. Sastri, ed., *South Indian Inscriptions*, vol. III, part III, no. 133, p. 279. The inscription is in the eighth year of a Parakesarivarman, most probably Uttama Chola, which would allow a fifty-year period to have intervened between the original engraving and its copy.

54. In citing Konerirajapuram and Kuttalam, Padma Kaimal, "Early Cola Kings and 'Early Cola Temples': Art and the Evolution of Kingship," *Artibus Asiae* 56, nos. 1/2 (1996): 63, suggests that the decision to have the temples facing west was due to their being funerary in character, one celebrating her husband Gandaraditya and the other her son Uttama Chola. However, there is also her west-facing temple, the Tiru-araneri at Tiruvarur, that has no funerary connotations.

55. West-facing temples include Konerirajapuram, Kuttalam, Tiruvarur, and Anangur; east-facing temples include Kurangaduturai, Sembiyan Mahadevi, Tirukodikaval, and Vriddhachalam.

56. See the inscription on the pedestal of the Dancing Shiva bronze in Tiruvenkadu temple that is discussed later in this chapter.

57. Sastri, ed., *South Indian Inscriptions*, vol. III, part III, no. 151A, pp. 312–322. See especially lines 80 and 82; a third image of Ganapati is mentioned on line 84. See Douglas Barrett, *Early Cola Bronzes* (Bombay: Bhulabhai Memorial Institute, 1965), plates 1–9, for superb details of these bronzes.

58. Douglas Barrett, *Early Cola Bronzes*, pp. 22–23.

59. Bernard Berenson, in a brilliant essay titled "The Rudiments of Connoisseurship" in *The Study and Criticism of Italian Art* (London: G. Bell and Sons, Ltd., 1903), pp. 111–148, speaks of drapery in painting as the perfect field for the intrusion of mannerisms ("Give a fold a turn that he is accustomed to give it"). He speaks of "one quirk, one curve, one line" as being as characteristic as strokes, curves, and pothooks in writing. Sydney J. Freedberg, writing about Berenson, demystified connoisseurship, writing: "Intuition is no more than the process by which a connoisseur acquires and enters data into his (her) mental bank of remembered similars, then compares, analyzes, and arrives at a solution." See his "Some Thoughts on Berenson, Connoisseurship, and the History of Art," in *I Tatti Studies: Essays in the Renaissance*, vol. 3 (Florence: Villa I Tatti, Harvard Center for Italian Renaissance Studies, 1989), pp. 11–26.

60. Douglas Barrett, *Early Cola Bronzes*, plate 10.

61. Sastri, ed., *South Indian Inscriptions*, vol. III, part III, no. 151A, p. 319: line 35.

62. Ibid., p. 319: line 37.
63. Ibid., p. 320: line 59.
64. Ibid., p. 321: line 85.
65. Ibid., p. 320: line 67.
66. Ibid., p. 319: line 40.
67. Ibid., p. 320: line 72.
68. Ibid., p. 321: lines 76 and 78.
69. Ibid., p. 319: line 46.
70. Ibid., p. 319: line 42.
71. Ibid., p. 319: line 48.
72. Ibid., p. 319: line 49.
73. Ibid., p. 320: line 58.
74. Ibid., p. 320: line 61.
75. Ibid., p. 321: line 75.
76. Ibid., p. 320: line 69.
77. Ibid., p. 320: line 70.
78. Ibid., pp. 321–322: lines 85–87, mentions all three gardens.

79. Swaminathan, ed., *South Indian Inscriptions*, vol. XXXII, part II, no. 137, p. 256f.

80. P. R. Srinivasan, *South Indian Inscriptions*, vol. XXVI (Madras: Superintendent, Government Press, 1978), no. 712. p. 502.

81. Temple of Vriddhachalam: Rao, ed., *South Indian Inscriptions*, vol. XIX, no. 302, pp. 149–150. For the gift at the temple of Sembiyan Mahadevi, see *Nagipattana Mavatta Kalvettukal (Inscriptions of Nagapattinam Dt)* (Chennai: State Dept of Archaeology, 2007): inscription no. 31/1999, p. 78f. Also Mahalingam, *A Topographical List: Thanjavur*, no. TJ 1572, p. 347, and *Annual Report on Indian Epigraphy*, 1925, no. 493.

82. Tiruvenkadu: Rao, ed., *South Indian Inscriptions*, vol. XIII, no. 144, pp. 73–76.

83. Tiruvalanjuli: K. V. Subrahmanya Aiyer, ed., *South Indian Inscriptions*, vol. VIII (Madras: Superintendent, Government Press, 1937), no. 236, p. 130.

84. E. Hultzsch, ed., *South Indian Inscriptions*, vol. II, part II (Madras: Superintendent, Government Press, 1891), no 2. 35 gold flowers: p. 19; 130 gold flowers: p. 20.

85. Sastri, ed., *South Indian Inscriptions*, vol. V (Madras: Superintendent, Government Press, 1925), no. 519, pp. 207–208.

86. S. Sambandhasivacarya, B. Dagens, M. L. Barazer-Billoret, and T. Ganesan, with the collaboration of J. M. Creismeas, *Suksmagama*, vol. II (Pondicherry: Institut Français de Pondichéry, 2012), chapter 37: English summary on pp. cxix–cxxi; Sanskrit text on pp. 232–240.

87. The date is arrived at from personal discussion with T. Ganesan, one of the scholars involved with the translation of the text. For the varieties of flowers, see Sambandhasivacarya, et al., *Suksmagama*, vol. II, n. 2 on p. cxix (English); text, verses 4, 5, 7, 8 on p. 234.

88. *Suksmagama*, vol. II, pp. 232–240.

89. B. A. Saletore, *Ancient Karnataka, vol. 1: History of Tuluva* (Poona: Oriental Book Agency, 1936), pp. 93–96.

90. Khasarpana Lokeshvara: See Benjamin Rowland, *The Art and Architecture of India: Buddhist, Hindu, Jain* (Harmondsworth; Baltimore: Penguin Books, 1953), plate 95, p. 147. See also John Irwin, "The Sanchi Torso," *Journal of the Indian Society of Oriental Art* 6 (1974): 52.

91. B. A. Saletore, *Ancient Karnataka*, pp. 94–95. Since the text of this inscription is not easy to access, I give it in its entirety here:

> Svasti. Sri. One who is a sun to the lotus that is the Lunar race, One with an effulgent body, One with his chest rubbed with saffron from the breast of Lakshmi, One who endowed with great physical strength protected the corners of the world shining in the moonlight of pure fame, One by whom the evil of drinking was made distant (i.e. removed), One who by his distinguished achievements released the earth for the sake of the agraharas of Brahmins, One who by his valour recovered his kingdom after defeating traitorous wicked enemy (to whom he had given land [formerly])—such an Alupendra ruler named Kundavarman was equal to Karna in liberality, to Arjuna in valour, to Indra in wealth, and to Brihaspati in wisdom. And (he was also) virtuous. He was like as bee at the lotus feet of Balacandra Sikhamani. When 4068 years and nine months had passed in the Kaliyuga, and Jupiter was in kanya in the Rohini nakshatra on the afternoon (of the day) in an auspicious moment, (he) set up the image of god Lokesvara in the beautiful vihara of Kadirika.

See also K. V. Subrahmanya Aiyer, ed., *South Indian Inscriptions*, vol. VII (Madras: Superintendent, Government Press, 1932), no. 191, p. 87.

92. The CMA Nataraja measures 44 inches, and inclusive of its pedestal and aureole, weighs 257 pounds. This image is 4 inches taller, more substantial, but minus an aureole. My estimate is a weight around 250 pounds.

93. Two boulders carrying brief inscriptions and found within a fort at Karadi along the banks of the Pennai river to the far north present us with an enigma. Both are dated in the reign of Parantaka, in his fortieth and forty-first year, and both use similar language to speak of the gift of ninety-six sheep to burn a *nonda vilakku* in the temple of Madapparai. The inscription of the forty-first year or 946 mentions the gift from Sembiyan Mahadevi, consort of prince (*pillaiyar*) Gandaraditya; that of the fortieth year or 945 speaks of Viranaraniyar, consort of prince (*pillaiyar*) Gandaraditya. I have checked both rubbings at Mysuru, and the reading, while not sharp, is quite clear. See *Annual Report on Indian Epigraphy*, 1937, nos. 220 and 221. Who is this Viranaraniyar who so totally disappears from the epigraphic record? Was she perhaps a princess who died young without bearing any children?

94. Mahalingam, *A Topographical List: Thanjavur*, no. TJ 151, p. 33, and TJ 2972, p. 669.

95. The nine other Parantaka queens, known from their gifts to various temples are:

> Tribhuvanamahadevi: Mahalingam, *A Topographical List: Thanjavur*, no. TJ 2781, pp. 631–632, and TJ 3017, pp. 678–679.
> Chola Sikhamaniyar, daughter of Nanguri Nangaiyar of Mayilappil: Mahalingam, *A Topographical List: Thanjavur*, no. TJ 3027, pp. 680–681, and TJ 2791, p. 633.
> Arinjikai, daughter of Iladaraiyar: Mahalingam, *A Topographical List: Thanjavur*, no. TJ 3031, p. 681.
> Tennavan Mahadeviyar alias Narayana Nangri Nangaiyar: Mahalingam, *A Topographical List: Thanjavur*, no. TJ 2738, p. 622.
> Trailokyamahadevi: Mahalingam, *A Topographical List: Thanjavur*, no. TJ 2800, p. 635.
> Cheyabhuvana Chinatamaniyar of Kaveripumpattinam: Mahalingam, *A Topographical List: Thanjavur*, no. TJ 2922, p. 659.
> Vallavan Mahadeviyar: Mahalingam, *A Topographical List: Thanjavur*, no. TJ 2328, p. 532.
> Arulmoli Nanagaiyar, daughter of Palavettaraiyar: Mahalingam, *A Topographical List: Thanjavur*, no. TJ 2874, p. 649.
> Cholamahadeviyar: Mahalingam, *A Topographical List: Thanjavur*, nos. TJ 2835, p. 642, and TJ 2991, p. 673.

96. Orattanan is known from several inscriptions, including Mahalingam, *A Topographical List: Thanjavur*, nos. TJ 1510, pp. 351–352; TJ 1564, pp. 363–364; and TJ 1574, p. 366.

97. A search through inscriptions reveals the names of as many as twelve other queens for Uttama Chola:

> Battan Danatongiyar: Rao, ed., *South Indian Inscriptions*, vol. XIX, no. 311, pp. 155–156, and Mahalingam, *A Topographical List: Thanjavur*, no. TJ 764, pp. 180–181.
> Malapadi Tennavan Mahadeviyar: Rao, ed., *South Indian Inscriptions*, vol. XIX, no. 311, pp. 155–156.
> Kilandigal, daughter of Vilupparaiyar: Ibid.
> Vanavan Mahadeviyar, daughter of Irungolar: Ibid.
> ———, daughter of Palavettaraiyar: Ibid.
> Viranaraniyar, daughter of Ilamukkaraiyar: Mahalingam, *A Topographical List: Thanjavur*, no. TJ 159, p. 35.
> Gopan Sakkapu: Rao, ed., *South Indian Inscriptions*, vol. XIX, no. 407, p. 214.
> Aruran Amabalattadigalar aka Ponamballattu-adigalar: Mahalingam, *A Topographical List: Thanjavur*, no. TJ 1298, p. 305.
> Minavan Madeviyar: Swaminathan, ed., *South Indian Inscriptions*, vol XXXII, part II, no. 54, p. 166.
> Siddhavadavan Chuttiyar, daughter of Miladu-udaiyar: Mahalingam, *A Topographical List: Thanjavur*, no. TJ 742, pp. 173–174.
> Panchavan Madeviyar: Mahalingam, *A Topographical List: Thanjavur*, no. TJ 1567, p. 364.
> Nakkan Tillai Alagiyar: Mahalingam, *A Topographical List: Tiruchirappalli*, no. Tp 1685, p. 372.

98. V. Vedachalam, "Pandiya Nattil Natarajisvaram," in *Tolliyal Nokkil Tamilakam* (Chennai: Tolpural Avya Turai,

1999), pp. 274–279. Vedachalam, epigraphist with the Tamil Nadu State Department of Archaeology, points out that this is the very first use of the term "Nataraja" in Tamil Nadu. A Pandya record of Vikrama Pandya, dated to the year 1245, records the dedication of a temple named Natarajisvaram, which enshrined an image of Nataraja at Tiruvekampattu near Shivaganga. The donor, Somanathadevar, was the family guru of king Vikrama Pandya.

99. This name is especially popular in all of Vikrama Chola's *meykirtis*, where Dancing Shiva is also referred to as the king's *kula nayakan*, or family deity. See E. Hultzsch, ed., *South Indian Inscriptions*, vol. III, part II, no. 79, "Inscription at Tirumalavadi," pp. 182–186, where line 16 refers to *kula-nayakan*, and line 20 to *Arbuda Kuttar*.

100. Mahalingam, *A Topographical List: Thanjavur*, no. TJ 646, p. 137.

101. Ibid., no. TJ 2221, p. 509.

102. Ibid., no. TJ 1061, pp. 247–248; Mahalingam, *A Topographical List: Tiruchchirappalli*, no. Tp 468, p. 101.

103. Mahalingam, *A Topographical List: Thanjavur*, no. TJ 612, p. 141.

104. See Padma Kaimal, "Shiva Nataraja: Shifting Meanings of an Icon," *Art Bulletin* 81, no. 3 (1999): 390–419.

105. Risha Lee, "Constructing Community: Tamil Merchant Temples in India and China, 850–1281," (PhD dissertation, Columbia University, 2012), especially p. 307.

106. Indira Peterson, *Poems to Śiva: The Hymns of the Tamil Saints* (Princeton, NJ: Princeton University Press, 1989), p. 183.

107. Ibid., p. 118.

108. For debates on the original and subsequent interpretations of the significance of Dancing Shiva, see Padma Kaimal, "Shiva Nataraja: Shifting Meanings of an Icon," *Art Bulletin* 81, no. 3 (1999): 390–419; and Vidya Dehejia, *The Sensuous and the Sacred: Chola Bronzes from South India* (New York: American Federation of Arts; Seattle: University of Washington Press, 2002), pp. 94–105.

109. Hultzsch, ed., *South Indian Inscriptions*, vol. II, no. 34, p. 145: line 7: "One solid aureole, covering the god, consisting of two pillars (*toranakal*) and one half-moon (*ardhachandra*), and measuring six muram and two viral in circumference."

110. Peterson, *Poems to Śiva*, p. 118.

111. Douglas Barrett, *Early Cola Bronzes* (Bombay: Bhulabhai Memorial Institute, 1965), plates 57, 58.

112. The bronze aureole was broken at some stage and repaired by the queen Kamakshi, wife of the Maratha king Shivaji in the year 1885. At that time, a *makara* head was introduced to disguise the repair, and it may be seen just below the flowing scarf where it joins the *tiruvatchi*. The leg of the Dancing Shiva also seems to have been damaged, and the bronze repair craftsman added a serpent to curl around his ankle and disguise the damage. The inscription in question, written in modern Nagari on the original pedestal, was noticed by R. Nagaswamy. It reads: "Under the order of queen Kamakshi, the wife of Sivaji, her agent Nagaraja repaired the worn out image of Natyaraja, in the temple of Brihadesvara, the Salivahana Saka 1807, equivalent to Tarana, on a full-moon day which fell on a Tuesday, and reconsecrated the image." See Nagaswamy, "Adavallan and Dakshinameruvitankar of the Tanjore Temple," *Lalit Kala* 12 (1962): 36–38.

113. K. Damodaran, "New Light on Thiruvenkadu Nataraja Bronze," in *South Indian Studies* (Madras: Society for Archaeological, Historical, and Epigraphical Research, 1978), pp. 150–156.

114. See chapter 3, earlier.

115. Aiyer, ed., *South Indian Inscriptions,* vol. VII, no. 972, p. 470.

116. Mahalingam, *A Topographical List: Thanjavur*, no. TJ 1023, p. 240. See Nicholas Cane, "Queen Cempiyan Mahadevi's Religious Patronage," especially pp. 358–365, for further examples.

117. Women singers of the saints' hymns are not something we come across often in the inscriptions of the Chola period.

118. Swaminathan, ed., *South Indian Inscriptions*, vol. XXXII, part I, no. 52, p. 66, in the year 41 of Madiraiyum Ilamum konda Ko Parakesari, i.e. Parantaka, and hence the year 947.

119. I am grateful to Dr. Chandramoorthy, who was in charge of registration of bronzes, for sharing with me his insights into the numbers of temple bronzes created during Chola times.

120. Mahalingam, *A Topographical List: Thanjavur*, no. TJ 612, p. 141. See also Rao, ed., *South Indian Inscriptions*, vol. XXIII, part II, no. 212, pp. 155–156.

121. Mahalingam, *A Topographical List: Thanjavur*, no. TJ 595, p. 137. See also Rao, ed., *South Indian Inscriptions*, vol. XIX, no. 90, p. 46.

122. Rao, ed., *South Indian Inscriptions*, vol. XIX, no. TJ 826, p. 196. Also Aiyer, ed., *South Indian Inscriptions*, vol. VII, no. 1031, pp. 488–489.

123. Mahalingam, *A Topographical List: Tiruchchirappalli*, no. 468, p. 101. See also *Annual Report on Indian Epigraphy* 1908, no. 597.

124. Swaminathan, ed., *South Indian Inscriptions*, vol. XXXII, part II, no. 156, p. 280f. The musician named Rajakesari Kodandaraman was originally from Nattarmangalam but had relocated to Thanjavur.

125. Hultzsch, ed., *South Indian Inscriptions*, vol. II, no. 25, p. 125. Engraved on inner *gopura*, left of entrance.

CHAPTER 5: THE TIRUVENKADU MASTER AND TEN THOUSAND PEARLS ADORN A BRONZE

1. I am grateful to the Epigraphical Survey of India for access to the copies of the Tiruvenkadu inscriptions in their Mysore office. *Annual Report on Indian Epigraphy*, 1918, no. 456.

2. The first verse of the first hymn of child saint Sambandar, which contains this phrase, reads thus:

Thodudaiya sheviyan, vidai eri, or thu venmadi shudi
Kadudaiya shudalai podi pushi, en ullam kavar kalvan.

He wears a woman's earring on one ear
riding on his bull,
crowned with the pure white crescent moon
body smeared with ash from the burning ground,
he is the thief who stole my heart.

See Indira Peterson, *Poems to Śiva: The Hymns of the Tamil Saints* (Princeton, NJ: Princeton University Press, 1989), pp. 270–271.

3. Job Thomas, *Tiruvenkadu Bronzes* (Madras: Cre-A, 1986) contains extracts of several of the relevant inscriptions in his footnotes.

4. Kazhamulam and Tonipuram are alternative names for Sirkali. See Peterson, *Poems to Śiva*, p. 68, which quotes, in translation, Appar hymns IV/82 and IV/83.

5. T. V. Mahalingam, *A Topographical List of Inscriptions in the Tamil Nadu and Kerala States*, vol. 7: *Thanjavur District* (New Delhi: Indian Council of Historical Research, 1992), no. TJ 1191, pp. 280–281. I am grateful to Dr. Muniratnam for access to the transcript of *Annual Report on Indian Epigraphy*, 1925, no. 182. The phrase literally translates as "in order to strengthen the king's arms/shoulders."

6. *ARE* 1918, no. 457. Courtesy Epigraphical Survey, Mysore. The names, extracted from the damaged inscription, are as follows:

Devar Sarpan, of the Sri Rajaraja Jananatha select military regiment, headman of Andanur, supervisor, leader, of the . . .
from north street of Nangur
Narayanan from Avishvaram
Ranganar svami
Nilakantha of the Shankara gotra
Butana, son of Satakarni from Talaishangatu
Shatanilayan, son of Satakarni
Shantanu, son of Satakarni
Kani-ilaiyan, son of Satakarni
. . . varan from Turukka
Vadakkan . . .
. . . from maran ko . . .

7. H. Krishna Sastri, ed., *South Indian Inscriptions*, vol. V (Madras: Superintendent, Government Press, 1925), no. 980, pp. 367–368.

8. For instance, speaking of a magnificent Dancing Shiva and consort in a temple at Kumbakonam, a knowledgeable and respected authority wrote: "I have no hesitation in concluding that both must be royal consecrations, so great is their majesty and power." R. Nagaswamy, "On Dating South Indian Bronzes," in *Indian Art & Connoisseurship: Essays in Honor of Douglas Barrett*, ed. John Guy (Chidambaram Ahmedabad, India: Indira Gandhi National Centre for the Arts in association with Mapin Publishing, 1995), p. 116.

9. E. Hultzsch, ed., *South Indian Inscriptions*, vol. II, part I (Madras: Superintendent, Government Press, 1891), no. 46, p. 187.

10. Pramod Chandra, *The Sculpture of India, 3000 BC–1300 AD* (Washington, DC; Cambridge, MA: National Gallery of Art; Harvard University Press, 1985).

11. See introduction, earlier.

12. Vidya Dehejia, *Slaves of the Lord: The Path of the Tamil Saints* (New Delhi: Mushiram Manoharlal, 1988), pp. 54–55.

13. T. V. Gopal Iyer and François Gros, eds., *Tēvāram: hymnes Śivaïtes du pays tamoul* (Pondicherry: Institut Français d'Indologie, 1984–1991), vol. 2, book 6, hymn 45, verse 8, p. 289. Translation is mine.

14. T. N. Ramachandran, "Bronze Images from Tiruvenkadu-Svetaranya (Tanjore District)," *Lalit Kala* 3/4 (April 1956–March 1957): 55–62; esp. p. 58. Also cited in Vidya Dehejia, *Art of the Imperial Cholas* (New York: Columbia University Press, 1990), p. 60. For Tamil text of hymn, see T. V. Gopal Iyer and François Gros, eds., *Tēvāram: hymnes Śivaïtes du pays tamoul*, book 1, hymn 87, verse 5, p. 9.

15. *ARE* 1918, no. 450, courtesy of the Epigraphical Survey, Mysore. We may assume him to be a person of some stature since he speaks of having obtained the lands he donated for the worship of *Pichcha Devar* from the king Rajendra I.

16. *ARE* 1918, no. 451, courtesy of the Epigraphical Survey, Mysore. He gave land to meet the regular expenses of worship of the bronze, and gold to replate the previously plated roof of the shrine of this bronze image. The lengthy inscription speaks also of a food hall instituted in the name of *Pichcha Devar*, of arrangements to feed brahmins, and of wages given to the women who worked in that hall.

17. *ARE* 1918, no. 451, courtesy of the Epigraphical Survey, Mysore.

18. Hultzsch, *South Indian Inscriptions*, vol. II, part I, no. 6, pp. 74–75. A long necklace of seventy-six *rudraksha* beads strung with gold was donated in that same year by a chieftain, Vanavan Pallavaraiyan, while a brahmin army general, Karikala Kanna Brahmadhirayan, gold-plated the roof of the dance hall and added various decorations to it. Gemstones were provided for embedding into the aureole. It speaks also of a gold and a silver plate for offering sacred food to the image.

19. *ARE* 1918, no. 451, courtesy of the Epigraphical Survey, Mysore.

20. Sastri, ed., *South Indian Inscriptions*, vol. V, no. 978, p. 366. Also *Annual Report on Indian Epigraphy*, 1896, no. 114.

21. *Annual Report on Indian Epigraphy*, 1986, no. 111. Also Sastri, ed., *South Indian Inscriptions*, vol. V, no. 974, p. 363.

22. This suggestion was first made by Job Thomas in his *Tiruvenkadu Bronzes*, p. 49.

23. G. V. Srinivasa Rao, ed., *South Indian Inscriptions*, vol. XIII (Madras: Government of India, Department of Archaeol-

ogy,1952), no. 33, p. 13–14. This record in the temple at Tirumalpuram in North Arcot district is in both Sanskrit and Tamil, and it clearly states his name as Rajaraja in the first line of Sanskrit. A second record, dated in his tenth year, speaks of a royal order to donate 900 sheep to the Kachchisvara temple in Little Kanchipuram, in order to burn a set of ten lamps named Rajarajan after the king. See Rao, ed., *South Indian Inscriptions*, vol. XIII, no. 149, pp. 78–79.

24. Hultzsch, ed., *South Indian Inscriptions*, vol. II, part I, no. 1, para. 2, p. 8.

25. T. V. Mahalingam, *A Topographical List of Inscriptions in the Tamil Nadu and Kerala States*, vol. 8: *Tiruchchirappalli District* (New Delhi: Indian Council of Historical Research, 1992), no. Tp 1687, p. 372, in Rajaraja's year 28 = 1013. See also Sastri, ed., *South Indian Inscriptions*, vol. V, no. 652/92, p. 275.

26. Mahalingam, *A Topographical List: Tiruchchirappalli*, no. Tp 1697, p. 374, in Rajendra's fourteenth year, or 1026. See also Sastri, ed., *South Indian Inscriptions*, vol. V, no. 652/91, p. 273.

27. Hultzsch, ed., *South Indian Inscriptions*, vol. II, part I, no. 66, pp. 259–303.

28. See for instance an inscription of the year 1229 that records a gift for rice offering to the consort of the bedroom chamber in the Mayuram temple. It specifies that after offering it to the goddess, the food was to be distributed among members of the temple establishment. G. V. Srinivasa Rao, ed., *South Indian Inscriptions*, vol. XXIII (Madras: Director-General, Archaeological Survey of India, 1979), no. 372, pp. 258–259.

29. Hultzsch, ed., *South Indian Inscriptions*, vol. II, part I, no. 6, pp. 74–75.

30. K. V. Subrahmanya Aiyer, ed., *South Indian Inscriptions*, vol. VII (Madras: Government of India, Department of Archaeology, 1932), no. 485, pp. 298–301. Also Mahalingam, *A Topographical List: Thanjavur*, no. TJ 1653, p. 386. The inscription is of Kulottunga II in the year 1145 CE.

31. The lists of ingredients, very similar in content, are repeated in their entirety for the daily worship of each saint, and for the festival of each saint.

32. There is some debate about a long and large green pepper that seems to find mention in certain early sources; it does not appear to be the same as the green chili.

33. The inscription repeats these closely similar lists for the various festivals and for each of the three saints' images.

34. Rao, ed., *South Indian Inscriptions*, vol. XXIII (Madras: Government of India, Department of Archaeology, 1979), no. 42, pp. 20–22. It is dated in the twenty-ninth year of Rajaraja, or 1014.

35. See Vidya Dehejia, "Assemblages of Sacred Bronzes," in Vidya Dehejia, ed., *The Sensuous and the Sacred: Chola Bronzes from South India* (New York: American Federation of Arts; Seattle: University of Washington Press, 2002), pp. 84–85. See also appendix B:I, in this book.

36. Josephine Shaya, "Greek Temple Treasures and the Invention of Collecting," in *Museum Archetypes and Collecting in the Ancient World*, ed. Maia Wellington Gahtan and Donatella Pegazzano (Leiden; Boston: Brill, 2014), pp. 24–32.

37. As first suggested by R. Nagaswamy.

38. Hultzsch, ed., *South Indian Inscriptions*, vol. II, part I, no. 51, pp. 203–217.

39. Ibid., vol. II, part I, no. 7, para. 10, pp. 73–74.

40. Ibid., vol. II, part I, nos. 1, 2, pp. 1–20.

41. Ibid., vol. II, part I, no. 3, pp. 21–42. Dakshina Meru Vitanker, or "Bronze lord of southern Meru (the sacred mountain)."

42. Mahalingam, *A Topographical List: Thanjavur*, no. TJ 2937, p. 662. Gift of the headman of Tonur, given to him from the booty of the Malainadu campaign, which he consecrated at Palanam.

43. Hultzsch, ed., *South Indian Inscriptions*, vol. II, part I, no. 7, p. 81, an inscription of Kundavai's gifts, is one example of such detailed specifications.

44. This is an abbreviated version of Hultzsch, ed., *South Indian Inscriptions*, vol. II, part II, no. 79, line 16, p. 399. The image was dedicated by a resident of the village of Nallur, and the sets of jewelry donated included 1,400 pearls.

45. On the basis of 2 1/2 *kalanju* = 1 sovereign = 8 grams.

6 *kalanju* = 1 troy ounce.
1 ounce = 28.3 grams.
100 *kalanju* = 16 2/3 ounces.
So 2 1/2 *kalanju* = 8 grams.

Rao, ed., *South Indian Inscriptions*, vol. XXIII, no. 42, pp. 20–22, dated in the twenty-ninth year of Rajaraja, which corresponds to 1014.

46. Hultzsch, ed., *South Indian Inscriptions*, vol. II, part I, no. 7, v. 10, p. 83.

47. Ibid., vol. II, part I, no. 39, p. 165f. This is a gift of general (*senapati*) Krishna Raman, who held the title Mummudi Chola Brahma-marayan.

48. Ibid., vol. II, part I, no. 38, pp. 152–161.

49. Ibid., vol. II, part I, no. 47, pp. 190–192. See also Mahalingam, *A Topographical List: Thanjavur*, no. TJ 2660, p. 604.

50. Mahalingam, *A Topographical List: Thanjavur*, no. TJ 881, p. 209. Also H. Krishna Sastri, ed., *South Indian Inscriptions*, vol. III, part IV (Madras: Superintendent, Government Press, 1920), no. 211, p. 273. The Tirukkalar Copper-Plate of Kulottunga III lists each item, its weight, and the specific fineness of the gold of which it was made. The first three plates belong respectively to the time of Rajendra Chola, Rajadhiraja, and Kulottunga.

51. Josephine Shaya, "Greek Temple Treasures," p. 25. See also her "The Greek Temple as Museum: The Case of the

Legendary Treasure of Athena from Lindos," *American Journal of Archaeology* 109, no. 3 (2005): 423–442.

52. Sastri, ed., *South Indian Inscriptions*, vol. V, no. 692, p. 289.

53. Mahalingam, *A Topographical List: Thanjavur*, no. TJ 412, p. 95, in the temple of Tirupanandal. Also *Annual Report on Indian Epigraphy*, 1914, no. 46.

54. Mahalingam, *A Topographical List: Thanjavur*, no. TJ 205, pp. 47–48. See also *Annual Report on Indian Epigraphy*, 1931–1932, no. 115.

55. See chapter 3, earlier.

56. K. V. Subrahmanya Aiyer, ed., *South Indian Inscriptions*, vol. VI (Madras: Superintendent, Government Press, 1928), no. 33, pp. 12–16. Thanks to Marxia Gandhi, this inscription is translated here for the first time. The inscription speaks of three major pieces of jewelry—a *kolkai, a kodukku*, and a *kosakam*.

57. *Kolkai* appears to be a linga cover, *kodukku* may be a curved ornament, and *kosakam* appears to be a garment for the bronze images. These terms remain untranslated and somewhat confusing. The inscription merits detailed translation and further study.

58. The group consisted of one image of Chandesha, one fallen father lying on the ground, one linga from which an arm protrudes, a second image of Chandesha kneeling to receive the grace of the lord, one flower garland that was given to him by Shiva and Uma, and one four-armed bronze Shiva accompanied by Uma. Hultzsch, ed., *South Indian Inscriptions*, vol. II, part I, no. 6, p. 68.

59. Ibid., vol. II, part I, no. 14, pp. 99–100.

60. Ibid., vol. II, part II, no. 24, pp. 121–124. Inscribed on inner *gopuram* of the temple.

61. Ibid., vol. II, part I, nos. 11–18, pp. 95–104.

62. Marxia Gandhi, ed., *Thanjavur Vattak Kalvattigal*, part II (Chennai: State Department of Archaeology, 2015–2016), no. 52/2014, part II, p. 83f.

63. Hultzsch, ed., *South Indian Inscriptions*, vol. II, part I, no. 67, p. 307.

64. See transcript of inscription 680 for year 1919 in the Mysore Epigraphical Survey Office (*Annual Report on Indian Epigraphy* 1919, no. 680). T. V. Mahalingam, *A Topographical List of Inscriptions in the Tamil Nadu and Kerala States*, vol. 7: *Thanjavur District* (New Delhi: Indian Council of Historical Research, 1992), no. TJ 1622, pp. 376–377. See also Kudavayil Balasubrahmaniam, *Tiruvarur Tirukoyil* (Tiruvarur: Arulmiku Tyagarajaswamy tirukkoil veliyidu, 1988), in Tamil: "Tiruvarur Tirukoyil Kalvettukal," no. 76, pp. 496–504.

65. See transcript of inscription 679 for year 1919 in the Mysore Epigraphical Survey Office (*Annual Report on Indian Epigraphy*, 1919, no. 679).

66. While the inscription commences with the familiar *meykirti* of Rajendra I, it moves in line 8, with little warning, to phraseology used in the *meykirti* of Rajendra II. The inscription thus dates to the time of Rajendra II.

67. H. Krishna Sastri, ed., *South Indian Inscriptions*, vol. IV (Madras: Superintendent, Government Press, 1923), no. 223, pp. 29–31.

CHAPTER 6: CHOLA OBSESSION WITH SRI LANKA AND HINDU BRONZES FROM THE ISLAND

1. While the first inscription has long been known, this second inscription was uncovered during recent clearance on the same rock surface, barely a meter lower down. See Rasika Muthucumarana, "Godawaya: An Ancient Port City (2nd Century CE) and the Recent Discovery of the Unknown Wooden Wreck," *Australian Institute of Maritime Archaeology Newsletter* 28, no. 3 (2009): 21–26. While underwater archaeologists are still working on the wreck, a preliminary estimate suggests that the ship was 75 feet in length. Recent radiocarbon dates from the wood of the sunken ship have yielded dates between the second century BCE and the first century CE.

2. See Andrew Lawler, "Seafaring in Ancient Sri Lanka," *Archaeology* (November–December 2014): 42–47; and Susanne Loos-Jayawickrame, "Digging Up a Maritime Past," *Sunday Times*, April 14, 2002. See also Osmund Bopearachchi, "Sites portuaires et emporia de l'ancien Sri Lanka: nouvelles donnees archeologiques," *Arts Asiatiques* 54 (1999): 5–22; and Osmund Bopearachchi, *Tamil Traders in Sri Lanka and Sinhalese Traders in Tamil Nadu: New Archaeological Evidence on Cultural and Commercial Relationships between Sri Lanka and Tamil Nadu* (Colombo: International Centre for Ethnic Studies, 2008), p. 32.

3. P. J. Cherian and Jaya Menon, *Unearthing Pattanam: Histories, Cultures, Crossings* (New Delhi: National Museum and Kerala Council for Historical Research, 2014).

4. Lionel Casson, "New Light on Maritime Loans: P. Vindob G 40822," in *Zeitschrift für Papyrologie und Epigraphik*, Band 84 (1990), pp. 195–206.

5. Lionel Casson, *The Periplus Maris Erythraei* (Princeton, NJ: Princeton University Press, 1989), introduction, p. 24.

6. *Akananuru* 149, trans. Vaidehi Herbert, quoted in *Unearthing Pattanam: Histories, Cultures, Crossings* (New Delhi: National Museum, 2014), p. 28.

7. R. Parthasarathy, trans. *The Tale of an Anklet: An Epic of South India. The Cilappatikaram of Ilanko Atikal* (New York: Columbia University Press, 1992), pp. 46–47.

8. Casson, *The Periplus*, introduction, pp. 23–24, and text, pp. 77–85.

9. An early Chinese commentary confirms such construction of non-Chinese ships in India, Sri Lanka, and southeast Asia: "With fibrous bark of the coconut they make cords which bind the parts of the ship together. And they caulk them with a paste made of ko-lan, stopping up the openings and preventing the water from coming in. Nails and clamps are not used." I Chieh Ching Yin I, as quoted from Joseph Needham in R.A.L.H. Gunawardana, "Seaways to Sielediba: Changing Patterns of Navigation in the Indian Ocean and Their Impact

on Pre-Colonial Sri Lanka," in *Sri Lanka and the Silk Road of the Sea*, ed. Senake Bandaranayake (Colombo: Sri Lanka National Commission for UNESCO and the Central Cultural Fund, 1990), p. 30.

10. Tom Vosner, "The Jewel of Muscat: Reconstructing a 9th c. Sewn-Plank Boat," in *Shipwrecked: Tang Treasures and Monsoon Winds*, by Regina Krahl, ed. John Guy, Julian Raby, and J. Keith Wilson (Washington, DC: Arthur M. Sackler Gallery, Smithsonian Institution; Singapore: National Heritage Board, Singapore Tourism Board, 2010). Sri Lankan scholar R.A.L.H. Gunawardana points out that a staggering 400 miles of rope were needed to construct the ship that Tom Severin built in 1980 to reenact the famous Sindbad voyage. See Gunawardana, "Seaways to Sielediba," p. 31. Tim Severin, *The Sindbad Voyage* (London: G. P. Putnam's Sons, 1983).

11. The bridge built by Rama's army of monkeys and bears relied on these sand banks to make their project feasible!

12. Pliny the Elder, *The Natural History*, ed. John Bostock and H. T. Riley (Somerville, MA: Perseus Digital Library, 2006), book 6, chapter 24.

13. Casson, *The Periplus*, introduction, p. 57, and text, p. 89.

14. Fa-Hsien, *The Travels of Fa-Hsien (A.D. 399–414) or Record of the Buddhistic Kingdoms*, trans. H. A. Giles (Cambridge: Cambridge University Press, 1923), chapter XXXVII, p. 101.

15. Henry Yule, trans. and ed., *The Book of Ser Marco Polo, the Venetian, Concerning the Kingdoms and Marvels of the East* (New York: Scribner, 1903), book 3, chapter 16.

16. John A. Legge, "The Ceylon Pearl Oyster Fisheries," *Spolia Zeylanica* 8 (1913): 201–202.

17. T. V. Mahalingam, *A Topographical List of Inscriptions in the Tamil Nadu and Kerala States*, vol. 7: *Thanjavur District* (New Delhi: Indian Council of Historical Research, 1992), no. TJ 3204, pp. 719–720; also K. G. Krishnan, ed., *South Indian Inscriptions*, vol. XVII (Madras: Superintendent, Government Press, 1957), no. 501, p. 207. Bitter battles between Parantaka and the Pandyas led the Pandya king to flee to Lanka with all his royal paraphernalia that included his crown, flag, parasol, and other such items; if these fell into enemy hands, it gave the possessor the right to claim victory over the dispossessed king. When circumstances forced the Pandya ruler to leave Lanka for the Chera country of Kerala, he left his regal insignia in the safekeeping of the Lanka ruler. Parantaka Chola waged war in an attempt to capture it, but was unable to do so, leaving it to Rajaraja to finally lay claim to it and through possession of the regalia to the Pandya kingdom.

18. Mahalingam, *A Topographical List: Thanjavur*, nos. TJ 2461, p. 559, and TJ 2288, p. 523.

19. G. V. Srinivasa Rao, ed., *South Indian Inscriptions*, XIII (Madras: Superintendent, Government Press, 1952), no. 281A, p. 149.

20. Mahalingam, *A Topographical List: Thanjavur*, nos. TJ 2254, p. 517, and TJ 2445, p. 556.

21. Ibid., nos. TJ 2277, p. 521, and TJ 2357, pp. 537–538.

22. E. Hultzsch, ed., *South Indian Inscriptions*, vol. II, part II (Madras: Superintendent, Government Press, 1891), no. 59, pp. 241–245. A second group of ornaments, presented up to his twenty-ninth year, is engraved on the north wall of the central shrine at Thanjavur: it similarly speaks of gifts made by Rajaraja prior to his twenty-ninth year and specifies that these gifts are in addition to those engraved on the Chandesha shrine and those engraved on the temple's base moldings. His total gifts of gold, gems, coral, and pearls is quite tremendous.

23. The first has 5,611 pearls, a second with 2,077 pearls, a third with 1,541 pearls, a fourth with 1,590 pearls, a fifth with 1,625 pearls, a sixth with over a thousand (there is some damage to the numbers), a seventh with 1,566, an eighth with over a thousand (damage once again), and a ninth with 1,566.

24. Hultzsch, ed., *South Indian Inscriptions*, vol. II, part II, no. 59, p. 242.

25. Ibid., vol. II, part II, no. 59, pp. 236–245.

26. Ibid., vol. II, part II, no. 3, pp. 35–42.

27. Meera Abraham, *Two Medieval Merchant Guilds of South India* (New Delhi: Manohar Publications, 1988), p. 140.

28. Ibid.

29. Ibid., p. 143.

30. Mahalingam, *A Topographical List: Thanjavur*, no. TJ 576, p. 131. The inscription contains the interesting information that 20 *Ilakkasu* was equivalent to 10 *kalanju* of gold. Also H. Krishna Sastri, ed., *South Indian Inscriptions*, vol. V (Madras: Superintendent, Government Press, 1925), no. 720, p. 303.

31. Mahalingam, *A Topographical List: Thanjavur*, no. TJ 249, p. 60.

32. Ibid., no. TJ 250, p. 60; G. V. Srinivasa Rao, ed., *South Indian Inscriptions*, vol. XIII (Madras: Superintendent, Government Press, 1952), no. 253, p. 135.

33. Mahalingam, *A Topographical List: Thanjavur*, no. TJ 329, p. 78. Rao, ed., *South Indian Inscriptions*, vol. XIII, no. 223, p. 120.

34. Mahalingam, *A Topographical List: Thanjavur*, no. TJ 2634, pp. 597–598. K. V. Subrahmanya Aiyer, ed., *South Indian Inscriptions*, vol. VI (Madras: Superintendent, Government Press, 1928), no. 443, p. 184.

35. Mahalingam, *A Topographical List: Thanjavur*, no. TJ 1619, pp. 375–376. Krishnan, ed., *South Indian Inscriptions*, vol XVII, no. 617, p. 282.

36. Hultzsch, ed., *South Indian Inscriptions*, vol. II, part II, no. 36, p. 149f.

37. I am grateful for this new translation kindly provided by Indira Peterson.

38. David Dean Shulman, *Songs of the Harsh Devotee: The Tevaram of Cuntaramurttinayanar* (Philadelphia: University of Pennsylvania, 1990), p. 510.

39. Shulman, *Songs of the Harsh Devotee*, song 80, end of verse 5, p. 511.

40. H.C.P. Bell, *Archaeological Survey of Ceylon Annual Report*, 1906, and continued in 1907–1913. See also C. E. Godakumbura, "Bronzes from Polonnaruwa," *Journal of the Ceylon Branch of the Royal Asiatic Society*, VII, part 2 (1961): 239–253.

41. H. Krishna Sastri, ed., *South Indian Inscriptions*, vol. IV (Madras: Superintendent, Government Press, 1923), nos. 1388–1392, pp. 489–491.

42. Ibid., vol. IV, no. 1390, p. 490.

43. Ibid., vol. IV, no. 1391, pp. 490–491.

44. Ibid., vol. IV, no. 1392, p. 491.

45. Ibid., vol. IV, nos. 1412–1414, pp. 495–496.

46. Ibid., vol. IV, no. 1412, pp. 495–496: The Rajarajishvaram temple at Matottam, alias Rajaraja-puram, was located in the Mummudicholamandalam of Ilam, and the donor Tari-Kumaran is described as headman of Tirukuttranallur in Chola-mandalam.

47. Ibid., vol. IV, no. 1414, p. 496. This refers to the god as *Ramishvaram Udaiyar*, and then says he rises and gives grace as *Rishabhavahana Devar* (Lord with the bull), suggesting a processional icon. A highly placed official gave money that, through the intervention of oil merchants, and betel and plantain merchants, was to be used for this lamp.

48. Known as Naipena vihara, this is the temple from which the large majority of bronzes were recovered.

49. Sastri, ed., *South Indian Inscriptions*, vol. IV, no. 1393, p. 491:

Tiruppuvanadevan of Mohanurudaiyan
Tillaiarasu Tiyaga Chintamani Muvendavelan
Karpagai, daughter of Mukarinadalvan
Panchnadivanan of Nallur

50. Such iconographic drawings are known in the context of Nepal but have not been found elsewhere in south Asia. See Pratapaditya Pal, *Art of Nepal* (Los Angeles: Los Angeles County Museum of Art, 1985).

51. C. E. Godakumbura, "Bronzes from Polonnaruwa," *Journal of the Ceylon Branch of the Royal Asiatic Society* VII, part 2 (1961): 239–253. See also P. Sarvesvara Iyer, "Puranic Saivism in Ceylon during the Polonnaruwa Period," in *Proceedings of the First International Conference Seminar of Tamil Studies, Kuala Lumpur, Malaysia, April 1966*, ed. X. S. Thani Nayagam, V. I. Subramoniam, R. E. Asher et al. (Kuala Lumpur: International Association of Tamil Research, 1968), pp. 462–474; esp. p. 471.

52. Godakumbura, "Bronzes from Polonnaruwa." See also Iyer, "Puranic Saivism."

53. Elaine Craddock, *Śiva's Demon Devotee: Kāraikkāl Ammaiyār* (Albany: State University of New York Press, 2010), p. 138.

54. Ibid., p. 141.

55. Ibid., p. 144.

56. See for instance Jean Boisselier, "Appendix I: The Buddha Image," in *The Heritage of Thai Sculpture* (New York and Tokyo: Weatherhill, 1975), pp. 195–196.

57. Iyer, "Puranic Saivism," p. 474.

58. The first letter is damaged. See Ananda Coomaraswamy, *Bronzes from Ceylon, Chiefly in the Colombo Museum*, series A, no. 1 (Ceylon: Colombo Museum, 1914). Also Iyer, "Puranic Saivism," reads it as Ganapati Usabha vamsa.

59. *Bronzes Bouddhiques et Hindous de l'antique Ceylan* (Paris: Musée National des Arts Asiatiques-Guimet, 1991), pp. 136–137.

60. Cited in S. Pathmanathan, "The Nanadesis of Anuradhapura: A Unique Bronze Image of Virabhadra," in *Ancient & Medieval Commercial Activities in the Indian Ocean: Testimony of Inscriptions and Ceramic-Sherds: Report of the Taisho University Research Project, 1997–2002*, ed. Noboru Karashima (Tokyo: Taisho University, 2002), p. 49. The first inscription is dated in the sixth and seventh years of Chankapotivarman (Samgha-poti-varman).

61. Sastri, ed., *South Indian Inscriptions*, vol. IV, no. 1403, p. 493.

62. S. Pathmanathan, "The Nanadesis of Anuradhapura: A Unique Bronze Image of Virabhadra," pp. 50–51: "We of the Nankunattu caused this inscription to be engraved so that the four persons appointed [by us] would in conjunction with the employees of the Makkotai-palli continue to perform this charity [dharma]."

63. Kanadar *korale*, Kunchuttu *korale*, Uddiyankulam *korale*, Kapla *korale*: Sastri, ed., *South Indian Inscriptions*, vol. IV, nos. 1406–1411, pp. 494–495. All records are fragmentary and damaged.

64. Sastri, ed., *South Indian Inscriptions*, vol. IV, no. 1408, p. 494. A slight problem exists with the plural use of the word *senapatikal*.

65. Sastri, ed., *South Indian Inscriptions*, vol. IV, nos. 1394–1395, p. 491.

66. Ibid., vol. IV, no. 1396, p. 492.

67. This body consisted of the Matantarattar, Valanjiyar (a merchant guild), and Nagarattar (local merchant community).

68. He is described as highly venerated and knowing the *sastras*, *agamas*, *silas*, and *achara*.

CHAPTER 7: THE SILK ROUTE OF THE OCEAN AND TEMPLE ART IN THE DAYS OF RAJARAJA II

1. Y. Subbarayulu, "The Tamil Merchant-Guild Inscription at Barus, Indonesia: A Rediscovery," in *Ancient & Medieval Commercial Activities in the Indian Ocean: Testimony of Inscriptions and Ceramic-Sherds: Report of the Taisho University Research Project, 1997–2002*, ed. Noboru Karashima (Tokyo: Taisho University, 2002), pp. 19–26.

2. Noboru Karashima and Y. Subbarayulu, "Ancient and Medieval Tamil and Sanskrit Inscriptions Relating to Southeast Asia and China," in *Nagapattinam to Suvarnadvipa:*

Reflections on the Chola Naval Expeditions to Southeast Asia, ed. Hermann Kulke, K. Kesavapany, and Vijay Sakhuja (Singapore: Institute of Southeast Asian Studies, 2009), appendix I, no. 13, pp. 285–286. Gold was pegged to the value of musk, a highly prized commodity used for medicinal purposes. See also Noboru Karashima, "Medieval Commercial Activities in the Indian Ocean as Revealed from Chinese Ceramic Sherds and South Indian and Sri Lankan Inscriptions," in Kulke et al., *Nagapattinam to Suvarnadvipa*, pp. 20–60.

3. Originally reported in 1892, the pillar was recently rediscovered in the Jakarta National Museum by the team of scholars brought together by Noboru Karashima, who has spent several decades on unearthing the connections between India, Southeast Asia, and China. See Karashima, "Medieval Commercial Activities," fig. 2.56, p. 56.

4. Meera Abraham, *Two Medieval Merchant Guilds of South India* (New Delhi: Manohar Publications, 1988), p. 41; also appendix A, "Inscriptions of Ayyavole," p. 183.

5. G. V. Srinivasa Rao, ed., *South Indian Inscriptions*, vol. XIX (Madras: Superintendent, Government Press, 1967), no. 170, pp. 86–87. The land endowment was to ensure the burning of a perpetual lamp.

6. Ibid., vol. XIX, no. 216, p. 110.

7. Ibid., vol. XIX, no. 459, p. 235. The Valanjiyar and the Disai Ayirattu Ainurruvar built a fourth part of the temple in stone, with the remaining three-fourths being built by an individual Srika, known as *Kattrali Pichchan*.

8. Ibid., vol. XIX, no. 4, p. 2. This record of the year 2 of Parakesarivarman has been assigned to Rajendra in Mahalingam. T. V. Mahalingam, *A Topographical List of Inscriptions in the Tamil Nadu and Kerala States*, vol. 7: *Thanjavur District* (New Delhi: Indian Council of Historical Research, 1992), no. TJ 620, p. 143. However, I am following *South Indian Inscriptions*, vol. XXIII, in assigning this record instead to Uttama Chola. G. V. Srinivasa Rao, ed., *South Indian Inscriptions*, vol. XXIII (Madras: Superintendent, Government Press, 1979), no. 253, p. 173.

9. Paul Wheatley, "Geographical Notes on Some Commodities Involved in Sung Maritime Trade," *Journal of the Malay Branch of the Royal Asiatic Society* 32, no. 2 (1959): 24ff.

10. Tansen Sen, "The Military Campaigns of Rajendra Chola and the Chola-Srivijaya-China Triangle," in Kulke et al., *Nagapattinam to Suvarnadvipa*, p. 62. Sen quotes Robert Hartwell, "Foreign Trade, Monetary Policy, and Chinese 'Mercantilism,'" in *Collected Studies on Sung History Dedicated to James T. C. Liu in Celebration of His Seventieth Birthday*, ed. Kinugawa Tsuyoshi (Kyoto: Dohosh, 1989), pp. 453–488; esp. p. 454.

11. Hartwell, "Foreign Trade," p. 454. Sen, "The Military Campaigns," p. 62, a specialist in the Chinese end of this trade route, points out that the increasing Chinese demand for foreign goods, which resulted in a negative balance of trade for China, caused the Song rulers to convert what had been a system of voluntary tribute to a mandatory source of income.

12. Sen, "Military Campaigns," p. 69, quotes a document in which the president of the Council of Rites in China objected to the Song emperor's order to receive the Pagan Burmese (Myanmar) envoys with the same lowly status given to the Cholas:

> The Chola kingdom is subject to Srivijaya, this is why . . . we wrote to its ruler on coarse paper with an envelope of plain stuff. Pagan, on the other hand, is a great kingdom and should not be perceived as a small tributary state.

13. For this apt designation, see Gungwiu Wang, "Introduction: Shops in the Nanhai," in *Shipwrecked: Tang Treasures and Monsoon Winds*, by Regina Krahl, ed. John Guy, Julian Raby, and J. Keith Wilson (Washington, DC: Arthur M. Sackler Gallery, Smithsonian Institution; Singapore: National Heritage Board, Singapore Tourism Board, 2010), p. 16.

14. This gift was recorded in a copper-plate grant by Rajaraja's son Rajendra only in the year 1019, when he already seems to have been contemplating a naval battle with Srivijaya. Karashima and Subbarayalu, "Ancient and Medieval Tamil and Sanskrit Inscriptions," appendix I, p. 273. See also K. V. Subrahmanya Aiyer, "The Larger Leiden Plates (of Rajaraja I)," in *Epigraphia Indica*, vol. XXII (1933–34), ed. N. P. Chakravarti (Delhi: Manager of Publications, 1938), no. 34, pp. 257. The inscription quotes Rajendra's words: "This lord of Kataha of great valour, the abode of virtues, thus prays to all future kings: protect (ye) for ever this my charity."

15. Hermann Kulke, "The Naval Expeditions of the Cholas," in Kulke et al., *Nagapattinam to Suvarnadvipa*, p. 6, quoting W. P. Groeneveldt, *Historical Notes on Indonesia and Malaysia: Compiled from Chinese Sources* (Djakarta: C. V. Bhratara, reprint 1960), p. 65.

16. Karashima and Subbarayalu, "Ancient and Medieval Tamil and Sanskrit Inscriptions," appendix I, no. 2, "Nagapattinam inscription (1)," p. 275f. The somewhat damaged inscription also lists silver vessels, brass lamps, and other ritual items gifted by Sri Mulan. See also Mahalingam, *A Topographical List: Thanjavur*, no. TJ 1547, p. 360.

17. Karashima and Subbarayalu, "Ancient and Medieval Tamil and Sanskrit Inscriptions," appendix I, no. 3, "Nagapattinam inscription (2)," pp. 276–277; also Mahalingam, *A Topographical List: Thanjavur*, no. TJ 1545, pp. 359–360. Both these gifts were engraved in stone by a certain Eran Sadaiyan of Nagapattinam.

18. Karashima and Subbarayalu, "Ancient and Medieval Tamil and Sanskrit Inscriptions," appendix I, no. 4, "Nagapattinam inscription (3)," pp. 277–278; also Mahalingam, *A Topographical List: Thanjavur*, no. TJ 1549, p. 360.

19. K. N. Chaudhuri, *Trade and Civilization in the Indian Ocean: An Economic History from the Rise of Islam to 1750*

(Cambridge: Cambridge University Press, 1985), p. 56, in which he cites an article by J. Kuwabara in the *Memoirs of the Toyo Bunko*, vol. 7, 1935.

20. Meera Abraham, *Two Medieval Merchant Guilds*, pp. 140ff.

21. E. Hultzsch, ed., *South Indian Inscriptions*, vol. II, part I (Madras: Superintendent, Government Press, 1891), no. 20, p. 105. The inscription is issued by Rajendra from his palace at his new capital, named after him as "Town of him who captured the Ganges," or Gangai-konda-chola-puram.

22. Karashima and Subbarayalu, "Ancient and Medieval Tamil and Sanskrit Inscriptions," appendix I, no. 6 (cited wrongly as Tirukkadaiyur inscription, Amritaghatesvara temple), pp. 279–280. Also Hultzsch, ed., *South Indian Inscriptions*, vol. II, part I, no. 20, p. 105.

23. Karashima and Subbarayalu, "Ancient and Medieval Tamil and Sanskrit Inscriptions," appendix I, no. 7, "Perumber Inscription of Virarajendra," p. 280. The editors add, "A different interpretation could be that he was pleased to give it back to the king who surrendered at his feet."

24. Karashima and Subbarayalu, "Ancient and Medieval Tamil and Sanskrit Inscriptions," appendix I, no. 8, "Smaller Leiden Copper-Plates of Kulottunga Chola I," pp. 280–282. The mention of the town of Karaikkal as constituting the boundaries of the monastery to north and west leave no doubt that this is the same monastery at Nagapattinam originally sanctioned by Rajaraja I; in 1090 a new chapel, the Rajendra-perum-palli, was added, taking the name of the current ruler Rajendra, who had assumed the title of Kulottunga, or the apex of the dynasty.

25. Karashima and Subbarayalu, "Ancient and Medieval Tamil and Sanskrit Inscriptions," appendix I, no. 5, "Karandai Copper-Plate Inscription of Rajendra I," pp. 278–279.

26. Karashima and Subbarayalu, "Ancient and Medieval Tamil and Sanskrit Inscriptions," appendix I, no. 9, "Chidambaram Inscription of Kulottunga I," p. 283; see also E. Hultzsch, ed., *Epigraphia Indica*, vol. V, 1898–99 (Ootacamund: Government Epigraphist for India, 1960), no. 13C, p. 106.

27. "Motupalli Pillar-Inscription of Ganapatideva, AD 1244–45," in *Epigraphia Indica*, vol. XII, 1913–14, ed. Sten Konow (Calcutta: Government of India, 1982), pp. 188ff. Sanskrit verses written in Telugu script.

28. S. D. Goitein and Mordechai A. Friedman, *Indian Traders of the Middle Ages: Documents from the Cairo Geniza "India Book"* (Leiden: Brill, 2011), part 2: letter III.1, pp. 554–563.

29. T. V. Gopal Iyer and François Gros, eds., *Tēvāram: hymnes Śivaïtes du pays tamoul*, vol. 2 (Pondicherry: Institut Français d'Indologie, 1985), p. 73: Appar IV, 73.6. Translation is mine.

30. The Cleveland Nataraja, 32.25 inches tall, weighs 100 pounds, and the rectangular pedestal on which he stands, accompanied by Uma, is another 86.5 pounds. The Valuvur Shiva is both larger and also has a more substantial pedestal.

31. The Asia Society Uma, 35 inches tall, weighs 93 pounds with her lotus base. Uma at Valuvur is further placed upon a large rectangular pedestal.

32. David Smith, *The Dance of Siva: Religion, Art and Poetry in South India* (Cambridge: Cambridge University Press, 2003), p. 8.

33. Mahalingam, *A Topographical List: Thanjavur*, nos. TJ 1500–1501, p. 349.

34. Ibid., no. TJ 1502, p. 349, dated in the fifth year of Rajadhiraja.

35. Ibid., no. TJ 1505, p. 350. The image was set up by a resident of Mulangudi.

36. Ibid., no. TJ 1506, p. 350. The inscription specifies the dimensions of the shrine as measuring 2 *pattis* (?) on the north and south sides, and five *pattis* on east and west.

37. Ibid., no. TJ 1509, p. 351.

38. While the temple at Melaikkadambur, built in the form of a chariot with wheels during the reign of Kulottunga I, carries a few select bas reliefs featuring the stories of the saints, a complete narrative, following the *Periya Purana*, appears first at Darasuram.

39. Françoise L'Hernault, with P. R. Srinivasan and Jacques Dumarçay, *Darasuram: Epigraphical Study: Etude Architecturale: Etude Iconographique* (Paris: École Française d'Extrême-Orient, 1987), pp. 135–136.

40. Mahalingam, *A Topographical List: Thanjavur*, no. TJ 1856, pp. 430–431. See also Marxia Gandhi and A. Padmavathy, eds., *Nannilam Kalvettukal* (Chennai: State Department of Archaeology, 1977), no. 71/1977, no page numbering.

41. Mahalingam, *A Topographical List: Thanjavur*, no. TJ 1857, p. 431. See also Gandhi and Padmavathy, eds., *Nannilam Kalvettukal*, no. 69/1977, no page numbering.

42. Mahalingam, *A Topographical List: Thanjavur*, no. TJ 1867, p. 433. See also Gandhi and Padmavathy, eds., *Nannilam Kalvettukal*, no. 5/1977, no page numbering.

43. David Dean Shulman, *Songs of the Harsh Devotee: The Tevaram of Cuntaramurttinayanar* (Philadelphia: University of Pennsylvania, 1990), hymn 72, verse 6, p. 465.

44. *Annual Report on Indian Epigraphy*, 1925, no. 223. The record, examined by courtesy of the Epigraphical Survey of India Office in Mysuru, commences with the *meykirti* of Rajadhiraja so that its content proper commences with line 8. Damage to the stone is largely along the start of each line, but it is also seen in its crucial phrase, which reads "vattanaigal padanadanda nada . . . ." The signatory of the deed that transfers land to the temple and outlines its boundaries is a certain Kalamulamudaiyan Adalvan Pillaialvan, alias Tiruvidhi Tiruvalampuram Nambi.

45. R. Nagaswamy, "Melaperumpallam Bronzes," in *Art and Culture of Tamil Nadu*, ed. R. Nagaswamy (Delhi: Sundeep Prakashan, 1980), pp. 95–100.

46. My translation. Iyer and Gros, *Tēvāram*, book 6, hymn 58, verses 6 and 7, pp. 310–311.

47. *ARE* 1925, no. 223. I am grateful to the Epigraphical

Survey of India in Mysuru for having made it possible for me to study the inscription in person.

48. Mahalingam, *A Topographical List: Thanjavur*, no. TJ 1694, p. 396. See also nos. TJ 1702 and 1703 for gifts to enable a festival for this swaying lord in the month of *Markali*, p. 398.

49. Ibid., no. 1704, pp. 398–399.

50. Ibid., no. TJ 1122, p. 265; ARE 1925, no. 222. He also gave an image of the goddess Uma as the lady of the bedroom chamber (*Tiru Palliarai Pirattiyar*). A second record of the same date speaks of a further gift of land by a private individual to ensure the adequate worship of the image of the Dancing Lord set up by the chieftain. Mahalingam, *A Topographical List: Thanjavur*, no. TJ 1124, p. 266; ARE 1925, no. 215.

51. For photo of image, see R. Nagaswamy, *Chola Bronzes* (Chennai: Tamil Arts Academy, 2011), plates 127 and 128.

52. One might note that inscriptions that record gifts from temple priests are few and far between.

53. Richard H. Davis, trans., *A Priest's Guide for the Great Festival: Aghorasiva's Mahotsavavidhi* (New York: Oxford University Press, 2010). Davis includes a gloss from a later commentary.

54. Ibid., p. 37.

55. Ibid., p. 50.

56. Ibid., p. 135.

57. Ibid., p. 128.

58. Ibid., p. 132.

59. Ibid., p. 133.

60. Ibid., pp. 134–136.

61. Ibid., p. 118.

62. Ibid., p. 123.

63. T. V. Mahalingam, *A Topographical List of Inscriptions in the Tamil Nadu and Kerala States*, vol. 8: *Tiruchchirappalli* (New Delhi: Indian Council of Historical Research, 1991), no. Tp 1254, pp. 277–278, at the Jambukeshvara temple at Tiruvannaikaval. (In a rare example of a citation error in Mahalingam's volumes, I found that his reference to *Ep. Ind.* VIII was incorrect; I have been unable to find the correct citation.)

64. Mahalingam, *A Topographical List: Thanjavur*, no. TJ 2011, p. 466.

65. Ibid., no. TJ 2041, p. 472.

66. See chapter 5, earlier.

67. Mahalingam, *A Topographical List: Thanjavur*, no. TJ 2010, p. 466; *Annual Report on Indian Epigraphy* 1927–28, no. 87.

68. Mahalingam, *A Topographical List: Thanjavur*, no. TJ 1376, p. 321.

69. Ibid., no. TJ 1128, p. 266.

70. Iyer and Gros, eds., *Tēvāram*, p. 404: III-126.

71. Mahalingam, *A Topographical List: Thanjavur*, no. TJ 2037, p. 472.

72. Sastri, ed., *South Indian Inscriptions*, vol. IV, no. 225, pp. 31–34. The inscription consists of thirty-one Sanskrit verses followed by thirty-six in Tamil.

73. Mahalingam, *A Topographical List: Thanjavur*, no. TJ 1376, p. 321.

74. Ibid., no. TJ 2503, p. 567.

75. Ibid., no. TJ 2390, pp. 545–546.

76. Mahalingam, *A Topographical List: Tiruchchirappalli*, no. Tp 141, pp. 29–30.

77. Ibid., no. Tp 1337, p. 294.

78. Tamara I. Sears, "Constructing the Guru: Ritual Activity and Architectural Space in Medieval India," *Art Bulletin* XC, no. 1 (March 2008): 9.

79. P. Acharya, *Sheaves of Tamil Muse* (Madras: n.d.), p. 54.

80. Vidya Dehejia, "Iconographic Transference between Krsna and Three Saiva Saints," in *Indian Art and Connoisseurship: Essays in Honour of Douglas Barrett*, ed. John Guy (Ahmedabad: Mapin Publishing, 1995), pp. 140–49.

81. Marxia Gandhi, ed., *Thanjavur Taluk Inscriptions*, vol. 1, 1979: no. 3/1979, no page numbering, dated to the year 1236 in the reign of Rajaraja III, speaks of the provision of sacred food for the dancing lord Sambandar (*Kuttadum Tirujnanasambanda Ishvaram Udaiyar*).

82. See chapter 2, earlier.

83. R. Nagaswamy, "Chidambaram Bronzes," *Lalit Kala* 19 (1979): 9–16, plus plates.

CHAPTER 8: EVOLVING MANIFESTATIONS OF THE GODDESS, THE GOD VISHNU, AND THE BUDDHA

1. S. Swaminathan, ed., *South Indian Inscriptions*, vol. XXXII (New Delhi: Director General, Archaeological Survey of India, 2012), part II, no. 167, p. 294, in temple at Kumaravayalur in Trichy district.

2. Ibid. *Stridhanam* is a gift from a woman's natal family to a bride and is intended solely for her personal use.

3. Swaminathan, ed., *South Indian Inscriptions*, vol. XXXII, part II, no. 147, p. 271. Apparently, the terms of the gift were not honored. Forty-two years later, in the fourteenth regnal year of Uttama Chola, or 985, when the written document was produced, the authorities ordered the gift to be engraved in stone, and four individuals gave their undertaking to see that her gift was correctly used.

4. Swaminathan, ed., *South Indian Inscriptions*, vol. XXXII, part II, no. 192, pp. 326–328.

5. H. Krishna Sastri, "The Tiruvalangadu Copper-Plates of the Sixth Year of Rajendra-Chola I," in *South Indian Inscriptions*, vol. III, part III (Madras: Superintendent, Government Press, 1920), no. 205, in particular, verse 46, p. 418.

6. R. Nagaswamy, "A Note on Nishumbhasudani Installed by Vijayalaya Chola in Tanjore," *Lalit Kala* 18 (1977): 39f and plate XVIII, fig. 1.

7. See Vidya Dehejia, *The Sensuous and the Sacred: Chola Bronzes from South India* (New York: American Federation of Arts; Seattle: University of Washington Press, 2002), p. 134.

8. Swaminathan, ed., *South Indian Inscriptions*, vol. XXXII,

part I, no. 76, p. 87. Engraved on a boulder near the Shiva temple at Timmichur, near Tirukkoyilur, South Arcot district. The curse reads thus: *ivai mattruvar ezhu narakkattu kizhanarakattu nirpan armaravarkku aramalladu tunai ellai.*

9. T. V. Mahalingam, *A Topographical List of Inscriptions in the Tamil Nadu and Kerala States*, vol. 8: *Tiruchchirappalli* (New Delhi: Indian Council of Historical Research, 1991), no. Tp 623, pp. 132–133, in the Arumbavur temple is one such example.

10. G. V. Srinivasa Rao, ed., *South Indian Inscriptions*, vol. XIII (Madras: Superintendent, Government Press, 1952), no. 149, pp. 78–79.

11. S. Sambandhasivacarya, B. Dagens, M. L. Barazer-Billoret, and T. Ganesan, with the collaboration of J. M. Creismeas, *Suksmagama*, vol. 2 (Pondicherry: Institut Français de Pondichéry, 2012), chapter 45: English summary on pp. cxli–cxliii; Sanskrit text on pp. 309–313.

12. T. V. Mahalingam, *A Topographical List of Inscriptions in the Tamil Nadu and Kerala States*, vol. 7: *Thanjavur* (New Delhi: Indian Council of Historical Research, 1992), no. TJ 1122, p. 265.

13. Ibid., no. TJ 1061, pp. 247–248.

14. Ibid., no. TJ 2157, p. 495; see also K. V. Subrahmanya Aiyer, ed., *South Indian Inscriptions*, vol. VIII (Madras: Superintendent, Government Press, 1937), no. 201, pp. 100–101.

15. G. V. Srinivasa Rao, ed., *South Indian Inscriptions*, vol. XXIII (Madras: Superintendent, Government Press, 1979), no. 372, pp. 258–259. See also Mahalingam, *A Topographical List: Thanjavur*, no. TJ 1113, p. 262, in the reign of Rajaraja III in 1229. While the surviving epigraphic record should be read with caution and should not be considered an accurate reflection of the popularity of images, it is nevertheless a source of considerable importance that should not be bypassed.

16. Vasudha Narayanan, *The Vernacular Veda: Revelation, Recitation, and Ritual* (Columbia: University of South Carolina Press, 1994): appendix, 3.3.3, p. 156.

17. These statistics are collected from Mahalingam, *A Topographical List: Thanjavur*.

18. Mahalingam, *A Topographical List: Thanjavur*, no. TJ 1267, p. 299: Tirukadaiyur temple. See also *Annual Report on Indian Epigraphy*, 1925, no. 257. The inscription also speaks of the crime of priests wearing or selling the lotus blossoms grown by the temple for Lord Shiva.

19. Mahalingam, *A Topographical List: Thanjavur*, no. TJ 1897, pp. 440–441. See also *Annual Report on Indian Epigraphy*, 1922, no. 503.

20. Discussed briefly by R. Nagaswamy, "On Dating South Indian Bronzes," in *Indian Art & Connoisseurship: Essays in Honor of Douglas Barrett*, ed. John Guy (Chidambaram Ahmedabad, India: Indira Gandhi National Centre for the Arts in association with Mapin Publishing, 1995), p. 104 and figs. 2a and 2b, where he assigns it to ca. 800. Nagaswamy's consistently early dates do not, I believe, hold up to close scrutiny.

21. R. Nagaswamy, *Masterpieces of Early South Indian Bronzes* (New Delhi: National Museum, 1983), catalogue no. 58, image nos. 155, 156, 157, pp. 149 and 150.

22. P. R. Srinvasan, *Bronzes of South India*, Bulletin of the Madras Government Museum (Madras: India Press, 1963), pl. XIX, fig. 96.

23. R. Nagaswamy, *Masterpieces*, figs. 164–166.

24. Vidya Dehejia, *Art of the Imperial Cholas* (New York: Columbia University Press, 1982), pp. 25–29.

25. My translation of *Periyalvar Tirumoli*, second decade, hymn 4, in *Nalayira Divya Prabandham* (Madras: V. N. Devanathan, 1971), verse 1, p. 9. See Vidya Dehejia, *Slaves of the Lord: The Path of the Tamil Saints* (Delhi: Munshiram Manoharlal, 1988), p. 100.

26. Swaminathan, ed., *South Indian Inscriptions*, vol. XXXII, part I, no. 20, p. 24f, dated in the year 15 of Parantaka. We are told that each local resident would voluntarily provide a set fee for food offerings to this bronze and for its regular worship. The exact amount of the fees, for each family, for each bride and bridegroom, and for cremation, are given. It is also specified that the administrative body of the *nadu* (district) ensured that the inscription was written in both copper and on stone (*shembilum silaiyilum sheydu kuduttom*).

27. "Six Inscriptions from Tirunamanallur," in *Epigraphia Indica*, vol. VII, 1902–03, ed. E. Hultzsch (New Delhi: Director-General, Archaeological Survey of India, 1981), no. 19 (B), p. 134f.

28. G. V. Srinivasa Rao, ed., *South Indian Inscriptions*, vol. XIX (Madras: Superintendent, Government Press, 1967), no. 196, p. 101, engraved on a pillar in a rock-cut cave at Tiruvellarai. See also Mahalingam, *A Topographical List: Tiruchchirappalli*, no. Tp 507, p. 108.

29. The only other figure in Tamil iconography with a hairdo resembling ringlet curls is Shiva saint Chandesha.

30. My translation of Sambandar hymn 1, verse 10.

31. Noboru Karashima and Y. Subbarayalu, "Goldsmiths and Padinen-vishayam: A Bronze Buddha Image of Nagapattinam," in *Ancient & Medieval Commercial Activities in the Indian Ocean: Testimony of Inscriptions and Ceramic-Sherds: Report of the Taisho University Research Project, 1997–2002*, ed. Noboru Karashima (Tokyo: Taisho University, 2002), pp. 57–61.

32. Alain Danielou, trans., *Manimekhalai (The Dancer with the Magic Bowl) by Merchant-Prince Shattan* (New York: New Direction Books, 1989), p. 143.

33. Samuel Beal, *Si-Yu-Ki: Buddhist Records of the Western World. Translated from the Chinese of Hiuen Tsiang AD 629* (London: Trubner & Co., Ltd, 1884), vol. II, p. 229.

34. Michael Lockwood and A. Vishnu Bhat, *King Mahendra's Mattavilasa* (Madras: Christian Literature Society, 1981).

35. K. R. Srinivasan, *Cave-Temples of the Pallavas* (New Delhi: Archaeological Survey of India, 1964), p. 173.

36. Vidya Dehejia, "The Persistence of Buddhism in Tamilnadu," in *A Potpourri of Indian Art*, ed. Pratapaditya Pal (Bombay: Marg Publications, 1988), pp. 53–74.

37. T. N. Ramachandran, *The Nagapattinam and Other Buddhist Bronzes in the Chennai Museum* (Chennai: Director of Museums, Government of Tamilnadu, 2005). M. A. Siddhique, Director of Museums, tells us in a single-paragraph foreword that about 350 bronzes have been unearthed from Nagapattinam since 1856.

38. As cited in Vidya Dehejia, "The Persistence of Buddhism in Tamilnadu," p. 60.

39. Vidya Dehejia, *The Sensuous and the Sacred: Chola Bronzes from South India* (New York: American Federation of Arts; Seattle: University of Washington Press, 2002), p. 210. See also Karashima and Subbarayalu, "Goldsmiths and Padinenvishayam," pp. 57–61. Both Karashima and Nagaswamy are confident that the inscription belongs to the early eleventh century and must refer to Rajendra I, and not to Kulottunga I (r. 1070–1120), who also assumed the title of Rajendra.

CHAPTER 9: WORSHIP IN UNCERTAIN TIMES AND THE SECRET BURIAL OF BRONZES

1. I have given a summarized version of a lengthy inscription: see *Annual Report on Indian Epigraphy*, 1904, no. 501, to which I had access courtesy of the Epigraphical Survey of India in Mysuru. See also K. G. Krishnan, ed., *South Indian Inscriptions*, vol. XVII (Madras: Superintendent, Government Press, 1957), no. 543, p. 225. Also T. V. Mahalingam, *A Topographical List of Inscriptions in the Tamil Nadu and Kerala States*, vol. 7: *Thanjavur* (New Delhi: Indian Council of Historical Research, 1992), no. TJ 3243, p. 729; and Krishnan, ed., *South Indian Inscriptions*, vol. XVII, no. 543, p. 225.

2. Mahalingam, *A Topographical List: Thanjavur*, no. TJ 2517, p. 570.

3. Ibid., no. TJ 2514, p. 570.

4. Ibid., no. TJ 2520, p. 571.

5. C. P. Rajendran, Kusala Rajendran, S. Srinivasalu, Vanessa Andrade, P. Aravazhi, and Jaishri Sanwal, "Geoarchaeological Evidence of a Chola-Period Tsunami from an Ancient Port at Kaveripattinam on the Southeastern Coast of India," *Geoarchaeology: An International Journal* 26, no. 6 (2011): 867–887.

6. Mahalingam, *A Topographical List of Inscriptions: Thanjavur*, no. TJ 1219, p. 288. This inscription is in the temple at Talachangadu.

7. I am grateful to Mr. Karuppiah of the Mysore Epigraphical Survey of India for access to the full transcript of the *Annual Report on Indian Epigraphy*, 1926, no. 141. See appendix B, IV. The inscription is somewhat damaged, and the exact relationship between the four images taken away for safekeeping and the rest of the images mentioned in the record remains unclear.

8. *Annual Report on Indian Epigraphy*, 1927, no. 308. Thanks to Dr. Muniratnam for access to the rubbing of this inscription (missing a section) that extends along the base moldings of the temple.

9. Mahalingam, *A Topographical List: Thanjavur*, no. TJ 783, p. 186. Also *Annual Report on Indian Epigraphy*, 1918, no. 1, to which I had access through the cooperation of Dr. Muniratnam.

10. Mahalingam, *A Topographical List: Thanjavur*, no. TJ 1582, p. 368. See also *Annual Report on Indian Epigraphy* 1925, no. 500.

11. See chapter 4, earlier.

12. Mahalingam, *A Topographical List: Thanjavur*, no. TJ 219, pp. 51–52. See *Annual Report on Indian Epigraphy* 1931–32, no. 89.

13. Mahalingam, *A Topographical List: Thanjavur*, no. TJ 833, p. 209. See also *South Indian Inscriptions*, vol. VI, no. 50, pp. 28–30 (in the Shiva temple), and 58 (in the Vishnu temple).

14. My thanks to Mr. Karuppiah of the Mysore Epigraphic Survey of India for making available the original transcript of *Annual Report on Indian Epigraphy*, 1925, no. 218.

15. *Annual Report on Indian Epigraphy*, 1925, no. 217.

16. Ibid., no. 216.

17. Ibid., no. 219.

18. Marxia Gandhi and A. Padmavathy, eds., *Nannilam Kalvettukal* (Chennai: State Department of Archaeology, 1977): N.K. 157/1977, no page numbering.

19. Krishnan, ed., *South Indian Inscriptions*, vol. XVII, no. 541, pp. 223–224.

20. Krishnan, ed., *South Indian Inscriptions*, vol. XVII, no. 544, pp. 225–226. Mahalingam, *A Topographical List: Thanjavur*, no. TJ 3239, p. 728.

21. *Annual Report on Indian Epigraphy*, 1911, no. 296. This same record is repeated also in *Annual Report on Indian Epigraphy*, 1921, no. 562.

22. *Annual Report on Indian Epigraphy*, 1913, no. 80; the inscription starts with a reference to her *stridhanam* (*stridhanam petrudaiyenay ennuday varukira adiyaril*), records the four names, and concludes on her selling them into service (*devar adimaiyay kodutta*). I have added the lady's name as Lakshmi; the phrase used is "she who rests on his sacred chest" (*tiru marbu idam kondal*). The sale is in the thirteenth year of Rajadhiraja II, or 1179. On the subject of *stridhanam*, we may note that when Sembiyan Mahadevi made a gift of land to the temple in the town of Sembiyan Mahadevi, her inscription specifies that she bought land from a mother and daughter who had, respectively, the right of *stridhanam*, and that the disposal of the lands devolved upon the mother's husband. *Annual Report on Indian Epigraphy*, 1925, no. 479.

23. I am grateful to Dr. Muniratnam for access to the transcript of *Annual Report on Indian Epigraphy*, 1917, no. 223.

24. Mahalingam, *A Topographical List: Thanjavur*, no. TJ 2520, p. 571.

25. Ibid., no. TJ 2532, p. 573. *Annual Report on Indian Epigraphy*, 1918, no. 511.

26. Mahalingam, *A Topographical List: Thanjavur*, no. TJ 2523, p. 572.

27. Ibid., no. TJ 2538, pp. 574–575.

28. Ibid., no. TJ 2542, pp. 575–576. Dated in the thirty-second year of Pandya king Srivallabha, the inscription gives us fascinating information about the decline of the Cholas. It tells us that commencing from the time Kopperunjingadeva, an unknown upstart who took the name Pallava to which he had no right, was fighting the Kannadiyas, festivals at the Tiruvenkadu temple ceased and had not been resumed as yet.

29. Ibid., no. TJ 2537, p. 574.

30. The merchant took the name of the child saint Sambandar, whose verses we have encountered often in these pages.

31. Risha Lee, "Rethinking Community: The Indic Carvings of Quanzhou," in *Nagapattinam to Suvarnadvipa: Reflections on the Chola Naval Expeditions to Southeast Asia*, ed. Hermann Kulke, K. Kesavapany, and Vijay Sakhuja (Singapore: Institute of Southeast Asian Studies, 2009), p. 250f.

32. Ibid., pp. 245–249.

33. S. Ratnasabapathy, *Divine Bronzes: The Thanjavur Art Gallery Bronze Sculptures* (Thanjavur: Thanjavur Art Gallery Administration, 1982 reprint), appendix III, p. 133.

34. T. N. Ramachandran, "Bronze Images from Tiruvenkadu-Svetaranya (Tanjore District)," *Lalit Kala* 3/4 (1956–1957): 55–62. See also Ratnasabapathy, *Divine Bronzes*.

35. R. Nagaswamy, "New Bronze Finds from Tiruvenkadu," *Transactions of the Archaeological Society of South India* 5 (1972): 109–122.

36. Ratnasabapathy, *Divine Bronzes*, p. 134.

37. C. Meenakshi, "Tandantottam Bronzes," *Journal of the Mythic Society* 28, 2 (1937): 89–93. R. Nagaswamy, "Some Adavallan and Other Bronzes of the Early Chola Period," *Lalit Kala* 10 (1961): 34–40.

38. Nagaswamy, "Some Adavallan and Other Bronzes of the Early Chola Period," fig. 2.

39. The copper plate itself is dated to the year 1036 but speaks of provisions that took effect from the year 1027, presumably the year when the Esalam temple was complete. R. Nagaswamy, "Archaeological Finds in South India: Esalam Bronzes and Copper-Plates," *Bulletin de l'École Française d'Extrême-Orient* 76 (1987): 1–68.

40. S. Sankaranarayana, Marxia Gandhi, A. Padmavathy, and R. Sivanantham, *Thiruvindalur Copper Plate* (Chennai: State Department of Archaeology, 2011); see last four pages of the plates. The images found are Ganesha, Shiva as *Chandrashekhara*, saint Sundarar together with his wives Paravai and Sangili, Karaikkal Ammaiyar, dancing child saint Sambandar, saint Appar, saint Manikkavachakar, Astra devar or Shiva's trident, plus a lamp, water vessels, and musical pipes.

41. See chapter 4, earlier.

42. R. Nagaswamy, "Nallur Bronzes," *Lalit Kala* 20 (1982): 9–11, plus plates. Three of the hidden bronzes are of a later sixteenth-century date, and reflect a second round of hiding bronzes after the arrival of the Portuguese.

43. See chapter 4, earlier.

44. H. Krishna Sastri, ed., *South Indian Inscriptions*, vol. III, part IV (Madras: Superintendent, Government Press, 1929), no. 211, p. 474.

45. R. Nagaswamy, "Chidambaram Bronzes," *Lalit Kala* 19 (1979): 9–16, plus plates.

46. Nagaswamy, "Archaeological Finds in South India," plate LXXVI, p. 198.

47. A group of Egyptian bronzes in the Freer Gallery of Art are so badly consumed by "bronze disease" that it is not possible even to identify the subject matter portrayed.

48. I thank Paul Jett, former head of the Conservation Center at the Freer Gallery of Art, Smithsonian Institution, for his input into this tricky problem.

49. Vidya Dehejia, *The Sensuous and the Sacred: Chola Bronzes from South India* (New York: American Federation of Arts; Seattle: University of Washington Press, 2002), chart on pp. 84–85. The royal images from the Calico Museum, Ahmedabad, recently claimed by the Tamil Nadu police, Idol Wing, to be those of emperor Rajaraja and his queen Lokamahadevi commissioned by Adittan Suriyan, temple manager of emperor Rajaraja (985–1012) prior to 1012, appear to belong a hundred years later to ca. 1125. See discussion of the queen in chapter 7, earlier.

50. See appendix B, II.

51. K. V. Subrahmanya Aiyer, ed., *South Indian Inscriptions*, vol. VIII (Madras: Superintendent, Government Press, 1937), no. 201, pp. 100–101.

52. *Vimanarcanakalpa* (Madras: Venkatesvara Mudralaya, 1926): ch. 70, "Bhaya Rakshastham Nishkritih," pp. 435–439. See also Richard Davis, *Lives of Indian Images* (Princeton, NJ: Princeton University Press, 1997), pp. 127–128.

53. Richard Davis, *Lives of Indian Images*, p. 127f.

54. Mehrdad Shokoohy, "Architecture of the Sultanate of Ma'bar and Other Muslim Monuments in South India," *Journal of the Royal Asiatic Society* 1, no. 1 (April 1991): 31–92. Shokoohy tells us that he is quoting one of the more modest of estimates, that of Muhammad Qasim, bin Hindu Shaha, known as Firishta; see *Tarikh-i-Firishta* (Lucknow, 1864), p. 60.

55. As quoted in Shakoohy, "Architecture of the Sultanate," p. 33.

56. Muhammad Habib, *The Campaigns of Ala-ud-din Khilji beng Hazrat Amir Khusrau's Khazainul Futuh, (Treasures of Victory)* (Madras: Cosmopolitan Publishers, 1931), pp. 106–107.

57. We should note, however, that there is reference to breaking stone idols that are referred to as "contaminated stones." See Muhammad Habib, *The Campaigns of Ala-ud-din Khilji*, p. 107.

58. *Annual Report on Indian Epigraphy*, 1916, no. 175.

59. This inscription is on the east wall of the *mandapa* in front of the central shrine in the Agnishvara temple; it speaks of the Kannanur perumal, or the Vishnu of Kannanur, who "during the time of the Turks, had proceeded to a safe place" (*turukkar kalamay shemattilai ezhundaruli irunda ivarai*). Courtesy

Epigraphical Survey of Mysuru; *Annual Report on Indian Epigraphy* 1935-1936, no. 144. We must remember that over half of Chola inscriptions remain unpublished and that other similar references are likely to emerge if the inscriptions are made readily available to scholars.

CHAPTER 10: REVIEWING THE CHOLA ACHIEVEMENT A MILLENNIUM LATER

1. *The Hindu*, Tiruchirappalli edition, July 1, 2015.
2. Indira Peterson, *Poems to Śiva: The Hymns of the Tamil Saints* (Princeton, NJ: Princeton University Press, 1989), Appar V: 207, p. 211.
3. Ibid., Appar IV: 15. The last lines are of verses 6, 7, and 8.

APPENDIX C: TENTH-CENTURY CHOLA YOGINIS IN CONTEXT

1. See Vidya Dehejia, *Yogini Cult & Temples: A Tantric Tradition* (New Delhi: The National Museum, 1986).
2. Padma Kaimal, *Scattered Goddesses: Travels with the Yoginis* (Ann Arbor, MI: Association of Asian Studies, 2012).
3. Melpadi is 40 kilometers from Kaveripakkam, the other possible site of the yogini temple.
4. To avoid identifying the yoginis by their current museum location, I am giving them names that largely follow those assigned by Padma Kaimal in her *Scattered Goddesses*.
5. Swaminathan, ed., *South Indian Inscriptions*, vol. XXXII (New Delhi: Archaeological Survey of India, 2012), appendix, nos. 5-10, pp. 390-396. Dated in Krishnadeva's regnal years 21 to 29, and thus from 960 to 968, these records extend the period during which he occupied Chola territory.
6. K. K. Handiqui, *Yaśastilaka and Indian Culture: or, Somadeva's Yaśastilaka and Aspects of Jainism and Indian Thought and Culture in the Tenth Century* (Sholapur: Jaina Saṁskṛti Saṁrakshaka Sangha, 1968).
7. Somadevasuri's *Yasatilaka Campu*. Originally translated with the help of Mrs. Manikuntala Bhowmik and cited in Dehejia, *Yogini Cult*, pp. 26-27, it has since been revised, with occasional corrections, by Tyler Richard.
8. Kaimal, *Scattered Goddesses*, p. 30, fig. 3. The images range in size from the smallest at 43.7 inches to the largest at 52.5 inches.
9. In my 1986 book on the yoginis, I described this as a winnower; while it resembles one, it is of the type used by temple priests even today as they ritually clear up after ceremonial rites.
10. The *hamsa* of the texts is a pecking goose and not a swan as the bird is often described. Yogini temples tend to carry an image of Shiva at the center of the circle of goddesses; see Dehejia, *Yogini Cult*, p. 104. Two male figures, one of Shiva and one identified as Shanmuga, the younger son of Shiva, may have belonged to this temple. See Padma Kaimal, *Scattered Goddesses*, ch. 1, esp. table 2, pp. 8-10.

APPENDIX D: TRACE METAL ANALYSIS ON FIVE CHOLA BRONZES}

1. Dharma P. Agrawal, *The Copper Bronze Age in India* (New Delhi: Munshiram Manoharlal, 1971); Ben B. Johnson, "Krishna Rajamannar Bronzes: An Examination and Treatment Report," in *Krishna: The Cowherd King, Museum of Art Monograph Series 1*, ed. Pratapaditya Pal (Los Angeles: Los Angeles County Museum of Art 1972), pp. 45-58; Otto Werner, *Spektralanalytische und Metallurgische Untersuchungen: an Indischen Bronzen*, vol. 2 (Leiden: Brill, 1972); Jonathon E. Ericson and Hiroshi Shirahata, "Lead Isotope Analysis of Ancient Copper and Base Metal Ore Deposits in Western India," in *Application of Science in Examination of Works of Art: Proceedings of the Seminar, September 7-9, 1983* (Boston: Museum of Fine Arts, 1985), pp. 207-212; Sharada Srinivasan, "Lead Isotope and Trace Element Analysis in the Study of Over a Hundred South Indian Metal Icons," *Archaeometry* 41, no. 1 (1999): 91-116; Paul Craddock and Duncan Hook, "The Bronzes of the South of India: A Continuing Tradition?" in *Scientific Research on the Sculptural Arts of Asia, Proceedings of the Third Forbes Symposium at the Freer Gallery of Art* (Washington, DC: Freer Gallery of Art, Smithsonian Institution, 2007), pp. 75-90; C. Reedy and Sherry Harlacher, "Elemental Composition of Sri Lankan Bronzes: Technological Style and Change," in *Scientific Research on the Sculptural Arts of Asia, Proceedings of the Third Forbes Symposium at the Freer Gallery of Art* (Washington, DC: Freer Gallery of Art, Smithsonian Institution, 2007), pp. 63-74; Arjuna Thantilage, "An Archaeo-metallurgical Investigation of Sri Lankan Historical Bronzes," PhD Thesis, Postgraduate Institute of Archaeology, University of Kelaniya, Sri Lanka, 2008; Sharada Srinivasan, "Tamil Chola Bronzes and Swamimalai Legacy: Metal Sources and Archaeotechnology," *Journal of the Minerals, Metals & Materials Society* 68, no. 8 (2016): 2207-2221.
2. S.M.M. Young, P. Budd, R. Haggerty, and A.M. Pollard, "Inductively Coupled Plasma-Mass Spectometry for the Analysis of Ancient Metals," *Archaeometry* 39, no. 2 (1997): 379-392.
3. Laure Dussubieux, Aurelie Deraisme, Gérard Frot, Christopher Stevenson, A.M.Y. Creech, and Yves Bienvenu, "LA-ICP-MS, SEM-EDS and EPMA Analysis of Eastern North American Copper-based Artefacts: Impact of Corrosion and Heterogeneity on the Reliability of the LA-ICP-MS Compositional Results," *Archaeometry* 50, no. 4: 643-657.
4. Young et al., "Inductively Coupled Plasma-Mass Spectometry for the Analysis of Ancient Metals."
5. Srinivasan, "Lead Isotope and Trace Element Analysis in the Study of Over a Hundred South Indian Metal Icons"; Thantilage, "An Archaeo-metallurgical Investigation of Sri Lankan Historical Bronzes."
6. Chandra L. Reedy, *Himalayan Bronzes: Technology, Style, and Choices* (Cranbury, NJ: Associated University Presses, 1997), pp. 85-86.
7. Craddock and Hook, "The Bronzes of the South of India: A Continuing Tradition?"; Srinivasan, "Lead Isotope and Trace Element Analysis in the Study of Over a Hundred South Indian Metal Icons," 91-116; and Srinivasan, "Tamil Chola Bronzes and Swamimalai Legacy: Metal Sources and Archaeotechnology."

Index

Note: Page numbers in italic type indicate illustrations.

Abraham, Meera, 170, 195
Aden, 4, 25–26, 114, 193, 196, 267
Agastya, 118
Aghora-Shivacharya, "Procedures for the Great Festival" (Mahotsava vidhi), 212–13
Ali, Daud, 84
alvars (saints of Vishnu), 21, 243, 263
Amarasimha's Sanskrit lexicon, 25
Anaimangalam (village), 194
Anjuvannam (guild), 193
anukkis (intimates), 5, 139, 162–63, 268; Nakkan Pavai, 162–63, 268; Paravai Nangaiyar, 162–63, 268; Tuppayan Uttamacholi, 139. See also bhogiyars
Appar (saint), 3, 12, 22, 41–42, 50, 51, 99, 118, 135, 149, 156, 184, 186, 186, 187, 197, 198, 208, 214, 216, 217, 219, 270–71, 291n19
Arjuna, 209, 223
attha virattanam (eight heroic forms), temples associated with, 198–206; Darasuram, 200, 203–5, 204; Kadaiyur, 202; map of, 203; Tiruchengatankudi, 205–6; Valuvur, 198, 202
Avalokiteshvara, 243, 246, 246 (detail), 247
ayyavole (guild). See disai ayirattu ainurruvar

Balasubrahmanyam, S. R., viii
Barrett, Douglas, viii
beauty: bodily, 1, 3–4, 114; in motion, 34, 292n54; of Shiva, 1, 3, 22, 34; spiritual/divine, 1, 4; of Uma, 3; vocabulary for, 292n54
Bell, H.P.C., 190
Berenson, Bernard, 6, 301n59
Bhasa, The Statue Play (Pratima Nataka), 91–92
bhogiyars (concubines), 45–46, 139; Nakkan Aiyaradigal, 45, 96; Nangai Chattapeymanar, 45. See also anukkis
body: Indian ideal of, 1, 3–4, 114; sacred and sensuous combined in, 4
Brahma, 84
Brahmadirayar (devotee), 142, 144
brahmotsavam (annual resanctification festival), 18, 19, 20, 269, 286, 290n10
bronze: composition of, 23; corrosion and protection of, 261
bronzes: adornment of, 28–30, 52, 89, 127, 131, 138, 150–58; buried, 258–65; earliest processional images, 33–34, 38; financing of, 4; groups of, owned by temples, 20, 216, 273–76; lost-wax process of making, 26, 30, 31, 32–33, 100, 267; as material objects, questions and issues, 4–5, 23–28, 61; missing, 261–62; numbers of, 4, 12; patronage of artists/workshops producing, 58, 114, 245, 247; purpose of, 4; removal of, from temple settings, 269; roles of, in temples and processions, 14; scholarship on, viii–ix; solid casting of, 23; Sri Lankan bronzes compared to, 175–89; stone sculptures compared to, 33, 64, 160–61; trace metal analysis of, 282–85; Western bronzes compared to, 32–33; wooden precursors of, 14, 23. See also Polonnaruwa, Sri Lanka: Hindu bronzes from; temples, cited primarily for their bronzes/architecture; Vijayanagara bronzes
Buddha, 175, 176, 184, 244
Buddhism, 171, 175, 190–91, 242–43
Buddhist imagery, 113–14, 113, 175, 176, 243–47, 244, 245, 246

Capital workshop/style, 51–52, 58–61, 59, 63–64, 63, 65, 281, 281
Casson, Lionel, 25, 165
celibacy, 216
Champakalakshmi, C., viii
Chandesha (saint), 158–60, 159, 160, 184, 185–86, 213, 258, 259, 261
Cheras, 147, 154
chieftans: Araiyan Tiruvegamanudaiyar, 229; Bhuti Vikarama Kesari, 41; Gangaikondachola Pallavaraiyan, 173; Iladaraiyar, 79; Kandan Maravan, 37, 42; Katanagan Nagattaraiyan, 61; Palavettaraiyars, 41, 49; Sundara Cholan, 133; Vels, 49; Villavan Peraraiyar, 72, 75
China: Chola-style temple built in, 257–58; and trade, 4, 114, 147, 165–67, 193–95
Chola dynasty: administration of, 157–58, 198, 251–52; calamities in thirteenth century for, 249, 251–53, 256–57; early history of, 37–39; end of, 84; expansion of, 9; father-son joint rule in, 38; global context for, 7; main rulers of, 272; maps of, 10, 12; marital alliances' role in, 44, 115; power-sharing with chieftains in, 96–97; scholarship on, viii–ix; and Sri Lanka, 12, 26, 147, 167–73, 191, 267, 307n17; and Srivijaya dynasty, 193–95, 197; trade's significance for, 4, 25–26, 193–97, 267; warfare commonplace for, 4, 37–38, 51, 64, 169, 249
coastal belt, south India, 17, 28, 32, 34, 52, 58, 59, 61, 64, 71, 198, 202, 249, 258–59, 267
Coastal workshop/style, 51–58, 59, 61, 62, 64, 65, 99, 109, 114, 208, 224, 226, 249
coins, Sri Lankan, 81–82, 170–71
concubines. See anukkis; bhogiyars
connoisseurship, 6–7, 289n16, 301n59
Consort of the Bedroom Chamber, 229, 260
contrapposto, 34, 54, 59, 131, 139, 142, 146, 160, 175, 182, 184, 186, 206, 217, 245
copper: chemical coloration of, 61; introduction of, 23; sources of, 5, 24–28, 171, 267; trade in, 25–26, 171. See also bronze
copper-plate inscriptions, 24, 37, 49, 67, 69, 84–87, 94–95, 156,

316

167, 194, 196, 259; Anbil plates, 8, 37, 85; Esalam plates, 41, 259; Tiruvalankadu plates, 8, 24, 37, 84, 85, 259; Tiruvindalur plates, 86, 87
Craddock, Paul, 26

Damodaran, K., 124
dance-drama performances, music, and performers, 18–19, 82, 213; Adalaiyur-chakkai, 18–19; ariya, 18–19, 82, 124; chakkai, 18–19, 82; dance masters, 83; in festivals, 5, 16, 18, 82, 213, 269; instruments used for, 5, 111, 269; Kirti Maraikandan, 82; local/vernacular (deshi), 82, 99, 124; payments to, 18, 82, 111, 148, 149; tamula, 18–19; Tiruvelai-arai-chakkai, 19; Vijaya Rajendran Achariyan, 161–62
Davis, Richard, ix, 262
Delhi Sultanate, 262–65
deshi (local/vernacular) music and dance, 82, 99, 124
Devi Mahatmyam ("Glory of the Goddess"), 221
Dhatuvamsa (Lineage of Relics), 27
disai ayirattu ainurruvar (Five Hundred of the Thousand Directions) [guild], 49, 83, 193, 309n7
donations. See gifts/donations
donors, female, 4–5, 46, 268; anukkis, 5, 162–63, 268; Ariyan Umaiyalvi, 229; bhogiyars, 45; Chitrakomalam, 79; Eran, 76; Irayiravan Devi, 235; Kadamba-vitari, 43; Kanari Tonri, 82, 127; Kundavai (Kundavaiyar), 91; Lady Kadamba, 37; Madevi Kadambadevi, 43; Mainjan Kavaiyan, 75; Mullai Nangaiyar, 44; Nakkan Aiyaradigal, 45; Nangai Bhuti, 41; Nangai Chattapeymanar, 45; Nanguri Nangaiyar, 44; Pandan Kali, 44; Pichchai, 190; queens, 5, 44, 97–117, 124–26, 268; Tuppayan Uttamacholi, 139; Uma as favorite of, 221, 268
donors, male: Amalan Sheyyavayar, 138; Amarakon, 262; Arinjikai Pirattiyar, 91; Aruran Kamban, 49; Bhattan Mahadevan Narayanan, 75, 76; Danapati Arangan, 74; Karrali Picchan, 12; Katanagan Nagattaraiyan, 61; Mavulavan Malayan, 249; Munrukai velaikkaran, 190; Muvendavelan, 206; Nripatunga, 42; Pudi Kuttan, 39; Sambanda-perumal, 258; Sarpan, 131; Sendan Kari, 221; Srika (Tirukattrali Pichchan), 49; Sundara Cholan, 133; Talikumaran, 173–74; Tiruvaiyaru Yogiyar, 49; Tiruvidhi Tiruvalampura Nambi, 208; Uttaman Nambi, 251; Vanavan Pallavariyan, 139; Villavan Peraraiyar, 72, 75
Durga-Uma, 221–26, 225, 227

epigraphs. See inscriptions
Eran Chadaiyan (carpenter/engraver), 194

Faxian (Chinese Buddhist pilgrim), 168
festivals and processions: Buddhist, 243; decline of, in present day, 269; descriptions of, 14, 16–21, 22–23, 212–14; earliest bronze images for, 33–34, 38; economic significance of, 18–19, 149; emergence of, 14; inscriptions about, 16–18, 67, 111; persistence of, into the present day, 20–21, 269; priests' role in, 212–14; Sacred Seven temples as subject of, 39; as subject of hymns, 22–23, 291n19; vehicles for carrying divine images in, 213, 213. See also dance-drama performances, music, and performers
Five Hundred of the Thousand Directions (guild). See disai ayirattu ainurruvar
flowers (fresh and artifical gold), as gifts for temples, 111–13
food offerings: contributors to preparation of, 18; distribution of, 5, 18, 77, 149, 269; types of, 5, 77, 149–50; typical Indian fare reflected in, 149–50
fortress of love (kamakottam), 227
Freedberg, David, 6
Freedberg, Sydney, 6, 301n59

Gajasura, 198
gana attendants, 182, 198, 199 (detail), 206, 209
Gandhi, Marxia, ix, 12, 86
Ganesha, 20, 102, 118, 187–88, 189, 213, 261
Ganga dynasty, 79
Ganges (river goddess), 121, 121, 122, 123, 123, 177
Garuda, 253
gifts/donations: for adornment of bronzes, 30, 89, 131, 138; of food, 149; inscriptions recording, 9, 17–19, 26–27, 37, 41–42, 45–46, 49–51, 67, 69, 70, 72, 75–87, 111–13, 127, 148–58, 169–70, 249, 251, 256; lamps as, 49–50; of land, 17–19, 37, 69, 72, 84–86, 111, 127, 249; to temples, 9, 37, 41–46, 49–51, 61, 67, 72, 75–84, 111–13, 127, 148–58, 162–63, 169–70, 249, 251, 256. See also donors, female; donors, male; lamps, gifts of
Glover, Ian, 26
gold, 127, 153–58
Grand Anicut dam, 93
Great Temple, Thanjavur, 5, 7, 12, 64, 65, 70, 127, 133, 147–50, 148, 154, 160–62, 161, 195, 261, 273–75
Gros, François, 215
guhais (monasteries), 214–16
Gulf of Mannar, 167–68, 168, 170, 267
Gunamenagaipuram (suburb of Chidambaram), 162–63, 268

Halayudha, 49
Hall, Kenneth, viii, 96
high officials: Adittan Suryan, 156; Aniruddha Brahmadhirayan, 85; Ariyan Pichchan, 253; Brahmamangalam, 85; Jayamuri-nadalvan, 190; Kadamban Kolakkavan, 131; Kadan Kanavadi, 158; Karikala Kanna Brahmadhirayan, 139; Koyil Mayilai (also known as Parantakan Muvendavelan or Madhurantaka Muvendavelan), 19, 77, 82; Minavan Muvendavelan, 83; Mummudi Chola Kadupatti, 226; Muvendavelan, 206; Nalayirattu Munurruvan, 126; Naralokaviran, 16, 215; Parantaka Siriyavelan, 49, 170; Rajendrachola Muvendavelan, 157; Sirandan Munaiadaraiyan, 251; Uttamachola Brahmamarayan, 148; Vagaiyili Muvendavelan, 40; Velan Gandaradittan, 229; Venbanattu Velan, 42; Vikki Annan, 37, 43; Vikrisinga Muvendavelan, 154; Villavan Muvendavelan, 227. See also srikaryam officers
history, Indian sense of, 69–70, 84
hook-and-eye closures, 154, 155

INDEX 317

hymns: Buddhism and Jainism mentioned in, 243; of the Muvar, 22–23, 42, 125–26, 214–15, 291n19; in ritual worship, 5, 148, 158, 219; sacred images described in, 111; Shiva as subject of, 1, 3–4, 22–23, 41–42, 49–50, 99, 118–19, 125–27, 129, 134–35, 171–72, 198, 208, 214–16, 227, 270–71; Vishnu as subject of, 230

Icon Centers, 261, 269
indentured service, 252–53; Araiyar Perungadi, 252; Kalaiyan Kumaran, 253; Namba Nambi Kadukkal Nangai, 253; Soman Tattan, 252
inductively coupled plasma (ICP) testing, 27, 282–85
inscriptions: absence of claims of patronage/authorship regarding temple construction, 48–49; archival function of, 67, 69–70, 76, 77–78, 84, 87, 150; bearing witness to thirteenth-century calamities, 249–53; bronzes as subject of, 12; as Chola characteristic, 9; extent of, 5, 9; festivals and processions as subject of, 16–18, 67, 111; gifts/donations recorded by, 9, 17–19, 26–27, 37, 41–46, 49–51, 67, 69, 70, 72, 75–87, 111–13, 127, 148–58, 169–70, 249, 251, 256; on government administration, 251–52; on Great Temple, 147–49, 148; irrigation-related, 95–96; jewelry as subject of, 150–58, 169–70; lamps as subject of, 50; palm leaves as surface for, 67, 72, 78, 83–84, 86, 157; placement of, 71–72, 75–78; of Sacred Seven temples, 38–49; scholarship on, 5–6; temple festivities as subject of, 17–18; on temples, 42, 67–84; temple servitude outlined in, 252–53; typical content of, 9, 70. See also copper-plate inscriptions; temples, cited primarily for their inscriptions
irrigation, 89, 92–96, 94, 268
Ishana Shiva Pandita (guru of Rajendra), 259

Jainism, 243
Jewish traders: Abraham Ben Yiju, 25, 196–97; Joseph Ben Abraham, 25, 196–97
jewelry and ornament: on Chola bronzes, 28–30, 52, 89, 127, 131, 138, 150–58; gold, 127, 153–58; jewelry, 89, 127, 169–70; pearls, 151, 167–70, 267

Kaimal, Padma, viii, 37, 293n5
Kali (goddess), 42, 44, 58, 83, 139, 221, 226–27, 226
kamakottam (fortress of love), 227
Kamboja (Cambodia), 196
Kanappan (saint), 142, 143, 143 (detail), 219, 264, 264
Karashima, Noboru, viii
Karikala Cholas (second-century ancestor of Chola kings), 93
Kasyapa (sage), 84
Kaveri river, 4, 5, 9, 23, 30, 34, 39, 39, 93–95, 94
Khusrau, Amir, 262–63
Khusrau Khan (Delhi Sultanate commander), 263
Kidaram, 195–96
King Parakrama's Ocean (lake), 172
kings and princes, Chola: Adirajendra, 173; Aditya, 8, 37, 38, 42–46, 64, 81; Aditya Karikala, 76, 77, 80, 169; Arikulakesari, 43–44, 46; Arinjaya (Arinjikai), 43–44, 46; Gandaraditya, ix, 43, 76, 97, 99, 111, 115, 118, 125–27; Jatavarman Sundara Pandya, 202, 256–57; Kannaradeva, 43, 46, 49; Ko Maran Sadaiyan (Jatavarman Pandya), 98; Ko Rajakesari, 44; Kulottunga, 16, 47, 80, 170, 195–96, 214; Kulottunga II, 17, 83, 149, 203, 261; Kulottunga III, 18, 71, 81, 83, 169, 202, 205, 249, 262; Maravarman Sundara Pandya I, 256; Parakrama Bahu, 172; Parantaka, 12, 37–38, 42–46, 48, 51–52, 61, 64, 67, 71–72, 76–79, 81, 94, 97, 115, 126, 169; Rajadhiraja, 24, 86, 139, 259; Rajadhiraja II, 169; Rajaditya, 38, 51, 78–82, 97, 115, 235, 277; Rajaraja, 5, 7, 12, 45, 46, 59, 64, 70, 76–77, 80–82, 92, 97, 119, 123, 127, 147–48, 150, 153–54, 157, 158, 160–62, 169–70, 172–73, 194, 196, 203, 206, 227, 249, 261, 268; Rajaraja II, 18, 157, 197–206, 227, 258; Rajaraja III, 81, 112, 208, 249, 251; Rajendra, 24, 37, 41, 71, 77, 80, 82, 84, 85, 91, 131, 148, 162–63, 169–70, 174, 180, 194–95, 203, 259, 268; Rajendra II, 86, 162–63, 268; Sundara, 8, 37, 43, 85, 97; Uttama, 76–77, 91, 97, 99, 111, 112, 115, 117, 193, 260; Uttamasili, 43–44, 46, 294n29; Vijayalaya, 8, 9, 37, 93, 221; Vikrama, 16, 80–83, 209; Virarajendra, 86
kings and princes, other: Chekachai Khan, 258; Gajabahu (Gamini Abhaya), 165; Ganapati, 196; Krishnadeva III, 79–80, 277; Kundavarman, 113, 114; Maranjadaiyan (Varaguna Pandya), 42; Maravarman Vikrama Pandya, 84; Nandivarma, 42; Sthanu Ravi, 37, 43; Varaguna Pandya (Maranjadaiyan), 42; Vijayabahu, 190, 193; Vikrama Pandya, 81; Vikrama Pandya III, 80
Kolar gold mine, 154
Kollidam stream, 18, 93, 94
Konulampallam, buried bronzes in, 260–61
Krishna: as avatar of Vishnu, 230, 234; dancing, 217, 234, 235; as King of Dwarka, 235, 239, 239 (rear view), 242, 253–54, 254, 255 (rear details); vanquishing Kaliya, 234–35, 236, 237 (rear view), 238, 238 (rear detail)
Kumaraganam (guild), 190

Lakshmana, 232
Lakshmi, 1, 2, 133
Lalitavistara, 243
lamps, gifts of, 9, 12, 16, 18, 42, 43, 45, 49–50, 70, 75, 76, 78, 80, 81, 82, 83, 88, 148, 162, 170, 197, 202, 203, 206, 212, 227, 235, 249, 259, 273
linga (symbol of Shiva), 14, 15, 22, 227
literacy, 76
Lokeshvara, 113–14, 113, 243
lost-wax process, 26, 30, 31, 32–33, 267

Madurai (town), 4, 10, 20, 27, 38, 44, 47, 79, 81, 168, 169, 263, 267, 287
Mahabharata, 209, 223
Mahalingam, T. V., 4, 5–6, 48, 70
Mahendravarman, Mattavilasa (Drunken Sport), 242
Maitreya, 243, 245, 245
Malik Kafur (Delhi Sultanate general), 262–63
Manigramam (guild), 28, 43, 193
Manikkavachakar (saint), 186, 202, 260; Tiruvempavai, 202
Manimekhalai, 242

Manu (mythical king), 84
marital alliances, 44, 115
Markandeya (devotee), 202
Master of the off-kilter substyle, 54, 57, 58, 109, 259
mathas (monasteries), 214–16
Mattusch, Carol, 32
Morelli, Giovanni, 6
Mother of Karaikkal (Karaikkal Ammaiyar) (saint), 180, 181, 182, 182, 259, 260
Mukund, Kanakalatha, viii
mula vigraha (root-image), 14
Mushalagan, 59, 150
music. See dance-drama performances, music, and performers
Muvar (Revered Three), 22, 23, 42, 125–26, 134, 184, 202, 216–17. See also Appar; Sambandar; Sundarar

Nagapattinam (district), 4, 5, 9, 48–49, 52, 243, 269; Buddhist monastery, 194, 195–96
Nagaswamy, R., viii, 208, 259
Nalvar (Sacred Four), 202
Naminandi (saint), 203, 204
Nammalvar (saint), 229, 230
Nandi, 213
Narasinga Munaiyaraiyar (saint), 203–4
Narayanan, Vasudha, ix
nayanmar (saints of Shiva), 21–23, 21, 41, 171, 184, 198, 202, 203, 216–19, 243. See also Muvar
novice devotee, 142, 144

officials. See high officials
ornament. See jewelry and ornament
Orr, Leslie, viii, 87, 291n19

Pallava dynasty, 7, 9, 23, 34, 37, 42, 205, 258, 267
palm leaves, inscriptions on, 67, 72, 78, 83–84, 86
Panchu, Sriram, x
Pandya dynasty, 4, 38, 51, 78, 147, 154, 169, 256–57, 307n17
Paravai (wife of Sundarar), 142, 144, 145, 145 (detail), 149, 210, 217, 260
Patanjali (sage), 260
patrons. See donors, female; donors, male
Pattinappalai, 95
pearls, 151, 167–70, 267
performers. See dance-drama performances, music, and performers
The Periplus of the Erythrean Sea, 25, 166–68
Periyalvar (saint), 234
Periya Puranam. See Sekkilar, Periya Puranam
Peterson, Indira, ix, 95, 126
Piggott, Vince, 26
Pliny, 165, 167
Polo, Marco, 168
Polonnaruwa, Sri Lanka, 172–75, 184, 186–87, 190–91; Hindu bronzes from, 175–89, 191; Shiva devale 1, 172; Shiva devale 2, 172–73, 173; Shiva devale 5, 174–75, 174, 179–80, 184, 186, 188

portraiture, 91–92
pradakshina (circumambulation), 75–76
priests, 161, 212–16, 212
processions. See festivals and processions

queens: Ahalaya (Sri Lankan), 165; Arinjikai, 115; Arulmoli Nanagaiyar, 115; Aruran Ambalattadigal (Aruran Ponnambalattadigal), 91, 115, 221; Battan Danatongiyar, 115; bronze statue, 210, 211; Cheyabhuvana Chinatamaniyar, 115; Cholamahadevi (Cholamahadeviyar), 44, 115, 133, 142; Chola Sikhamaniyar, 44, 115; Dantisakti (Dantishakti Vilangi), 49, 112; Gopan Sakkapu, 115; Kadupattigal Tamaramettiyar, 44; Kokkilanadigal (Kokkilan, Kilanadigal), 51, 78–79, 81, 82, 115, 170, 235, 268; Kundavai (Kundaviyar), 91, 112, 153, 155, 158; Lokamahadevi, 150; Mahadeviadigal, 79; Malapadi Tennavan Mahadeviyar, 115; Minavan Madeviyar, 115; Nakkan Tillai Alagiyar, 116; Orattanan Solabbaiyar (Tribhuvanamahadevi), 115; Panchavan Madeviyar, 116; Panchavan Mahadevi, 83, 150–51, 153; of Parantaka, 115; Sembiyan Mahadevi, 46, 49, 83, 89, 90, 91–93, 97–99, 111, 115, 117–18, 124–27, 147, 162, 223, 251, 259–60, 268; Siddhavadavan Chuttiyar, 115; Sonna Mahadeviyar, 91; Sorabbiyar Tribhuvanamadevi, 112; Tennavan Mahadeviyar, 44, 115; Trailokyamahadevi, 115; Tribhuvanamahadevi, 115; Tribhuvana mulududaiyal, 83; Urattayan Sorabbai, 91, 115; of Uttama Chola, 115–16; Vallavan Mahadeviyar, 115; Vanavan Mahadevi (Madevi), 82, 112, 115, 172; Vayiriakkan Tribhuvanamahadevi, 44; Viranaraniyar, 76–77, 115

Rajarajesvara Natakam ("Rajaraja Play"), 162
Rajendran, Dr., x
Ram, N., x
Rama (avatar of Vishnu), 223, 230, 232, 232, 233
Ramachandran, T. N., 243
Ramanujan, A. K., ix
Ramayana, 48, 91–92, 223
Rasa-Ratna-Samuchchaya, 25
Rashtrakuta dynasty, 38, 51, 79–80, 82, 154, 277
Ratnasabhapati Bronze Workshop, xi
Revered Three. See Muvar
rice farming, 4, 93–95
Rodin, Auguste, 32
Rukmini (consort of Krishna), 235, 253, 255 (rear view), 257

Sacred Seven temples, 38–49; Aiyaru (Pancha-nadishvara) (Tiruvaiyaru), 39, 40, 42, 45, 112; Chottruturai, 40, 40, 42, 44–45, 50; Kandiyur, 40, 44; map of, 39; Neyttanam, 6, 36, 37, 41, 42–45, 50, 66–67, 68, 69; Palanam, 39, 40, 42, 44, 154, 157; photographs of, 40–41; Poonturutti, 40, 44–45, 51, 63–64, 161; Vedikudi, 41, 42, 45–48, 47, 50
Sagar, Jyoti, x
saints. See Muvar; nayanmar
Sambandar (saint), ix, xii, 4, 12, 22–23, 34, 99, 121, 123, 129, 135, 149, 156, 171–72, 184, 186, 214–17, 217, 218, 242, 243, 259, 261, 270–71, 291n19, 293n15

INDEX 319

Saraswati, Mrs., x
Sastri, Nilakantha, viii
Satakopa. See Nammalvar
Satyabhama (consort of Krishna), 253, 255 (rear view)
Sekkilar, Periya Puranam, 126, 172, 203, 214
Sembiyan Mahadevi (queen), 46, 49, 83, 89, 90, 91–93, 97–99, 111, 115, 117–18, 124–27, 147, 162, 223, 251, 259–60, 268
Sembiyan Mahadevi (town), 89, 91, 112, 251
Sen, Tansen, viii, 194
Seneviratne, Sudarshan, x, 26
Seruwila copper belt, x, 26, 27, 171, 267
Shaya, Josephine, 156
shipbuilding, 167
Shiva: beauty of, 1, 3–4, 22, 34; Chandesha's relationship to, 158–60; Chola worship of, 9, 230, 270–71; eight heroic forms of, 198; sacred symbolic images of, 14, 15; in Sanskrit texts, 22; as subject of hymns, 1, 3–4, 22–23, 41–42, 49–50, 99, 118–19, 125–27, 129, 134–35, 171–72, 198, 208, 214–16, 227, 270–71, 291n19; Tamil concept of, 22, 34, 38, 124; temples dedicated to, 38; Uma as consort of, 1, 20, 28–30, 216, 221, 227, 229; as Victor of Three Forts, 51. See also Shiva, images of
Shiva, images of: aureoles surrounding, 119, 120; Begging Lord, 12, 14, 133–35, 136, 137 (details), 137 (rear view), 138–39, 160, 161, 202, 206–9, 207, 249, 250, 258; Bhairava, 139, 141, 142; with bull, 12, 99–100, 100, 101, 129, 130, 130 (details), 131, 214, 258–59; Chandrashekhara (the Lord crowned with the Crescent Moon), 19, 39, 260; Dancing Shiva, 12, 16, 17, 23, 89, 99, 112, 116–27, 116, 117 (rear view), 119–25, 122 (detail), 124 (details), 175, 176 (detail), 176–78, 177–80, 179 (rear view), 181, 209, 209, 213, 260, 261; in early Chola dynasty, 38; eight heroic forms, 198–206, 203, 227; flames emerging from hands of, 123–24, 124; Half Woman (Ardhanari), 63–64, 65, 76, 100, 101, 139, 140, 140 (detail), 140 (rear detail), 156, 160, 161, 258, 264, 264; Hunter, 209–10, 210; Kalyanasundarar (as bridegroom), 2, 2, 3, 3, 29, 30, 33, 35, 133, 134; portable, 16, 38, 118; seated, 52, 53; series of, owned by temples, 20, 216; similarity of, 38; "with swaying gait," 206–9, 207; trident weapon personified as Astra Devar, 19, 19; with Uma and Skanda (Somaskanda), 32, 32, 106, 108, 186-187, 188; Uma as consort, xii (detail), 1, 2, 3 (rear detail), 16, 20, 28, 29, 33, 35, 52, 102, 104, 105, 105 (rear detail), 131, 132, 133, 134 (detail), 151, 153, 161, 199, 200, 200 (detail), 210, 210, 213, 254, 256, 256, 258–59; Victor of Three Forts (Tripura Vijaya), 12, 35, 38, 50–64, 55–57, 60, 102, 103, 106, 109, 109 (detail), 110 (rear detail), 110 (rear view), 150–51, 152, 198, 239, 240, 241 (rear view), 259, 261; Victor over Elephant Demon, 198, 199, 199 (detail), 200, 201, 201 (detail), 202; Victor over Yama, 202; Wondrous Dancer, 16, 116, 116, 117, 119, 124–25. See also linga
Shulman, David, ix
Silappadikaram (The Tale of the Anklet), 165–66
silk route, 147, 193, 195, 258
Sirala (son of Siruttondar), 204–6, 205
Siruttondar (saint), 204–6, 205, 253
Sita (wife of Rama), 232, 232
Sivanandh, Aarthi, x

Sivaramamurti, C., viii
Skanda, 20, 20, 106, 108, 186–87, 198, 212, 217, 256, 260
Somadevasuri, Yasastilaka, 277, 279
Spencer, George, viii
sribali puja, 19–20, 19, 50, 80
srikaryam officers: Ayyan Kamakkodanar, 45; Battan Kannan, 111; duties of, 45, 46, 111, 157, 171, 260; Minavan Villattur Nattukon, 45, 50; Pallavaraiyar of Inganadu, 82; titles of, 96–97. See also high officials
Sri Lanka: Buddhism in, 171, 175, 190–91; Chola dynasty and, 12, 26, 147, 167–73, 191, 267, 307n17; coins from, 81–82, 170–71; as copper source, 26–28, 27, 171, 267; Hindu bronzes from, 175–89, 191; Hindu temples in, 172–75, 173, 174; pearl fisheries of, 167–70; Tamil patronage of Buddhist shrines in, 190; trade's significance for, 4, 165, 167, 191, 193, 267
Srinivas, K., 25
Srinivasan, P. R., viii
Sri Rajaraja Vijayam ("Victory of Sri Rajaraja"), 161–62
Srivijaya dynasty, 9, 167, 193–95, 197
stone sculptures: bronze sculptures compared to, 61, 64; Great Temple, Thanjavur, 64, 160–61, 161; Nageshvara temple, 61, 62, 71, 73, 74
Strahan, Donna, x, 27, 282
Subbarayulu, Y., viii
Subrahmanya, 144, 146
Suksmagama, 112, 229
Sumatra, 9, 167
Sundarar (saint), 12, 80, 134–35, 142, 144, 145, 149, 155 (detail), 156, 169, 172, 173, 186, 187, 202–4, 206, 214, 217, 219, 219
Swaminathan, M. S., x

Tagore, Rabindranath, 35
Tamil language, character of, 34–35
Tamil Liberation Army, 52
temple priests, 212–16, 212; Suvarnan Narayana Bhattadittan, 161
temples: description of, 9; in early Chola dynasty, 37–49, 293n5; early south Indian, 22; festivities associated with, 17–21, 212–14; financing of, 4; flowers as gifts for, 111–13; gifts/donations to, 9, 37, 41–46, 49–51, 61, 67, 72, 75–84, 111–13, 127, 148–58, 162–63, 169–70, 249, 251, 256; groups of bronzes owned by, 20, 216, 273–76; images in, 4, 12, 15; inscriptions on, 67–84; jewelry as gifts for, 150–58; lamps as gifts for, 49–50; management of, 70, 111–12, 148–49, 156–57; map of, 11; numbers of, 4; priests of, 212–16; Sembiyan's patronage of, 97–117, 124–26; Shiva as chief dedicatee of, 38; terminology related to, 293n15. See also attha vivattanam (eight heroic forms), temples associated with; Great Temple, Thanjavur; Sacred Seven temples; temples, cited primarily for their bronzes/architecture; temples, cited primarily for their inscriptions
temples, cited primarily for their bronzes/architecture: Aiyaru (Pancha-nadishvara), 39, 40, 42, 45; Anangur, 98; Chidambaram, 16, 118, 163, 171, 196, 203, 215, 216, 219, 260; Darasuram, 49, 197, 227, 228, 258; Esalam, 259,

262; Gangaikondacholapuram, 41, 180; Kadiri Manjunath, 113, 113; Kapalishvara, 14; Karaiyaviram, 61; Keelaiyur, 52, 61; Kilapaluvur, 15, 18; Konerirajapuram, 86, 91, 99–105, 109, 111–12, 125–26; Lalgudi, 68; map of, 11; Minakshi, 20; Nallur, 259–60; Pullamangai, 13, 48; Shivapuram, 70, 157; Tandantottam, 34, 54, 258–59, 269; Tirucherai, 232; Tiruvaduturai, 12, 261, 275; Tiruvalankadu, 182; Tiruvarur, 22, 162; Tiruvaymur, 18, 208; Tiruvenkadu, 83, 112, 124, 128–46, 249, 256, 258; Tiruvidaimaradur, 19, 21, 81–84, 127, 170, 193; Tiruvindalur, 259; Tribhuvanam, 49, 249, 250, 262; Vadakkalathur, 28, 33, 52, 269; Valampuram, 206–9, 249, 252; Vriddhachalam, 88, 112

temples, cited primarily for their inscriptions: Avalivanallur, 229, 262, 275; Chidambaram, 126; Kalitattai, 170; Karuttangudi, 221; Kovilvenni, 127; Kumaravayalur, 220, 221; Manambadi, 19; Mannargudi, 252; map of, 11; Maraikkadu (Vedaranyam), 52, 80–81, 193, 248, 253; Mayuram, 229; Muvar Koil, 41; Nageshvara, 13, 61, 69, 71–78, 72–75, 157; Panaiyur, 229; Pandanallur, 157; Senganur, 252; Somanathadeva, 71; Sulamangalam, 253; Tiruchendurai, 41; Tiruchengatankudi, 253; Tirukkalitattai, 49; Tirukkarkuti, 97; Tirukkodikaval, 98; Tirumalavadi, 147; Tirumananjeri, 49; Tirumandurai, 170; Tirunavalur (Tirunamanallur), 78–80, 268; Tirupamburam, 253; Tirupannandal, 18, 157; Tirupattur, 127; Tirupugalur, 214; Tiruvalanjuli, 112; Tiruvellarai, 235; Tiruvidavayil, 50, 214; Tiruvilakudi (Tiruvelvikudi), 49, 106, 118, 193, 249, 251, 262, 269, 275–76; Tiruvisalur, 127; Tyagaraja, 17–18; Udaiyalur, 251; Ukkachi, 251

Tevaram (hymns of Appar, Sambandar, and Sundarar), 22, 42, 214–15

Thailand, 28

Thanjavur (city), 9, 37, 39, 41, 42

Thanjavur (district), 4–7, 9, 12, 37, 38, 43, 48–49, 52, 58–59, 221

Thantilage, Arjuna, x, 26, 27

Thomas, Job, 129

tin, 23–24, 28

Tiruchirappalli. See Trichy

Tirumurai (Tamil sacred "canon" that includes Tevaram), 126, 203, 214–15

Tiruvenkadu Master, 92, 129–46, 146, 160, 206, 219, 258

Tiruvenkadu workshop, 142, 144–46, 206–11, 249

Tiruvidaimaradur Master, 197–206

trade: China and, 4, 114, 147, 165–67, 193–95; Chola dynasty and, 4, 25–26, 193–97, 267; in copper, 25–26, 171; routes for, 165–67, 166; shipping of bronzes linked to, 114; Sri Lanka and, 4, 165, 167, 191, 193, 267; Srivijaya dynasty and, 193–95. See also Aden; Jewish traders

Trivedi, Sanjeev, xi

Uma: bodily beauty of, 3; power of, 221; Shiva as consort of, 1, 20, 28–30, 216, 221, 227, 229; temples dedicated to, 227, 228; Vishnu as brother of, 1, 133, 224; women's patronage in honor of, 221, 268. See also Durga-Uma; Uma, images of

Uma, images of: Bhoga Shakti (pleasure force), 227, 260; Conqueror of Buffalo-Demon Mahisa, 223–24, 223, 224, 224 (details); Consort of the Bedroom Chamber, 229, 260; Destroyer of Nishumba, 221, 222, 222 (detail), 223; Sembiyan image modeled on, 89, 91–92; Shiva as consort, xii (detail), 1, 2, 3 (rear view detail), 12, 16, 19, 20, 28, 29, 33, 35, 52, 102, 104, 105, 105 (rear detail), 131, 132, 133, 134 (detail), 151, 153, 161, 199, 200, 200 (detail), 210, 210, 213, 254, 256, 256, 258–59; with Skanda, 20, 20, 106, 108, 198, 212, 256, 260; solid vs. hollow versions of, 32; standing, 33, 61, 62, 63–64, 63, 100, 102, 102, 106, 106 (detail), 107, 108, 182, 183, 183 (rear detail), 184, 185–86, 191, 191, 257, 259, 281

Umapati Sivacharya (poet), 200

Valanjiyar (guild), 49

Vijayanagara bronzes, 263–64, 264

Vijayanagara dynasty, 9, 263

Vijayanagara King Krishnadevaraya and His Two Queens, 265

Vimanarcanakalpa, 262

Vishnu: avatars of, 230, 232, 234–35, 242–43, 254; bronzes of, 2, 23, 24, 229–42, 231, 233 (detail), 254; Chola dynasty traced to, 84; as Narasimha, 254, 255; as subject of hymns, 229, 230; temples dedicated to, 230; Uma as sister of, 1, 133, 224; as Varaha, 254, 255

Weerasinghe, Jagath, x, 26

Wentworth, Blake, 29

women. See anukkis; bhogiyars; donors, female; queens

workshops, 58

Xuanxang (Chinese pilgrim), 242

yoginis, 277–81

Photography and Copyright Credits

Photo: American Institute of Indian Studies: 5.4 (e)
Courtesy of Archaeological Survey of India: 7.10
Art Gallery, Thanjavur; photo by Sanjeev Trivedi: 0.1 (a, b), 2.3, 2.4, 2.8, 5.1, 5.2, 5.3, 5.4 (a-d), 5.6, 5.7 (a, b), 5.8 (a, b), 5.9 (a-c), 5.10, 5.12, 5.13, 5.14, 7.19, 7.20, 7.21, 8.10 (b), 9.9 (a, b)
Arthur M. Sackler Gallery, Smithsonian Institution, Washington, DC: C.8
Courtesy of The Calico Museum of Textiles and The Sarabhai Foundation Collections, Ahmedabad: 2.5 (a, b), 4.6 (a, b), 4.9, 7.14 (a, b), 8.4 (a-c)
Courtesy of the Cleveland Museum of Art: 1.5, 1.6, 4.13, 4.14 (a), 9.7
Creative Commons-BY, photo: Brooklyn Museum, 1992.142_SL1.jpg: 8.5 (a, b)
Courtesy of Dallas Museum of Art: 4.18 (b), 4.22 (b)
Courtesy of Department of National Museums, Sri Lanka; photo by Jagath Weerasinghe: 6.14 (b)
Courtesy of Department of National Museums, Sri Lanka; photo by Vidya Dehejia: 6.3, 6.5, 6.6, 6.14 (a), 6.15 (a, b), 6.16, 6.17, 6.20
Courtesy Detroit Institute of Arts, Bridgeman Images: C.7
Courtesy of Director General, Central Cultural Fund; photo by Vidya Dehejia: 6.1, 6.2 (a, b), 6.4 (b), 6.7, 6.11 (b), 6.12, 6.18 (a, b), 6.19
Courtesy of Director General, Central Cultural Fund; photo by K. Rajapaksha: 6.4 (a), 6.9, 6.11 (a), 6.13
Freer Gallery of Art and Arthur M. Sackler Gallery, Smithsonian Institution, Washington, DC; photo by Neil Greentree: 1.13 (a, b, d, e)
Freer Gallery of Art, Smithsonian Institution, Washington, DC: 4.1 (a-e), 4.16 (a, b)
Government Museum, Chennai; photo by Christine Guidolotti: 5.5 (a-c)
Government Museum, Chennai; photo by Vidya Dehejia: 7.11, 8.1 (a, b), 8.18 (a, b)
The Hindu Photo Library: 3.11, 9.10 (a, b)
Photo courtesy of Institut français de Pondichéry / École française d'Extrême-Orient: 7.2, 7.5, 8.19 (a, b)

Photo by Jamison Miller; image courtesy Nelson-Atkins Museum of Art, Media Services: C.5
Los Angeles County Museum of Art: 4.21, 8.14, 9.3, 9.4, 9.5, 9.9 (d, right)
The Metropolitan Museum of Art, New York: 2.11 (a, b), 8.8 (b)
Photo by Minneapolis Institute of Art: C.6
Courtesy Musée guimet, photo by Hervé Lewandowski, © RMN-Grand Palais / Art Resource, NY: C.1 (a-c)
Courtesy Museum Rietberg, Zurich; photo by Rainer Wolfsberger: 8.6 (a, b), C.4
National Museum, New Delhi: 8.12 (a, b), 8.15 (a, b), 9.11, 9.12
© The Norton Simon Foundation: 1.16, 2.6, 4.11, 4.12, 4.20 (a, b), 4.22 (a), 9.8
© The Norton Simon Foundation; photo by Vidya Dehejia: 7.17 (a, b)
The Philadelphia Museum of Art / Art Resource, NY: 8.10 (a)
Prasad Pawar: 5.16, 5.17, 5.18
Private collection: 1.7, 4.18 (c)
Private collection; photo by Vidya Dehejia: 1.11, 7.18
Courtesy of R. Nagaswamy: 1.12, 1.15, 1.17, 2.10 (a, b), 4.8 (a), 4.10 (a-c)
Photo by Richard Davis: 1.9
With permission of the Royal Ontario Museum © ROM: C.3
Courtesy of Sowparnika Balaswaminathan: 1.13 (c)
Courtesy of Surendra Kumar: 9.13
Photo by Synthescape; courtesy of Asia Society, Asia Society / Art Resource, NY: 1.14, 4.18 (a), 8.13 (a, b), 8.16
© Victoria and Albert Museum, London: 4.19, 8.17, 9.6
Photo by Vidya Dehejia: 1.1, 1.2, 1.3, 1.4, 1.8, 1.10, 2.1 (a-g), 2.2, 2.7, 2.9, 2.12, 2.13, 2.14, 3.1, 3.2, 3.3, 3.4, 3.5, 3.6, 3.7, 3.8, 3.9, 3.10, 4.2 (a-b), 4.3, 4.4 (a-c), 4.5, 4.7, 4.8 (b), 4.14 (b), 4.15, 4.17, 4.23, 5.11, 5.15, 6.8, 6.10, 7.1, 7.3, 7.4, 7.6, 7.7, 7.8 (a, b), 7.9, 7.12, 7.13, 7.15, 7.16 (a, b), 8.2, 8.3, 8.7 (a, b), 8.8 (a), 8.9, 8.13(c), 9.1, 9.2, 9.9 (c), C.2, C.9, C.10
The Walters Art Museum, Baltimore: 8.11 (a, b)

A. W. Mellon Lectures in the Fine Arts 1952—2021

1952 Jacques Maritain, *Creative Intuition in Art and Poetry*
1953 Sir Kenneth Clark, *The Nude: A Study of Ideal Art* (published as *The Nude: A Study in Ideal Form*, 1956)
1954 Sir Herbert Read, *The Art of Sculpture* (published 1956)
1955 Etienne Gilson, *Art and Reality* (published as *Painting and Reality*, 1957)
1956 E. H. Gombrich, *The Visible World and the Language of Art* (published as *Art and Illusion: A Study in the Psychology of Pictorial Representation*, 1960)
1957 Sigfried Giedion, *Constancy and Change in Art and Architecture* (published as *The Eternal Present: A Contribution on Constancy and Change*, 1962–1964)
1958 Sir Anthony Blunt, *Nicolas Poussin and French Classicism* (published as *Nicolas Poussin*, 1967)
1959 Naum Gabo, *A Sculptor's View of the Fine Arts* (published as *Of Divers Arts*, 1962)
1960 Wilmarth Sheldon Lewis, *Horace Walpole* (published 1960)
1961 André Grabar, *Christian Iconography and the Christian Religion in Antiquity* (published as *Christian Iconography: A Study of Its Origins*, 1968)
1962 Kathleen Raine, *William Blake and Traditional Mythology* (published as *Blake and Tradition*, 1968)
1963 Sir John Pope-Hennessy, *Artist and Individual: Some Aspects of the Renaissance Portrait* ((published as *The Portrait in the Renaissance*, 1966)
1964 Jakob Rosenberg, *On Quality in Art: Criteria of Excellence, Past and Present* (published 1967)
1965 Sir Isaiah Berlin, *Sources of Romantic Thought* (published as *The Roots of Romanticism*, 1999)
1966 Lord David Cecil, *Dreamer or Visionary: A Study of English Romantic Painting* (published as *Visionary and Dreamer: Two Poetic Painters, Samuel Palmer and Edward Burne-Jones*, 1969)
1967 Mario Praz, *On the Parallel of Literature and the Visual Arts* (published as *Mnemosyne: The Parallel between Literature and the Visual Arts*, 1970)
1968 Stephen Spender, *Imaginative Literature and Painting*
1969 Jacob Bronowski, *Art as a Mode of Knowledge* (published as *The Visionary Eye: Essays in the Arts, Literature, and Science*, 1978)
1970 Sir Nikolaus Pevsner, *Some Aspects of Nineteenth-Century Architecture* (published as *A History of Building Types*, 1976)
1971 T. S. R. Boase, *Vasari: The Man and the Book* (published as *Giorgio Vasari: The Man and the Book*, 1979)
1972 Ludwig H. Heydenreich, *Leonardo da Vinci*
1973 Jacques Barzun, *The Use and Abuse of Art* (published 1974)
1974 H. W. Janson, *Nineteenth-Century Sculpture Reconsidered* (published as *The Rise and Fall of the Public Monument*)
1975 H. C. Robbins Landon, *Music in Europe in the Year 1776*
1976 Peter von Blanckenhagen, *Aspects of Classical Art*
1977 André Chastel, *The Sack of Rome: 1527* (published 1982)
1978 Joseph W. Alsop, *The History of Art Collecting* (published as *The Rare Art Traditions: The History of Art Collecting and Its Linked Phenomena Wherever These Have Appeared*, 1982)
1979 John Rewald, *Cézanne and America* (published as *Cézanne and America: Dealers, Collectors, Artists, and Critics, 1891–1921*, 1989)
1980 Peter Kidson, *Principles of Design in Ancient and Medieval Architecture*
1981 John Harris, *Palladian Architecture in England, 1615–1760*
1982 Leo Steinberg, *The Burden of Michelangelo's Painting*
1983 Vincent Scully, *The Shape of France* (published as *Architecture: The Natural and the Manmade*)
1984 Richard Wollheim, *Painting as an Art* (published 1987)
1985 James S. Ackerman, *The Villa in History* (published as *The Villa: Form and Ideology of Country Houses*, 1990)
1986 Lukas Foss, *Confessions of a Twentieth-Century Composer*
1987 Jaroslav Pelikan, *Imago Dei: The Byzantine Apologia for Icons* (published 1990)
1988 John Shearman, *Art and the Spectator in the Italian Renaissance* (published as *Only Connect...: Art and the Spectator in the Italian Renaissance*, 1992)
1989 Oleg Grabar, *Intermediary Demons: Toward a Theory of Ornament* (published as *The Mediation of Ornament*, 1992)
1990 Jennifer Montagu, *Gold, Silver, and Bronze: Metal Sculpture of the Roman Baroque* (published 1996)
1991 Willibald Sauerländer, *Changing Faces: Art and Physiognomy through the Ages*
1992 Anthony Hecht, *The Laws of the Poetic Art* (published as *On the Laws of the Poetic Art*, 1995)
1993 John Boardman, *The Diffusion of Classical Art in Antiquity* (published 1994)
1994 Jonathan Brown, *Kings and Connoisseurs: Collecting Art in Seventeenth-Century Europe* (published 1995)
1995 Arthur C. Danto, *Contemporary Art and the Pale of History* (published as *After the End of Art: Contemporary Art and the Pale of History*, 1997)
1996 Pierre M. Rosenberg, *From Drawing to Painting: Poussin, Watteau, Fragonard, David, Ingres* (published as *From Drawing to Painting: Poussin, Watteau, Fragonard, David, and Ingres*, 2000)
1997 John Golding, *Paths to the Absolute* (published as *Paths to the Absolute: Mondrian, Malevich, Kandinsky, Pollock, Newman, Rothko, and Still*, 2000)
1998 Lothar Ledderose, *Ten Thousand Things: Module and Mass Production in Chinese Art* (published 2000)
1999 Carlo Bertelli, *Transitions*
2000 Marc Fumaroli, *The Quarrel between the Ancients and the Moderns in the Arts, 1600–1715*

2001	Salvatore Settis, *Giorgione and Caravaggio: Art as Revolution*	2011	Mary Beard, *The Twelve Caesars: Images of Power from Ancient Rome to Salvador Dalí*
2002	Michael Fried, *The Moment of Caravaggio* (published 2010)	2012	Craig Clunas, *Chinese Painting and Its Audiences* (published 2017)
2003	Kirk Varnedoe, *Pictures of Nothing: Abstract Art since Pollock* (published 2006)	2013	Barry Bergdoll, *Out of Site in Plain View: A History of Exhibiting Architecture since 1750*
2004	Irving Lavin, *More than Meets the Eye*	2014	Anthony Grafton, *Past Belief: Visions of Early Christianity in Renaissance and Reformation Europe*
2005	Irene J. Winter, *"Great Work": Terms of Aesthetic Experience in Ancient Mesopotamia*	2015	Thomas Crow, *Restoration as Event and Idea: Art in Europe, 1814–1820* (published as *Restoration: The Fall of Napoleon in the Course of European Art, 1812–1820*)
2006	Simon Schama, *Really Old Masters: Age, Infirmity, and Reinvention*	2016	Vidya Dehejia, *The Thief Who Stole My Heart: The Material Life of Chola Bronzes from South India, c. 855–1280*
2007	Helen Vendler, *Last Looks, Last Books: The Binocular Poetry of Death* (published as *Last Looks, Last Books: Stevens, Plath, Lowell, Bishop, Merrill*, 2010)	2017	Alexander Nemerov, *The Forest: America in the 1830s*
2008	Joseph Leo Koerner, Bosch and Bruegel: *Parallel Worlds* (published as *Bosch and Bruegel: From Enemy Painting to Everyday Life*, 2016)	2018	Hal Foster, *Positive Barbarism: Brutal Aesthetics in the Postwar Period* (published as *Brutal Aesthetics: Dubuffet, Bataille, Jorn, Paolozzi, Oldenburg*)
2009	T. J. Clark, *Picasso and Truth* (published as *Picasso and Truth: From Cubism to Guernica*, 2013)	2019	Wu Hung, *End as Beginning: Chinese Art and Dynastic Time*
2010	Mary Miller, *Art and Representation in the Ancient New World*	2021	Jennifer Roberts, *Contact: Art and the Pull of Print*